Macromedia® Flash™ MX 2004 ActionScript 2.0 Dictionary

Contents at a Glance

Macromedia®
Flash™ MX 2004
ActionScript 2.0
Dictionary

Macromedia Inc.
Articles by Flash Experts

macromedia®
PRESS

1249 Eighth Street, Berkley, CA 94710
An Imprint of Pearson Education
Boston • Indianapolis • London • Munich • New York • San Francisco

Macromedia® Flash™ MX 2004 ActionScript 2.0 Dictionary

Macromedia Press books are published in association with:

Peachpit Press
1249 Eighth Street
Berkeley, CA 94710
510/524-2178 ■ 800-283-9444
510/524-2221 (fax)

Find us on the World Wide Web at:
http://www.peachpit.com
To report errors, please send a note to errata@peachpit.com

International Standard Book Number: 0-3212-2841-3

06 05 04   7 6 5 4 3

Printed and bound in the United States of America

Third-Party Information

This guide contains links to third-party websites that are not under the control of Macromedia, and Macromedia is not responsible for the content on any linked site. If you access a third-party website mentioned in this guide, then you do so at your own risk. Macromedia provides these links only as a convenience, and the inclusion of the link does not imply that Macromedia endorses or accepts any responsibility for the content on those third-party sites.

Speech compression and decompression technology licensed from Nellymoser, Inc. (www.nellymoser.com).

sorenson media. Sorenson™ Spark™ video compression and decompression technology licensed from Sorenson Media, Inc.

Opera ® browser Copyright © 1995-2002 Opera Software ASA and its suppliers. All rights reserved.

Apple Disclaimer

Peachpit Press

Acquisitions Editors:
Linda Anne Bump, Angela Kozlowski

Development Editors:
Fred Speers, Chris Zahn

Senior Project Editor:
Kristy Hart

Copy Editor:
Ben Lawson

Technical Reviewers:
Michael Grunding, Robert Hall

Interior Design:
Louisa Adair

Compositors:
Mark Shirar, Ron Wise

Cover Design/Layout:
Alan Clements

Index:
Cheryl Lenser

Acknowledgments

Peachpit Press wishes to acknowledge the assistance of the Macromedia Instructional Media Development Group.
Director: Erick Vera
Project Management: Stephanie Gowin, Barbara Nelson
Writing: Jody Bleyle, Mary Burger, Kim Diezel, Stephanie Gowin, Dan Harris, Barbara Herbert, Barbara Nelson, Shirley Ong, Tim Statler
Managing Editor: Rosana Francescato
Editing: Linda Adler, Mary Ferguson, Mary Kraemer, Noreen Maher, Antonio Padial, Lisa Stanziano, Anne Szabla
Production Management: Patrice O'Neill
Media Design and Production: Adam Barnett, Christopher Basmajian, Aaron Begley, John Francis, Jeff Harmon

Table of Contents

IV Working with External Data and Media   379

10 Working with External Data   381

About the Authors

aYo Binitie II, artist and multimedia designer/developer, is Creative Director for Room99 Limited (www.room99.co.uk) and DesignStreet London (www.designstreet.net). He is co-author of *Reality Macromedia: Flash Communication Server MX Strategic Solutions For Online Interaction* (Macromedia Press, 2003). An artist by training, his search for new dynamic forms of expression has resulted in experiments with Flash and other rich media and web technologies. He continues to extend the ethos of "renaissance man," by integrating art and new media technology.

Jeremy Brown has had an intimate relationship with Flash, and the flash community since 1998. A student of philosophy and music, he enjoys pondering over ways to simplify his programming thought process, and applying the disciplines of musical study to his methodology. When not hunched over the keyboard, Jeremy unwinds behind his drum set or at the pool hall. Born and raised in Washington D.C., Jeremy now lives in Malmö, Sweden, where he runs his own company J3R. Jeremy's web site is located at http://www.j3r.com.

Randy H. Drisgill is the Chief Technology Officer for Vshift (http://www.vshift.com), a Macromedia Alliance Solution Provider Partner located in Orlando, Florida. At Vshift, he has been architecting and developing dynamic web applications for companies throughout the country. Randy completed his Bachelor's degree in Management Information Systems from the University of Central Florida. From there, he started his IT career at Lockheed Martin's Enterprise Information Systems in Orlando Florida, working with several enterprise-level initiatives including being lead developer for LockheedMartin.com. With over seven years working on the web, Randy has co-authored a previous book on ColdFusion and Flash integration, and has given presentations at MXNorth and at the Orlando Macromedia User Group.

Alistair McLeod is Development Director at iteration::two, a Scottish Software Consultancy focused on delivering pervasive, interactive applications using agile development methods. With extensive experience in the financial sector, Alistair has a proven track record in delivering performant, scalable and robust enterprise solutions. Alistair now drives the development of rich client enterprise solutions using Flash MX 2004 and Enterprise Java. Alistair developed the Actionscript 2 testing framework, AS2Unit, available at www.as2unit.org, which has been released as an open source project to the Flash community. Alistair also contributes Rich Internet articles to flashmagazine.com.

Dr. William B. Sanders is a Professor of Interactive Information Technology at the University of Hartford. He has been involved with Flash since Flash 3 and has published six previous books on Flash and Flash Communication Server. His interests are in creating highly interactive and dynamic forms of web-based communication for interpersonal contacts, business, and education. Central to these interests is the development of concepts that can be applied to enhance seamless interaction for multi-sited task performance, developing and maintaining relationships, and international understandings and coordination. Because of the strong interactive tools in Flash, it has become the preferred tool to accomplish these goals. He is currently working on a book on Flash MX Professional 2004.

Jeff Tapper is the Chief Technologist for Tapper.net Consulting. He has been developing internet based applications since 1995, for a myriad of clients including Toys R Us, IBM, Allaire, Dow Jones, American Express, M&T Bank, Verizon, and Allied Office Supplies, among others. As a Macromedia Instructor, he is currently certified to teach all of Macromedia's courses on ColdFusion and Flash development. Jeff has worked as author and technical editor for several books on technologies including Flash and ColdFusion, including the soon to be released *Object Oriented Programming with ActionScript 2.0* (New Riders, 2004). He is also a frequent speaker at Macromedia Development Conferences and user groups. Jeff formed Tapper.net Consulting to focus on developing Rich Internet Applications and empowering clients through mentoring.

Steven Webster is Technical Director at iteration::two, a Scottish Software Consultancy focused on delivering pervasive, interactive applications using agile development methods. As a founder of iteration::two, Steven is recognized as a Software Engineer with a strong understanding of J2EE Design, Architecture, and development methodologies, working at the forefront of mobile application development and rich-client development using Flash MX and J2EE. Recognized within the development community as an authority on Rich Internet Application development using Flash and J2EE, Steven is the author of *Reality J2EE: Architecting for Flash MX* (Macromedia Press, 2003) and a regular contributor to the "Engineering RIAs" column at flashmagazine.com.

Introduction

I have never been a big fan of shipping products at the end of the summer, for I love the California sun. The team has been working through weekends and until midnight for months now. Just a few hundred more bugs to fix, and Macromedia Flash MX 2004 (code named "Matador") and Macromedia Flash MX 2004 Professional (code named "Toreador") will be in customers' hands. I have an enormous velvet painting of a matador, the fruit of some forgotten garage sale, hanging over my cubicle for moral support. Someone has kidnapped the Director of QA's plastic puppy and is holding it for ransom; its plastic ear was sent through by FedEx with a list of demands. So, everyone is getting tired, but we're still having some fun. By the time you read this, our team's very own puppy, Matador, will be unveiled to the world.

Flash as a Paintbrush

I have said before that we like to think of what we do as making paintbrushes, the essential tools by which artists ply their trade. I like to think that if Rembrandt or Monet were alive today, they would be using Macromedia Flash MX and would be amazed by the level of creative expression they could achieve. Flash is a paintbrush that advances exponentially every year, always becoming more streamlined and versatile and bristling with more features. It's also a paintbrush that has been fabricated not by a single artisan, but rather by hundreds of people who have contributed to make it the product it is today. It's no surprise that it's perhaps one of the most advanced tools that a creative professional has ever had at his or her disposal.

Flash has become such an essential part of the Internet that it's come to be accepted as part of daily electronic life. However, take a step back and think about what it means: Moving graphics, synchronized with sound, integrated video and interactivity, viewable simultaneously by millions of people all over the world! It's a pretty amazing communications medium with unrivaled reach.

Of course, nobody remembers who crafted paintbrushes for Monet and Rembrandt. What really matters is the art that is created with these tools, not the tools themselves. So although we're proud of our achievement with Flash, what is truly inspiring is seeing what our customers do with Flash. Whenever we are feeling weary after a long day of bug fixing, we take a few moments to look at some hot new Flash content coming out of the community. Incredible work is being done out there. When we see something really fabulous, we marvel at the hard work that went into making it happen, but we also take a bit of pride in knowing that some of our code is making it all possible under the hood. Everyone on the team feels the same way. It's the creativity and energy of the Flash community that really keeps us going.

We've come a long way. Flash is everywhere! Flash is everything that is dynamic on the web. It is great design, subtle and beautiful. It is great, responsive applications. Sometimes it is gratuitous and jolting, but every new world comes with its share of good and bad. It is and will continue to be everywhere. It has become as much a part of the web as HTML. Flash is now a part of standalone applications. It's also making inroads into new realms: Flash is coming soon to your cell phone (if it isn't there already) and to a myriad of other mobile devices. Flash is everywhere, and yet it's also still growing.

A Little Flash History

There are a lot of new faces on the Flash engineering team, and some of the new faces from a few years ago are now veterans who have been through multiple releases of the product. My own story with Flash now goes back pretty far. I've been working on Flash for five years, starting with Flash 4, and this is my fourth major release of the product. So, I can tell you that Flash didn't just burst onto the scene one day. It has grown and matured into each of its uses over time. Early versions featured only simple drawing and animation. Then came Flash 4, along with a little interactivity with the introduction of scripting. This enabled people to make interactive designs, and Flash branding really took off. After all, interacting with content is more engaging than simply watching content. Thus, ActionScript was born, and from that time on, scripting has made all the difference in Flash.

Initially, ActionScript was a simple language that enabled the creation of only the most basic events and actions. The promise, however, was clearly visible. As ActionScript evolved through subsequent releases, its capabilities increased. Flash designers and developers could create ever more engaging interfaces.

It wasn't only the capabilities of ActionScript that evolved the state of the art. Legions in the Flash community did amazing things, showing the world what could be done and challenging each other in the process. Each month, a new web site took Flash to a new level and applied Flash to a new problem. The biggest difference that enabled people to create and evolve was the evolving capability of ActionScript. What would take people months to animate using the Timeline took weeks to program in ActionScript. The end result was a user experience that really raised the bar for the overall standard of user interfaces on the web.

When Flash MX hit, Flash developers rose to the Rich Internet Application challenge. The Macromedia Flash development team had produced a tool that, for the first time, started to feel like a development environment that was familiar to programmers. It had components and a far more mature, sophisticated programming language.

The Macromedia MX release was the most successful release for Macromedia customers. The integrated toolset, Macromedia Studio, really proved a great hit with customers because they could buy one box and get all the products they needed to build a complete web site.

Flash designers and developers took up Flash MX and produced great web site experiences, great application interfaces for the server side, great client-side applications, beautiful data visualizations, and on and on. All this was made possible in large part by the matured language called ActionScript.

Along with these new capabilities came challenges. For example, when people started writing a lot of code, standards and best practices had to be established. Macromedia defined some standards, but the community of Flash developers defined the best practices as a result of their many hours of dedicated experimenting and improving. Those coding standards were communicated through books, web sites, discussion postings, and an endless stream of conversations everywhere Flashers got together. As important as the language's capabilities, those standards helped to drive a capable and efficient community to create, share, and improve.

Some Final Thoughts

While I sit late at night in the wee hours and contemplate the release, I have no way of knowing the great and incredible things Flash programmers will create. There is one thing we have come to respect without question, though. Each great Flash interface is as much about the creator as it is about the information it delivers. The community of Flash developers prizes invention and creativity. Macromedia Flash gives them a tool that uncorks their design statements while providing solid ground to develop hard-core applications with complete server-side integration. Flash is unique that way, and those who have rallied around it are unique in their ability to react to that opportunity and do great things. With this release, we will see a huge number of programmers pick up Flash for the first time, and their voices will join the Flash experts in creating great online experiences. ActionScript 2.0 will be behind every one of them.

Have a great time and impress us all!

Gary Grossman, Director of Engineering

About this Book

This book serves as both an ActionScript 2.0 language reference and an edited volume containing the thinking of some leading members of the Flash community. The first part of the book contains a series of articles written by Flash community leaders about Flash MX 2004 and ActionScript 2.0 that run the gamut from design patterns to code style to the creation of an entire site. The ActionScript Dictionary presented in the second part of the book is for people who want the full language reference in hard copy format.

The language reference is invaluable for any programmer. If you are like many, you like to read your language reference, quickly skipping around, annotating the pages, and comparing it to other books. Although this is the same language reference that can be found online in the Flash product, the productivity of having a few books open while you code can be irreplaceable. In book form, you may find the language reference more useful and thus may find yourself more effective.

In the MX 2004 release of Flash and Flash Professional, ActionScript has taken another leap forward, and we expect to see great things from the Flash community. Learning from MX, Macromedia found the limits, ceilings, workarounds, and speed bumps in the MX version and worked on them. The result of that work was a huge amount of headroom for those doing the biggest projects. For the average person who wants simple interactivity, the original roots of the language are still there to keep it as approachable as possible.

The new language adds a full object-oriented paradigm to ActionScript. Now, ActionScript enables programmers to build a complete catalog of hierarchical classes and modify those classes for specific purposes. These new ActionScript classes are the equivalent of classes in any fully matured OOP language such as C++ or Java. Rather than going into a lot of detail here, we recommend you check out Jeff Tapper's article, Article 5, "Understanding Object-Oriented

Programming in Macromedia Flash MX 2004." You will learn the values of this new language and how to use object-oriented programming to your benefit.

When you are ready to plunge into the new syntax of all this new functionality, take a look at William B. Sanders's article, Article, 1, "Converting from ActionScript to ActionScript 2.0." You'll get caught up on the fundamental differences in ActionScript 2.0, and with the language reference, you'll have a great head start on your next project.

When Macromedia listened to the web development community and took a hard look at what people are doing out there, they heard and saw that there was a lot developed in HTML and a lot developed in Flash, but the two were rarely integrated well. All too often, a great Flash interface is launched off an HTML page, and the two windows exist separately. That's a great opportunity for a better, more integrated user experience. A new area for Flash developers is building *hybrid* applications. These applications integrate HTML and Flash content seamlessly so that the user has a great experience throughout the web site or application, regardless of technology. This way, you can focus on using the technology that's best for the situation.

Several articles in this book will help you learn the skills and techniques to create a great hybrid experience. Randy H. Drisgill's article, Article 3, "Macromedia Flash MX 2004 HTML TextField Enhancements," shows you how to build HTML into Flash so that you can bring the HTML world into Flash and blend the experiences of each technology better. aYo Benitie's article, Article 4, "Creating Hybrid Flash Applications (HTML, JavaScript, and Flash)," then takes the whole view of integrating Flash content throughout HTML content to create a complete web site. Using these resources and the language reference, you will have a much more complete picture of how to build hybrid HTML-Flash and Flash-HTML experiences.

When you are ready to dive in and build a Rich Internet Application, read up on patterns that will provide the best practices and approaches to integrating your client-side logic and display with your server-side logic and data. You will find Article 6, "ActionScript Design Patterns for Rich Internet Application Development," by Steven Webster and Alistair Mcleod, very helpful in introducing you to building architected rich Internet applications.

None of this works very well without a standardized set of assumptions, standards, and best practices. These are sometimes invented, sometimes the result of a large community of input, and sometimes only exhibit themselves over a long time. Jeremy Brown distills some of the most important elements of programming style for success in his article, Article 2, "The Power of Style: Writing Clean Code." If you follow his methods, your code will be more understandable, which equates to fewer programming mistakes over time. Standards are a powerful and important positive factor in a programming community. The standards in "The Power of Style" will do wonders for the entire Flash community that follows them.

Lucian Beebe, Senior Product Manager

I

Articles

Article 1

Converting from ActionScript to ActionScript 2.0

by William B. Sanders

Developers who have used ActionScript from its inception have seen it grow in size and complexity from a few actions to a complete lexicon rivaling even the most developed scripting languages. It has eclipsed languages like JavaScript 1.5 in its scope and size. (ActionScript 2.0 will look very much like JavaScript 2.0, though.) In this latest version of ActionScript, Macromedia has made enough fundamental changes to warrant a change in reference from ActionScript to ActionScript 2.0. All previous versions of ActionScript, but most significantly the version released with Flash MX, are now called ActionScript 1.0.

ActionScript 2.0 can be called an object-oriented programming (OOP) language, whereas previous versions were more modestly referred to as an object-*based* programming language, and that was only with the Flash MX version. Such distinctions are perhaps more hair-splitting than necessary because OOP is as much an attitude toward programming as it is the built-in features of a language used to generate OOP structures in a script. (See Article 5, "Understanding Object-Oriented Programming in Macromedia Flash MX 2004," by Jeffery Tapper) The change in ActionScript's form is due to the OOP embedded in the ECMA-262 standard, out of which emerged

ECMAScript Edition 4—the proposal for Internet scripting languages. (The latest version of ECMAScript standards is referred to as "Edition" or "proposal" by ECMA. A shorthand for ECMAScript proposal 4 is ECMAScript 4.)

For those familiar with the early days of personal computers, you may remember that every different brand of computer had its own version of the BASIC programming language. Among others were Atari, Commodore, Texas Instruments, Timex-Sinclair, Apple, and IBM. A program developed on an Atari could not be run on an IBM. Instead of coming up with a standard for all PC BASIC languages, the different companies just went their own way until the only ones left were Apple and IBM (running Microsoft BASIC). When the Internet came along, Netscape developed a new language called JavaScript that ran on its browser. Microsoft then developed a slightly different version of JavaScript to run on its browser, Internet Explorer, and so the developers had to write different scripts for the two different browsers.

Wisely, the European Computer Manufacturers' Association (ECMA) encouraged that a standard be developed so that the Internet would not become the Tower of Babel that the early personal computer languages were. Because ECMA sets standards for a number of different computer-related tasks, they number them, and ECMA-262 represents the standard for Internet scripting languages, most notably JavaScript. However, instead of calling it JavaScript, they called it ECMAScript, and the current edition is ECMAScript 4.

The new version of JavaScript under development to conform with ECMAScript 4 is called JavaScript 2.0, and so Macromedia followed suit and called the ECMA standard-meeting version of ActionScript "ActionScript 2.0." (See `http://www.mozilla.org/js/language/es4/index.html` for the full standard.) To be sure, you will find differences between ActionScript 2.0 and the ECMAScript 4 standard. For example, Flash has certain built-in non-ECMA classes such as MovieClip and LoadVars because it *remains* the scripting language for Flash and not something more generic. Otherwise, the language is very close to the ECMAScript 4 standard.

So why bother to adopt a standard that has nothing to do with Flash? Well, ActionScript could either remain a language unlike any other, or it could adopt a way of programming that is familiar to other programmers. By taking the latter course of action, ActionScript can be learned readily by programmers who already know OOP languages such as C++ and Java. Likewise, because JavaScript 2.0 is taking the same route, JavaScript 2.0 programmers will be able to pick up ActionScript quickly as well.

The key to this new direction is the object-oriented model of programming, and by making ActionScript more OOP-like and suitable for object-oriented programming, ActionScript provides a stronger base for well-structured programs with code that is:

- Reusable
- Modular
- Scalable
- Maintainable
- Secure
- Robust

Beginning with Flash MX and the introduction of *prototype* structures, ActionScript began migrating toward the ECMASCript 4 proposal, and that journey is now more complete with ActionScript 2.0. So although the change from ActionScript 1.0 to ActionScript 2.0 is a major one, the result should not be wholly unfamiliar.

As you read the rest of the article, you will find a discussion of what is new with ActionScript 2.0 and tools related to the new ActionScript. First, the article examines the new tools and procedures that affect all ActionScript programming in Flash. You will learn about changes to the Actions panel and the addition of the Behaviors panel and integrated Script window. Also in the initial section you will learn about the new case-sensitivity in writing script and how to create classes and strong data typing. No matter what you're doing with ActionScript 2.0, these new procedures and tools will affect the results.

Second, you will find that several new terms have been added to ActionScript 2.0. Some of these terms are new statements, objects, or general properties. For example, MovieClipLoader is a new class. Other terms, though, are properties or methods added to existing terms, such as the Systems object's new methods and properties. In addition, this section shows whole new ways of doing things in ActionScript 2.0. One of the major additions is the use of a subset of Cascading Style Sheets (CSS) to style text.

Finally, the article briefly examines using ActionScript 2.0 with components. You will find very few of the Flash MX ActionScript techniques for styling components still extant. Using ActionScript 2.0, you will find other fundamental approaches to using components as well. For example, instead of using the setHandler() method, listeners are now employed as event detectors.

The purpose of this section is to expand on and more fully examine what you will find in the main dictionary. It also serves as a quick look-up of what's new in ActionScript 2.0. Because the bulk of ActionScript 2.0 is virtually identical to ActionScript 1.0, if you already know ActionScript, this article will show the critical differences and new procedures to be followed, which will save you time and frustration. When you finish this article, you should have a good understanding of the new direction ActionScript 2.0 takes and how to use and integrate it with ActionScript 1.0.

Actions Panel

One of the first things you will notice about the Actions panel is that it is no longer divided into expert and normal modes. In most respects, the expert mode was really a normal mode, and the normal mode was really a learning mode. Most developers never used the normal mode and were glad to see it eliminated. However, many designers relied heavily on it, and even developers used it occasionally to straighten out code formatting.

To get a quick overview of the new Actions panel and the new ActionScript terms, open up a new page using File > General Tab > New Flash Document and press F9 to open the Actions panel. (You will notice that you can open a lot more than just a document.) Now select File > Publish Settings > Flash and change the version to Flash Player 6 and the ActionScript version to ActionScript 1.0. By doing so, all the new ActionScript terms in the Actions toolbox will be highlighted in yellow. Figure 1.1 shows what you can expect to see in the Actions toolbox when new terms are encountered.

The Actions panel itself has changed little from the expert mode of Flash MX. However, some important changes have been introduced, including the following:

- Placement of the Script navigator in the bottom left pane
- Addition of tabs to select ActionScript in different frames and objects
- Placement of the Script Pin button at the bottom of the panel
- Addition of code line markers (red dots that can be toggled on and off by clicking the line numbers)

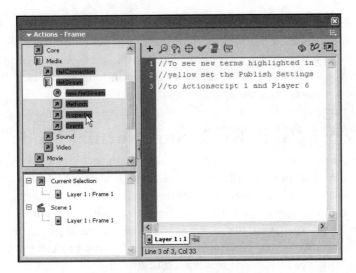

Figure 1.1   By setting the Publish Settings to the previous version of Flash, all the new terms are highlighted in yellow.

Otherwise, the Actions panel is the same as in Flash MX. Figure 1.2 shows the panel with the Publish Settings set to ActionScript 2.0 and Player 7 with code using the new NetConnection and NetStream classes.

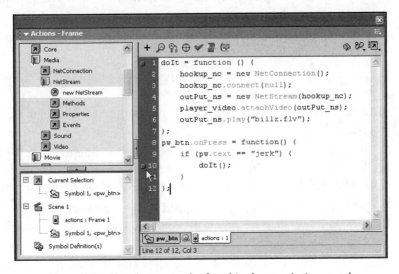

Figure 1.2   Key changes can be found in the new Actions panel.

Designers who have become accustomed to using the helpful normal mode can either transition to the new Actions panel using code hints to help, or they can use the new Behaviors panel. For additional help in creating code and as a substitute for the normal mode, the next section introduces the new Behaviors panel that generates code for specific tasks.

Behaviors Panel Replacing Normal Mode

To aid those who are not developers, the new Flash includes a Behaviors panel. Rather than just helping the user to write code, the Behaviors panel writes chunks of code to accomplish different tasks. For example, the `gotoAndPlay()` and `gotoAndStop()` actions need some kind of event to fire them. Using the Behaviors panel, the user just has to select the object or frame that will use the code, and the Behaviors panel does the rest. For example, consider a typical Flash application that is designed to give the user a choice using buttons. One choice will be correct and the other incorrect, and so one button will order the playhead to go to and stop at the incorrect answer frame and the other to go to and stop at the frame representing the correct answer. Follow these steps to create a simple quiz movie using the Behaviors panel:

1. Open a new Flash document.
2. Create a total of three layers, naming them from top to bottom Items, Buttons, Background.
3. Add a total of ten frames to each layer, and add keyframes in Frames 5 and 10 of each layer.
4. Select the first frame of the Buttons layer, create a button object, and make a copy of it. Place one above the other.
5. Click the first frame of the Items layer, and in the Actions panel, type `stop();`.
6. In the Background layer in the first frame, type the question, **Q: Which version of ActionScript has classes?** Next to the top button, type **ActionScript 1**, and next to the bottom button, type **ActionScript 2**.
7. In the Items layer, click on Frame 5, and in the middle of the stage, type **Incorrect.** Then, click on Frame 10 and type **Correct** in the middle of the stage.
8. Click on the first frame of the Buttons layer and click on the top button. Open the Behaviors panel, click on the "+" button to open a popup menu, and select Movieclip > Goto and Stop at frame or label, as illustrated in Figure 1.3.

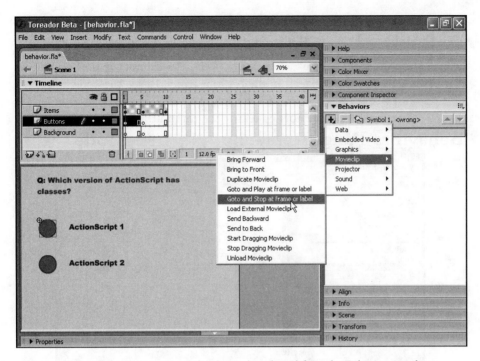

Figure 1.3   Different sets of code can be selected from the Behaviors panel.

9. The Goto and Stop at frame or label dialog box opens. Type the number 5 in the Frame(label) text box, as shown in Figure 1.4.

Figure 1.4   All the user has to include is the frame number to create the necessary script.

10. Repeat Steps 8 and 9 for the bottom button, but type 10 for the frame instead of 5. That's it. All the necessary script for the quiz is complete.

When using the Behaviors panel to create code, you cannot see the script, but it is being generated and placed in the Actions panel. To see the code, select the top button and press F9 to open the Actions panel. Figure 1.5 shows the code generated by the Behaviors panel for the top button:

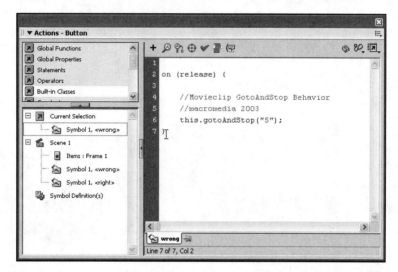

Figure 1.5   Scripts generated with the Behaviors panel appear in the Actions panel.

Although many may miss the helpful structure elements in the normal mode from previous versions of Flash, the Behaviors panel makes it very easy to generate code in much bigger chunks.

When the Behaviors panel generates code, it does so in a case-sensitive manner. As you will see in the next section on case sensitivity, all ActionScript 2.0, no matter how it is generated, (unlike ActionScript 1.0) is case sensitive.

Case Sensitivity

In ActionScript 1.0, all code is case-insensitive. That is, a variable named `alpha` can be accessed as `Alpha` or `aLpHa` or any combination of cases that spell "alpha." However, in ActionScript 2.0, the code is case-sensitive. For example, if you type the code

```
var alpha="Call me, Alphie"
trace(Alpha);
```

instead of seeing "Call me, Alphie" in the Output panel, you will see "undefined." That's because `Alpha` is not defined, even though `alpha` is. If your ActionScript 1.0 files have not paid attention to case sensitivity, you will have to rewrite them if you want to convert your code into files that will run on the Flash 7 player. Otherwise, they will only be able to run on the Flash 6 player.

The change from case-insensitive to case-sensitive code is a *crucial* matter, and until you get used to being sure that all references, definitions, and assignments are case-sensitive, you are likely to encounter bugs in your scripts.

In the same way that ActionScript 2.0 requires you to pay attention to cases in naming and referencing, it has also tightened up on the way data types are employed. The next section explains the entire process of data typing, and although it is not difficult to understand, it requires you to pay attention to a detail not required with ActionScript 1.0.

Strong Data Typing

You may not have been aware of the fact that all data typing prior to ActionScript 2.0 uses *weak data typing*. That means variables and properties can be assigned different types of data at different times, and ActionScript is perfectly happy. That is good because if you want to change a variable from a numeric variable to a string variable, all you needed to do was assign the variable a string value. For example, in ActionScript 1.0 the following script works just fine:

```
var alpha = 521;
trace(2 + alpha); //Output shows: 523
var alpha = "Bloomfield Rocks!";
trace (2 + alpha); //Output shows: 2Bloomfield Rocks!
```

The code also works in ActionScript 2.0, but it's a fairly sloppy practice because the variable changes from one type to another. Also, none of the type checking will be in place. Using *strongly typed data*, however, you are required to include the type of data when you declare a variable. For example, the following declaration creates a numeric variable:

```
var priceItem:Number = 14.95;
```

The variable named `priceItem` is now a numeric (number) variable and cannot be a string or some other kind of variable unless it is retyped. ("Retyping" refers to *providing* a new data type and not keyboard efforts.)

However, if you enter

```
var item:Number = "Hot Dog";
```

you will encounter an error message because the assigned value "Hot Dog" is a string instead of a number.

If you are familiar with languages like Java, numeric variables are broken down into finer categories such as double and integer, but ActionScript 2.0 simply uses Number for any type of numeric value. You can assign the following data types in ActionScript 2.0:

- Accordion
- Alert
- Array
- Binding
- Boolean
- Button
- Camera
- CheckBox
- Color
- ComboBox
- ComponentMixing
- CustomActions
- DataField
- DataGrid
- DataHolder
- DataSet
- DataType
- Date
- DateChooser
- Delta
- DeltaItem
- DeltaPacket
- Endpoint
- Error
- Function
- Label
- LoadVars
- LocalConnection
- Log
- MediaController
- MediaDisplay
- MediaPlayback
- Menu
- MenuBar
- Microphone
- MovieClip
- MovieClipLoader
- NetConnection
- NetStream
- Number
- Object
- PendingCall
- PopUpManager
- PrintJob
- ProgressBar
- RadioButton
- RadioButtonGroup
- RDBMSResolver
- ScrollPane
- SharedObject
- Slide
- SOAPCall
- Sound
- String
- TextArea
- TextField
- TextFormat
- TextInput

- TextSnapshot
- Tree
- TypedValue
- Video
- Void
- WebServiceConnector

- Window
- XML
- XMLConnector
- XMLNode
- XMLSocket
- XUpdateResolver

In addition, all built-in classes and all custom classes and interfaces can be data types as well.

Most of the new features, including strong typing and the use of classes and OOP, are best understood by seeing how they work in the new integrated Script window, a feature only in the Professional version of Flash. So we now will turn to a discussion of how to use this new editing tool to optimize your use of ActionScript 2.0.

Using the Integrated Script Window to Create a Class

To facilitate coding in ActionScript 2.0, there are now two different scripting windows. First, you have the familiar Actions panel, which is almost identical to the expert mode of the Actions panel in Flash MX. The second one, called the Integrated Script window, works very much like a text editor, such as Notepad. You can write code in it that is saved and used outside of the FLA or SWF file, and that code is addressed and used in the Actions panel. However, unlike Notepad, the Integrated Script window has many of the error-checking and formatting features of the Actions panel. In fact, most of the code editing features found in the Actions panel are duplicated in the Integrated Script window.

You can write external scripts in the Integrated Script window and bring them into the movie using the `#include` action. However, the key purpose of this new script editor is to create classes. Flash MX uses the `prototype` and the `registerClass` functions to create classes, but that method is a bit awkward and divergent from the way classes are created in most other OOP-based languages. So, now classes are created in separate .as files written in the Integrated Script window. A single class is all that can be created in a single .as file, and the .as file name must match the class name. Furthermore, the .as file must be in the same folder as the FLA file that uses the class. The information in the .as file is compiled into the SWF file. Generally, development takes place with the FLA, SWF, and .as file all residing in the same folder, as shown in Figure 1.6.

Figure 1.6   Class definitions saved as .as files must be in the same folder as the .FLA files that use the classes.

When you define a class, you can make it part of the authoring environment by placing it in the Classes folder within the First Run folder. The full path in Windows XP, for example, is Program Files > Macromedia > Flash 2004 > en > First Run > Classes. So if you create a class you're likely to use in several different programs, you can save time by placing it in the Classes folder.

To see how to use the Integrated Script window and create and use a class in ActionScript 2.0, follow these steps to create a simple movie:

1. Open a new Flash document and create a total of three layers, naming them from top to bottom Actions, Text field, and Background.
2. In the Text field layer, add two dynamic text fields next to one another, naming the one on the left itemOut and the one on the right checkOut.
3. In the Background layer, type the label **Product** over the left text field and the label **Total** over the right text field. Save the file as classItem.fla in a folder named ItemClass.
4. Select File > New > ActionScript File and enter the following script in Listing 1.1:

Listing 1.1   **Creating a Class**

```
class Item {
    var describe:String;
    var price:Number;
    var tax:Number;
    function Item(describe, price, tax) {
        this.describe = describe;
        this.price = price;
        this.tax = tax;
    }
function selectedItem() {
        return describe;
    }
    function kaChing():Number {
        return price += (price*tax);
    }
}
```

5. Save the file as Item.as in the ItemClass folder. Note that the class name "Item" must match the name of the file. Figure 1.7 shows the completed Integrated Script window with the Actions panel ghosted in the foreground.

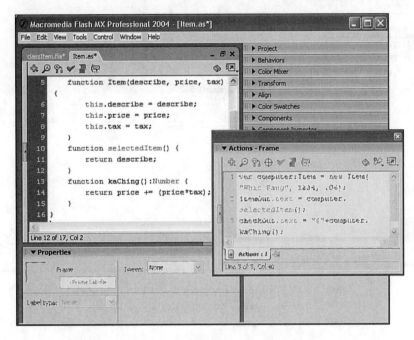

Figure 1.7   All class definitions must be created in the Integrated Script window.

6. Click the classItem.fla tab at the bottom of the Integrated Script window to select the FLA document and open the Actions panel. Type the following script:

```
var computer:Item = new Item("Whiz Bang", 1234, .06);
itemOut.text = computer.selectedItem();
checkOut.text = "$"+computer.kaChing();
```

Figure 1.8 shows the FLA document window with the related code and stage. Note the tab in the upper left corner to toggle back to the Integrated Script window. (The Macintosh version of Flash has separate windows with no tabs.)

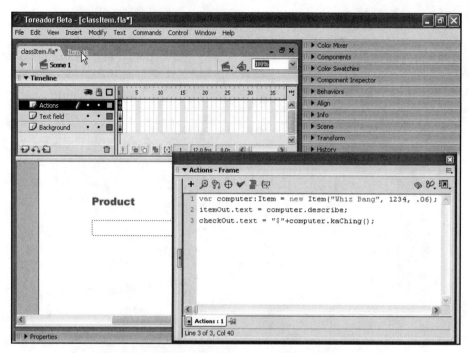

Figure 1.8　Only the Actions panel can be used to instantiate
the class developed in the Integrated Script Window.

7. Save the script and press Ctrl+Enter to test the movie (Command-Return on the Mac). You should see the current value of the Item.describe property in the left window and the output of the Item.kaChing() method in the right window. Figure 1.9 shows the output of testing the movie. Note the tabs in the lower left corner of the figure.

After going through all that for the simple output and calculations, the new system for creating classes may seem to be a step backwards in both productivity and coding. However, one of the main purposes of OOP is to encourage reusable code. The Item class can be called by any script simply by placing the Item.as file in the same folder as the SWF file calling it. By creating a library of classes in this fashion, production time can be reduced considerably.

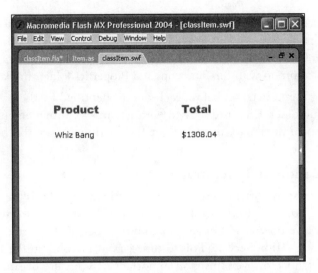

Figure 1.9   The output requires both the code from the .as file and the Actions panel.

Using the New Terms and Term Groups

In addition to new tools and procedures, ActionScript 2.0 has several new terms, and the terms are grouped differently in the Actions toolbox in the Actions panel. The groupings of the different terms are now in the following top-level folders in the Actions toolbox:

- Global Functions
- Global Properties
- Statements
- Operators
- Built-in Classes
- Constants
- Compiler Directives
- Types
- Deprecated
- Data
- Components

In rethinking the top-level folders and their subfolders, Macromedia completely restructured the organization of the Actions toolbox. So, instead of being able to provide a set of equivalence folders to Flash MX, you have to go through the different folders and see how the terms are organized. Some folders like Constants and Operators are almost identical to Flash MX, and Objects in Flash MX are now Built-in Classes. However, Global Functions and Global Properties have very little in common with the Functions and Properties folders in Flash MX.

In discussing the new terms below, each one is identified by the path to its folder and subfolder. Each is discussed with examples to supplement its discussion in the main dictionary portion (Part II, "Dictionary") of this book.

NetConnection and NetStream

One of the most important new features of ActionScript 2.0 is the addition of terms that can be used to stream Flash Video (FLV) files. The streaming is actually a progressive download but appears indistinguishable from streaming with Flash Communication Server. (This feature is available only in the Professional version of Flash.) However, this is an important new feature because it means that you no longer have to place an external video directly into a Flash movie or movie clip. Instead, all you have to do is call up the video like you would an external text or graphic file.

Two key objects are involved: NetConnection and NetStream (Built-in Classes > Media). NetConnection has a single method, `connect`. However, NetStream is a bit more robust, and its features are summarized in Table 1.1.

Table 1.1   **NetStream Properties, Methods and Event**

Methods	Description
`close()`	Stops play altogether, and resumption of play starts at the beginning of the file.
`pause()`	A toggle method that stops and resumes play of stream in position where stop/start occurs.
`play()`	Begins streaming play to designated output device.
`seek(n)`	Moves to the stream position in seconds (n).
`setBufferTime(n)`	Establishes the number of seconds (n) the stream is placed into buffer before dropping frames.
Properties	**Description**
`bufferLength`	Current number of seconds in the buffer.
`bufferTime`	Seconds specified in the `setBufferTime()` method.
`currentFps`	Frames per second in current stream.
`time`	How long in seconds the stream has been playing.
Event handler	**Description**
`onStatus`	Whenever an error or status change occurs, this event fires.

To see how the two new media objects work in a Flash movie, this next example uses all the objects' methods, properties, and events. All the code is in Frame 1. Figure 1.10 shows the stage running a video with the different objects and their instance names.

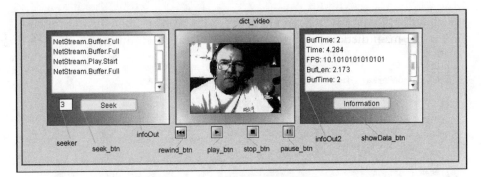

Figure 1.10   A good deal of information about the status
of a stream is available using the NetStream class.

The embedded video object shown in Figure 1.10 is named `dict_video` and is shown as a rectangle with an "X" in the middle when viewed on the development stage. The two text boxes to the left and right of the video are TextArea components, but the text field named `seeker` is simply an input text field. The Seek and Information buttons are Button components, and the four buttons beneath the video are modified button symbols found in Window > Other Panels > Common Libraries > Buttons > Playback. (The pause button was created by removing the arrow from the playback-loop button and replacing it with the parallel vertical bars.)

Add five layers—Actions, Video, Text fields, Buttons, and Background. Place the elements shown in Figure 1.10 on an 800×600 stage and add the following script in Listing 1.2 to Frame 1 of the Actions layer.

Listing 1.2   **Playing an FLV File**

```
//Make a connection
var hookup_nc:NetConnection = new NetConnection();
hookup_nc.connect(null);
//Create a NetStream instance
var showTime_ns:NetStream = new NetStream(hookup_nc);
//Attach the NetStream to the video on stage
dict_video.attachVideo(showTime_ns);
//Set buffer to 2 seconds
```

continues

Listing 1.2 **Continued**

```
showTime_ns.setBufferTime(2);
//Play video
play_btn.onPress = function() {
     showTime_ns.play("dict.flv");
};
//Rewind
rewind_btn.onPress = function() {
     showTime_ns.seek(0);
};
//Stop video
stop_btn.onPress = function() {
     showTime_ns.close();
};
//Pause video (toggle)
pause_btn.onPress = function() {
     showTime_ns.pause();
};
//Seek position
seek_btn.label = "Seek";
seekVid = new Object();
seekVid.click = function() {
     showTime_ns.seek(parseInt(seeker.text));
};
seek_btn.addEventListener("click", seekVid);
//Check the current NetStream status
showTime_ns.onStatus = function(info) {
     infoOut.text += info.code+newline;
     infoOut.vPosition = infoOut.maxVPosition;
};
showStream = new Object();
showStream.click = function() {
     infoOut2.text += "Time: "+showTime_ns.time+newline;
     infoOut2.text += "FPS: "+showTime_ns.currentFps+newline;
     infoOut2.text += "BufLen: "+showTime_ns.bufferLength+newline;
     infoOut2.text += "BufTime: "+showTime_ns.bufferTime+newline;
};
showData_btn.addEventListener("click", showStream);
showData_btn.label = "Information";
```

The only other piece required is an FLV file. I created one using Sorensen Squeeze, but they can be generated using Flash Communication Server directly from camera input as well. If you have an existing movie file, such as AVI or MOV, you can use Flash to transform it to an FLV file. Import the file into the Library panel, select the icon in the Library panel, and right-click (Control-click on the Mac) it to open the context menu. In the context menu, select Properties > Export, and the movie will be saved in FLV format.

ID3

MP3 files may contain information tags known as ID3 tags. These tags were originally 256 bytes, but now the latest version of the tag, known as ID3v2, can be up to 256 megabytes. Located at the beginning of the audio file, the ID3v2 tag can have a good deal of information, including encapsulated pictures. In the latest version of Flash, you can access up to 39 of the properties that make up ID3v2 files, as shown in Table 1.2.

Table 1.2   **ID3v2 Properties**

Property	Description	Property	Description
COMM *comment	Comment	TALB *album	Album/Movie/Show title
TBPM	beats per minute	TCOM *artist	Composer
TCON *genre	Content type	TCOP	Copyright message
TDAT	Date	TDLY	Play list delay
TENC	Encoded by	TEXT	Lyricist/Text writer
TFLT	File type	TIME	Time
TIT1	Content group description	TIT2 *songname	Title/song name/ content description
TIT3	Subtitle/ Description refinement	TKEY	Initial key
TLAN	Language(s)	TLEN	Length
TMED	Media type	TOAL	Original album/ movie/ show title
TOFN	Original filename	TOLY	Original lyricist/ text writer
TOPE	Original artist/ performer	TORY	Original release year
TOWN	File owner/licensee	TPE1 *artist	Lead performer Soloist
TPE2	Band/orchestra/ accompaniment	TPE3	Conductor/performer refinement
TPE4	Interpreted, remixed, or otherwise modified by	TPOS	Part of a set
TPUB	Publisher	TRCK *track	Track number/Position in set
TRDA	Recording dates	TRSN	Internet radio station name
TRSO	Internet radio station owner	TSIZ	Size
TSRC ISRC	International Standard Recording Code	TSSE	Software/Hardware and settings used for encoding
TYER *year	Year	WXXX	URL link frame

*Backward compatibility to IDv1 properties in Flash 6 player.

The two new ID3 terms are `Sound.id3.property` and `onID3`, (Built-in Classes > Media > Sound > Objects). Both terms are used with the Sound object using MP3 files. The new terms can be employed to provide the viewer more information about an MP3 file when it begins to be played.

To see how to use both the `id3` property and the `onID3` event handler, the following example uses three objects on the stage (the italicized word is the instance name).

- 1 button   *showIt*
- 1 input text field   *feature*
- 1 dynamic text field   *showFeature*

The whole movie can be done in two layers. Place the button and text field in the bottom layer and the code in the top layer. When you test the script, use the property names from Table 1.2 to examine the different elements of the MP3 file embedded in the ID3 tag (see Listing 1.3).

Listing 1.3 **ID3 Feature Display**

```
showIt.onPress = function() {
    coolBreeze_sound = new Sound();
    id3Feature = feature.text;
    coolBreeze_sound.onID3 = function() {
        showFeature.text = coolBreeze_sound.id3[id3Feature];
    };
    coolBreeze_sound.loadSound("chillyJazz.mp3", true);
};
```

Context Menu

The context menu appears when a menu-sensitive element is right-clicked (Control-clicked on the Mac) in a Flash movie. ActionScript 2.0 provides objects, properties, methods, and event handlers for context menus. The ContextMenu and ContextMenuItem classes are at the crux of the context menu usage in ActionScript 2.0. Table 1.3 provides a summary of the objects and their respective properties, methods, and event handlers.

Specialized context menus and their specified items can be added to any `MovieClip.menu`, `Button.menu` or `TextField.menu`. After instantiating a ContextMenu class, using the `customItems` array property, you can add different labels (captions) and callbacks to the menu that uses the ContextMenuItem class.

Table 1.3   **ContextMenu and ContextMenuItem Class Properties, Methods and Event Handlers**

ContextMenu	Description
new ContextMenu ([callBackFunction])	Constructor.
copy()	Copies the specified ContextMenu class.
hideBuiltInItems()	Hides the built-in items.
builtInItems	Object members corresponds to built-in menu items.
customItems	An undefined array containing ContextMenuItem classes.
onSelect	The callback handler called when the context menu object invoked.

ContextMenuItem	Description
new ContextMenuItem (caption, callBack, [separatorBefore,] [enabled,] [visible])	Constructor.
copy()	Copies the specified ContextMenuItem class.
caption	Provides a label for the menu item.
enabled	Boolean value that determines whether item is enabled or not.
separatorBefore	Boolean value that determines if a separator bar appear above the menu item.
visible	Boolean value that determines whether the item is visible or not.
onSelect	The callback handler called when the menu item is selected.

To see how to use the context menu terms, the following example uses a single movie clip with the instance name star_mc. Place a star-shaped movie clip in the middle of the stage, and in Frame 1, add the following script in Listing 1.4.

Listing 1.4   **Movie Clip Context Menu**

```
//Create Context Menu
var starMen_cm = new ContextMenu();
//Hide the built-in items in context menu
starMen_cm.hideBuiltInItems();
//Add custom items
starMen_cm.customItems.push(new ContextMenuItem("Left Corner", lefty));
starMen_cm.customItems.push(new ContextMenuItem("Right Corner", righty));
starMen_cm.customItems.push(new ContextMenuItem("Center", center));
```

continues

Listing 1.4 **Continued**

```
//Set up functions that fire with item selection
function lefty(obj:Object, item) {
    star_mc._x = 0;
    star_mc._y = 0;
}
function righty(obj:Object, item) {
    star_mc._x = 550;
    star_mc._y = 400;
}
function center(obj:Object, item) {
    star_mc._x = 165.2;
    star_mc._y = 90.5;
}
//Connect the menu to Object.menu
_level0.star_mc.menu = starMen_cm;
```

When you test the movie, place the cursor and right-click (Control-click on the Mac) on the movie clip object. As you can see in Figure 1.11, a context menu appears with the new items added in the script. Even though most of the built-in items are hidden because of the line `starMen_cm.hideBuiltInItems()`, in the script, the Settings and Debugger items remain. (The Debugger menu item will appear only if you have the debugger plug-in installed in your browser.)

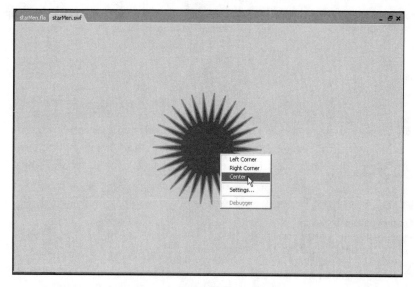

Figure 1.11 The customized menu items can be used to launch any function required.

TextField.StyleSheet

An important addition to ActionScript 2.0 is the TextField.StyleSheet built–in class. Using this new class, you can create a style sheet or even use a Cascading Style Sheet (CSS). The new class has five methods and a callback handler, as shown in Table 1.4.

Table 1.4   **TextField.StyleSheet Methods and Callback Handler**

Method	Description
getStyle(styleName)	Gets the named style (for example, "bodyText") and its property names and values.
getStyleNames()	Gets the array containing the style names.
load()	Begins loading CSS file into StyleSheet.
parseCSS(cssSheet)	Parses CSS in cssSheet and loads style sheet.
setStyle(name, style)	Inserts a new style with [name] and given characteristics [style].
Callback Handler	**Description**
onLoad	Used in conjunction with StyleSheet.load() indicating a successful load with a Boolean true.

The importance of using CSS style sheets is that they are standardized as part of the ECMA proposal, not only for HTML, but for XML and other ECMA languages. At this time, though, Flash supports only a subset of the full CSS set of formats. Table 1.5 shows the CSS formatting terms and acceptable values.

Table 1.5   **CSS Terms and Flash Values**

CSS Format	Flash Assignment and Values
text-align	Alignment to left, center, and right.
font-size	Use only numeric value. (Points/pixels work the same.)
text-decoration	Only values are none and underline.
margin-left	Use only numeric value. (Points/pixels work the same.)
margin-right	Use only numeric value. (Points/pixels work the same.)
font-weight	Recognized values are normal and bold.
font-style	Recognized values are normal and italic.
text-indent	Use only numeric value. (Points/pixels work the same.)
font-family	Mono, sans-serif, and serif are available. Mono is converted to _typewriter (courier-like), sans-serif is converted to _sans (Arial-like), and serif is converted to _serif (Times-like).
color	Use #hhhhhh hexadecimal values only. Names (for example, green) are not supported.
display	Only values are inline, block, and none.

To see how to integrate CSS with a Flash movie, first create a CSS file. Listing 1.5 uses a Flash-legal set of terms and associated values. (Save the file as dictStyle.css.)

Listing 1.5   **CSS Style Sheet**

```
.highLight {
        color: #983803;
        font-family: sans-serif;
        font-weight: bold;
        font-size: 11;
}
.bodyFont {
        margin-left: 9;
        font-family: serif;
        color: #000000;
        font-size: 12;
}
.header {
        color: #983803;
        text-align: center;
        font-weight: bold;
        font-size: 16;
        font-family: sans-serif;
}
```

To apply the CSS external style sheet, it must be loaded using the `TextField.StyleSheet.load("fileName.css")` method. So, first create an instance of the TextField.StyleSheet class, and then using the instance, use the `load()` method to set the style to the contents of the CSS file. To check to see if the CSS file loads successfully, you can use the `onLoad` event handler to create a function that passes a Boolean true if the file loads. In Listing 1.6, a small dynamic text field (instance name "loadMe") and a large dynamic text field (instance name "praise") serve to display whether the file loaded successfully and to display the CSS-formatted text on the screen.

Listing 1.6   **Applying CSS Style Sheet to Text**

```
//Create StyleSheet
var willStyleSheet = new TextField.StyleSheet();
willStyleSheet.onLoad = function(cssUp) {
    if (cssUp) {
        _level0.loadMe.text = "CSS is Up";
    } else {
        _level0.loadMe.text = "Load Error";
    }
};
```

```
praise.styleSheet = willStyleSheet;
var speech:String = '<p class=\"header\">Mark Antony on Making a Point</p>';
speech += '<p class=\"bodyFont\">';
speech += "<br>I am no orator, as Brutus is;\n";
speech += "But, as you know me all, a plain blunt man, \n";
speech += "That love my friend; and that they know full well \n";
speech += "That gave me public leave to speak of him:\n";
speech += "For I have neither wit, nor words, nor worth,\n";
speech += "Action, nor utterance, nor the power of speech,\n";
speech += 'To stir men\'s blood: I only speak <span class=\"highLight\"> right on;
➥</span>\n';
speech += "I tell you that which you yourselves do know;";
speech += "</p>";
praise.htmlText = speech;
willStyleSheet.load("dictStyle.css");
```

Figure 1.12 shows the output. Note the different fonts and font styles used in the output.

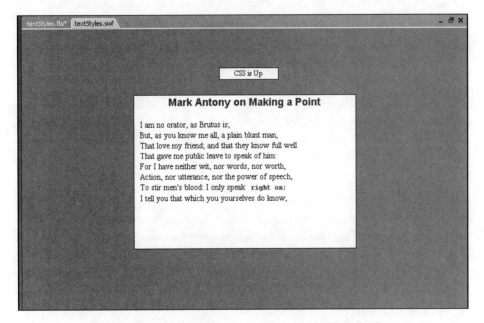

Figure 1.12   Text is formatted using an external CSS Style Sheet.

In addition to using external CSS style sheets, ActionScript 2.0 enables the user to employ the same style sheet characteristics using a special set of terms similar to those in Table 1.5. Table 1.6 shows the Flash inline terms used to assign CSS-like values to different text properties.

Table 1.6   **Flash CSS Inline Terms**

textAlign	fontSize	textDecoration	marginLeft
marginRight	fontWeight	fontStyle	textIndent
fontFamily	color	display	

To see how to employ the inline CSS terms, Listing 1.7 shows how to create a user-class and how to assign a value to a tag. Also, it illustrates how to use some of the other ActionScript 2.0 terms associated with the TextField.StyleSheet class.

Listing 1.7   **Inline Styles Applied to Text**

```
//Dynamic Example
var dynamicSheet = new TextField.StyleSheet();
dynamicSheet.setStyle("a:hover", {color:"#009966"});
dynamicSheet.setStyle(".noted", {fontFamily:'Verdana', fontSize:24,
fontWeight:'bold'});
createTextField("dreamField", 0, 200, 150, 200, 35);
dreamField.html = true;
dreamField.styleSheet = dynamicSheet;
dreamField.htmlText = "<p class='noted'><a
href='http://www.sandlight.com'>Sandlight</a></p>";
```

When you test the movie, you will see that a single word, "Sandlight," appears in the middle of the page. When you pass the mouse pointer over it, it turns from black to green, demonstrating the hover effect. The "noted" class is applied over the <a> tag style.

PrintJob Class

The PrintJob class is the central class for printing out dynamically generated materials, including databases and user-generated information. The class has a constructor and three methods shown in Table 1.7.

Table 1.7   **PrintJob Methods**

Method	Description
addPage()	Specifies the print target and optional print area, a bitmap Boolean, and frame number.
send()	Spooled pages sent to printer.
start()	Opens the OS's print dialog window and initiates spooling.

Of these three methods, only `addPage()` needs more than a little explanation. At its most simple use, a single parameter prints the entire current page. For example, the following script prints the entire page:

```
printNow_pj = new PrintJob();
printNow_.pj.addPage(0);
```

However, you can specify a movie clip as a target and further specify what area is to be printed. For example, in the PrintJob script below, the print area for the movie clip is

```
{xMin:0, xMax:225, yMin:0, yMax:200},
```

Those parameters outline the upper left print area beginning at 0,0 and the lower right at 225,200 of the target—not the page. The `addPage()` bitmap parameter is an option triggered by `{printAsBitmap:true}` that enables bitmap printing for those pages with bitmap graphics. If the option is not used, the default printing uses vector graphics.

Listing 1.8 shows how a user can enter dynamic information through UI Components (InputText and Radio Buttons), which is then displayed to the screen in a movie clip and printed out (see Figure 1.13):

Listing 1.8   **Printing Dynamic Data**

```
//Initialize Radio Buttons
la_rb.label = la_rb.data="Los Angeles";
ny_rb.label = ny_rb.data="New York";
at_rb.label = at_rb.data="Atlanta";
bf_rb.label = bf_rb.data="Bloomfield";
//Hide Print Button
purchase_btn._visible = false;
//Register
register_btn.onRelease = function() {
    //Generate Registration number
    var conNum:Number = Math.round(Math.random(1)*1000000);
    level0.ticketClip_mc.confirm.text = "Confirmation number: FL-AS2"+conNum;
    //Place information into MC that will be printed
    ticketClip_mc.ticket.text += name_ip.text+newline;
    ticketClip_mc.ticket.text += address_ip.text+newline;
    ticketClip_mc.ticket.text += CtStZp_ip.text+newline;
    ticketClip_mc.ticket.text += email_ip.text+newline;
    ticketClip_mc.ticket.text += "Location: "+radioGroup.selection.data;
    //Show Print Button
    purchase_btn._visible = true;
};
//Print
purchase_btn.onRelease = function() {
```

continues

Listing 1.8 **Continued**

```
ticketPrint_pj = new PrintJob();
var confirmRes = ticketPrint_pj.start();
confirmRes = ticketPrint_pj.addPage("ticketClip_mc", {xMin:0, xMax:225,
➥yMin:0, yMax:200}, {printAsBitmap:false}, 1);
ticketPrint_pj.send();
delete ticketPrint_pj;
};
```

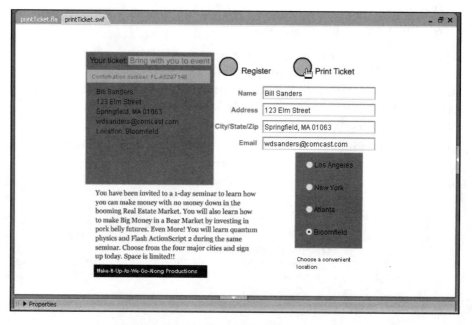

Figure 1.13   Text in a movie clip to be printed.

MovieClipLoader

The new MovieClipLoader class provides a new way of loading and "listening to" a movie being loaded. The MovieClipLoader is instantiated exactly like any other class using the new statement. As is the case with several of the new classes, a listener callback is used in conjunction with the class and related methods and properties. Table 1.8 shows the methods, properties, and listener callback functions used with the MovieClipLoader class.

Table 1.8 **MovieClipLoader Methods, Properties, and Listener Callback Functions**

Method	Description
loadClip(url,target)	Begins the process of loading an SWF file into the movie clip target.
unloadClip(target)	Terminates a current download.
getProgress(target)	Retrieves the current number of bytes loaded and total number of bytes.

Properties	Description
bytesLoaded	Returned object property of getProgress method of current number of bytes loaded.
bytesTotal	Returned object property of getProgress method of current number of bytes loaded.

Listener Callback Functions	Description
onLoadStart(target)	Called when download begins.
onLoadProgress(target,BL,BT)	Implemented as an alternative to getProgress method and can be used as single function for tracking bytes loaded (BL) and progress meters needing the total number of bytes (BT).
onLoadComplete(target)	Called when the download is finished.
onLoadInit(target)	Called when the download is complete *and* the actions in the first frame are complete.
onLoadError(target, errorCode)	Called when download fails or is terminated by unloadClip method.

To see how the MovieClipLoader class is instantiated and used to load an external movie into an existing movie clip, this next movie loads three different movies. As each movie is loaded, the listeners display the beginning and end of the load and the name of the loaded movie (see Listing 1.9).

Listing 1.9 **Loading a Movie Clip**

```
//Instantiate the MovieClipLoader
var mcLoader:MovieClipLoader = new MovieClipLoader();
var loadListner:Object = new Object();
//Listen for Start
loadListner.onLoadStart = function(movieClip) {
    _level0.loadInfo.text = "Begin";
};
loadListner.onLoadComplete = function(movieClip) {
    _level0.loadInfo.text += "--Complete " + launch;
};
mcLoader.addListener(loadListner);
```

continues

Listing 1.9   **Continued**

```
//Establish Functions for ComboBox
alpha = function () {
    mcLoader.loadClip("alpha.swf", loader_mc);
};
beta = function () {
    mcLoader.loadClip("beta.swf", loader_mc);
};
gamma = function () {
    mcLoader.loadClip("gamma.swf", loader_mc);
};
//Set up the ComboBox
var comboListener:Object = new Object();
chooseLoad_cb.addItem("Select One");
chooseLoad_cb.addItem("Alpha", "alpha");
chooseLoad_cb.addItem("Beta", "beta");
chooseLoad_cb.addItem("Gamma", "gamma");
comboListener.change = function(eventObj) {
    launch = chooseLoad_cb.selectedItem.data;
    if (launch == "alpha") {
        alpha();
    } else if (launch == "beta") {
        beta();
    } else if (launch == "gamma") {
        gamma();
    }
};
chooseLoad_cb.addEventListener("change", comboListener);
```

Figures 1.14 and 1.15 show how the different movies are loaded using the combo box UI component.

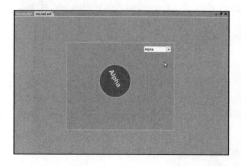 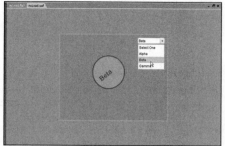

Figures 1.14 and 1.15   Different movie clips loaded into the screen.

Exceptions and the Error Class

In the Exceptions folder in the Actions panel, you will find the terms that are used with the Error class in ActionScript 2.0. The statements in the Exceptions folder are used in conjunction with the Error class instances. When an error occurs, an Error object is thrown using a `throw` statement. A `catch` statement is used to handle the error, typically with a statement specifying the error. A `try` statement looks for the error condition, and within the `try` block, the `throw` statement is initiated if the error condition is met. The `try` and `catch` statements are bound with a `finally` statement; thus, an exception is composed of three blocks. The `catch` statement contains an error argument, typically `e` or `error`. Within the `try...catch...finally` sequence, the `finally` block always executes whether the error condition is met or not.

The Error object is instantiated not with a variable, but with a message argument using the format

```
throw new Error("Error message");
```

within a `try` block.

The Error class has a single method and two properties, as shown in Table 1.9.

Table 1.9   **Error Method and Properties**

Method	Description
toString()	Transforms the Error object into a string.

Properties	Description
message	The error message associated with the error.
name	Exception type or name of error.

The Error class can be used to report built-in errors, such as the failure of an external file to load, or you can create user errors. In Listing 1.10, a new user error is created that traps numeric values under 65. It employs a UI List component for obtaining the data that will or will not create the error conditions. Two dynamic text fields display the data value (`data_txt`) and the error message, plus the ever-present value generated in the finally block (`errorMsg_txt`).

Listing 1.10   **Catching Defined Errors**

```
_global.style.setStyle("color", 0xa699e6);
_global.style.setStyle("highlightColor", 0xa6a6a6);
_global.style.setStyle("shadowColor", 0xa6a6a6);
```

continues

Listing 1.10 **Catching Defined Errors**

```
_global.style.setStyle("fontWeight", "bold");
//List box labels and data
errList_lb.addItem("Name", "Clark Kent");
errList_lb.addItem("Address", "123 Elm");
errList_lb.addItem("Age", 64);
errList_lb.addItem("Weight", 160);
//Create listener object
errorListen = new Object();
errorListen.change = function(eventObject) {
    errorMsg_txt.text = "";
    data_txt.text = errList_lb.selectedItem.data;
    var tester = errList_lb.selectedItem.data;
    //Exception
    try {
        //This next line is the custom error condition
        if (tester<=64 && typeof (tester) != "string") {
            throw new Error("Under the limit");
        }
    } catch (error) {
        if (error.message == "Under the limit") {
            errorMsg_txt.text = "Must 65 or older.";
        }
    } finally {
        errorMsg_txt.text += "Ok";
    }
};
errList_lb.addEventListener("change", errorListen);
```

Figure 1.16 shows how the error message is displayed, along with the "Ok" from the `finally` block:

Figure 1.16 The error throw is displayed in a text field.

Other New Terms in ActionScript 2.0

In addition to the new classes, ActionScript 2.0 has some other new key terms, some of which are associated with other classes. Each is reviewed briefly with examples and explanations. They are covered in the main dictionary but like the other new terms are given further attention here.

The following section examines the different classes with new properties, methods, or other features in no special order. They are discussed here because they are new in some fashion and constitute enhancements to existing classes.

Array Constants

Five new constants are associated with the Array class and are used in conjunction with `Array.sort()` and `Array.sortOn()` methods. The constants are all uppercase, and because ActionScript 2.0 is case-sensitive, this feature is important. The following provides a brief description of each.

- **CASEINSENSITIVE**. Ignores case sensitivity when sorting, so words beginning with lowercase letters are not all placed after words beginning with uppercase letters. For example, Listing 1.11 generates two sorts with different outcomes, depending on whether the CASEINSENSITIVE constant is employed:

Listing 1.11   **A Case Insensitive Sort**

```
var folks:Array = new Array();
folks.push("Jesse", "Bill", "Linda", "Jeff", "aYo")
trace("First: " + folks.sort())
var newOrder:Array = folks.sort(Array.CASEINSENSITIVE);
trace("Second: " + newOrder);
_lockroot property
```

The following output is generated:

```
First: Bill,Jeff,Jesse,Linda,aYo
Second: aYo,Bill,Jeff,Jesse,Linda
```

As can be seen, the second sort puts the names in correct alphabetical order because the case is ignored.

- **DESCENDING**. Basically, this is a backward sort. The highest value is placed first and the lowest last. You can use the constants with `Array.sortOn()` as well, as Listing 1.12 shows:

Listing 1.12   **Sorting in Descending Order**

```
var cowPokes:Array = new Array();
cowPokes.push({name:"Wild Bill Hitchcock", classify:"Lawman"});
cowPokes.push({name:"Billy the Kid", classify:"Outlaw"});
cowPokes.push({name:"Wyatt Earpp", classify:"Lawman"});
```

continues

Listing 1.12 **Continued**

```
cowPokes.push({name:"Jesse James", classify:"Outlaw"});
cowPokes.push({name:"Sundance Kid", classify:"Outlaw"});
var cowboy:Array = cowPokes.sortOn ("name",Array.DESCENDING);
for (x=0; x<cowboy.length; x++) {
trace(cowboy[x]["name"]);
}
```

The script generates the following output:

```
Wyatt Earpp
Wild Bill Hitchcock
Sundance Kid
Jesse James
Billy the Kid
```

Note that in using a constant with `Array.sortOn()` that the field name precedes the constant.

```
var cowboy = cowPokes.sortOn ("name",Array.DESCENDING);
```

- **NUMERIC.** The numeric sort is designed for sorting when numbers are being compared, but if numbers are not in the array, string comparisons are used.

- **RETURNINDEXEDARRAY.** This constant keeps the array in unsorted order but returns the index value of each element in the position it will be in when sorted. For example, the following script

```
var folks:Array = new Array();
folks.push("Jesse", "Bill", "Linda", "Jeff", "aYo")
trace(folks.sort(Array.RETURNINDEXEDARRAY));
```

would display the following in the Output panel:

```
1,3,0,2,4
```

using a case-sensitive sort.

Keeping in mind that "aYo" begins with a lowercase letter and will be last in a sorted list where all the other names begin with an uppercase letter, you can see how this index works. The following shows the sorted list of names with the original index value next to each name:

Bill	[1]
Jeff	[3]
Jesse	[0]
Linda	[2]
aYo	[4]

- **UNIQUESORT.** Every element in the array must be unique or an error is thrown. For example, if you have an array with the elements Jones, Smith, Jones, Allen, Johnson, and use the UNIQUESORT constant, instead of getting a sorted output, a 0 is returned.

_lockroot

When using several levels created by having multiple movie clips, it can be easy to make a call to the root level, forgetting that the root may be several levels up. To make life easier, especially when loading SWF files into movie clips using MovieClipLoader class, use _lockroot. To keep the root level where you want it, you can use the new _lockroot property. For example, if the following were put into the first frame of a movie and then loaded into another movie, the root target would be the movie that was loaded, not the movie into which it is loaded:

```
this._lockroot = true;
if (x == undefined || x>80) {
        var x:Number = 0;
}
x++;
_root.cool_mc._alpha = x+20;
_root.cool_mc._rotation = x;
```

To test the use of _lockroot, create a movie with two frames with a movie clip with the instance name "cool_mc" that can be seen to rotate—a simple line is fine. Test it using the above script so that you can see the movie clip in the movie rotate and change alpha levels. Then load the movie into another movie using MovieClipLoader. You should see the same actions. Then comment out the first line as shown:

```
//this._lockroot = true;
```

Now try it again. Without the _lockroot statement, neither the change in rotation nor the alpha level operate correctly when the movie is loaded into another movie clip.

MouseWheel

The addition of a mouse wheel event handler provides a mechanism to build movies that recognize and use the input from a mouse wheel. The onMouseWheel event handler recognizes changes in the mouse wheel position. The amount and direction (positive or negative) of the mouse wheel value can be passed to a function and captured in the function argument. The following script shows how a movie clip object on the stage can be moved left and right using the script:

```
wheelMover = new Object();
wheelMover.onMouseWheel = function(mover) {
        bar_mc._x += mover;
};
Mouse.addListener(wheelMover);
```

In addition to the event handler, the TextField class includes a new property, mouseWheelEnabled. The line

```
someTextField.mouseWheelEnabled=true;
```

will enable the scroll bar to move when the mouse wheel is turned.

Movie Clip Depths

Two new movie clip methods are getNextHighestDepth() and getInstanceAtDepth(). The former method is employed to find what the next highest depth is for a loading movie clip. If no movie clip has been loaded, the next depth is 0. As each new movie clip is loaded, the depth increases by 1. The latter method, expressed as movieClipName.getInstanceAtDepth(), finds the name of the movie clip loaded at the specified depth. To see how the methods work, Listing 1.13 has a single movie clip on the stage with the instance name pinkie_mc and movie clips in the Library panel with the linkage names grayguy and greenie.

Listing 1.13   **Dynamically Changing Movie Clip Depths**

```
depth1_btn.onPress = function() {
    var someDepth = pinkie_mc.getNextHighestDepth();
    pinkie_mc.attachMovie("grayguy", "grayguyUp", someDepth);
    first_txt.text = pinkie_mc.getInstanceAtDepth(someDepth);
    trace(someDepth);
};
depth2_btn.onPress = function() {
    var someDepth = pinkie_mc.getNextHighestDepth();
    pinkie_mc.attachMovie("greenie", "greenieUp", someDepth)._x = -20;
    second_txt.text = pinkie_mc.getInstanceAtDepth(someDepth);
    trace(someDepth);
};
```

Figure 1.17 shows the results of pressing the top and bottom buttons several times. Each time the buttons are pressed, the depth increases by one, and the two movie clips loaded from the Library take turns overlapping each other.

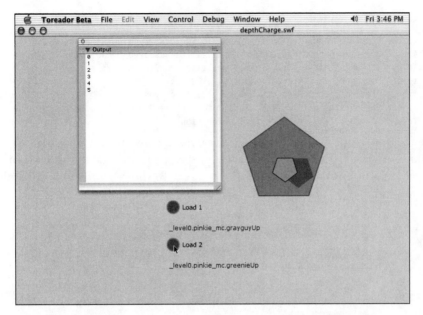

Figure 1.17   The Output panel shows the increasing depths each time the functions are fired.

Getting the Player Version

Another new movie clip method is `getSWFVersion`. It returns an integer with the player version (for example, 5, 6, or 7) the SWF was published as. For instance,

```
trace(_root.getSWFVersion());
```

shows the version of the SWF file in the Output panel.

Added System Capabilities Properties

Flash MX introduced `System.capabilities` to the ActionScript lexicon, and the new properties in ActionScript 2.0 primarily add to those capabilities. Like the original, many return a Boolean value. In Listing 1.14, six of the nine properties displayed have Boolean values.

Listing 1.14   **System Capabilities Displayed**

```
trace("Printing: "+System.capabilities.hasPrinting);
trace("Screen playback: "+System.capabilities.hasScreenPlayback);
```

continues

Listing 1.14   **Continued**

```
trace("Streaming audio: "+System.capabilities.hasStreamingAudio);
trace("Screen Broadcast: "+System.capabilities.hasScreenBroadcast);
trace("Streaming video: "+System.capabilities.hasStreamingVideo);
trace("Debugger: "+System.capabilities.isDebugger);
trace("Player type: "+System.capabilities.playerType);
trace("Server string: "+System.capabilities.serverString);
trace("Version: "+System.capabilities.version);
```

In addition to the Boolean values, `playerType` and `version` return fairly terse values. However, the new `serverString` property specifies values for each of the capabilities in URL-encoded format. Figure 1.18 shows all the output for the above script:

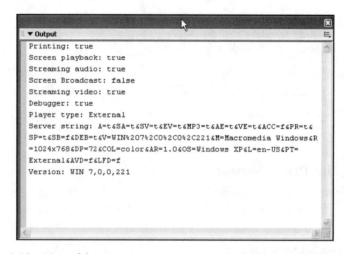

Figure 1.18   Most of the new `System.capabilities` properties are Boolean values.

Another new property added to the System class is `useCodePage`. This property is assigned a Boolean value to determine whether the system uses Unicode or the operating system's code page. The default setting is *not* to use Unicode, and so if you want to use Unicode, use the following script:

```
System.useCodepage=true;
```

The property is treated separately because it is not part of the properties belonging to the `System.capabilities`.

New System Methods

Two new System methods have been introduced in ActionScript 2.0. First, `System.security.allowDomain()` provides a way to override the default security system that disallows inter-domain scripting. For example, if your domain is www.domainAlpha.com and you have an SWF file in www.domainBeta.com, you can allow access so that you can load the movie in www.domainBeta.com using the line

```
System.security.allowDomain("domainBeta.com")
```

You can also use the formats "`http://domain`" or "`http://ip address`."

A second new System method, the `showSettings()` method, allows access to the different Macromedia Flash Player Settings for privacy, local storage, microphone, and camera. You can set your script to call one of the specific settings, as illustrated in Listing 1.15:

Listing 1.15   **Viewing System Settings**

```
//Privacy=0
priv_btn.onPress = function() {
     System.showSettings(0);
};
//Local Storage=1
store_btn.onPress = function() {
     System.showSettings(1);
};
//Microphone=2
mic_btn.onPress = function() {
     System.showSettings(2);
};
//Camera=3
cam_btn.onPress = function() {
     System.showSettings(3);
};
```

Each of the different settings is addressed by a value from 0 to 3 as indicated in the script. Figure 1.19 shows the setting shown when the Camera button is pressed.

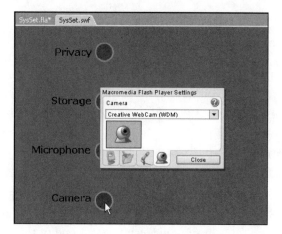

Figure 1.19 Each of the four different Macromedia Flash Player
Settings can be displayed with the `showSettings()` method.

Adding and Changing HTTP Request Headers

Both the LoadVars and XML classes have a new method, `addRequestHeader()`.
Using an instance of either class, you can add or change HTTP request headers. The method accepts two arguments: a header name and a header value
associated with the header name. For example,

```
var Loadie_0 = new LoadVars();
Loadie_0.addRequestHeader("Content-Type", "'Special'");
```

would specify "Content-Type" in the HTTP header with the value "Special."
The XML class uses identical formatting with the LoadVars class.

All the new terms discussed in this section apply to existing classes. In the next
section, ActionScript 2.0 has been applied to UI components as well; however,
you will see that ActionScript 2.0 usage with UI components is very different
from Flash MX.

UI Components and ActionScript 2.0

ActionScript 2.0 has several new terms and changes in addressing UI components. Also, several new UI component classes have their own ActionScript 2.0
methods, properties, and event handlers, and many of the old UI components
have changed the ActionScript associated with their class as well. Rather than

attempting to examine all the terms associated with all the UI components, this section will focus on key new ActionScript 2.0 ways of dealing with UI components.

Styling UI Components

One of the major changes in ActionScript 2.0 in dealing with components is how they are styled, especially on a global level. Each of the UI components can be considered a class, and so global styles are assigned to the class. You can now assign a class style sheet for any class of component. Using the format

```
var comStyleSheetName = _global.styles.UIComponent=new
mx.styles.CSSStyleDeclaration();
```

you set the style sheet for the class. Table 1.10 shows the UI component class names that you can assign.

Table 1.10   **Component Coding Names**

Alert	Button	CheckBox	ComboBox	DataGrid
Label	List	Menu	NumericStepper	ProgressBar
RadioButton	ScrollPane	TextArea	TextInput	Tree
Window				

Listing 1.16 shows examples of scripting the Button, CheckBox, and ComboBox classes:

Listing 1.16   **CSS Styling Buttons**

```
//Button Styles
var btnStyle = _global.styles.Button=new mx.styles.CSSStyleDeclaration();
btnStyle.color = 0xBF3F00;
btnStyle.fontFamily = "Verdana";
btnStyle.fontWeight = "bold";
//Check Box Styles
var ckBxStyle = _global.styles.CheckBox=new mx.styles.CSSStyleDeclaration();
ckBxStyle.color = 0xA8C2B5;
ckBxStyle.fontFamily = "Georgia";
ckBxStyle.fontWeight = "bold";
//Combo Box Styles
comBx_cb.addItem("Alpha");
comBx_cb.addItem("Beta");
comBx_cb.addItem("Gamma");
var comBxStyle = _global.styles.ComboBox=new mx.styles.CSSStyleDeclaration();
comBxStyle.color = 0xBF3F00;
```

continues

Listing 1.16 **Continued**

```
comBxStyle.backgroundColor = 0xA8C2B5;
comBxStyle.background = 0xD4BBA1;
comBxStyle.fontFamily = "Courier";
comBxStyle.fontWeight = "bold";
```

Individual Style Settings

The ActionScript 2.0 for individual component styling is little changed from ActionScript 1.0. However, you will find a few changes. ActionScript 1.0 used the method

```
componentInName.setStyleProperty(styleProp, value);
```

However, ActionScript 2.0 uses

```
componentInName.setStyle(styleProp, value);
```

The difference is small, but small differences are the kinds that cause the most trouble because they are so difficult to detect. The following script shows how color and background color in a TextArea UI component are changed.

```
write_txt.text = "Nothing is perfect, and so nothing can be perfectly imperfect.";
write_txt.setStyle("color", 0xdddd00);
write_txt.setStyle("backgroundColor", 0xaa0000);
```

As can be seen, the difference is quite small. In the above example, the text colored is that assigned to the instance of the TextArea class, whereas in most other UI components the colored text is its label.

Styles Supported in ActionScript 2.0

The UI component style properties in ActionScript 2.0 have followed the general CSS style format adopted in other ActionScript 2.0 style properties. For example, instead of using the following line to set text color

```
light_btn.setStyleProperty("textColor", 0xdd00dd);
```

as is done in ActionScript 1.0, the line

```
light_btn.setStyle ("color", 0xdd00dd);
```

uses the color property, a term familiar to CSS users. Table 1.11 shows the complete set of UI component styles supported in ActionScript 2.0.

Table 1.11   **ActionScript 2.0 Component Style Names**

backgroundColor	component's background color
borderColor	3-D border's black section or 2-D section's color
borderStyle	*none, inset, outset,* or *solid* are recognized styles
buttonColor	3-D section and button face color
color	text color
disabledColor	color when text disabled
fontFamily	font family name, in quotes (for example, "Verdana," "Georgia")
fontSize	numeric value only for font size—no unit of measure (for example, pt or px)
fontStyle	*italic* or *normal* are recognized styles
fontWeight	*bold* or *normal* are recognized styles
highlightColor	three-dimensional border section
marginLeft	a numeric value only for left margin—no unit of measure (for example, pt or px)
marginRight	a numeric value only for right margin—no unit of measure (for example, pt or px)
scrollTrackColor	track color in a scrollbar
shadowColor	3-D border section
symbolBackgroundColor	radio button or check box background color
symbolBackgroundDisabledColor	radio button or check box background color when disabled
symbolBackgroundPressedColor	radio button or check box background color when pressed
symbolColor	color of radio button dot or check box check
symbolDisabledColor	disabled color of radio button or check box
textAlign	*left, right,* or *center* are acceptable values
textDecoration	*none* or *underline* are acceptable values
textIndent	a numeric value only for text indent—no unit of measure (for example, em, pt or px)

Making the Transition

The two primary areas of significant change between ActionScript 1.0 and ActionScript 2.0 can be found in the use of classes and CSS-like style terminology. This shift reflects the maturation of ActionScript into an ECMAScript 4-compliant language. As an object-oriented language, ActionScript now has the framework for building structures using encapsulated code, inheritance, and polymorphism.

This newest version of Flash, besides introducing ActionScript 2.0, can be used in interaction with other languages, primarily JavaScript, to create other structures that interact with ActionScript 2.0. See Article 4, "Creating Hybrid Flash Applications (HTML, JavaScript, and Flash)" by aYo Binitie on using Flash with multiple languages.

In this article, we have seen that although ActionScript 2.0 has different features and tools than ActionScript 1.0, the differences can be broken down into a few simple categories. First, we have the new tools like the Actions panel without the normal mode, the Integrated Script window (Flash Professional Only), and the Behaviors panel. Second, a few new classes have been added, and instead of using the `prototype` function, you can now create and reference classes in true object-oriented programming style. Third, some new features have been added to the existing classes you were familiar with from Flash MX. Finally, the UI components use ActionScirpt in their styling.

To help guide you through the transition, we have focused on the new features in ActionScript 2.0. And, for your convenience, all the scripts in this article are available online at `www.sandlight.com`; you can freely download them from there. I think you'll find that ActionScript 2.0 contains a number of welcomed changes to make your Flash creations even better.

Article 2

The Power of Style: Writing Clean Code

by Jeremy Brown

Code that only you can understand does not make you an advanced coder; code that your grandmother can understand does!

Jeremy Brown—www.j3r.com

Programming with Good Style

With the release of Flash MX 2004, one may feel overwhelmed with the vast amount of new information that needs to be absorbed. Whether we are professional programmers or designers trying to get a simple script to work, it is useful to take a step back and look at the most basic way to improve our abilities. I would like you to take a deep breath, relax, and read about a gem that I call programming style.

Back to Basics

There is currently a strong focus in the Flash community on object-oriented programming and other advanced programming methodologies. Before learning these advanced concepts, it is important to make sure that we first understand the fundamentals that these concepts build on, so as not to drown in the ocean before we have bothered learning to swim. Programming fundamentals are often ignored because of a lack of available information, thereby leaving programmers with many technical examples but no real understanding of the underlying fundamental concepts. For example, we are told to use certain syntax with no explanation as to why it is beneficial. Without any real rationale, we find that we have been coding for years without using simple fundamentals to make our work easier.

The most powerful and advantageous step I took in my development as a programmer was when I looked closely at *how* I program. By examining how I program, I learned that the written style of my code had a direct impact on the quality of my code. By studying my own coding habits, I realized that coding style, the *way we write code*, is one of the most valuable, yet sadly overlooked aspects of programming. Unlike traditional arts in which style defines the artists' work (often by breaking away from the mainstream), we programmers want to develop our style to conform to a common, recognizable standard. By focusing on readability, organization, and simplicity, we create code that is always familiar in style and easy to work with.

The importance of good style is usually realized over time; hence, this article can be seen as a shortcut that will help you avoid the pitfalls of poor coding and place you on the right path. Even if you are an experienced programmer and are familiar with many of the following ideas, analysis of coding style should be a regular practice, and I hope this article will serve as a reminder to take a step back and spend a little time on your coding style.

Style as Part of Our Programming Thought Process

The examination of style is not the analysis of any particular implementation or technique. Formulating a unique coding style requires a thought process that takes place when writing code. Instead of thinking in terms of conventions, standards, and rules, which tends to make life feel rather stiff, we can approach this subject simply as a means of improving our style. Just as we choose what clothes to wear in the morning and how to comb our hair, it will be up to each individual in the end to choose how to fashion his or her code. It is not important that we all have the exact same coding style, but it is essential that we develop a clean and consistent style that is easy to understand.

By using prefixes, thoughtful naming, useful comments, and white space, our code will become self-documented. Self-documented code means that the actual code has a high level of readability. Any nonprofessional should be able to read our code and get a feeling for what it does, even if they have no programming background. This may sound like a lofty goal, but if we keep this thought in the back of our minds, the result will be significant.

As an example, when I am coding, I often pretend that I will have to explain my code to my grandmother at the end of each day. This may sound ridiculous, but it keeps me focused on making my code as clear as possible. To test code for readability, it is useful to have other programmers review our code and point out parts that they have trouble understanding. For the ultimate test of self-documentation, we can try explaining our code to people who do not know anything about programming. Often in this process, we realize which sections of code need work due to our inability to explain them.

From Knowledge to Understanding

There is an enormous difference between knowledge and understanding. A musician can become well versed in music theory by reading a few books and committing the knowledge to memory. However, without picking up an instrument and applying this knowledge, the musician's performance will not improve. By applying theoretical knowledge when playing, the theory will transcend the musician's conscious mind and become part of the subconscious and be incorporated into motor skills and hearing. This transformation is one of knowledge into understanding.

In this same way, programmers must practice to transform theoretical knowledge into understanding. If you apply the following ideas to your code, you will not only have more readable, portable, and reliable code, but you will gain a better understanding of programming in general. You will also spend much less time debugging!

Coding Conventions: Setting Our Own Standards

Whether we are just getting started with programming or have been coding for some time, the topic of coding conventions may never be encountered, or perhaps the idea is tossed aside and deemed unnecessary. I remember that when I was first introduced to coding conventions, they seemed redundant—something that would slow me down and complicate things. On the contrary, after forcing them into my work, I have found using them to be one of the most valuable assets for simplification, clarity, and speed of production.

I feel that in any art (as I consider programming to be an art), the basics are the most important aspect to master. Just as martial arts students will never perform black belt moves with grace if they have not mastered the white belt requirements, programmers will have great difficulty when programming complex applications if they do not have a firm grasp of the fundamentals. After learning the syntax of a programming language, it is beneficial to focus on our style of coding before jumping directly into advanced programming methodologies. Focusing on how to style our code will help us gain a better understanding of programming and prepare us for more advanced topics. The idea of coding conventions traditionally refers to using a naming convention, so we will begin by looking at the use of prefixes and suffixes.

Coding style, the theme of this article, is really an extension of coding conventions. Coding style includes naming conventions and goes a step further by examining the aesthetics of coding beyond the actual *working code*. After examining naming conventions, we will move on to these other aspects of style.

Setting Your Own Standards

Coding conventions, or naming conventions, are one of the fundamentals of good programming style. The word "convention" in this context can be replaced with "standard." Using a coding standard simply means that we make some decisions about how we write code. For example, we may decide that we will always use prefixes or suffixes in variable names to help us understand them better or that we will always begin method names with a verb to symbolize that they represent the behavior of objects.

We want to make comprehensive decisions about our coding style so that our work is consistent and uniform. A standard within one project will help keep things under control in that project; a standard that is consistent in all our projects will make reuse of code much easier. Sometimes when freelancing or working with a team, we will have to break away from our own standard and code in the "style" or standard of the head developer or according to a company guideline. This type of situation is inevitable, but it will not present a problem if we understand the importance of standards, have fine-tuned our own standard, and feel comfortable using it. By establishing a comfort level within our own standard, we will easily be able to adopt and understand standards of other programmers when we need to.

The First Step: Prefixes or Suffixes

The first and most basic step we can take to improve our coding style is to use prefixes or suffixes. In addition to the fact that this will enable code hinting in

Flash, it will also improve our understanding of data types and help us catch errors before they happen.

In Flash, we can take a variable of any type and change it to another type. For example, in Listing 2.1 we take a variable of type `Number` and change it to a variable of type `String`.

Listing 2.1   **Lacking a Prefix, We Are Not Reminded of the Data Type**

```
// there is no prefix in the name of the variable to indicate its data type
var age = 28;

// 100 lines later in the code the variable's data type is changed to String;
age = "29";
```

This code is legal in Flash as far as the compiler is concerned. Whether the data type change was on purpose or accidental, it is best to avoid changing a data type in this manner, as doing so causes uncertainty in our code. What would happen now if we were to perform a calculation with the age variable?

To remind ourselves of what type of data we are working with and to gain a better understanding of data types, we can add a prefix to our variable names. Let's use the prefix "num" for `Number` types and try this example again in Listing 2.2.

Listing 2.2   **Using a Prefix, We Are Reminded of the Data Type**

```
// there is a prefix in the name of the variable indicating its data type;
var numAge = 28;

// 100 lines later in the code we are reminded of the data type;
numAge =  29;
```

The difference in Listing 2.2 is that the prefix "num" reminds us of the variable's data type. In Listing 2.1 we change the variable "age" from a `Number` type to a `String` type, which will most certainly cause problems in our hypothetical program. In Listing 2.2 we change the variable "numAge" from a `Number` type to another `Number` type because we are reminded by the prefix that we are working with a `Number` type. It may seem like this mistake would never happen, but believe me, it happens *all the time*. By adding prefixes to our variable names, we gain a better understanding of data types, and we become more conscious of what we are doing when we code.

Strong typing, which we will cover next, can be used to *prevent* the changing of data types. Even though strong typing is an established practice whereas naming conventions is a controversial subject, prefixes are introduced first in this article because they are a familiar practice from Flash MX, and they are also a relevant element of coding style. By first examining the importance of knowing about data types, then the advantages of using prefixes, and finally the advantages of using strong typing, I felt it would be easier to follow the logic behind these practices.

However, now that ActionScript supports strong typing, we have a dilemma. In Flash MX, the use of prefixes was the only way to get code hints, and it was also the only reminder we had if we wanted our variables to stay the same type. In Flash MX 2004, strong typing solves both of these problems, so we are left wondering whether we should continue using prefixes at all.

Some programmers frown on the use of prefixes in strongly typed object-oriented languages that keep track of type information automatically. For one reason, strongly typing a variable prevents its type from being changed, which makes prefixes seem redundant. Another reason is that in a totally object-oriented environment, all variables hold *references* to objects, and it should be the responsibility of the object to know its type, not the variable, because the variable is just a logical reference used to manipulate the object.

To add to the confusion about whether to use prefixes, strong typing is optional in ActionScript. If we use prefixes without strong typing as is done in Listing 2.2, a variable's type might *still* be accidentally changed, and the name will then be even more misleading than if there was no prefix at all. This was a problem in Flash MX; there was no *real* way to prevent type mismatch errors. It is important to remember that prefixes are only a cosmetic reminder, whereas strong typing is an active prevention. Now that we have strong typing, I recommend using both. Prefixes improve our understanding and awareness, and strong typing prevents errors. We will now examine how to use strong typing to prevent type changes and then explore the practice of combining strong typing with prefixes.

Using Strong Typing to Catch Type Mismatch Errors

Strong typing is now a part of the ActionScript 2.0 language. If we use strong typing, the compiler will give mismatch errors when we try to change a data type. By using strong typing, we are also provided with code hints without the need for prefixes or suffixes. This is very different from how things worked in Flash MX, where we *needed* prefixes or suffixes to enable code hinting. On one hand, this is a blessing because the compiler protects us from making type mismatch errors; on the other hand, it may lead us to believe that using prefixes or suffixes is no longer useful. In Listing 2.3 we use strong typing without prefixes.

Listing 2.3   **Relying on the Compiler: Strong Typing Without Prefixes**

```
// relying on strong typing to catch errors
var age:Number = 28;

// 100 lines later the variable name does not remind us of the data type
age = "29";
```

This code gives us an error when we test our movie because we strongly typed the age variable as a type `Number`, and the compiler will not let us assign a different data type later in our code. The problem in this example is that this code is blindly relying on the compiler. Even when using strong typing, it is still beneficial to use a prefix to remind us of the data type as is done in Listing 2.4.

Listing 2.4   **Best Practice: Strong Typing with Prefixes**

```
// best practice because we use a prefix together with strong typing;
var numAge:Number = 28;

// 100 lines later in the code we are reminded of the data type;
numAge = 29;
```

This way, we will catch our mistakes *before* testing our program because we are reminded of the data type based on the prefix. At the same time, because the variable is strongly typed, it will be impossible to change the data type, so there is no risk that the prefix will become misleading, which could happen if we *only* used prefixes as was done in Listing 2.2.

You may be asking yourself why the prefix is needed at all, as long as the compiler catches the mistake. It matters because by using the prefix, we force ourselves to take responsibility. By taking responsibility, our coding becomes more reflective; we gain a deeper mental connection with our code, which results in a deeper level of understanding.

How to Get Started with Prefixes or Suffixes

If these ideas seem totally unimportant or abstract, don't worry; it takes some real use to understand why they are valuable. If you do not use prefixes and strong typing already, I recommend that you start taking advantage of the benefits they provide. You will gain a better understanding of your code and most likely have far fewer bugs!

Feel free to make up your own prefixes or suffixes. I like prefixes better, but this is just a personal preference. You can change the ActionScript hinting that Flash uses by editing the AsCodeHints.xml file on your computer. For more information on how to do this, refer to Listing 2.5.

Listing 2.5   **ActionScript Hinting**

You can change the ActionScript hinting that Flash uses by editing this file:

```
PC:
C:\Documents and Settings\USERNAME\Local Settings\Application
Data\Macromedia\Flash MX 2004\en\Configuration\ActionsPanel\AsCodeHints.xml

Mac:
~/Users/USERNAME/Library/Application Support/Macromedia/Flash
2004/en/Configuration/Actions Panel/AsCodeHints.xml
```

Be sure to replace USERNAME with your own username. I have edited my code hints to look like this:

```
<typeinfo pattern="mc*" object="MovieClip" />
<typeinfo pattern="array*" object="Array" />
<typeinfo pattern="str*" object="String" />
<typeinfo pattern="num*" object="Number" />
<typeinfo pattern="btn*" object="Button" />
<typeinfo pattern="txt*" object="TextField" />
<typeinfo pattern="fmt*" object="TextFormat" />
<typeinfo pattern="date*" object="Date" />
<typeinfo pattern="sound*" object="Sound" />
<typeinfo pattern="xml*" object="XML" />
<typeinfo pattern="xmlnode*" object="XMLNode" />
<typeinfo pattern="xmlsocket*" object="XMLSocket" />
<typeinfo pattern="color*" object="Color" />
<typeinfo pattern="cm*" object="ContextMenu" />
<typeinfo pattern="cmi*" object="ContextMenuItem" />
<typeinfo pattern="pj*" object="PrintJob" />
<typeinfo pattern="mcl*" object="MovieClipLoader" />
<typeinfo pattern="err*" object="Error" />
<typeinfo pattern="cam*" object="Camera"/>
<typeinfo pattern="lv*" object="LoadVars" />
<typeinfo pattern="lc*" object="LocalConnection"/>
<typeinfo pattern="mic*" object="Microphone"/>
<typeinfo pattern="nc*" object="NetConnection"/>
<typeinfo pattern="ns*" object="NetStream"/>
<typeinfo pattern="so*" object="SharedObject"/>
<typeinfo pattern="video*" object="Video"/>
<typeinfo pattern="_level*" object="MovieClip" />
<typeinfo pattern="_parent" object="MovieClip" />
<typeinfo pattern="_root" object="MovieClip" />
```

The position of the asterisk determines the usage of prefixes or suffixes. Keep in mind that you can add prefixes or suffixes for types that are not in this list; for example, "num" is not present by default. Using prefixes or suffixes together with strong typing is the first step toward gaining a better understanding of our code, improving our style, and preventing type mismatch errors. In the next section, we will examine how we can make our code more readable and easier to maintain.

Readability: Understanding Our Code

Coding with good style involves discipline. We have to force ourselves at first to abide by self-imposed rules and restrictions in order to improve. It is important to keep in mind that the point of this work is to make our lives easier. It is sometimes hard to believe that rules and restrictions will make things easier, and for this reason, we often come up with rationalizations for not working on our coding style. Before examining how to make our code self-documenting, we will look at some of these rationalizations, and hopefully you will decide in the end that working on your coding style is a worthwhile effort.

A Battle Against Carelessness

Well-styled code has a clean appearance—it is easy to read, comprehend, reuse, and modify. Poorly-styled code is sloppy, cryptic, and often impossible to reuse or maintain. The main reason poorly-styled code finds its way into our programs is carelessness. Perhaps we feel stressed, so we pump out code as fast as we can, hoping that we will save time. In reality, if we take it easy and write our code with good style, we save much more time because the result of our efforts is a program built with nails of titanium, as opposed to a program held together by tape and glue.

Before handing you a box of titanium nails and a nail gun, let's look at some common reasons that people build programs with tape and glue.

Lack of Knowledge

Lack of knowledge is, perhaps, the most acceptable excuse. If we are new to Flash, it is difficult to appreciate the importance of making our code understandable right from the start. We may start using Flash with the goal of accomplishing a set task as fast as possible, using code as a means to an end. Perhaps we just want to set up a simple personal web page to show our friends. The ad hoc approach is a natural way to learn something new and is fine if we are just dabbling in the realm. However, Flash is an addictive creature; that first web page may inspire us to take a shot at re-creating a favorite childhood game, or perhaps that personal page leads to a job offer, and suddenly we are working professionally. If we take this step from casual play to serious programming, it is a good idea to start examining our coding style.

A Waste of Time

Sometimes an informal or improvised approach is faster, but this is only true on the smallest projects. Creating a simple banner ad is not an involved project, and the speed advantage of just hacking it together will probably not have a drastic effect on the project. However, if our client asks us to turn that banner ad into a banner game, the complexity suddenly rises. When the level of complexity rises, having good style will speed our programming up tremendously. It may take a little bit longer to code with good style, but we will spend much less time hunting bugs.

My Flash File Is So Advanced that I Hardly Understand It Myself

If we open up an old Flash project and do not understand our code because it is written with poor style, then there is no point in saving any project that we work on. If we code with good style, we are able to reuse old code easily. Sometimes our lack of understanding of code is caused by trying to program far beyond our level, but more commonly our difficulties with programming are a result of sloppy coding style.

Admitting the limitations of the human brain is imperative to becoming a good programmer. We are only fooling ourselves if we believe that we can retain a medium-sized system in our heads. There is no shame in using a clean programming style as a crutch for the brain's limited capacity. We have examined the use of prefixes to remind ourselves of data types, and we will shortly examine other techniques to improve readability, organization, and simplification.

Programming Bugs

Sometimes there are bugs in software, but most of the time, bugs are a result of programming errors, not the programming environment. Writing with poor style and then blaming Flash for the bugs is just a way to rationalize poor style. If we want to improve our debugging ability by two hundred percent, we need only admit to ourselves that we are not perfect and that there is a ninety-nine percent chance the bug is in our code. Even if we are positive that a bug in Flash is causing problems, it is essential to remember that an important part of programming is figuring things out anyway! The ability to think outside the box and create a workaround to a problem is vital.

Intentional Sloppiness

This is the most inexcusable reason of them all. If we intentionally make our code impossible for others to understand in an attempt to appear advanced, to hold onto our job, or to avoid sharing our ideas and techniques, we are only hurting ourselves. The following paragraph describes some reasons why.

If we code in an obscure manner in an attempt to appear advanced or to hold onto our job, eventually people will realize that the reason no one else can work on "that crazy project" is not that our code is so sophisticated, but that it is so cryptic and sloppy. Do not confuse sloppy or confusing with advanced— no one else does. Eventually this type of code will catch up to us and damage our professional image. In my time as a professional, I have worked on complex code that is completely understandable at first glance, and I have run into simple code that is so cryptic I cannot even guess what the programmer's intentions were. The former is preferable in every way; the latter merely points out an obvious lack of work ethics and is a good way to lose your job. If you decide to share your files as open source, then props to you for contributing to the flash community. Just be sure to make your shared code understandable, or you defeat the purpose entirely. If you have never shared your code as open source, I suggest trying it. When I first started making my code public, I was anxious about potential criticism as well as the idea of losing my precious tricks and secrets. I realized quickly that making code public is one of the best ways to improve. People are very generous with their ideas, and chances are someone else out there has that same "secret" and is willing to work together to create an optimal solution. Such collaboration is most often beneficial for both parties. The more you share, the more you get back. It's a karma thing.

Performance

The argument that well-styled code may slow down application performance is valid. However, in most cases, the tradeoff is worthwhile, as certain performance issues can be pinpointed and optimized without damaging the overall style of the code. We will revisit this subject next in our discussion of readability.

Readability

Now that we are beyond the common excuses for not working on our coding style, we can dig in and look at other ways to improve it. Making our code more readable is a key point of coding style. The result of working toward readability is self-documented code. Self-documented code is created mainly by picking good names for our variables, methods, parameters, and classes.

Variables

Besides using prefixes to keep track of data types, we can implement other techniques to make our variables more useful. Most important is to give our variables names that represent exactly what they are. For example, "x" is an enigmatic variable name, whereas "`numStartPosistionX`" tells us a lot more. It is much more helpful to have a long variable name that describes the exact contents and usage of a variable than to have a short name that is vague. Variables can also be used for the sole purpose of making code more comprehensible by breaking up complicated operations into more understandable pieces. By taking a complex expression and breaking it into several smaller, simpler expressions, we improve both the readability and the maintainability of our code.

Be wary of magic strings and numbers. These are literal strings and numbers found throughout our programs such as "English" and 6. Instead of having these literal values spread throughout our programs, we should assign them to static class properties, instance properties, or temporary variables, depending on the scope that is needed.

> **Note**
>
> Scope refers to the accessibility and lifetime of data. The larger the scope, the easier it is for other objects to access the data, and in most cases data with a larger scope has a longer lifetime. In Flash, the _global object has the largest scope. By putting data in the _global object, we can access it from anywhere in our application at any time. An example of smaller scope is the scope of a temporary variable declared inside a method. Such a variable exists within that method when the method is called, and it is destroyed when the method is finished executing. The concept of scope is mainly about *where* and *for how long* data exists. When we use variables to break things up within methods, which we do in Listing 2.10, we will be working with variables that have a small scope.

To get rid of magic strings and numbers such as "English" and 6, we can examine what these literal values represent; in this case they represent "language" and "minimum version." These values will probably need a larger scope because it is probable that many other classes within our system will need access to this information, and we will need this information to be available for the lifetime of our application. In an object-oriented system, we should take advantage of the organization that classes and objects provide. Instead of putting "language" and "minimum version" in the _global object or on the _root, we can make these static properties of a Constants class. This way, our data is still accessible, and at the same time, it is encapsulated in a class. Let's look at how we can implement this idea in Listing 2.6. In Listing 2.7 we look at how to access static properties of a Constants class.

Listing 2.6 **Creating a Constants Class**

```
class Constants {
    static var strLANGUAGE:String = "English";
    static var numMINIMUM_VERSION_NEEDED:Number = 6;
}
```

Listing 2.7   **To Access Static Properties of a Constants Class, We Refer to These Properties Directly Through the Class Name (Note that Constants are Traditionally Written in Uppercase with Words Separated by Underscores.)**

```
var strVersion = getVersion().charAt(4);
var numVersion = parseInt(strVersion);
var bolCorrectFlashVersion = numVersion >= Constants.numMINIMUM_VERSION_NEEDED;
var strTextsFileName = Constants.strLANGUAGE + ".xml";
if(bolCorrectFlashVersion){
     trace("The version of Flash is correct, time to load " + strTextsFileName);
}else{
     trace("The version of Flash is too low");
}
```

The advantage of using a Constants class instead of "hard coding" these values throughout our program is that if we change the language or the minimum player version requirement, we only have to do it in one place, as opposed to running through a thousand lines of code in all our classes looking for "English" and 6. It is important to remember that we should always try to place data in the smallest possible scope, which is why we use a Constants class instead of just putting this in the _global object. At the same time, we do not want to put unnecessary data in our Constants class, only data that is truly *constant*. In other words, it is not only important to figure out *what* our data represents, but also to think about *where* our data should reside in our program.

Methods

Everyone is familiar with the MovieClip class; it is a very powerful and robust class that enables us to do all kinds of interesting things from the day we pick up Flash. Let's take a look at what makes the MovieClip class so handy. The sheer amount of functionality it has to offer through its properties and methods, although impressive, is not the reason it is so useful. What makes it useful is the fact that the property, method, and parameter names are so easy to understand and use. Take a look at the MovieClip methods in Listing 2.8.

Listing 2.8   **Good Method Names**

```
mcMyClip.getURL("www.j3r.com","_blank");
mcMyClip.startDrag();
```

The fact that the method names are very clear enables us to use them without knowing or needing to care about how they work. They just work! The implementation is hidden from us, and the functionality is provided through a simple interface. If we had to know *how* every MovieClip method worked internally, we would get bogged down in code and be unable to think on an abstract level. With the implementation hidden, we are able solve our problems rather than getting lost in the technicalities of how our tools work. We should build our own classes in this same manner, with the goal of encapsulating the complexity involved and providing an interface that is easy to use.

Seeing that the usefulness of any class relies on the usefulness of its interface, let's take a look at why method names are the final decisive aspect in determining a class's usefulness. Imagine if the Flash development team decided that ATM was a great acronym for "attach to mouse," so they decided to use the method name ATM instead of `startDrag`. ATM would have been a dreadful name for this method because ATM by itself means nothing of importance and has no relevance to the behavior that the method actually provides. No matter how great a method's purpose and functionality, if it has a bad name, it deteriorates in value astronomically. Give each method a name that represents exactly what it does—nothing more and nothing less.

Traditionally, method names should begin with a verb, and class names should be nouns. This is because methods represent the behavior of objects, which are "things," and behavior is the action of a "thing." In other words, methods "do stuff" to "things" that are nouns, so a verb in the method name just makes sense. There are of course exceptions to this rule, but if you write a method and the name does not begin with a verb, it is worthwhile to spend a little extra time pondering the name, making sure it fits the behavior. Parameter names should provide any information needed that the method name does not provide. Keep in mind that a long method name that is accurate is much better than a short one that is not.

Creating good method names will not only make our classes easy to use, it will force us to rethink our class structures before things get out of hand. For example, if we run into a method named `doAllThatStuffToTheXml`, we realize that the bad name is a warning signal, a sign that the method name is insufficient and will cause problems later on. Knowing this, we break up all that "stuff" into smaller, more precise methods with unambiguous names.

This may all seem obvious to more experienced programmers, but in the rush of trying to get things done, it can be tempting to use the first names that come to mind. I suggest investing as much time as it takes to think through your names. Ask yourself if the method name, together with its parameter names, fully represents exactly what the method does. If so, then move on to the next line of code; if not, grab a cup of coffee and rethink the names. Spending time to create good names is a worthwhile activity, so remember to take your time when thinking up any other names, such as class or property names. Good naming will improve your coding substantially, and creating good names from the beginning will prevent timely and costly rewriting and reworking of code.

A Real World Example

I think the best way to understand the usefulness of a clean coding style is by comparing examples. Let's examine a class written with poor style and then examine the same class written with good style. Suppose we found the code in Listing 2.9 while browsing around an open source site on the Internet:

Listing 2.9   **A Usable but Cryptic Class**

```
//Bad style: a usable but cryptic class with one method
dynamic class myC extends MovieClip {
    public function getD(o:Object):Number {
        return Math.sqrt((this._x-o._x)*(this._x-o._x)+(this._y-o._y)*(this._y-
        ➥o._y));
    }
}
```

Technically, there is nothing wrong with this class. The problem is that for anyone but the author of the class, it appears rather cryptic, and it is therefore difficult to figure out its purpose. If we write our code in this manner, we will probably be lost when we try to modify it a year later. Let's examine what is wrong with this code in order to figure out how to write it with good style:

- The class name "myC" tells us nothing about the purpose of the class.
- The method name "getD" tells us very little about the method—what does D stand for?
- The parameter "o" is obscure; all we know is that it is some sort of object, which means it could be anything in Flash.
- We can see that the method returns a value of type Number, but because the expression is so cryptic, it is hard to guess what this number represents.

Now let's take this same example and code with good style. We will discuss the differences between Listing 2.9 and Listing 2.10 after Listing 2.10. Keep in mind, both of these classes are identical as far as functionality is concerned.

Listing 2.10   **Example of Good Style**

```
/*********************************************************************
CLASS MovieClipWithExtraMethods
Extends MovieClip with user defined methods:
```

continues

Listing 2.10 **Continued**

```
getDistance(refToWhatObject) // returns distance to the reference object
*********************************************************************/
dynamic class MovieClipWithExtraMethods extends MovieClip {

    /****************************************************************
    PUBLIC METHODS
    ****************************************************************/

    /*— — — — — — — — — — — — — — — — — — — — — — — — — — — ·
    getDistance
    returns the distance from this MovieClip to any other Object with _x and _y
    properties
    — — — — — — — — — — — — — — — — — — — — — — — — — — — .*/
    public function getDistance(refToWhatObject:Object):Number {

        var numDistanceX:Number = this._x - refToWhatObject._x;
        var numDistanceY:Number = this._y - refToWhatObject._y;

        var numDistanceSquaredX:Number = numDistanceX * numDistanceX;
        var numDistanceSquaredY:Number = numDistanceY * numDistanceY;
        var numDistance:Number = Math.sqrt(numDistanceSquaredX +
        ➥numDistanceSquaredY);

        return numDistance;
    }
}
```

Now we can examine the differences:

- The class name now provides a hint about the purpose of the class: This class is a subclass of the MovieClip class and will provide everything the MovieClip class provides plus one or more user-defined methods.

- The method name "getDistance" insinuates that this method calculates some sort of distance.

- The incoming parameter "refToWhatObject" suggests two things: The "ref" prefix suggests that we are to pass a reference to an object as an argument. The "To" in the name "ToWhatObject" suggests something together with the name of the method "getDistance." Together, the name of the method and the name of the parameter tell us that this method will *get the distance to another object.* In other words, the method documents itself!

Note

The parameter is typed as an Object so that we can send in a reference to any object that has an _x and _y property such as a MovieClip, Button, or TextField.

- The expression that calculates the return value is broken down into simple steps with temporary variables. The temporary variables have descriptive names that explain each step of the process. This makes it much easier to understand what is going on and to make modifications later if needed. For example, perhaps we would want to make sure that the incoming object has an _x and _y property, and if not, display an error message.

Note

The temporary variables in this method are an example of small scope. These variables are created, used, and destroyed within the method each time the method is called. No other part of the application has access to these variables because their scope is strictly declared within the method, and they exist for a *very* short time.

Performance

If you're thinking to yourself that these techniques will slow down performance, you are correct. Performance will slow down a bit, but in most cases, readability is much more important than speed. If you guarantee that your code is easy to understand, you will have a much better time when you or someone else needs to go back and fix something or make enhancements. If you design your application well, you will be able to go through your project when you are finished and pinpoint a specific speed problem, *if* you are having one. In that case, fine, optimize the code, but do this only *after* you have noticed a speed problem and only where needed. Readability is king when it comes to modification and reuse of code.

We have covered a lot of material in this section. Armed with prefixes, strong typing, good naming, and good use of temporary variables to break things up, we have the necessary knowledge to improve our style to the point that our code is self-documenting. Try to keep in mind that knowledge becomes understanding through application. I find it useful to put Post-it notes on my monitor to remind myself of new concepts so that I can apply them to my code. Over time, the information on the notes becomes second nature, a part of my understanding. I then rip the notes down and put up new ones.

Now that we know how to make our code self-documenting, let's take a break from talking about the actual code and explore the topics of documentation and organization.

Comments, White Space, and Barriers

Our next step is to look at the elements that surround our code, namely comments and white space, and examine how we can use these to our advantage. By looking at other aspects of coding besides the actual code, we find ways to improve our style of programming without actually touching the "working code."

Comments are one of those tricky subjects that can lead to heated debates among programmers. It is rather obvious why we should comment our code: It helps us and others who work on our code understand its purpose. It can be argued, however, that if the code is written in a self-documented manner with good class, method, parameter, property, and variable names, comments will become obsolete and possibly get in the way. This can be true when we really get the hang of writing self-documented code, but even then, comments can be useful.

A good comment tells something that may not be obvious. For example, we might want to comment a complicated section of our code so that it is understandable in the future. It is of course best to avoid complicated code, but in some situations, complicated code is the only way to solve a problem. In such circumstances, it is important to document the intention of the code, not the code itself. In other words, we do not want to reiterate our code in our comments or explain our syntax; instead, we want to explicate the purpose of the code.

Another way to improve our code without actually touching the "working code" is to use white space generously. White space is a valuable tool to separate different sections of code. White space is especially useful in class declarations, but it can be used anywhere to make distinct separations between coding structures. Just as any author uses white space between chapters, sections, and paragraphs to delineate chapters or shifting thoughts, programmers can and should use white space to achieve readability.

Together with white space, we can use comments to make barriers between different sections in our code. These barriers can also be used for detailed documentation. Important sections of a class, such as the constructor, class properties, instance properties, private methods, and public methods, can all be clearly separated with white space and barriers.

I think it is useful to understand a bad example before examining a good one, so in the next section we will learn how poor comments, lack of white space, and lack of barriers can really mess up our code.

Comments that Destroy

Earlier we created a subclass that inherits from the MovieClip class and provides an extra method that calculates the distance to another object with _x and _y properties. We wrote this class using good variable names, descriptive method and parameter names, white space, and barriers. In other words, the class is self-documented and organized. Before we learn how to destroy a well-written class, let's take a look at the original self-documented class in Listing 2.11 so that we are familiar with it.

Listing 2.11   **A Self-Documented Class**

```
/******************************************************************
CLASS MovieClipWithExtraMethods
Extends MovieClip with user defined methods:
getDistance(refToWhatObject) // returns distance to the reference object
******************************************************************/
dynamic class MovieClipWithExtraMethods extends MovieClip {

    /**************************************************************
    PUBLIC METHODS
    **************************************************************/

    /*- - - - - - - - - - - - - - - - - - - - - - - - - - - - -·
    getDistance
    returns the distance from this MovieClip to any other Object with _x and _y
    properties
    - - - - - - - - - - - - - - - - - - - - - - - - - - - - -·*/
    public function getDistance(refToWhatObject:Object):Number {

        var numDistanceX:Number = this._x - refToWhatObject._x;
        var numDistanceY:Number = this._y - refToWhatObject._y;

        var numDistanceSquaredX:Number = numDistanceX * numDistanceX;
        var numDistanceSquaredY:Number = numDistanceY * numDistanceY;
        var numDistance:Number = Math.sqrt(numDistanceSquaredX +
        ➡numDistanceSquaredY);

        return numDistance;
    }
}
```

Listing 2.12 shows this same class, still written with self-documenting code, but diminished in quality due to redundant comments, lack of white space, and lack of barriers.

Listing 2.12   **Self-Documenting Code Diminished in Quality Due to Redundant Comments, Lack of White Space, and Lack of Barriers**

```
dynamic class MovieClipWithExtraMethods extends MovieClip {
    // getDistance
    public function getDistance(refToWhatObject:Object):Number {
        // distance x
        var numDistanceX:Number = this._x - refToWhatObject._x;
        // distance y
        var numDistanceY:Number = this._y - refToWhatObject._y;
        // square distance x
        var numDistanceSquaredX:Number = numDistanceX * numDistanceX;
        // square distance y
        var numDistanceSquaredY:Number = numDistanceY * numDistanceY;
        // square root
        var numDistance:Number = Math.sqrt(numDistanceSquaredX +
        ➡numDistanceSquaredY);
        // return
        return numDistance;
    }
}
```

The comments in this class are so redundant it might make you giggle. However, running into comments such as this is not very amusing when you are trying to get your job done. Seeing that this type of commenting is useless, let's move on and explore how comments can be meaningful.

Comments that are Meaningful

Our goal is to make our code so self-documenting that comments are not needed. Sometimes, however, there is no getting around the need for certain comments. If we find that we need some comments, we shouldn't use too many. Chances are, if there is a problem with our code, a maintenance programmer will want to know what we were *trying* to do, not a reiteration of our code. Here is a list of things to keep in mind when commenting:

- Comment your intentions, not the code itself.
- Point out any future updates that need to be implemented.
- Point out any resources, theories, formulas, theorems, or design patterns that you have used or based your code on.

Let's take the original self-documented class in Listing 2.11 and see if we can improve it with meaningful comments in Listing 2.13.

Listing 2.13   **The Final Class: Self-Documenting Code Combined with
Meaningful Comments**

```
/*********************************************************************
CLASS MovieClipWithExtraMethods
Extends MovieClip with user defined methods:
getDistance(refToWhatObject) // returns distance to the reference object
*********************************************************************/
dynamic class MovieClipWithExtraMethods extends MovieClip {

    /************************************************************
    PUBLIC METHODS
    ************************************************************/

    /*- - - - - - - - - - - - - - - - - - - - - - - - - - - - - .
    getDistance
    returns the distance from this MovieClip to any other Object with _x and _y
    properties
    DEVELOPER NOTE: needs protection against objects with no _x and _y properties
    - - - - - - - - - - - - - - - - - - - - - - - - - - - - - .*/
    public function getDistance(refToWhatObject:Object):Number {

        // get the difference in _x position from this MovieClip to the
        // reference object
        var numDistanceX:Number = this._x - refToWhatObject._x;
        // get the difference in _y position from this MovieClip to the
        // reference object
        var numDistanceY:Number = this._y - refToWhatObject._y;

        // calculate the birds eye distance between this MovieClip
        // and the reference object using Pythagorean Theorem (a2 + b2 = c2)
        var numDistanceSquaredX:Number = numDistanceX * numDistanceX;
        var numDistanceSquaredY:Number = numDistanceY * numDistanceY;
        var numDistance:Number = Math.sqrt(numDistanceSquaredX +
        ➥numDistanceSquaredY);

        return numDistance;
    }
}
```

Let's take a look at why the comments in Listing 2.13 are useful:

- The comments in this class describe the intentions of the code, not the
  code itself.
- There is a developer note suggesting how the class can be improved. This
  type of information is very useful when we have to work on several
  classes at a time or have to update classes that were written long ago or
  by another developer.

- There is a reference to a theorem that is used in the calculation, which might prove to be useful if someone else needs to update this code because he or she will know where to look if he or she needs help understanding it.

Now that we know how to make use of the space surrounding our code without destroying the self-documentation, there is nothing stopping us from developing a good programming style. In the next section, we will move even further away from code and learn how to design a system in Flash.

Simplification—Design Your System

We have all seen code that goes on forever in an endless spider web of if/else statements for a hundred lines, all bundled inside an `onEnterFrame` event. This type of code is usually hacked together by beginners but surprisingly finds its way into professional-level projects. Updating and fixing programs written in this manner is a nightmare.

Even if we are just making a small web page and want to get it done as quickly as possible, devoting a little time to planning in the beginning will save much more time than jumping right into the coding process. If you have ever completed a project and wanted to start over, saying to yourself, "Now I know how I should have done it," then this section is for you.

The size and complexity of any given problem does not necessarily determine the complexity of its solution. Designing a program can take from an hour to several months, depending on what we are building. In its basic form, making a system design just means that we design our system on paper at a higher level of abstraction, away from code. By designing on paper, we can rewrite the system in many different ways, making changes quickly and easily.

Don't be concerned that designing your system will take the fun out of it; after a while, it's likely you will have just as much fun in the planning process as you do with the implementation. Designing your system is imperative. Imagine if architects just improvised—our cities would be falling to the ground.

Designing a system mainly consists of breaking larger problems into smaller problems—breaking advanced entities into simpler entities. There are many different ways to design: from the top down, from the bottom up, one piece at a time, in stages, or a combination of these and many other methodologies. You can purchase books on this subject, and I stress that this will just be a very general overview on how to get started with system design. It is better, however, to write out a simple design than to forge ahead with no written plan. The following section of this article contains a design and implementation guideline that I find works well for small- to medium-sized projects in Flash.

Top Down Design, Bottom Up Implementation

This guideline is pretty straightforward: We will design our system from the top down, and then build it from the bottom up. In other words, we will start designing by analyzing the largest parts of the system and then work our way to the smaller more hidden parts. When we are finished with the design, we will then start building the smallest parts and work our way to the larger ones.

If you are unfamiliar with classes and components, you can use this guideline with just MovieClips. The important thing here is not what implementation you use but that you design the system before coding.

Design Your Application from the Top Down

First, grab a notepad and a pencil with a good eraser. Alternatively, you can use a deck of index cards because they work very well for object-oriented systems: You can treat each card as a class, component, or MovieClip and move them around as you make changes to the system design.

1. First, you want to break your application down into main entities. If you are building a web page for a band, your main entities might be a navigation bar, a news section, a guest book, and an MP3 player. If you are building a racing game, your main entities might be a car, a track, a map, and a scoreboard.

2. Draw a design for your application, pretending that all these main entities are complete. Each entity will be a class, component, or MovieClip. At this stage, pretend that they are already built; all the complicated programming is hidden inside them, and now you are just going to put together your application using public properties, methods, and events. Write down what public properties, methods, and events you will need. Specify method parameters and put the application together on paper using these imaginary entities. Change whatever you need to! Rewriting an imaginary entity on paper is a lot easier than rewriting a real one, so take your time and do as many versions as you need. Stay at this stage until you are so sure your design is perfect that you start getting a warm and fuzzy feeling.

3. Look at these main entities from a higher level. Imagine you could pull already-made classes, components, and MovieClips out of a magic hat and start building these entities. What would these classes, components, and MovieClips look like? What would they be called? What properties and methods would they have? What parameters would each method have? Break each main entity down into these imaginary pre-made classes, components, and MovieClips.

4. Draw a design for each main entity using these imaginary classes, components, and MovieClips. If you are missing anything, or if the properties and methods you have chosen for these classes, components, and MovieClips do not solve all your problems, go back to step three and repeat this process until you feel you know exactly what you need to create each main entity.

5. Look to see if any of the classes or components you need are available for purchase or for free on the Internet. Many professional level classes, components, and code libraries are on the market. Paying for professional-level code ensures quality and brings both costs and production time down drastically.

6. Continue with this process, but now start breaking down the complex classes, components, and MovieClips that will make up each main entity. Break them down into less complicated classes, components, and MovieClips. Continue breaking everything down until you are at the absolute "nuts and bolts" level.

Building Each Entity from the Bottom Up

I have always had a rule that I take at least a one-day break between the design phase and the implementation phase, otherwise known as the building or production phase. During this break, I let the design flow freely through my mind as I do other things—not focusing on it, but just letting it rest in my mind. The result is that I often end up going back to the design and changing things. Inevitably, I end up changing enough of the design that I take another break. I continue this process until I can go back to my design without needing to make changes. This process may take a week, and it may push the production back a week, but on larger projects, this saves immense amounts of time. The earlier you catch mistakes in the design, the more time you save. That being said, let's take a look at how to build our system.

1. Start building the "nuts and bolts" classes, components, and MovieClips for one of your main entities. These should be the simplest classes,

components, and MovieClips that you will need to build the next level of complexity within one of your main entities.

2. Build the next level of complexity with these new "nuts and bolts" you have just created.

3. Keep moving upward until you have completed one main entity, one of the top-level entities from step one.

4. Move back to the "nuts and bolts" level and work upwards to build another of the main entities, from small simple parts to a large complex one.

5. Continue this process until all the main entities are built.

6. Now put the system together based on the design you wrote in step two. You did write it out, didn't you? At this point, your main entities will provide public properties and methods that enable you to put your system together with a high level of abstraction. All the complicated code will be encapsulated in the entities. The code that puts your main entities together can be on Frame 1 of the Timeline, or in a System class.

You may have to run through this process a few times before you really get the hang of it, and by that time, you will probably have your own process that is slightly different, which is great. Whatever approach to designing your system works for you is the one you should use because it is important that you enjoy doing this work. If you don't enjoy it, chances are you will skip it, so work with it and come up with your own way that is enjoyable.

One alternative way to design your system would be to start building your main entities from the top and work your way down. You can then use "dummy" lower level classes, components, and MovieClips to build main entities with an extremely limited functionality. This way, you get a version of the system together quickly that has pseudo functionality. You would then start replacing the "dummy" lower level classes, components, and MovieClips with real implementations as needed. There are advantages to this approach if you need to release the application in stages or need to have a version up half-way through the production phase to show your client that you are in fact working on their project.

I prefer the "Top Down Design, Bottom Up Implementation" that I have outlined in detail because I find it to produce systems that are more reliable. In addition, by creating each main entity individually, I am much more likely to end up with a reusable component, rather than one that is strongly coupled to the rest of a specific system. Lastly, by designing from the highest level of abstraction and then programming one main entity at a time from the bottom up, I reach small rewarding goals on completion of each main entity, which motivates me to dig into the "nuts and bolts" of the next one.

There are many other ways to design a system. Look into other ways and combine your favorite aspects of each into your own methodology. It is not important that you design your system in any particular manner, as long as you write out some sort of design before you start programming and have a planned approach for the building process as well. Careful planning and building will save many hours of programming and create applications that are more reliable.

To gain a deeper understanding of system design, I suggest learning about object-oriented systems. Object-oriented techniques and metaphors such as information hiding through encapsulation, abstraction, reusability, robustness, maintainability, and flexibility really simplify your life. If you have not already studied these concepts in depth, go out and buy a book on object-orientation. This will help your design immensely! If you get into creating large object-oriented systems, you might also want to learn UML, the Unified Modeling Language, which is the standard language, often used within a visual modeling environment, for designing object-oriented systems.

We have covered a lot of material. To wrap things up, I would like to share some final thoughts that I find useful in my daily life as a programmer.

General Tips

The largest problem with programming is handling complexity. Any project that takes longer than a week or two to program can quickly become a disordered mess. When I realized the tendency for programs to become so complex, I began looking for ways to simplify my code and my thought processes. After focusing on my coding style, my programming skills and my ability to handle complex applications developed rapidly. In this last section, we examine the use of abstraction in reducing complexity, as well as the importance of our working environment, taking breaks, and being resourceful.

Highest Level of Abstraction

Always work at the highest level of abstraction possible. If you get confused while writing your code, stop and write it all out in your native language. It's a lot easier to think logically in your native language than it is to think in a programming language. It's also a lot faster to rethink and rewrite when there is no code involved.

We have worked a good deal with the example class called MovieClipWithExtraMethods. Let's take a look at how I first wrote this class declaration in English. The final class can be found back in Listing 2.13. The following pseudocode shows the original thought process behind the class.

By thinking things through in our native language, we save a lot of time, not having to waste our mental energy on coding syntax:

```
declare a dynamic class that extends MovieClip

    declare a public method called getDistance that receives another object
    ➥reference as a parameter
        get the difference in _x position from this MovieClip to the reference
        ➥object
        get the difference in _y position from this MovieClip to the reference
        ➥object

        calculate the birds eye distance between this MovieClip
        ➥and the reference object using Pythagorean Theorem (a2 + b2 = c2)

        square the X difference
        square the Y difference
        add these squares together
        take the square root of this sum to find the birds eye distance

        return this distance

    end of method

end of class declaration
```

After thinking through what we want to do in our native language, it is much easier to implement the code. You may notice that some of these sentences made their way into the final class in Listing 2.13 as comments; this is an extra benefit of thinking things through in our native language first. By writing things out in our native language, we end up with nice sentences that can be turned into comments. This way, the comments always explain the intention of the code, not the code itself.

Another form of abstraction, which we have already discussed, involves encapsulating complexity into objects and then using the objects' interface to get our work done. Abstraction should take place within our objects as well. If your public methods start becoming too intricate, break the complexity out of the public methods into private ones. If the entire class becomes too complex, build a new class to encapsulate that complexity. Whenever you feel things are becoming too complex, it's a good idea to stop and ask why. Break it down;

hide the complexity.

Find the Right Level of Complexity

If you have chosen a programming profession, you will remain a student for the duration of your career; the technology will continue to change, and you will have to keep up or bail out. Just when you think you really understand everything, you realize that you don't understand very much. Just when you finally feel you have mastered the newest technologies, everything is flipped upside down, and there is a completely new set of technologies to learn.

With so much new material to cover, there is always the danger that we might take on too much. We try to implement too many new methodologies in our current projects and end up getting lost in things that we do not really understand. The right level of complexity for any project depends on many factors, such as your current level of ability, your desire to push yourself beyond your level, and your deadline. Find a balance; do not overshoot and get stuck a day before deadline with a half-finished project that is over your head and out of control.

Pay Attention to Your Environment

A comfortable working environment enables productivity. Keep your computer meticulously organized, clean your desk and the room you work in, purchase a comfortable chair and a plant. Small comforts make a difference, and outward organization helps promote organization of thought.

Perhaps you cannot change the fact that there is a freeway right outside the window, but you can limit self-imposed distractions. We all like to think that we can do many things at once, but in actuality, the more we do simultaneously, the less attention we give to each task. Music, for example, often helps me think creatively, yet lyrics draw too much of my attention, so I often listen to instrumental jazz when I work. When things get complicated, I find that absolute silence is golden. I try to habitually observe my environment and change any distracting factors that are within my control.

Take Breaks

Sometimes the best thing you can do is get up and walk away from your computer. When I am stuck on something, I usually start feeling frustrated. This frustration often leads to some sort of ignorant blindness, trying the same thing repeatedly, insisting that it *should* work, refusing to accept the fact that it is *not* working. Often just leaving the computer and doing something else leads my mind to a solution. While shooting a game of pool or making a good meal, an idea will suddenly pop into my head that fixes the problem I was having.

Be Resourceful

Be your own teacher. If you find yourself always running to a forum or emailing an acquaintance for help, you will not develop as quickly as you would by trying to figure things out for yourself. It's not a bad thing to ask people in the community for help, but it is beneficial to first try to find the answer yourself. Here are some key reasons for this:

- Any answer to a problem that is handed to you on a silver platter will at best remain knowledge. In the process of hunting down an answer yourself, you gain a deeper comprehension of the problem, and the potential arises for understanding the solution.

- While trying to solve one problem, you will run across other useful information. Each time you explore one subject that you do not understand, you will likely learn about another subject as well.

- If you always send your scripts to an acquaintance or post them on a forum for help, and it is obvious that you have not even tried to figure out the problem yourself, people will get tired of doing your work for you and will likely stop helping you.

Keep in mind that the Internet has vast amounts of useful information. Before running for help, open up your favorite search engine and spend a good hour trying to find your own answers. Another great way to learn is to start helping other people. By explaining things to others, you deepen your own understanding of the subject matter.

Enjoy the Process

It's so easy to get caught up in our goals and desires that we often forget to enjoy the process. I don't know how many times I have thought that if only I was "this good," I would be happy, but as soon as one goal is reached, another is set. There is always more to learn and accomplish.

It is important to have goals, but it is also important to pay attention to where we are now. If we get too caught up in everything we want to learn, we will not be able to focus on what we are doing. Enjoy not knowing everything—some of the most fun you may ever have is when you know the least about what you are doing. Some of my most exciting experiences have been with

Flash when I picked up version 3 and started to *play*. Back then, I didn't care if I was doing things correctly; I just had fun being creative. If your mind is burdened with too much information, it is hard to find that magic creative feeling. For this reason, I usually divide personal projects into three main stages. When I have an idea for a new site, I first sit down with Flash and let myself play freely with no rules. I continue in this way, letting the creative juices flow, until I feel that the creative development of the idea is complete. Usually at the end of this stage I have a working prototype of my new site. I then commit to a formal design phase, followed by a production phase as outlined in the section "Top Down Design, Bottom Up Implementation." It's important to get serious about your programming if you want to improve, but don't forget to let go every now and then and just have fun!

Conclusion

If you integrate the contents of this article into your thought process while coding, it will all become second nature in no time. It's inevitable that each person ends up creating their own style and developing their own methodologies, and this is a part of what makes the Flash organism evolve. It's not necessary for everyone to have the same style, as long as we are all striving toward a similar goal.

As much as good style will improve your programming, it is not the answer to all problems. There are many methodologies out there; try to avoid turning any methodology into a dogmatic religion. To prevent falling into this type of mental trap, it is helpful to think of each methodology as a tool. Just as Flash components are a set of tools, and we use only the components we *need* for each project we work on, we can think of methodologies as tools in the same way, using the ones that we need on a project-by-project basis. Choose the tools you find appropriate and do not buy into late night commercials that sell *the one and only tool you will ever need!* Learn about many different methodologies, combine them into your own, and always be willing to alter your programming belief system.

Pay attention when you code and keep in mind that any technique that reduces complexity is worth looking into. Two years ago, I jotted down one word on a Post-it note and stuck it on my monitor as a constant reminder. When things start getting stressful and over-complicated, I look up and read that note, a friendly reminder to myself:

Simplify!

Article 3

Macromedia Flash MX 2004 HTML TextField Enhancements

by Randy H. Drisgill

IF YOU'VE SPENT TIME CHECKING out all the new features available in Flash MX 2004 and in the Flash Player 7, you will have undoubtedly noticed the new HTML feature enhancements. These enhancements allow for a more robust utilization of common HTML techniques. I have always thought that it was interesting how some things in Flash were so much easier to accomplish than in HTML (such as content layout and application updating without refreshing the browser), yet some of the most basic HTML features (such as scrolling and right-clicking) actually have been more difficult. Thankfully, with this latest Flash version, we can now easily perform these tasks as well as other typically simple HTML techniques, such as image placement and Cascading Style Sheets (CSS). In this article we will be discussing how to interact with these features through ActionScript. We will be looking at the changes to Flash's TextField HTML capabilities, including images, Cascading Style Sheets, scroll wheel support, and right-click support. We will accomplish this while building a company contact list application with images, links, and stylistic decorations created entirely with HTML in Flash TextFields. For those of you in a hurry, the full source code for this application is available at the end of the article (see Listings 3.12-3.14).

Automatic HTML Enhancements—Scrolling and Right-Clicking

The first two HTML enhancements that we will be learning about are automatically accessible when using TextFields in the new version of Flash. All we need to see them in action is to start building our application and get a TextField with some data and links in it. Because we are starting from scratch, we need to open Flash MX 2004 and create a new Flash document. Let's save the document right away; otherwise, when it comes time to test the application, our images will not be found (because Flash tests unsaved movies from your temp directory). For this application, let's save the document as textfield.fla in a directory called htmlexample.

Let's begin by placing a large TextField on the stage. In the Properties panel, name the TextField instance content_txt and make it Dynamic Text, multiline, render text as HTML, selectable, and show border around text (see Figure 3.1). With the TextField properly set up, we can begin the ActionScript that will create the contact list.

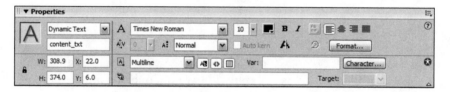

Figure 3.1 The properties of the TextField show all the required selections.

Assume a database connection has already been made and an array has been created to hold each of the contact objects. For simplicity's sake, in Listing 3.1 we create this array ourselves (rather than actually make a database connection). Note that database connections can be made using web services (more info can be found by reading Article 6, "ActionScript Design Patterns for Rich Internet Application Development," by Steven Webster and Alistair McLeod) or through the use of Flash Remoting (check out Macromedia's DevNet web site at http://www.macromedia.com/devnet/mx/flashremoting/).

Listing 3.1 **An Array Is Created to Hold All the Contact Objects**

```
//create empty array to hold fake database query
var db_array:Array = new Array();

//populate the array with objects that include name, email, web site, and picture
db_array[0] = {name:'Randy
Drisgill',email:'randy@vshift.com',website:'http://www.monkeytongue.com',picture:'
➥images/randy.jpg'};
db_array[1] = {name:'Chip
Wiggins',email:'chip@vshift.com',website:'http://www.vshift.com',picture:'images/
➥chip.jpg'};
db_array[2] = {name:'Omar W.',email:'omar@vshift.com',website:'',picture:''};
db_array[3] = {name:'Nik M.',email:'nik@vshift.com',website:'',picture:''};
db_array[4] = {name:'Kevin B.',email:'kevin@vshift.com',website:'',picture:''};
db_array[5] = {name:'Ambrose
F.',email:'ambrose@vshift.com',website:'',picture:''};
db_array[6] = {name:'John C.',email:'john@vshift.com',website:'',picture:''};
db_array[7] = {name:'Henry D.',email:'henry@vshift.com',website:'',picture:''};
db_array[8] = {name:'Marcela
E.',email:'marcela@vshift.com',website:'',picture:''};
```

You'll see in Listing 3.1 that we have created an object for each element in the array, and we have simply used an empty string for the contacts that don't have web sites or pictures. Now in Listing 3.2 we will loop through this array and add each result to a new line in a temporary variable.

Listing 3.2 **An Empty String Is Created and Populated By the Contents of the Contacts Array**

```
//create empty variable to hold the display text
var displaytext:String = '';

//loop through the array and add each line to displaytext
for(var i:Number=0;i<db_array.length;i++){
    displaytext += db_array[i].picture + '<br>';
    displaytext += db_array[i].name + '<br>';
    displaytext += db_array[i].email + '<br>';
    displaytext += db_array[i].website + '<br><br>';
}
```

For each line in Listing 3.2, we are adding a <br> to force a break in our HTML, and on the last line we have two
s to make a large break between each contact. In Listing 3.3, we set the contents of our TextField to the HTML stored in the variable. This variable will be used to display the HTML in Flash.

Listing 3.3   **The TextField Content Is Updated with the HTML to be Displayed**

```
//set our TextField content equal to that of the displaytext variable
content_txt.htmlText = displaytext;
```

If we test our movie now, we will see that we have a very simple output of the text name of each picture, along with contact name, email, and web site on separate lines. So far, this isn't very impressive, but we can show one new feature of Flash right now. If the amount of text we are trying to add is larger than our TextField, we can test Flash Player 7's new mouse scroll wheel support by simply clicking on the TextField in the tested movie and rotating the scroll wheel up and down. This feature is great, and we didn't even have to add any code. Next, let's start adding some HTML to make things more interesting. We will add a `mailto:` link to the email line and a standard link to the web site line. This will enable us to link users to the contact's email address and web site. While we are at it, let's place an `if` statement around the web site line so that only contacts with web sites will have a line shown for them.

Listing 3.4   **Mail and Web Site Links Are Added to the HTML**

```
//loop through the array and add each line to displaytext
for(var i:Number=0;i<db_array.length;i++){
    displaytext += db_array[i].picture + '<br>';
    displaytext += db_array[i].name + '<br>';
displaytext += '<a href="mailto:' + db_array[i].email + '">' + db_array[i].email +
➥'</a><br>';
    if(db_array[i].website != ''){
        displaytext += '<a target="_blank" href="' + db_array[i].website + '">'
➥+ db_array[i].website + '</a><br><br>';
    } else {
        displaytext += '<br><br>';
    }
}
```

With this code in place, we can now click the links and see the resulting web site. This will let us test another great automatic feature of the Flash Player 7—right-click support. If you test the movie and right-click one of our links, you will see the new options Copy and Open Link. If you were playing this through a browser, you would also get a third option, Open in new window (my favorite new Player feature). Next, we will take a look at Flash's new HTML image capabilities.

Adding Images

So far, we really haven't done anything new with ActionScript, so let's start by adding some newly supported HTML. We can now add an image to the HTML. In previous versions of ActionScript, we would have had to create a new movie clip and placed it dynamically next to the text item before changing its content to that of a .jpg on our system. With Flash MX 2004, we can just add the image with an HTML <img> tag, and Flash automatically flows the text around the image. In Listing 3.5 we are adding an if statement and the <img> tag that will point to an image stored in the same directory as our application.

Listing 3.5   **Images Are Added to the HTML for Each Available Contact.**

```
//if the user has a picture we will show it with the html img tag
if(db_array[i].picture != ''){
    displaytext += '<img src="' + db_array[i].picture + '" id="image' + i + '"
    ➥align="right" height="60" width="60"><br>';
}
```

For this to work, we will have to add corresponding JPGs to the images subdirectory under our main directory. Because only the first two contacts in this application have images, you will only need two. You should notice in Listing 3.5 that we can control the size of the image through the use of the height and width properties. You must include both height and width for the size change to work, and percentages are ignored. We can also control alignment via the align property, and a movie clip id can be assigned with the HTML id property. When we test the movie, we can see that our images appear exactly where we want them (see Figure 3.2).

Some other requirements of note when using images—there must be more than one line of text for them to show up, and they appear on the line below the one with their <img> tag (unless they are the first item in the HTML). Also, note that links can be placed around images, but border and alt properties are ignored. The image tag does not support GIFs, PNGs, or progressive JPGs, but interestingly enough, it does support URL references to SWFs or references to the names of SWFs that are located in the Flash file's library. If you want to try something really neat, replace your contact pictures with animated SWFs. These previous requirements are specific to using images in Flash and are somewhat different from standard HTML, so watch out for them in your code.

Figure 3.2   Our images appear to the right of the corresponding HTML lines.

Now let's add some HTML by loading it directly from an existing HTML document. Although this concept hasn't changed since the previous version of Flash, it may be more useful now with the new capability to have images in your imported HTML. In practice, using an existing HTML document can be valuable for repurposing existing web content in Flash (such as a common footer file). For this we will create our HTML document called footer.html and place it in our project root directory. The contents of this file are shown in Listing 3.6.

Listing 3.6   **The Contents of the footer.html File**

```
textvar=<img src="images/logo.jpg" width="144" height="56"><br>
<font face="arial">Copyright ©2003<br>Vshift. All rights reserved.<br>
<a href="http://www.vshift.com/privacy.html">Privacy Policy</a> - <a
href="http://www.vshift.com/terms.html">Terms of Use</a></font>
```

Notice in Listing 3.6 that we are loading a logo image, and there are two links to existing HTML documents (you can make your own image and links to whatever you want). In addition, we have added textvar= to the front of our HTML. This is needed by Flash to read in the HTML as a variable. If you were repurposing existing HTML content for this, you may have to use a scripting language such as ColdFusion MX to add this variable to the HTML content on the fly (to avoid including it in your standard footer file for your web site).

Now to hold this HTML in Flash, we will add a new TextField below our existing one with an instance name of footer_txt. You can leave off the show border around text property this time because we don't want a border around our footer. To read the HTML, we will use the ActionScript in Listing 3.7.

Listing 3.7   **A *LoadVars* Object is Used to Load the HTML into the Footer TextField**

```
//make a new LoadVars object
var loader:Object = new LoadVars();

//read footer.html into the object
loader.load("footer.html");

//when loaded, write it to the footer_txt field
loader.onLoad = function():Void {
     footer_txt.htmlText = loader.textvar;
};
```

Listing 3.7 creates a LoadVars object and reads footer.html into it, and then when the loading is complete, it writes the HTML to the footer_txt TextField. If we test the movie now, we should see our common footer with its logo and common links at the bottom (see Figure 3.3).

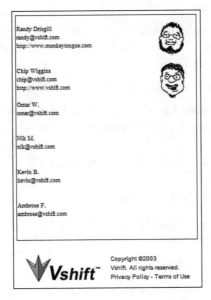

Figure 3.3   Our footer HTML is shown at the bottom of the screen.

Cascading Style Sheet (CSS)

Now that we have explored the image enhancements to the HTML supported in the new version of Flash, we can begin to explore the powerful new Cascading Style Sheet (CSS) features. If you have ever wished you had more control over the look of Flash text or the ability to change it on the fly via quick changes to an external text file, this enhancement is for you. With CSS and Flash, we will do just that, by creating an external style sheet and attaching it to our TextField in ActionScript. The CSS supported in the Flash Player 7 is a subset of the actual CSS standard (much as Flash's support for HTML is a small subset of the actual HTML language). To implement this feature, we use the new StyleSheet subclass of the TextField class in ActionScript. Style sheets can be implemented in three ways:

- Load the CSS from a URL using `StyleSheet.load`.
- Parse the CSS from strings using `StyleSheet.parseCSS`.
- Set a style object for the style sheet using `StyleSheet.setStyle`.

We will be using the first method to add styles to our ActionScript. The first thing we need to do is create a new StyleSheet object on the TextField. Therefore, we add this line to the top of the ActionScript.

```
content_txt.styleSheet = new TextField.StyleSheet();
```

Note the difference in the capitalization of the two style sheets here, which is critical because of the way Macromedia coded the style sheets to work. Next, we replace our previous code:

```
content_txt.htmlText = displaytext;
```

We replace the code with Listing 3.8 , which has a loader that calls our CSS file (we will create this CSS file in a moment).

Listing 3.8 **A Style Sheet Is Loaded into the TextField**

```
//load our stylesheet
content_txt.styleSheet.load("style.css");

//when stylesheet loads, check for error finding CSS
content_txt.styleSheet.onLoad = function(result:Boolean):Void{
    if(result){
        content_txt.htmlText = displaytext;
    } else {
        //display error message in textfield if CSS is not found
        content_txt.htmlText = 'Error loading CSS';
    }
}
```

Listing 3.8 loads our CSS and either sets the `displaytext` to the `content_txt` (thus showing us the styled HTML) or displays a simple error message. Next, we need to change our loop that creates `displaytext` to include some style classes, as shown in Listing 3.9.

Listing 3.9   **The Loop Is Updated to Include Style Classes**

```
for(var i:Number=0;i<db_array.length;i++){
    if(db_array[i].picture != ''){
        displaytext = displaytext + '<img src="' + db_array[i].picture + '"
        ➥id="image' + i + '" align="right" height="60" width="60"><br>';
    }
    displaytext += '<p class="nametext">' + db_array[i].name + '</p>';
    displaytext += '<a class="emailtext" href="mailto:' + db_array[i].email +
    ➥'">' + db_array[i].email + '</a><br>';
    if(db_array[i].website != ''){
        displaytext += '<a class="websitetext" target="_blank" href="' +
        ➥db_array[i].website + '">' + db_array[i].website + '</a><br><br>';
    } else {
        displaytext += '<br><br>';
    }
}
```

Notice in Listing 3.9 that our classes for this HTML are called `nametext`, `emailtext`, and `websitetext`. These classes are attached to either a `<p>` tag in the case of `nametext`, or `<a href>` tags in the case of `emailtext` and `websitetext`. Lastly, we need to create our CSS file. We will name it style.css and place it in our project root directory. To begin the CSS file, let's just place some simple font and text styles in it. Listing 3.10 shows how we can use basic font and alignment styles to help us control the design of the displayed text.

Listing 3.10   **The Style.css File Begins with Font and Alignment Styles**

```
.nametext {
    font-family: sans-serif; font-size: 24px; font-weight: bold; text-align:
    ➥left;
}
.emailtext {
    font-family: Arial; font-size: 19px; font-weight: normal; text-align: left;
}
.websitetext {
    font-family: Arial; font-size: 10px; font-weight: normal; text-align: left;
}
```

If we save our style.css file and then test our movie, we should see that our text is now sized in a nice way. Now to complete our CSS, let's add the link styles in Listing 3.11 to the bottom of the existing style.css. With link styles, we can create very useful visual indicators for the links in our application.

Listing 3.11 **The Style.css File Concludes with Link Hover and Active Styles**

```
a {
    color: #600000; text-decoration: none;
}
a:hover {
    color: #ff0000; text-decoration: underline;
}
a:active {
    color: #cccccc;
}
```

If we save our style.css file one more time and retest our Flash file, we can see that the links are now colored red, they have underlines only when the mouse hovers over them, and they turn grey when they are clicked (see Figure 3.4).

Figure 3.4 Our finished contact list application with all our styles applied.

To fully understand the concept of CSS in Flash, we need to learn the specifics of how Flash handles CSS. In Flash, TextFields go into a special mode (Style Sheet Mode) when they have a style sheet assigned to them. When in Style Sheet Mode, the `.text` and `.htmlText` properties of the TextField are the same. This is different from the way HTML text is handled in standard TextFields for the previous version of Flash (in standard mode it is harder to switch back and forth between `.htmlText` and `text` properties because HTML is added directly to the text). Also, this mode causes input TextFields to become dynamic variables. This means that an input TextField will switch to a regular dynamic variable and will not display as an editable text field when the movieclip is tested. The only way to set a value for these TextFields is through the traditional dynamic TextField properties of `.text` and `.htmlText` (both `setTextFormat` and `replaceSel` no longer function after Style Sheet Mode is implemented).

The CSS that is supported in the latest version of Flash is shown in Table 3.1.

Table 3.1   **Supported CSS Properties and Values**

CSS property	ActionScript property	Usage and supported values
`text-align`	`textAlign`	Recognized values are left, center, and right.
`font-size`	`fontSize`	Only numeric part of value is used; units (px, pt) are not parsed; pixels and points are equivalent.
`text-decoration`	`textDecoration`	Recognized values are none and underline.
`margin-left`	`marginLeft`	Only numeric part of the value used. Units (px, pt) are not parsed; pixels and points are equivalent.
`margin-right`	`marginRight`	Only numeric part of the value used. Units (px, pt) are not parsed; pixels and points are equivalent.
`font-weight`	`fontWeight`	Recognized values are normal and bold.
`font-style`	`fontStyle`	Recognized values are normal and italic.
`text-indent`	`textIndent`	Only numeric part of the value used. Units (px, pt) are not parsed; pixels and points are equivalent.
`font-family`	`fontFamily`	A comma-separated list of fonts to use, in descending order of desirability. The following font conversions are available: mono is converted to _typewriter, sans-serif is converted to _sans, and serif is converted to _serif.
`Color`	`color`	Only hexadecimal color values are supported. Named colors (such as blue) are not supported.
`display`	`display`	Supported values are inline, block, and none.

These styles can be applied to a subset of the HTML tags that are available in Flash. Table 3.2 shows which tags can be styled and how the style is applied.

Table 3.2   **Supported HTML Tags for CSS Styles**

Style name	How the Style Is Applied
P	The CSS supported in the Flash Player 7 is a subset of the actual CSS standard (much as Flash's support for HTML is). Affects all <p> tags.
Body	Affects all <body> tags. The p style, if specified, takes precedence over the body style.
Li	Affects all <li> bullet tags.
A	Affects all <a> anchor tags.
a:link	Affects all <a> anchor tags. This style is applied after any a style.
a:hover	Applied to an <a> anchor tag when the mouse is hovering over the link. This style is applied after any a and a:link style. After the mouse moves off the link, the a:hover style is removed from the link.
a:active	Applied to an <a> anchor tag when the mouse is pressed on the link. This style is applied after any a and a:link style. After the mouse button is released, the a:active style is removed from the link.

The following list shows some specific nuances of working with Flash's implementation of CSS:

- a:visited is not supported for technical reasons.
- Fonts that have spaces in them need to have quotes around them.
- Complex fonts such as WingDings are not supported in TextFields; they convert to Times.
- Colors need to be represented in their hex values (for example, #000000 is ok, but "black" is not).
- Multiple selectors on one rule set is not supported (for example, p, a, li { font-family: Arial } does not work).
- The style attribute in HTML is unsupported (for example, <p style="{ font-weight: bold }"> does not work).
- Generic font names relate to the Flash generic fonts (for example, mono converts to _typewriter, sans-serif converts to _sans, and serif converts to _serif).
- Sometimes the last semicolon is needed in a rule set, or else the rule will be ignored (for example, color: #ff0000; text-decoration: underline would ignore the underline)
- When changing the font size, Flash ignores the unit of measure (for example, "px", "pt", and so on) and simply applies the numeric value to the size shown.

- CSS allows dashes, but ActionScript converts them to non-dashed names automatically (for example, `font-weight` will be represented as `fontWeight`).

You can use CSS in your Flash applications to control many of their design aspects, while enabling them to be very easily changed on the fly without having to recompile your Flash application.

Wrap Up

The HTML enhancements available in the new version of Flash are quite powerful. We used them to create a contact list application that used a TextField with HTML containing images and links that supported mouse scrolling and right-clicking and that had a dynamic style sheet associated with it. There are still a few other things worth exploring with regard to these new features. You could experiment with including SWFs in your HTML instead of images to give your application movement or to have a refresh animation when the database content is updating. You could try styling raw XML data for use in an application where a data feed is provided in XML, such as a syndicated WebBlog like Macromedia's `markme.com` web site. You could also try implementing the other style loading techniques such as the `parseCSS` and `setStyle` functions, which enable different ways of accomplishing the type of styling we have reviewed in this article (for more on these topics, consult the Help files included with Flash MX 2004). You can use the techniques learned in this article to create a variety of Rich Internet Applications, anything from email browsers to stock quotes, all of which could benefit from an HTML user interface implemented in Macromedia Flash MX 2004.

Listing 3.12 **The Complete Code Listing for textfield.fla**

```
//create stylesheet object for content_txt
content_txt.styleSheet = new TextField.StyleSheet();

//create the array to hold all the contact objects
var db_array:Array = new Array();

//populate the array with objects that include name, email, website, and picture
db_array[0] = {name:'Randy Drisgill',email:'randy@vshift.com',website:
➥'http://www.monkeytongue.com',picture:'images/randy.jpg'};
db_array[1] = {name:'Chip
Wiggins',email:'chip@vshift.com',website:'http://www.vshift.com',picture:'images/
➥chip.jpg'};
db_array[2] = {name:'Omar W.',email:'omar@vshift.com',website:'',picture:''};
```

continues

Listing 3.12 **Continued**

```
db_array[3] = {name:'Nik M.',email:'nik@vshift.com',website:'',picture:''};
db_array[4] = {name:'Kevin B.',email:'kevin@vshift.com',website:'',picture:''};
db_array[5] = {name:'Ambrose F.',email:'ambrose@vshift.com',website:'',
➥picture:''};
db_array[6] = {name:'John C.',email:'john@vshift.com',website:'',picture:''};
db_array[7] = {name:'Henry D.',email:'henry@vshift.com',website:'',picture:''};
db_array[8] = {name:'Marcela E.',email:'marcela@vshift.com',website:'',
➥picture:''};

//create empty variable to hold the display text
var displaytext:String = '';

//loop throught the array and add each line to displaytext
for(var i:Number=0;i<db_array.length;i++){
    //if the user has a picture we will show it with the html img tag
    if(db_array[i].picture != ''){
        displaytext += '<img src="' + db_array[i].picture + '" id="image' + i +
        ➥'" align="right" height="70" width="70"><br>';
    }
    displaytext += '<p class="nametext">' + db_array[i].name + '</p>';
    displaytext += '<a class="emailtext" href="mailto:' + db_array[i].email +
    ➥'">' + db_array[i].email + '</a><br>';
    if(db_array[i].website != ''){
        //add href to website
        displaytext += '<a class="websitetext" target="_blank" href="' +
        ➥db_array[i].website + '">' + db_array[i].website + '</a><br><br>';
    } else {
        displaytext += '<br><br>';
    }
}

//load our stylesheet
content_txt.styleSheet.load("style.css");

//when stylesheet loads, check for error finding css
content_txt.styleSheet.onLoad = function(result:Boolean):Void{
    if(result){
        content_txt.htmlText = displaytext;
    } else {
        //display error message in textfield if css is not found
        content_txt.htmlText = 'Error loading CSS';
    }
}

//make a new LoadVars object
var loader:Object = new LoadVars();

//read footer.html into the object
loader.load("footer.html");
```

Listing 3.12   **Continued**

```
//when loaded, write it to the footer_txt field
loader.onLoad = function():Void{
    footer_txt.htmlText = loader.textvar;
};
```

Listing 3.13   **The Complete Code Listing for footer.html.**

```
textvar=<img src="images/logo.jpg" width="144" height="56"><br>
<font face="arial">Copyright ©2003<br>Vshift. All rights reserved.<br>
<a href="http://www.vshift.com/privacy.html">Privacy Policy</a> - <a
➥href="http://www.vshift.com/terms.html">Terms of Use</a></font>
```

Listing 3.14   **The complete code listing for style.css.**

```
.nametext {
    font-family: sans-serif; font-size: 24px; font-weight: bold; text-align:
    ➥left;
}
.emailtext {
    font-family: Arial; font-size: 19px; font-weight: normal; text-align: left;
}
.websitetext {
    font-family: Arial; font-size: 10px; font-weight: normal; text-align: left;
}
a {
    color: #600000; text-decoration: none;
}
a:hover {
    color: #ff0000; text-decoration: underline;
}
a:active {
    color: #cccccc;
}
```

Article 4

Creating Hybrid Macromedia Flash Applications (HTML, JavaScript, and Flash)

by aYo Binitie

CYBERSPACE; THE INTERNET; THE WORLD WIDE WEB; the new information superhighway. In the words of the Sony Playstation legend, "The 3rd Place." Here interactivity, information, communication, business, trade, art, design, games, and a whole lot more are all made available to the user with voice activation, motion activation, or the click of a mouse. This new world is made possible by the interaction and synergy of a myriad of multimedia and scripting technologies, media that, when interwoven and integrated, form vital components that fuse their unique substrings of data into a coherent interactive tapestry. These composites of various media and technologies constitute what we know as the web page or the web application, our portal into cyberspace.

The heterogeneous mix of technologies occurs primarily because each technology has its forte. Each technology is best suited to complete certain tasks or achieve certain aims. Consider the case of a basic static web page. A web page is, at its most basic, a script of HTML tags saved as an HTML document and displayed with a web browser. Such a basic document displays text data and performs a few interactive functions, such as linking one HTML document to another and showing flat planes of color. To create mood and improve the user experience, the web page may need to incorporate a few graphics, namely,

GIF, PNG, or JPEG image files. Such files are not native to HTML and will have to be created in an image editor (such as Macromedia Fireworks). The images are then embedded in the HTML document to achieve improved visual presentation. Thus, at this very basic level, we have a simple hybrid document, a fusion of two separate media—HTML script and image files.

Contemporary demands on the Internet, however, require a far greater level of sophistication, involving multimedia and dynamic server technologies. These demands have pushed the envelope and scope of hybridization to enable the development of intuitive web sites called Rich Media Applications. These web sites are robust and intelligent enough to cope with the interactive, informative, visual, and secure requirements of Internet users. A web site like Macromedia.com succinctly illustrates the concept of web hybridization. This web site incorporates the use of Flash applications as a multimedia vehicle to deliver sophisticated animated graphics, intuitive navigation, video, and sound as well as to transfer data. ColdFusion server technology provides connectivity between the client interface, server, and database, generates the HTML display pages, sends email, and effects various events. Flash Communication Server technology streams audio and video data. JavaScript, Quicktime, XML, and probably a few other covert technologies also contribute. These media are all interwoven to create the final web site. This is the reality of contemporary web site development and the level of development and creativity the average web user has come to expect.

To further explore web hybridization, we need to examine some of the more common web programming languages and see how they are incorporated in the development of a hybrid application in relation to ActionScript 2.0 and Flash MX 2004 technology. JavaScript, HTML, and CSS (Cascading Style Sheets) are our selected programming formats. The purpose of this article is to individually examine their spheres of operation, and then explore how they all come together in the development of a web site.

HTML

Internet.com's Webopedia defines the HTML programming language as "...*HyperText Markup Language,* the authoring language used to create documents on the World Wide Web."

HTML defines the structure and layout of a web document by using a variety of tags and attributes. The correct structure for an HTML document starts with `<html><head></head><body>` and ends with `</body></html>`. All the information you want to include in your web page belongs between the `<body>` and `</body>` tags.

There are hundreds of other tags used to format and layout the information in a web page. Tags are also used to specify hypertext links. These enable web developers to direct users to other web pages with only a click of the mouse on an image or word.

The most common way that Flash applications are displayed is in a browser window on a web site. To display a Flash document in a web page, HTML code is written to embed the Flash document (SWF) in it. This hybrid document is the most basic form of interaction between a Flash file (SWF) and an HTML document. A document such as this can be hand-coded by a developer with a basic knowledge of HTML in a text editor such as Notepad or Homesite 5.0, generated from within the Flash authoring interface using the Publish feature (see Listing 4.1), or created with the use of a web editing tool like Dreamweaver MX 2004 to embed the SWF file and publish the HTML document.

Listing 4.1   **FlashMX 2004-Generated HTML Code**

```
<OBJECT classid="clsid:D27CDB6E-AE6D-11CF-96B8-444553540000"
 codebase="http://download.macromedia.com/pub/shockwave/cabs/flash/
 ➥swflash.cab#version=7,0,0,0"
 WIDTH="100%" HEIGHT="100%" id="quiet_room" ALIGN="middle">
 <PARAM NAME="allowScriptAccess" VALUE="sameDomain">
  <PARAM NAME=application VALUE="quiet_room.swf">
 <PARAM NAME=quality VALUE=high>
 <PARAM NAME=scale VALUE=exactfit>
 <PARAM NAME=bgcolor VALUE=#666666>
 <EMBED src="quiet_room.swf" quality=high scale=exactfit bgcolor=#666666
 ➥WIDTH="100%"
 HEIGHT="100%" NAME="quiet_room" ALIGN="middle" swLiveConnect=true
 ➥allowScriptAccess="sameDomain"
  TYPE="application/x-shockwave-flash" PLUGINSPAGE="http://www.macromedia.com/go/
  ➥getflashplayer"></EMBED>
 </OBJECT>
```

The browser, in addition to its role as a display platform, can also provide the means by which data transfers can be made to and from the embedded Flash (SWF) document. For instance, variables can be passed to the embedded SWF document from HTML tags using the FlashVars parameter of the Macromedia Flash Player (see Listing 4.2).

Listing 4.2   **Embedded Tag Examples**

```
<PARAM NAME=FlashVars VALUE="fooBar=Hello Flash User&">
<EMBED FlashVars="fooBar=Hello Flash User"> </EMBED>
```

Data transfers (such as the ones in Listing 4.2) may still be in the domain of a static web page if the name–value pairs (`FlashVar` variables) are hard-coded in the HTML document.

In many cases, dynamic server technology may be involved in the development and deployment of a web site with embedded Flash files. Under these circumstances, the web pages may likely be server-generated, sending and/or receiving a variety of unique client data. Let's take the example of a web site that sends stock quotes to its users. It is without question that each of the messages received will need to have a unique tag so that updates go to the right recipient. Thus, the server will have to generate a unique set of variables for each recipient that logs on to the site to view his or her messages based on the user's input. This is a case where the HTML environment can be used to send variables to the Flash document to search for the right video to play back. A common way is to encode the data into the URL, thus making it accessible to the `FlashVars` property and thus the SWF file. Interactivity can be further enhanced by the addition of JavaScript code to the browser environment.

Cascading Style Sheets (CSS)

CSS is a mechanism for adding style (for example, fonts, colors, and spacing) to web documents. CSS was developed to deal with the problems of formatting HTML and XML documents, and it provides a tool by which formatting can be accomplished ubiquitously across the myriad of browsers used in the Internet environment. CSS uses rules to dictate the mode of formating. Each rule has a style name called a selector. The selector has one or many properties. Designing a CSS style sheet is easy. All that is required is a little knowledge of HTML. For example:

```
H4 { color: #FFFFFF }
```

This example is a simple CSS rule. This rule consists of two main parts: a selector (H4) and a declaration of the color white as a hexadecimal (#FFFFFF). The declaration has two parts: property (color) and value (#FFFFFF). Although this example influences only one of the properties needed for rendering an HTML document, it qualifies as a style sheet on its own. Combined with other style sheets (one fundamental feature of CSS is that style sheets are combined), it determines the final presentation of the document. A common example of CSS is the use of styles to match browser scrollbars to the color of the main HTML document.

ActionScript 2.0 supports CSS within the Flash authoring environment. Working with CSS in FlashMX 2004, it is possible to create styles that redefine built-in HTML formatting tags used by Flash Player (such as <p> and <li>), create style "classes" that can be applied to specific HTML elements using the <p> or <span> tags' class attribute, or define new tags. The Flash Player supports a subset of properties in the original CSS1 specification. This means that during the development of a web site, a style sheet can be written that deals with the problems of formatting in the web page as a whole HTML document and embedded Flash file. This will result in a seamless user interface, where the display within the Flash file carries a similar formatting style as the rest of the content displayed in HTML document.

Cascading Style Sheets are represented in ActionScript by the TextField.StyleSheet class. This class is only available for SWFs that target Flash Player 7 or later. To create a new style sheet object, you call the TextField.StyleSheet class's constructor.

```
var myCSSStyle = new TextField.StyleSheet();
```

To add styles to a style sheet object, you can either load an external CSS file into the object or define the styles in ActionScript. For information on loading an external style sheet, see Article 3, "Macromedia Flash MX 2004 HTML TextField Enhancements," by Randy Drisgill.

> **Note**
>
> Note that ActionScript property names are derived by removing the dashes from the corresponding CSS property and capitalizing the subsequent character.
>
> More information on the use of CSS in Flash is available from Article 1, "Converting from ActionScript to ActionScript 2.0," by William Sanders, and the ActionScript documentation.

JavaScript

JavaScript is an object-oriented language. As a standard web scripting language, its use is quite common in web pages. If you have seen a rollover button on an HTML page or have been irritated by an advertising pop-up window, then you have experienced JavaScript. Used sensibly, JavaScript can be a powerful ally of ActionScript, working in sync to produce effects and procedures that are useful and even breathtaking. An example of the usefulness of JavaScript is the fact that it can be used on web site index pages to check for the correct Flash Player on the user's browser and, depending on the results, redirect the user to the Macromedia web site to download a newer Flash Player. JavaScript can also be used to create visual effects in the browser window. For example, it is possible to trigger an effect to simulate an earthquake on the browser from within the embedded Flash application. ActionScript and JavaScript have a lot in common because they are both based on the ECMA-262 standard, the international standard for JavaScript. In fact, ActionScript is a derivative of JavaScript. This provides much potential for interaction between ActionScript in the SWF document and JavaScript in the browser environment.

Flash MX 2004 ActionScript 2.0 Classes

Flash MX 2004 ActionScript 2.0 has a variety of built-in classes designed to enable seamless integration with external data sources. Taking a cursory look at the available classes, the most obvious are the Databinding, WebServices, LoadVars, XML, NetConnection, NetServices (used with Flash Remoting), LocalConnection, and TextField classes. There are many more, and they all provide a means of interacting with external data sources to create a Rich Internet Application (RIA). (See also Article 6, "ActionScript Design Patterns for Rich Internet Application Development," by Steven Webster and Alistair McLeod.) These classes contain the methods and properties needed to make the development of a hybrid application possible. The structures examined here will require in-depth studying from more appropriate sources.

- **XML (Extensible Markup Language)**—XML is a powerful and ubiquitous medium that facilitates the transfer of data across various platforms. Most existing web technologies use this standard because of its capability to create bridges between differing system architectures and document object models (DOMs). Flash MX 2004 is no different, and the XML class provides the prerequisite tool to deal with XML data transfers. An XML document may, for instance, hold the data for a slide show. If this data is made available to a Flash application, the required slides can be shown when activated. If our slide XML document is made available to a ColdFusion template that is associated with our Flash application, it can date the server with any changes made to the slide content or select the appropriate slide show for the client based on client specifications. To create an instance of the XML object in Flash 2004, type the following code in the Actions Panel:

```
var aYoXML:XML= new XML()
```

- **Databinding**—The Flash Databinding class provides a powerful way by which Flash applications can send, receive, and update data from external and internal sources. Databinding creates a link between a data source and an endpoint. This data source may be the contents of a TextField object or an XML or a WebServices document. The point at which the data is retrieved or updated is called an endpoint. Endpoints can be Flash UI components or Flash objects. The binding listens for changes in the data-source and updates the endpoint. A weather update feature on a web site can be auto-updated from a public WebServices weather document using databinding. For more information about databinding, see Article 6.

- **getURL()**—The `getURL()` method enables the developer to load a document from a specific mapped URL into a window. It can also send variables to another application at a defined URL. This URL may be locally mapped or may be an absolute URL. The method can be used in isolation or attached to a movie clip. When using `getURL()` to send variables, there are two options available: the GET and POST methods. The GET method sends data attached to the end of a URL, whereas the POST method sends all the variables attached to the movie clip with a separate HTTP header. If no variables are to be sent, the `getURL()` method can be used without the optional parameters:

```
getURL("http://www.macromedia.com");

var firstName:String = "James";
var useGet = getURL (http://ww.macromedia.com?firstName=" + firstName, "_blank",
➥"GET");

var usePost =  my_mc.getURL("http://www.designstreet.net/send_email.cfm",
➥"_blank", POST)
```

- **LoadVars()**—The LoadVars class enables the developer to transfer variables between a Flash file and a server. Using the LoadVars class, verification of successful data transfers, progress indications, and stream data during downloads can be monitored and achieved. The LoadVars class uses the methods `load()`, `send()`, and `sendAndLoad()` to communicate with servers. LoadVars transfers ActionScript name and value pairs. A LoadVars class must be instantiated first before it can be used. The following code creates an instance of the LoadVars class.

```
var MyVarLoader = new LoadVars()
```

- **LocalConnection()**—The LocalConnection class provides a browser-to-browser line of communication between two different applications residing on the same computer. Although this can be achieved with JavaScript, LocalConnection is the Flash authoring environment's native method of achieving this communication. A good example of this is the case of a main application with another application in a separate browser that is used as a remote control. The remote control application can, using JavaScript, activate the launch of the main application in a larger browser window and control all the events and actions therein, thus freeing up the real estate of the main window for display purposes only.

- **NetConnection()**—The NetConnection class works in two different modes: locally within the Flash application and remotely with Flash Communication Server and Flash Remoting. Locally, the NetConnection class provides a means by which FLV files can be accessed, controlled, and played through their absolute or relative URL. It is required that this class be defined to use the NetStream class. Where the NetConnection object is used remotely, it manages a bidirectional connection between the client and Flash Communication Server or Flash Remoting. The Flash Communication Server enables you to share audio, video, and data using the Macromedia Real-Time Messaging Protocol (RTMP). Flash Remoting on the other hand makes Action Messaging Format (AMF) connections to application servers via the NetConnection class using the HTTP protocol. The NetConnection class makes its connections, local or otherwise with the `NetConnection.connect()` method. The following lines of code illustrate three different ways in which instances of the NetConnection class are created:

```
var my_local _nc:NetConnection = new NetConnection(); my_local_nc.connect(null);

var my_FCS _nc = new NetConnection(); my_local_nc.connect("rtmp:/myConnection");

var my_remoting _nc = new NetConnection(); my_local_nc.connect
➥("http://mysite.com");
```

- **NetStream()**—Using the NetStream object, it is possible to play back audio, video, and text data streams. Used natively, this class provides a means by which FLV files can be streamed and played in the Flash application. The NetStream object works with the NetConnection object. When FLV video streaming is involved, a video object is required to display the streaming data. The NetStream object is also used with the Flash Communication Server. It creates a monodirectional connection between the server and the Flash application to stream FLV data to and from the client. Educational web sites can use the NetStream object to play recorded FLV video files as online tutorials and lectures for students. The following code creates an instance of the NetStream:

```
var my_local _nc:NetConnection = new NetConnection();
my_local_nc.connect(null);
var my_local_ns:NetStream= new NetStream(myNetConnection);
my_local_ns.play("http://my.site.com/ AS-II-documentation/ayo.flv");
```

- **Shared Objects**—A shared object is a data storage feature. There are two types: the local shared object and the remote shared object.

  A *local* shared object is the Flash equivalent of a cookie, though it is more intuitive. It enables data to be stored for individual clients on their hard drives. In its most basic application, it provides a means by which data unique to each client can be stored on the client machine for use any time the client logs in to the web site. A local SharedObject can be used, for instance, to keep a user's personal login details for a site on his hard drive. The following syntax creates a local shared object:

```
var zainab_so = SharedObject.getLocal("foo");
```

  On the other hand, a *remote* shared object is used in Flash Communication Server applications. With a remote shared object, data can be stored or used to facilitate real time transfer of information across connected users. An example of such a transfer is real time text updates during a real time web chat session. During a session, when the connected client types a message and sends it, all connected clients see the updated message on their screens. Remote shared objects are created using the following syntax:

```
var bill_remote_so= SharedObject.getRemote("sanders", my_nc.uri, false)
```

- **System**—The System object contains the capabilities object and the security object. Using the System object, a developer can write code that checks for the capabilities of the client's system. By so doing, it is possible to customize the user's interface. For instance, a Flash file could check if the client's system can stream video and encode video using the `System.hasStreamingVideo` and `System.hasVideoEncoder` properties. If the client can neither stream nor encode video, the Flash file does not trigger structures in it that use these capabilities. The following function block uses a property of the System.capabilities object to check for the presence of a video encoder.

```
Check4Video= function(){
if (System.capabilities.hasVideoEncoder) {
    trace("$");
//display site to suit client status
}
}
```

- **Stage**—The Stage class gives the developer access to the size of the browser in pixels. It can be an invaluable tool in the placement of a Flash file in the browser environment. With the Stage class, you can determine from within the Flash file how the document responds to changes in browser size. In real terms, it gives the developer the power to determine what part of the SWF is resized with the browser and what is not. To utilize this class, the `Stage.scaleMode` needs to be set to `"noScale."` A listener object is then initialized to trigger the `Stage.onResize` method, which is triggered when the browser is resized. The following code sets the Stage.scaleMode property to "noScale".

```
Stage.scaleMode= "noScale"
```

- **TextField**—The TextField class provides the means by which text data can be displayed to the user. It is an extremely powerful and fluid class that gives the developer a myriad of ways to display and control text and visual data. TextFields can be created in development time or at runtime. They can be editable, as with input fields, or they can act as containers to deal with text or visual data transfer. CSS formatting can be implemented on the TextField class, which can be achieved from within the Flash file or by loading an external CSS document. In a basic scenario, content for a Flash application can be displayed from data received from an XML or WSDL document.

  HTML pages, supported image files (JPG and SWF), and other web documents (CFM) can be embedded in text fields. This feature can be set up in the authoring environment or generated at runtime. The text field must be a dynamic text field and must be set to accept HTML tags. After this is done, whole HTML pages can be imported into the Flash application. If the correct id tags are set, it is possible to control Flash applications embedded in a web page that is imported into the Flash application.

- **fsCommand**— This is a function which allows the SWF file to communicate with either Flash Player or the program hosting Flash Player, such as a web browser. With the `fsCommand`, a Flash application can communicate with the Flash Player and the web browser. `fsCommand` comes into its own when there is the need to run executable programs from the Flash application. It has properties to manage the Flash Player aspect ratio in the browser. The `fsCommand` creates a point of interaction between Flash ActionScript and browser-embedded JavaScript.

The tools listed above are perhaps the most obvious tools Flash provides for dealing with external data sources. However, they are just a few in a whole arsenal of tools available to the Flash developer. The reason for this stock-taking is simple. Flash provides many options for development purposes. These tools work independently and in correlation with each other to produce a variety of results. Take the example of an Array, which may hold data used to provide the names for a set of MovieClip buttons and assign them the functions or events they are required to trigger. The data used to populate such an array may be provided by an XML document. To transfer the required data to the buttons, the XML object is needed to load the XML document, parse the required data from it, and then assign the results to an Array object. It is therefore good practice to lay all your development cards on the table. A useful analogy is the idea of a painter laying out all his paints on the palette before mixing paint and starting work on a canvas. In this manner, the developer can make an educated choice of tools and decide on the various combinations and permutations in which those tools will be deployed, depending on the other technologies being deployed. Having looked at the tools at our disposal, we can examine the processes involved in the development of a web site.

Developing a Hybrid Application: A Case Study (The Quiet Room)

The most useful way to explore the possibilities of web hybridization is to examine a case study and analyze the way such an application is conceived and developed. To do this, we will create a fictional project. By nature of its requirements, this application needs to use a combination of the languages we have outlined above. A fictitious design firm Company A has decided to develop a web site as an online showpiece to demonstrate novel ways in which they develop web applications. At a creative huddle, the design team comes up with a concept web site called "The Quiet Room." The Quiet Room will utilize multimedia elements like audio and video. The web site will be intuitive enough to check for the latest Macromedia Flash Player and, based on the result, instruct the user to download the player or enter the site. To make it more interesting, it is agreed that navigation should be done from a small remote control, giving the user the ability to launch the site to access the innards or close the site when it is not needed. The development team then creates a draft with the following specifications. This design brief will serve as a reference point to keep the goals of the project in sight during development.

Quiet Room Design Outline

The Quiet Room is an attempt to create a functional piece of conceptual art that showcases the variety of multimedia resources and artistic and technical ability available at Company A. The concept is to build an online environment where digital art will merge with various web technologies to achieve a unique yet functional web application. This experimental web site incorporates Flash technology as its core medium, while its supporting structures are built with other web scripting technology combined to create a complete, seamless unit. Creative yet functional ways of displaying text and visual data need to be explored. The site will make use of multimedia elements (sound, video, movement) to heighten the sensory levels of user experience and will experiment with unusual methods to navigate through the site.

Having an outline gives the developer a creative direction to help channel design and development ideas. Web sites succeed best when there is proper planning. It is good practice to have a provisional blueprint drawn up before the design/development process starts. It enables the developer to take stock of the various technologies and elements that will need to be orchestrated as the site is built. As the site is developed, the provisional architecture will inevitably change to incorporate new ideas, but this method gives the project a sound basis on which to begin.

The Provisional Blueprint

In his book *MTIV: Process, Inspiration and Practice for the New Media Designer* (New Riders, 2002), Hillman Curtis quotes the Bauhaus maxim, "form follows function." Every designer and developer should adhere to this concept in the development of any project. It keeps you focused on the site goals and serves as a constant reminder of the creative direction during site development. Our brief has given us the general direction that the site development should take, so let's now take stock of the tools and elements required to design and develop the site.

Site Elements

The site elements include:

- **Graphics**—To be imported into the Flash file for background and other graphic elements within the site
- **FLV files**—Video files
- **MP3 files**—Sound
- **Text or XML files**—For the text content within the site
- **HTML documents**—index.html, remote.html and quiet_room.html

Site Technologies

The site technologies include:

- **ActionScript 2.0**—The native Flash coding language, akin to JavaScript, will enable the developer to construct the actions and events in the Flash file and enable interaction with the Javascript embedded in the HTML document, ColdFusion scripting, and the CSS document required for site formatting.
- **JavaScript**—This will enable the developer to check if the client has the right player and redirect the client to the Macromedia download page if necessary. It will also enable the Flash application to trigger various effects in the browser.
- **Cascading Style Sheet (CSS)**—The style sheet will enable us to format the HTML document text fields in the Flash application (if required).

Tools Required

The tools required include:

- Flash MX 2004
- Fireworks MX 2004
- Dreamweaver MX 2004 or Homesite 5.0

Site Layout

Based on the brief, the site will utilize HTML documents for the browser environment. There will be an opening page to check for the correct Flash player, a remote control, and a main viewing area. Both documents will have

Flash applications embedded in them. A couple things need to be done before the development process starts. First, we need to take a complete look at the site in its entire context, taking into consideration the way the Flash applications will sit in both HTML documents. Second, a procedure that deals with the way the user accesses and navigates through the site needs to be crafted.

The required user experience is vital, so the client browser must be checked for the correct player to view the site. The index page of the site must have the capacity to check for the appropriate player when the connection is made to the web site. If this is unsuccessful, the client will be redirected or informed to download the right player. If, on the other hand, the client has the right player, then the remote control HTML page is activated, from where the main application is triggered. Figure 4.1 shows the procedural logic of the Quiet Room index page.

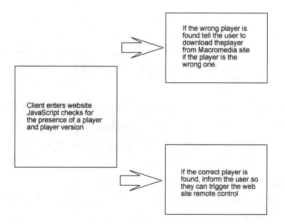

Figure 4.1 Procedural logic of The Quiet Room index page.

Two HTML documents will form the main part of this application. One will hold a Flash application that will perform the duties of a remote control, and the other will contain the main viewing window for the site. Figure 4.2 supplies the procedural logic of the Quiet Room application.

Figure 4.2 Procedural logic of the Quiet Room application.

Remote Control (remote.html)

The remote control application is the main navigation structure of the application. It will be opened as a pop-up window from the index page and will serve two main functions. First, it will launch the viewing area of the application, and second, it will control general navigation within the viewing window. The user will be able to close the main viewing window from the remote control.

JavaScript controls from the index page will control the size of the remote control browser window and the size of the main browser window when launched from the remote control.

Remote controls need to be small and portable, so the remote control HTML document, which we will call "remote.html," needs to be of a relatively small size. In the spirit of exploring novel methods of expression, the remote control panel will be designed in a landscape format rather than the traditional portrait format (see Figure 4.3).

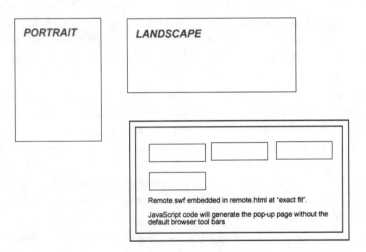

Figure 4.3   Exploring design formats for the remote control application.

Using the Publish feature in the Flash authoring environment, the remote control Flash application will be set to "exact fit" in remote.html. This will have the effect of filling the entire browser window with the Flash application, thus giving it the proper feel of a remote control. A JavaScript function will generate the page and ensure that the page is launched without the browser toolbars and that it is set to the right size.

Main Viewing Window (quiet_room.html)

The main window, quiet_room.html, houses the main Flash application, quiet_room.swf. The placement of the Flash application in the browser window needs to be considered. However, to plan for this, a number of factors needs to be considered.

First, to ensure that the web page is viewed in the manner determined by the developer, the HTML page has to have its size fixed, and the browser resizing properties must be disabled. The browser resize property will be disabled by the JavaScript code that launches it from the remote control module, remote.html. The Flash application, quiet_room.swf, will be published with the "no scale" property so that its aspect ratio remains fixed.

The web site will be seen on a variety of monitors of varying sizes and screen resolutions. The average computer monitor screen size varies between 15 inches and 21 inches, with the majority usually being between 15 inches and 19 inches. Screen resolutions of between 800×600 and 1024×768 pixels are the usual status quo. It is therefore a good practice to ensure that the main view browser size is set to no greater than 800×600 pixels (preferably a little less), enabling the majority of users view the web site without running out of viewing space.

Considerations of site weight are very important. The Internet works with telecommunications, and there are constraints and limitations on bandwidth. This factor is further exacerbated by peak Internet usage periods. Optimization of graphic and text content is therefore imperative to ensure speedy loading times. The development logic for the Flash application also needs to be well thought out to prevent needless code and the accompanying excess application weight. Where necessary, files will be imported into the application at runtime rather than embedded during authoring.

The background graphic, bg_4.jpg, has a canvas size of 1000×880 pixels, our Flash application quiet_room.swf is set to 640×480 pixels, and the HTML document quiet_room.html has an aspect ratio of 800×600 pixels. To create a seamless feel to the site, all these elements need to be arranged like a jigsaw puzzle to work in concert.

For exact placement, the HTML document will be divided up using a couple tables. The background graphic first has to be cropped to fit the size of the browser window. It will then be sliced into three parts. One slice will form the background for the Flash application, and the other pieces will fit in tables in the HTML document, quiet_room.html. A CSS document will provide the appropriate classes to ensure proper formatting of the HTML document and table structures. JavaScript code integrated into the HTML file will have functions that can be called from the Flash application to trigger effects on the browser if so desired by the user. These functions will be called from the remote control.

Figure 4.4 illustrates the manner in which the HTML document will be split up in the browser window.

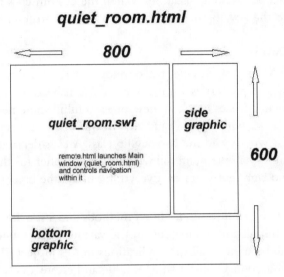

Figure 4.4   Table structure and dimensions of the Quiet Room application.

The preceding ideas and suggestions will form the provisional draft for the development of the Quiet Room. These ideas will be developed and expanded as the creation of the site progresses. Armed with this blueprint and having all the necessary tools and elements, the project can now begin. A good practice is to have these ideas written or typed on a sheet of paper and stuck on a wall close by, scribbled on a white board, or printed and distributed to the development team. This gives the developer or team a constant point of reference during the project development period.

Having a project procedure does two things. First, it enables an effective division of labor strategy by which various design and development assignments can be apportioned to members of a team. If, on the other hand, there is only one developer, it allows for the prioritizing of the various parts of the project. It also creates a documented plan of attack and lists the jobs to be done so that various parts are not overlooked.

Building the Sample Web Site

For the Quiet Room project, Flash applications form the core components of the web site, so it is a good idea to start by developing the Flash applications and then building the other features around them as supporting structures. To begin, a custom class needs to be written to provide certain methods necessary to the development of the two Flash applications. We will start by defining the custom class for both Flash applications. When the custom class is defined, we will move on to the development of the rest of the site structures.

Setting Up a Custom Class

Although Flash MX 2004 provides the developer with a variety of built-in classes, methods, and properties, on many occasions it becomes necessary to extend these default classes or create new ones to fulfill some need in the Flash application. We will be doing just that in this instance—creating a new custom class that will extend the MovieClip class. A class declaration consists minimally of the `class` statement, followed by an identifier for the class name, and then left and right curly braces. Everything inside the braces is the class body.

This will provide us with some modified methods and a few new methods to enable easier manipulation of elements in the various Flash applications. Our custom class will be used by all the applications in this project. To begin, create a folder and call it code. Open Flash MX 2004 and create a new ActionScript document. Save this document as QKlass.as.

> **Note**
>
> Classes can only be defined in ActionScript (AS) files. A class cannot be declared on a frame script in an FLA file. The specified class name must match the name of the AS file that contains it.

Open the document QKlass.as. We will be extending the MovieClip class to create three new methods and to extend two existing ones. First we need to define the class, declare a few constants, and create the class constructor function. To do this, type the following code in QKlass.as:

```
dynamic class QKlass extends MovieClip {

function QKlass() {}
}
```

The above declaration means that the class QKlass is a subclass of the MovieClip class and will inherit all its properties and methods. Let's start by extending certain methods of the MovieClip class.

Extending the Methods of a Built-in Class

The style sheet will enable us to format the HTML document holding the Flash application. A modified form of this method will be created to enable attached application clips to be positioned on the Stage with precision from one method, rather than having to set up their x and y coordinates separately. In the QKlass class definition block and underneath the QKlass contructor, we will create a new method called `newAttachMovie`. This method will extend the `attachMovie` method and is defined as shown in Listing 4.3.

Listing 4.3 **Extending the *MovieClip*.Class**

```
(C2) //------------------------------
     // Extends Application clip method attachMovie
     //------------------------------

     function newAttachMovie(attacher:MovieClip, idName:Object, newname:Object,
     ➡depth:Number, PosX:Number, PosY:Number) {
         attacher.attachMovie(idName, newname, depth);
         attacher[newname]._x = PosX;
         attacher[newname]._y = PosY;
     }
```

The first line, `function newAttachMovie(attacher, idName, newname, depth, posX, posY)`, defines the new method's name and the variables required to execute the rest of the function block. The "attacher" is the _level or the movieClip where the new movie clip will be placed. `idName` is the identifier of the application clip to be generated from within the Flash application library. `depth` is the depth at which this application clip will be set. The variables `PosX` and `PosY` are the x and y coordinates of the application clip on the Stage. When this new method is called at runtime, attached application clips will be placed precisely at the appropriate location.

The MovieClip class method `createEmptyMovieClip` enables the creation of new MovieClips at runtime. This method also has no provision for the exact placement of newly-created application clips on the Stage. A new method, `newCreateMovieClip`, will be written to enable newly-created application clips to be positioned on the Stage from one method. This is an improvement on the conventional method of creating the MovieClip and then defining its position on the Stage separately. The new method has all the parameters of the original method with a few new ones to enable exact placement. Type the code in Listing 4.4 underneath the previously created method `newAttachMovie()`.

Listing 4.4   **Extending the *MovieClip.createEmptyMovieClip()* Method**

```
//------------------------------
// Extends Application clip method createEmptyMovieClip
//------------------------------
function newCreateEmptyMovieClip(applicationLoc:MovieClip, newname:Object,
➥depth:Number, posX:Number, posY:Number) {
    applicationLoc.createEmptyMovieClip(newname, depth);
    applicationLoc[newname]._x = posX;
    applicationLoc[newname]._y = posY;
}
```

In a similar manner to the previous code, applicationLoc defines the target application where the new application clip will be created. newname provides the name of the MovieClip, depth is the depth it should be placed at, and posX and posY are its x and y coordinates.

Creating New Custom Methods

A few custom methods need to be defined. It makes sense to create a custom method when many instances of a class are required to do the same job. For instance, we have a function fadeIn() that fades in any application clip that calls it. This means that for every application clip that uses the function, the function is reinterpreted. It is therefore more efficient to define such a function as a method of the required class.

Four custom methods will be built here for the QKlass class: doFadeIn, doFadeOut, doScaleIn, and doScaleOut. As their names imply, the first two methods will effect _alpha changes on a target object, causing it to fade in or out. The last two will effect changes on the _xscale property of a target object, causing it to, well, scale in and out.

doFadeIn

Beneath the previous method, type the following code. The first line declares the method name, doFadeIn, and the method parameter, my_mc. Here, strong data typing is used to declare the parameter, my_mc (my_mc:MovieClip). This ensures that the Flash compiler knows that the information sent for processing is of the MovieClip class, thereby saving valuable processing time. ActionScript 2.0 strict data typing also provides you the ability to explicitly specify the data type for variables, as shown in Listing 4.5.

Listing 4.5 **Custom Method to Increase the _alpha Value of a Movieclip**

```
//------------------------------
// fadeIn
//------------------------------

function doFadeIn(my_mc:MovieClip) {
    my_mc._alpha = 2;
    my_mc.onEnterFrame = function() {
        var alphaVal = 5;
        if (this._alpha<99) {
            return this._alpha += alphaVal;
        }else {
            delete this.onEnterFrame();
        }
    };
}
```

Explaining the method above, we see that the method is sent the parameter of a target application clip, my_mc:MovieClip. This application clip is then given an alpha value of 2 (my_mc._alpha=2), thus making it virtually transparent. The QKlass inherits from the MovieClip class and therefore possesses all its properties and methods. At the top of the script, just after the class definition, define a variable constant alphaVal:Number. This constant will determine the amount by which the alpha level of my_mc will be increased until the if condition is resolved. The value of alphaVal is set to 5. Next, my_mc uses the onEnterFrame method to check for its _alpha value. It does this using the if conditional statement if (this._alpha<99). Because my_mc._alpha is set to 2, the if condition is not satisfied; therefore the alpha value of my_mc is increased by a constant of 5 (alphaVal) until the alpha value exceeds 99. To the viewer, the application clip fades in.

doFadeout

The doFadeOut method follows the same construct, except for the fact that the conditional statement checks to see if the _alpha is greater than a value of zero, and if so, it implements a decrement of the alphaVal until the condition is met. Type the code shown in Listing 4.6 underneath the previous function, doFadeIn.

Listing 4.6 **Custom Method to Decrease the _alpha Value of a Movieclip**

```
() //------------------------------.
    // fadeOut
    //------------------------------
    function doFadeOut(my_mc:MovieClip) {
```

continues

Listing 4.6 **Continued**

```
my_mc.onEnterFrame = function() {
    var alphaVal = 5;
    if (this._alpha>0) {
        //trace(this._alpha+" : "+alphaVal);
        this._alpha -= alphaVal;
    }else {
        delete this.onEnterFrame();
    }
};
}
```

doScaleIn and doScaleOut

The doScaleIn and doScaleOut methods follow a similar construct as the doFadeIn and doFadeOut methods. The only difference is the variable constant, scaleVal:Number, which needs to be defined underneath the alphaVal constant. The methods in this case deal with the _xscale property of the target application clip my_mc. To define these methods, type the code shown in Listings 4.7 and 4.8 beneath the previously defined functions.

Listing 4.7 **Custom Method to Increase the** _xscale **Value of a Movie Clip**

```
//------------------------------
// ScaleIn
//------------------------------
function doScaleIn(my_mc:MovieClip) {
    my_mc._xscale = 1;
    my_mc.onEnterFrame = function() {
        //trace("&^%");
        var scaleVal=2;
        if (this._xscale<99) {
            this._xscale += scaleVal;
        }else {
            delete this.onEnterFrame();
        }
    };
}
```

Listing 4.8 **Custom Method to Decrease the** _xscale **Value of a Movie Clip**

```
//------------------------------
// ScaleOut
//------------------------------
function doScaleOut(my_mc:MovieClip) {
    my_mc.onEnterFrame = function() {
        if (this._xscale>2) {
```

continues

Listing 4.8 **Continued**

```
            this._xscale -= scaleVal;
        }else {
            delete this.onEnterFrame();
        }
    };
  }

}
```

doButtonAction

The remote control uses custom-built movie clip buttons. These will be application clips tailored to suit the background visuals. As there will be more than one button, it makes sense to create a custom method that will deal with the button actions and behavior. The method will be called doButtonAction. It will require one parameter, my_mc:Object, the target application clip. This parameter will then utilize the ActionScript application clip methods onRollOver and onRollOut to trigger the required events. Create this method underneath the doScaleOut method as shown in Listing 4.9.

Listing 4.9 **Custom Method to Affect Button Actions on a Movie Clip**

```
//----------------------------------
    //doButtonAction
    //---------------------------------.
    function doButtonAction(my_mc:Object) {
        my_mc.onRollOver = function() {
            this.gotoAndStop(2);
        };
            my_mc.onRollOut= function() {
            this.gotoAndStop(1);
        };
    }
```

Save the document QKlass.as.

The custom class QKlass takes into consideration all the probable custom methods that may be needed to create elements and assign to them various events, actions, and properties. This enables the developer to concentrate on the business of developing each part of the application without having to toggle back and forth from the class definition to add a new method or property. With the custom class QKlass in place, the rest of the development process can continue. The remote control application seems to be the next application to tackle because it will control all the events and actions in the main application.

The Remote Control Module

The remote control module is an HTML document called remote.html. In it is embedded a Flash application, remote.swf. This application contains the navigation for the main application document, quiet_room.html. The application clip buttons in the remote control bill are used to open or close the main application, as well as trigger events within it.

The following are the functions required of the remote control:

- Launch the main viewing window.
- Play the video in the main viewer.
- Open text information.
- Play sound from the main viewer.
- Toggle an email module.
- Close the main viewing window.

Here, as before, the Flash application is the main resource of the remote control module. Other scripting features will be built around its functionality. Therefore, we will address the development of the remote control application first before addressing anything else

Remote Control Application

Open Flash MX 2004 and create a new Flash document. Save it as remote.fla. Click on the Publish option in the File menu (File > Publish). In the Publish Settings panel, click on the Flash tab. In this panel, select ActionScript 2.0 as the scripting language. Click on the Settings button and create a class path by browsing to the code folder where QKlass.as is saved and selecting it. Click OK and exit the Publish Settings panel. This way, the Flash application is mapped to have access to the custom class QKlass (see Figure 4.5).

Create a new Flash ActionScript document. Save it in the code folder as r_1.as. All the code for remote.fla will be done in this document. Select the first frame of the first layer of the Flash application, and in the Actions panel, type **#include ./code/r_1.as**. This will load the code in r_1.as into remote.fla. Open the ActionScript document, r_1.as, and type:

```
Stage.scaleMode = "noScale";
```

This indicates the current scaling of the Flash application in the Stage. The scaleMode property forces the application into a specific scaling mode. In this case, no scaling will be done.

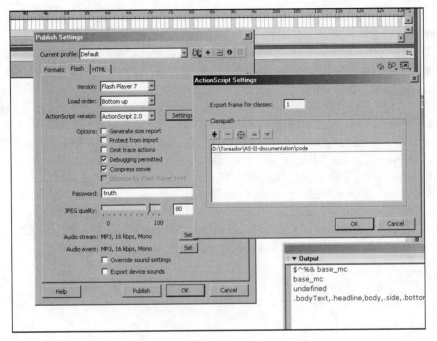

Figure 4.5 Setting the class path in Flash.

Background and Animation

In the images folder is the background image (see Figure 4.6) for the remote control. The path to the image is assigned to the variable bg. This variable will provide the information with which the Flash application will load its background.

```
var bg:String = "./images/r1.jpg";
```

Figure 4.6 Remote control background image.

Create `remoteBase`, an instance of the QKlass class. With the custom method `newCreateEmptyMovieClip`, create a new application clip `base_mc`. Position the application clip at x and y coordinates of 0 and 0, respectively. Load `base_mc` with the variable `bg`. Type the following code underneath the previously typed code.

```
remoteBase = new QKlass();
remoteBase.newCreateEmptyMovieClip(_level0, "base_mc", 1, 0, 0);
base_mc.loadMOvie(bg);
```

Open up the file remote.fla. On the Stage, go to the toolbar and select the "Oval tool". Create a disc. Using the Oval tool, create a series of concentric circles. With the Line tool, draw a few lines to cut across the circles. Use the Selection tool to delete sections of the image, and use the Fill tool to fill out sections. You should end up with something like what is shown in Figure 4.7. Press the F8 key to open the Convert to Symbol panel and convert the image into an application clip. Call it disc and delete it from the Stage.

Figure 4.7   Disc image.

Go to the library, right-click the image, and open the Linkage Properties dialog box (see Figure 4.8). Select the Export for ActionScript option and leave the identifier as disc. Close the Linkage Properties dialog box.

Linkage Properties	
Identifier: disc	OK
AS 2.0 Class:	Cancel
Linkage: ☑ Export for ActionScript	
☐ Export for runtime sharing	
☐ Import for runtime sharing	
☑ Export in first frame	
URL:	Help

Figure 4.8   The Linkage Properties dialog box.

Switch tabs in your Flash authoring interface and bring up r_1.as. Using the modified `attachApplication` method defined in QKlass, attach an application to the Stage. Use the identifier disc and name the new application `d1_mc`.

```
remoteBase.newAttachMovie(_level0, "disc", "d1_mc", 2, 130, 80);
```

Create a rotary effect for the newly attached movie clip using the _rotation property. This sorts out the background for the remote control application.

```
d1_mc.onEnterFrame = function() {
    this._rotation += 3;
};
```

Remote Control Application Buttons: Remote Navigation for the Quiet Room

The main components for the remote control application consist of application clip buttons generated at runtime. The button labels will be supplied by variables from an imported text file. These variables will be used also as a control by which various functions will be assigned to the different buttons. Keeping the variables in an external text file separates editable content of the remote control from the application structure. By separating the content, changes can be made quickly outside the authoring interface and effected at runtime. We begin by creating this text document. To do this, open Notepad (Win OS) and type the following text:

```
bVar0=Launch&bVar1=Info&bVar2=Video&bVar3=Sound&bVar4=eMail&bVar5=Close
```

Save the document in the code folder as rB_names.txt. This text file will be imported into the Flash application and will provide the data required to name the navigation structures. It will also provide information necessary to trigger various actions and events.

Using the tabs in Flash MX 2004, bring up remote.fla. Select the Rectangle tool. Click on the "Rectangle tool" and select the "Round Rectangle Radius" option. Set the value to 5 and draw a rectangle. Select the Text tool and create a dynamic text field over the rectangle.

In the Properties Inspector, select the dynamic option and give the text object the instance name of qLabel_txt. Select the rectangle and text and convert them to a MovieClip. Call the MovieClip qBtn, and before you close the panel, click on the Advanced button and select the Export for ActionScript option. Leave the identifier name as it is. The remote control movie clip button is shown in Figure 4.9.

Assign the text file path to the variable rBtnNames.

```
var rBtnNames:String = "code/rB_names.txt";
```

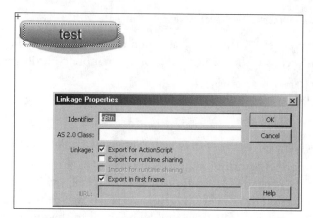

Figure 4.9   The remote control movie clip button.

Create a new LoadVars class instance and call it rBdata. Use the onLoad method to assign a function fooLoaded to rBData. The function fooLoaded will validate loading of the text file, assign names to the buttons, and allocate the required events and functions to the various buttons based on data supplied from the loaded text file. Load rBData with the variable rBtnNames using the Loadvars.load method. This will provide rBData with the directory map for the text file. Next, create a new Array class instance, rBDataArr, which will have the data retrieved from the text file allocated indices in its structure.

```
var rBData:LoadVars = new LoadVars();
rBData.onLoad = fooLoaded;
rBLoad = rBData.load(rBtnNames);
var rBDataArr:Array = new Array();
```

Define a new function, fooLoaded. Set its parameter as success. The Boolean success is a property that validates the success of an event or argument. Using the if condition, check whether the text file has been loaded with a trace.

```
function fooLoaded(success) {
    if (success) {
        trace("loaded");
```

Collect all the variables loaded from the text file and convert them to a string. To do this, use the String class method toString() and assign the value to a variable istring. When this is done, separate the string into substrings with the String.split method, using & as the delimiter. Assign the value to a variable iSplit.

```
//collect all the variables , convert to string and assign to dataArr
var iString:String=rBData.toString();
 iSplit=iString.split("&");
 trace(iSplit.length);
```

The substring will now be assigned to rBDataArr. This will be done using the for loop sequence. The loop will use a variable i set to zero to intialize it, the length of the variable iSplit subtracted by 1 will be the condition, and an increment of i will evaluate the loop.

```
for (var i = 0; i<iSplit.length-1; i++) {
     _level0.rBDataArr[i] = rBData["bVar"+i];
```

Using the remoteBase class newAttachMovie method, buttons will be attached to the Stage, and their positions will be plotted. The buttons' application clip text object qLabel_txt will be assigned their names from the data supplied by the rBDataArr.

Due to the size of the buttons, it will not be possible to place all the buttons on the same x or y coordinates; therefore, an if condition needs to be written into the code to reposition buttons that extend beyond the Stage size.

```
remoteBase.newAttachMovie(_level0, "qBtn", "b"+i+"_tbtn", 7+i, 25+(105*i),
➡50);
_level0["b"+i+"_tbtn"].qLabel_txt.text = _level0["b"+i+"_tbtn"].qLabels_txt.
➡text=_level0.rBDataArr[i];
trace(i);
remoteBase.doButtonAction(_level0["b"+i+"_tbtn"]);
     if (i>2) {
     _level0["b"+i+"_tbtn"]._x=25+(105*(i-3));
     _level0["b"+i+"_tbtn"]._y=100;
          }
```

To attach the functions to the respective buttons, we use a series of if conditional statements. Looking at the first button, the label value is validated against the required string, in this case "Launch." If there is a strict equality, the button uses an onRelease function to launch the function launchQuietRoom().

```
if (_level0["b"+i+"_tbtn"].qLabel_txt.text == "Launch") {
_level0["b"+i+"_tbtn"].onRelease = function() {
          launchQuietRoom();
               };
     }
```

The labels for all the other buttons are used in the same manner to validate and assign functions to all the other buttons. Therefore, the label "Info" will assign the function that will trigger the information panel on the main window to the "Info" button. The "Video" button will trigger the video, the

"Sound" will play an MP3 file, "eMail" will trigger an email panel in the main window, and "Close" will close the main viewer. Unlike the previous conditional statement, each of the MovieClip buttons will use the Local Connection Object remoteCon_lc to make a call to another local connection object (quietroom_lc) in the main Flash application quiet_room.swf. The functions attached to the LocalConnection object, quietroom_lc, will then be fired. Let us examine in detail the arguments that are assigned to the "Info" button. The arguments used for this button are used for all the other buttons. First, as with the launch button, the value of the text object in the button is compared against the string "Info." If this is so, the button is assigned an onRelease method that triggers the arguments within its function block. In this case, it uses the remote_lc LocalConnection object to make a function call in the quiet_room.swf. All the other buttons are assigned their events in the same way. The code is shown in Listings 4.10 through 4.14.

Listing 4.10   **Open the Information Panel in quiet_room.swf**

```
if (_level0["b"+i+"_tbtn"].qLabel_txt.text == "Info") {
        _level0["b"+i+"_tbtn"].onRelease = function() {
            _level0.remoteCon_lc.send("quietroom_lc", "doQInfo");
            };
        }
```

Listing 4.11   **Play Video in quiet_room.swf**

```
if (_level0["b"+i+"_tbtn"].qLabel_txt.text == "Video") {
            _level0["b"+i+"_tbtn"].onRelease = function() {
                _level0.remoteCon_lc.send("quietroom_lc", "doQVideo");
            };
        }
```

Listing 4.12   **Play mp3 in quiet_room.swf**

```
if (_level0["b"+i+"_tbtn"].qLabel_txt.text == "Sound") {
    _level0["b"+i+"_tbtn"].onRelease = function() {
        _level0.remoteCon_lc.send("quietroom_lc", "doQSound");
            };
        }
```

Listing 4.13   **Open Email Panel in quiet_room.swf**

```
if (_level0["b"+i+"_tbtn"].qLabel_txt.text == "eMail") {
        _level0["b"+i+"_tbtn"].onRelease = function() {
            _level0.remoteCon_lc.send("quietroom_lc", "doQMail");
            };
        }
```

Listing 4.14   **Close quiet_room.html**

```
if (_level0["b"+i+"_tbtn"].qLabel_txt.text == "Close") {
        _level0["b"+i+"_tbtn"].onRelease = function() {
            _level0.remoteCon_lc.send("quietroom_lc", "doQClose");
                };
        }
    }
        trace(_level0.rBDataArr[5]);
    }
}
```

The arguments above set up the all the buttons to control events in the quiet_room.html. However, to actually launch the main application window, a launch function needs to be defined. This function calls a function embedded in the remote.html document. This opens a browser window with the requested URL.

Define the launch function, launchQuietRoom. This function uses the getURL function to call a JavaScript function embedded in remote.html. This function, openNewWindow, uses the parameters sent from launchQuietRoom to open quiet_room.html. The browser window will be of a specific size and have both its toolbars and its resizing properties disabled. (The resulting browser window may not obey some of the instructions, depending on the document object model (DOM) of the browser. The script in Listing 4.15 is guaranteed to work in Internet Explorer browser from version 4+)

Listing 4.15   **Using a Flash Function to Call a Browser Embedded JavaScript Function**

```
launchQuietRoom = function () {
getURL("javascript:openNewWindow('quiet_room.html';'q_room','height=600,width=800,
➥toolbar=no,scrollbars=no')");
};
```

To facilitate interaction between the remote control and the main window, a LocalConnection class instance needs to be defined. This will be called remoteCon_lc.

```
remoteCon_lc = new LocalConnection();
```

This finishes the development of the remote control application. It needs to be embedded in an HTML document. When this is done, we will open up the HTML document and add a few lines of JavaScript to it. This JavaScript function will enable us to open the quiet_room.html when it is needed, at the correct specified size. To publish remote.html and remote.swf, go to the File menu and select Publish Settings (File > Publish Settings). Select the HTML tab and choose pixels from the dimension option. Select noScale for the Scale option, click Publish, and click OK.

Remote.html

Open Dreamweaver MX 2004, Homesite 5.0, or the HTML editor of your choice and open the HTML document remote.html. Between the `<head>` tags, type `<script language= "JavaScript"> </script>`. Define the JavaScript function openNewWindow between the tags. The Window class of the JavaScript language provides the open() method (`window.open(URL, Name,Features, Replace)`) that can be used to open browser windows and define required properties of the browser window. Listing 4.16 provides an example.

Listing 4.16   **HTML Script *<head>* Tags for Remote.html with JavaScript Function**

```
<HTML>
<HEAD>
<meta http-equiv=Content-Type content="text/html;  charset=ISO-8859-1">
<TITLE>remote control</TITLE>
<script language="JavaScript">
function openNewWindow(URLtoOpen, windowName, windowFeatures) {
newWindow=window.open(URLtoOpen, windowName, windowFeatures);
}
</script>
```

In the top `<body>` tag, type the parameters **leftmargin=0** and **topmargin=0**. This will enable the Flash application remote.swf to fit snugly within the borders with no margins. The code shown in Listing 4.17 is generated by the Flash MX 2004 authoring API during publishing to embed the remote.swf into remote.html.

Listing 4.17   **HTML Script *<body>* Tags and Script for remote.html**

```
</HEAD>
<BODY bgcolor="#666666" leftmargin=0 topmargin=0 >
<!— URL's used in the application—>
<!— text used in the application—>
<OBJECT classid="clsid:D27CDB6E-AE6D-11CF-96B8-444553540000"
 codebase="http://download.macromedia.com/pub/shockwave/cabs/flash/
 ➥swflash.cab#version=7,0,0,0"
 WIDTH="350" HEIGHT="150" ALIGN="middle">
<PARAM NAME="allowScriptAccess" VALUE="sameDomain">
 <PARAM NAME=application VALUE="remote.swf"> <PARAM NAME=quality VALUE=high>
 ➥<PARAM NAME=bgcolor VALUE=#666666> <EMBED src="remote.swf" quality=high
 ➥bgcolor=#666666  WIDTH="350" HEIGHT="150" ALIGN="middle" allowScriptAccess=
 ➥"sameDomain"
TYPE="application/x-shockwave-flash" PLUGINSPAGE="http://www.macromedia.com/go/
 ➥getflashplayer"></EMBED>
</OBJECT>
</BODY>
</HTML>
```

This completes the remote control application. At this point, if the HTML document is previewed, it will have the browser toolbars and have its default resizing properties (see Figure 4.10). The final look of the remote control will be completed with a JavaScript function call, which will trigger it from the web site index page (the page that performs the Flash Player check). From there, its aspect ratio, browser properties, and placement on the screen will be defined. Our next step is developing the main part of this application, quiet_room.html.

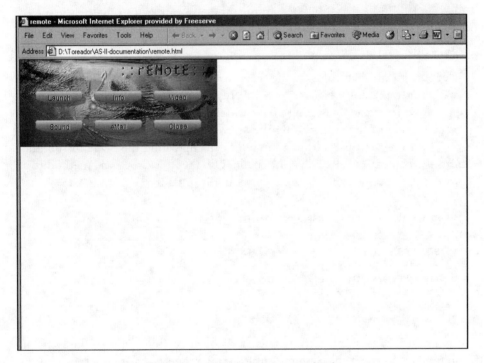

Figure 4.10   The finished remote.html.

The Main Viewing Window_ the qUiET room

The quiet_room is the main component of our hybrid application. In it are various features designed to play audio and video files. The quiet_room.html file is launched from the remote control. JavaScript functions set the browser size and features and set off special effects that affect the browser. All its features are controlled from the remote control application. A local connection class object is used to create a communication link between the remote control and the quiet_room application. As with the remote control application,

Flash technology is the core component for this application, and as such, we will begin by developing the quiet_room application.

Create a new Flash document and call it quiet_room.fla. This application needs to have its aspect ratio completely under control, which is effectively done using the Stage properties from within the Flash application. Create a new Flash ActionScript document, call it qr_1.as, and save it in the code folder. Open quiet_room.fla and qr_1.as.

Use the tabs in Flash MX 2004 and open quiet room.fla. On the first frame of layer 1, type the following code in the Actions panel.

```
#include "qr_1.as"
```

Select qr_1.as. To begin, assign the Stage width and height properties to the variables qStageX and qStageY, respectively. Disable the capability for the Flash application to rescale by setting Stage.scaleMode to zero. Align the application to the top left of the screen using the Stage.align property and set the value to "TL." To prevent users from zooming or manipulating the Stage in runtime from the context panel, disable the menu. Use the Stage.showMenu method to prevent the options from showing by setting it to false (see Listing 4.18).

Listing 4.18 **Setting the Stage Properties for the quiet_room**

```
//- - - - - - - - - - - - - - - - - - - - - - - - - - - - - - - - - - -
//STAGE PROPERTIES
//- - - - - - - - - - - - - - - - - - - - - - - - - - - - - - - - - - -
qStageX=Stage.width, qStageY=Stage.height;
Stage.scaleMode = "noScale";
Stage.align = "TL";
Stage.showMenu = false;
```

It is a neat idea to show each user what his or her system supports in terms of multimedia, so using the Systems capabilities property, create a series of if conditional statements to search for the user's capability to support video and audio. The results, if true, will be assigned to a series of set variables. Type the code shown in Listing 4.19 to achieve this:

Listing 4.19 **Setting the System Checks for the quiet_room**

```
if (System.capabilities.hasVideoEncoder) {
    var sysvid:String = "VIDEO";
}else {
    sysvid= " no VIDEO";
    }
```

continues

Listing 4.19   **Continued**

```
if (System.capabilities.hasAudio) {
    var sysaud:String = "AUDIO";
}else {
    sysaud= " no AUDIO";
    }

if (System.capabilities.hasMP3) {
    var sysmp3:String = "MP3";
}else {
    sysmp3= " no MP3";
    }

if (System.capabilities.hasStreamingVideo) {
    var syssvid:String = "STREAMING VIDEO";
}else {
    syssvid= " no STREAMINGVIDEO";
    }

if (System.capabilities.hasStreamingAudio) {
    var syssaud:String = "STREAMING AUDIO";
}else {
    syssaud= " no STREAMINGAUDIO";
    }

var sysos:String = System.capabilities.os;
```

This system check tells users what their system supports. This way, they can make repairs or download the right drivers to fully experience the features in the web site.

Creating the Backdrop for the Quiet_room

A bitmap image created to give the quiet room its artsy backdrop will be imported at runtime into the application. This is the point at which the custom class Qklass will be needed to create and postion the MovieClip container for the bitmap image.

Define a new instance of the QKlass.

```
//----------------------------------
//QKLASS
//----------------------------------
var quietRoomBase = new QKlass();
```

To begin, assign the paths to the background and the email module for the application to the variables bg and mailmod, respectively. Create a new empty application clip to hold the background image. Call this application clip base_mc.

```
//—————————————————————————————————————
//BACKGROUND
//—————————————————————————————————————
bg = "./images/bg_4.jpg";
mailmod="mailer1.swf";
quietRoomBase.newCreateEmptyMovieClip(_level0, "base_mc", 1, 0, 0);
```

The background image needs to be loaded into the application clip base_mc. To do this, create a new instance of the MovieClipLoader class and call it qLoader. To use the application clip loader, a listener object needs to be pressed into service. Define a new Object, assign it listener properties, and call it qEavesDropper. Load the background image.

```
qLoader = new MovieClipLoader();
qEavesDropper = new Object();
qLoader.addListener(qEavesDropper);
qLoader.loadClip(bg, base_mc);
```

Confirm the beginning of the loading sequence by using MovieClipLoader. onLoadStart to verify success with a trace. The onLoadStart parameter clip inherits its value from the target file to be loaded, as specified in the loadClip method. Check the progress of the loading process with the onLoadProgress method. Its parameters bytesLoaded and bytesTotal are inherited from getBytesLoaded and getBytesTotal of the clip parameter. Assign the loading percentage to a new variable, _level0.qPercent.

```
qEavesDropper.onLoadStart = function(clip) {
    trace("$^%& "+clip._name);
};
//——————————————————————————————————————·
qEavesDropper.onLoadProgress = function(clip, bytesLoaded, bytesTotal) {
    _level0.qPercent = Math.round(100*(bytesLoaded/bytesTotal));
};
```

Create a new application clip to contain the email module. Call this application clip mailbase_mc. Define a new loading sequence for the mail module and create a listener to apply the MovieClipLoader methods. Call the new listener qMEavesDropper.

```
//—————————————————————————————————————
//LOAD EMAIL
//—————————————————————————————————————
quietRoomBase.newCreateEmptyMovieClip(_level0, "mailbase_mc", 14, 0, 0);
qMLoader = new MovieClipLoader();
qMEavesDropper = new Object();
qMLoader.addListener(qMEavesDropper);
//qMLoader.loadClip(mailmod, mailbase_mc);
qMEavesDropper.onLoadStart = function(clip) {
    trace("$^%& "+clip._name);
};
```

The Flash application will verify that the loading sequence for the background is complete. If this is so, all the logic for the application will be initialized for use by the remote control. Use the `MovieClipLoader.onLoadComplete` method to confirm completion. Within the function block, all the arguments for the application will be defined. This will ensure that no major element is initialized in the application until the background is set. Set a `trace` to confirm success.

```
//------------------------------------------------
//COMPLETE BACKGROUND AND ACTIVATE Q-ROOM
//------------------------------------------------
qEavesDropper.onLoadComplete = function(clip) {
    trace(clip._name), trace(bytesTotal);
    _level0.qPercent = "/\\/\\/\\^~#_!_**___!/\\/\\/\\";
```

A text display will inform the Flash client (user) of the multimedia status of the user machine. The data displayed here will be supplied by the results of the systems check performed earlier by the Systems class. This text field will be generated at runtime. Define the text field using the `createTextField` method and call the text class instance `qSystemsCheck`. Set the text field properties and assign to the `*.text` property the combined value of the variables defined in the Systems check arguments. Use an instance the TextFormat class, `q_txt_format`, to format the style of the text field, and assign the new text format to `qSystemCheck`. See Listing 4.20 for an example.

Listing 4.20   **Creating the Text Field that Will Display the System Check**

```
    _level0.createTextField("qSystemCheck", 4, 130, 370, 350, 350);
    qSystemCheck.html = true;
    qSystemCheck.multiline = false;
    qSystemCheck.selectable = true;
    qSystemCheck.type = "dynamic";
    qSystemCheck.text = ":::qUieT roOM nAtive SystEMs:::"+newline
+"------·/\\/\\/\\/\\/\\------------------."
+newline+sysvid+newline+sysaud+newline
+sysmp3+newline+syssvid+newline+syssaud
+newline+sysos+newline+_level0.qPercent;

    q_txt_format = new TextFormat("Arial", 10, 0xFFCC00, true, false);
    qSystemCheck.setTextFormat(q_txt_format);
```

Now the backdrop for the application and the system check readout have been developed. The information panel is the next feature of the quiet room to which we turn our attention. The info panel will display data from an HTML document. The capability to load and display HTML documents with embedded JPG or SWF files is a new feature of Flash, and we will be using it in this application.

Information Display Module

The first application clip module for the quiet room is the information display. Any text data for the site will be displayed from a text field within this application clip.

The text display device will slide out of a recess in one of the walls of the quiet room when needed and slide back after use. It will have three arms that will unfold to reveal a display field. It will be controlled from the Info button in the remote control. This will enable the user to activate it or put it away. It is shown in Figure 4.11.

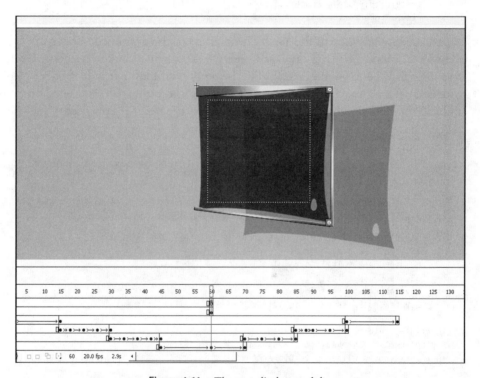

Figure 4.11   The text display module.

First, the graphics and animation for this application clip need to be created. To begin, open quiet_room.fla. Select the Rectangle tool and draw three bars. Using the Selection tool, modify the shapes of the bars to the shape in the illustration. Use the Color Mixer to create a metallic linear gradient fill and apply the fill to the bars. Select each bar and convert them the MovieClips. Call them bar, bar1 and bar2, respectively (see Figure 4.12).

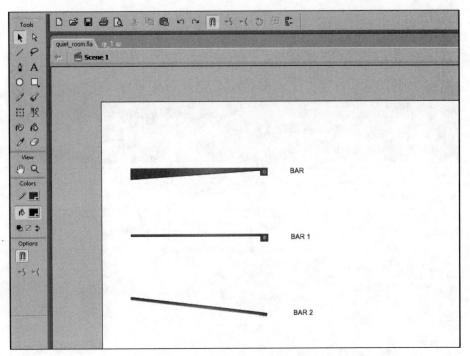

Figure 4.12 Bars for the text display module.

Select all three bars and convert them to an application clip with the name
slideBack. Give the application a linkage identifier of slideBack. Using all three
application clips, create a simple animation using key frames and tweens. First
create a layer, label it toparm, and place "bar" in the first frame. Create another
keyframe on Frame 15. Place the instance on bar on Frame 15 about 350 pixels
further than its original position. Apply a motion tween. Create two more layers below the layer toparm and call them centrearm and bottomarm. Place bar1
on Frame 15 and create a new keyframe at Frame 30. At Frame 30, rotate bar1
ninety degrees. Do the same for bar2, which is placed in the bottomarm layer,
but start at Frame 30 and finish at Frame 45. Apply tweens to both.

Create three new layers, two at the top and the other at the bottom. Call the
bottom field "Text back," and on Frame 45, draw a new rectangle. Using the
Selection tool, shape the rectangle to give the appearance of a rubber film
stretched between the arms of the animated bars. Convert the vector into an
application clip. Apply a tween between Frames 46 and 60. At Frame 45, set
the MovieClip _alpha properties to zero. The Timeline for the text display
module is shown in Figure 4.13.

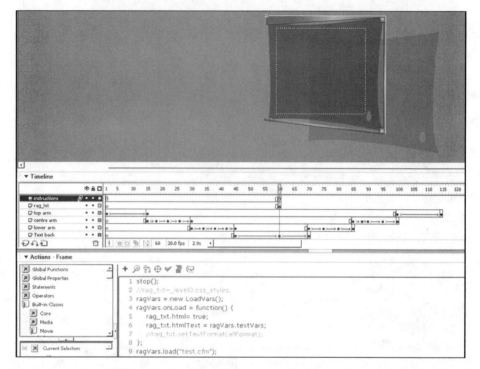

Figure 4.13 Timeline for the text display module.

Call one of the two new top layers rag_txt and the topmost layer instructions. At Frame 60 of layer rag_txt, use the Text tool to create a dynamic multiline text field. In the Properties field, select the HTML option. Call the text instance rag_txt. At Frame 60 of the instructions layer, type the following code in the Actions panel. The data to be displayed in rag_txt will be imported from a web document. A new LoadVars object, ragVars, will enable the Flash application to load the web document into the web page. Define the LoadVars object and define the properties for the text instance rag_txt. Create a new TextFormat object, r_txt_fmt to format rag_txt. Listing 4.21 illustrates the text formatting for the information panel text field.

Listing 4.21 **Setting the Text Formatting for the Information Panel Text Field**

```
stop();
ragVars = new LoadVars();
ragVars.onLoad = function() {
rag_txt.html= true;
rag_txt.htmlText = ragVars.textVars;
```

continues

Listing 4.21   **Continued**

```
rag_txt.setTextFormat(r_txt_fmt);
trace(rag_txt.htmlText)
};
    r_txt_fmt = new TextFormat("Arial", 10, 0xFFCC00, true, false);
    r_txt_fmt.leading=r_txt_fmt.leftMargin= r_txt_fmt.rightMargin=2;
    rag_txt.setTextFormat(r_txt_fmt);
```

At Frame 1 of the instructions layer, type **stop()** in the actions panel. Reverse the tweens to fold back the bars on their respective layers. Close the MovieClip and delete it from the main Stage. Create a large rectangle on the main Stage, convert it to an application clip, and call it quietmask. Delete it from the Stage. Select quietMask from the library, open its properties, and give it a linkage identifier of quietMask.

Open the qr_1.as document. Use the newAttachMovie method to attach instances of the MovieClips slideback and quietMask to the Stage. Call these instances sb_mc and qm_mc, respectively. Set their depths to 8 and 9, respectively, as well as the position coordinates (_x and _y). Assign the directory path for the web document to be loaded into the text display field of the application clip, sb_mc, to a variable, ragval. To create the effect of the text display module coming out of the slot in the wall, use the setMask method to create a mask for sb_mc with the MovieClip qm_mc.

```
//— — — — — — — — — — — — — — — — — — — — — — — — — — — — — — ·
//INFORMATION MACHINE
//— — — — — — — — — — — — — — — — — — — — — — — — — — — — — —
quietRoomBase.newAttachMovie(_level0, "slideBack", "sb_mc", 8, 115, 120);
quietRoomBase.newAttachMovie(_level0, "quietMask", "qm_mc", 9, 246, 240);
sb_mc.setMask(_level0.qm_mc);
ragval="http://localhost:8500/AS-II-documentation/test.cfm";
```

This completes the information display panel. The mask prevents the user from seeing the initial part of the info panel animation, thereby creating the illusion of the info panel sliding out of a recess in the wall when activated. Loading the content from an external HTML source enables easy updates of visual and textual content.

Video Playback Module

The video playback module is simply an application clip created at runtime to load a video object with a MovieClip wrapper from the library. The video object will enable the playback of FLV audio and video files through the HTTP or RTMP protocols. The video playback and closure will be triggered from the Video button on the remote control.

To create the video object, open quiet_room.fla and go to the library. In the library menu, click on New Video, which creates an embedded video in the application library. Drag an instance of the video object onto the Stage and give it an instance name of q_video. Select the video object and convert it to an application clip symbol. Name the application clip qVid. Delete the application clip from the Stage, select it from the library, and give it a linkage identifier of qVid.

Go back to qr_1.as. Create a new application clip, which will house the video application, and call it vidbase_mc. Attach the video application clip to this application clip and give it an instance name of vid_mc.

```
//-------------------------------------.
//VIDEO and MASK
//-------------------------------------.
quietRoomBase.newCreateEmptyMovieClip(_level0, "vidbase_mc", 5, 0, 0);
quietRoomBase.newAttachMovie(_level0.vidbase_mc, "qVid", "vid_mc", 1, 300,
➥180);
```

To play FLV files, create an instance of the NetConnection class, qConnection. The video files will be retrieved using the HTTP protocol. To do this, NetConnection.connect is set a "null" parameter. Next, create an instance of the NetStream object, and give it an instance name of q_ns. Attach the NetStream object to the video object with the attachVideo method. To create a transparent effect for the video, set the alpha value of the video application clip to 30.

```
//-------------------------------------
//NET CONNECTION
//-------------------------------------
qConnection = new NetConnection();
qConnection.connect(null);
q_ns = new NetStream(qConnection);
q_ns.SetBufferTime(5);
qvNum = 0;
_level0.vidbase_mc. vid_mc.q_video.attachVideo(q_ns);
_level0.vidbase_mc.vid_mc._alpha = 30;
```

To complete the background for the MovieClip, open the quiet room and select the Oval tool. Draw a circle with no fill. Convert the circle to a MovieClip and call it qDisc. Give the application identifier the name of qDisc. Import a couple of these clips to the Stage and use the onEnterFrame method to create a rotary effect for the discs.

```
for (var k = 0; k<2; k++) {
quietRoomBase.newAttachMovie(_level0, "qDisc", "qDisc"+k+"_mc", 10+k,
➥400+(k*20), 320);
_level0["qDisc"+k+"_mc"].onEnterFrame = function() {
```

```
        this._rotation += 1;
    };
}
```

In qr_1.as, create two new instances of the sound object, q_sound and quake_sound.

```
//-----------------------------------------
//SOUNDs
//-----------------------------------------
q_sound = new Sound();
quake_sound = new Sound();
```

The q_sound instance will initialize playback of a streamed MP3 file. Audio playback will be triggered by the remote control's sound button. The other sound instance, quake_sound, will play as soon as the web page is launched. This will be in sync with an earthquake effect, triggered from a JavaScript function in the browser page. The quake_sound will take its sound file from a WAV file imported into the library, and q_sound will be getting its source files from an HTTP map to the MP3 file directory.

Open quiet_room.fla and using File > Import, import thunder.wav into the library. Select it and give it a linkage identifier of thunder.

Open qr_1.as and attach the thunder sound file to the quake_sound object using the attachSound method. To start play, use the sound.start method. Now, after the application clip is launched and the background is loaded, there will be a crash of thunder.

```
quake_sound.attachSound("thunder");
quake_sound.start();
```

The LocalConnection class is the core structure facilitating the transfer of information between the remote control application and the main browser window. Using the LocalConnection class, actions and events can be triggered on the main viewer from the remote control. So the remote control and the main application must have an instance of the LocalConnection class to communicate. An instance of the LocalConnection class has already been defined for the remote control application. The main application, quiet_room.fla, needs to have a similar instance defined in it to create a communication link.

To begin, define three variables, qsNum, qvNum, and qmNum. Set the values of all three to zero. These variables will all be assigned initial values of zero. They will all serve as toggle controls to enable activation and deactivation of certain structures within the main viewer.

```
qsNum=0, qvNum=0, qmNum=0;
```

Define an instance of the LocalConnection class and call it `quietroom_lc`.

```
//------------------------------.
//LOCAL CONNECTION / functions
//------------------------------.
quietroom_lc = new LocalConnection();
```

Define a function, `doQInfo`, which will activate the text display panel from the remote control. This function will be associated with the quietroom_lc local connection. In the function block, type the argument `sb_mc.play();`.

```
quietroom_lc.doQInfo = function() {
sb_mc.play();
};
```

Beneath the `quietroom_lc.doQInfo` function block, define a new function, `quietroom_lc.doQVideo`. This function will verify the value of the variable `qvNum`. If the value equals zero, the NetStream object `q_ns` will activate playback of the stipulated video. If, on the other hand, the variable equals one, then the NetStream object closes, and the video is cleared from the screen using the `clear()` method. Listing 4.22 shows the code.

Listing 4.22   **The *quietroom_lc.doQVideo* Function**

```
quietroom_lc.doQVideo = function() {
if (qvNum == 0) {
//q_ns.play("http://localhost/Toreador/AS-II-documentation/ayo.flv");
q_ns.play("aa.flv");
            qvNum = 1;
        } else if (qvNum == 1) {
myNetStream.close();
_level0.vidbase_mc.vidbaseBack_mc.vid_mc.q_video.clear();
qvNum = 0;
            }
    };
```

The commented argument is there to illustrate that the FLV path can be defined relatively to the folder on the hard drive or by using an HTTP map.

Define a new function, `quietroom_lc.doQSound`, to control and toggle the sound from the remote control. Here, the arguments within the function block check for the value of the variable `qsNum`, and depending on whether the value equals zero or one, an MP3 file is streamed for audio playback. An animated application clip is also faded in or faded out, depending on whether there is audio playback (see Listing 4.23).

Listing 4.23   **The *quietroom_lc.doQSound* Function**

```
quietroom_lc.doQSound = function() {
if (qsNum == 0) {
q_sound.loadSound("./sound/ jazz.mp3", true), q_sound.start();
quietRoomBase.newAttachMovie(_level0, "mouth", "qmouth_mc", 12, 400, 400);
quietRoomBase.doFadeIn(_level0.qmouth_mc);
qsNum = 1;
          } else if (qsNum == 1) {
q_sound.stop(), qsNum=0;
quietRoomBase.doFadeOut(_level0.qmouth_mc);
          }
     };
```

The function `quietroom_lc.doQMail` triggers the loading of an SWF from an external directory. The arguments in the function block check for the value of the variable `qmNum`, and depending on whether the value equals zero or one, the mail module is loaded or unloaded (see Listing 4.24).

Listing 4.24   **The *quietroom_lc.doQMail* Function**

```
quietroom_lc.doQMail = function() {
          if (qmNum == 0) {
qMLoader.loadClip(mailmod, mailbase_mc);
qmNum = 1;
          } else if (qvNum == 1) {
mailbase_mc.unloadClip();
qmNum = 0;
          }
     };
```

The last function, `quietroom_lc.doQClose`, sends a message to a JavaScript function in the main browser and closes the browser (see Listing 4.25).

Listing 4.25   **The *quietroom_lc.doQClose* Function**

```
quietroom_lc.doQClose = function() {
     getURL("javascript:closeWindow()");
     };
```

To activate the LocalConnection instance, use the `connect` method to prepare it to receive commands.

```
quietroom_lc.connect("quietroom_lc");
```

Let us examine the unique way in which the LocalConnection object, `quietroom_lc`, receives instructions from `remote_lc`. The `remote_lc` object first makes sure of the link by using the `send` method and defining the `quiet_lc` object as its target recipient object. For the `quiet_lc` object to receive instructions, it needs to use the `connect` method to create a bridge with the local connection object defined in `remote_lc`, in this case, itself. Voila, that's it.

Pause a bit here and review the design brief again before proceeding. A little artistic touch might be needed to finish off the application. Open quiet_room.fla and, using the Pencil tool, set to free form to sketch a fly. Convert the image into a application clip and animate the fly to create a flapping motion. Create a new application clip, call it fly, and use a curved motion guide to tween the insect between about 40 frames. Delete the fly from the Stage, and from the library, set its linkage id as fly. Define a count variable j and set its value as zero. Using the `onMouseMove` method and an `if` condition, check for the value of the count j. If it is less than 30, attach instances of the fly application clip to `_level0` and set their `+rotation` property to a random value between 0 and 290 degrees. Listing 4.26 presents the code.

On the Stage, it appears that flies come in through the window every time the user moves the mouse on the main viewing window (see Figure 4.14).

Listing 4.26 **Code for the Termites Flying-Through-the-Window Animation**

```
//- - - - - - - - - - - - - - - - - - - - - - - - - - - - - .
//TERMITES
//- - - - - - - - - - - - - - - - - - - - - - - - - - - - - .
    j = 0;
    _level0.onMouseMove = function() {
        j++;
        if (j<30) {
            //trace(j);
            quietRoomBase.newAttachMovie(_level0, "fly", ["fly"+j], 40+j,
            ➡526, 60);
            //_level0.attachApplication("fly", ["fly"+j], 40+j);
            level0["fly"+j]._rotation = Math.random()*-290;
        }
        if (j>30) {
            j = 0;
        }
    };

};
```

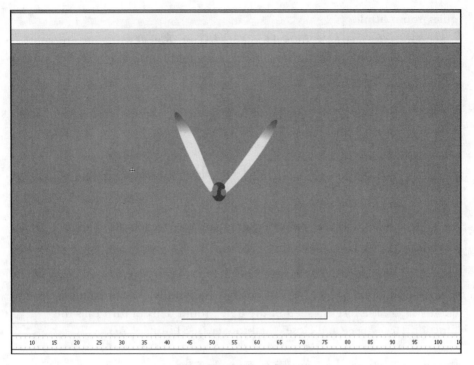

Figure 4.14   The Termite.

To achieve the insect animation code above, assign j (the previously initialized variable) an increment property (j++). This is triggered whenever the mouse moves on the Stage. Next, we use a conditional statement to limit the number of flies at any one time to no more than 30. If that condition is satisfied, and the mouse is in motion, then using the newAttachMovie method, flies are placed at the location of the window in the application. The multidirectional movement of the flies is addressed by assigning random values to the _rotation property of the application clips.

The insect touch completes the code for the quiet_room.swf. Save quiet_room.fla and publish quiet_room.swf and quiet_room.html. Go to the File menu and select Publish Settings (File > Publish Settings). Select the HTML tab and choose pixels for the dimension option. Select noScale for the Scale option, click Publish, and click OK. Next, we need to address quiet_room.html and add to it a style sheet and JavaScript features.

quiet_room.html

Open Dreamweaver MX 2004, Homesite 5.0, or the HTML editor of your choice and open the HTML document quiet_room.html. Between the `<head>` tags, type `<script language= "JavaScript"> </script>`.

Two functions need to be defined here. One of them, `closeWindow`, will receive instructions from the Flash application causing the browser window to close. The other function, `qQuake`, will trigger an earthquake effect in the browser window after the browser window is launched.

The HTML document published by Flash MX 2004 will need to be edited to include the JavaScript.

Begin by defining the JavaScript function `closeWindow` between the `<script>` tags. The Window class of the JavaScript language provides the method `close()` defined as `window.close()`. The `close()` method is used to close browser windows. A window can be close itself by calling `self.close`, or it can be closed from the parent document. Assign the argument `self.close` to a variable `closeIt`. Now, when the close button is clicked in the remote control, `quietroom_lc.doQClose` is called in the quiet_room. This in turn calls the function `closeWindow` and closes the browser (see Listing 4.27).

Listing 4.27 **JavaScript Function to Close the Window**

```
<HTML>
<HEAD>
<meta http-equiv=Content-Type content="text/html; charset=iso-8859-1">
<TITLE>quiet_room</TITLE>
<script language="JavaScript">
function closeWindow(){closeIt=self.close();
}
```

The earthquake effect "qQuake" takes a random number that is assigned to a variable called the `quakeIndex`. The `Math.floor` method is used to ensure that the number is an integer. A series of arguments using the `window.moveBy()` method moves the browser window to a series of positions back and forth between the _x and _y coordinates (see Listing 4.28).

Listing 4.28 **JavaScript Function to Create an Earthquake Effect**

```
function qQuake(){
quakeIndex=Math.floor(Math.random()*10)
for (i=0;i,i<20;i++){
window.moveBy(0,quakeIndex)
```

continues

Listing 4.28   **Continued**

```
    window.moveBy(quakeIndex,0)
    window.moveBy(0,-quakeIndex)
    window.moveBy(-quakeIndex,0)
}}
```

Fix the window position to a spot on the user's screen when the page is launched (see Listing 4.29):

Listing 4.29   **Fix the Window Position to a Spot on the User's Screen When the Page Is Launched**

```
    winPos=window.moveTo(100,100);
</script>
```

Underneath the `</script>`, use the HTML `<link>` tag to import an external CSS document

```
<link href="code/quiet.css" type="text/css" rel="stylesheet">
```

Open a new style sheet document and create a simple style sheet that will deal with the formatting for all the HTML documents associated with this application. Type the following CSS selectors (see Listing 4.30). The `body` selector defines the margins for all web documents associated with this document. It also sets the background color.

Listing 4.30   **Creating a Simple Stylesheet**

```
body {
    margin-left: 0px;
    margin-top: 0px;
    margin-right: 0px;
    margin-bottom: 0px;
    background-color: #666666;
}
```

The `side` and `bottom` selectors are custom CSS classes that will set the format of any HTML tag that has its class attribute set to it, `class= 'side'`. The important property here is the `background-image`. This property is mapped to a bitmap image that will provide the background of the table cells beside and below the quiet_room.swf. Setting the width and height of the classes ensures that the table cells will keep a predefined size (see Listing 4.31).

Listing 4.31 **CSS Class Rules**

```
.side {
    background-image: url(../images/side.jpg);
    background-repeat: no-repeat;
    width: 160px;
    border: 0px;
    margin-left: 0px;
    margin-top: 0px;
    margin-right: 0px;
    margin-bottom: 0px;
}
 bottom {
    background-image: url(../images/bottom.jpg);
    background-repeat: no-repeat;
    height: 120px;
    margin-left: 0px;
    margin-top: 0px;
    margin-right: 0px;
    margin-bottom: 0px;
    vertical-align: top;
}
```

Save the style sheet in the code folder as quiet.css.

Just for purposes of comparison, Figure 4.15 shows the quiet_room.html page without CSS formatting and tables.

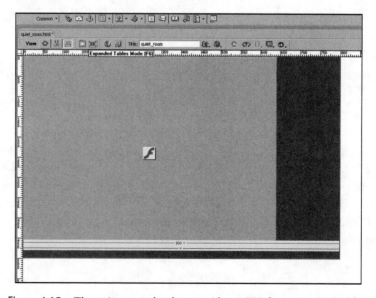

Figure 4.15 The quiet_room.html page without CSS formatting and tables.

Open quiet_room.html. In the `<body>`, edit the tag by typing the following code within its angled brackets `bgcolor="#666666" onLoad="qQuake()"`. The `bgcolor` attribute within the "body" tag sets the hexadecimal for the background color of the browser page. Ideally the CSS document defines the web page color, however setting the background color provides a backup, in the event that the CSS document does not load quickly. The JavaScript `onLoad` method calls the function `qQuake` when the window is launched (see Listing 4.32).

Listing 4.32   **Calling the Quake Effect**

```
</HEAD>
<BODY bgcolor="#666666" onLoad="qQuake()">
```

Create a table with two rows of cells. If Dreamweaver MX 2004 is your tool of choice, use the Table tool on the Common panel. Set the table width to 800 and its border, cell spacing, and cellpadding to 0. Set the width of the first cell column `<td>` to 640, the exact size of quiet_room.swf. Select all the code generated by Flash MX 2004 and put the code between the tags of this cell (see Listing 4.33).

Listing 4.33   **Inserting the Code in the Table Cell**

```
<table width="800" border="0" cellpadding="0" cellspacing="0" >
  <tr>
    <td width="640">

<!— URL's used in the application—>
<!— text used in the application—>

<OBJECT classid="clsid:D27CDB6E-AE6D-11CF-96B8-444553540000"
 codebase="http://download.macromedia.com/pub/shockwave/cabs/flash/swflash.cab#
 ➥version=7,0,0,0"
 WIDTH="640" HEIGHT="480" id="quiet_room" ALIGN="middle">
<PARAM NAME="allowScriptAccess" VALUE="sameDomain">
 <PARAM NAME=application VALUE="quiet_room.swf">
<PARAM NAME=quality VALUE=high>
<PARAM NAME=scale VALUE=noscale>
<PARAM NAME=bgcolor VALUE=#666666>
<EMBED src="quiet_room.swf" quality=high scale=noscale bgcolor=#666666
➥WIDTH="640" HEIGHT="480" NAME="quiet_room" ALIGN="middle" swLiveConnect=true
➥allowScriptAccess="sameDomain"
 TYPE="application/x-shockwave-flash" PLUGINSPAGE="http://www.macromedia.com/go/
 ➥getflashplayer"></EMBED>
</OBJECT>

<!— Bookmarks used in the application—>

</td>
```

Edit the next cell and set its class attribute to side. The side class selector of the CSS document will format these cells, setting their aspect ratio and giving them the specified background image.

```
<td class="side"></td></tr></table>
```

Create a new table with one cell underneath the previous one. Set its width to 800, select its single cell tag <td>, and set its class attribute to the string bottom.

```
<table width="800" border="0" cellpadding="0" cellspacing="0" >
    <tr>
      <td class="bottom"> </td>
    </tr>
  </table>

</BODY>
</HTML>
```

Figure 4.16 shows the completed quiet_room.html page.

Figure 4.16   The completed quiet_room.html in Dreamweaver showing active CSS and tables.

Save quiet_room.html.

Preview the HTML document remote.html and click the launch button. The quiet_room.html document will be launched at an aspect ratio of 800×600 pixels with a seamless integration of Flash application and background graphics. On launch, the browser will vibrate, and the sound of thunder will be heard. The completed quiet_room.html shows how a Flash application works in harmony with JavaScript and HTML. The capability for instructions to be sent from the Flash application to the browser creates a unified application were all elements work in concert.

Index.html

The application requires an index page where users trying to access the site can have their machines checked for the correct Flash Player. This page opens the remote control application in the specified size and browser attributes. The browser window will have a Flash button that will open the remote.html document. JavaScript code will be used to check for browser compatibility. Open a new HTML document and save it as index.html. Define a new JavaScript function, openNewWindow. Beneath it, define the window position by assigning the window.moveTo argument to a variable, winPos.

```
<?xml version="1.0" encoding="iso-8859-1"?><!DOCTYPE html PUBLIC "-//W3C//DTD
➥XHTML 1.0 Transitional//EN"
    "http://www.w3.org/TR/xhtml1/DTD/xhtml1-transitional.dtd">
<html>
<head>
<title>qUiet roOM</title>
<script language="JavaScript">
function openNewWindow(URLtoOpen, windowName, windowFeatures) {
newWindow=window.open(URLtoOpen, windowName, windowFeatures);
}
winPos=window.moveTo(400,300);
</script>
```

Import the CSS document quiet.css using the following code.

```
<link href="code/quiet.css" type="text/css" rel="stylesheet">
</head>
<body leftmargin=0 topmargin=0 >
```

Within the <body> tags, using Dreamweaver MX 2004, import a Flash button using the Flash Button tool (see Figure 4.17). In the Insert Flash Button panel, select a button of your choice. Type "**launch Remote**" in the Button Text option. In the Link option, type the following instructions:

```
"javascript:openNewWindow('remote.html';'remote,'height=150,width=350,toolbar=no,
➥scrollbars=no".
```

Click Apply and OK.

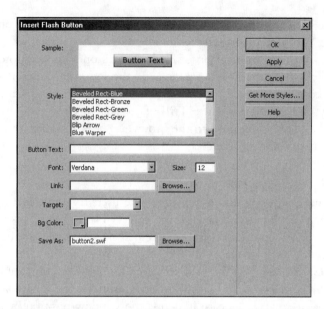

Figure 4.17   DreamweaverMX 2004 Insert Flash Button panel.

The code in Listing 4.34 is generated by Dreamweaver as a result.

Listing 4.34   **Dreamweaver-Generated Code for the Flash Button**

```
<object classid="clsid:D27CDB6E-AE6D-11cf-96B8-444553540000" codebase=
➥"http://download.macromedia.com/pub/shockwave/cabs/flash/swflash.cab#version=
➥7,0,0,0" width="100" height="22">
  <param name="BGCOLOR" value="" />
  <param name="application" value="button1.swf" />
  <param name="quality" value="high" />
  <embed src="button1.swf" quality="high" pluginspage="http://www.macromedia.com/
  ➥shockwave/download/index.cgi?P1_Prod_Version=ShockwaveFlash" type=
  ➥"application/x-shockwave-flash" width="100" height="22" ></embed>
</object>
```

Initalize two variables, `hasFlash` and `hasFlashActiveX,` as in Listing 4.35. Set their value to zero. These variables will act as controls to validate the presence of the Flash Player and Flash Active X.

Listing 4.35   **Initializing the Variables to Check for the Flash Player and Flash Active X**

```
<script language=JavaScript>
<!— //initialize variable
    var hasFlash = 0;
```

continues

Listing 4.35 **Continued**

```
    var hasFlashActiveX = 0;
//->
    </script>
```

Use the script below to check for the ActiveX controls:

```
    <script language=VBScript>
<!- // this checks for the availability of the activeX control
    on error resume next
        hasFlashActiveX = (IsObject(CreateObject
        ➥("ShockwaveFlash.ShockwaveFlash.7")))
//->
    </script>
```

Create a <font> tag and specify its font type and color. This will overwrite the CSS style.

```
<font face="Verdana" size="1" color="#FFFFFF">
```

Between the font tags, define the following arguments (see Listing 4.36). Begin by defining a variable, "Flashplugin". We assign to this variable the values of the navigator.mimeTypes array and supported x-shockwave or x-shockwave Flash plug in type objects. The Navigator mimeTypes[] is a JavaScript array objects of supported MIME types. MIME is the short for *Multipurpose Internet Mail Extensions,* a specification for formatting non-ASCII messages so that they can be sent over the Internet. MIME support enables browsers to send and receive graphics, audio, and video files via the Internet (see Listing 4.24).

Listing 4.36 **Assigning MIME types to the Variable** *plugin*

```
<script language="JavaScript">

<!- // this checks for the availability of the plugin...

    var FlashPlugin = (navigator.mimeTypes && navigator.mimeTypes["application/
    ➥x-shockwave-flash"] ? navigator.mimeTypes["application/
    ➥x-shockwave-flash"].enabledFlashPlugin : 0);
```

A condition now checks to see if the plugin exists on the clients computer and parses a substring of the plugin description. The result is converted to an integer using the parseInt method. If this is greater than or equal to 7, then the hasFlash variable is given a value of one, and a welcome message is displayed. The plugin.description method is a read-only string that gives a description of the specified plugin (see Listing 4.37).

Listing 4.37 **Checking for the Presence of the Flash player**

```
        if (FlashPlugin &&  parseInt(FlashPlugin.description.substring
    ➥(FlashPlugin.description.indexOf(".")-1)) >= 7) {
            hasFlash = 1;
        }


// if they pass either activeX or FlashPlugin test, welcome them
        if (hasFlash || hasFlashX) {
            document.write("Welcome to the QuiEt roOM!<br/>");
        }


        else {
// the check has failed they need to get the player to see the site
            document.write("<br>You need to install Flash 7 Player.<br>(ignore if
        ➥IE user)<br><br/>");
            //document.write(navigator.FlashPlugin.description);
            document.write("<a href=http://www.macromedia.com/shockwave/download/
        ➥index.cgi?P1_Prod_Version=ShockwaveFlash> Download FlashPlugin</a>");
```

If the plugin search is unsuccessful, a link to the Macromedia site to enable download appears. The majority of the preceding code deals with Netscape browsers. The code to check for the correct Flash player on Internet Explorer is similar and is also included. These browsers auto-install the correct player if they do not exist (see Listing 4.38).

Listing 4.38 **Checking for the Presence of the Flash Player for IE and AOL**

```
            //check for IE/AOL on Win32, because they'll do autoinstall of ActiveX
            ➥control
    if((navigator.appName == "Microsoft Internet Explorer" || navigator.appName.
    ➥indexOf("AOL") != -1) && (navigator.appVersion.indexOf("Win") != -1)) {
                var iewin32 = 1;
            }


        if (!iewin32) { // if not IE for windows, it's a manual download.
            document.write("<a href=http://www.macromedia.com/shockwave/
            ➥download/index.cgi?P1_Prod_Version=ShockwaveFlash> Download
            ➥Plugin</a>");
            document.write("");
        }

    }
//—></script>
</body>
</html>
```

Save the page.

Preview the index page, and if the right player exists, click on the "Launch Remote" button. The remote control will open at 350×150 pixels at the specified position on the screen. From the remote control, launch the main browser window and access information in the quiet room.

Wrap Up: A Recap of the Quiet Room

The quiet room illustrates the manner in which various web technologies can be brought together with Flash applications to create an application (see Figure 4.18). The application used five mainstream technologies to make it work: HTML, JavaScript, Flash, CSS, and text files. JavaScript dealt with browser effects triggered by the Flash applications, and HTML provided the base and some of the content, as did the text files. The CSS was used to format the HTML documents. Hybridization of this nature can be used on an even larger scale, incorporating many more technologies. Using various technologies to build an application is the equivalent of selecting the right tool for the right job. As was stated early in this article, each medium has its place and function and, if used in the right manner, can assist developers in creating very exciting applications.

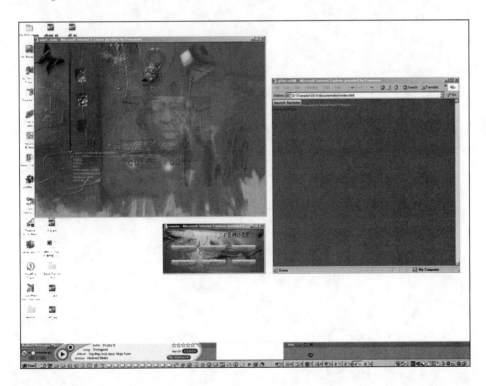

Article 5

Understanding Object-Oriented Programming in Macromedia Flash MX 2004

by Jeff Tapper—Tapper.net Consulting

THIS ARTICLE APPROACHES ACTIONSCRIPT from the point of view of object-oriented programming. It begins with a little history and then launches into a discussion of the object-oriented qualities of Flash ActionScript.

Welcome to the World of Objects

Flash ActionScript started down the road toward becoming an object-oriented (OO) language back in the days of Flash 5, when it was an object-*based* language. An object-based language is one that uses objects as its core building block. A true OO language takes that concept much further by incorporating concepts such as classes, inheritance, polymorphism, inheritance, and encapsulation, each of which are described in more detail in this article.

Flash MX extended the language much further, adding more OO concepts, although many argued that it was still object-based. With the proper coding discipline, it was possible to build OO systems, but there was nothing native to the language to enforce the OO concepts. The reality of Flash MX was that it was used "prototypes" to achieve its OO constructs. In ActionScript 2.0, however, the language can now force OO behaviors, which enables developers to harness ever-greater power. Additionally, ActionScript 2.0 has become a "class-based" language, bringing it more in line with the coding styles of most other OO languages. Among the many benefits of these changes are reduced development time and more extensible applications.

At the core of this revolutionary new way of building applications is, simply enough, the object.

Why Objects?

With all this talk about extending the OO nature of ActionScript, one is left to ask the question, "What is an object-oriented language, and why is it so important?"

OO systems take a revolutionary approach to the software development paradigm. Rather than being organized by logic rules or actions, OO systems are organized by discrete objects representing the real-world entities that the system will use. The result is that an OO system acts as a scale model of the business entity for which it was built, rather than a long list of logical rules. By designing the system this way, the system can be adaptive to the business it is built to serve.

Studies have repeatedly shown that 70-80% of all costs throughout the life-cycle of a software project come after the software has been launched. Specifically, these costs result from maintenance and changes to the software. OO systems by their nature are more adaptable to change and therefore can reduce these costs significantly. Let's consider an example of a human resources system. In a traditional procedural language, there would be several routines, including:

- Hire an employee.
- Fire an employee.
- Adjust an employee's salary.
- Promote employee.
- Demote employee.

In the equivalent OO system, there would simply be an "employee" object. The employee object would be aware of its properties (name, date of birth, salary, title, department, and so on), and there would be methods for interacting with the employee object. There would be only one place in the system where each task would be performed. These places are usually "methods." One such method would be the "adjust salary" method. This method would take an argument to describe the change in the employee's salary. The method would take the argument and adjust the salary by that amount. With this method in place, any of the other actions that might affect an employee object could use this method. Therefore, the "promote employee" method could call the "adjust salary" method to give the user a raise commensurate with his or her new job. Equally, the "demote employee" method could call the same "adjust salary" method to reduce the employee's salary. Even the "hire employee" and "fire employee" methods could make use of this method to set the initial salary for the employee or to reduce it to zero on the employee's termination date. In a procedural system, changes to the way an employee's salary is adjusted need to be coded in several places. In the OO system described here, only a single place needs to be modified, without the need to give thought to how it will affect the rest of the system.

What Is an Object?

An object is the main building block of an object-oriented programming (OOP) application. It is an entity in the system that can be uniquely described, has specific capabilities, has the ability to broadcast messages to other objects, and has the ability to listen to others broadcasting messages to it.

A well-designed OO system should closely mirror the world in which it will work. For example, the following are types of objects one might find in a human resources application.

- Employee
- Department
- Job
- Manager

In the next section, we will examine how these "classes" of objects are implemented in ActionScript 2.0.

ActionScript 2.0

It was certainly possible to build OO systems in Flash MX; however, the latest release includes a revision to the language, now called ActionScript 2.0. ActionScript 2.0 is an alternate set of syntax that can be used to enforce OO constructs in a Flash application. Using Flash MX 2004 does not force a developer to use ActionScript 2.0, as the traditional AS syntax will still work fine; however, ActionScript 2.0 opens new worlds not previously available to Flash developers. Among the new features are strong data typing (enabling Flash to enforce that variables, arguments, or return values of a function will only be of a certain data type), static methods and properties for classes (covered later), inheritance, interfaces, and much more. It is important to understand that this "enforcement" occurs as the .fla is compiled into an .swf. By enforcing it at that time, the Flash Player can run the movie far more efficiently, as it does not need to do runtime conversions between datatypes.

> **Note**
>
> For more details on strong data typing, see Article 1, "Converting from ActionScript to ActionScript 2.0," by William Sanders.

Other improvements in ActionScript 2.0 include the new "class-based" syntax. Aside from bringing a more standardized interface to ActionScript, the new syntax also enables "class paths" to be set in each application, allowing for easier reuse of class files between applications. Another difference is the case sensitivity of ActionScript 2.0. In Flash MX, the language was selectively case-sensitive, with most internal commands being case-sensitive and most developer-created ones being non-case-sensitive. In ActionScript 2.0, all commands are now case-sensitive, enabling greater efficiency in the compiler and Player.

Classes

A class is a blueprint that defines how objects of a particular type are built. In traditional ActionScript, a class was defined by its constructor function, and then it could have additional properties and methods prototyped onto it (see Listing 5.1).

Listing 5.1 **Code Creating a Constructor Function and Defining the Method** *adjustSalary*

```
var Employee = function(id, firstname, lastname, salary){
  this.id = id;
  this.firstname = firstname;
  this.lastname = lastname;
  this.salary = salary;
}
Employee.prototype.adjustSalary = function(amt){
  this.salary += amt;
}
```

The first block of code in Listing 5.1 is a constructor function that determines how an employee object will be created. This is followed by the definition of a method called adjustSalary. Implementing this in ActionScript 2.0 could look like Listing 5.2.

Listing 5.2   **ActionScript 2.0 Allows for More Robust Class Definitions**

```
class Employee {
    private var firstName:String;
    private var lastName:String;
    private var salary:Number;
    private var id:Number;

    public function
Employee(id:Number,firstname:String,lastname:String,salary:Number){
        this.id = id;
        this.firstName = firstname;
        this.lastName = lastname;
        this.salary = salary;
    }

    public function adjustSalary(amt:Number):Void{
        this.salary += amt;
    }
}
```

You'll notice that the class definition is now more robust, beginning with the class keyword and followed by the name of the class. Next, the properties of the class are declared (the new private keyword keeps them from being made available outside of the class), along with their "visibility" (the concept of data-hiding is covered in more detail in the "Delegation" section of this article). Next, a constructor function is defined (the function that has the same name as the class itself). This constructor is very similar in structure to the earlier example, with the addition of the new data typing of arguments (id and salary are defined as numeric, while firstName and lastName are defined as strings). The adjustSalary method is also defined here in the class, removing the need to prototype it onto the class afterward.

Objects

An object is an instance of a particular class. In Flash, anything with which a developer and designer can interact is an object. This includes buttons, movie clips, text fields, and so on. As a member of a class, an object has the characteristics of that class. For example, a movie clip, as a member of the MovieClip class, will have a Timeline with commands (called methods) to interact with the Timeline (`play()`, `stop()`, `gotoFrame()`, and so on). Just like in ActionScript 1.0, in ActionScript 2.0 there are three fundamental ways an object can come into existence:

- **Visual Creation**—This includes text fields, graphics, buttons, movie clips, and any other object that can be drawn or dragged onto the Stage.
- **Method Creation**—Movie clips and text fields can be created using methods of the movie clip, including `duplicateMovieClip`, `createEmptyMovieClip`, `attachMovie`, `createTextfield`, and so on.
- **Explicit Instantiation** (with the `new` keyword)—This is the programming standard for object creation. For example, `var myObject:Object = new Object();`.

A fourth type of class also exists and is referred to as "top level" or "static" classes. These special classes include Math, Key, and other static classes, whose methods can be invoked directly against the class without first instantiating the object. The idea of classes with static methods such as these is discussed later in this article.

In ActionScript, the vast majority of objects are created by invoking the class constructor with the `new` keyword.

```
var me:Employee = new Employee(12,"jeff","tapper",10000000);
```

In this example, a new object named `me` is instantiated by invoking the constructor of the Employee class and passing in arguments that will be used to populate the properties (see below) of the new object.

Properties

A property is nothing more than a variable belonging to an object. Built-in visual objects such as buttons and movie clips have a series of properties including `_x`, `_y`, `_height`, and `_width`, which serve to describe aspects of the objects. Custom objects, such as the Employee class described above, can have their own properties as well. In the case of the Employee class, the properties are `id`, `firstName`, `lastName`, and `salary`. We create a new member of the Employee class like this:

```
var me:Employee = new Employee(12,"jeff","tapper",10000000);
```

Attributes are passed to the constructor and are then used to populate the properties of the new objects. In this case, we have a new employee object named `me`. Me has an id of 12, a `firstName` of "jeff," a `lastName` of "Tapper," and a salary of `10000000` (I think it's time for a raise). These properties describe the instance of an object in the system. Although we can have several different employees, each of which will an `id`, `firstName`, `lastName`, and `salary`, they can have individual values for each. (It wouldn't be pleasant to work in an office where everyone had exactly the same name. Although it would be easier to remember folks' names, other dilemmas would likely ensue.)

Here we notice that, with the exception of the new strong data typing syntax, this is identical to how properties would be passed to a constructor in ActionScript 1.0.

```
me = new Employee(12,"jeff","tapper",10000000);
```

ActionScript 2.0 has also added a concept known as "static" properties. A static property is a property that is assigned to the class, as opposed to being assigned to individual instances of the class. In ActionScript 1.0, the properties of the Math class (`pi`, `ln2`, and so on) were all static properties. To use the value of `pi` in our applications, we could refer to:

```
var circumference = Math.pi*diameter;
```

where `pi` is referred to directly from the Math class, not from an object. In ActionScript 2.0, we can still use the static properties of the Math class, but we are also free to create static properties of our own classes. To do this, we can use the `static` keyword.

```
class Triangle {
    public static var numSides:Number=3;
    ...
}
```

In this example, the property `numSides` is set as a static property, meaning it will be available from the class, not from instances of the class. With this definition, this code will run properly and return the number 3:

```
trace(Triangle.numSides);
```

The following code will throw an error message because static members cannot be accessed through objects of a class, but only through the class itself.

```
var test:Triangle = new Triange();
trace(test.numSides);
```

Methods

In the same way that a property is nothing but a variable assigned to an object, a method is simply a function tied to an object. The methods of an object describe its behavior—what the object can do or what can be done to the object. In the example of an employee, a method has been defined to adjust the employee's salary.

Listings 5.3 and 5.4 show the ActionScript 1.0 (Listing 5.3) and ActionScript 2.0 (Listing 5.4) approaches to add methods to a class.

Listing 5.3   **Prototype Was Used to Add Methods to a Class in ActionScript 1.0**

```
Employee.prototype.adjustSalary = function(amt){
  this.salary += amt;
}
```

Listing 5.4   **As of ActionScript 2.0, Methods Can Now be Added Within the Class Definition as a Function.**

```
class Employee {
    ...

    public function adjustSalary(amt:Number):Void{
        this.salary += amt;
    }
}
```

Among the other new changes for methods seen here are the strong data typing (for more on strong data typing in ActionScript 2.0 see Article 1). It is now possible to define both the data type of arguments (as seen in Listing 5.4 with the argument amt defined as a number) as well as the data type of the variable being returned (in Listing 5.4, the `adjustSalary` method is set to return nothing, for which we use the term "Void."

With the addition of ActionScript 2.0, there is a new way to create a "static method."

Note

A static method is a method tied to a class, not to members of the class. The methods of the built-in Math object are static methods.

ActionScript 1.0 version of a static method:

```
MyClass = function(){
    //
}
MyClass.myStaticMethod = function(){
    trace("hi");
}
```

ActionScript 2.0 version of a static method:

```
class MyClass{
    public static function myStaticMethod():Void{
        trace("hi");
    }
}
```

Both the ActionScript 1.0 and ActionScript 2.0 syntax allow for attaching methods to the class, as opposed to instances. Just like static properties, ActionScript 2.0 will throw an error if a static method is accessed through an instance, whereas ActionScript 1.0 would simply return `undefined`.

Another change in ActionScript 2.0 is the ability to define functions and properties as either public or private. If not specified, any created properties and methods will be created as public. A public method can be called from other objects, wheras a private method can only be accessed from within the same object. For more on public and private methods, see the "Delegation" section.

With the concepts of classes, properties, and methods as a solid foundation, the fundamental concepts of OOP can be built upon them.

OO Concepts

Aside from having objects and methods, there are many other OO concepts that are now available to ActionScript developers. Chief among these are encapsulation (the ability to centralize all aspects of an entity in the system into an object), inheritance (the ability for one type of object to be an extension of another type of object), and polymorphism (the ability of an object to take many forms). These three concepts form the basis of OOP. This section will explore some of these concepts and how they can help with development of applications.

Encapsulation

The most basic concept of OO design is encapsulation. Encapsulation is nothing more than designing a system with objects that contain all the data of an entity in the system (properties) as well as all the actions that can be done to or by the entity (methods).

Delegation

Another benefit of OO systems is the concept of delegation. Although not unique to the OO world, it is a nice side-effect of encapsulation. The procedural world was able to implement delegation through the use of sub-routines, whereas the OO world achieves delegation through methods. One of the key benefits of an OO system is the ease of maintenance. There are many reasons why these systems become easier to maintain, but key among them is the idea that each operation that occurs within a system happens in one and only one place. By *delegating* responsibility this way, when changes become necessary in the system, the scale of change will be small, as each change only necessitates a single alteration of the system.

Delegation becomes possible through the effective use of methods in the system. By building granular methods that perform only one task each, the idea of delegation becomes simpler. The core of granular tasks for methods begins with the idea of each property of an object having a "getter" and "setter" method. These methods are solely responsible for enabling other objects in the system to interact with an object's properties. By declaring an object's properties as private (as seen in Listing 5.2), outside objects are forbidden from interacting directly with the properties. The only way for outside objects to interact with these properties becomes through the "getter" and "setter" methods. Listing 5.5 shows the Employee class modified so that all properties are marked as private and so that public methods are available for retrieving any property.

Listing 5.5   **Several Methods Are Added to the Employee Class to Delegate Interaction with Its Properties to Various Methods**

```
class Employee {
    private var firstName:String;
    private var lastName:String;
    private var salary:Number;
    private var id:Number;

    function Employee(id:Number,firstname:String,lastname:String,salary:Number){
        setID(id);
        setFirstName(firstname);
        setLastName(lastname);
        setSalary(salary);
    }

    public function adjustSalary(amt:Number):Void{
        setSalary(getSalary()+amt);
    }
```

continues

Listing 5.5   **Continued**

```
    // getter functions
    public function getID():Number{
        return this.id;
    }
    public function getFirstName():String{
        return this.firstName;
    }
    public function getLastName():String{
        return this.lastName;
    }
    public function getSalary():Number{
        return this.salary;
    }


    //setter functions
    private function setID(ID:Number):Boolean{
        this.id = ID;
        return true;
    }
    public function setFirstName(fname:String):Boolean{
        this.firstName = fname;
        return true;
        }
    public function setLastName(lname:String):Boolean{
        this.lastName = lname;
        return true;
    }
    private function setSalary(num:Number):Boolean{
        this.salary = num;
        return true;
    }

    function serializeInfo():Employee{
        var obj = new
  Employee(getID(),getFirstName(),getLastName(),getSalary());

        return obj;
    }
}
```

Although all the getter methods are publicly available, the setID and setSalary
methods are marked as private. This ensures that those methods can only be
called from within this class. The only place in the system that should be calling setID is the constructor, as an employee's id is their unique identifier in the
system. To allow anything other than the constructor to set an employee's ID
could potentially wreak havoc on the system, so it is marked as private. The
setSalary method is also set as private, as there is another method (adjustSalary)

that is the public interface to change an existing employee's salary. An extra method, `serializeInfo`, has also been added with the sole purpose of creating a new object that contains a snapshot of the employee object. This can easily enable other objects to work on a copy of an employee without affecting the actual employee object.

By delegating the responsibilities this way, the system has become more maintainable. Should the underlying data structure of an employee need to change, as long as the getter and setter methods are correctly maintained, the rest of the system doesn't need to be aware of the changes to the structure of the object.

ActionScript 2.0 has also introduced a new concept with getter and setter functions that enables developers to define a series of functions that can be called as if they were properties. This is done with the keywords `get` and `set` used in function definitions. Listing 5.6 shows a sample of these special `get` and `set` functions in use.

Listing 5.6 **A Sample of the Employee Object with *get* and *set* functions.**

```
public function get fname():String{
    return this.firstName;
}
public function set fname(fname:String):Void{
    this.firstName = fname;
}
```

These functions can then be called as if they were properties in themselves, as seen in Listing 5.7.

Listing 5.7 **Using the *get* and *set* Function**

```
var me:Employee = new Employee(1,"Jeff","Tapper",120);
me.fname = "Jeffrey";
trace(me.fname);
```

In this example, the set function `fname` is invoked by simply assigning a value to it, as if it were a simple property. The `trace` action is then shown invoking the get function. Using this methodology, all data members of an object can be set to `private`, and a series of `get` and `set` functions can be written and made publicly available, effectively implementing the data hiding concept. One limitation to be aware of with this style of implicit getters and setters is that the `get` and `set` method names cannot be the same as the property names. This is due to a limitation resulting from ActionScript 2.0 actually being compiled into traditional AS for implementation. For this reason, the examples in Listing 5.6 and 5.7 show a `get` and `set` function named `fname` to enable developers to work with the `firstName` property.

> **Note**
> The idea of delegation can go far beyond simple getter and setter methods. There exist OO purists in the world who believe that in a well-designed system, each method should contain one and only one line of code. Although it is not necessary to take OO design to this extreme, keeping it in mind helps to keep designs clean and granular in the system.

A well-designed OO system is incredibly bureaucratic in its nature, and that is not a bad thing. Although bureaucracy in business can lead to bottlenecks and inefficiencies, in an OO system, it helps ensure the maintainability of the system.

Considering the effort usually associated with maintenance and adaptation of a launched software project, the fewer places in a system that need to be recoded for every change, the quicker (and therefore cheaper) it will be to maintain the system. Therefore, by building OO systems with proper delegation, the total cost of ownership can be dramatically reduced.

With the concepts of encapsulation and delegation firmly in hand, it's time to look into other OO constructs that can determine how our objects are designed.

Polymorphism

The term *polymorphism* comes from the Greek roots *poly* meaning "many" and *morph* meaning "shape" or "form." So, polymorphism is a way of describing something that can take many forms, meaning that it can react differently in different contexts. In the next few sections, inheritance and interfaces will be discussed as a means to achieve polymorphistic behaviors.

Inheritance

As we model our objects based on the real-world objects they mimic, we will find relations of objects that can be defined by the model "x is a y." One example of this is "an Employee is a Human." In the OO world, we could implement this type of relationship with inheritance. So, any properties and methods of the Human class would be inherited by the Employee class. Let's look at a simpler example: shapes.

Triangles come in many varieties: isosceles (where 2 sides have equal lengths), equilateral (where all 3 sides have equal lengths), right triangles (two sides meet at a 90 degree angle), and triangles that meet none of these conditions.

It is safe to say that all four types of triangles described above share the properties and methods of a triangle. One of these similarities is the number of sides a triangle has. For this reason, we want to implement a Triangle class, which might look like Listing 5.8.

Listing 5.8 **ActionScript 2.0 Syntax for Creating a Triangle Class**

```
class Triangle {
    private var numSides:Number=3;
    private var sideLengths:Array;
    private var height:Number;
    private var base:Number;
    //constructor
    public function Triangle(side0:Number,side1:Number,side2:Number){
        this.sideLengths = new Array(side0,side1,side2);
    }
    public function getSides():Array{
        return this.sideLengths;
    }
    private function getHypotenuse(a:Number,b:Number):Number{
        var cSquared = Math.pow(a,2)+Math.pow(b,2);
        return Math.sqrt(cSquared);
    }
    private function getBaseOrHeight(side:Number,hyp:Number):Number{
        var aSquared = Math.pow(hyp,2) - Math.pow(side,2);
        return Math.sqrt(aSquared);
    }
      public function calculateArea(height:Number,width:Number){
            return (.5*height*width);
      }

}
```

Based on the geometric rules for triangles, we know that each type of triangle, while still having three sides, has differences that will dictate that they are created differently (for example, an equilateral triangle only needs to have one side length provided, as all sides are equal length, whereas an isosceles triangle needs to have two side lengths provided, one for the base, one for the two matching sides). Another key difference is the mechanism we will use to calculate the area of the triangle. By creating subclasses of the Triangle class to represent each subset of triangles, the calculateArea method for each subclass can override the method of the same name of the Triangle class. In this way, calculateArea is a polymorphistic method—it has many forms, one for a generic triangle, another for the an equilateral triangle, and so on. Below are the three subclasses of the Triangle class: EquilateralTriangle, RightTriangle, and IsoscelesTriangle.

Listing 5.9 **Using Inheritance, the Triangle Class is Extended with Subclasses EquilateralTriangle, RightTriangle, and IsoscelesTriangle**

```
class EquilateralTriangle extends Triangle{
    public function EquilateralTriangle(side:Number){
```

```
            this.sideLengths[0] = side;
            this.base = side;
            this.sideLengths[1] = side;
            this.sideLengths[2] = side;
            this.height = getBaseOrHeight(side/2,side);
        }
        public function calculateArea():Number{
            return this.base*this.height;
        }
    }
    class IsoscelesTriangle extends Triangle{
        public function IsoscelesTriangle(base:Number,matchingSideLength:Number){
            this.sideLengths[0] = base;
            this.base = base;
            this.sideLengths[1] = matchingSideLength;
            this.sideLengths[2] = matchingSideLength;
            this.height = getBaseOrHeight(base/2,matchingSideLength);
        }
        public function calculateArea():Number{
            return this.base*this.height;
        }
    }
    class RightTriangle extends Triangle{
        public function RightTriangle(base:Number,height:Number){
            this.sideLengths[0] = base;
            this.base = base;
            this.sideLengths[1] = height;
            this.height=height;
            this.sideLengths[2] =
    getHypotenuse(this.sideLengths[0],this.sideLengths[1]);
        }

        public function calculateArea():Number{
            return .5*this.sideLengths[0]*this.sideLengths[1];
        }
    }
}
```

In this example, it becomes clear that although there are several different types of triangles, they are all similar at their core. The similarities can be shared from the superclass, whereas the differences can be implemented with subclasses.

Note

This example assumes that the creator of the object knows what type of triangle it will be. Using a "design pattern" known as the "Factory Pattern," it is possible to build a single method of the Triangle class that will determine which type of Triangle is being created and return that newly created triangle. For details on design patterns, see Steven Webster and Alistair McLeod's Article 6, "ActionScript Design Patterns for Rich Internet Application Development."

Those familiar with OO languages will find similarities between inheritance in ActionScript 2.0 and inheritance in Java. Chief among these similarities is that the language does not support "multiple inheritance," which is the ability of a class to inherit from more than one class. Languages such as C++ do allow this, but it adds greater complexity to the implementation. ActionScript 2.0 solves this problem in the same way as Java—rather than allowing a class to inherit from multiple classes, the concept of "interfaces" was introduced.

Interfaces

An interface is a special OO construct that is like a class but contains no methods or properties of its own. Instead it dictates the methods that classes implementing the interface must have. Unlike other OO languages, an ActionScript 2.0 interface cannot declare properties.

Interfaces act like a contract. When a class is declared as implementing an interface, that class is signing on to the concept that it will implement all the methods defined in the interface. This will guarantee the polymorphism of the methods in the interface because each class implementing it will have its own means to implement the methods described in the interface. This becomes worthwhile when there are several related classes, and inheritance is not appropriate. In the classic OO example of shapes, a Shape interface can be designed, declaring that all shapes will have a method to determine how to calculate the area for that shape. This may be more appropriate than having a base class named Shape, as each subclass of Shape (Circle, Triangle, Trapezoid, and so on) would need to override the `calculateArea` method of the Shape class, as no two shapes have the same formula for calculating the area. Listing 5.10 below shows an interface Shape that indicates a method that all shapes implementing the interface must have.

Listing 5.10 **The Shape Interface Defines a Method that All Shapes Must Implement**

```
interface Shape{
    function calculateArea():Number;
}
```

Next, the triangle class needs to be informed that it will implement this interface. This is done with the `implements` keyword, as seen in Listing 5.11.

Listing 5.11   **The Triangle Class Declares that it Will Implement the Shape Interface and Therefore Must Include a** *calculateArea* **Method**

```
class Triangle implements Shape{
    var numSides:Number=3;
    var sideLengths:Array;
    public function calculateArea(height:Number,width:Number):Number{
            return (.5*height*width);
    }
...
```

If more classes were to be created to represent other shapes (rectangle, circle, trapezoid, and so on), each could also implement this interface, which would require that they all have a calculateArea method that returns a number.

After the concepts of encapsulation, inheritance, and polymorphism are understood, OO systems can be designed to be extremely flexible and maintainable. It can also be seen why OO systems require more initial design. By understanding the encapsulation of entities of the problem domain into objects, the hierarchy (superclasses and subclasses) of the classes, and interfaces needed for a system, significantly less time can be spent implementing the design of the classes. After the basic design of the objects is understood, the next logical leap is understanding how objects interact with each other.

Messages—Communicating Between Objects

Just as efficient communications within a company are integral to the success of the company, communications between objects in an OO system are integral to that system functioning properly. Generally, communications between objects are referred to as "messages." If the employees of a company are unable to communicate effectively amongst themselves, the efficiency of operation of the company will be significantly reduced. Likewise, a well-designed system needs to consider exactly how the objects of that system will interact. Fortunately, OO systems are designed to mirror real-world entities; therefore, the first clues about messages that will be sent and received by objects can come from observing their real-world counterparts.

Events and Event Handlers

At the core of the messages an object will send and receive is the concept of an "event." An event is something that can happen to an object and to which it can react. Nearly every observable real-world object has events that can be described. A door understands the "open" and "close" events; a light bulb understands the "power on" and "power off" events. Likewise, objects in OO systems have a series of events they too can understand. A button in a Flash application can respond to a "mouse over" event (among others).

For each event, an event handler can be defined. An event handler is a method of the object that will be fired when the object "hears" that a certain event has occured. In Flash, it is not uncommon to build an `onRelease`, `onKillFocus`, or even `onLoad` event handler to react to those specific events. These methods are defined just like any others, with the only difference being the naming convention (usually starting with the prefix "on") that determines that the method will be automatically invoked when the object detects the occurrence of a particular event.

An `onRollover` event handler for a button:

```
my_btn.onRollover = function(){
    trace ("you have rolled over the button");
}
```

In Flash, there are generally two types of events to which objects can react: user events, such as `onClick`, `onRollover`, and so on, and system events, such as `onEnterFrame`, `onResult`, and `onLoad`. The concepts behind both types of events and how they are handled are almost identical, with the only fundamental difference being that one is specifically created by an action of the user, whereas the other is created by an action of the system.

Broadcasting Custom Messages

Although it is useful to be able to react to predefined events such as a mouse rolling over a button or a LoadVars object receiving data, it can be far more powerful to define custom events that are unique to the problem domain of the application. Consider a technology development project. When a project is started, several things need to happen simultaneously: the billing department needs to be notified of the terms of the contract, a development team needs to be assembled, network services teams need to be notified of the requirements for development servers, and so on. This can be built linearly, such that the billing department is first notified, and when it completes its process, it notifies the development manger, who completes his process and notifies network services. This, however, is not terribly efficient. If the billing department is overworked and does get around to processing the request, the other departments' notifications will be greatly delayed. A better idea is that of broadcasting a custom message and setting all three departments as listeners for that message.

Therefore, a project object can broadcast a "startProject" message, and any object that listens to the project object can have its own custom response to the message. In terms of extensibility, it now becomes much easier to modify the business rules surrounding the start of a project. Should the business require a legal team to be notified of the project start so they can review all contracts, they can be added as a listener as well.

In ActionScript, we can implement custom broadcasters and listeners with the use of the AsBroadcaster class. To do this, we need to add the broadcasting methods to an object. We do that with the `AsBroadcaster.initialize()` method, which looks like this:

```
AsBroadcaster.initialize(sales_mc);
```

When initialized, the object specified as the argument of the initialize method (in this case, `sales_mc`) has two new methods added to it: `addListener` and `broadcastMessage`. Using the `addListener` method, we can specify other objects to listen for events being broadcast by this object:

```
sales_mc.addListener(netops_mc);
```

When an object is set as a listener (as `netops_mc` is in the above example), it can respond to events broadcast to it with its own custom event handler. Listing 5.12 and Figure 5.1 show AsBroadcaster in action.

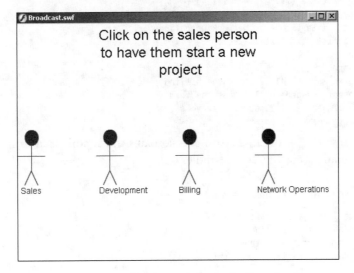

Figure 5.1 The broadcasting test movie clip as it starts.

In this example, we have a Flash application with four identical movie clips on the stage. Each of the four movie clips is an instance of the "mcPerson" clip, which has a dynamic text box below it and a stick figure. They also have another dynamic text box in a "word bubble," but those are hidden at the start of the movie.

Each of the four movie clips represents a member of the consulting team. From left to right, we have: The Salesperson, The Development Manager, The Billing Supervisor, and The Network Operations Manager. They each have corresponding instance names: sales_mc, development_mc, billing_mc, and netops_mc.

Listing 5.12 **When Clicked, the Salesperson Broadcasts the *onStartJob* Event to All the Departments**

```
sales_mc.onRelease = function(){
    this.broadcastMessage("onJobStart");
}
// establish broadcast and listeners
AsBroadcaster.initialize(sales_mc);
sales_mc.addListener(billing_mc);
sales_mc.addListener(development_mc);
sales_mc.addListener(netops_mc);
sales_mc.addListener(sales_mc);

// show job titles
billing_mc.title_txt.text = "Billing";
development_mc.title_txt.text = "Development";
netops_mc.title_txt.text="Network Operations";
sales_mc.title_txt.text="Sales";

//set words
billing_mc.words = "I'll start the billing";
development_mc.words = "I'll get the team";
netops_mc.words = "I'll get the servers";
sales_mc.words = "We got the job!";
```

The Actions layer of the mcPerson clip contains the actions seen in Listing 5.13, including a custom event handler.

Listing 5.13 *title_txt.autosize = true;*

```
words_mc._visible = false;
this.onJobStart = function(){
    words_mc._visible = true;
    words_mc.words_txt.text = this.words;
}
```

Looking through Listing 5.12, we can see that this starts with a simple onRelease event handler for the sales_mc movieClip. After the event handler declaration, `sales_mc` is initialized with the methods of AsBroadcaster. This makes the `addListener` and `broadcastMessage` methods available to it. When it has been initialized, each of the four movie clips (`sales_mc`, `development_mc`, `billing_mc`, and `netops_mc`) are set as listeners to it. A custom property, `words`, is assigned to each of the four movie clips, designating what each will say when hired for a job. Lastly, the job titles of each of the movie clips is shown in the `title_txt` field.

Looking more closely at the `onRelease` event handler for `sales_mc`, we can see that a single action, `broadcastMesssage("onJobStart")`, is all that occurs. The `broadcastMessage` action tells each object listening to `sales_mc` to invoke its `onJobStart` event handler. As each of the four movie clips has been assigned as listeners, each of their `onJobStart` event handlers (shown in Listing 5.13) will be invoked. Figure 5.2 shows the Flash application after `sales_mc` has been clicked and released.

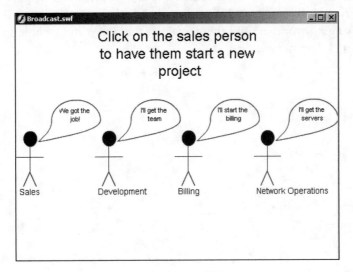

Figure 5.2 The broadcasting test movie clip when the person on the left is clicked.

Although this is a very simplistic example of broadcasting custom messages, the power it represents should be clear. Not only can Flash applications react to events from users, but also a robust framework exists for them to react to our own custom events.

Conclusion

The Object revolution brings a very different approach to the world of software development. Although this article is not designed to make readers experts in OOP, hopefully it gave readers the foundation they need to understand OO development and to start putting some of the best practices into every day use.

Using the principles of OOP (encapsulation, polymorphism, and inheritance), systems can be designed as scale models of the world they represent. By encapsulating entities into objects, they can closely mirror their real-world counterparts, making them more adaptable to the changes their counterparts encounter. Through the use of inheritance, it's not necessary to force a round peg into a square hole; rather than fitting the job to the object, the object can be extended to match the needs of the job. With polymorphism, the objects can take the shape they need at the time they need it.

As is often the case, businesses that are rigid and resistant to change tend to die off quickly. A well-designed OO system can enable business systems to adapt to the changing world around them, making them free and flexible to address challenges as they occur.

Article 6

ActionScript Design Patterns for Rich Internet Application Development

by Steven Webster and Alistair McLeod

THE RICH INTERNET APPLICATION (RIA) is a term coined by Macromedia to describe an application with the look, feel, interactivity, and experience of a desktop application that is delivered with the same advantages and benefits of a more traditional HTML-based web application.

The development of Rich Internet Applications is being driven by the fusion of secure, stable, and performant server-side technologies such as J2EE (and ColdFusion MX, which is deployed on J2EE) and .NET, with Macromedia Flash MX providing the interactive presentation tier experience.

iteration::two is a software consultancy based in Edinburgh, Scotland that is applying its expertise in the development of Enterprise Internet Applications using J2EE technologies to the development of RIAs using a fusion of Flash MX and J2EE on the client and server. Intent on delivering an improved user experience to our clients, iteration::two have delivered RIAs to some of the largest media, entertainment, and financial services clients in Europe. Further information on the company can be found at http://www.iterationtwo.com/.

An example Rich Internet Application, the fictional "Bank of Edinburgh" online bank, is discussed in *Reality J2EE: Architecting for Macromedia Flash MX* (Macromedia Press, 2003), and we have more recently completed Opal, a desktop RIA providing mobile messaging for global corporations. This development is the result of twelve development months of effort, an achievement made possible only through the re-application of our experience in delivering complex J2EE web applications to the field of RIA development. The Opal application can be seen in Figure 6.1.

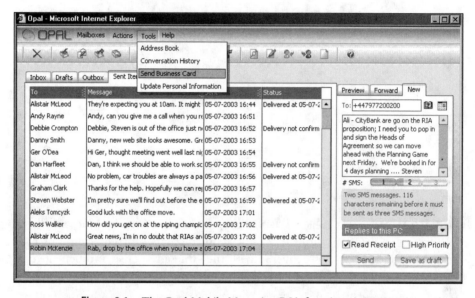

Figure 6.1 The Opal Mobile Messaging RIA from iteration::two.

Traditionally, dynamic applications built in Macromedia Flash would employ a moderate amount of ActionScript, often enabling simple integration with a server-side script. However, RIA development raises the complexity of the server-side development, which correspondingly affects the complexity of the client-side application. To deliver scalable and performant RIAs into production with predictable quality, we must address this increasing complexity.

Though the number of lines of code is a very arbitrary metric of complexity, it is worth realising that the Opal application, from which the iteration::two pattern catalog is born, comprises approximately 65,000 lines of Java code on the server and 25,000 lines of ActionScript code on the client.

In this article, we will introduce software design patterns as a design concept that has been successfully applied in software engineering for a number of years. We will learn a little about the inherent complexity of Rich Internet Application development and learn the design patterns that iteration::two have adopted from the various pattern communities, most notably the J2EE community (Alur, Deepak, Crupi, John, and Malks, Dan. *Core J2EE Patterns: Best Practices and Design Strategies*. Prentice Hall PTR, 2003). We will learn how ActionScript 2.0, with its improved support for an object-oriented approach to software development, lends itself particularly well to implementing the iteration::two pattern catalog.

Our aim is to cover this subject through the development of a simple RIA browser for the Amazon.com book catalog. Our aim is not to demonstrate an appropriate application of RIA technologies, but rather to demonstrate the engineering of an RIA application using ActionScript 2.0 design patterns through the development of a simple application that is easily understandable. We chose Amazon for our example because Amazon has exposed the back-end logic for their business through Web Services, enabling us to focus our discussion on the client-side development without having to cover the server-side implementation.

We will introduce each pattern in turn, focusing on the development problem that must be addressed before introducing the design pattern as a candidate solution. After we are comfortable with the concept of the design pattern, we will discuss how ActionScript 2.0 can be used to implement the solution.

Technologies for RIA Development

Before delving into ActionScript 2.0, design patterns, and the development of our RIA Amazon browser using the iteration::two pattern catalog, we will first revise the technologies involved in a Rich Internet Application.

The presentation tier of a Rich Internet Application is a Macromedia Flash movie (SWF) that may be run from any device with the Flash 6 Player or greater. These devices obviously include web browsers, but they also include mobile phones, PDAs, interactive television consoles, and so on.

The "business logic" of a Rich Internet Application resides on an application server, using an appropriate server-side technology. The technologies that Macromedia has elected to support for RIA development are J2EE (Enterprise Java), CFMX (Coldfusion MX), and .NET.

So that binary data may be exchanged between the client and server, we have chosen to employ Flash Remoting MX. With Flash Remoting deployed in the application server, business methods on the server may be exposed as "services" that the Flash client can remotely invoke through ActionScript. This enables a Flash client to request that some server-side functionality be invoked using Flash Remoting, and the results are returned to the client through Flash Remoting before being prepared for display on the client.

In our experience, with appropriate architecture on the client and the server, Flash Remoting is well suited to the development of large-scale enterprise Rich Internet Applications.

Flash MX Professional 2004 introduces Web Services as another candidate technology for client-server integration that can be treated as any other service, accessed through a service-oriented architecture exposed on the server. The Service Locator pattern enables choices on the technology for client-server integration to be localized to a single class. Encapsulation of this technology choice not only abstracts the details of the technology used to the developer, but it enables alternative technologies to be swapped in without impacting the rest of the application.

An overview of a Rich Internet Application component architecture is given in Figure 6.2.

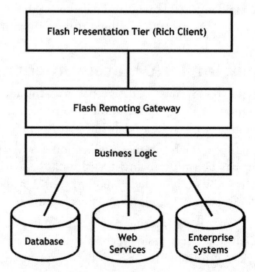

Figure 6.2 Rich Internet Application architecture using Flash, Flash Remoting, and Server-Side Application.

Now that we have discussed Rich Internet Applications and the technologies for RIA development, let's move on to consider what design patterns are and how they can help us in our development of RIAs.

Design Patterns and Pattern Catalog

The seminal book on design patterns is the aptly-titled "Design Patterns," by Erich Gamma, Richard Helm, Ralph Johnson, and John Vlissides, known more commonly throughout the software engineering community as the "Gang of Four" or GoF.

In their own words, "designing object-oriented software is hard, and designing reusable object orient-software is even harder. You must find pertinent objects…and establish key relationships between them. Your design should be specific to the problem at hand but also general enough to address future problems and requirements."

In object-oriented analysis and design, a software application is described as a system of collaborating objects, each object playing a well-defined role within the collaboration. A design pattern can be considered as a solution to a recurring design problem. A design pattern is most often a description of a collaboration of objects, rather than a strategy for designing an object itself.

The Gang of Four pattern catalog contains 12 design patterns that outline common solutions to three types of problems:

- **Creational Patterns**—These address the creation of classes, such as the Singleton pattern that ensures creation of an object occurs once and once only.
- **Structural Patterns**—These address the composition of classes or objects, such as the Façade pattern, which presents a higher-level interface to a series of subsystems.
- **Behavioral Patterns**—These address the ways in which classes or objects interact and distribute responsibility, such as the Command pattern, which encapsulates a request as an object, enabling support for parameterizing requests, logging requests, and supporting undoable operations.

At the Java One conference in 2001, Deepak Alur, John Crupi, and Dan Malks of Sun Microsystems presented their own "Core J2EE Patterns." The Core J2EE Pattern catalog represents solutions to the recurring problems faced by the Sun Java Center consultants during the development of enterprise web applications. J2EE developers have successfully developed systems with attention to the Core J2EE pattern catalog. When a collection of patterns is repeatedly used to solve a higher-level problem, a software framework emerges. In the J2EE community, many frameworks now exist as implementations of these best-practice design patterns.

At iteration::two, we have applied our experience in developing complex enterprise web applications to the development of Rich Internet Applications. The Core J2EE pattern catalog from Sun Professional Services has proven an excellent set of patterns that can be adapted for Flash MX Rich Internet Applications. We have successfully developed our own ActionScript framework, resulting from the collaboration of these design patterns.

We will now move ahead and further describe the core components of the framework used by iteration::two.

ActionScript 2.0 and Design Patterns

ActionScript 1.0, which is the ActionScript language that has existed up to and including the release of Flash MX, has a pseudo-object-oriented development model, based on the notion of objects and object prototypes.

With the emergence of ActionScript 2.0, which implements much of the ECMA4.0 standard, object-oriented language features have been introduced that enable the ActionScript developer to think of his or her system development in terms of classes, instances of objects, and the collaborations or passing of messages between these objects.

Though it has been possible to implement design patterns to a fashion using ActionScript 1.0, with ActionScript 2.0, we can now more naturally express an architectural framework as a series of collaborating design patterns.

We will now examine some of the key patterns in a framework that support the rapid development of RIAs and examine how these patterns can be naturally and effectively implemented in an object-oriented fashion using ActionScript 2.0.

We will use UML (Unified Modeling Language) notation to describe our patterns, borrowing on two important UML diagrams—the class diagram and the sequence diagram.

The UML class diagram will enable us to document patterns as classes and document those classes in terms of their relationship with other classes. The class diagram will give us a static, stationary view of the system.

Meanwhile, the sequence diagram will enable us to describe how the classes in a particular design pattern interact together and how they interact with the classes involved in other patterns. The sequence diagram will give us a dynamic, living, breathing view of the system.

Let's now jump into the actual discussion of the patterns for our Rich Internet Amazon example.

Rich Internet Amazon Application

Rather than present the patterns in an academic fashion, we will instead follow a simple example of a RIA that enables us to demonstrate the patterns in context.

We will build an RIA browser for the Amazon.com book catalog that enables us to search for relevant titles by keyword, to display the book jackets on our desktop, and to interact with the books before purchasing them from the Amazon site itself. Amazon exposes their product catalog as a set of Web Services, which enables us to demonstrate the pattern catalog without having to perform a significant amount of back-end development.

Flash MX Professional 2004 makes it possible for a Flash client to hook directly to Web Services, using data binding to bind UI controls to the results passed back from a Web Service call. However, this data binding is only supported for web services running on the same server as the one from which the Flash application was served. To access remote Web Services, such as the Amazon Web Services, a "proxy" Web Service must be supplied, which provides a local interface to the remote service. Rather than provide a Web Service proxy in this manner, we have taken the simpler approach of hiding the Web Service implementation behind a Java application running on a Tomcat application server. If you visit `http://aspatterns.iterationtwo.com/`, you can download the full source code for the application, including the server-side implementation. Alternatively, you can learn how to point your client at another server hosting the back-end.

Similarly, we have provided very little functionality on the user interface, limiting the example to the behavior necessary to explore each of the design patterns in context. This enables us to keep the focus of this article on the framework of collaborating ActionScript patterns that enable the engineering of Rich Internet Applications using ActionScript 2.0.

A screenshot of the iteration::two Amazon RIA browser can be seen in Figure 6.3.

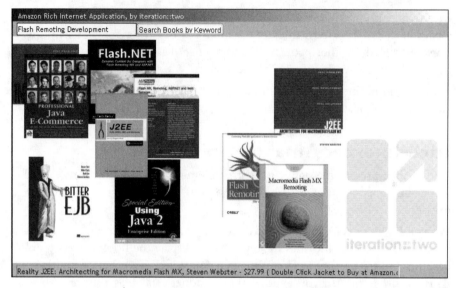

Figure 6.3 Amazon RIA browser showing results of a keyword search.

The iteration::two ActionScript 2.0 Pattern Catalog

Let's now take a look at the iteration::two ActionScript pattern catalog. This catalog represents the ActionScript implementation of some core design patterns that provide a framework for the development of Rich Internet Applications.

If we consider the "back-end" or server-side of an enterprise RIA to be the "bottom," and the presentation tier to be the "top," then we will take a "bottom-up" approach to studying these design patterns. In turn, we will look at the following patterns:

- Service Locator
- Value Object
- Business Delegate
- Front Controller
- Command Pattern
- View Helper

Let's summarise how we'll tackle each of these design patterns. For each pattern, we will first identify the recurring design problem that the pattern addresses. We'll then consider how the pattern may be implemented using ActionScript 2.0, and further consider how the pattern collaborates with other design patterns to provide a structure in our framework. Using our Amazon RIA application, we will explore some concrete examples of how the pattern can be used to solve a real-world problem.

> **Note**
>
> ActionScript 2.0 encourages us to elaborate the best practice of keeping all ActionScript code in external text files by packaging code into namespaces that correspond to a directory structure. All code for our Amazon RIA will exist under the com.iterationtwo.amazonria namespace in the corresponding com/ iterationtwo/amazonria directories. Different patterns in the framework will reside in different packages underneath this framework, as will be seen in the class definitions.

Let's start with the first of our patterns—the Service Locator.

Service Locator

When building a Rich Internet Application, we naturally adopt a Service-Oriented Architecture (SOA). A SOA is an application architecture that consists of a set of loosely coupled business services that may be accessed by a range of clients. Assembled together, these services may be aggregated to solve a particular business problem.

As previously discussed, we have made a decision in our Amazon RIA to use Flash Remoting as our technology for client-server integration. The Service Locator class will encapsulate all the details of Flash Remoting. Should we decide at a later stage to use a different technology for passing data between client and server, the Service Locator class will be the only class that we have to change to reflect this decision.

Flash Remoting enables a Flash presentation tier to act as a client to a service-oriented architecture. For a ColdFusion developer, services may include ColdFusion pages or ColdFusion Components. A .NET developer may want to expose ASPX pages, DLL files, or .NET Web Services, while a J2EE developer might choose to expose their plain old Java Classes, Servlets, JSP, Enterprise JavaBeans, or JMX Mbeans as services. And for all these technologies, SOAP Web Services are an emerging standard that enable application functionality to be exposed to third-party clients as services.

In fact, the only thing that all these disparate services have in common is that they are remote and that, to use them, we must first locate them and connect to them.

Though Flash Remoting provides a uniform means of connecting to these disparate services, how we do that depends upon knowing their location, the type of service they are, and how a connection to that type of service is established.

For instance, to connect to a Java class that has been exposed to Flash Remoting as a service, we must know the URL of the application server on which the Flash gateway is running, we must know that the service is indeed a Java class, and we must know the fully qualified path name (such as `com.iterationtwo.amazonria.flash.AmazonService`) of that Java class.

Problem

Looking up and creating connections to a series of different services that may be implemented with different technologies is not the concern of the Flash client application developer. When developing the client-side logic for a Rich Internet Amazon browser, the developer really doesn't care whether the books written by a particular author are located using a SOAP Web Service, a Java application, or a .NET DLL. More importantly, he or she doesn't care about the different ways in which they should locate the service, depending on how the service is implemented.

The developer just wants the service handed to him or her on a plate so that he or she can call the "findBooksWrittenByAuthor" method that does exactly what it says on the tin.

This is a commonly recurring problem. This is a job for the Service Locator pattern.

Solution

The Service Locator provides a uniform means of locating server-side services for use by a client-side client. We can extend the utility of the Service Locator by ensuring that attempts are made to locate only real and existing services. The Service Locator can be created with a lookup table of known services—when an application demands the use of a new service, this service is registered with the Service Locator so that it may be available for use by the client.

As discussed previously, the name by which a service is located depends on its implementation. A plain Java object on the server is looked up by its fully qualified class name, whereas an Enterprise JavaBean service is located by the fully qualified class name of its home interface. A Web Service may be located by the location of its WSDL file, whereas a ColdFusion component may be located by a combination of the directory from the root web directory in which it is located along with the component's filename. The Service Locator can provide a useful abstraction here—when services are registered with the Service Locator, they are given a "canonical name," such as "AmazonService." Whether "AmazonService" is a Web Service, a Java class, or a ColdFusion Component is of interest only when the service is first registered with the Service Locator. Clients of the service need only locate the service using its simpler name, "AmazonService."

ActionScript 2.0 Implementation

The Service Locator hides from its clients (usually the Business Delegate pattern, which will be discussed later) the details of locating and connecting to a service. In our Amazon RIA, this is making a connection through the Flash Remoting server to the J2EE application responsible for interrogating the Amazon catalog through Web Services.

The creation of connections is always one of the most expensive operations in distributed systems and is a well-established problem in database systems, for instance. Creating a new connection each time a service is to be called can be expensive, both in terms of memory (connections essentially eat up resources) and in speed (opening a connection to a server is usually the critical operation). A Connection Pool is a strategy used in database designs to alleviate this problem. By opening a number of connections on startup and then reusing these connections among all service requests, we can eliminate both the expense of creating connections and the bottleneck of sharing a single connection.

In our Service Locator, we have implemented a very basic Connection Pool by creating a single connection that is reused by all instances of the Service Locator. We implement this using a private static class attribute.

Should we want to implement a more complete Connection Pool strategy, it can be achieved in the Service Locator, to the ignorance of all other parts of the service. This is a perfect example of good object granularity.

Within our Amazon RIA application, the ServiceLocator class is used only in the AmazonDelegate (which is explained later in this article). When creating a ServiceLocator, we provide a reference to a responseHandler. We discuss the need for response handlers in Flash Remoting in more detail in Reality J2EE—Architecting for Flash MX. In summary, however, the response handler is the class that contains the methods that will be called when a service call has completed and the results are available, such as a list of books in response to a keyword search.

Rich client applications, such as those developed with Flash MX presentation tiers, advertise "responsiveness" as one of the key benefits. To ensure that the application is responsive, when data is fetched from the server, the application should not "hang" until the server has passed its result back to the client. Instead, the request is made to the server, and the client application is immediately available. The server then passes data back to the client later, when it is available. This is known as an "asynchronous response," which is achieved using a response handler to receive the response at this future point in time.

The response handler strategy can be used whenever the client-server communication is asynchronous, including Flash Remoting and Web Service integration.

> **Note**
>
> ActionScript 2.0 introduces object-oriented features not available in ActionScript 1.0, such as private functions and private class attributes. We use these features in our Amazon RIA example class to encapsulate its implementation.

As can be seen in the ServiceLocator constructor that follows, not only do we store the response handler, but we also create a directory of service names—simple names to map to server-side services—as well as a cache for services that have previously been instantiated.

We also specify the default URL for the NetServices gateway URL. In a production-strength system, this URL would not be hard-wired into the class.

```
public function ServiceLocator( responseHandler )
{
    this.responseHandler = responseHandler;
    serviceDirectory = new Array();
    serviceCache = new Array();

    NetServices.setDefaultGatewayUrl( "http://127.0.0.1:8080/amazonria/gateway" );

    initialiseServices();
}
```

The ServiceLocator constructor calls `initialiseServices()` to add the mappings of the canonical service names to their fully qualified name. In our implementation, the private function `addService()` does the actual work of storing the mapped values together.

```
private function initialiseServices()
{
        addService( "AmazonService", "com.iterationtwo.amazonria.flash.
        ➥AmazonService" );
}
```

The only other public function of the ServiceLocator is `getService()`, which enables classes using the ServiceLocator to retrieve a service for a given canonical service name:

```
public function getService( serviceName:String )
{
        if ( serviceExists( serviceName ) )
            return getServiceInstance( serviceName );
        else
            trace( "ServiceLocator: No Such Service - " + serviceName );
}
```

The `serviceExists()` method returns a Boolean to indicate whether the canonical service name has been defined to the ServiceLocator. The `getServiceInstance()` method returns the service for the canonical name and handles the creation and caching of the services. Subsequent requests for the same service will result in the service being retrieved from the cache rather than the construction of a new object and the performance hit that this incurs.

If no service exists for the provided service name, we throw an error to the Output panel. In a production-strength system, we would introduce the Exception processing available with ActionScript 2.0.

From this simple example, we can already see how the ServiceLocator encapsulates the retrieval of services using an easy-to-remember canonical name that isn't tied to the implementation of the service, enabling clients of business services to locate and use them in a simple, scalable, and maintainable fashion.

Let's move on to discuss the next design pattern—the Value Object.

Value Object

In an enterprise application, several tiers exist in the architecture. Architects will often talk of a 3-tier or even n-tier design to describe the layers of architecture that are decoupled from each other. In an RIA, we will typically have a 3-tier design, comprising our presentation tier, business tier, and integration or service tier.

The presentation tier is a Flash application implementing the user interface. The business tier will typically cross the chasm between ActionScript and the server-side technology, with Flash Remoting providing the bridge. At the back-end, the integration tier will hook the business logic into databases, message queues, LDAP servers, legacy systems, and so on, and it will expose these as services to the business logic.

Problem

An application developer needs not concern himself or herself with the complexities of the integration tier. When asking to find all books written by Webster, the business logic developer cares little for whether these are returned as an SQL ResultSet, a collection of container-managed entity beans, or XML from an object persistence engine. Rather, the business logic developer wants "books" that have "titles," "cover images," and a "price."

Similarly, our presentation tier developer wants to build a user interface without having to worry whether changes to how author data is represented in the database requires changes to how author data is presented on the user interface.

Rather, within each tier of the application, the various developers are interested only in the "currency" of books, authors, publishers—or objects, to be more precise. They are not concerned about how these objects are represented internally at various places in the application architecture, nor do they want to be exposed to the results of a change in the underlying object representation. They care about the value of the data, not the way it is represented.

This is a commonly recurring problem. This is a job for the Value Object pattern.

Solution

The Value Object is simply a container for the data that represents an entity in the system, such as a book, and the attributes of that entity, such as the ISBN number, the author, and the publisher.

The Value Object should be able to carry this data around between application tiers. Clients should be able to populate Value Objects to pass as arguments to method calls further down the architecture. Services should be able to return results as Value Objects or as collections of Value Objects (typically as arrays).

Consequently, the Value Object can contain the attributes representing its data, methods to populate or "set" the data, and methods to fetch or "get" the data.

It is also worth considering that in a complex system, a Value Object may contain other Value Objects—a Book Value Object may contain an array of Review Value Objects, for instance, to represent the different reviews of a particular book.

ActionScript 2.0 Implementation

ActionScript 2.0's new object-oriented features enable us to implement a
"proper" object model in our client side application. For example, the following is one possible implementation of a KeywordRequest Value Object that
can be used as the "currency" in a request to an Amazon Service.

```
class com.iterationtwo.amazonria.vo.KeywordRequest
{
     public function KeywordRequest()
     {
     }

     public function getKeyword():String
     {
          return keyword;
     }

     public function setKeyword( keyword:String )
     {
          this.keyword = keyword;
     }

     private var keyword:String;
}
```

This class definition enables client code to construct a KeywordRequest Value
Object and use it as follows.

```
var keywordRequest:KeywordRequest = new KeywordRequest();
keywordRequest.setKeyword( "harry potter goblet of fire" );
var keyword:String = keywordRequest.getKeyword();
```

Because we have defined the `keyword` attribute within the KeywordRequest
class as being `private`, the compiler prohibits attempts to do the following:

```
var keyword:String = keywordRequest.keyword;
```

The above notation to access class attributes (often called the "dot-notation")
is the manner in which many ActionScript developers normally write their
client code. However, it is considered bad practice to have class members as
public scope.

ActionScript 2.0 has introduced implicit getters and setters to help with this
issue. Implicit getters and setters can be defined within a class using the following format:

```
class com.iterationtwo.amazonria.vo.KeywordRequest
{
     public function KeywordRequest()
     {
```

```
        }

        public function get keyword():String
        {
                return theKeyword;
        }

        public function set keyword( keyword:String )
        {
                this. theKeyword = keyword;
        }

        private var theKeyword:String;
}
```

> **Note**
> Due to the manner in which the implicit getters and setters are compiled, their function names cannot be the same name as an attribute of the class. For this reason, we have had to rename the keyword class attribute to theKeyword.

Defining a class with implicit getters and setters enables clients of that class to use the dot–notation to access the class attributes through those functions:

```
var keyword:String = keywordRequest.keyword;
keywordRequest.keyword = "new keyword";
```

Although the implicit getters and setters may seem a useful addition to ActionScript 2.0, the enforced renaming of attributes affects the readability of our code when we are using Flash Remoting.

> **Using Getters and Setters with Flash Remoting**
> When data is passed through Flash Remoting, the attribute names are used to determine the data to be transferred, so a server-side class has to refer to the attributes in their renamed form. This enforces an inconsistency between the attributes in the server and client-side models, which we do not consider a good practice. Consequently, we have chosen not to use implicit getters and setters in our Value Object implementations. However, so that the client-side developers can still use the notation they are most familiar with, that is, `var keyword:String = keywordRequest.keyword`, we pragmatically mark our Value Object class attributes as public in scope.

In our Amazon RIA, we have created Value Objects to capture the information required for the service request to the Amazon Web services and to capture the information returned from those services.

All Amazon search requests contain some basic information required for all requests and additional information depending on the specific request. The

creation of a base class is the ideal fit for this model. We have created the
AmazonBaseRequest class:

```
class com.iterationtwo.amazonria.vo.AmazonBaseRequest
{
        public function AmazonBaseRequest()
        {
                tag = "webservices-20";
                devtag = "<amazon-devtag>";
        }

        private var tag:String;
        private var devtag:String;
        public var locale:String;
}
```

Note

A base class is a class that will be extended by other classes, known as derived classes. Derived classes
inherit all functions and attributes of the base class they extend. This class hierarchy is a principal tenet
of object-oriented development.

Note

As explained previously, we have decided to keep our class attributes public in scope so that clients of
this class can use the "dot-notation" to access the class data.

However, two class attributes, tag and devtag, have the same value for all
Amazon requests. We set their values in the class constructor and defined those
attributes as private in the class so that classes external to the
AmazonBaseRequest class cannot access or change their values.

Note

The Amazon Web Service requires the tag and devtag attributes. You can receive your own free
devtag (also called a Token) by registering to use the Amazon Web Service at http://
www.amazon.com/gp/aws/landing.html.

Individual service requests to the Amazon Web Service require additional information, and we have created individual Value Object classes for these. For example, to perform a keyword search, we have created the KeywordRequest class:

```
class com.iterationtwo.amazonria.vo.KeywordRequest extends AmazonBaseRequest
{
        public function KeywordRequest()
        {
        }

        public var keyword:String;
        public var page:String;
```

```
public var mode:String;
public var type:String;

private static var registered:Boolean = Object.registerClass(
"com.iterationtwo.amazonria.vo.KeywordRequest", KeywordRequest );
}
```

As can been seen in Figure 6.4, the KeywordRequest class extends the AmazonBaseRequest class, so it picks up all the attributes of the latter through the class hierarchy.

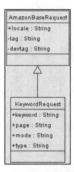

Figure 6.4   UML Class Diagram, showing the KeywordRequest Value Object class as a child of the AmazonBaseRequest parent base class.

The final attribute of the class, `registered`, requires further explanation. `Object.registerClass()` is used to assign a Symbol ID (in this case, `com.iterationtwo.amazonria.vo.KeywordRequest`) to a given function (in this case, our class constructor, `KeywordRequest`). With Flash Remoting, the Symbol ID is available as a `getType()` method in our server-side code. We use this `getType()` method to map the client-side class data onto an instance of the server-side class as specified by the Symbol ID. This provides a neat mapping between client-side and server-side Value Objects.

Note

For the J2EE backend to our Amazon RIA, we use the ASTranslator project (http://carbonfive.sourceforge.net/astranslator to perform Value Object translation from client to server. This is discussed in detail in *Reality J2EE: Architecting for Flash MX* (Macromedia Press, 2003), by Steven Webster.

We have used a static class attribute to execute the `Object.registerClass` method so that it is executed at most once only for each Value Object class in our application, not once per instance of class construction.

As well as the request Value Objects, we have also created Value Objects to store the results of the Amazon Web Service calls. For example, searches are returned in a ProductInfo class:

```
class com.iterationtwo.amazonria.vo.ProductInfo
{
      public function ProductInfo()
      {
      }

      public var details:Array;
      public var totalresults:String;
      public var totalpages:String;
      public var listname:String;
}
```

`Object.registerClass()` is not required for Value Objects where the data is only populated from the result of a service request.

ProductInfo contains the primitive attributes `totalresults`, `totalpages`, and `listname`, and an Array of another Value Object, Details. The Details class is also defined as a Value Object.

This "deep" Value Object enables the detailed results of a search to be fetched by clients of the ProductInfo class in various ways:

```
// Get the ProductInfo from the Service Result
var productInfo:ProductInfo = getProductInfo();
var firstDetails:Details = productInfo.details[0];
var productName:String = firstDetails.productName;
```

or

```
var productInfo:ProductInfo = getProductInfo();
var productName:String = productInfo.details[0].productName;
```

The Value Object pattern enables us to contain the data that represents an entity in the system in a single class. Use of this pattern enables client-side and server-side developers to use a common vocabulary when discussing the overall business model and simplifies the communication of information between the different layers of an application.

Now that we can locate remote services and describe system objects on the client and the server with a common vocabulary, let's study the Business Delegate pattern to see how we can make our business logic available to clients.

Business Delegate

When building a Rich Internet Application, the Flash client will inevitably request that some data is fetched, some new data is created on the server, or some existing data is updated on the server. Additionally, the Flash client may ask that some other service is performed, such as sending an email from the server, querying the parcel track number at UPS, and so on.

Problem

When developing an RIA, the application developer does not want to be concerned with the specific implementation details of a particular business service. Furthermore, the application developer does not want to expose himself or herself to the implementation details of a business service any more than he or she wanted to expose himself or herself to the representation of the underlying model (which the Value Object pattern solved).

Solution

The Business Delegate pattern, borrowed from the Core J2EE Pattern catalog, reduces the coupling between the Flash client and business services, hiding the implementation details of the service.

Where there may be volatility in the implementation of the business service API, the Business Delegate is able to shield this volatility somewhat from the client. In the context of our Amazon RIA, we cannot assume that Amazon will not make changes to the API for searching titles. The Business Delegate pattern will ensure that the Flash user interface is isolated from such changes—the presentation tier relies only on the services exposed to the Business Delegate, delegating responsibility for the actually business service integration to the aptly-named Business Delegate.

The Business Delegate is a close friend of the Service Locator pattern—indeed, the Service Locator is likely only to be used by the Business Delegate and no other classes. Acting as a middleman on behalf of the presentation tier, when the Business Delegate is asked to provide a business service, such as returning all book titles by Steven Webster, it will likely call on its colleague the Service Locator to locate the AmazonService so that the Business Delegate may then perform the search.

Furthermore, the Business Delegate will negotiate with its clients using Value Objects. If asked for a list of books written by Steven Webster, the Business Delegate will accept an Author Value Object, representing Steven Webster as the author. The Business Delegate will then ask the Service Locator to find the AmazonService and perform its searchByAuthor method using the relevant information extracted from the Author Value Object. As results are returned to the Business Delegate in whichever form the particular service dictates, the

Business Delegate will construct a collection of Book Value Objects, populating each Book with the pertinent details.

Consequently, the presentation tier will "deal in Authors and Books" with the Business Delegate, ambivalent to the implementation details of the search service, the underlying representation of books and authors, and the location of the service itself. Figure 6.5 is a UML sequence diagram demonstrating the collaboration of the Value Object, Business Delegate, and Service Locator patterns to invoke a server-side service.

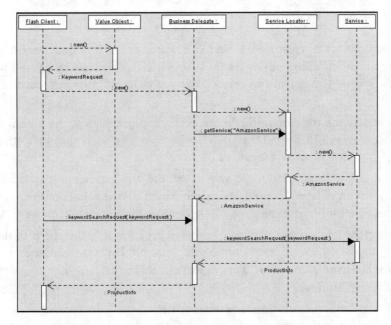

Figure 6.5   Sequence Diagram demonstrating collaboration of
Business Delegate, Service Locator, and Value Objects.

A key benefit of the Business Delegate pattern is that it provides a logical place for optimization such as result caching to be performed. If a particular search pattern is likely to be a common one, such as "fetch all books in the Java Programming department," then the Business Delegate may invoke the service the first time only, caching the results. Subsequent requests by the Flash client for Java Programming books will no longer need to perform a remoting call to a remote service and can instead instantaneously return the books that were previously cached.

ActionScript 2.0 Implementation

In ActionScript 2.0, the Business Delegate is implemented in its own class, exposing the business methods as public functions.

The Business Delegate is a close collaborator with the Service Locator pattern that we introduced earlier. When the delegate is created, it immediately creates a new Service Locator and fetches any services it knows it is going to require.

```
public function AmazonDelegate()
{
    var serviceLocator:ServiceLocator = new ServiceLocator( this );
    service = serviceLocator.getService( "AmazonService" );
}
```

Furthermore, when creating the Service Locator, the delegate assumes responsibility for the handling of any results passed back by services by passing itself as the response handler to the Service Locator using the `this` reference to refer to itself.

However, having the AmazonDelegate as the response handler has implications on the use of the Business Delegate class because it restricts the application to a single action following a service call.

If we want our application to be able to call the same service in two different scenarios with different actions being performed on the results of that service call, then we cannot use the AmazonDelegate as the response handler.

We therefore refactor our AmazonDelegate class to enable the client of the class to define which object should be the response handler. Thus, the AmazonDelegate constructor dictates that clients of the class have to provide the response handler:

```
public function AmazonDelegate( responseHandler )
{
    var serviceLocator:ServiceLocator = new ServiceLocator( responseHandler );
    service = serviceLocator.getService( "AmazonService" );
}
```

With this implementation, when service calls have been made, methods on the response handler passed into the AmazonDelegate are executed on completion of service calls.

For example, our delegate could have the following business method used by clients to do a keyword search:

```
public function keywordSearchRequest( keywordRequest:KeywordRequest )
{
        service.keywordSearchRequest( keywordRequest );
}
```

The `keywordSearchRequest()` function of this class is provided with a instance of the KeywordRequest Value Object. The delegate method uses the `service` instance that was created in the AmazonDelegate constructor to call the `keywordSearchRequest()` service, passing it the `keywordRequest` Value Object.

On completion of the `keywordSearchRequest()` service, either `keywordSearchRequest_Result()` or `keywordSearchRequest_Status()` will be called, depending on the success of the service. This function call will be made on the object passed into the AmazonDelegate constructor.

We have elected not to use strict typing on the response handler so that the framework does not control which classes are allowed to be response handlers. Industrial implementations of a pattern-based framework would likely specify an interface or base class of suitable response handlers to enforce compile-time checking of the object being passed to the Service Locator.

The Business Delegate pattern provides a simple interface through which business logic can be exposed. Use of this pattern enables us to hide the internals of service lookup through the Service Locator and enables the client of the delegate to manage the response from the service as it requires.

Let's now move ahead and take a look at how we incorporate the Front Controller pattern into our architecture.

Front Controller

In a complex Rich Internet Application, the user interface is likely to service a vast number of types of requests. A simple application, sometimes called a "Flashlet" or "Applet," is likely to have a single job such as "fetch weather given zip code," or "fetch stock quote for ticker." An application of this complexity is really a "single use-case" application.

However, with an RIA that may have tens or even hundreds of use-cases, the application architecture needs to support the systematic handling of user gestures, such as menu selections, toolbar button presses, form submissions, drag and drops, and so on.

Problem

When the number of use-cases increases, the number of common system services that must be performed can scale terribly unless there is some centralized control for handling these requests.

Consider an online banking application in which all requests to perform some action on an account first require that the currently logged-in user is authenticated. As the number of use-cases increases, for example, "Add Account," "View Transactions," and "Transfer Money between Accounts," then the number of occurrences of authentication code splattered around the architecture will increase as well.

Furthermore, as the number of use-cases increases, it becomes necessary to have a centralized means of deciding which use-cases must be executed as a result of the gestures made by the user (button clicks, menu selections) and the current state of the application.

This is a problem that we can choose to solve with the Front Controller pattern.

Solution

The Front Controller is the initial point of contact for handling a request. In a Rich Internet Application, a request can be considered a menu selection, a press of a toolbar button, the submission of a form, the dragging and dropping of an item from one area to another, and so on. A request is initiated by a "user gesture."

The Front Controller manages the handling of each request, invoking centralized services such as authentication or logging on each request. The Front Controller is then responsible for ensuring that the control logic necessary to complete a particular request is carried out.

ActionScript 2.0 Implementation

The Front Controller pattern could be implemented in a number of ways in ActionScript 2.0. We have chosen to present a simplified implementation in this article.

A first-cut implementation of the Front Controller could be as follows:

```
class com.iterationtwo.amazonria.control.AmazonController
{
        public function AmazonController()
        {
        }

        public function performAction( action:String )
        {
                if ( action == "keywordSearch" )
                        doKeywordSearch();
                else if ( action == "authorSearch" )
                        doAuthorSearch();
        }
}
```

Although this code would work as a Front Controller, it is hardly extensible. This implementation forces clients of the Front Controller to construct a new instance of the controller and to call a function each time an action is to be performed. Also, as the application grows, the `performAction()` method would grow, until it reached an unmanageable state.

A more scalable solution is to use an event-driven Front Controller. ActionScript 2.0 introduces the EventDispatcher class to help with this. Using the EventDispatcher, we can decouple the Front Controller from its clients. Rather than expect explicit function calls, the controller listens for defined events and performs actions on the arrival of those events.

We have created a new class, the EventBroadcaster, to handle the event processing on behalf of the Front Controller. The EventBroadcaster class uses the EventDispatcher to provide a mechanism to broadcast events and also to keep a record of the classes that have registered an interest in specific events. Our implementation is as follows:

```
class com.iterationtwo.amazonria.control.EventBroadcaster
{
        public static function getInstance()
        {
                if ( eventBroadcaster == undefined )
                        eventBroadcaster = new EventBroadcaster();

                return eventBroadcaster;
        }

        private function EventBroadcaster()
        {
                EventDispatcher.initialize( this );
        }

        public function broadcastEvent( eventName:String )
        {
                var event:Event = new Event();
                event.type = eventName;

                dispatchEvent( event );
        }

        private static var eventBroadcaster;

        public var dispatchEvent:Function;
        public var addEventListener:Function;
        public var removeEventListener:Function;
}
```

We have implemented the EventBroadcaster using the Singleton pattern. The Singleton pattern ensures that one and only one instance of the EventBroadcaster class can exist in the system.

> **Note**
>
> The Singleton pattern is implemented by having a `static` `getInstance()` method on the class and by making the constructor `private`. A `private` `static` variable in the class stores the only instance of the EventBroadcaster, which is created using "lazy instantiation" the first time `getInstance()` is executed.

By initializing itself with the EventDispatcher in its own constructor, the EventBroadcaster is furnished with the implementations of the `dispatchEvent()`, `addEventListener()`, and `removeEventListner()` functions declared at the end of the class. These functions are defined in the EventDispatcher class.

Clients of the EventBroadcaster, such as our Front Controller, can broadcast events of a given type by using the `broadcastEvent()` method. The `broadcastEvent()` method creates an instance of the ActionScript 2.0 Event class and dispatches that event to interested objects using the `dispatchEvent()` method. Objects can register their interest in an event by using the `addEventListener()` function, as follows:

```
EventBroadcaster.getInstance().addEventListener( "eventName", responseHandler );
```

In the example above, when an event "eventName" is broadcast, an appropriate method on the `responseHandler` will be invoked.

Which method is invoked on the `responseHandler` is governed by the following rules defined in the EventDispatcher class.

If the `typeof` the `responseHandler` is Object or MovieClip, the EventDispatcher first checks if the `responseHandler` has a `handleEvent()` function. If it exists, that function is called with the event object. If no `handleEvent()` function exists, the EventDispatcher will call a function on the `responseHandler` with the name of the event. In the example above, a call will be made to `responseHandler.eventName()`, passing the event object.

If the `responseHandler` is a function, that function will be invoked and will be passed the event object.

With the functionality provided in the EventBroadcaster, client classes can register themselves as being interested in specific events, and other client classes can broadcast those events.

We will now see how the Front Controller can use the EventBroadcaster to act on broadcasted events:

```
class com.iterationtwo.amazonria.control.AmazonController
{
      public function AmazonController()
      {
            EventBroadcaster.getInstance().addEventListener( "keywordSearch",
            ➥this );
            EventBroadcaster.getInstance().addEventListener( "authorSearch",
            ➥this );
      }

      public function keywordSearch( event:Event )
      {
            doKeywordSearch();
      }

      public function authorSearch( event:Event )
      {
            doAuthorSearch();
      }
}
```

The AmazonController constructor registers itself as the response handler for the events named keywordSearch and authorSearch through the addEventListener() function.

If another class in the application, perhaps as the result of the user pressing a "Search" push button, broadcasts the keywordSearch event, as follows:

```
EventBroadcaster.getInstance().broadcastEvent( "keywordSearch" )
```

then because the AmazonController has registered an interest in keywordSearch events, the keywordSearch() function of the AmazonController class will be invoked when the event is broadcast. This demonstrates the collaboration between the EventBroadcaster, which ensures that user gesture events are broadcast, and the AmazonController, which ensures that user gesture events are handled.

The collaboration of the Front Controller and the Event Broadcaster classes also enables finer control over an application. A single application could choose to have more than one controller to manage separate parts of an application (for example, if the system was modular in design with pluggable components, each component might have its own controller).

In such an application, each controller can register with the Singleton EventBroadcaster for its own set of events. For example, controller1 might be interested in events authorSearch and keywordSearch, whereas controller2 might be interested in events authorSearch and asinSearch.

Although the event-driven Front Controller described above is better than the function-based one described initially, it still has the same problem of extensibility. Over time, as more events are added to the system, the class will turn into a "Fat Controller," bloated with additional logic. Let's take a look now at the Command Pattern—a diet pill for a fat Front Controller!

Command Pattern

In many strategies for object-oriented analysis of a system, some form of "Use-Case Analysis" is performed. A use-case can be considered a typical interaction between one or more users and the system to carry out a specific task. In agile development, a use-case is typically a "user story," or in feature-driven development, we could call a use-case a "feature."

In the context of our Amazon RIA, a use-case might include "fetch all books by author," "fetch product specific details given ISBN," or "keyword search for books."

Martin Fowler describes refactoring as "improving the design of existing code." In an RIA, the typically large number of use-cases means that a commonly applied J2EE refactoring becomes necessary in the ActionScript world as well.

In refactoring, code that is getting a little stale, a little moldy, and is generally becoming unhealthy for us is identified by its "code smell." A common code smell in presentation-tier design is that of the "Fat Controller."

Problem

As more and more code is added to the controller to handle the different events pertaining to different use-cases, the controller grows in complexity. When any individual class in the system grows in complexity, it becomes difficult to test, difficult to maintain, and a target for failure.

Solution

Refactoring of this bad practice is achieved by introducing the Command pattern. The Command pattern enables us to "shed weight from the controller," reducing the controller's task to centralized request handling. The Front Controller handles incoming requests but acts as a delegation point with specific Command classes containing control code to which the controller delegates.

In our previous description of the Front Controller pattern, we allowed the controller itself to handle the control logic for each particular use-case by implementing an appropriate event-handling method for each event broadcast as a result of a user gesture.

By introducing the Command pattern, the Front Controller can perform that essential skill of management—delegating someone else to do all the hard work! The Front Controller can then specialize in determining what needs to be done and by whom in response to a user gesture, and then it can leave a utility class—the Command class—to actually perform the control logic pertaining to a particular use-case.

A use-case will require the invocation of business services, the handling of results of these service method calls, and the updating of the view with these results. Encapsulation of the control code that uses the Business Delegate to invoke services, that handles the Business Delegate results, and that both interrogates and updates the view is a problem solved by the Command pattern.

Another benefit emerges with this strategy. In our initial discussion of the Business Delegate pattern, the delegate invoked server-side methods and then handled the results of those methods. A side effect of this was that each call to a server-side method could only be used in a single context. If we wanted to call a `fetchBooksByAuthor()` method and display the results in both a tabular view and an interactive jacket cover view, we would need two methods on our Business Delegate, each using the results from the `fetchBooksByAuthor()` method in different contexts.

When we introduce the Command pattern, however, each command pertains to the appropriate context. We would likely have a `ViewBookListCommand` and a `ViewBookCoversCommand`. Each Command class can now invoke the same `fetchBooksByAuthor()` method on the Business Delegate and provide the handler methods for the service results. The Business Delegate is then simplified dramatically, delegating the result handling to the Command classes, rather than having to deal with results itself.

As shown in Figure 6.6, this collaboration of the Front Controller, Command pattern, and Business Delegate pattern becomes a very powerful collaboration indeed when we start to build large-scale RIAs.

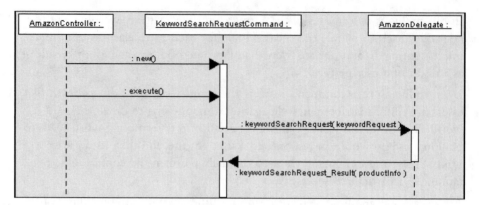

Figure 6.6   Command Pattern handling results passed back from Business Delegate.

ActionScript 2.0 Implementation

In ActionScript 2.0, we implement each command in its own class. The command's responsibility is to prepare a request for a server-side service, make the request to the Business Delegate, and handle the response. The command should prepare the response for the presentation tier, ensuring that the view is updated with the results of the server-side method call.

In our Amazon RIA, all concrete command classes must implement the Command interface. This enables us to use the Command interface in our Front Controller, which needs not concern itself with the detailed implementation of each concrete command.

Interfaces are another new feature of ActionScript 2.0. Interfaces force the addition of functions onto the classes that implement that interface.

Our Command interface is defined as follows:

```
interface com.iterationtwo.amazonria.commands.Command
{
        function execute():Void;
}
```

This interface ensures that each command class that implements the interface must include an execute() function.

Individual Command classes are used to perform single pieces of business logic. For example, the following is a possible definition of the command used to perform a keyword search:

```
class com.iterationtwo.amazonria.commands.KeywordSearchRequestCommand implements
➥Command
```

```
{
        public function KeywordSearchRequestCommand()
        {
                delegate = new AmazonDelegate( this );
        }

        public function execute():Void
        {
                delegate.keywordSearchRequest();
        }

        public function keywordSearchRequest_Result( productInfo:ProductInfo )
        {

                new AmazonViewHelper().setUserMessage( "Found " +
                ➥productInfo.totalresults + " items in " + productInfo.totalpages
                ➥+ " pages" );
        }

        public function keywordSearchRequest_Status( status )
        {
                new AmazonViewHelper().setUserMessage( "The keyword search failed"
                ➥);
        }

        private var delegate:AmazonDelegate
}
```

As you can see from above, the `KeywordSearchRequestCommand` implements the
Command interface, which enforces the inclusion of an `execute()` method.
This class relationship is shown in Figure 6.7.

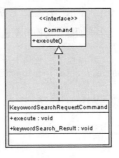

Figure 6.7 Command interface as a contract to concrete command classes.

The KeywordSearchRequestCommand constructor creates a new
AmazonDelegate class and registers itself with the delegate as the response
handler. This enables each command to take responsibility for the handling
of service method results, such as a list of books.

The main `execute()` method of KeywordSearchRequestCommand uses the delegate created in the constructor to make a `keywordSearchRequest()` call to the server. Results from the service call are handled by the response handler:

```
public function keywordSearchRequest_Result( productInfo:ProductInfo )
```

This handler expects a ProductInfo Value Object from the server. ProductInfo contains an array of Details Value Objects. The result handler ensures that the results of the keyword search are reported to the user using a View Helper class that will be discussed in the next section.

In our Amazon RIA, failures are handled simply by tracing status messages to the Output panel in the following method:

```
public function keywordSearchRequest_Status( status )
```

Now that we have our individual commands all implementing the Command interface, we can refactor the Front Controller to uses these classes. Having the Front Controller deal with the Command interface means it needs not be aware of the internal workings of each individual command implementation. The AmazonController is able to assume that every command, because it implements the Command interface, will have an `execute()` method that it can call.

Our implementation of the Front Controller listens for appropriate events, enabling it to decide which command class it should be telling to execute. The Front Controller decides which command class to delegate to by a simple mapping between event names and concrete Command classes. This mapping means we no longer need to handle the events in their individual callback functions (for example, `keywordSearch()`). Instead, we can handle all events in the global `handleEvent()` function used by the EventDispatcher.

Here is our new Front Controller class, refactored to include the Command pattern.

```
class com.iterationtwo.amazonria.control.AmazonController
{
        public function AmazonController()
        {
            commands = new Array();
            initialiseCommands();
        }

        private function initialiseCommands()
        {
            addCommand( "authorSearch", new AuthorSearchRequestCommand() );
            addCommand( "keywordSearch", new KeywordSearchRequestCommand() );
        }
```

```
public function handleEvent( event:Event )
{
      executeCommand( event.type );
}

private function executeCommand( commandName:String )
{
      var command:Command = getCommand( commandName );
      command.execute();
}

private function addCommand( commandName:String, commandRef:Command )
{
      commands[ commandName ] = commandRef;
      EventBroadcaster.getInstance().addEventListener( commandName,
      ➥this );
}

private function getCommand ( commandName ):Command
{
      var command:Command = commands[ commandName ];
return command;
}

private var commands:Command;
}
```

The AmazonController uses initialiseCommands() to map the event names to the individual commands and registers those events with the EventBroadcaster. On receipt of an event in its handleEvent() function, the AmazonController retrieves the command delegated to manage that event and invokes its execute() function.

As can be seen, the Command pattern is a close friend of the Front Controller, taking responsibility for performing use-case specific work while letting the Front Controller get on with its job of capturing events and controlling the application workflow by orchestrating the commands.

The one task that our framework isn't very good at right now, however, is preparing the results that the command has returned to it from the server for the view. The View Helper pattern comes along to make the job of each Command easier in this regard. We shall now discuss the View Helper in more detail.

View Helper

One of the key tenets of user interface development is that of "separation of content and code." This idea is central to many development practices that ensure that the responsibilities of the user interface designer and the application developer are kept discrete. Changes to the user interface in the way information is presented to the user should not have any negative effects on the implementation of the application.

Looking at this from the other direction, a trap that many developers fall into is that of embedding business logic in the presentation logic. For web application developers, placing business logic as script intermingled with HTML has been a bad habit that many have not realized until too late that they should break. Java has always promoted the separation of business logic into tag libraries and external classes, ColdFusion has promoted tag libraries and more recently ColdFusion Components (which are essentially external Java classes), and .NET now recommends the use of "code-behinds" to separate business logic from the HTML content and layout in an ASPX page.

Problem

With a Flash user interface, the temptation for developers to scatter code around the Timeline or place code on movie clips and components does little to help achieve a clean separation. As the size of an application scales up, it is important that a solution is found to solve this recurring presentation problem.

Interweaving presentation and business logic in this manner is the foundation of a system that becomes less flexible, less reusable, and less resilient to change. Modularity of the application becomes dramatically reduced, while separation of the roles in the development team becomes increasingly difficult.

Solution

The view (user interface) should be responsible only for the formatting of data. All responsibility for the fetching of data, the processing of data, and the preparation of data in a model ready to be consumed by the view should be implemented in a standalone class known as a View Helper. The View Helper stores an intermediate data model and serves as an adapter for the business data on behalf of the view.

The View Helper is able to decouple an application's presentation tier from the business tier. A business tier service call, such as "fetch book information by title," may be used in several different contexts. A shopping cart view may want simply to display a summary of the book information, whereas a product view may want to display a detailed page with all the information about the book. Specific View Helpers, such as a ShoppingCartViewHelper or ProductViewHelper, can extract the appropriate information from a book object and set the various elements on the page—dynamic text fields or movie clips containing images, for instance—accordingly, preparing the same model for different views.

Additionally, it is often the case that to invoke a service call, we need to fetch some information from the view. For instance, to search for a book by author, we need to take the author's name from somewhere on the view. In a search page, the name may be provided in a search box, whereas a product view may make a hyperlink out of the author's name to initiate the search. In this scenario, the View Helper would be used to fetch the author's name from a particular view.

Described above, the View Helper forms a contract between the user interface developer and the application developer. The application developer doesn't care how to display the information pertaining to a product or how to fetch the author's name to perform a search. Likewise, the user interface developer doesn't care how a book is stored on the server or how it is fetched; he or she simply cares that it has a title, an author, a jacket cover, and an ISBN number, so that he or she can display its details on screen.

This contract between the user interface and the business logic is achieved using the View Helper pattern.

ActionScript 2.0 Implementation

In our Amazon RIA, we create the AmazonViewHelper class to retrieve information from the user interface to pass to service requests or to display book information back on the user interface.

Part of its implementation is as follows:

```
class com.iterationtwo.amazonria.view.AmazonViewHelper
{
        public function AmazonViewHelper()
        {
        }

        public function getKeywordRequest():KeywordRequest
        {
                var keywordRequest:KeywordRequest = new KeywordRequest();

                keywordRequest.keyword = getSearchTerm();
                keywordRequest.page = "1";
                keywordRequest.mode = "books";
                keywordRequest.type = "heavy";

                return keywordRequest;
        }

        public function setUserMessage( userMessage:String )
```

```
        {
                _root.userMessage.text = userMessage;
        }

        private function getSearchTerm():String
        {
                return _root.searchField.text;
        }
    }
```

The getKeywordRequest() function in AmazonViewHelper is used by the AmazonDelegate to create and populate a KeywordRequest Value Object. This Value Object is required to perform a keyword search service. In our example implementation, we have hard-coded some of the values while retrieving the search text from the entry field on the user interface via the getSearchTerm() private function.

The setUserMessage() function is used to update a status message on the user interface and can be called by any Command class to advise the user as to the results of any user gestures.

The View Helper pattern abstracts the user interface implementation from the command performing the business logic. It enables the creative designer and client-side ActionScript developer to work in tandem, with the View Helper defining the "contract" between the members of the team.

RIA development necessarily involves collaboration between the user interface designer and the developer responsible for implementing the Command classes in ActionScript. On a large-scale RIA development, it is unlikely that these will be the same person. It is our experience at iteration::two that the Command class developer will create the View Helper classes and provide empty methods that he requires to fetch information from the user interface or to populate the user interface. The user interface designer can consequently "flesh out" these methods to work with his or her particular user interface design. If the design changes, then the View Helper methods can be updated, and the Command classes remain oblivious to the user interface changes.

This also makes it much easier to test the command logic independently of the user interface. We discuss test-driven development and unit-testing of ActionScript in *Reality J2EE: Architecting for Macromedia Flash MX* (Macromedia Press, 2003), and we encourage the reader to adopt this practice.

Pattern Framework in Action

So far we have looked at a small number of design patterns in the context of

RIA development and discussed the problems that each pattern circumvents. Remember that a pattern is a recognized solution to the problem, but it says nothing about the implementation of that solution. In developing your own RIAs, it is likely that you will use the implementations given here as starting points for your own implementations of the patterns.

The collaboration of the patterns given here is the makings of a framework for the rapid development of Rich Internet Applications. Let's quickly summarize how the patterns all interoperate, from the front to the back.

Everything starts with a user gesture; perhaps the user has entered a keyword into a search box and clicked on the search button. Clicking the button generates an event that has been previously registered with the EventBroadcaster class. This event now arrives at the AmazonController, which is acting as a single point of contact for all user gestures. The controller recognizes the event and dispatches the responsibility for handling that event to a specific Command class, calling the `execute()` method on the Command class. The Command class, recognizing that it's handling a keyword search, asks for help from the appropriate AmazonViewHelper to get the keyword that was typed into the search box on the UI. The Command class then creates a KeywordRequest Value Object, which it passes as an argument to the `keywordSearchRequest()` method on the AmazonDelegate. This method on the Business Delegate requires the Amazon Service, which the Business Delegate locates simply by asking the ServiceLocator class for "AmazonService." Oblivious to whether this is a Web Service, a Java class, or even a dummy back-end being used during development, the Business Delegate uses the KeywordRequest Value Object to request a list of matching books.

The service on the server-side returns a ProductInfo Value Object. Because the Business Delegate might be asked to use the keyword search method in many different contexts, rather than make any guesses about what it should do with the results it has, it simply passes them back to the Command class that called it. The Command class, on receiving the results, then uses an AmazonViewHelper class to update the view to the search results page before using a method on the View Helper to set the results to those it has received from the Business Delegate.

From clicking "search" and having typed in an author, our pattern-based framework has collaborated to fetch the results from the server and display them back on the UI.

More importantly, with this framework in place, development can proceed at an increasing pace. Each new use-case requires the creation of a Command class, reusing or creating Value Objects and methods on the Business Delegate as required.

Though our application may grow in complexity, our code doesn't.

What We Have Learned

Developing enterprise RIAs needs not be complex when the power of ActionScript 2.0 is leveraged to implement a collaboration of tried-and-tested software design patterns.

The pattern framework that has been presented is a loose coupling of patterns—each Rich Internet Application that you develop may use a simplified pattern framework or may demand that other design problems are solved using other design patterns, such as the Mediator, the Observer, or an implementation of the Factory pattern. It is as important to know when not to use a design pattern as it is to know when one can improve the design of your existing code. Refactoring your Rich Internet Application toward a pattern-based architecture is a way of ensuring that your intent is expressed clearly.

There are numerous other considerations in the correct engineering of Rich Internet Applications, many of which are solved by features of the Flash MX Professional 2004 environment, and many of which are solved simply through the re-application of experience gained in traditional enterprise software development.

The Amazon RIA developed in this chapter, and the full source code and Flash movies, are available for download at `http://aspatterns.iterationtwo.com/`, where the team at iteration::two openly share their experiences in Rich Internet Application engineering.

We hope that many of you share our experiences through the web site and are encouraged to explore how ActionScript 2.0 and design patterns can help you to better engineer your own Rich Internet Applications.

Further Reading

Webster, Steven. *Reality J2EE: Architecting for Macromedia Flash MX*, Macromedia Press, 2003.

Alur, Deepak, Crupi, John, and Malks, Dan. *Core J2EE Patterns: Best Practices and Design Strategies*. Prentice Hall PTR, 2003.

II

ActionScript Reference Guide

INTRODUCTION
Getting Started with ActionScript

Macromedia Flash MX 2004 and Flash MX Professional 2004 are the professional standard authoring tools for producing high-impact web experiences. ActionScript is the language you use when you want to develop an application within Flash. You don't have to use ActionScript to use Flash, but if you want to provide user interactivity, work with objects other than those built into Flash (such as buttons and movie clips), or otherwise turn a SWF file into a more robust user experience, you'll probably want to use ActionScript.

Intended audience

This book assumes that you already have Flash MX 2004 or Flash MX Professional 2004 installed and know how to use it. You should know how to place objects on the Stage and manipulate them in the Flash authoring environment. If you have written programs before, ActionScript will feel familiar. But even if you haven't, ActionScript isn't hard to learn. It's easy to start with very simple commands and build more complexity as you go along.

System requirements

ActionScript does not have any system requirements in addition to Flash MX 2004 or Flash MX Professional 2004. However, the documentation assumes that you are using the default publishing settings for your Flash files: Flash Player 7 and ActionScript 2.0. If you change either of these settings, explanations and code samples shown in the documentation may not work correctly.

Using the documentation

This document provides an overview of ActionScript syntax, information on how to use ActionScript when working with different types of objects, and details on the syntax and usage of every language element. Start by learning the terminology and basic concepts used in the rest of the document (see Chapter 2, "ActionScript Basics," on page 229). Next, learn the mechanics of writing and debugging Flash scripts (see Chapter 3, "Writing and Debugging Scripts," on page 259).

Before writing your own scripts, you should complete the lessons "Write Scripts with ActionScript" and "Create a Form with Conditional Logic and Send Data," which provide a hands-on introduction to working with ActionScript. To find these lessons, select Help > How Do I > Quick Tasks.

After you understand the basics, you are ready to use the information in the rest of this document as it applies to the specific effect you are trying to achieve. For example, if you want to learn how to write a script that performs a certain action when a user clicks the mouse, see Chapter 4, "Handling Events," on page 287.

When you find information about a certain command you want to use, you can look up its entry in Chapter 12, "ActionScript Dictionary," on page 409; every language element is listed there in alphabetical order.

Typographical conventions

The following typographical conventions are used in this book:

- `Code font` indicates ActionScript code.
- *Code font italic* indicates an element, such as an ActionScript parameter or object name, that you replace with your own text when writing a script.

Terms used in this document

The following terms are used in this book:

- *You* refers to the developer who is writing a script or application.
- *The user* refers to the person who will be running your scripts and applications.
- *Compile time* is the time at which you publish, export, test, or debug your document.
- *Runtime* is the time at which your script is running in Flash Player.

ActionScript terms such as *method* and *object* are defined in Chapter 2, "ActionScript Basics," on page 229.

Additional resources

Specific documentation about Flash and related products is available separately.

- For information about working in the Flash authoring environment, see Using Flash Help. For information about working with components, see Using Components Help.
- For information about creating communication applications with Flash Communication Server, see *Developing Communications Applications* and *Managing Flash Communication Server*.
- For information about accessing web services with Flash applications, see *Using Flash Remoting*.

The Macromedia DevNet website (www.macromedia.com/devnet) is updated regularly with the latest information on Flash, plus advice from expert users, advanced topics, examples, tips, and other updates. Check the website often for the latest news on Flash and how to get the most out of the program.

The Macromedia Flash Support Center (www.macromedia.com/support/flash) provides TechNotes, documentation updates, and links to additional resources in the Flash community.

PART I
Welcome to ActionScript

This part includes basic information on the ActionScript language.

Chapter 1 includes information on what is new or changed in ActionScript and Flash Player 7. If you have used ActionScript before, be sure to review this information carefully.

If you are new to ActionScript, read Chapters 2 and 3 to get a good foundation for understanding ActionScript terminology and syntax and for learning how to write and debug your scripts.

CHAPTER 1
What's New in Flash MX 2004 ActionScript

Macromedia Flash MX 2004 and Macromedia Flash MX Professional 2004 provide several enhancements that make it easier for you to write more robust scripts using the ActionScript language. These new features, which are discussed in this chapter, include new language elements, improved editing and debugging tools (see "ActionScript editor changes" on page 225 and "Debugging changes" on page 226), and the introduction of a more object-oriented programming model (see "New object-oriented programming model" on page 226).

This chapter also contains an extensive section that you should read carefully if you plan to publish any of your existing Flash MX or earlier files to Flash Player 7 (see "Porting existing scripts to Flash Player 7" on page 219).

New and changed language elements

This section describes the ActionScript language elements that are new or changed in Flash MX 2004. To use any of these elements in your scripts, you must target Flash Player 7 (the default) when you publish your documents.

- The `Array.sort()` and `Array.sortOn()` methods let you add parameters to specify additional sorting options, such as ascending and descending sorting, whether to consider case sensitivity when sorting, and so on.
- The `Button.menu`, `MovieClip.menu`, and `TextField.menu` properties work with the new ContextMenu and ContextMenuItem classes to let you associate context menu items with Button, MovieClip, or TextField objects.
- The `ContextMenu class` and `ContextMenuItem class` let you customize the context menu that is displayed when a user right-clicks (Microsoft Windows) or Control-clicks (Macintosh) in Flash Player.
- The Error class and the `throw` and `try..catch..finally` commands let you implement more robust exception handling.
- The `LoadVars.addRequestHeader()` and `XML.addRequestHeader()` methods add or change HTTP request headers (such as `Content-Type` or `SOAPAction`) sent with `POST` actions.
- The `MMExecute()` function lets you issue Flash JavaScript API commands from ActionScript.
- (Windows only) The `Mouse.onMouseWheel` event listener is generated when the user scrolls using the mouse wheel.

- The `MovieClip.getNextHighestDepth()` method lets you create MovieClip instances at runtime and be guaranteed that their objects render in front of the other objects in a parent movie clip's *z*-order space. The `MovieClip.getInstanceAtDepth()` method lets you access dynamically created MovieClip instances using the depth as a search index.
- The `MovieClip.getSWFVersion()` method lets you determine which version of Flash Player is supported by a loaded SWF file.
- The `MovieClip.getTextSnapshot()` method and the `TextSnapshot object` let you work with text that is in static text fields in a movie clip.
- The `MovieClip._lockroot` property lets you specify that a movie clip will act as _root for any movie clips loaded into it, or that the meaning of _root in a movie clip won't change if that movie clip is loaded into another movie clip.
- The MovieClipLoader class lets you monitor the progress of files as they are being loaded into movie clips.
- The NetConnection class and NetStream class let you stream local video files (FLV files).
- The PrintJob class gives you (and the user) more control over printing from Flash Player.
- The `Sound.onID3` event handler provides access to ID3 data associated with a Sound object that contains an MP3 file.
- The `Sound.ID3` property provides access to the metadata that is part of an MP3 file.
- The `System class` has new objects and methods, and the System.capabilities object has several new properties.
- The `TextField.condenseWhite` property lets you remove extra white space from HTML text fields that are rendered in a browser.
- The `TextField.mouseWheelEnabled` property lets you specify whether a text field's contents should scroll when the mouse pointer is positioned over a text field and the user rolls the mouse wheel.
- The `TextField.StyleSheet class` lets you create a style sheet object that contains text formatting rules such as font size, color, and other formatting styles.
- The `TextField.styleSheet` property lets you attach a style sheet object to a text field.
- The `TextFormat.getTextExtent()` method accepts a new parameter, and the object it returns contains a new member.
- The `XML.addRequestHeader()` method lets you add or change HTTP request headers (such as `Content-Type` or `SOAPAction`) sent with `POST` actions.

New security model and legacy SWF files

Rules for how Flash Player determines whether two domains are the same have changed in Flash Player 7. In addition, rules that determine whether and how a SWF file served from an HTTP domain can access a SWF file or load data from an HTTPS domain have changed. In most cases, these changes won't affect you unless you are porting your existing SWF files to Flash Player 7.

However, if you have SWF files published for Flash Player 6 or earlier that load data from a file stored on a server, and the calling SWF is playing in Flash Player 7, the user might see a dialog box that didn't appear before, asking whether to allow access. You can prevent this dialog box from appearing by implementing a *policy file* on the site where the data is stored. For more information on this dialog box, see "About compatibility with previous Flash Player security models" on page 395.

You might also need to implement a policy file if you are using runtime shared libraries. If either the loading or loaded SWF file is published for Flash Player 7 and the loading and loaded files aren't served from the exact same domain, use a policy file to permit access. For more information on policy files, see "About allowing cross-domain data loading" on page 394.

Porting existing scripts to Flash Player 7

As with any new release, Flash Player 7 supports more ActionScript commands than previous versions of the player; you can use these commands to implement more robust scripts. (See "New and changed language elements" on page 217.)However, if you used any of these commands in your existing scripts, the script might not work correctly if you publish it for Flash Player 7.

For example, if you have a script with a function named Error, the script might appear to compile correctly but might not run as expected in Flash Player 7, because Error is now a built-in class (and thus a reserved word) in ActionScript. You can fix your script by renaming the Error function to something else, such as ErrorCondition.

Also, Flash Player 7 implements a number of changes that affect how one SWF file can access another SWF file, how external data can be loaded, and how local settings and data (such as privacy settings and locally persistent shared objects) can be accessed. Finally, the behavior of some existing features has changed.

If you have existing scripts written for Flash Player 6 or earlier that you want to publish for Flash Player 7, you might need to modify the scripts so they conform with the implementation of Flash Player 7 and work as designed. These modifications are discussed in this section.

ECMA-262 Edition 4 compliance

Several changes have been implemented in Flash Player 7 to conform more closely to the ECMA-262 Edition 4 proposal (see www.mozilla.org/js/language/es4/index.html). In addition to the class-based programming techniques available in ActionScript 2.0 (see "New object-oriented programming model" on page 226), other features have been added and certain behaviors have changed. Also, when publishing for Flash Player 7 and using ActionScript 2.0, you can cast one object type to another. For more information, see "Casting objects" on page 243. These capabilities don't require you to update existing scripts; however, you may want to use them if you publish your scripts to Flash Player 7 and then continue to revise and enhance them.

Unlike the changes mentioned above, the changes listed in the following table (some of which also improve ECMA compliance) may cause existing scripts to work differently than they did previously. If you used these features in existing scripts that you want to publish to Flash Player 7, review the changes to make sure your code still works as intended or to determine whether you need to rewrite your code. In particular, because undefined is evaluated differently in certain cases, you should initialize all variables in scripts that you port to Flash Player 7.

SWF file published for Flash Player 7	SWF file published for earlier versions of Flash Player
Case sensitivity is supported (variable names that differ only in capitalization are interpreted as being different variables). This change also affects files loaded with #include and external variables loaded with LoadVars.load(). For more information, see "Case sensitivity" on page 233.	Case sensitivity is not supported (variable names that differ only in capitalization are interpreted as being the same variable).

Evaluating undefined in a numeric context returns NaN.
`myCount +=1;`
`trace(myCount); // NaN`
	Evaluating undefined in a numeric context returns 0.
	`myCount +=1;`
	`trace(myCount); // 1`

When undefined is converted to a string, the result is undefined.
`firstname = "Joan ";`
`lastname = "Flender";`
`trace(firstname + middlename + lastname);`
`// Joan undefinedFlender`
	When undefined is converted to a string, the result is "" (an empty string).
	`firstname = "Joan ";`
	`lastname = "Flender";`
	`trace(firstname + middlename +`
	`    lastname);`
	`// Joan Flender`

When you convert a string to a Boolean value, the result is true if the string has a length greater than zero; the result is false for an empty string.	When you convert a string to a Boolean value, the string is first converted to a number; the result is true if the number is nonzero, false otherwise.

When setting the length of an array, only a valid number string sets the length. For example, " 6" works but " 6" or "6xyz" does not.
`my_array=new Array();`
`my_array[" 6"] ="x";`
`trace(my_array.length); // 0`
`my_array["6xyz"] ="x";`
`trace(my_array.length); // 0`
`my_array["6"] ="x";`
`trace(my_array.length); // 7`
	When setting the length of an array, even a malformed number string sets the length:
	`my_array=new Array();`
	`my_array[" 6"] ="x";`
	`trace(my_array.length); // 7`
	`my_array["6xyz"] ="x";`
	`trace(my_array.length); // 7`
	`my_array["6"] ="x";`
	`trace(my_array.length); // 7`

Domain-name rules for settings and local data

In Flash Player 6, superdomain matching rules are used by default when accessing local settings (such as camera or microphone access permissions) or locally persistent data (shared objects). That is, the settings and data for SWF files hosted at here.xyz.com, there.xyz.com, and xyz.com are shared, and are all stored at xyz.com.

In Flash Player 7, exact-domain matching rules are used by default. That is, the settings and data for a file hosted at here.xyz.com are stored at here.xyz.com, the settings and data for a file hosted at there.xyz.com are stored at there.xyz.com, and so on.

A new property, `System.exactSettings`, lets you specify which rules to use. This property is supported for files published for Flash Player 6 or later. For files published for Flash Player 6, the default value is `false`, which means superdomain matching rules are used. For files published for Flash Player 7, the default value is `true`, which means exact-domain matching rules are used.

If you use settings or persistent local data and want to publish a Flash Player 6 SWF file for Flash Player 7, you might need to set this value to `false` in the ported file.

For more information, see `System.exactSettings` on page 866.

Cross-domain and subdomain access between SWF files

When you develop a series of SWF files that communicate with each other—for example, when using `loadMovie()`, `MovieClip.loadMovie()`, `MovieClipLoader.LoadClip()`, or Local Connection objects—you might host the movies in different domains, or in different subdomains of a single superdomain.

In files published for Flash Player 5 or earlier, there were no restrictions on cross-domain or subdomain access.

In files published for Flash Player 6, you could use the `LocalConnection.allowDomain` handler or `System.security.allowDomain()` method to specify permitted cross-domain access (for example, to let a file at someSite.com be accessed by a file at someOtherSite.com), and no command was needed to permit subdomain access (for example, a file at www.someSite.com could be accessed by a file at store.someSite.com).

Files published for Flash Player 7 implement access between SWF files differently from earlier versions in two ways. First, Flash Player 7 implements exact-domain matching rules instead of superdomain matching rules. Therefore, the file being accessed (even if it is published for a Player version earlier than Flash Player 7) must explicitly permit cross-domain or subdomain access; this topic is discussed below. Second, a file hosted at a site using a secure protocol (HTTPS) must explicitly permit access from a file hosted at a site using an insecure protocol (HTTP or FTP); this topic is discussed in the next section (see "HTTP to HTTPS protocol access between SWF files" on page 223).

Because Flash Player 7 implements exact-domain matching rules instead of superdomain matching rules, you might have to modify existing scripts if you want to access them from files that are published for Flash Player 7. (You can still publish the modified files for Flash Player 6.) If you used any `LocalConnection.allowDomain()` or `System.security.allowDomain()` statements in your files and specified superdomain sites to permit, you must change your parameters to specify exact domains instead. The following code shows an example of the kinds of changes you might have to make:

```
// Flash Player 6 commands in a SWF file at www.anyOldSite.com
// to allow access by SWF files that are hosted at www.someSite.com
// or at store.someSite.com
System.security.allowDomain("someSite.com");
my_lc.allowDomain = function(sendingDomain) {
   return(sendingDomain=="someSite.com");
}
// Corresponding commands to allow access by SWF files
// that are published for Flash Player 7
System.security.allowDomain("www.someSite.com", "store.someSite.com");
my_lc.allowDomain = function(sendingDomain) {
   return(sendingDomain=="www.someSite.com" ||
     sendingDomain=="store.someSite.com");
}
```

You might also have to add statements like these to your files if you aren't currently using them. For example, if your SWF file is hosted at www.someSite.com and you want to allow access by a SWF file published for Flash Player 7 at store.someSite.com, you must add statements like the following to the file at www.someSite.com (you can still publish the file at www.someSite.com for Flash Player 6):

```
System.security.allowDomain("store.someSite.com");
my_lc.allowDomain = function(sendingDomain) {
   return(sendingDomain=="store.someSite.com");
}
```

To summarize, you might have to modify your files to add or change `allowDomain` statements if you publish files for Flash Player 7 that meet the following conditions:

- You implemented cross-SWF scripting (using `loadMovie()`, `MovieClip.loadMovie()`, `MovieClipLoader.LoadClip()`, or Local Connection objects).
- The called SWF file (of any version) is not hosted at a site using a secure protocol (HTTPS), or the calling and called SWF files are both hosted at HTTPS sites. (If only the called SWF file is HTTPS, see "HTTP to HTTPS protocol access between SWF files" on page 223.)
- The SWF files are not in same domain (for example, one file is at www.domain.com and one is at store.domain.com).

You have to make the following changes:

- If the called SWF file is published for Flash Player 7, include `System.security.allowDomain` or `LocalConnection.allowDomain` in the called SWF file, using exact domain-name matching.

- If the called SWF file is published for Flash Player 6, modify the called file to add or change a `System.security.allowDomain` or `LocalConnection.allowDomain` statement, using exact domain-name matching, as shown in the code examples earlier in this section. You can publish the modified file for either Flash Player 6 or 7.

- If the called SWF file is published for Flash Player 5 or earlier, port the called file to Flash Player 6 or 7 and add a `System.security.allowDomain` statement, using exact domain-name matching, as shown in the code examples earlier in this section. (LocalConnection objects aren't supported in Flash Player 5 or earlier.)

HTTP to HTTPS protocol access between SWF files

As discussed in the previous section, rules for cross-domain and subdomain access have changed in Flash Player 7. In addition to the exact-domain matching rules now being implemented, you must explicitly permit files hosted at sites using a secure protocol (HTTPS) to be accessed by files hosted at sites using an insecure protocol. Depending on whether the called file is published for Flash Player 7 or Flash Player 6, you must implement either one of the `allowDomain` statements (see "Cross-domain and subdomain access between SWF files" on page 221), or use the new `LocalConnection.allowInsecure Domain` or `System.security.allowInsecureDomain()` statements.

Warning: Implementing an `allowInsecureDomain()` statement compromises the security offered by the HTTPS protocol. You should make these changes only if you can't reorganize your site so that all SWF files are served from the HTTPS protocol.

The following code shows an example of the kinds of changes you might have to make:

```
// Commands in a Flash Player 6 SWF file at https://www.someSite.com
// to allow access by Flash Player 7 SWF files that are hosted
// at http://www.someSite.com or at http://www.someOtherSite.com
System.security.allowDomain("someOtherSite.com");
my_lc.allowDomain = function(sendingDomain) {
  return(sendingDomain=="someOtherSite.com");
}
// Corresponding commands in a Flash Player 7 SWF file
// to allow access by Flash Player 7 SWF files that are hosted
// at http://www.someSite.com or at http://www.someOtherSite.com
System.security.allowInsecureDomain("www.someSite.com",
  "www.someOtherSite.com");
my_lc.allowInsecureDomain = function(sendingDomain) {
  return(sendingDomain=="www.someSite.com" ||
    sendingDomain=="www.someOtherSite.com");
}
```

You might also have to add statements like these to your files if you aren't currently using them. A modification might be necessary even if both files are in same domain (for example, a file in http://www.domain.com is calling a file in https://www.domain.com).

To summarize, you might have to modify your files to add or change statements if you publish files for Flash Player 7 that meet the following conditions:

- You implemented cross-SWF scripting (using `loadMovie()`, `MovieClip.loadMovie()`, `MovieClipLoader.LoadClip()`, or Local Connection objects).
- The calling file is not hosted using an HTTPS protocol, and the called file is HTTPS.

You must make the following changes:

- If the called file is published for Flash Player 7, include `System.security.allowInsecureDomain` or `LocalConnection.allowInsecureDomain` in the called file, using exact domain-name matching, as shown in the code examples earlier in this section. This statement is required even if the calling and called SWF files are in same domain.
- If the called file is published for Flash Player 6 or earlier, and both the calling and called files are in same domain (for example, a file in http://www.domain.com is calling a file in https://www.domain.com), no modification is needed.
- If the called file is published for Flash Player 6, the files are not in same domain, and you don't want to port the called file to Flash Player 7, modify the called file to add or change a `System.security.allowDomain` or `LocalConnection.allowDomain` statement, using exact domain-name matching, as shown in the code examples earlier in this section.
- If the called file is published for Flash Player 6 and you want to port the called file to Flash Player 7, include `System.security.allowInsecureDomain` or `LocalConnection.allowInsecureDomain` in the called file, using exact domain-name matching, as shown in the code examples earlier in this section. This statement is required even if both files are in same domain.
- If the called file is published for Flash Player 5 or earlier, and both files are not in the same domain, you can do one of two things. You can either port the called file to Flash Player 6 and add or change a `System.security.allowDomain` statement, using exact domain-name matching, as shown in the code examples earlier in this section, or you can port the called file to Flash Player 7, and include a `System.security.allowInsecureDomain` statement in the called file, using exact domain-name matching, as shown in the code examples earlier in this section.

Server-side policy files for permitting access to data

A Flash document can load data from an external source by using one of the following data loading calls: `XML.load()`, `XML.sendAndLoad()`, `LoadVars.load()`, `LoadVars.sendAndLoad()`, `loadVariables()`, `loadVariablesNum()`, `MovieClip.loadVariables()`, `XMLSocket.connect()`, and Macromedia Flash Remoting (`NetServices.createGatewayConnection`). Also, a SWF file can import runtime shared libraries (RSLs), or assets defined in another SWF file, at runtime. By default, the data or RSL must reside in the same domain as the SWF file that is loading that external data or media.

To make data and assets in runtime shared libraries available to SWF files in different domains, you should use a *cross-domain policy file*. A cross-domain policy file is an XML file that provides a way for the server to indicate that its data and documents are available to SWF files served from certain domains, or from all domains. Any SWF file that is served from a domain specified by the server's policy file is permitted to access data or RSLs from that server.

If you are loading external data, you should create policy files even if you don't plan to port any of your files to Flash Player 7. If you are using RSLs, you should create policy files if either the calling or called file is published for Flash Player 7.

For more information, see "About allowing cross-domain data loading" on page 394.

ActionScript editor changes

The ActionScript editor has been updated in a number of ways to make it more robust and easier to use. These changes are summarized in this section.

Word wrapping   You can now use the Options pop-up menu in the Script pane, Debugger panel, and Output panel to enable or disable word wrapping. You can also toggle word wrapping using the pop-up menu in the Actions panel. The keyboard shortcut is Control+Shift+W (Windows) or Command+Shift+W (Macintosh).

Viewing context-sensitive help   When your pointer is positioned over an ActionScript language element in the Actions toolbox or in the Script pane, you can use the View Help item in the context menu to display a help page about that element.

Importing scripts   When you select Import Script from the pop-up menu in the Actions panel, the imported script is copied into the script at the insertion point in your code file. In previous versions of Flash, importing a script overwrote the contents of the existing script.

Single-click breakpoints   To add a debugging breakpoint before a line of code in the Debugger panel or the Script pane of the Actions panel, you can click in the left margin. In previous versions of Flash, clicking in the left margin selected a line of code. The new way to select a line of code is to Control-click (Windows) or Command-click (Macintosh).

Normal and expert modes no longer in Actions panel   In previous versions of Flash, you could work in the Actions panel either in normal mode, in which you filled in options and parameters to create code, or in expert mode, in which you added commands directly into the Script pane. In Flash MX 2004 and Flash MX Professional 2004, you can work in the Actions panel only by adding commands directly to the Script pane. You can still drag commands from the Actions toolbox into the Script pane or use the Add (+) button above the Script pane to add commands to a script.

Pinning multiple scripts   You can pin multiple scripts within a FLA file along the bottom of the Script pane in the Actions panel. In previous versions of Flash, you could pin only one script at a time.

Script navigator   The left side of the Actions panel now contains two panes: the Actions toolbox and a new Script navigator. The Script navigator is a visual representation of the structure of your FLA file; you can navigate through your FLA file here to locate ActionScript code.

Integrated Script window for editing external files (Flash Professional only)   You can use the ActionScript editor in a Script window (separate from the Actions panel) to write and edit external script files. Syntax coloring, code hinting, and other preferences are supported in the Script window, and the Actions toolbox is also available. To display the Script window, use File > New and then select the type of external file you want to edit. You can have multiple external files open at the same time; filenames are displayed on tabs across the top of the Script window. (The tabs appear only in Windows.)

Debugging changes

This section describes changes that improve your ability to debug your scripts.

Output window changed to Output panel   You can now move and dock the Output panel in the same way as any other panel in Flash.

Improved error reporting at compile time   In addition to providing more robust exception handling, ActionScript 2.0 provides a number of new compile-time errors. For more information, see Appendix A, "Error Messages," on page 987.

Improved exception handling   The Error class and the `throw` and `try..catch..finally` commands let you implement more robust exception handling.

New object-oriented programming model

The ActionScript language has grown and developed since its introduction several years ago. With each new release of Flash, additional keywords, objects, methods, and other language elements have been added to the language. However, unlike earlier releases of Flash, Flash MX 2004 and Flash MX Professional 2004 introduce several new language elements that implement object-oriented programming in a more standard way than before. Because these language elements represent a significant enhancement to the core ActionScript language, they represent a new version of ActionScript itself: ActionScript 2.0.

ActionScript 2.0 is not a new language. Rather, it comprises a core set of language elements that make it easier to develop object-oriented programs. With the introduction of keywords such as `class`, `interface`, `extends`, and `implements`, ActionScript syntax is now easier to learn for programmers familiar with other languages. New programmers can learn more standard terminology that they can apply to other object-oriented languages they may study in the future.

ActionScript 2.0 supports all the standard elements of the ActionScript language; it simply enables you to write scripts that more closely adhere to standards used in other object-oriented languages, such as Java. ActionScript 2.0 should be of interest primarily to intermediate or advanced Flash developers who are building applications that require the implementation of classes and subclasses. ActionScript 2.0 also lets you declare the object type of a variable when you create it (see "Strict data typing" on page 242) and provides significantly improved compiler errors (see Appendix A, "Error Messages," on page 987).

The language elements that are new in ActionScript 2.0 are listed below.

- `class`
- `extends`
- `implements`
- `interface`
- `dynamic`
- `static`
- `public`
- `private`
- `get`
- `set`
- `import`

Key facts about ActionScript 2.0 include the following points:

- Scripts that use ActionScript 2.0 to define classes or interfaces must be stored as external script files, with a single class defined in each script; that is, classes and interfaces cannot be defined in the Actions panel.

- You can import individual class files implicitly (by storing them in a location specified by global or document-specific search paths and then using them in a script) or explicitly (by using the `import` command); you can import packages (collections of class files in a directory) by using wildcards.

- Applications developed with ActionScript 2.0 are supported by Flash Player 6 and later.

Caution: The default publish setting for new files created in Flash MX 2004 is ActionScript 2.0. If you plan to modify an existing FLA file to use ActionScript 2.0 syntax, ensure that the FLA file specifies ActionScript 2.0 in its publish settings. If it does not, your file will compile incorrectly, although Flash will not generate compiler errors.

For more information on using ActionScript 2.0 to write object-oriented programs in Flash, see Chapter 9, "Creating Classes with ActionScript 2.0," on page 359.

CHAPTER 2
ActionScript Basics

ActionScript has rules of grammar and punctuation that determine which characters and words are used to create meaning and in which order they can be written. For example, in English, a period ends a sentence. In ActionScript, a semicolon ends a statement.

The following general rules apply to all ActionScript. Most ActionScript terms also have individual requirements; for the rules for a specific term, see its entry in Chapter 12, "ActionScript Dictionary," on page 409.

Differences between ActionScript and JavaScript

ActionScript is similar to the core JavaScript programming language. You don't need to know JavaScript to use and learn ActionScript; however, if you know JavaScript, ActionScript will appear familiar.

This manual does not attempt to teach general programming. There are many resources that provide more information about general programming concepts and the JavaScript language.

- The European Computers Manufacturers Association (ECMA) document ECMA-262 is derived from JavaScript and serves as the international standard for the JavaScript language. ActionScript is based on the ECMA-262 specification.

- Netscape DevEdge Online has a JavaScript Developer Central site (http://developer.netscape.com/tech/javascript/index.html) that contains documentation and articles useful for understanding ActionScript. The most valuable resource is the *Core JavaScript Guide.*

Some of the differences between ActionScript and JavaScript are as follows:.

- ActionScript does not support browser-specific objects such as Document, Window, and Anchor.

- ActionScript does not completely support all the JavaScript built-in objects.

- ActionScript does not support some JavaScript syntax constructs, such as statement labels.

- In ActionScript, the `eval()` action can perform only variable references.

Unicode support for ActionScript

Macromedia Flash MX 2004 and Macromedia Flash MX Professional 2004 support Unicode text encoding for ActionScript. This means that you can include text in different languages in an ActionScript file. For example, you could include text in English, Japanese, and French in the same file.

You can set ActionScript preferences to specify the type of encoding to use when importing or exporting ActionScript files. You can select either UTF-8 encoding or Default Encoding. UTF-8 is 8-bit Unicode format; Default Encoding is the encoding form supported by the language your system is currently using, also called the *traditional code page*.

In general, if you are importing or exporting ActionScript files in UTF-8 format, use the UTF-8 preference. If you are importing or exporting files in the traditional code page in use on your system, use the Default Encoding preference.

If text in your scripts doesn't look as expected when you open or import a file, change the import encoding preference. If you receive a warning message when exporting ActionScript files, you can change the export encoding preference or turn this warning off in ActionScript preferences.

To select text encoding options for importing or exporting ActionScript files:

1 In the Preferences dialog box (Edit > Preferences), click the ActionScript tab.

2 Under Editing Options, do one or both of the following:

- For Open/Import, select UTF-8 to open or import using Unicode encoding, or select Default Encoding to open or import using the encoding form of the language currently used by your system.

- For Save/Export, select UTF-8 to save or export using Unicode encoding, or select Default Encoding to save or export using the encoding form of the language currently used by your system.

To turn the export encoding warning off or on:

1 In the Preferences dialog box (Edit > Preferences), click the Warnings tab.

2 Select or deselect Warn on Encoding Conflicts When Exporting .as Files.

Caution: The Test Movie command (see "Debugging your scripts" on page 272) will fail if any part of the SWF file path has characters that cannot be represented using the MBCS encoding scheme. For example, Japanese paths on an English system will not work. All areas of the application that use the external player are subject to this limitation.

Terminology

As with any scripting language, ActionScript uses its own terminology. The following list provides an introduction to important ActionScript terms.

Actions are statements that instruct a SWF file to do something while it is playing. For example, `gotoAndStop()` sends the playhead to a specific frame or label. In this manual, the terms *action* and *statement* are interchangeable.

Boolean is a `true` or `false` value.

Classes are data types that you can create to define a new type of object. To define a class, you use the `class` keyword in an external script file (not in a script you are writing in the Actions panel).

Constants are elements that don't change. For example, the constant Key.TAB always has the same meaning: it indicates the Tab key on a keyboard. Constants are useful for comparing values.

Constructors are functions that you use to define the properties and methods of a class. By definition, constructors are functions within a class definition that have the same name as the class. For example, the following code defines a Circle class and implements a constructor function:

```
// file Circle.as
class Circle {
   private var radius:Number
   private var circumference:Number
// constructor
   function Circle(radius:Number) {
      circumference = 2 * Math.PI * radius;
   }
}
```

The term *constructor* is also used when you create (instantiate) an object based on a particular class. The following statements are constructors for the built-in Array class and the custom Circle class:

```
my_array:Array = new Array();
my_circle:Circle = new Circle();
```

Data types describe the kind of information a variable or ActionScript element can hold. The ActionScript data types are String, Number, Boolean, Object, MovieClip, Function, null, and undefined. For more information, see "About data types" on page 238.

Events are actions that occur while a SWF file is playing. For example, different events are generated when a movie clip loads, the playhead enters a frame, the user clicks a button or movie clip, or the user types on the keyboard.

Event handlers are special actions that manage events such as mouseDown or load. There are two kinds of ActionScript event handlers: event handler methods and event listeners. (There are also two event handlers, on() and onClipEvent(), that you can assign directly to buttons and movie clips.) In the Actions toolbox, each ActionScript object that has event handler methods or event listeners has a subcategory called Events or Listeners. Some commands can be used both as event handlers and as event listeners and are included in both subcategories.

Expressions are any legal combination of ActionScript symbols that represent a value. An expression consists of operators and operands. For example, in the expression x + 2, x and 2 are operands and + is an operator.

Functions are blocks of reusable code that can be passed parameters and can return a value. For more information, see "Creating functions" on page 255.

Identifiers are names used to indicate a variable, property, object, function, or method. The first character must be a letter, underscore (_), or dollar sign ($). Each subsequent character must be a letter, number, underscore, or dollar sign. For example, firstName is the name of a variable.

Instances are objects that belong to a certain class. Each instance of a class contains all the properties and methods of that class. For example, all movie clips are instances of the MovieClip class, so you can use any of the methods or properties of the MovieClip class with any movie clip instance.

Instance names are unique names that let you target movie clip and button instances in scripts. You use the Property inspector to assign instance names to instances on the Stage. For example, a master symbol in the library could be called `counter` and the two instances of that symbol in the SWF file could have the instance names `scorePlayer1_mc` and `scorePlayer2_mc`. The following code sets a variable called `score` inside each movie clip instance by using instance names:

```
_root.scorePlayer1_mc.score += 1;
_root.scorePlayer2_mc.score -= 1;
```

You can use special suffixes when naming instances so that code hints (see "Using code hints" on page 267) appear as you type your code. For more information, see "Using suffixes to trigger code hints" on page 266.

Keywords are reserved words that have special meaning. For example, `var` is a keyword used to declare local variables. You cannot use a keyword as an identifier. For example, `var` is not a legal variable name. For a list of keywords, see "Keywords" on page 237.

Methods are functions associated with a class. For example, `getBytesLoaded()` is a built-in method associated with the MovieClip class. You can also create functions that act as methods, either for objects based on built-in classes or for objects based on classes that you create. For example, in the following code, `clear()` becomes a method of a `controller` object that you have previously defined:

```
function reset(){
   this.x_pos = 0;
   this.x_pos = 0;
}
controller.clear = reset;
controller.clear();
```

Objects are collections of properties and methods; each object has its own name and is an instance of a particular class. Built-in objects are predefined in the ActionScript language. For example, the built-in Date object provides information from the system clock.

Operators are terms that calculate a new value from one or more values. For example, the addition (+) operator adds two or more values together to produce a new value. The values that operators manipulate are called *operands*.

Parameters (also called *arguments*) are placeholders that let you pass values to functions. For example, the following `welcome()` function uses two values it receives in the parameters `firstName` and `hobby`:

```
function welcome(firstName, hobby) {
   welcomeText = "Hello, " + firstName + "I see you enjoy " + hobby;
}
```

Packages are directories that contain one or more class files, and reside in a designated classpath directory (see "Understanding the classpath" on page 373).

Properties are attributes that define an object. For example, `_visible` is a property of all movie clips that defines whether a movie clip is visible or hidden.

Target paths are hierarchical addresses of movie clip instance names, variables, and objects in a SWF file. You name a movie clip instance in the movie clip Property inspector. (The main Timeline always has the name _root.) You can use a target path to direct an action at a movie clip or to get or set the value of a variable. For example, the following statement is the target path to the variable volume inside the movie clip stereoControl:

```
_root.stereoControl.volume
```

For more information on target paths, see "Absolute and relative target paths" in Using Flash Help.

Variables are identifiers that hold values of any data type. Variables can be created, changed, and updated. The values they store can be retrieved for use in scripts. In the following example, the identifiers on the left side of the equal signs are variables:

```
var x = 5;
var name = "Lolo";
var c_color = new Color(mcinstanceName);
```

For more information on variables, see "About variables" on page 244.

Syntax

As with any language, ActionScript has syntax rules that you must follow in order to create scripts that can compile and run correctly. This section describes the elements that comprise ActionScript syntax.

Case sensitivity

In a case-sensitive programming language, variable names that differ only in case (book and Book) are considered different from each other. Therefore, it's good practice to follow consistent capitalization conventions, such as those used in this manual, to make it easy to identify names of functions and variables in ActionScript code.

When you publish files for Flash Player 7 or later, Flash implements case sensitivity whether you are using ActionScript 1 or ActionScript 2.0. This means that keywords, class names, variables, method names, and so on are all case sensitive. For example:

```
// In file targeting Flash Player 7
// and either ActionScript 1 or ActionScript 2.0
//
// Sets properties of two different objects
cat.hilite = true;
CAT.hilite = true;

// Creates three different variables
var myVar=10;
var myvar=10;
var mYvAr=10;
// Does not generate an error
var array = new Array();
var date = new Date();
```

This change also affects external variables loaded with LoadVars.load().

In addition, case sensitivity is implemented for external scripts, such as ActionScript 2.0 class files or scripts that you import using the #include command. If you are publishing files for Flash Player 7 and have previously created external files that you add to your scripts by using the #include statement, you should review each file and confirm that you used consistent capitalization throughout. One way to do this is to open the file in the Script window (Flash Professional only) or, in a new FLA file, set your publish settings to Flash Player 7 and copy the file's contents into the Actions panel. Then use the Check Syntax button (see "Checking syntax and punctuation" on page 270) or publish your file; errors that are caused by naming conflicts appear in the Output panel.

When Syntax coloring is enabled, language elements written with correct capitalization are blue by default. For more information, see "Keywords" on page 237 and "Syntax highlighting" on page 265.

Dot syntax

In ActionScript, a dot (.) is used to indicate the properties or methods related to an object or movie clip. It is also used to identify the target path to a movie clip, variable, function, or object. A dot syntax expression begins with the name of the object or movie clip followed by a dot, and ends with the element you want to specify.

For example, the _x movie clip property indicates a movie clip's *x* axis position on the Stage. The expression ballMC._x refers to the _x property of the movie clip instance ballMC.

As another example, submit is a variable set in the form movie clip, which is nested inside the movie clip shoppingCart. The expression shoppingCart.form.submit = true sets the submit variable of the instance form to true.

Expressing a method of an object or movie clip follows the same pattern. For example, the play() method of the ball_mc movie clip instance moves the playhead in the Timeline of ball_mc, as shown in the following statement:

```
ball_mc.play();
```

Dot syntax also uses two special aliases, _root and _parent. The alias _root refers to the main Timeline. You can use the _root alias to create an absolute target path. For example, the following statement calls the function buildGameBoard() in the movie clip functions on the main Timeline:

```
_root.functions.buildGameBoard();
```

You can use the alias _parent to refer to a movie clip in which the current object is nested. You can also use _parent to create a relative target path. For example, if the movie clip dog_mc is nested inside the movie clip animal_mc, the following statement on the instance dog_mc tells animal_mc to stop:

```
_parent.stop();
```

Slash syntax

Slash syntax was used in Flash 3 and 4 to indicate the target path of a movie clip or variable. This syntax is still supported by Flash Player 7, but its use is not recommended, and slash syntax is not supported in ActionScript 2.0. However, if you are creating content intended specifically for Flash Player 4, you must use slash syntax. For more information, see "Using slash syntax" on page 1001.

Curly braces

ActionScript event handlers, class definitions, and functions are grouped together into blocks with curly braces ({ }). You can put the opening brace on the same line as your declaration or on the next line, as shown in the following examples. To make your code easier to read, it's a good idea to choose one format and use it consistently.

```
// Event handler
on(release) {
  myDate = new Date();
  currentMonth = myDate.getMonth();
}

on(release)
{
  myDate = new Date();
  currentMonth = myDate.getMonth();
}

// Class
class Circle(radius) {
}

class Square(side)
{
}

// Function
circleArea = function(radius) {
  return radius * radius * MATH.PI;
}
squareArea = function(side)
{
  return side * side;
}
```

You can check for matching curly braces in your scripts; see "Checking syntax and punctuation" on page 270.

Semicolons

An ActionScript statement is terminated with a semicolon (;), as shown in these examples:

```
var column = passedDate.getDay();
var row    = 0;
```

If you omit the terminating semicolon, Flash still compiles your script successfully. However, using semicolons is good scripting practice.

Parentheses

When you define a function, place any parameters inside parentheses:

```
function myFunction (name, age, reader){
    // your code here
}
```

When you call a function, include any parameters passed to the function in parentheses, as shown here:

```
myFunction ("Steve", 10, true);
```

You can also use parentheses to override the ActionScript order of precedence or to make your ActionScript statements easier to read. (See "Operator precedence and associativity" on page 249.)

You also use parentheses to evaluate an expression on the left side of a dot in dot syntax. For example, in the following statement, the parentheses cause `new Color(this)` to evaluate and create a Color object:

```
onClipEvent(enterFrame) {
    (new Color(this)).setRGB(0xffffff);
}
```

If you don't use parentheses, you must add a statement to evaluate the expression:

```
onClipEvent(enterFrame) {
    myColor = new Color(this);
    myColor.setRGB(0xffffff);
}
```

You can check for matching parentheses in your scripts; see "Checking syntax and punctuation" on page 270.

Comments

Using comments to add notes to scripts is highly recommended. Comments are useful for keeping track of what you intended and for passing information to other developers if you work in a collaborative environment or are providing samples. Even a simple script is easier to understand if you make notes as you create it.

To indicate that a line or portion of a line is a comment, precede the comment with two forward slashes (//):

```
on(release) {
    // create new Date object
    myDate = new Date();
    currentMonth = myDate.getMonth();
    // convert month number to month name
    monthName = calcMonth(currentMonth);
    year = myDate.getFullYear();
    currentDate = myDate.getDate();
}
```

When Syntax coloring is enabled (see "Syntax highlighting" on page 265), comments are gray by default. Comments can be any length without affecting the size of the exported file, and they do not need to follow rules for ActionScript syntax or keywords.

If you want to "comment out" an entire portion of your script, place it in a comment block rather than adding // at the beginning of each line. This technique is easier and is useful when you want to test only parts of a script by commenting out large chunks of it.

To create a comment block, place /* at the beginning of the commented lines and */ at the end. For example, when the following script runs, none of the code in the comment block is executed:

```
// The code below runs
var x:Number = 15;
var y:Number = 20;
// The code below doesn't run
/*
on(release) {
    // create new Date object
    myDate = new Date();
    currentMonth = myDate.getMonth();
    // convert month number to month name
    monthName = calcMonth(currentMonth);
    year = myDate.getFullYear();
    currentDate = myDate.getDate();
}
*/
// The code below runs
var name:String = "My name is";
var age:Number = 20;
```

Keywords

ActionScript reserves words for specific use within the language, so you can't use them as identifiers, such as variable, function, or label names. The following table lists all ActionScript keywords:

break	case	class	continue
default	delete	dynamic	else
extends	for	function	get
if	implements	import	in
instanceof	interface	intrinsic	new
private	public	return	set
static	switch	this	typeof
var	void	while	with

Constants

A constant is a property whose value never changes.

For example, the constants BACKSPACE, ENTER, QUOTE, RETURN, SPACE, and TAB are properties of the Key object and refer to keyboard keys. To test whether the user is pressing the Enter key, you could use the following statement:

```
if(Key.getCode() == Key.ENTER) {
    alert = "Are you ready to play?";
    controlMC.gotoAndStop(5);
}
```

About data types

A data type describes the kind of information a variable or ActionScript element can hold. There are two kinds of data types built into Flash: primitive and reference. The primitive data types—String, Number, and Boolean—have a constant value and therefore can hold the actual value of the element they represent. The reference data types—MovieClip and Object—have values that can change and therefore contain references to the actual value of the element. Variables containing primitive data types behave differently in certain situations than those containing reference types. (See "Using variables in a program" on page 247.) There are also two special data types: null and undefined.

In Flash, any built-in object that isn't a primitive data type or a movie clip data type, such as Array or Math, is of the Object data type.

Each data type has its own rules and is described in the following topics:

- "String" on page 238
- "Number" on page 239
- "Boolean" on page 239
- "Object" on page 240
- "MovieClip" on page 240
- "Null" on page 240
- "Undefined" on page 240

When you debug scripts, you may need to determine the data type of an expression or variable to understand why it is behaving a certain way. You can do this with the `typeof` operator (see "Determining an item's data type" on page 241).

You can convert one data type to another using one of the following conversion functions: `Array()`, `Boolean()`, `Number()`, `Object()`, `String()`.

String

A string is a sequence of characters such as letters, numbers, and punctuation marks. You enter strings in an ActionScript statement by enclosing them in single or double quotation marks. Strings are treated as characters instead of as variables. For example, in the following statement, `"L7"` is a string:

```
favoriteBand = "L7";
```

You can use the addition (+) operator to *concatenate*, or join, two strings. ActionScript treats spaces at the beginning or end of a string as a literal part of the string. The following expression includes a space after the comma:

```
greeting = "Welcome," + firstName;
```

To include a quotation mark in a string, precede it with a backslash character (\). This is called *escaping* a character. There are other characters that cannot be represented in ActionScript except by special escape sequences. The following table provides all the ActionScript escape characters:

Escape sequence	Character
\b	Backspace character (ASCII 8)
\f	Form-feed character (ASCII 12)
\n	Line-feed character (ASCII 10)
\r	Carriage return character (ASCII 13)
\t	Tab character (ASCII 9)
\"	Double quotation mark
\'	Single quotation mark
\\	Backslash
\000 - \377	A byte specified in octal
\x00 - \xFF	A byte specified in hexadecimal
\u0000 - \uFFFF	A 16-bit Unicode character specified in hexadecimal

Number

The number data type is a double-precision floating-point number. You can manipulate numbers using the arithmetic operators addition (+), subtraction (-), multiplication (*), division (/), modulo (%), increment (++), and decrement (--). You can also use methods of the built-in Math and Number classes to manipulate numbers. The following example uses the sqrt() (square root) method to return the square root of the number 100:

```
Math.sqrt(100);
```

For more information, see "Numeric operators" on page 249.

Boolean

A Boolean value is one that is either true or false. ActionScript also converts the values true and false to 1 and 0 when appropriate. Boolean values are most often used with logical operators in ActionScript statements that make comparisons to control the flow of a script. For example, in the following script, the SWF file plays if the variable password is true:

```
onClipEvent(enterFrame) {
  if (userName == true && password == true){
    play();
  }
}
```

See "Using built-in functions" on page 255 and "Logical operators" on page 251.

Object

An object is a collection of properties. Each property has a name and a value. The value of a property can be any Flash data type, even the object data type. This allows you to arrange objects inside each other, or *nest* them. To specify objects and their properties, you use the dot (.) operator. For example, in the following code, `hoursWorked` is a property of `weeklyStats`, which is a property of `employee`:

```
employee.weeklyStats.hoursWorked
```

You can use the built-in ActionScript objects to access and manipulate specific kinds of information. For example, the Math object has methods that perform mathematical operations on numbers you pass to them. This example uses the `sqrt()` method:

```
squareRoot = Math.sqrt(100);
```

The ActionScript MovieClip object has methods that let you control movie clip symbol instances on the Stage. This example uses the `play()` and `nextFrame()` methods:

```
mcInstanceName.play();
mc2InstanceName.nextFrame();
```

You can also create custom objects to organize information in your Flash application. To add interactivity to an application with ActionScript, you'll need many different pieces of information: for example, you might need a user's name, the speed of a ball, the names of items in a shopping cart, the number of frames loaded, the user's ZIP Code, or the key that was pressed last. Creating custom objects lets you organize this information into groups, simplify your scripting, and reuse your scripts.

MovieClip

Movie clips are symbols that can play animation in a Flash application. They are the only data type that refers to a graphic element. The MovieClip data type allows you to control movie clip symbols using the methods of the MovieClip class. You call the methods using the dot (.) operator, as shown here:

```
my_mc.startDrag(true);
parent_mc.getURL("http://www.macromedia.com/support/" + product);
```

Null

The null data type has only one value, `null`. This value means "no value"—that is, a lack of data. The `null` value can be used in a variety of situations. Here are some examples:

- To indicate that a variable has not yet received a value
- To indicate that a variable no longer contains a value
- As the return value of a function, to indicate that no value was available to be returned by the function
- As a parameter to a function, to indicate that a parameter is being omitted

Undefined

The undefined data type has one value, `undefined`, and is used for a variable that hasn't been assigned a value.

Determining an item's data type

While testing and debugging your programs, you may discover problems that seem to be related to the data types of different items. In these cases, you may want to determine an item's data type. To do so, use the `typeof` operator, as shown in this example:

```
trace(typeof(variableName));
```

For more information on testing and debugging, see Chapter 3, "Writing and Debugging Scripts," on page 259.

Assigning data types to elements

Flash automatically assigns data types to the following kinds of language elements, as discussed in the next section, "Automatic data typing":

- Variables
- Parameters passed to a function, method, or class
- Values returned from a function or method
- Objects created as subclasses of existing classes

However, you can also explicitly assign data types to items, which can help prevent or diagnose certain errors in your scripts. For more information, see "Strict data typing" on page 242.

Automatic data typing

In Flash, you do not need to explicitly define an item as holding either a number, a string, or other data type. Flash determines the data type of an item when it is assigned:

```
var x = 3;
```

In the expression `var x = 3`, Flash evaluates the element on the right side of the operator and determines that it is of the number data type. A later assignment may change the type of x; for example, the statement `x = "hello"` changes the type of x to a string. A variable that hasn't been assigned a value has a type of `undefined`.

ActionScript converts data types automatically when an expression requires it. For example, when you pass a value to the `trace()` action, `trace()` automatically converts the value to a string and sends it to the Output panel. In expressions with operators, ActionScript converts data types as needed; for example, when used with a string, the + operator expects the other operand to be a string.

```
"Next in line, number " + 7
```

ActionScript converts the number 7 to the string "7" and adds it to the end of the first string, resulting in the following string:

```
"Next in line, number 7"
```

Strict data typing

ActionScript 2.0 lets you explicitly declare the object type of a variable when you create it; this is called *strict data typing*. Because data type mismatches trigger compiler errors, strict data typing helps prevent you from assigning the wrong type of data to an existing variable. To assign a specific data type to an item, specify its type using the var keyword and post-colon syntax:

```
// strict typing of variable or object
var x:Number = 7;
var birthday:Date = new Date();

// strict typing of parameters
function welcome(firstName:String, age:Number){
}

// strict typing of parameter and return value
function square(x:Number):Number {
  var squared = x*x;
  return squared;
}
```

Because you must use the var keyword when strictly typing variable, you can't strictly type a global variable (see "Scoping and declaring variables" on page 245).

You can declare the data type of objects based on built-in classes (Button, Date, MovieClip, and so on) and on classes and interfaces that you create. For example, if you have a file named Student.as in which you define the Student class, you can specify that objects you create are of type Student:

```
var student:Student = new Student();
```

You can also specify that objects are of type Function or Void.

Using strict typing helps ensure that you don't inadvertently assign an incorrect type of value to an object. Flash checks for typing mismatch errors at compile time. For example, suppose you type the following code:

```
// in the Student.as class file
class Student {
  var status:Boolean; // property of Student objects
}

// in a script
var studentMaryLago:Student = new Student();
studentMaryLago.status = "enrolled";
```

When Flash compiles this script, a "Type mismatch" error is generated.

Another advantage of strict data typing is that Flash MX 2004 automatically displays code hints for built-in objects when they are strictly typed. For more information, see "Strictly typing objects to trigger code hints" on page 266.

Files published using ActionScript 1 do not respect strict data typing assignments at compile time. Thus, assigning the wrong type of value to a variable that you have strictly typed doesn't generate a compiler error.

```
var x:String = "abc"
x = 12 ; // no error in ActionScript 1, type mismatch error in ActionScript 2
```

The reason for this is that when you publish a file for ActionScript 1, Flash interprets a statement such as var x:String = "abc" as slash syntax rather than as strict typing. (ActionScript 2.0 doesn't support slash syntax.) This behavior can result in an object that is assigned to a variable of the wrong type, causing the compiler to let illegal method calls and undefined property references pass through unreported.

Therefore, if you are implementing strict data typing, make sure you are publishing files for ActionScript 2.0.

Casting objects

ActionScript 2.0 lets you cast one data type to another. The cast operator that Flash uses takes the form of a function call and is concurrent with *explicit coercion*, as specified in the ECMA-262 Edition 4 proposal. Casting lets you assert that an object is of a certain type so that when type-checking occurs, the compiler treats the object as having a set of properties that its initial type does not contain. This can be useful, for example, when iterating over an array of objects that might be of differing types.

In files published for Flash Player 7 or later, cast statements that fail at runtime return null. In files published for Flash Player 6, no runtime support for failed casts is implemented.

The syntax for casting is *type(item)*, where you want the compiler to behave as if the data type of *item* is *type*. Casting is essentially a function call, and the function call returns null if the cast fails. If the cast succeeds, the function call returns the original object. However, the compiler doesn't generate type mismatch errors when you cast items to data types that you created in external class files, even if the cast fails at runtime.

```
// in Animal.as
class Animal {}

// in Dog.as
class Dog extends Animal { function bark (){} }

// in Cat.as
class Cat extends Animal { function meow (){} }

// in FLA file
var spot:Dog = new Dog();
var temp:Cat = Cat (spot);  // assert that a Dog object is of type Cat
temp.meow(); // doesn't do anything, but no compiler error either
```

In this situation, you asserted to the compiler that temp is a Cat object, and, therefore, the compiler assumes that temp.meow() is a legal statement. However, the compiler doesn't know that the cast will fail (that is, that you tried to cast a Dog object to a Cat type), so no compile-time error occurs. If you include a check in your script to make sure that the cast succeeds, you can find type mismatch errors at runtime.

```
var spot:Dog = new Dog();
var temp:Cat = Cat (spot);
trace(temp);  // displays null at runtime
```

You can cast an expression to an interface. If the expression is an object that implements the interface or has a base class that implements the interface, the object is returned. If not, null is returned.

The following example shows the results of casting built-in object types. As the first line in the with(results) block shows, an illegal cast—in this case, casting a string to a movie clip—returns null. As the last two lines show, casting to null or undefined returns undefined.

```
var mc:MovieClip;
var arr:Array;
var bool:Boolean;
var num3:Number;
var obj:Object;
var str:String;
_root.createTextField("results",2,100,100,300,300);
with(results){
text = "type MovieClip : "+(typeof MovieClip(str));        // returns null
text += "\ntype object : "+(typeof Object(str));          // returns object
text += "\ntype Array : "+(typeof Array(num3));           // returns object
text += "\ntype Boolean : "+(typeof Boolean(mc));         // returns boolean
text += "\ntype String : "+(typeof String(mc));           // returns string
text += "\ntype Number : "+(typeof Number(obj));          // returns number
text += "\ntype Function : "+(typeof Function(mc));       // returns object
text += "\ntype null : "+(typeof null(arr));              // returns undefined
text += "\ntype undefined : "+(typeof undefined(obj));    // returns undefined
}
//Results in Output panel
type MovieClip : null
type object : object
type Array : object
type Boolean : boolean
type String : string
type Number : number
type Function : object
type null : undefined
type undefined : undefined
```

You can't override primitive data types such as Boolean, Date, and Number with a cast operator of the same name.

About variables

A *variable* is a container that holds information. The container itself is always the same, but the contents can change. By changing the value of a variable as the SWF file plays, you can record and save information about what the user has done, record values that change as the SWF file plays, or evaluate whether a condition is true or false.

It's a good idea always to assign a variable a known value the first time you define the variable. This is known as *initializing a variable* and is often done in the first frame of the SWF file. Initializing a variable helps you track and compare the variable's value as the SWF file plays.

Variables can hold any type of data (see "About data types" on page 238). The type of data a variable contains affects how the variable's value changes when it is assigned in a script.

Typical types of information that you can store in a variable include a URL, a user's name, the result of a mathematical operation, the number of times an event occurred, or whether a button has been clicked. Each SWF file and movie clip instance has a set of variables, with each variable having a value independent of variables in other SWF files or movie clips.

To test the value of a variable, use the trace() action to send the value to the Output panel. For example, trace(hoursWorked) sends the value of the variable hoursWorked to the Output panel in test mode. You can also check and set the variable values in the Debugger in test mode. For more information, see "Using the trace statement" on page 283 and "Displaying and modifying variables" on page 276.

Naming a variable

A variable's name must follow these rules:

- It must be an identifier (see "Terminology" on page 230).
- It cannot be a keyword or an ActionScript literal such as true, false, null, or undefined.
- It must be unique within its scope (see "Scoping and declaring variables" on page 245).

Also, you should not use any element in the ActionScript language as a variable name; doing so can cause syntax errors or unexpected results. For example, if you name a variable String and then try to create a String object using new String(), the new object is undefined.

```
hello_str = new String();
trace(hello_str.length); // returns 0

String = "hello"; // Giving a variable the same name as a built-in class
hello_str = new String();
trace(hello_str.length); // returns undefined
```

The ActionScript editor supports code hints for built-in classes and for variables that are based on these classes. If you want Flash to provide code hints for a particular object type that is assigned to a variable, you can strictly type the variable or name the variable using a specific suffix.

For example, suppose you type the following code:

```
var members:Array = new Array();
members.
```

As soon as you type the period (.), Flash displays a list of methods and properties available for Array objects. For more information, see "Writing code that triggers code hints" on page 265.

Scoping and declaring variables

A variable's *scope* refers to the area in which the variable is known and can be referenced. There are three types of variable scope in ActionScript:

- Local variables are available within the function body in which they are declared (delineated by curly braces).
- Timeline variables are available to any script on that Timeline.
- Global variables and functions are visible to every Timeline and scope in your document.

Note: ActionScript 2.0 classes that you create support public, private, and static variable scopes. For more information, see "Controlling member access" on page 368 and "Creating class members" on page 369.

Local variables

To declare local variables, use the `var` statement inside the body of a function. A local variable is scoped to the block and expires at the end of the block. A local variable not declared within a block expires at the end of its script.

For example, the variables `i` and `j` are often used as loop counters. In the following example, `i` is used as a local variable; it exists only inside the function `makeDays()`:

```
function makeDays() {
  var i;
  for( i = 0; i < monthArray[month]; i++ ) {

    _root.Days.attachMovie( "DayDisplay", i, i + 2000 );

    _root.Days[i].num = i + 1;
    _root.Days[i]._x = column * _root.Days[i]._width;
    _root.Days[i]._y = row * _root.Days[i]._height;

    column = column + 1;

    if (column == 7 ) {

      column = 0;
      row = row + 1;
    }
  }
}
```

Local variables can also help prevent name conflicts, which can cause errors in your application. For example, if you use `name` as a local variable, you could use it to store a user name in one context and a movie clip instance name in another; because these variables would run in separate scopes, there would be no conflict.

It's good practice to use local variables in the body of a function so that the function can act as an independent piece of code. A local variable is only changeable within its own block of code. If an expression in a function uses a global variable, something outside the function can change its value, which would change the function.

You can assign a data type to a local variable when you define it, which helps prevent you from assigning the wrong type of data to an existing variable. For more information, see "Strict data typing" on page 242.

Timeline variables

Timeline variables are available to any script on that Timeline. To declare Timeline variables, initialize them on any frame in the Timeline. Be sure to initialize the variable before trying to access it in a script. For example, if you put the code `var x = 10;` on Frame 20, a script attached to any frame before Frame 20 cannot access that variable.

Global variables

Global variables and functions are visible to every Timeline and scope in your document. To create a variable with global scope, use the _global identifier before the variable name, and do not use the var = syntax. For example, the following code creates the global variable myName:

```
var _global.myName = "George"; // syntax error
_global.myName = "George";
```

However, if you initialize a local variable with the same name as a global variable, you don't have access to the global variable while you are in the scope of the local variable:

```
_global.counter = 100;
counter++;
trace(counter); // displays 101
function count(){
  for( var counter = 0; counter <= 10 ; counter++ ) {
  trace(counter); // displays 0 through 10
  }
}
count();
counter++;
trace(counter); // displays 102
```

Using variables in a program

You must declare a variable in a script before you can use it in an expression. If you use an undeclared variable, as shown in the following example, the variable's value will be NaN or undefined, and your script might produce unintended results:

```
var squared = x*x;
trace(squared); // NaN
var x = 6;
```

In the following example, the statement declaring the variable x must come first so that squared can be replaced with a value:

```
var x = 6;
var squared = x*x;
trace(squared); // 36
```

Similar behavior occurs when you pass an undefined variable to a method or function:

```
getURL(myWebSite); // no action
var myWebSite = "http://www.macromedia.com";

var myWebSite = "http://www.macromedia.com";
getURL(myWebSite); // browser displays www.macromedia.com
```

You can change the value of a variable many times in a script. The type of data that the variable contains affects how and when the variable changes. Primitive data types, such as strings and numbers, are passed by value. This means that the actual content of the variable is passed to the variable.

In the following example, x is set to 15 and that value is copied into y. When x is changed to 30 in line 3, the value of y remains 15 because y doesn't look to x for its value; it contains the value of x that it received in line 2.

```
var x = 15;
var y = x;
var x = 30;
```

As another example, the variable inValue contains a primitive value, 3, so the actual value is passed to the sqrt() function and the returned value is 9:

```
function sqrt(x){
  return x * x;
}

var inValue = 3;
var out = sqrt(inValue);
```

The value of the variable inValue does not change.

The object data type can contain such a large and complex amount of information that a variable with this type doesn't hold the actual value; it holds a reference to the value. This reference is like an alias that points to the contents of the variable. When the variable needs to know its value, the reference asks for the contents and returns the answer without transferring the value to the variable.

The following is an example of passing by reference:

```
var myArray = ["tom", "josie"];
var newArray = myArray;
myArray[1] = "jack";
trace(newArray);
```

The above code creates an Array object called myArray that has two elements. The variable newArray is created and is passed a reference to myArray. When the second element of myArray is changed, it affects every variable with a reference to it. The trace() action sends tom, jack to the Output panel.

In the following example, myArray contains an Array object, so it is passed to function zeroArray() by reference. The zeroArray() function changes the content of the array in myArray.

```
function zeroArray (theArray){
  var i;
  for (i=0; i < theArray.length; i++) {
    theArray[i] = 0;
  }
}

var myArray = new Array();
myArray[0] = 1;
myArray[1] = 2;
myArray[2] = 3;
zeroArray(myArray);
```

The function zeroArray() accepts an Array object as a parameter and sets all the elements of that array to 0. It can modify the array because the array is passed by reference.

Using operators to manipulate values in expressions

An expression is any statement that Flash can evaluate and that returns a value. You can create an expression by combining operators and values or by calling a function.

Operators are characters that specify how to combine, compare, or modify the values of an expression. The elements that the operator performs on are called *operands*. For example, in the following statement, the + operator adds the value of a numeric literal to the value of the variable foo; foo and 3 are the operands:

```
foo + 3
```

This section describes general rules about common types of operators, operator precedence, and operator associativity. For detailed information on each operator mentioned here, as well as special operators that don't fall into these categories, see the entries in Chapter 12, "ActionScript Dictionary," on page 409.

Operator precedence and associativity

When two or more operators are used in the same statement, some operators take precedence over others. ActionScript follows a precise hierarchy to determine which operators to execute first. For example, multiplication is always performed before addition; however, items in parentheses take precedence over multiplication. So, without parentheses, ActionScript performs the multiplication in the following example first:

```
total = 2 + 4 * 3;
```

The result is 14.

But when parentheses surround the addition operation, ActionScript performs the addition first:

```
total = (2 + 4) * 3;
```

The result is 18.

When two or more operators share the same precedence, their associativity determines the order in which they are performed. Associativity can be either left-to-right or right-to-left. For example, the multiplication operator has an associativity of left-to-right; therefore, the following two statements are equivalent:

```
total = 2 * 3 * 4;
total = (2 * 3) * 4;
```

For a table of all operators and their precedence and associativity, see Appendix B, "Operator Precedence and Associativity," on page 991.

Numeric operators

Numeric operators add, subtract, multiply, divide, and perform other arithmetic operations.

The most common usage of the increment operator is i++ instead of the more verbose i = i+1. You can use the increment operator before or after an operand. In the following example, age is incremented first and then tested against the number 30:

```
if (++age >= 30)
```

In the following example, age is incremented after the test is performed:

```
if (age++ >= 30)
```

The following table lists the ActionScript numeric operators:

Operator	Operation performed
+	Addition
*	Multiplication
/	Division
%	Modulo (remainder of division)
-	Subtraction
++	Increment
- -	Decrement

Comparison operators

Comparison operators compare the values of expressions and return a Boolean value (true or false). These operators are most commonly used in loops and in conditional statements. In the following example, if the variable score is 100, a certain SWF file loads; otherwise, a different SWF file loads:

```
if (score > 100){
    loadMovieNum("winner.swf", 5);
} else {
    loadMovieNum("loser.swf", 5);
}
```

The following table lists the ActionScript comparison operators:

Operator	Operation performed
<	Less than
>	Greater than
<=	Less than or equal
>=	Greater than or equal

String operators

The + operator has a special effect when it operates on strings: it concatenates the two string operands. For example, the following statement adds "Congratulations," to "Donna!":

```
"Congratulations, " + "Donna!"
```

The result is "Congratulations, Donna!" If only one of the + operator's operands is a string, Flash converts the other operand to a string.

The comparison operators >, >=, <, and <= also have a special effect when operating on strings. These operators compare two strings to determine which is first in alphabetical order. The comparison operators only compare strings if both operands are strings. If only one of the operands is a string, ActionScript converts both operands to numbers and performs a numeric comparison.

Logical operators

Logical operators compare Boolean values (`true` and `false`) and return a third Boolean value. For example, if both operands evaluate to `true`, the logical AND operator (`&&`) returns `true`. If one or both of the operands evaluate to `true`, the logical OR operator (`||`) returns `true`. Logical operators are often used with comparison operators to determine the condition of an `if` action. For example, in the following script, if both expressions are true, the `if` action will execute:

```
if (i > 10 && _framesloaded > 50){
  play();
}
```

The following table lists the ActionScript logical operators:

Operator	Operation performed
&&	Logical AND
||	Logical OR
!	Logical NOT

Bitwise operators

Bitwise operators internally manipulate floating-point numbers to change them into 32-bit integers. The exact operation performed depends on the operator, but all bitwise operations evaluate each binary digit (bit) of the 32-bit integer individually to compute a new value.

The following table lists the ActionScript bitwise operators:

Operator	Operation performed
&	Bitwise AND
|	Bitwise OR
^	Bitwise XOR
~	Bitwise NOT
<<	Shift left
>>	Shift right
>>>	Shift right zero fill

Equality operators

You can use the equality (`==`) operator to determine whether the values or identities of two operands are equal. This comparison returns a Boolean (`true` or `false`) value. If the operands are strings, numbers, or Boolean values, they are compared by value. If the operands are objects or arrays, they are compared by reference.

It is a common mistake to use the assignment operator to check for equality. For example, the following code compares *x* to 2:

```
if (x == 2)
```

In that same example, the expression `x = 2` is incorrect because it doesn't compare the operands, it assigns the value of 2 to the variable `x`.

The strict equality (===) operator is like the equality operator, with one important difference: the strict equality operator does not perform type conversion. If the two operands are of different types, the strict equality operator returns `false`. The strict inequality (`!==`) operator returns the inversion of the strict equality operator.

The following table lists the ActionScript equality operators:

Operator	Operation performed
==	Equality
===	Strict equality
!=	Inequality
!==	Strict inequality

Assignment operators

You can use the assignment (=) operator to assign a value to a variable, as shown in the following example:

```
var password = "Sk8tEr";
```

You can also use the assignment operator to assign multiple variables in the same expression. In the following statement, the value of a is assigned to the variables b, c, and d:

```
a = b = c = d;
```

You can also use compound assignment operators to combine operations. Compound operators perform on both operands and then assign the new value to the first operand. For example, the following two statements are equivalent:

```
x += 15;
x = x + 15;
```

The assignment operator can also be used in the middle of an expression, as shown in the following example:

```
// If the flavor is not vanilla, output a message.
if ((flavor = getIceCreamFlavor()) != "vanilla") {
    trace ("Flavor was " + flavor + ", not vanilla.");
}
```

This code is equivalent to the following slightly more verbose code:

```
flavor = getIceCreamFlavor();
if (flavor != "vanilla") {
    trace ("Flavor was " + flavor + ", not vanilla.");
}
```

The following table lists the ActionScript assignment operators:

Operator	Operation performed
=	Assignment
+=	Addition and assignment
-=	Subtraction and assignment
*=	Multiplication and assignment

Operator	Operation performed
%=	Modulo and assignment
/=	Division and assignment
<<=	Bitwise shift left and assignment
>>=	Bitwise shift right and assignment
>>>=	Shift right zero fill and assignment
^=	Bitwise XOR and assignment
|=	Bitwise OR and assignment
&=	Bitwise AND and assignment

Dot and array access operators

You can use the dot operator (.) and the array access operator ([ ]) to access built-in or custom ActionScript object properties, including those of a movie clip.

The dot operator uses the name of an object on its left side and the name of a property or variable on its right side. The property or variable name can't be a string or a variable that evaluates to a string; it must be an identifier. The following examples use the dot operator:

```
year.month = "June";
year.month.day = 9;
```

The dot operator and the array access operator perform the same role, but the dot operator takes an identifier as its property, whereas the array access operator evaluates its contents to a name and then accesses the value of that named property. For example, the following expressions access the same variable velocity in the movie clip rocket:

```
rocket.velocity;
rocket["velocity"];
```

You can use the array access operator to dynamically set and retrieve instance names and variables. For example, in the following code, the expression inside the [ ] operator is evaluated, and the result of the evaluation is used as the name of the variable to be retrieved from movie clip name:

```
name["mc" + i]
```

You can also use the eval() function, as shown here:

```
eval("mc" + i)
```

The array access operator can also be used on the left side of an assignment statement. This allows you to dynamically set instance, variable, and object names, as shown in the following example:

```
name[index] = "Gary";
```

You create multidimensional arrays in ActionScript by constructing an array, the elements of which are also arrays. To access elements of a multidimensional array, you can nest the array access operator with itself, as shown in the following example:

```
var chessboard = new Array();
for (var i=0; i<8; i++) {
  chessboard.push(new Array(8));
}
function getContentsOfSquare(row, column){
  chessboard[row][column];
}
```

You can check for matching [ ] operators in your scripts; see "Checking syntax and punctuation" on page 270.

Specifying an object's path

To use an action to control a movie clip or loaded SWF file, you must specify its name and its address, called a *target path*.

In ActionScript, you identify a movie clip by its instance name. For example, in the following statement, the _alpha property of the movie clip named star is set to 50% visibility:

```
star._alpha = 50;
```

To give a movie clip an instance name:

1 Select the movie clip on the Stage.

2 Enter an instance name in the Property inspector.

To identify a loaded SWF file:

- Use _levelX, where X is the level number specified in the loadMovie() action that loaded the SWF file.

   For example, a SWF file loaded into level 5 has the target path _level5. In the following example, a SWF file is loaded into level 5 and its visibility is set to false:

```
onClipEvent(load) {
    loadMovieNum("myMovie.swf", 5);
}
onClipEvent(enterFrame) {
    _level5._visible = false;
}
```

To enter a SWF file's target path:

- In the Actions panel (Window > Development > Actions), click the Insert Target Path button and select a movie clip from the list that appears.

For more information on target paths, see "Absolute and relative target paths" in Using Flash Help.

Using built-in functions

A function is a block of ActionScript code that can be reused anywhere in a SWF file. If you pass values as parameters to a function, the function will operate on those values. A function can also return values.

Flash has built-in functions that let you access certain information and perform certain tasks, such as getting the version number of Flash Player hosting the SWF file (getVersion()). Functions that belong to an object are called *methods*. Functions that don't belong to an object are called *top-level functions* and are found in the Functions category of the Actions panel.

Each function has its own characteristics, and some functions require you to pass certain values. If you pass more parameters than the function requires, the extra values are ignored. If you don't pass a required parameter, the empty parameters are assigned the undefined data type, which can cause errors when you export a script. To call a function, it must be in a frame that the playhead has reached.

To call a function, simply use the function name and pass any required parameters:

```
isNaN(someVar);
getTimer();
eval("someVar");
```

For more information on each function, see its entry in Chapter 12, "ActionScript Dictionary," on page 409.

Creating functions

You can define functions to execute a series of statements on passed values. Your functions can also return values. After a function is defined, it can be called from any Timeline, including the Timeline of a loaded SWF file.

A well-written function can be thought of as a "black box." If it has carefully placed comments about its input, output, and purpose, a user of the function does not need to understand exactly how the function works internally.

Defining a function

Functions, like variables, are attached to the Timeline of the movie clip that defines them, and you must use a target path to call them. As with variables, you can use the _global identifier to declare a global function that is available to all Timelines without using a target path. To define a global function, precede the function name with the identifier _global, as shown in the following example:

```
_global.myFunction = function (x) {
    return (x*2)+3;
}
```

To define a Timeline function, use the function action followed by the name of the function, any parameters to be passed to the function, and the ActionScript statements that indicate what the function does.

The following example is a function named areaOfCircle with the parameter radius:

```
function areaOfCircle(radius) {
    return Math.PI * radius * radius;
}
```

You can also define a function by creating a *function literal*—an unnamed function that is declared in an expression instead of in a statement. You can use a function literal to define a function, return its value, and assign it to a variable in one expression, as shown in the following example:

```
area = (function() {return Math.PI * radius *radius;})(5);
```

When a function is redefined, the new definition replaces the old definition.

Passing parameters to a function

Parameters are the elements on which a function executes its code. (In this manual, the terms *parameter* and *argument* are interchangeable.) For example, the following function takes the parameters initials and finalScore:

```
function fillOutScorecard(initials, finalScore) {
   scorecard.display = initials;
   scorecard.score = finalScore;
}
```

When the function is called, the required parameters must be passed to the function. The function substitutes the passed values for the parameters in the function definition. In this example, scorecard is the instance name of a movie clip; display and score are input text fields in the instance. The following function call assigns the value "JEB" to the variable display and the value 45000 to the variable score:

```
fillOutScorecard("JEB", 45000);
```

The parameter initials in the function fillOutScorecard() is similar to a local variable; it exists while the function is called and ceases to exist when the function exits. If you omit parameters during a function call, the omitted parameters are passed as undefined. If you provide extra parameters in a function call that are not required by the function declaration, they are ignored.

Using variables in a function

Local variables are valuable tools for organizing code and making it easy to understand. When a function uses local variables, it can hide its variables from all other scripts in the SWF file; local variables are scoped to the body of the function and ceases to exist when the function exits. Any parameters passed to a function are also treated as local variables.

You can also use global and regular variables in a function. However, if you modify global or regular variables, it is good practice to use script comments to document these modifications.

Returning values from a function

Use the `return` statement to return values from functions. The `return` statement stops the function and replaces it with the value of the `return` action. The following rules govern the use of the `return` statement in functions:

- If you specify a return type other than void for a function, you must include a `return` statement in the function.
- If you specify a return type of void, you should not include a `return` statement.
- If you don't specify a return type, including a `return` statement is optional. If you don't include one, an empty string is returned.

For example, the following function returns the square of the parameter x and specifies that the returned value must be a Number:

```
function sqr(x):Number {
   return x * x;
}
```

Some functions perform a series of tasks without returning a value. For example, the following function initializes a series of global variables:

```
function initialize() {
   boat_x = _global.boat._x;
   boat_y = _global.boat._y;
   car_x = _global.car._x;
   car_y = _global.car._y;
}
```

Calling a user-defined function

You can use a target path to call a function in any Timeline from any Timeline, including from the Timeline of a loaded SWF file. If a function was declared using the `_global` identifier, you do not need to use a target path to call it.

To call a function, enter the target path to the name of the function, if necessary, and pass any required parameters inside parentheses. For example, the following statement invokes the function `sqr()` in the movie clip `MathLib` on the main Timeline, passes the parameter 3 to it, and stores the result in the variable `temp`:

```
var temp = _root.MathLib.sqr(3);
```

The following example uses an absolute path to call the `initialize()` function that was defined on the main Timeline and requires no parameters:

```
_root.initialize();
```

The following example uses a relative path to call the `list()` function that was defined in the `functionsClip` movie clip:

```
_parent.functionsClip.list(6);
```

CHAPTER 3
Writing and Debugging Scripts

In Macromedia Flash MX 2004 and Macromedia Flash MX Professional 2004, you can write scripts that are embedded in your FLA file or stored externally on your computer. (If you are writing ActionScript 2.0 class files, you must store each class as an external file that has the same name as the class.) To write embedded scripts, use the Actions panel and attach the action to a button or movie clip, or to a frame in the Timeline (see "Controlling when ActionScript runs" on page 260). To write external script files, you can use any text editor or code editor. In Flash Professional, you can also use the built-in Script window. For more information, see "Using the Actions panel and Script window" on page 262.

When using the ActionScript editor, you can also check syntax for errors, automatically format code, and use code hints to help you complete syntax. In addition, the punctuation balance feature helps you pair parentheses, braces, or brackets. For more information, see "Using the ActionScript editor" on page 265.

As you work on a document, test it often to ensure that it plays as smoothly as possible and that it plays as expected. You can use the Bandwidth Profiler to simulate how your document will appear at different connection speeds (see "Testing document download performance" in Using Flash Help). To test your scripts, you use a special debugging version of Flash Player that helps you troubleshoot. If you use good authoring techniques in your ActionScript, your scripts will be easier to troubleshoot when something behaves unexpectedly. For more information, see "Debugging your scripts" on page 272.

Controlling when ActionScript runs

When you write a script, you use the Actions panel to attach the script to a frame on a Timeline, or to a button or movie clip on the Stage. Scripts attached to a frame run, or *execute*, when the playhead enters that frame. However, scripts attached to the first frame of a SWF file may behave differently from those attached to subsequent frames, because the first frame in a SWF file is rendered incrementally—objects are drawn on the Stage as they download into Flash Player—and this can affect when actions execute. All frames after the first frame are rendered all at once, when every object in the frame is available.

Scripts attached to movie clips or buttons execute when an event occurs. An *event* is an occurrence in the SWF file such as a mouse movement, a keypress, or a movie clip being loaded. You can use ActionScript to find out when these events occur and execute specific scripts depending on the event. For more information, see Chapter 4, "Handling Events," on page 287.

To perform an action depending on whether a condition exists, or to repeat an action, you can use `if`, `else`, `else if`, `for`, `while`, `do while`, `for..in`, or `switch` statements, which are briefly described in the rest of this section.

Checking a condition

Statements that check whether a condition is `true` or `false` begin with the term `if`. If the condition exists, ActionScript executes the statement that follows. If the condition doesn't exist, ActionScript skips to the next statement outside the block of code.

To optimize your code's performance, check for the most likely conditions first.

The following statements test three conditions. The term `else if` specifies alternative tests to perform if previous conditions are false.

```
if (password == null || email == null) {
    gotoAndStop("reject");
} else if (password == userID){
    gotoAndPlay("startMovie");
}
```

If you want to check for one of several conditions, you can use the `switch` statement instead of using multiple `else if` statements.

Repeating an action

ActionScript can repeat an action a specified number of times or while a specific condition exists. Use the `while`, `do..while`, `for`, and `for..in` actions to create loops.

To repeat an action while a condition exists:

* Use the `while` statement.

A `while` loop evaluates an expression and executes the code in the body of the loop if the expression is `true`. After each statement in the body is executed, the expression is evaluated again. In the following example, the loop executes four times:

```
i = 4;
while (var i > 0) {
    my_mc.duplicateMovieClip("newMC" + i, i );
    i--;
}
```

You can use the `do..while` statement to create the same kind of loop as a `while` loop. In a `do..while` loop, the expression is evaluated at the bottom of the code block so the loop always runs at least once, as shown in the following example:

```
i = 4;
do {
    my_mc.duplicateMovieClip("newMC" +i, i );
    i--;
} while (var i > 0);
```

To repeat an action using a built-in counter:

- Use the `for` statement.

Most loops use a counter of some kind to control how many times the loop executes. Each execution of a loop is called an *iteration*. You can declare a variable and write a statement that increases or decreases the variable each time the loop executes. In the `for` action, the counter and the statement that increments the counter are part of the action. In the following example, the first expression (`var i = 4`) is the initial expression that is evaluated before the first iteration. The second expression (`i > 0`) is the condition that is checked each time before the loop runs. The third expression (`i--`) is called the *post expression* and is evaluated each time after the loop runs.

```
for (var i = 4; i > 0; i--){
    myMC.duplicateMovieClip("newMC" + i, i + 10);
}
```

To loop through the children of a movie clip or object:

- Use the `for..in` statement.

Children include other movie clips, functions, objects, and variables. The following example uses the `trace` statement to print its results in the Output panel:

```
myObject = { name:'Joe', age:25, city:'San Francisco' };
for (propertyName in myObject) {
    trace("myObject has the property: " + propertyName + ", with the value: " +
    myObject[propertyName]);
}
```

This example produces the following results in the Output panel:

```
myObject has the property: name, with the value: Joe
myObject has the property: age, with the value: 25
myObject has the property: city, with the value: San Francisco
```

You may want your script to iterate over a particular type of child—for example, over only movie clip children. You can do this with `for..in` in conjunction with the `typeof` operator.

```
for (name in myMovieClip) {
    if (typeof (myMovieClip[name]) == "movieclip") {
        trace("I have a movie clip child named " + name);
    }
}
```

For more information on each action, see individual entries in Chapter 12, "ActionScript Dictionary," on page 409.

Using the Actions panel and Script window

You can embed Flash scripts in your FLA file or store them as external files. It's a good idea to store as much of your ActionScript code in external files as possible. This makes it easier to reuse code in multiple FLA files. Then, in your FLA file, create a script that uses #include statements to access the code you've stored externally. Use the .as suffix to identify your scripts as ActionScript (AS) files. (If you are writing custom class files, you must store them as external AS files.)

Note: ActionScript code in external files is compiled into a SWF file when you publish, export, test, or debug a FLA file. Therefore, if you make any changes to an external file, you must save the file and recompile any FLA files that use it.

When you embed ActionScript code in your FLA file, you can attach code to Frames and to objects. Try to attach embedded ActionScript to the first frame of the Timeline whenever possible. That way, you won't have to search through a FLA file to find all your code; it is centralized in one location. Create a layer called "Actions" and place your code there. That way, even if you do place code on other Frames or attach it to objects, you'll have to look at only one layer to find it all.

To create scripts that are part of your document, you enter ActionScript directly into the Actions panel. To create external scripts, use your preferred text editor or, in Flash Professional, you can use the Script window. When you use the Actions panel or Script window, you are using the same ActionScript editor, and are typing your code in the Script pane at the right side of the panel or window. To reduce the amount of typing you have to do, you can also select or drag actions from the Actions toolbox to the Script pane.

To display the Actions panel, do one of the following:

- Select Window > Development Panels > Actions.
- Press F9.

(Flash Professional only) To display the Script window, do one of the following:

- To begin writing a new script, select File > New > ActionScript File.
- To open an existing script, select File > Open, and then open an existing AS file.
- To edit a script that is already open, click the document tab that displays the script's name. (Document tabs are supported only in Microsoft Windows.)

About the ActionScript editor environment

The ActionScript editor environment consists of two sections. The section on the right is the Script pane, the area where you type your code. The section on the left is an Actions toolbox that contains an entry for each ActionScript language element.

In the Actions panel, the Actions toolbox also contains a Script navigator, which is a visual representation of the locations in the FLA file that have associated ActionScript; you can navigate through your FLA file here to locate ActionScript code. If you click an item in the Script navigator, the script associated with that item appears in the Script pane, and the playhead moves to that position on the Timeline. If you double-click an item in the Script navigator, the script gets pinned (see "Managing scripts in a FLA file" on page 264).

Actions toolbox   Script navigator*   Pop-up menu*

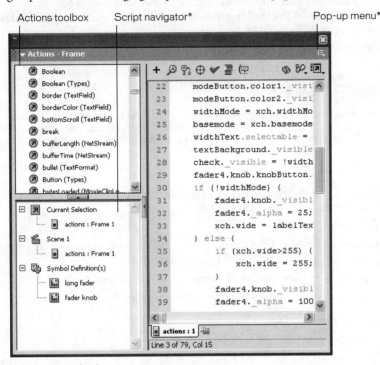

* Actions panel only

There are also several buttons above the Script pane:

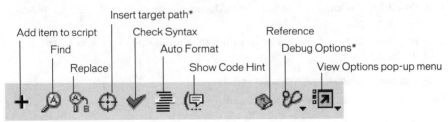

* Actions panel only

You edit actions, enter parameters for actions, or delete actions directly in the Script pane. You can also double-click on an item in the Actions toolbox or the Add (+) button above the Script pane to add actions to the Script pane.

Managing scripts in a FLA file

If you don't centralize all your code within a FLA file in one location, you can *pin* (lock in place) multiple scripts in the Actions panel to make it easier to move among them. In the following figure, the script associated with the current location on the Timeline is on Frame 1 of the layer named Cleanup. (The tab at the far left always follows your location along the Timeline.) That script is also pinned (it is shown as the rightmost tab). Two other scripts are pinned; one on Frame 1 and the other on Frame 15 of the layer named Intro. You can move among the pinned scripts by clicking on the tabs or by using keyboard shortcuts. Moving among pinned scripts does not change your current position on the Timeline.

Tip: If the content displayed in the Script pane isn't changing to reflect the location that you are selecting on the Timeline, the Script pane is probably displaying a pinned script. Click the leftmost tab at the lower left of the Script pane to display the ActionScript associated with your location along the Timeline.

To pin a script:

1 Position your pointer on the Timeline so the script appears in a tab at the lower left of the Script pane in the Actions panel.

2 Do one of the following:

- Click the pushpin icon to the right of the tab. (If the pushpin looks like the icon at the far left, the script is already pinned; clicking that icon unpins it.)
- Right-click (Windows) or Control-click (Macintosh) on the tab, and select Pin Script.
- Select Pin Script from the Options pop-up menu (at the upper right of the panel).

To unpin one or more scripts:

- Do one of the following:

  - If a pinned script appears in a tab at the lower left of the Script pane in the Actions panel, click the pushpin icon to the right of the tab. (If the pushpin looks like the icon on the far left, the script is already unpinned; clicking that icon pins it.)
  - Right-click (Windows) or Control-click (Macintosh) on a tab, and select Close Script or Close All Scripts.
  - Select Close Script or Close All Scripts from the Options pop-up menu (at the upper right of the panel).

To use keyboard shortcuts with pinned scripts:

- You can use the following keyboard shortcuts to work with pinned scripts:

Action	Windows shortcut key	Macintosh shortcut key
Pin script	Control-= (equal sign)	Command-=
Unpin script	Control-- (minus sign)	Command--
Move focus to tab on the right	Control-Shift-. (period)	Command-Shift-.

Action	Windows shortcut key	Macintosh shortcut key
Move focus to tab on the left	Control-Shift-, (comma)	Command-Shift-,
Unpin all scripts	Control-Shift-- (minus)	Command-Shift--

Using the ActionScript editor

Flash MX 2004 and Flash MX Professional 2004 provide several tools to help you write syntactically correct code and lets you set preferences for code formatting and other options. These capabilities are discussed in this section.

Syntax highlighting

In ActionScript, as in any language, *syntax* is the way elements are put together to create meaning. If you use incorrect ActionScript syntax, your scripts will not work.

When you write scripts in Flash MX 2004 and Flash MX Professional 2004, commands that are not supported by the version of the player you are targeting appear in yellow in the Actions toolbox. For example, if the Flash Player SWF version is set to Flash 6, ActionScript that is supported only by Flash Player 7 appears in yellow in the Actions toolbox. (For information on setting the Flash Player SWF version, see "Setting publish options for the Flash SWF file format" in Using Flash Help.)

You can also set a preference to have Flash "color-code" parts of your scripts as you write them, to bring typing errors to your attention. For example, suppose you set your Syntax coloring preference to have keywords appear in deep green. While you are typing code, if you type `var`, the word `var` appears in green. However, if you mistakenly type `vae`, the word `vae` remains black, providing you with an immediate clue that you made a typing error.

To set preferences for syntax coloring as you type, do one of the following:

- Select Edit > Preferences, and specify Syntax coloring settings on the ActionScript tab.
- In the Actions panel, select Preferences from the Options pop-up menu (at the upper right of the panel) and specify Syntax coloring settings on the ActionScript tab.

Writing code that triggers code hints

When you work in the ActionScript editor (either in the Actions panel or Script window), Flash can detect what action you are entering and display a *code hint*—a tooltip that contains the complete syntax for that action, or a pop-up menu that lists possible method or property names. Code hints appear for parameters, properties, and events when you strictly type or name your objects so that the ActionScript editor knows which code hints to display, as discussed in the rest of this section. For information on using code hints when they appear, see "Using code hints" on page 267.

Note: Code hinting is enabled automatically for native classes that don't require you to create and name an object of the class, such as Math, Key, Mouse, and so on.

Strictly typing objects to trigger code hints

When you use ActionScript 2.0, you can strictly type a variable that is based on a built-in class, such as Button, Array, and so on. If you do so, the ActionScript editor displays code hints for the variable. For example, suppose you type the following:

```
var names:Array = new Array();
names.
```

As soon as you type the period (.), Flash displays a list of methods and properties available for Array objects, because you have typed the variable as an array. For more information on data typing, see "Strict data typing" on page 242. For information on using code hints when they appear, see "Using code hints" on page 267.

Using suffixes to trigger code hints

If you use ActionScript 1 or you want to display code hints for objects you create without strictly typing them (see "Strictly typing objects to trigger code hints" on page 266), you must add a special suffix to the name of each object when you create it. For example, the suffixes that trigger code hinting for the Array class and the Camera class are _array and _cam, respectively. If you type the following code:

```
var my_array = new Array();
var my_cam = Camera.get();
```

and then type either of the following (the variable name followed by a period), code hints for the Array and Camera object, respectively, appear.

```
my_array.
my_cam.
```

For objects that appear on the Stage, use the suffix in the Instance Name text box in the Property inspector. For example, to display code hints for MovieClip objects, use the Property inspector to assign instance names with the suffix _mc to all MovieClip objects. Then, whenever you type the instance name followed by a period, code hints appear.

Although suffixes are not required for triggering code hints when you strictly type an object, using them consistently helps you and others understand your scripts.

The following table lists the suffixes required for support of automatic code hinting:

Object type	Variable suffix
Array	_array
Button	_btn
Camera	_cam
Color	_color
ContextMenu	_cm
ContextMenuItem	_cmi
Date	_date
Error	_err
LoadVars	_lv

Object type	Variable suffix
LocalConnection	_lc
Microphone	_mic
MovieClip	_mc
MovieClipLoader	_mcl
PrintJob	_pj
NetConnection	_nc
NetStream	_ns
SharedObject	_so
Sound	_sound
String	_str
TextField	_txt
TextFormat	_fmt
Video	_video
XML	_xml
XMLNode	_xmlnode
XMLSocket	_xmlsocket

For information on using code hints when they appear, see "Using code hints" on page 267.

Using comments to trigger code hints

You can also use ActionScript comments to specify an object's class for code hinting. The following example tells ActionScript that the class of the instance theObject is Object, and so on. If you were to enter mc followed by a period after these comments, a code hint would display the list of MovieClip methods and properties; if you were to enter theArray followed by a period, a code hint would display a list of Array methods and properties; and so on.

```
// Object theObject;
// Array theArray;
// MovieClip mc;
```

However, Macromedia recommends using strict data typing (see "Strictly typing objects to trigger code hints" on page 266) or suffixes (see "Using suffixes to trigger code hints" on page 266) instead of this technique, because those techniques enable code hinting automatically and make your code more understandable.

Using code hints

Code hints are enabled by default. By setting preferences, you can disable code hints or determine how quickly they appear. When code hints are disabled in preferences, you can still display a code hint for a specific command.

To specify settings for automatic code hints, do one of the following:

- Select Edit > Preferences, and then enable or disable Code Hints on the ActionScript tab.
- In the Actions panel, select Preferences from the Options pop-up menu (at the upper right of the panel) and enable or disable Code Hints on the ActionScript tab.

If you enable code hints, you can also specify a delay in seconds before the code hints should appear. For example, if you are new to ActionScript, you might prefer no delay so that code hints always appear immediately. However, if you usually know what you want to type and only need hints when you use unfamiliar language elements, you can specify a delay so that code hints don't appear when you don't plan to use them.

To work with tooltip-style code hints:

1   Display the code hint by typing an open parenthesis [(] after an element that requires parentheses, such as a method name, a command such as `if` or `do while`, and so on.

    The code hint appears.

    Note: If a code hint doesn't appear, make sure you haven't disabled code hints on the ActionScript tab. If you want to display code hints for a variable or object you created, make sure that you have named your variable or object correctly (see "Using suffixes to trigger code hints" on page 266) or that you have strictly typed your variable or object (see "Strictly typing objects to trigger code hints" on page 266).

2   Enter a value for the parameter. If there is more than one parameter, separate the values with commas.

    Overloaded commands such as `gotoAndPlay()` or `for` (that is, functions or methods that can be invoked with different sets of parameters) display an indicator that allows you to select the parameter you want to set. Click the small arrow buttons or press Control+Left Arrow and Control+Right Arrow to select the parameter.

    ```
    for (
        ◄ 1 of 2 ► for ( init; condition; next ) {
                 }
    ```

3   To dismiss the code hint, do one of the following:

    - Type a closing parenthesis [)].
    - Click outside the statement.
    - Press Escape.

To work with menu-style code hints:

1 Display the code hint by typing a period after the variable or object name.

The code hint menu appears.

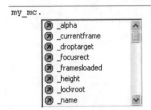

Note: If a code hint doesn't appear, make sure you haven't disabled code hints on the ActionScript tab. If you want to display code hints for a variable or object you created, make sure that you have named your variable or object correctly (see "Using suffixes to trigger code hints" on page 266) or that you have strictly typed your variable or object (see "Strictly typing objects to trigger code hints" on page 266).

2 To navigate through the code hints, use the Up and Down Arrow keys.

3 To select an item in the menu, press Return or Tab, or double-click the item.

4 To dismiss the code hint, do one of the following:

- Select one of the menu items.
- Click outside the statement.
- Type a closing parenthesis [ )] if you've already typed an open parenthesis.
- Press Escape.

To manually display a code hint:

1 Click in a code location where code hints can appear. Here are some examples:

- After the dot following a statement or command, where a property or method must be entered
- Between parentheses in a method name

2 Do one of the following:

- Click the Show Code Hint button above the Script pane.
- Press Control+Spacebar (Windows) or Command+Spacebar (Macintosh).
- If you are working in the Actions panel, open the pop-up menu (at the right side of the title bar), and select Show Code Hint.

Using Escape shortcut keys

You can add many elements to a script by using shortcut keys—pressing the Escape key and then two other keys. (These shortcuts are different from the keyboard shortcuts that initiate certain menu commands.) For example, if you are working in the Script pane and type Escape+d+o, the following code is placed in your script, and the insertion point is placed immediately following the word `while`, so you can begin typing your condition:

```
do {
} while ();
```

Similarly, if you type Escape+c+h, the following code is placed in your script, and the insertion point is placed between the parentheses, so you can begin typing your condition:

```
catch () {
}
```

If you want to learn (or be reminded) which commands have Escape shortcut keys, you can display them next to elements in the Actions panel.

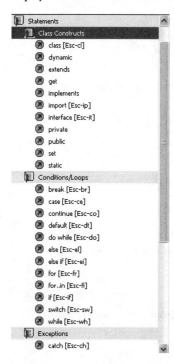

To display or hide Escape shortcut keys:

- From the View Options pop-up menu, enable or disable View Escape Shortcut Keys.

Checking syntax and punctuation

To thoroughly determine whether the code you wrote performs as planned, you need to publish or test the file. However, you can do a quick check of your ActionScript code without leaving the FLA file. Syntax errors are listed in Output panel. (When you check syntax, only the current script is checked; other scripts that may be in the FLA file are not checked.) You can also check to see if a set of parentheses, curly braces, or brackets (array access operators) around a block of code is balanced.

To check syntax, do one of the following:

- Click the Check Syntax button above the Script pane.
- In the Actions panel, display the pop-up menu (at the upper right of the panel) and select Check Syntax.
- Press Control+T (Windows) or Command+T (Macintosh).

To check for punctuation balance:

1 Click between braces ({ }), array access operators ([ ]), or parentheses (( )) in your script.

2 Press Control+' (Windows) or Command+' (Macintosh) to highlight the text between braces, brackets, or parentheses.

The highlighting helps you check whether opening punctuation has correct corresponding closing punctuation.

Formatting code

You can specify settings to determine if your code is formatted and indented automatically or manually. You can also choose whether to view line numbers and whether to wrap long lines of code.

To set format options:

1 Do one of the following

- In the Actions panel, select Auto Format Options from the Options pop-up menu (at the upper right of the panel).
- (Flash Professional only) In an external script file, choose Edit > Auto Format Options.

The Auto Format Options dialog box appears.

2 Select any of the check boxes. To see the effect of each selection, look in the Preview pane.

After you set Auto Format Options, your settings are applied automatically to code you write, but not to existing code. To apply your settings to existing code, you must do so manually. You might use this procedure to format code that was formatted using different settings, that you imported from another editor, and so on.

To format code according to Auto Format Options settings, do one of the following:

- Click the Auto Format button above the Script pane.
- Select Auto Format from the Actions panel pop-up menu.
- Press Control+Shift+F (Windows) or Command+Shift+F (Macintosh).

To use automatic indentation:

- Automatic indentation is turned on by default. To turn it off, deselect Automatic Indentation in ActionScript preferences.

When automatic indentation is turned on, the text you type after (or { is automatically indented according to the Tab Size setting in ActionScript preferences. To indent another line, select the line and press Tab. To remove the indent, press Shift+Tab.

To enable or disable line numbers and word wrap:

- From the View Options pop-up menu, enable or disable View Line Numbers and Word Wrap.

Debugging your scripts

Flash provides several tools for testing ActionScript in your SWF files. The Debugger, discussed in the rest of this section, lets you find errors in a SWF file while it's running in Flash Player. Flash also provides the following additional debugging tools:

- The Output panel, which displays error messages and lists of variables and objects (see "Using the Output panel" on page 281)
- The `trace` statement, which sends programming notes and values of expressions to the Output panel (see "Using the trace statement" on page 283)
- The `throw` and `try..catch..finally` statements, which let you test and respond to runtime errors from within your script
- The availability of comprehensive compiler error messages, which let you diagnose and fix problems more readily (see Appendix A, "Error Messages," on page 987)

You must be viewing your SWF file in a special version of Flash Player called Flash Debug Player. When you install the authoring tool, Flash Debug Player is installed automatically. So if you install Flash and browse a website that has Flash content, or do a Test Movie, then you're using Flash Debug Player. You can also run the installer in the <app_dir>\Players\Debug\ directory, or launch the stand-alone Flash Debug Player from the same directory.

When you use the Test Movie command to test movies that implement keyboard controls (tabbing, keyboard shortcuts created using `Key.addListener()`, and so on), select Control > Disable Keyboard Shortcuts. Selecting this option prevents the authoring environment from "grabbing" keystrokes, and lets them pass through to the player. For example, in the authoring environment, Control+U opens the Preferences dialog box. If your script assigns Control+U to an action that underlines text onscreen, when you use Test Movie, pressing Control+U will open the Preferences dialog box instead of running the action that underlines text. To let the Control+U command pass through to the player, you must select Control > Disable Keyboard Shortcuts.

Caution: The Test Movie command fails if any part of the SWF file path has characters that cannot be represented using the MBCS encoding scheme. For example, Japanese paths on an English system do not work. All areas of the application that use the external player are subject to this limitation.

The Debugger shows a hierarchical display list of movie clips currently loaded in Flash Player. Using the Debugger, you can display and modify variable and property values as the SWF file plays, and you can use breakpoints to stop the SWF file and step through ActionScript code line by line.

You can use the Debugger in test mode with local files, or you can use it to test files on a web server in a remote location. The Debugger lets you set breakpoints in your ActionScript that stop Flash Player and step through the code as it runs. You can then go back to your scripts and edit them so that they produce the correct results.

After it's activated, the Debugger status bar displays the URL or local path of the file, tells whether the file is running in test mode or from a remote location, and shows a live view of the movie clip display list. When movie clips are added to or removed from the file, the display list reflects the changes immediately. You can resize the display list by moving the horizontal splitter.

To activate the Debugger in test mode:

- Select Control > Debug Movie.

  This opens the Debugger. It also opens the SWF file in test mode.

Status bar   Watch list
    Display list   Code view

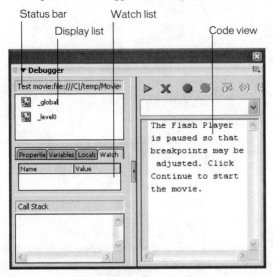

Debugging a SWF file from a remote location

You can debug a remote SWF file using the stand-alone, ActiveX, or plug-in versions of Flash Player. When exporting a SWF file, you can enable debugging in your file and create a debugging password. If you don't enable debugging, the Debugger will not activate.

To ensure that only trusted users can run your SWF files in the Flash Debug Player, you can publish your file with a debugging password. As in JavaScript or HTML, it's possible for users to view client-side variables in ActionScript. To store variables securely, you must send them to a server-side application instead of storing them in your file. However, as a Flash developer, you may have other trade secrets, such as movie clip structures, that you do not want to reveal. You can use a debugging password to protect your work.

When you export, publish, or test a movie, Flash creates a SWD file that contains debug information. To debug remotely, you must place the SWD file in the same directory as the SWF file on the server.

To enable remote debugging of a Flash movie:

1 Select File > Publish Settings.

2 On the Flash tab of the Publish Settings dialog box, select Debugging permitted.

```
Options:  ☐ Generate size report
          ☐ Protect from import
          ☐ Omit trace actions
          ☑ Debugging permitted
          ☐ Compress movie
          ☐ Optimize for Flash Player 6 r65

Password: [                    ]
```

3 To set a password, enter a password in the Password box.

After you set this password, no one can download information to the Debugger without the password. However, if you leave the Password box blank, no password is required.

4 Close the Publish Settings dialog box, and select one of the following commands:

- Control > Debug Movie
- File > Export Movie
- File > Publish Settings > Publish

Flash creates a debugging file with the .swd extension and saves it alongside the SWF file. The SWD file contains information that allows you to use breakpoints and step through code.

5 Place the SWD file in the same directory as the SWF file on the server.

If the SWD file is not in the same directory as the SWF file, you can still debug remotely, but the Debugger ignores breakpoints and you can't step through code.

6 In Flash, select Window > Development Panels > Debugger.

- In the Debugger, select Enable Remote Debugging from the Options pop-up menu (at the upper right of the panel).

To activate the Debugger from a remote location:

1 Open the Flash authoring application.

2 In a browser or in the stand-alone player, open the published SWF file from the remote location.

   The Remote Debug dialog box appears.

   If that dialog box doesn't appear, Flash can't find the SWD file. In this case, right-click (Windows) or Control-click (Macintosh) in the SWF file to display the context menu, and select Debugger.

3 In the Remote Debug dialog box, select Localhost or Other Machine:

   ▪ Select Localhost if the Debug player and the Flash authoring application are on the same computer.

   ▪ Select Other Machine if the Debug player and the Flash authoring application are not on the same computer. Enter the IP address of the computer running the Flash authoring application.

4 When a connection is established, a password prompt appears. Enter your debugging password if you set one.

   The display list of the SWF file appears in the Debugger.

Displaying and modifying variables

The Variables tab in the Debugger displays the names and values of any global and Timeline variables in the SWF file. If you change the value of a variable on the Variables tab, you can see the change reflected in the SWF file while it runs. For example, to test collision detection in a game, you can enter the variable value to position a ball in the correct location next to a wall.

The Locals tab in the Debugger displays the names and values of any local variables that are available wherever the SWF file has stopped at a breakpoint or anywhere else within a user-defined function.

To display a variable:

1   Select the movie clip containing the variable from the display list.

    To display global variables, select the _global clip in the display list.

2   Click the Variables tab.

The display list updates automatically as the SWF file plays. If a movie clip is removed from the SWF file at a specific frame, that movie clip, along with its variable and variable name, is also removed from the display list in the Debugger. However, if you mark a variable for the Watch list (see "Using the Watch list" on page 277), that variable is not removed.

To modify a variable value:

* Double-click the value, and enter a new value.

The value cannot be an expression. For example, you can use "Hello", 3523, or "http:// www.macromedia.com", and you cannot use x + 2 or eval("name:" +i). The value can be a string (any value surrounded by quotation marks), a number, or a Boolean value (true or false).

Note: To write the value of an expression to the Output panel in test mode, use the trace statement. See "Using the trace statement" on page 283.

Using the Watch list

To monitor a set of critical variables in a manageable way, you can mark variables to appear in the Watch list. The Watch list displays the absolute path to the variable and the value. You can also enter a new variable value in the Watch list the same way as in the Variables tab.

If you add a local variable to the Watch list, its value appears only when Flash Player is stopped at a line of ActionScript where that variable is in scope. All other variables appear while the SWF file is playing. If the Debugger can't find the value of the variable, the value is listed as Undefined.

The Watch list can display only variables, not properties or functions.

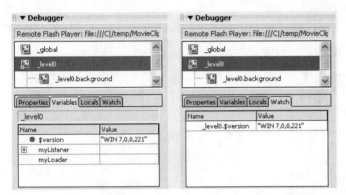

Variables marked for the Watch list and variables in the Watch list

To add variables to the Watch list, do one of the following:

- On the Variables or Locals tab, right-click (Windows) or Control-click (Macintosh) a selected variable and then select Watch from the context menu. A blue dot appears next to the variable.
- On the Watch tab, right-click (Windows) or Control-click (Macintosh) and select Add from the context menu. Enter the target path to the variable name and the value in the fields.

To remove variables from the Watch list:

- On the Watch tab, right-click (Windows) or Control-click (Macintosh) and select Remove from the context menu.

Displaying movie clip properties and changing editable properties

The Debugger's Properties tab displays all the property values of any movie clip on the Stage. You can change a value and see its effect in the SWF file while it runs. Some movie clip properties are read-only and cannot be changed.

To display a movie clip's properties in the Debugger:

1 Select a movie clip from the display list.

2 Click the Properties tab in the Debugger.

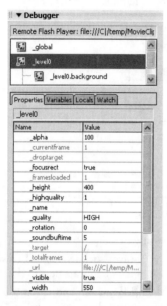

To modify a property value:

• Double-click the value, and enter a new value.

The value cannot be an expression. For example, you can enter 50 or "clearwater", but you cannot enter x + 50. The value can be a string (any value surrounded by quotation marks), a number, or a Boolean value (true or false). You can't enter object or array values (for example, {id: "rogue"} or [1, 2, 3]) in the Debugger.

For more information, see "String operators" on page 250 and "Using operators to manipulate values in expressions" on page 249.

Note: To write the value of an expression to the Output panel in test mode, use the trace statement. See "Using the trace statement" on page 283.

Setting and removing breakpoints

A breakpoint lets you stop a SWF file running in Flash Player at a specific line of ActionScript. You can use breakpoints to test possible trouble spots in your code. For example, if you've written a set of if..else if statements and can't determine which one is executing, you can add a breakpoint before the statements and step through them one by one in the Debugger.

You can set breakpoints in the Actions panel or in the Debugger. (To set breakpoints in external scripts, you must use the Debugger.) Breakpoints set in the Actions panel are saved with the Flash document (FLA file). Breakpoints set in the Debugger are not saved in the FLA file and are valid only for the current debugging session.

To set or remove a breakpoint in the Actions panel, do one of the following:

- Click in the left margin. A red dot indicates a breakpoint.
- Click the Debug options button above the Script pane.
- Right-click (Windows) or Control-click (Macintosh) to display the context menu, and select Breakpoint, Remove Breakpoint, or Remove All Breakpoints.
- Press Control+Shift+B (Windows) or Command+Shift+B (Macintosh).

Note: In previous versions of Flash, clicking in the left margin of the Script pane selected the line of code; now it adds or removes a breakpoint. To select a line of code, use Control-click (Windows) or Command-click (Macintosh).

To set and remove breakpoints in the Debugger, do one of the following:

- Click in the left margin. A red dot indicates a breakpoint.
- Click the Toggle Breakpoint or Remove All Breakpoints button above the code view.
- Right-click (Windows) or Control-click (Macintosh) to display the context menu, and select Breakpoint, Remove Breakpoint, or Remove All Breakpoints.
- Press Control+Shift+B (Windows) or Command+Shift+B (Macintosh).

  Once Flash Player is stopped at a breakpoint, you can step into, step over, or step out of that line of code. If you set a breakpoint in a comment or on an empty line in the Actions panel, the breakpoint is ignored.

Stepping through lines of code

When you start a debugging session, Flash Player is paused. If you set breakpoints in the Actions panel, you can simply click the Continue button to play the SWF file until it reaches a breakpoint. For example, in the following code, suppose a breakpoint is set inside a button on the line `myFunction()`:

```
on(press){
  myFunction();
}
```

When you click the button, the breakpoint is reached and Flash Player pauses. You can now step in to bring the Debugger to the first line of `myFunction()` wherever it is defined in the document. You can also step through or out of the function.

If you didn't set breakpoints in the Actions panel, you can use the jump menu in the Debugger to select any script in the movie. Once you've selected a script, you can add breakpoints to it. After adding breakpoints, you must click the Continue button to start the movie. The Debugger stops when it reaches the breakpoint.

As you step through lines of code, the values of variables and properties change in the Watch list and in the Variables, Locals, and Properties tabs. A yellow arrow along the left side of the Debugger's code view indicates the line at which the Debugger stopped. Use the following buttons along the top of the code view:

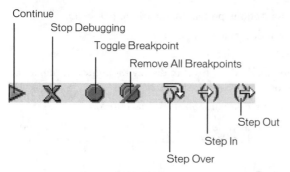

Step In advances the Debugger (indicated by the yellow arrow) into a function. Step In works only for user-defined functions.

In the following example, if you place a breakpoint at line 7 and click Step In, the Debugger advances to line 2, and a subsequent click of Step In will advance you to line 3. Clicking Step In for lines that do not have user-defined functions in them advances the Debugger over a line of code. For example, if you stop at line 2 and select Step In, the Debugger advances to line 3, as shown in the following example:

```
1 function myFunction() {
2 x = 0;
3 y = 0;
4 }
5
6 mover = 1;
7 myFunction();
8 mover = 0;
```

Step Out advances the Debugger out of a function. This button works only if you are currently stopped in a user-defined function; it moves the yellow arrow to the line after the one where that function was called. In the example above, if you place a breakpoint at line 3 and click Step Out, the Debugger moves to line 8. Clicking Step Out at a line that is not within a user-defined function is the same as clicking Continue. For example, if you stop at line 6 and click Step Out, the player continues executing the script until it encounters a breakpoint.

Step Over advances the Debugger over a line of code. This button moves the yellow arrow to the next line in the script and ignores any user-defined functions. In the example above, if you are stopped at line 7 and click Step Over, you go directly to line 8, and `myFunction()` is ignored.

Continue leaves the line at which the player is stopped and continues playing until a breakpoint is reached.

Stop Debugging makes the Debugger inactive but continues to play the SWF file in Flash Player.

Using the Output panel

In test mode, the Output panel displays information to help you troubleshoot your SWF file. Some information, such as syntax errors, is displayed automatically. You can display other information by using the List Objects and List Variables commands. (See "Listing a SWF file's objects" on page 281 and "Listing a SWF file's variables" on page 282.)

If you use the `trace` statement in your scripts, you can send specific information to the Output panel as the SWF file runs. This could include notes about the SWF file's status or the value of an expression. (See "Using the trace statement" on page 283.)

To display the Output panel, select Window > Development Panels > Output or press F2.

Note: If there are syntax errors in a script, the Output panel appears automatically when you check syntax or test your SWF file.

To work with the contents of the Output panel, use the Options pop-up menu in the upper right corner.

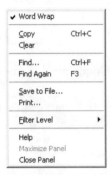

Listing a SWF file's objects

In test mode, the List Objects command displays the level, frame, object type (shape, movie clip, or button), target paths, and instance names of movie clips, buttons, and text fields in a hierarchical list. This is especially useful for finding the correct target path and instance name. Unlike the Debugger, the list does not update automatically as the SWF file plays; you must select the List Objects command each time you want to send the information to the Output panel.

The List Objects command does not list all ActionScript data objects. In this context, an object is considered to be a shape or symbol on the Stage.

To display a list of objects in a movie:

1 If your movie is not running in test mode, select Control > Test Movie.

2 Select Debug > List Objects.

A list of all the objects currently on the Stage is displayed in the Output panel, as shown in this example:

```
Level #0: Frame=1 Label="Scene_1"
  Button: Target="_level0.myButton"
    Shape:
  Movie Clip: Frame=1 Target="_level0.myMovieClip"
    Shape:
  Edit Text: Target="_level0.myTextField" Text="This is sample text."
```

Listing a SWF file's variables

In test mode, the List Variables command displays a list of all the variables currently in the SWF file. This is especially useful for finding the correct variable target path and variable name. Unlike the Debugger, the list does not update automatically as the SWF file plays; you must select the List Variables command each time you want to send the information to the Output panel.

The List Variables command also displays global variables declared with the _global identifier. The global variables are displayed at the top of the List Variables output in a "Global Variables" section, and each variable is prefixed with _global.

In addition, the List Variables command displays getter/setter properties—properties that are created with the Object.addProperty() method and invoke get or set methods. A getter/setter property is displayed alongside any other properties in the object it belongs to. To make these properties easily distinguishable from ordinary variables, the value of a getter/setter property is prefixed with the string [getter/setter]. The value displayed for a getter/setter property is determined by evaluating the get function of the property.

To display a list of variables in a SWF file:

1 If your SWF file is not running in test mode, select Control > Test Movie.

2 Select Debug > List Variables.

A list of all the variables currently in the SWF file is displayed in the Output panel, as shown in this example:

```
Global Variables:
  Variable _global.MyGlobalArray = [object #1] [
     0:1,
     1:2,
     2:3
  ]
Level #0:
  Variable _level0.$version = "WIN 6,0,0,101"
  Variable _level0.RegularVariable = "Gary"
  Variable _level0.AnObject = [object #1] {
    MyProperty: [getter/setter] 3.14159
  }
```

Displaying text field properties for debugging

To get debugging information about TextField objects, you can use the Debug > List Variables command in test movie mode. The Output panel uses the following conventions in displaying TextField objects:

- If a property is not found on the object, it is not displayed.
- No more than four properties are displayed on a line.
- A property with a string value is displayed on a separate line.
- If there are any other properties defined for the object after the built-in properties are processed, they are added to the display using the rules in the second and third points above.
- Color properties are displayed as hexadecimal numbers (0x00FF00).
- The properties are displayed in the following order: variable, text, htmlText, html, textWidth, textHeight, maxChars, borderColor, backgroundColor, textColor, border, background, wordWrap, password, multiline, selectable, scroll, hscroll, maxscroll, maxhscroll, bottomScroll, type, embedFonts, restrict, length, tabIndex, autoSize.

The Debug > List Objects command in test mode lists TextField objects. If an instance name is specified for a text field, the Output panel displays the full target path including the instance name in the following form:

```
Target = "target path"
```

Using the trace statement

When you use the `trace` statement in a script, you can send information to the Output panel. For example, while testing a movie or scene, you can send specific programming notes to the panel or have specific results appear when a button is pressed or a frame is played. The `trace` statement is similar to the JavaScript `alert` statement.

When you use the `trace` statement in a script, you can use expressions as parameters. The value of an expression is displayed in the Output panel in test mode, as shown here:

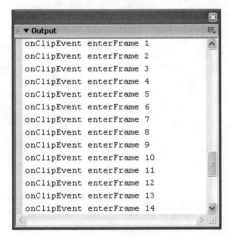

The `trace` statement returns values that appear in the Output panel.

```
onClipEvent(enterFrame){
   trace("onClipEvent enterFrame " + enterFrame++)
}
```

Updating Flash Player for testing

You can download the latest version of Flash Player from the Macromedia Support Center at www.macromedia.com/support/flash and use it to test your SWF files with the most recent version of Flash Player.

PART II
Handling Events and Creating Interaction

Events can be user-generated, such as mouse clicks or keypresses, or can occur as a result of some other process, such as an XML file loading over the network. The first chapter in this part describes the different types of events in Macromedia Flash and discusses how to handle them in ActionScript. The second chapter shows how to apply these principles to create simple interactive presentations, applications, and animations.

An *event* is a software or hardware occurrence that requires a response from a Macromedia Flash application. For example, an event such as a mouse click or a keypress is called a *user event*, since it occurs as a result of direct user interaction. An event generated automatically by Flash Player, such as the initial appearance of a movie clip on the Stage, is called a *system event*, because it isn't generated directly by the user.

In order for your application to react to events, you must use *event handlers*—ActionScript code associated with a particular object and event. For example, when a user clicks a button on the Stage, you might advance the playhead to the next frame. Or when an XML file finishes loading over the network, you might display the contents of that file in a text field.

ActionScript provides a few different ways to handle events: event handler methods, event listeners, and button and movie clip event handlers.

Using event handler methods

An event handler method is a class method that is invoked when an event occurs on an instance of that class. For example, the Button class defines an `onPress` event handler that is invoked whenever the mouse is pressed on a Button object. Unlike other methods of a class, however, you don't invoke an event handler directly; Flash Player invokes it automatically when the appropriate event occurs.

By default, event handler methods are undefined: when a particular event occurs, its corresponding event handler is invoked, but your application doesn't respond further to the event. To have your application respond to the event, you define a function with the function statement and then assign that function to the appropriate event handler. The function you assign to the event handler is then automatically invoked whenever the event occurs.

An event handler consists of three parts: the object to which the event applies, the name of the object's event handler method, and the function you assign to the event handler. The following example shows the basic structure of an event handler.

```
object.eventMethod = function () {
  // Your code here, responding to event
}
```

For example, suppose you have a button named next_btn on the Stage. The following code assigns a function to the button's onPress event handler; this function advances the playhead to the next frame in the Timeline.

```
next_btn.onPress = function ()
  nextFrame();
}
```

In the above code, the nextFrame() function is assigned directly to onPress. You can also assign a function reference (name) to an event handler method and then define the function later.

```
// Assign a function reference to button's onPress event handler method
next_btn.onPress = goNextFrame;

// Define doSubmit() function
function goNextFrame() {
  nextFrame();
}
```

Notice that you assign the function reference, not the function's return value, to the onPress event handler.

```
// Incorrect!
next_btn.onPress = goNextFrame();
// Correct.
next_btn.onPress = goNextFrame;
```

Some event handlers receive passed parameters that provide information about the event that occurred. For example, the TextField.onSetFocus event handler is invoked when a text field instance gains keyboard focus. This event handler receives a reference to the text field object that previously had keyboard focus.

For example, the following code inserts some text into the text field that just lost keyboard focus.

```
userName_txt.onSetFocus = function(oldFocus_txt) {
  oldFocus_txt.text = "I just lost keyboard focus";
}
```

The following ActionScript classes define event handlers: Button, ContextMenu, ContextMenuItem, Key, LoadVars, LocalConnection, Mouse, MovieClip, MovieClipLoader, Selection, SharedObject, Sound, Stage, TextField, XML, and XMLSocket. For more information about the event handlers they provide, see these class entries in Chapter 12, "ActionScript Dictionary," on page 409.

You can also assign functions to event handlers for objects you create at runtime. For example, the following code creates a new movie clip instance (newclip_mc) and then assigns a function to the clip's onPress event handler.

```
_root.attachMovie("symbolID", "newclip_mc", 10);
newclip_mc.onPress = function () {
  trace("You pressed me");
}
```

For more information, see "Creating movie clips at runtime" on page 330.

Using event listeners

Event listeners let an object, called a *listener object*, receive events generated by another object, called a *broadcaster object*. The broadcaster object registers the listener object to receive events generated by the broadcaster. For example, you could register a movie clip object to receive `onResize` notifications from the Stage, or a button instance could receive `onChanged` notifications from a text field object. You can register multiple listener objects to receive events from a single broadcaster, and you can register a single listener object to receive events from multiple broadcasters.

The event model for event listeners is similar to that of event handlers (see "Using event handler methods" on page 287), with two main differences:

- The object to which you assign the event handler is not the object that emits the event.
- You call a special method of the broadcaster object, `addListener()`, which registers the listener object to receive its events.

To use event listeners, you create a listener object with a property that has the name of the event being generated by the broadcaster object. You then assign a function to the event listener that responds in some way to the event. Lastly, you call `addListener()` on the object that's broadcasting the event, passing it the name of the listener object. The following code outlines the event listener model.

```
listenerObject.eventName = function(){
    // your code here
};
broadcastObject.addListener(listenerObject);
```

The specified listener object can be any object, such as a movie clip or button instance on the Stage, or an instance of any ActionScript class. The event name is an event that occurs on *broadCastObject*, which then broadcasts the event to *listenerObject*. You can register multiple listeners to one event broadcaster.

The following example shows how to use the `Selection.onSetFocus` event listener to create a simple focus manager for a group of input text fields. In this case, the border of the text field that receives keyboard focus is enabled (displayed), and the border of the text field that lost focus is disabled.

To create a simple focus manager with event listeners:

1 Using the Text tool, create a text field on the Stage.

2 Select the text field and, in the Property inspector, select Input from the Text Type pop-up menu, and select the Show Border Around Text option.

3 Create another input text field below the first one.

Make sure the Show Border Around Text option is not selected for this text field. Continue to create input text fields if desired.

4 Select Frame 1 in the Timeline and open the Actions panel (Window > Development Panels > Actions).

5 To create an object that listens for focus notification from the Selection class, enter the following code in the Actions panel:

```
var focusListener = new Object();
focusListener.onSetFocus = function(oldFocus_txt, newFocus_txt) {
    oldFocus_txt.border = false;
    newFocus_txt.border = true;
}
```

This code creates a new (generic) ActionScript object named focusListener. This object defines for itself an onSetFocus property, to which it assigns a function. The function takes two parameters: a reference to the text field that lost focus, and one to the text field that gained focus. The function sets the border property of the text field that lost focus to false, and sets the border property of the text field that gained focus to true.

6 To register the focusListener object to receive events from the Selection object, add the following code to the Actions panel:

```
Selection.addListener(focusListener);
```

7 Test the movie (Control > Test Movie), click in the first text field, and press Tab to switch focus between fields.

To unregister a listener object from receiving events, you call the removeListener() method of the broadcaster object, passing it the name of the listener object.

```
broadcastObject.removeListener(listenerObject);
```

Event listeners are available to objects of the following ActionScript classes: Key, Mouse, MovieClipLoader, Selection, TextField, and Stage. For a list of event listeners available to each class, see these class entries in Chapter 12, "ActionScript Dictionary," on page 409.

Using button and movie clip event handlers

You can attach event handlers directly to a button or movie clip instance by using the
`onClipEvent()` and `on()` handlers. The `onClipEvent()` handler handles movie clip events, and
the `on()` handler handles button events. You can also use `on()` with movie clips to create movie
clips that receive button events. For more information, see "Creating movie clips with button
states" on page 292.

To use an `on()` or `onClipEvent()` handler, attach it directly to an instance of a button or movie
clip on the Stage and specify the event you want to handle for that instance. For example, the
following `on()` event handler executes whenever the user clicks the button that the handler is
attached to.

```
on(press) {
  trace("Thanks for pressing me.");
}
```

You can specify two or more events for each `on()` handler, separated by commas. The
ActionScript in a handler executes when either of the events specified by the handler occurs. For
example, the following `on()` handler attached to a button executes whenever the mouse rolls over
out of the button.

```
on(rollOver, rollOut) {
  trace("You rolled over, or rolled out");
}
```

You can also attach more than one handler to an object if you want different scripts to run when
different events occur. For example, you could attach the following `onClipEvent()` handlers to
the same movie clip instance. The first executes when the movie clip first loads (or appears on the
Stage); the second executes when the movie clip is unloaded from the Stage.

```
onClipEvent(load) {
  trace("I've loaded");
}
onClipEvent (unload) {
  trace("I've unloaded");
}
```

For a complete list of events supported by the `on()` and `onClipEvent()` event handlers, see `on()`
on page 787 and `onClipEvent()` on page 788.

Event handling through `on()` and `onClipEvent()` doesn't conflict with event handling through
event handler methods that you define. For example, suppose you have a button in a SWF file;
the button can have an `on(press)` handler that tells the SWF file to play, and the same button
can have an `onPress` method, for which you define a function that tells an object on the Stage to
rotate. When the button is clicked, the SWF file plays and the object rotates. Depending on your
preference, you can use `on()` and `onClipEvent()`, event handler methods, or both types of event
handling. However, the scope of variables and objects in `on()` and `onClipEvent()` handlers is
different than in event handler and event listeners. (See "Event handler scope" on page 292.)

You can attach `onClipEvent()` and `on()` only to movie clip instances that have been placed on
the Stage during authoring. You cannot attach `onClipEvent()` or `on()` to movie clip instances
that are created at runtime (using the `attachMovie()` method, for example). To attach event
handlers to objects created at runtime, use event handler methods or event listeners. (See "Using
event handler methods" on page 287 and "Using event listeners" on page 289.)

Creating movie clips with button states

When you attach an `on()` handler to a movie clip, or assign a function to one of the MovieClip mouse event handlers for a movie clip instance, the movie clip responds to mouse events in the same way as a button does. You can also create automatic button states (Up, Over, and Down) in a movie clip by adding the frame labels _up, _over, and _down to the movie clip's Timeline.

When the user moves the mouse over the movie clip or clicks it, the playhead is sent to the frame with the appropriate frame label. To designate the hit area used by a movie clip, you use the `hitArea` property of the MovieClip class.

To create button states in a movie clip:

1 Select a frame in a movie clip's Timeline to use as a button state (Up, Over, or Down).

2 Enter a frame label in the Property inspector (_up, _over, or _down).

3 To add additional button states, repeat steps 1–2.

4 To make the movie clip respond to mouse events, do one of the following:

- Attach an `on()` event handler to the movie clip instance, as discussed in "Using button and movie clip event handlers" on page 291.

- Assign a function to one of the movie clip object's mouse event handlers (`onPress`, `onRelease`, and so forth), as discussed in "Using event handler methods" on page 287.

Event handler scope

The scope, or context, of variables and commands that you declare and execute within an event handler depends on the type of event handler you're using: event handlers or event listeners, or `on()` and `onClipEvent()` handlers.

Functions assigned to event handler methods and event listeners (like all ActionScript functions that you write) define a local variable scope, but `on()` and `onClipEvent()` handlers do not.

For example, consider the following two event handlers. The first is an `onPress` event handler associated with a movie clip named `clip_mc`. The second is an `on()` handler attached to the same movie clip instance.

```
// Attached to clip_mc's parent clip Timeline:
clip_mc.onPress = function () {
   var color; // local function variable
   color = "blue";
}
// on() handler attached to clip_mc:
on(press) {
   var color; // no local variable scope
   color = "blue";
}
```

Although both event handlers contain the same code, they have different results. In the first case, the `color` variable is local to the function defined for `onPress`. In the second case, because the `on()` handler doesn't define a local variable scope, the variable scopes to the Timeline of the movie clip `clip_mc`.

For `on()` event handlers attached to buttons, rather than to movie clips, variables (as well as function and method calls) are scoped to the Timeline that contains the button instance.

For instance, the following on() event handler will produce different results depending on whether it's attached to a movie clip or button object. In the first case, the play() function call starts the playback head of the Timeline that contains the button; in the second case, the play() function call starts the Timeline of the movie clip to which the handler is attached.

```
// Attached to button
on(press) {
   play(); // plays parent Timeline
}
// Attached to movie clip
on(press) {
   play(); // plays movie clip's Timeline
}
```

That is, when attached to a button object, the play() method call applies to the Timeline that contains the button—that is, the button's parent Timeline. But when the same handler is attached to a movie clip object, then the play() applies to the movie clip that bears the handler.

Within an event handler or event listener function definition, the same play() function would apply to the Timeline that contains the function definition. For example, suppose the following MovieClip.onPress event handler function were declared on the Timeline that contains the movie clip instance myMovieClip.

```
// Function defined on movie clip Timeline:
myMovieClip.onPress = function () {
   play(); // plays Timeline that contains the function definition
}
```

If you want to play the movie clip that defines the onPress event handler, then you have to refer explicitly to that clip using the this keyword, as follows:

```
myMovieClip.onPress = function () {
   this.play(); // plays Timeline of clip that defines the onPress handler
}
```

Scope of the "this" keyword

The this keyword refers to the object in the currently executing scope. Depending on what type of event handler technique you're using, this can refer to different objects.

Within an event handler or event listener function, this refers to the object that defines the event handler or event listener method. For example, in the following code this refers to myClip itself.

```
// onPress() event handler attached to _level0.myClip:
myClip.onPress = function () {
   trace(this); // displays '_level0.myClip'
}
```

Within an on() **handler attached to a movie clip**, this refers to the movie clip to which the on() handler is attached.

```
// Attached to movie clip named 'myClip'
on(press) {
   trace(this); displays '_level0.myClip'
}
```

Within an on() **handler attached to a button**, this refers to the Timeline that contains the button.

```
// Attached to button on main Timeline
on(press) {
   trace(this); // displays '_level0'
}
```

CHAPTER 5
Creating Interaction with ActionScript

In simple animation, Macromedia Flash Player plays the scenes and frames of a SWF file sequentially. In an interactive SWF file, your audience uses the keyboard and mouse to jump to different parts of a SWF file, move objects, enter information in forms, and perform many other interactive operations.

You use ActionScript to create scripts that tell Flash Player what action to perform when an event occurs. Some events that can trigger a script occur when the playhead reaches a frame, when a movie clip loads or unloads, or when the user clicks a button or presses a key.

A script can consist of a single command, such as instructing a SWF file to stop playing, or a series of commands and statements, such as first evaluating a condition and then performing an action. Many ActionScript commands are simple and let you create basic controls for a SWF file. Other actions require some familiarity with programming languages and are intended for advanced development.

About events and interaction

Whenever a user clicks the mouse or presses a key, an event is generated. These types of events are generally called *user events*, because they are generated in response to some action by the end user. You can write ActionScript to respond to, or *handle*, these events. For example, when a user clicks a button, you might want to send the playhead to another frame in the SWF file or load a new web page into the browser.

In a SWF file, buttons, movie clips, and text fields all generate events to which you can respond. ActionScript provides three ways to handle events: event handler methods, event listeners, and `on()` and `onClipEvent()` handlers. For more information about events and handling events, see Chapter 4, "Handling Events," on page 287.

Controlling SWF file playback

The following ActionScript functions let you control the playhead in the Timeline and load a new web page into a browser window:

- The `gotoAndPlay()` and `gotoAndStop()` functions send the playhead to a frame or scene. These are global functions that you can call from any script. You can also use the `MovieClip.gotoAndPlay()` and `MovieClip.gotoAndStop()` methods to navigate the Timeline of a specific movie clip object.
- The `play()` and `stop()` actions play and stop movies.
- The `getURL()` action jumps to a different URL.

Jumping to a frame or scene

To jump to a specific frame or scene in the SWF file, you can use the `gotoAndPlay()` and `gotoAndStop()` global functions or the equivalent `gotoAndPlay()` and `gotoAndStop()` methods of the MovieClip class. Each function or method lets you specify a frame to jump to in the current scene. If your document contains multiple scenes, you can specify a scene and frame to jump to.

The following example uses the global `gotoAndPlay()` function within a button object's `onRelease` event handler to send the playhead of the Timeline that contains the button to Frame 10.

```
jump_btn.onRelease = function () {
  gotoAndPlay(10);
}
```

In the next example, the `MovieClip.gotoAndStop()` method sends the Timeline of a movie clip named `categories_mc` to Frame 10 and stops. When you use the MovieClip methods `gotoAndPlay()` and `gotoAndStop()`, you must specify an instance to which the method.

```
jump_btn.onPress = function () {
  categories_mc.gotoAndStop(10);
}
```

Playing and stopping movie clips

Unless instructed otherwise, after a SWF file starts, it plays through every frame in the Timeline. You can stop or start a SWF file by using the `play()` and `stop()` global functions or the equivalent MovieClip methods. For example, you can use `stop()` to stop a SWF file at the end of a scene before proceeding to the next scene. After a SWF file stops, it must be explicitly started again by calling `play()`.

You can use the `play()` and `stop()` functions or MovieClip methods to control the main Timeline or the Timeline of any movie clip or loaded SWF file. The movie clip you want to control must have an instance name and must be present in the Timeline.

The following `on(press)` handler attached to a button starts the playhead moving in the SWF file or movie clip that contains the button object.

```
// Attached to a button instance
on(press) {
  // Plays the Timeline that contains the button
  play();
}
```

This same `on()` event handler code will produce a different result when attached to a movie clip object rather than a button. When attached to a button object, statements made within an `on()` handler are applied to the Timeline that contains the button, by default. However, when attached to a movie clip object, statements made within an `on()` handler are applied to the movie clip to which the `on()` handler is attached.

For example, the following `on()` handler code stops the Timeline of the movie clip to which the handler is attached, not the Timeline that contains the movie clip.

```
on(press) {
   stop();
}
```

The same conditions apply to `onClipEvent()` handlers attached to movie clip objects. For instance, the following code stops the Timeline of the movie clip that bears the `onClipEvent()` handler when the clip first loads or appears on the Stage.

```
onClipEvent(load) {
   stop();
}
```

Jumping to a different URL

To open a web page in a browser window, or to pass data to another application at a defined URL, you can use the `getURL()` global function or the `MovieClip.getURL()` method. For example, you can have a button that links to a new website, or you can send Timeline variables to a CGI script for processing in the same way as you would an HTML form. You can also specify a target window, just as you would when targeting a window with an HTML anchor (`<a></a>`) tag.

For example, the following code opens the macromedia.com home page in a blank browser window when the user clicks the button instance named `homepage_btn`.

```
homepage_btn.onRelease = function () {
   getURL("http://www.macromedia.com", _blank);
}
```

You can also send variables along with the URL, using `GET` or `POST`. This is useful if the page you are loading from an application server, like a ColdFusion Server (CFM) page, expects to receive form variables. For example, suppose you want to load a CFM page named addUser.cfm that expects two form variables, `name` and `age`. To do this, you could create a movie clip named `variables_mc` that defines those two variables, as shown below.

```
variables_mc.name = "Francois";
variables_mc.age = 32;
```

The following code then loads addUser.cfm into a blank browser window and passes to the CFM page `variables_mc.name` and `variables_mc.age` in the `POST` header.

```
variables_mc.getURL("addUser.cfm", "_blank", "POST");
```

For more information, see `getURL()` on page 598.

Creating interactivity and visual effects

To create interactivity and other visual effects, you need to understand the following techniques:

- Creating a custom mouse pointer
- Getting the mouse position
- Capturing keypresses
- Setting color values
- Creating sound controls
- Detecting collisions
- Creating a simple line drawing tool

Creating a custom mouse pointer

A standard mouse pointer is the operating system's onscreen representation of the position of the user's mouse. By replacing the standard mouse pointer with one you design in Flash, you can integrate the user's mouse movement within the SWF file more closely. The sample in this section uses a custom pointer that looks like a large arrow. The power of this feature, however, lies in your ability to make the custom pointer look like anything—for example, a football to be carried to the goal line or a swatch of fabric pulled over a couch to change its color.

To create a custom pointer, you design the pointer movie clip on the Stage. Then, in ActionScript, you hide the standard pointer and track its the movement. To hide the standard pointer, you use the Mouse.hide() method of the built-in Mouse class. To use a movie clip as the custom pointer, you use the startDrag() action.

To create a custom pointer:

1 Create a movie clip to use as a custom pointer, and place an instance of the clip on the Stage.

2 Select the movie clip instance on the Stage.

3 Select Window > Development Panels > Actions to open the Actions panel if it is not already visible.

4 Type the following in the Actions panel:

```
onClipEvent (load) {
  Mouse.hide();
  startDrag(this, true);
}
onClipEvent(mouseMove){
  updateAfterEvent();
}
```

The first onClipEvent() handler hides the mouse when the movie clip first appears on the Stage; the second handler calls updateAfterEvent whenever the user moves the mouse.

The updateAfterEvent function immediately refreshes the screen after the specified event occurs, rather than when the next frame is drawn, which is the default behavior. (See updateAfterEvent() on page 947.)

5 Select Control > Test Movie to test your custom pointer.

Buttons still function when you use a custom pointer. It's a good idea to put the custom pointer on the top layer of the Timeline so that it moves in front of buttons and other objects as you move the mouse in the SWF file. Also, the tip of a custom mouse pointer is the registration point of the movie clip you're using as the custom pointer. Therefore, if you want a certain part of the movie clip to act as the mouse tip, set the registration point coordinates of the clip to be that point.

For more information about the methods of the Mouse class, see the Mouse class entry in Chapter 12, "ActionScript Dictionary," on page 409.

Getting the mouse position

You can use the _xmouse and _ymouse properties to find the location of the mouse pointer (cursor) in a SWF file. Each Timeline has an _xmouse and _ymouse property that returns the location of the mouse within its coordinate system. The position is always relative to the registration point. For the main Timeline (_level0), the registration point is the upper left corner.

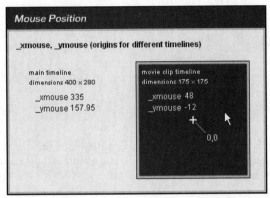

The _xmouse and _ymouse properties within the main Timeline and a movie clip Timeline

The following procedures show two ways to get the mouse position.

To get the current mouse position within the main Timeline:

1 Create two dynamic text boxes, and name them x_pos and y_pos.

2 Select Window > Development Panels > Actions to open the Actions panel if it is not already visible.

3 To return the mouse position within the main Timeline, add the following code to any frame in the _level0 SWF file:

```
x_pos = _root._xmouse;
y_pos = _root._ymouse;
```

The variables x_pos and y_pos are used as containers to hold the values of the mouse positions. You could use these variables in any script in your document. In the following onClipEvent() handler, the values of x_pos and y_pos update every time the user moves the mouse.

```
onClipEvent(mouseMove){
    x_pos = _root._xmouse;
    y_pos = _root._ymouse;
}
```

To get the current mouse position within a movie clip:

1 Create a movie clip.

2 Select the movie clip instance on the Stage. Using the Property inspector, name it `myMovieClip`.

3 Select Window > Development Panels > Actions to open the Actions panel if it is not already visible.

4 Use the movie clip's instance name to return the mouse position within the main Timeline.

For example, the following statement could be placed on any Timeline in the `_level0` SWF file to return the `_ymouse` position in the `myMovieClip` instance:

```
x_pos = _root.myMovieClip._xmouse
y_pos = _root.myMovieClip._ymouse
```

The code returns the `_xpos` and `_ypos` of the mouse, relative to the registration point.

5 Select Control > Test Movie to test the movie.

You can also determine the mouse position within a movie clip by using the `_xmouse` and `_ymouse` properties in a clip event, as shown in the following code:

```
onClipEvent(enterFrame){
  xmousePosition = this._xmouse;
  ymousePosition = this._ymouse;
}
```

For more information about the `_xmouse` and `_ymouse` properties, see `MovieClip._xmouse` on page 745 and `MovieClip._ymouse` on page 747.

Capturing keypresses

You can use the methods of the built-in Key class to detect the last key pressed by the user. The Key class does not require a constructor function; to use its methods, you simply call the methods on the class itself, as shown in the following example:

```
Key.getCode();
```

You can obtain either virtual key codes or ASCII (American Standard Code for Information Interchange) values of keypresses:

• To obtain the virtual key code of the last key pressed, use the `getCode()` method.

• To obtain the ASCII value of the last key pressed, use the `getAscii()` method.

A virtual key code is assigned to every physical key on a keyboard. For example, the Left Arrow key has the virtual key code 37. By using a virtual key code, you ensure that your SWF file's controls are the same on every keyboard, regardless of language or platform.

ASCII values are assigned to the first 127 characters in every character set. ASCII values provide information about a character on the screen. For example, the letter "A" and the letter "a" have different ASCII values.

To decide which keys to use and determine their virtual key codes, use one of these approaches:

• See the list of key codes in Appendix C, "Keyboard Keys and Key Code Values," on page 993.

• Use a Key class constant. (In the Actions toolbox, click the Built-in Classes category, click Movie, click Key, and click Constants.)

- Assign the following `onClipEvent()` handler to a movie clip, then select Control > Test Movie and press the desired key.

```
onClipEvent(keyDown) {
    trace(Key.getCode());
}
```

The key code of the desired key appears in the Output panel.

A common place to use Key class methods is within an event handler. In the following example, the user moves the car using the arrow keys. The `Key.isDown()` method indicates whether the key being pressed is the right, left, up, or down arrow. The event handler, `onEnterFrame`, determines the `Key.isDown(keyCode)` value from the `if` statements. Depending on the value, the handler instructs Flash Player to update the position of the car and to display the direction.

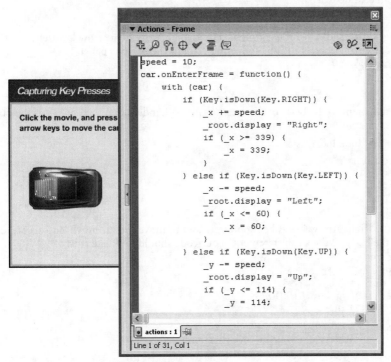

The input from the keyboard keys moves the car.

The following procedure shows how to capture keypresses to move a movie clip up, down, left, or right on the Stage, depending on which corresponding arrow key (up, down, left, or right) is currently pressed. The movie clip is confined to an arbitrary area that is 400 pixels wide and 300 pixels high. Also, a text field displays the name of the pressed key.

To create a keyboard-activated movie clip:

1 On the Stage, create a movie clip that will move in response to keyboard arrow activity.

In this example, the movie clip instance name is `car`.

2 On the Stage, create a dynamic text box that will be updated with the direction of the car. Using the Property inspector, give it an instance name of `display_txt`.

Note: Don't confuse variable names with instance names. For more information, see "About text field instance and variable names" on page 340.

3 Select Frame 1 in the Timeline; then select Window > Development Panels > Actions to open the Actions panel if it is not already visible.

4 To set how far the car moves across the screen with each keypress, define a `distance` variable and set its initial value to 10.

```
var distance = 10;
```

5 To create the event handler for the car movie clip that checks which arrow key (left, right, up, or down) is currently pressed, add the following code to the Actions panel:

```
car.onEnterFrame = function() {

}
```

6 Add a `with` statement to the body of the `onEnterFrame` handler, and specify `car` as the object of the `with` statement.

Your code should look like this:

```
var distance = 10;
car.onEnterFrame = function() {
    with (car) {
    }
}
```

7 To check if the Right Arrow key is being pressed, and to move the car movie clip accordingly, add code to the body of the `with` statement. Your code should look like this:

```
distance = 10;
car.onEnterFrame = function() {
  with (car) {
    if (Key.isDown(Key.RIGHT)) {
      _x += distance;
      if (_x >= 400) {
        _x = 400;
      }
      _root.display_txt.text = "Right";
    }
  }
}
```

If the Right Arrow key is down, the car's _x property is increased by the amount specified by the `distance` variable. The next `if` statement tests if the value of the clip's _x property is greater than or equal to 400 (if(_x >=400)); if so, its position is fixed at 400. Also, the word *Right* should appear in the SWF file.

8 Use similar code to check if the Left Arrow, Up Arrow, or Down Arrow key is being pressed. Your code should look like this:

```
var distance = 10;
car.onEnterFrame = function() {
  with (car) {
    if (Key.isDown(Key.RIGHT)) {
      _x += distance;
      if (_x >= 400) {
        _x = 400;
      }
      _root.display_txt.text = "Right";
    } else if (Key.isDown(Key.LEFT)) {
      _x -= distance;
      if (_x < 0) {
        _x = 0;
      }
      _root.display_txt.text = "Left";
    } else if (Key.isDown(Key.UP)) {
    _y -= distance;
      if (_y < 0) {
        _y = 0 ;
      }
    _root.display_txt.text = "Up";
    } else if (Key.isDown(Key.DOWN)) {
      _y += distance;
      if (_y > 300) {
        _y = 300;
      }
    _root.display_txt.text = "Down";
    }
  }
}
```

9 Select Control > Test Movie to test the file.

For more information about the methods of the Key class, see the Key class entry in Chapter 12, "ActionScript Dictionary," on page 409.

Setting color values

You can use the methods of the built-in Color class to adjust the color of a movie clip. The setRGB() method assigns hexadecimal RGB (red, green, blue) values to the movie clip. The following example uses setRGB() to change an object's color based on user input.

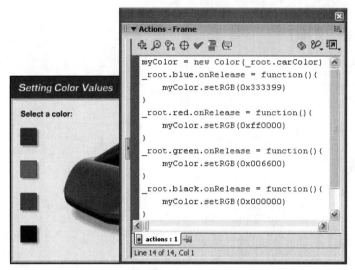

The button action creates a Color object and changes the color of the car based on user input.

To set the color value of a movie clip:

1 Select a movie clip on the Stage.

2 In the Property inspector, enter carColor as the instance name.

3 Create a button named color chip, place four instances of the button on the Stage, and name them red, green, blue, and black.

4 Select Frame 1 in the main Timeline, and select Window > Development Panels > Actions.

5 To create a Color object that targets the carColor movie clip, add the following code to the Actions panel:

```
myColor = new Color(_root.carColor);
```

6 To make the blue button change the color of the carColor movie clip to blue, add the following code to the Actions panel:

```
_root.blue.onRelease = function(){
  myColor.setRGB(0x0000ff)
}
```

The hexadecimal value 0x0000ff is blue. The following table displays the other colors you'll use and their hexadecimal values:

7 Repeat step 6 for the other buttons (red, green, and black) to change the color of the movie clip to the corresponding color. Your code should now look like this:

```
myColor = new Color(_root.carColor)
_root.blue.onRelease = function(){
  myColor.setRGB(0x0000ff)
}
_root.red.onRelease = function(){
  myColor.setRGB(0xff0000)
}
_root.green.onRelease = function(){
  myColor.setRGB(0x00ff00)
}
_root.black.onRelease = function(){
  myColor.setRGB(0x000000)
}
```

8 Select Control > Test Movie to change the color of the movie clip.

For more information about the methods of the Color class, see the Color class entry in Chapter 12, "ActionScript Dictionary," on page 409.

Creating sound controls

You use the built-in Sound class to control sounds in a SWF file. To use the methods of the Sound class, you must first create a Sound object. Then you can use the `attachSound()` method to insert a sound from the library into a SWF file while the SWF file is running.

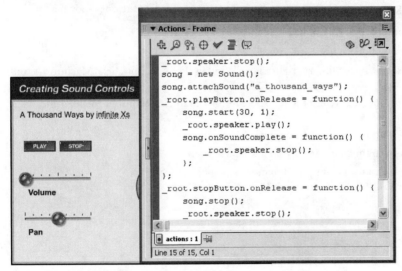

When the user releases the Play button, a song plays through the speaker.

The Sound class's setVolume() method controls the volume, and the setPan() method adjusts the left and right balance of a sound.

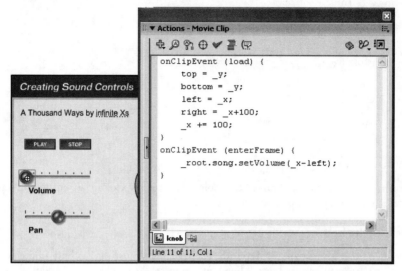

When the user drags the volume slider, the setVolume() method is called.

The following procedures show how to create sound controls like the ones shown above.

To attach a sound to a Timeline:

1 Select File > Import to import a sound.

2 Select the sound in the library, right-click (Windows) or Control-click (Macintosh), and select Linkage.

3 Select Export for ActionScript and Export in First Frame; then give it the identifier a_thousand_ways.

4 Add a button to the Stage and name it playButton.

5 Add a button to the Stage and name it stopButton.

6 Add a movie clip to the Stage and name it speaker.

7 Select Frame 1 in the main Timeline, and select Window > Development Panels > Actions. Add the following code to the Actions panel:

```
speaker.stop();
song = new Sound();
song.onSoundComplete = function() {
   speaker.stop();
};
song.attachSound("a_thousand_ways");
playButton.onRelease = function() {
   song.start();
   speaker.play();

};
stopButton.onRelease = function () {
   song.stop();
   speaker.stop();
}
```

This code first stops the speaker movie clip. It then creates a new Sound object (song) and attaches the sound whose linkage identifier is a_thousand_ways. Next, it defines an onSoundComplete handler for the song object, which stops the speaker movie clip once the sound has finished. Lastly, onRelease handlers associated with the playButton and stopButton objects start and stop the sound using the Sound.start() and Sound.stop() methods, and also play and stop the speaker movie clip.

8 Select Control > Test Movie to hear the sound.

To create a sliding volume control:

1 Drag a button to the Stage.

2 Select the button and select Modify > Convert to Symbol. Be careful to select the movie clip behavior.

   This creates a movie clip with the button on its first frame.

3 Select the movie clip and select Edit > Edit Selected.

4 Select the button and select Window > Development Panels > Actions.

5 Enter the following actions:

```
on (press) {
    startDrag(this, false, left, top, right, bottom);
}
on (release) {
    stopDrag();
}
```

The startDrag() parameters left, top, right, and bottom are variables set in a clip action.

6 Select Edit > Edit Document to return to the main Timeline.

7 Select the movie clip on the Stage.

8 Enter the following actions:

```
onClipEvent (load) {
    top = _y;
    bottom = _y;
    left = _x;
    right = _x+100;
    _x += 100;
}
onClipEvent (enterFrame) {
    _parent.song.setVolume(_x-left);
}
```

9 Select Control > Test Movie to use the volume slider.

To create a sliding balance control:

1 Drag a button to the Stage.

2 Select the button and select Insert > Convert to Symbol. Select the movie clip property.

3 Select the movie clip and select Edit > Edit Symbol.

4 Select the button and select Window > Development Panels > Actions.

5 Enter the following actions:

```
on (press) {
    startDrag ("", false, left, top, right, bottom);
    dragging = true;
}
on (release, releaseOutside) {
    stopDrag ();
    dragging = false;
}
```

The startDrag() parameters left, top, right, and bottom are variables set in a clip action.

6 Select Edit > Edit Document to return to the main Timeline.

7 Select the movie clip on the Stage.

8 Enter the following actions:

```
onClipEvent(load){
    top=_y;
    bottom=_y;
    left=_x-50;
    right=_x+50;
    center=_x;
}

onClipEvent(enterFrame){
    if (dragging==true){
        _parent.setPan((_x-center)*2);
    }
}
```

9 Select Control > Test Movie to use the balance slider.

For more information about the methods of the Sound class, see the Sound class entry in Chapter 12, "ActionScript Dictionary," on page 409.

Detecting collisions

The hitTest() method of the MovieClip class detects collisions in a SWF file. It checks to see if an object has collided with a movie clip and returns a Boolean value (true or false).

There are two cases in which you would want to know whether a collision has occurred: to test if the user has arrived at a certain static area on the Stage, and to determine when one movie clip has reached another. With hitTest(), you can determine these results.

You can use the parameters of hitTest() to specify the *x* and *y* coordinates of a hit area on the Stage, or use the target path of another movie clip as a hit area. When specifying *x* and *y*, hitTest() returns true if the point identified by (*x*, *y*) is a nontransparent point. When a target is passed to hitTest(), the bounding boxes of the two movie clips are compared. If they overlap, hitTest() returns true. If the two boxes do not intersect, hitTest() returns false.

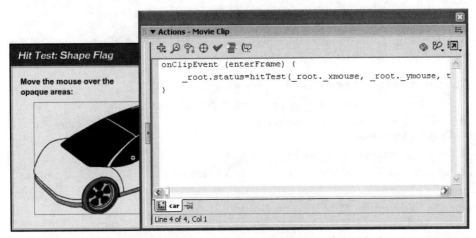

"True" appears in the text field whenever the mouse pointer is over the car body.

You can also use hitTest() to test a collision between two movie clips.

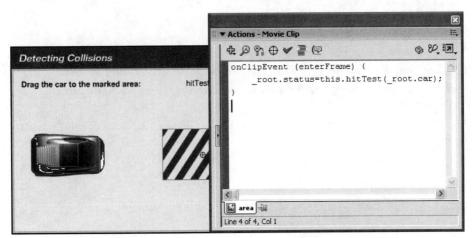

"True" appears in the text field whenever one movie clip touches the other.

The following procedures show how to detect collision using the car example.

To perform collision detection between a movie clip and a point on the Stage:

1 Create a new movie clip on the Stage, and enter box as the instance name in the Property inspector.

2 Create a dynamic text box on the Stage, and enter status as the instance name in the Property inspector.

3 Select the first frame on Layer 1 in the Timeline.

4 Select Window > Development Panels > Actions to open the Actions panel, if it is not already visible.

5 Add the following code in the Actions panel:

```
box.onEnterFrame = function () {
   status.text = this.hitTest(_xmouse, _ymouse, true);
}
```

6 Select Control > Test Movie, and move the mouse over the movie clip to test the collision.

The value true is displayed whenever the mouse is over a nontransparent pixel.

To perform collision detection on two movie clips:

1 Drag two movie clips to the Stage, and give them the instance names car and area.

2 Create a dynamic text box on the Stage, and enter status as the instance name in the Property inspector.

3 Select the first frame on Layer 1 in the Timeline.

4 Select Window > Development Panels > Actions to open the Actions panel, if it is not already visible.

5 Enter the following code in the Actions panel:

```
area.onEnterFrame = function () {
   status.text=this.hitTest(car);
}
car.onPress = function (){
   this.startDrag(false);
   updateAfterEvent();
}
car.onRelease = function () {
   this.stopDrag();
}
```

6 Select Control > Test Movie, and drag the movie clip to test the collision detection.

Whenever the bounding box of the car intersects the bounding box of the area, the status is true.

For more information, see MovieClip.hitTest() in Chapter 12, "ActionScript Dictionary," on page 409.

Creating a simple line drawing tool

You can use methods of the MovieClip class to draw lines and fills on the Stage as the SWF file plays. This allows you to create drawing tools for users and to draw shapes in the SWF file in response to events. The drawing methods are `beginFill()`, `beginGradientFill()`, `clear()`, `curveTo()`, `endFill()`, `lineTo()`, `lineStyle()`, and `moveTo()`. You can apply these methods to any movie clip instance (for instance, `myClip.lineTo()`) or to a level (`_root.curveTo()`).

The `lineTo()` and `curveTo()` methods let you draw lines and curves, respectively. You specify a line color, thickness, and alpha setting for a line or curve with the `lineStyle()` method. The `moveTo()` drawing method sets the current drawing position to *x* and *y* Stage coordinates you specify.

The `beginFill()` and `beginGradientFill()` methods fill a closed path with a solid or gradient fill, respectively, and `endFill()` applies the fill specified in the last call to `beginFill()` or `beginGradientFill()`. The `clear()` method erases what's been drawn in the specified movie clip object.

For more information, see `MovieClip.beginFill()` on page 693, `MovieClip.beginGradientFill()` on page 694, `MovieClip.clear()` on page 697, `MovieClip.curveTo()` on page 700, `MovieClip.endFill()` on page 703, `MovieClip.lineTo()` on page 715, `MovieClip.lineStyle()` on page 714, and `MovieClip.moveTo()` on page 720.

To create a simple line drawing tool:

1 In a new document, create a button on the Stage, and enter `clear_btn` as the instance name in the Property inspector.

2 Select Frame 1 in the Timeline; then select Window > Development Panels > Actions to open the Actions panel if it's not already visible.

3 In the Actions panel, enter the following code:

```
_root.onMouseDown = function() {
    _root.lineStyle(5, 0xFF0000, 100);
    _root.moveTo(_root._xmouse, _root._ymouse);
    isDrawing = true;
};
_root.onMouseMove = function() {
    if (isDrawing == true) {
        _root.lineTo(_root._xmouse, _root._ymouse);
        updateAfterEvent();
    }
};
_root.onMouseUp = function() {
    isDrawing = false;
};
clear_btn.onRelease = function() {
    _root.clear();
};
```

4 Select Control > Test Movie to test the movie. Click and drag your mouse to draw a line on the Stage. Click the button to erase what you've drawn.

Deconstructing a sample script

In the sample SWF file zapper.swf (which you can view in Using Flash Help), when a user drags the bug to the electrical outlet, the bug falls and the outlet shakes. The main Timeline has only one frame and contains three objects: the ladybug, the outlet, and a reset button. Each of these objects is a movie clip instance.

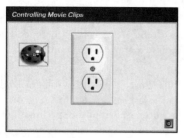

There is one script in the SWF file; it's attached to the bug instance, as shown in the following Actions panel:

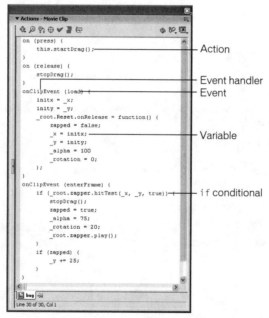

The Actions panel with the script attached to the bug instance

The bug's instance name is bug, and the outlet's instance name is zapper. In the script, the bug is referred to as this because the script is attached to the bug and the reserved word this refers to the object that contains it.

There are two `onClipEvent()` handlers with two different events: `load` and `enterFrame`. The actions in the `onClipEvent(load)` statement execute only once, when the SWF file loads. The actions in the `onClipEvent(enterFrame)` statement execute every time the playhead enters a frame. Even in a one-frame SWF file, the playhead still enters that frame repeatedly and the script executes repeatedly. The following actions occur within each `onClipEvent()` handler:

onClipEvent(load)   Two variables, `initx` and `inity`, are defined to store the initial *x* and *y* positions of the `bug` movie clip instance. A function is defined and assigned to the `onRelease` event of the Reset instance. This function is called each time the mouse button is pressed and released on the Reset button. The function places the ladybug back in its starting position on the Stage, resets its rotation and alpha values, and resets the `zapped` variable to `false`.

onClipEvent(enterFrame)   A conditional `if` statement uses the `hitTest()` method to check whether the bug instance is touching the outlet instance (`_root.zapper`). There are two possible outcomes of the evaluation, `true` or `false`:

```
onClipEvent (load) {
  initx = _x;
  inity = _y;
  _root.Reset.onRelease = function() {
    zapped = false;
    _x = initx;
    _y = inity;
    _alpha = 100
    _rotation = 0;
  };
}
```

If the `hitTest()` method returns `true`, the `stopDrag()` method is called, the `zapper` variable is set to `true`, the alpha and rotation properties are changed, and the `zapped` instance is told to play.

If the `hitTest()` method returns `false`, none of the code within the curly braces ({ }) immediately following the `if` statement runs.

There are two `on()` handlers attached to the `bug` instance with two different events: `press` and `release`. The actions in the `on(press)` statement execute when the mouse button is pressed over the bug instance. The actions in the `on(release)` statement execute when the mouse button is released over the bug instance. The following actions occur within each `onClipEvent()` handler:

on(press)   A `startDrag()` action makes the ladybug draggable. Because the script is attached to the `bug` instance, the keyword `this` indicates that it is the `bug` instance that is draggable:

```
on (press) {
  this.startDrag();
}
```

on(release)   A `stopDrag()` action stops the drag action:

```
on (release) {
  stopDrag();
}
```

To watch the SWF file play, see ActionScript Reference Guide Help.

PART III
Working with Objects and Classes

This part discusses the Macromedia Flash runtime object model and its capabilities, focusing on working with movie clips and text. This part also describes how to create your own classes and interfaces with ActionScript 2.0.

CHAPTER 6
Using the Built-In Classes

In addition to the ActionScript core language elements and constructs (`for` and `while` loops, for example) and primitive data types (numbers, strings, and arrays) described earlier (see "ActionScript Basics" on page 229), ActionScript also provides a number of built-in classes, or *complex data types*. These classes provide you with a variety of scripting features and functionality.

Some of these classes are based on the ECMAScript specification and are referred to as *core ActionScript classes*. These classes include the Array, Boolean, Date, and Math classes. For more information, see "Core classes" on page 319.)

The rest of the built-in ActionScript classes are specific to Macromedia Flash and Flash Player object model. To understand the distinction between core ActionScript classes and those specific to Flash, consider the distinction between core and client-side JavaScript: just as client-side JavaScript classes provide control over the client environment (the web browser and web page content), the classes specific to Flash provide runtime control over the appearance and behavior of a Flash application.

This chapter introduces the built-in ActionScript classes, describes common tasks you can perform with these classes, and provides code examples. For an overview of these classes, see "Overview of built-in classes" on page 319. For an overview of working with classes and objects in object-oriented programming, see "About classes and instances" on page 318.

About classes and instances

In object-oriented programming, a *class* defines a category of object. A class describes the properties (data) and behavior (methods) for an object, much like an architectural blueprint describes the characteristics of a building. To use the properties and methods defined by a class, you must first create an *instance* of that class. The relationship between an instance and its class is similar to the relationship between a house and its architectural blueprints.

Creating a new object

To create an instance of an ActionScript class, use the new operator to invoke the class's constructor function. The constructor function always has the same name as the class, and returns an instance of the class, which you typically assign to a variable.

For example, the following code creates a new Sound object.

```
var song:Sound= new Sound();
```

In some cases, you don't need to create an instance of a class to use it. For more information, see "About class (static) members" on page 318.

Accessing object properties

Use the dot (.) operator to access the value of a property in an object. Put the name of the object on the left side of the dot, and put the name of the property on the right side. For example, in the following statement, myObject is the object and name is the property:

```
myObject.name
```

The following code creates a new TextField object, and then sets its autoSize property to true.

```
var my_text = new TextField();
my_text.autoSize = true;
```

You can also use the array access operator ([]) to access the properties of an object. See "Dot and array access operators" on page 253.

Calling object methods

You call an object's method by using the dot (.) operator followed by the method. For example, the following code creates a new Sound object and calls its setVolume() method.

```
mySound = new Sound(this);
mySound.setVolume(50);
```

About class (static) members

Some built-in ActionScript classes have what are called *class members* (or *static members*). Class members (properties and methods) are accessed or invoked not on an instance of the class but on the class name itself. That is, you don't create an instance of the class in order to use those properties and methods.

For example, all of the properties of the Math class are static. The following code invokes the max() method of the Math class to determine the larger of two numbers.

```
var largerNumber = Math.max(10, 20);
```

Overview of built-in classes

This section lists all the ActionScript classes, including a brief description of each class and cross-references to other relevant sections of the documentation.

Core classes

The core ActionScript classes are those borrowed directly from ECMAScript. In the Actions toolbox, these classes are located in the Built-in Classes > Core subfolder.

Class	Description
Arguments	An array that contains the values that were passed as parameters to any function. See the Arguments class entry in Chapter 12, "ActionScript Dictionary," on page 409.
Array	The Array class contains methods and properties for working with array objects. See the Array class entry in Chapter 12, "ActionScript Dictionary," on page 409.
Boolean	The Boolean class is a wrapper for Boolean (`true` or `false`) values. See the Boolean class entry in Chapter 12, "ActionScript Dictionary," on page 409.
Button	The Button class provides methods and properties for working with button objects. See the Button class entry in Chapter 12, "ActionScript Dictionary," on page 409.
Date	The Date class provides access to date and time values relative to universal time (Greenwich Mean Time) or relative to the operating system on which Flash Player is running. See the Date class entry in Chapter 12, "ActionScript Dictionary," on page 409.
Error	The Error class contains information about errors that occur in your scripts. You typically use the `throw` statement to generate an error condition, which you can then handle using a `try..catch..finally` statement. See `try..catch..finally` and the Error class entries in Chapter 12, "ActionScript Dictionary," on page 409.
Function	The Function class is the class representation of all ActionScript functions, including those native to ActionScript and those that you define. See the Function class entry in Chapter 12, "ActionScript Dictionary," on page 409.
Math	The Math class lets you access and manipulate mathematical constants and functions. All of the properties and methods of the Math class are static, and must be called with the syntax `Math.method(parameter)` or `Math.constant`. See the Math class entry in Chapter 12, "ActionScript Dictionary," on page 409.
Number	The Number class is a wrapper for the primitive number data type. See the Number class entry in Chapter 12, "ActionScript Dictionary," on page 409.
Object	The Object class is at the root of the ActionScript class hierarchy; all other classes inherit its methods and properties. See the Object class entry in Chapter 12, "ActionScript Dictionary," on page 409.
String	The String class is a wrapper for the string primitive data type, which allows you to use the methods and properties of the String object to manipulate primitive string value types. See the String class entry in Chapter 12, "ActionScript Dictionary," on page 409.

Classes specific to Flash Player

The following tables list the classes that are specific to Flash Player and the Flash runtime model. These classes are typically split into four categories: movie classes (which provide overall control of SWF files and Flash Player), media classes (for working with sound and video), client-server classes (for working with XML and other external data sources), and authoring classes (which provide control over the Flash authoring environment).

Note: This categorization affects the locations of the classes in the Actions toolbox, but not how you use the classes.

Movie classes

The movie classes provide control over most visual elements in a SWF file, including movie clips, text fields, and buttons. The movie classes are located in the Actions toolbox in the Built-in Classes > Movie subfolder.

Class	Description
Accessibility	The Accessibility class manages communication between SWF files and screen reader applications. You use the methods of this class together with the global _accProps property to control accessible properties for movie clips, buttons, and text fields at runtime. See _accProps and the Accessibility class entries in Chapter 12, "ActionScript Dictionary," on page 409.
Button	Every button in a SWF file is an instance of the Button class. The Button class provides methods, properties, and event handlers for working with buttons. See the Button class entry in Chapter 12, "ActionScript Dictionary," on page 409.
Color	The Color class lets you get and set RGB color values for movie clip objects. For more information, see the Color class entry in Chapter 12, "ActionScript Dictionary," on page 409. For an example of using the Color class to change the color of movie clips, see "Setting color values" on page 304.
ContextMenu	The ContextMenu class lets you control the contents of the Flash Player context menu. You can associate separate ContextMenu objects with MovieClip, Button, or TextField objects by using the menu property available to those classes. You can also add custom menu items to a ContextMenu object by using the ContextMenuItem class. See the ContextMenu class and ContextMenuItem class entries in Chapter 12, "ActionScript Dictionary," on page 409.
ContextMenuItem	The ContextMenuItem class lets you create new menu items that appear in the Flash Player context menu. You add new menu items that you create with this class to the Flash Player context menu by using the ContextMenu class. See the ContextMenu class and ContextMenuItem class entries in Chapter 12, "ActionScript Dictionary," on page 409.
Key	The Key class provides methods and properties for getting information about the keyboard and keypresses. For more information, see the Key class entry in Chapter 12, "ActionScript Dictionary," on page 409. For an example of capturing keypresses to create an interactive SWF file, see "Capturing keypresses" on page 300.

Class	Description
LocalConnection	The LocalConnection class lets two SWF files running on the same computer communicate. See the LocalConnection class entry in Chapter 12, "ActionScript Dictionary," on page 409.
Mouse	The Mouse class provides control over the mouse in a SWF file; for example, this class lets you hide or show the mouse pointer. For more information, see the Mouse class entry in Chapter 12, "ActionScript Dictionary," on page 409. For an example of using the Mouse class, see "Creating a custom mouse pointer" on page 298.
MovieClip	Every movie clip in a Flash movie is an instance of the MovieClip class. You use the methods and properties of this class to control movie clip objects. See Chapter 7, "Working with Movie Clips," on page 325 and the MovieClip class entry in Chapter 12, "ActionScript Dictionary," on page 409.
MovieClipLoader	The MovieClipLoader class lets you track the download progress of SWF and JPEG files using an event listener mechanism. See "Preloading SWF and JPEG files" on page 403 and the MovieClipLoader class entry in Chapter 12, "ActionScript Dictionary," on page 409.
PrintJob	The PrintJob class lets you print content that is rendered dynamically and multipage documents. See the PrintJob class entry in Chapter 12, "ActionScript Dictionary," on page 409 and "Using the ActionScript PrintJob class" in Using Flash Help.
Selection	The Selection class lets you get and set text field focus, text field selection spans, and text field insertion points. See the Selection class entry in Chapter 12, "ActionScript Dictionary," on page 409.
SharedObject	The SharedObject class provides local data storage on the client computer. See the SharedObject class entry in Chapter 12, "ActionScript Dictionary," on page 409.
Stage	The Stage class provides information about a SWF file's dimensions, alignment, and scale mode, and reports Stage resize events. See the Stage class entry in Chapter 12, "ActionScript Dictionary," on page 409.
System	The System class provides information about Flash Player and the system on which Flash Player is running (for example, screen resolution and current system language). It also lets you show or hide the Flash Player Settings panel and modify SWF file security settings. See the System class entry in Chapter 12, "ActionScript Dictionary," on page 409.
TextField	The TextField class provides control over dynamic and input text fields. See Chapter 8, "Working with Text," on page 339 and the TextField class entry in Chapter 12, "ActionScript Dictionary," on page 409.
TextField.StyleSheet	The TextField.StyleSheet class (an "inner class" of the TextField class) lets you create and apply CSS text styles to HTML- or XML-formatted text. See "Formatting text with Cascading Style Sheets" on page 343 and the TextField.StyleSheet class entry in Chapter 12, "ActionScript Dictionary," on page 409.
TextFormat	The TextFormat class lets you apply formatting styles to characters or paragraphs in a TextField object. See "Using the TextFormat class" on page 341 and the TextFormat class entry in Chapter 12, "ActionScript Dictionary," on page 409.

Media classes

The media classes provide playback control of sound and video in a SWF file, as well as access to the user's microphone and camera, if they are installed. These classes are located in the Built-In Classes > Media subfolder in the Actions toolbox.

Class	Description
Camera	The Camera class provides access to the user's camera, if one is installed. When used with Flash Communication Server MX, your SWF file can capture, broadcast, and record images and video from a user's camera. See the Camera class entry in Chapter 12, "ActionScript Dictionary," on page 409.
Microphone	The Microphone class provides access to the user's microphone, if one is installed. When used with Flash Communication Server MX, your SWF file can broadcast and record audio from a user's microphone. See the Microphone class entry in Chapter 12, "ActionScript Dictionary," on page 409.
NetConnection	The NetConnection class is used to establish a local streaming connection for playing a Flash Video (FLV) file from an HTTP address or from the local file system. For more information, see the NetConnection class entry in Chapter 12, "ActionScript Dictionary," on page 409. For more information on playing FLV files over the Internet, see "Playing back external FLV files dynamically" on page 401.
NetStream	The NetStream class is used to control playback of FLV files. For more information, see the NetStream class entry in Chapter 12, "ActionScript Dictionary," on page 409. For more information on playing FLV files over the Internet, see "Playing back external FLV files dynamically" on page 401.
Sound	The Sound class provides control over sounds in a SWF file. For more information, see the Sound class entry in Chapter 12, "ActionScript Dictionary," on page 409. For an example of using the Sound class to create volume and balance controllers, see "Creating sound controls" on page 305.
Video	The Video class is used to display video objects in a SWF file. See the Video class entry in Chapter 12, "ActionScript Dictionary," on page 409.

Client-server classes

The following table lists classes that let you send and receive data from external sources or communicate with application servers over FTP, HTTP, or HTTPS.

Note: In Flash Player 7, a SWF file can load data only from exactly the same domain from which it was served. For more information, see "Flash Player security features" on page 392 and "About allowing cross-domain data loading" on page 394.

These classes are located in the Built-In Classes > Client/Server subfolder in the Actions panel.

Class	Description
LoadVars	The LoadVars class is an alternative to the `loadVariables()` action for transferring variables between a SWF file and a server in name-value pairs. See "Using the LoadVars class" on page 384 and the LoadVars class entry in Chapter 12, "ActionScript Dictionary," on page 409.
XML	The XML class extends the XMLNode class and provides methods, properties, and event handlers for working with XML-formatted data, including loading and parsing external XML, creating new XML documents, and navigating XML document trees. See "Using the XML class" on page 385 and the XML class entry in Chapter 12, "ActionScript Dictionary," on page 409.
XMLNode	The XMLNode class represents a single node in an XML document tree. It is the XML class's superclass. See the XMLNode class entry in Chapter 12, "ActionScript Dictionary," on page 409.
XMLSocket	The XMLSocket class lets you create a persistent socket connection with another computer for low-latency data transfer, like that required for real-time chat applications. See "Using the XMLSocket class" on page 388 and the XMLSocket class entry in Chapter 12, "ActionScript Dictionary," on page 409.

Authoring classes

The authoring classes are available only in the Flash authoring environment. These classes are found in the Built-In Classes > Authoring subfolder in the Actions toolbox.

Class	Description
CustomActionsg	The CustomActions class lets you manage any custom actions that are registered with the authoring tool. See the CustomActions class entry in Chapter 12, "ActionScript Dictionary," on page 409.
Live Preview	The Live Preview feature (listed under Built-in Classes in the Actions toolbox, though not a class) provides a single function called `onUpdate` that is used by component developers. See `onUpdate` in Chapter 12, "ActionScript Dictionary," on page 409.

CHAPTER 7
Working with Movie Clips

Movie clips are self-contained miniature SWF files that run independently of each other and the Timeline that contains them. For example, if the main Timeline has only one frame and a movie clip in that frame has ten frames, each frame in the movie clip plays when you play the main SWF file. A movie clip can, in turn, contain other movie clips, or *nested clips*. Movie clips nested in this way have a hierarchical relationship, where the *parent clip* contain one or more *child clips*.

Every movie clip instance has a name, called its *instance name*, that uniquely identifies it as an object that can be controlled with ActionScript. Specifically, the instance name identifies it as an object of the MovieClip class type. You use the properties and methods of the MovieClip class to control the appearance and behavior of movie clips at runtime.

You can think of movie clips as autonomous objects that can respond to events, send messages to other movie clip objects, maintain their state, and manage their child clips. In this way, movie clips provide the foundation of *component-based architecture* in Macromedia Flash MX 2004 and Macromedia Flash MX Professional 2004. In fact, the components available in the Components panel (Window > Development Panels > Components) are sophisticated movie clips that have been designed and programmed to look and behave in certain ways. For information on creating components, see *Using Components*.

About controlling movie clips with ActionScript

You can use global ActionScript functions or the methods of the MovieClip class to perform tasks on movie clips. Some MovieClip methods perform the same tasks as functions of the same name; other MovieClip methods, such as hitTest() and swapDepths(), don't have corresponding function names.

The following example illustrates the difference between using a method and using a function. Both statements duplicate the instance my_mc, name the new clip newClip, and place it at a depth of 5.

```
my_mc.duplicateMovieClip("newClip", 5);
duplicateMovieClip("my_mc", "newClip", 5);
```

When a function and a method offer similar behaviors, you can choose to control movie clips by using either one. The choice depends on your preference and familiarity with writing scripts in ActionScript. Whether you use a function or a method, the target Timeline must be loaded in Flash Player when the function or method is called.

To use a method, invoke it by using the target path of the instance name, a dot, and then the method name and parameters, as in the following statements:

```
myMovieClip.play();
parentClip.childClip.gotoAndPlay(3);
```

In the first statement, `play()` moves the playhead in the `myMovieClip` instance. In the second statement, `gotoAndPlay()` sends the playhead in `childClip` (which is a child of the instance `parentClip`) to Frame 3 and continues to move the playhead.

Global functions that control a Timeline have a *target* parameter that allows you to specify the target path to the instance that you want to control. For example, in the following script `startDrag()` targets the `customCursor` instance and makes it draggable:

```
on(press){
   startDrag("customCursor");
}
```

The following functions target movie clips: `loadMovie()`, `unloadMovie()`, `loadVariables()`, `setProperty()`, `startDrag()`, `duplicateMovieClip()`, and `removeMovieClip()`. To use these functions, you must enter a target path for the function's *target* parameter to indicate the target of the function.

The following MovieClip methods can control movie clips or loaded levels and do not have equivalent functions: `MovieClip.attachMovie()`, `MovieClip.createEmptyMovieClip()`, `MovieClip.createTextField()`, `MovieClip.getBounds()`, `MovieClip.getBytesLoaded()`, `MovieClip.getBytesTotal()`, `MovieClip.getDepth()`, `MovieClip.getInstanceAtDepth()`, `MovieClip.getNextHighestDepth()`, `MovieClip.globalToLocal()`, `MovieClip.localToGlobal()`, `MovieClip.hitTest()`, `MovieClip.setMask()`, `MovieClip.swapDepths()`.

For more information about these functions and methods, see Chapter 12, "ActionScript Dictionary," on page 409.

Calling multiple methods on a single movie clip

You can use the `with` statement to address a movie clip once, and then execute a series of methods on that clip. The `with` statement works on all ActionScript objects (for example, Array, Color, and Sound), not just movie clips.

The `with` statement takes an object as a parameter. The object you specify is added to the end of the current target path. All actions nested inside a `with` statement are carried out inside the new target path, or scope. For example, in the following script, the `with` statement is passed the object `donut.hole` to change the properties of `hole`:

```
with (donut.hole){
   _alpha = 20;
   _xscale = 150;
   _yscale = 150;
}
```

The script behaves as if the statements inside the `with` statement were called from the Timeline of the `hole` instance. The above code is equivalent to the following:

```
donut.hole._alpha = 20;
donut.hole._xscale = 150;
donut.hole._yscale = 150;
```

The above code is also equivalent to the following:

```
with (donut){
    hole._alpha = 20;
    hole._xscale = 150;
    hole._yscale = 150;
}
```

Loading and unloading additional SWF files

To play additional SWF files without closing Flash Player, or to switch SWF files without loading another HTML page, you can use the global `loadMovie()` function or `loadMovie()` method of the MovieClip class. You can also use `loadMovie()` to send variables to a CGI script, which generates a SWF file as its CGI output. When you load a SWF file, you can specify a level or movie clip target into which the SWF file will load. If you load a SWF file into a target, the loaded SWF file inherits the properties of the targeted movie clip. Once the movie is loaded, you can change those properties.

The `unloadMovie()` method removes a SWF file previously loaded by `loadMovie()`. Explicitly unloading SWF files with `unloadMovie()` ensures a smooth transition between SWF files and may decrease the memory required by Flash Player.

Use `loadMovie()` to do any of the following:

- Play a sequence of banner ads that are SWF files by placing a `loadMovie()` function at the end of each SWF file to load the next SWF file.
- Develop a branching interface that lets the user choose among several different SWF files.
- Build a navigation interface with navigation controls in level 0 that load other levels. Loading levels produces smoother transitions than loading new HTML pages in a browser.

For more information on loading movies, see "Loading external SWF and JPEG files" on page 398.

Specifying a root Timeline for loaded SWF files

The `_root` ActionScript property specifies or returns a reference to the root Timeline of a SWF file. If a SWF file has multiple levels, the root Timeline is on the level that contains the currently executing script. For example, if a script in level 1 evaluates `_root`, `_level1` is returned. However, the Timeline specified by `_root` can change depending on whether a SWF file is running independently (in its own level) or has been loaded into a movie clip instance by a `loadMovie()` call.

For example, consider a file named container.swf that has a movie clip instance named `target_mc` on its main Timeline. The container.swf file declares a variable named `userName` on its main Timeline; the same script then loads another file called contents.swf into the movie clip `target_mc`.

```
// In container.swf:
_root.userName = "Tim";
target_mc.loadMovie("contents.swf");
```

The loaded SWF file, contents.swf, also declares a variable named `userName` on its root Timeline.

```
// In content.swf:
_root.userName = "Mary";
```

When contents.swf loads into the movie clip in container.swf, the value of userName that's attached to the root Timeline of the hosting SWF file (container.swf) would be set to "Mary". This could cause code in container.swf (as well as contents.swf) to malfunction.

To force _root to always evaluate to the Timeline of the loaded SWF file, rather than the actual root Timeline, use the _lockroot property. This property can be set either by the loading SWF file or the SWF file being loaded. When _lockroot is set to true on a movie clip instance, that movie clip will act as _root for any SWF file loaded into it. When _lockroot is set to true within a SWF file, that SWF file will act as its own root, no matter what other SWF file loads it. Any movie clip, and any number of movie clips, can set _lockroot to true. By default, this property is false.

For example, the author of container.swf could attach the following code to the target_mc movie clip:

```
// Attached to target_mc movie clip:
onClipEvent (load) {
    this._lockroot = true;
}
```

This would ensure that references to _root in contents.swf—or any SWF file loaded into target_mc—will refer to its own Timeline, not the actual root Timeline of container.swf.

Equivalently, the author of contents.swf could add the following code to its main Timeline.

```
// Within contents.swf:
this._lockroot = true;
```

This would ensure that no matter where contents.swf is loaded, any reference it makes to _root will refer to its own main Timeline, not that of the hosting SWF file.

For more information, see MovieClip._lockroot on page 719.

Loading JPEG files into movie clips

You can use the loadMovie() function, or the MovieClip method of the same name, to load JPEG image files into a movie clip instance. You can also use the loadMovieNum() function to load a JPEG file into a level.

When you load an image into a movie clip, the upper left corner of the image is placed at the registration point of the movie clip. Because this registration point is often the center of the movie clip, the loaded image may not appear centered. Also, when you load an image to a root Timeline, the upper left corner of the image is placed on the upper left corner of the Stage. The loaded image inherits rotation and scaling from the movie clip, but the original content of the movie clip is removed.

For more information, see "Loading external SWF and JPEG files" on page 398, loadMovie() on page 624, MovieClip.loadMovie() on page 716, and loadMovieNum() on page 625.

Changing movie clip position and appearance

To change the properties of a movie clip as it plays, write a statement that assigns a value to a property or use the `setProperty()` function. For example, the following code sets the rotation of instance mc to 45:

```
mc._rotation = 45;
```

This is equivalent to the following code, which uses the `setProperty()` function:

```
setProperty("mc", _rotation, 45);
```

Some properties, called *read-only properties,* have values that you can read but not set. (These properties are specified as read-only in their ActionScript Dictionary entries.) The following are read-only properties: `_currentframe`, `_droptarget`, `_framesloaded`, `_parent`, `_target`, `_totalframes`, `_url`, `_xmouse`, and `_ymouse`.

You can write statements to set any property that is not read-only. The following statement sets the `_alpha` property of the movie clip instance wheel, which is a child of the car instance:

```
car.wheel._alpha = 50;
```

In addition, you can write statements that get the value of a movie clip property. For example, the following statement gets the value of the `_xmouse` property on the current level's Timeline and sets the `_x` property of the `customCursor` instance to that value:

```
onClipEvent(enterFrame){
    customCursor._x = _root._xmouse;
}
```

This is equivalent to the following code, which uses the `getProperty()` function:

```
onClipEvent(enterFrame){
    customCursor._x = getProperty(_root, _xmouse);
}
```

The `_x`, `_y`, `_rotation`, `_xscale`, `_yscale`, `_height`, `_width`, `_alpha`, and `_visible` properties are affected by transformations on the movie clip's parent, and transform the movie clip and any of the clip's children. The `_focusrect`, `_highquality`, `_quality`, and `_soundbuftime` properties are global; they belong only to the level 0 main Timeline. All other properties belong to each movie clip or loaded level.

For a list of movie clip properties, see "Property summary for the MovieClip class" on page 688.

Dragging movie clips

You can use the global `startDrag()` function or the `MovieClip.startDrag()` method to make a movie clip draggable. For example, you can make a draggable movie clip for games, drag-and-drop functions, customizable interfaces, scroll bars, and sliders.

A movie clip remains draggable until explicitly stopped by `stopDrag()`, or until another movie clip is targeted with `startDrag()`. Only one movie clip can be dragged at a time.

To create more complicated drag-and-drop behavior, you can evaluate the `_droptarget` property of the movie clip being dragged. For example, you might examine the `_droptarget` property to see if the movie clip was dragged to a specific movie clip (such as a "trash can" movie clip) and then trigger another action. For detailed information, see `startDrag()` on page 849 or `MovieClip.startDrag()` on page 738.

Creating movie clips at runtime

Not only can you create movie clip instances in the Flash authoring environment, but you can also create them at runtime. ActionScript provides three ways to create new movie clips at runtime:

- By creating a new, empty movie clip instance
- By duplicating an existing movie clip instance
- By attaching an instance of a movie clip library symbol to the Stage

Each movie clip instance you create at runtime must have an instance name and a depth (stacking, or z-order) value. The depth you specify determines how the new clip overlaps with other clips on the same Timeline. (See "Managing movie clip depths" on page 333.)

Creating an empty movie clip

To create an empty movie clip on the Stage, use the `createEmptyMovieClip()` method of the MovieClip class. This method creates a movie clip as a child of the clip that calls the method. The registration point for a newly created empty movie clip is the upper left corner.

For example, the following code creates a new child movie clip named `new_mc` at a depth of 10 in the movie clip named `parent_mc`.

```
parent_mc.createEmptyMovieClip("new_mc", 10);
```

The following code creates a new movie clip named `canvas_mc` on the root Timeline of the SWF file in which the script is run, and then invokes `loadMovie()` to load an external JPEG file into itself.

```
_root.createEmptyMovieClip("canvas_mc", 10);
canvas_mc.loadMovie("flowers.jpg");
```

For more information, see `MovieClip.createEmptyMovieClip()` on page 698.

Duplicating or removing a movie clip

To duplicate or remove movie clip instances, use the `duplicateMovieClip()` or `removeMovieClip()` global functions, or the MovieClip class methods of the same name. The `duplicateMovieClip()` method creates a new instance of an existing movie clip instance, assigns it a new instance name, and gives it a depth, or z-order. A duplicated movie clip always starts at Frame 1 even if the original movie clip was on another frame when duplicated, and is always in front of all previously defined movie clips placed on the Timeline.

To delete a movie clip you created with `duplicateMovieClip()`, use `removeMovieClip()`. Duplicated movie clips are also removed if the parent movie clip is deleted.

For more information, see `duplicateMovieClip()` on page 577 and `removeMovieClip()` on page 809.

Attaching a movie clip symbol to the Stage

The last way to create movie clip instances at runtime is to use `attachMovie()`. The `attachMovie()` method attaches an instance of a movie clip symbol in the SWF file's library to the Stage. The new clip becomes a child clip of the clip that attached it.

To use ActionScript to attach a movie clip symbol from the library, you must export the symbol for ActionScript and assign it a unique linkage identifier. To do this, you use the Linkage Properties dialog box.

By default, all movie clips that are exported for use with ActionScript load before the first frame of the SWF file that contains them. This can create a delay before the first frame plays. When you assign a linkage identifier to an element, you can also specify whether this content should be added before the first frame. If it isn't added in the first frame, you must include an instance of it in some other frame of the SWF file; if you don't, the element will not be exported to the SWF file.

To assign a linkage identifier to movie clip:

1 Select Window > Library to open the Library panel.

2 Select a movie clip in the Library panel.

3 In the Library panel, select Linkage from the Library panel options menu.

 The Linkage Properties dialog box appears.

4 For Linkage, select Export for ActionScript.

5 For Identifier, enter an ID for the movie clip.

 By default, the identifier is the same as the symbol name.

6 You can optionally assign an ActionScript 2.0 class to the movie clip symbol. (See "Assigning a class to a movie clip symbol" on page 337.)

7 If you don't want the movie clip to load before the first frame, deselect the Export in First Frame option.

 If you deselect this option, place an instance of the movie clip on the frame of the Timeline where you'd like it to be available. For example, if the script you're writing doesn't reference the movie clip until Frame 10, then place an instance of the symbol at or before that frame in the Timeline.

8 Click OK.

After you've assigned a linkage identifier to a movie clip, you can attach an instance of the symbol to the Stage at runtime by using `attachMovie()`.

To attach a movie clip to another movie clip:

1 Assign a linkage identifier to a movie clip library symbol, as described above.

2 With the Actions panel open (Window > Development Panels > Actions), select a frame in the Timeline.

3 In the Actions panel's Script pane, type the name of the movie clip or level to which you want to attach the new movie clip. For example, to attach the movie clip to the root Timeline, type `_root`.

4 In the Actions toolbox (at the left of the Actions panel), click the Built-in Classes category, the Movie category, and the MovieClip category, and double-click `attachMovie()`.

5 Using the code hints that appear as a guide, enter values for the following parameters:

- For `idName`, specify the identifier you entered in the Linkage Properties dialog box.

- For `newName`, enter an instance name for the attached clip so that you will be able to target it.

- For `depth`, enter the level at which the duplicate movie clip will be attached to the movie clip. Each attached movie clip has its own stacking order, with level 0 as the level of the originating movie clip. Attached movie clips are always on top of the original movie clip. Here is an example:

  ```
  myMovieClip.attachMovie("calif", "california", 10);
  ```

For more information, see `MovieClip.attachMovie()` on page 692.

Adding parameters to dynamically created movie clips

When you create or duplicate a movie clip dynamically using `MovieClip.attachMovie()` and `MovieClip.duplicateMovie()`, you can populate the movie clip with parameters from another object. The *initObject* parameter of `attachMovie()` and `duplicateMovie()` allows dynamically created movie clips to receive clip parameters. The *initObject* parameter is optional.

For more information, see `MovieClip.attachMovie()` on page 692 and `MovieClip.duplicateMovieClip()` on page 702.

To populate a dynamically created movie clip with parameters from a specified object, do one of the following:

- Use the following syntax with `attachMovie()`:
  ```
  myMovieClip.attachMovie(idName, newName, depth [, initObject])
  ```

- Use the following syntax with `duplicateMovie()`:
  ```
  myMovieClip.duplicateMovie(idName, newName, depth [, initObject])
  ```

The *initObject* parameter specifies the name of the object whose parameters you want to use to populate the dynamically created movie clip.

To populate a movie clip with parameters by using `attachMovie()`:

1 In a new Flash document, create a movie clip symbol by selecting Insert > New Symbol. Type `dynamic` in the Symbol Name text box and select the Movie Clip behavior.

2 Inside the symbol, create a dynamic text field on the Stage with an instance name of `name_txt`.

3 Select the first frame of the movie clip's Timeline and open the Actions panel (Window > Development Panels > Actions).

4 Create a new variable called `name`, and then assign its value to the `text` property of `name_txt`, as shown here:

```
var name:String;
name_txt.text = name;
```

5 Select Edit > Edit Document to return to the main Timeline.

6 Select the movie clip symbol in the library and select Linkage Properties from the Library panel's options menu.

The Linkage Properties dialog box appears.

7 Select the Export for ActionScript option, and click OK.

8 Select the first frame of the main Timeline and add the following code to the Actions panel's Script pane:

```
_root.attachMovie("dynamic", "newClipName", 10, {name:"Erick"});
```

9 Test the movie (Control > Test Movie). The name you specified in the `attachMovie()` call appears inside the new movie clip's text field.

Managing movie clip depths

Every movie clip has its own *z*-order space that determines how objects overlap within its parent SWF file or movie clip. Every movie clip has an associated depth value, which determines if it will render in front of or behind other movie clips in the same movie clip Timeline. When you create a movie clip at runtime using `MovieClip.attachMovie()`, `MovieClip.duplicateMovieClip()`, or `MovieClip.createEmptyMovieClip()`, you always specify a depth for the new clip as a method parameter. For example, the following code attaches a new movie clip to the Timeline of a movie clip named `container_mc` with a depth value of 10.

```
container_mc.attachMovie("symbolID", "clip_1", 10);
```

This creates a new movie clip with a depth of 10 within the *z*-order space of `container_mc`.

For example, the following code attaches two new movie clips to `container_mc`. The first clip, named `clip_1`, will render behind `clip_2`, because it was assigned a lower depth value.

```
container_mc.attachMovie("symbolID", "clip_1", 10);
container_mc.attachMovie("symbolID", "clip_2", 15);
```

Depth values for movie clips can range from -16384 to 1048575.

The MovieClip class provides several methods for managing movie clip depths: see `MovieClip.getNextHighestDepth()` on page 708, `MovieClip.getInstanceAtDepth()` on page 707, `MovieClip.getDepth()` on page 707, and `MovieClip.swapDepths()` on page 739.

Determining the next highest available depth

To determine the next highest available depth within a movie clip, use
`MovieClip.getNextHighestDepth()`. The integer value returned by this method indicates the
next available depth that will render in front of all other objects in the movie clip.

The following code creates a new movie clip, with a depth value of 10, on the Timeline of the
movie clip named `menus_mc`. It then determines the next highest available depth in that same
movie clip, and creates a new movie clip at that depth.

```
menus_mc.attachMovie("menuClip","file_menu", 10);
var nextDepth = menus_mc.getNextHighestDepth();
menus_mc.attachMovie("menuClip", "edit_menu", nextDepth);
```

In this case, the variable named `nextDepth` contains the value 11, because that's the next highest
available depth for the movie clip `menus_mc`.

To obtain the current highest occupied depth, subtract 1 from the value returned by
`getNextHighestDepth()`, as shown in the next section (see "Determining the instance at a
particular depth" on page 334).

Determining the instance at a particular depth

To determine the instance at particular depth, use `MovieClip.getInstanceAtDepth()`. This
method returns a reference to the instance at the specified depth.

The following code combines `getNextHighestDepth()` and `getInstanceAtDepth()` to
determine the movie clip at the (current) highest occupied depth on the root Timeline.

```
var highestOccupiedDepth = _root.getNextHighestDepth() - 1;
var instanceAtHighestDepth = _root.getInstanceAtDepth(highestOccupiedDepth);
```

For more information, see `MovieClip.getInstanceAtDepth()` on page 707.

Determining the depth of an instance

To determine the depth of a movie clip instance, use `MovieClip.getDepth()`.

The following code iterates over all the movie clips on a SWF file's main Timeline and displays
each clip's instance name and depth value in the Output panel.

```
for(each in _root) {
  var obj = _root[each];
  if(obj instanceof MovieClip) {
    var objDepth = obj.getDepth();
    trace(obj._name + ":" + objDepth)
  }
}
```

For more information, see `MovieClip.getDepth()` on page 707.

Swapping movie clip depths

To swap the depths of two movie clips on the same Timeline, use `MovieClip.swapDepths()`. For
more information, see `MovieClip.swapDepths()` on page 739.

Drawing shapes with ActionScript

You can use methods of the MovieClip class to draw lines and fills on the Stage. This allows you to create drawing tools for users and to draw shapes in the movie in response to events. The drawing methods are `beginFill()`, `beginGradientFill()`, `clear()`, `curveTo()`, `endFill()`, `lineTo()`, `lineStyle()`, and `moveTo()`.

You can use the drawing methods with any movie clip. However, if you use the drawing methods with a movie clip that was created in authoring mode, the drawing methods execute before the clip is drawn. In other words, content that is created in authoring mode is drawn on top of content drawn with the drawing methods.

You can use movie clips with drawing methods as masks; however, as with all movie clip masks, strokes are ignored.

To draw a shape:

1 Use `createEmptyMovieClip()` to create an empty movie clip on the Stage.

The new movie clip is a child of an existing movie clip or of the main Timeline, as in the following example:

```
_root.createEmptyMovieClip ("triangle", 1);
```

2 Use the empty movie clip to call drawing methods.

The following example draws a triangle with 5-point magenta lines and no fill:

```
with (_root.triangle) {
    lineStyle (5, 0xff00ff, 100);
    moveTo (200, 200);
    lineTo (300, 300);
    lineTo (100, 300);
    lineTo (200, 200);
}
```

For detailed information on these methods, see their entries in Chapter 12, "ActionScript Dictionary," on page 409.

Using movie clips as masks

You can use a movie clip as a mask to create a hole through which the contents of another movie clip are visible. The mask movie clip plays all the frames in its Timeline, just like a regular movie clip. You can make the mask movie clip draggable, animate it along a motion guide, use separate shapes within a single mask, or resize a mask dynamically. You can also use ActionScript to turn a mask on and off.

You cannot use a mask to mask another mask. You cannot set the _alpha property of a mask movie clip. Only fills are used in a movie clip that is used as a mask; strokes are ignored.

To create a mask:

1 On the Stage, select a movie clip to be masked.

2 In the Property inspector, enter an instance name for the movie clip, such as image.

3 Create a movie clip to be a mask. Give it an instance name in the Property inspector, such as mask.

   The masked movie clip will be revealed under all opaque (nontransparent) areas of the movie clip acting as the mask.

4 Select Frame 1 in the Timeline.

5 Open the Actions panel (Window > Development Panels > Actions) if it isn't already open.

6 In the Actions panel, enter the following code:

   image.setMask(mask);

For detailed information, see MovieClip.setMask() on page 737.

About masking device fonts

You can use a movie clip to mask text that is set in a device font. In order for a movie clip mask on a device font to work properly, the user must have Flash Player 6 release 40 or later.

When you use a movie clip to mask text set in a device font, the rectangular bounding box of the mask is used as the masking shape. That is, if you create a nonrectangular movie clip mask for device font text in the Flash authoring environment, the mask that appears in the SWF file will be the shape of the rectangular bounding box of the mask, not the shape of the mask itself.

You can mask device fonts only by using a movie clip as a mask. You cannot mask device fonts by using a mask layer on the Stage.

Handling movie clip events

Movie clips can respond to user events, such as mouse clicks and keypresses, as well as system-level events, such as the initial loading of a movie clip on the Stage. ActionScript provides two ways to handle movie clip events: through event handler methods and through onClipEvent() and on() event handlers. For more information, see Chapter 4, "Handling Events," on page 287.

Assigning a class to a movie clip symbol

Using ActionScript 2.0, you can create your own class that extends the behavior of the built-in MovieClip class, and then assign that class to a movie clip library symbol using the Linkage Properties dialog box. Whenever you create an instance of the movie clip to which the class is assigned, it assumes the properties and behaviors defined by the class assigned to it. (For more information about ActionScript 2.0, see Chapter 9, "Creating Classes with ActionScript 2.0," on page 359.)

In a subclass of the MovieClip class, you can provide method definitions for the built-in MovieClip methods and event handlers, like `onEnterFrame` and `onRelease`. In the following procedure, you'll create a class called MoveRight that extends the MovieClip class; MoveRight defines an `onPress` handler that moves the clip 20 pixels to the right whenever the user clicks the movie clip. In the second procedure, you'll create a movie clip symbol in a new Flash (FLA) document and assign the MoveRight class to that symbol.

To create a movie clip subclass:

1 Create a new directory called BallTest.

2 Create a new ActionScript file by doing one of the following:

   ■ (Flash MX Professional 2004) Select File > New, and select ActionScript file from the list of document types.

   ■ (Flash MX 2004) Create a text file in your preferred text editor.

3 Enter the following code in your script:

```
// MoveRight class -- moves clip to the right 5 pixels every frame
class MoveRight extends MovieClip {
    function onPress() {
        this._x += 20;
    }
}
```

4 Save the document as MoveRight.as in the BallTest directory.

To assign the class to a movie clip symbol:

1 In Flash, select File > New, select Flash Document from the list of file types, and click OK.

2 Using the Oval tool, draw a circle on the Stage.

3 Select the circle, then select Modify > Convert to Symbol. In the Convert to Symbol dialog box, select Movie Clip as the symbol's behavior and enter `Ball` in the Name text box.

4 Open the Library panel (Window > Library) and select the Ball symbol.

5 Select Linkage from the Library panel's options menu to open the Linkage Properties dialog box.

6 In the Linkage Properties dialog box, select the Export for ActionScript option, and type `MoveRight` in the AS 2.0 Class text box. Click OK.

7 Save the file as Ball.fla in the BallTest directory (the same directory that contains the MoveRight.as file).

8 Test the movie (Control > Test Movie).

Each time you click the ball movie clip, it moves 20 pixels to the right.

Initializing class properties

In the example presented earlier, you added the instance of the Ball symbol to the Stage manually—that is, while authoring. As discussed previously (see "Adding parameters to dynamically created movie clips" on page 332), you can assign parameters to clips you create at runtime using the *initObject* parameter of attachMovie() and duplicateMovie(). You can use this feature to initialize properties of the class you're assigning to a movie clip.

For example, the following class named MoveRightDistance is a variation of the MoveRight class discussed earlier (see "Assigning a class to a movie clip symbol" on page 337). The difference is a new property named distance, whose value determines how many pixels a movie clip moves each time it is clicked.

```
// MoveRightDistance class -- moves clip to the right 5 pixels every frame
class MoveRightDistance extends MovieClip {
  // distance property determines how many
  // pixels to move clip each mouse press
  var distance:Number;
  function onPress() {
    this._x += distance;
  }
}
```

Assuming this class is assigned to a symbol with a linkage identifier of Ball, the following code creates two new instances of the symbol on the root Timeline of the SWF file. The first instance, named ball_50, moves 50 pixels each time it is clicked; the second, named ball_125, moves 125 pixels each time its clicked.

```
_root.attachMovie("Ball", "ball_50", 10, {distance:50});
_root.attachMovie("Ball", "ball_125", 20, {distance:125});
```

A dynamic or input text field is a TextField object (an instance of the TextField class). When you create a text field, you can assign it an instance name in the Property inspector. You can use the instance name in ActionScript statements to set, change, and format the text field and its content using the TextField and TextFormat classes.

The methods of the TextField class let you set, select, and manipulate text in a dynamic or input text field that you create during authoring or at runtime. For more information, see "Using the TextField class" on page 339. For information on debugging text fields at runtime, see "Displaying text field properties for debugging" on page 282.

ActionScript also provides several ways to format your text at runtime. The TextFormat class lets you set character and paragraph formatting for TextField objects (see "Using the TextFormat class" on page 341). Flash Player also supports a subset of HTML tags that you can use to format text (see "Using HTML-formatted text" on page 351). Flash Player 7 and later supports the `<img>` HTML tag, which lets you embed not just external images, but also external SWF files, as well as movie clips that reside in the library *see "Image tag (<img>)" on page 353).

In Flash Player 7 and later, you can apply Cascading Style Sheets (CSS) styles to text fields using the TextField.StyleSheet class. You can use CSS to style built-in HTML tags, define new formatting tags, or apply styles. For more information on using CSS, see "Formatting text with Cascading Style Sheets" on page 343.

You can also assign HTML formatted text, which may optionally use CSS styles, directly to a text field. In Flash Player 7 and later, HTML text that you assign to a text field can contain embedded media (movie clips, SWF files, and JPEG files). The text will wrap around the embedded media, just as a web browser wraps text around media embedded in an HTML document. For more information, see "Image tag (<img>)" on page 353.

Using the TextField class

The TextField class represents any dynamic or selectable (editable) text field you create using the Text tool in Flash. You use the methods and properties of this class to control text fields at runtime. TextField objects support the same properties as MovieClip objects, with the exception of the `_currentframe`, `_droptarget`, `_framesloaded`, and `_totalframes` properties. You can get and set properties and invoke methods for text fields dynamically.

To control a dynamic or input text field using ActionScript, you must assign it an instance name in the Property inspector. You can then reference the text field with the instance name, and use the methods and properties of the TextField class to control the contents or basic appearance of the text field. You can also create TextField objects at runtime, and assign them instance names, using the `MovieClip.createTextField()` method. For more information, see "Creating text fields at runtime" on page 341.

Assigning text to a text field at runtime

To assign text to a text field, use the `TextField.text` property.

To assign text to a text field at runtime:

1 Using the Text tool, create a text field on the Stage.

2 With the text field selected, in the Property inspector (Window > Properties), enter `headline_txt` in the Instance Name text box, directly below the Text Type pop-up menu on the left side of the inspector.

Instance names can consist only of letters, underscores (_), and dollar signs ($).

3 In the Timeline, select the first frame in Layer 1 and open the Actions panel (Window > Development Panels > Actions).

4 Type the following code in the Actions panel:

```
headline_txt.text = "Brazil wins World Cup";
```

5 Select Control > Test Movie to test the movie.

About text field instance and variable names

In the Property inspector, you can also assign a variable name to a dynamic or input text field, as well as an instance name. You can then refer to the text field's variable name in ActionScript, whose value determines the text field's contents. A text field's instance name and variable name should not be confused, however.

You use the instance name assigned to a text field to invoke methods and get and set properties on that text field. A text field's variable name is simply a variable reference to the text contained by that text field; it is not a reference to an object.

For example, if you assigned a text field the variable name `mytextVar`, you could then set the contents of the text field using the following code:

```
var mytextVar = "This is what will appear in the text field";
```

However, you couldn't use the `mytextVar` variable to set the same text field's text property to some text.

```
//This won't work
myTextVar.text = "A text field variable is not an object reference";
```

In general, use the `TextField.text` property to control the contents of a text field, unless you're targeting a version of Flash Player that doesn't support the TextField class. This will lessen the chances of a variable name conflict, which could result in unexpected behavior at runtime.

Creating text fields at runtime

You can use the `createTextField()` method of the MovieClip class to create an empty text field on the Stage at runtime. The new text field is attached to the Timeline of the movie clip that calls the method. The `createTextField()` method uses the following syntax:

```
movieClip.createTextField(instanceName, depth, x, y, width, height)
```

For example, the following code creates a 300 x 100 pixel text field named `test_txt` at point (0,0) and a depth (z-order) of 10.

```
_root.createTextField("test_txt", 10, 0, 0, 300, 100);
```

You use the instance name specified in the `createTextField()` call to access the methods and properties of the TextField class. For example, the following code creates a new text field named `test_txt`, and then modifies its properties to make it a multiline, word-wrapping text field that expands to fit inserted text. Lastly, it assigns some text to the text field's `text` property.

```
_root.createTextField("test_txt", 10, 0, 0, 100, 50);
test_txt.multiline = true;
test_txt.wordWrap = true;
test_txt.autoSize = true;
test_txt.text = "Create new text fields with the MovieClip.createTextField
  method.";
```

You can use the `TextField.removeTextField()` method to remove a text field created with `createTextField()`. The `removeTextField()` method does not work on a text field placed by the Timeline during authoring.

For more information, see `MovieClip.createTextField()` on page 698 and `TextField.removeTextField()` on page 902.

Using the TextFormat class

You can use the ActionScript TextFormat class to set formatting properties of a text field. The TextFormat class incorporates character and paragraph formatting information. Character formatting information describes the appearance of individual characters: font name, point size, color, and an associated URL. Paragraph formatting information describes the appearance of a paragraph: left margin, right margin, indentation of the first line, and left, right, or center alignment.

To use the TextFormat class, you first create a TextFormat object and set its character and paragraph formatting styles. You then apply the TextFormat object to a text field using the `TextField.setTextFormat()` or `TextField.setNewTextFormat()` methods.

The `setTextFormat()` method changes the text format applied to individual characters, to groups of characters, or to the entire body of text in a text field. Newly inserted text, however— such as that entered by a user or inserted with ActionScript—does not assume the formatting specified by a `setTextFormat()` call. To specify the default formatting for newly inserted text, use `TextField.setNewTextFormat()`. For more information, see `TextField.setTextFormat()` on page 906 and `TextField.setNewTextFormat()` on page 905.

To format a text field with the TextFormat class:

1 In a new Flash document, create a text field on the Stage using the Text tool. Type some text in the text field on the Stage, like "Bold, italic, 24 point text".

2 In the Property inspector, type `myText_txt` in the Instance Name text box, select Dynamic from the Text Type pop-up menu, and select Multiline from the Line Type pop-up menu.

3 In the Timeline, select the first frame in Layer 1 and open the Actions panel (Window > Development Panels > Actions).

4 Enter the following code in the Actions panel to create a TextFormat object, and set its `bold` and `italic` properties to `true`, and its `size` property to 24.

```
// Create a TextFormat object
var txtfmt_fmt = new TextFormat();
// Specify paragraph and character formatting
txtfmt_fmt.bold = "true";
txtfmt_fmt.italic = "true";
txtfmt_fmt.size = "24"
```

5 Apply the TextFormat object to the text field you created in step 1 using `TextField.setTextFormat()`.

```
myText_txt.setTextFormat(txtfmt_fmt);
```

This version of `setTextFormat()` applies the specified formatting to the entire text field. There are two other versions of this method that let you apply formatting to individual characters or groups of characters. For example, the following code applies bold, italic, 24-point formatting to the first four characters you entered in the text field.

```
myText_txt.setTextFormat(txtfmt_fmt, 0, 3);
```

For more information, see `TextField.setTextFormat()` on page 906.

6 Select Control > Test Movie to test the movie.

Default properties of new text fields

Text fields created at runtime with `createTextField()` receive a default TextFormat object with the following properties:

```
font = "Times New Roman"
size = 12
textColor = 0x000000
bold = false
italic = false
underline = false
url = ""
target = ""
align = "left"
leftMargin = 0
rightMargin = 0
indent = 0
leading = 0
bullet = false
tabStops = [] (empty array)
```

For a complete list of TextFormat methods and their descriptions, see the TextFormat class entry in Chapter 12, "ActionScript Dictionary," on page 409.

Getting text metric information

You can use the `TextFormat.getTextExtent()` method to obtain detailed text measurements for a text string with specific formatting applied. For example, suppose you need to create, at runtime, a new TextField object containing an arbitrary amount of text that is formatted with a 24-point, bold, Arial font, and a 5-pixel indent. You need to determine how wide or high the new TextField object must be to display all of the text. The `getTextExtent()` method provides measurements such as ascent, descent, width, and height.

For more information, see `TextFormat.getTextExtent()` on page 923.

Formatting text with Cascading Style Sheets

Cascading Style Sheets are a mechanism for creating text styles that can be applied to HTML or XML documents. A style sheet is a collection of formatting rules that specify how to format HTML or XML elements. Each rule associates a style name, or *selector*, with one or more style properties and their values. For example, the following style defines a selector named `bodyText`.

```
bodyText { text-align: left}
```

You can create styles that redefine built-in HTML formatting tags used by Flash Player (such as `<p>` and `<li>`), create style "classes" that can be applied to specific HTML elements using the `<p>` or `<span>` tag's `class` attribute, or define new tags.

You use the TextField.StyleSheet class to work with text style sheets. You can load styles from an external CSS file or create them natively using ActionScript. To apply a style sheet to a text field that contains HTML- or XML-formatted text, you use the `TextField.styleSheet` property. The styles defined in the style sheet are mapped automatically to the tags defined in the HTML or XML document.

Using styles sheets involves three basic steps:

- Create a style sheet object from the TextField.StyleSheet class. See "Creating a style sheet object" on page 344.
- Add styles to the style sheet object, either by importing them from an external CSS file or by defining them with ActionScript. See "Loading external CSS files" on page 345 and "Creating new styles with ActionScript" on page 346.
- Assign the style sheet object to a text field that contains XML- or HTML-formatted text. See "Applying styles to a TextField object" on page 346, "An example of using styles with HTML" on page 348, and "An example of using styles with XML" on page 350.

Supported CSS properties

Flash Player supports a subset of properties in the original CSS1 specification (www.w3.org/TR/REC-CSS1). The following table shows the supported CSS properties and values, and their corresponding ActionScript property names. (Each ActionScript property name is derived from the corresponding CSS property name; the hyphen is omitted and the subsequent character is capitalized.)

CSS property	ActionScript property	Usage and supported values
text-align	textAlign	Recognized values are `left`, `center`, and `right`.
font-size	fontSize	Only the numeric part of the value is used; units (px, pt) are not parsed; pixels and points are equivalent.
text-decoration	textDecoration	Recognized values are `none` and `underline`.
margin-left	marginLeft	Only the numeric part of the value is used. Units (px, pt) are not parsed; pixels and points are equivalent.
margin-right	marginRight	Only the numeric part of the value is used. Units (px, pt) are not parsed; pixels and points are equivalent.
font-weight	fontWeight	Recognized values are `normal` and `bold`.
font-style	fontStyle	Recognized values are `normal` and `italic`.
text-indent	textIndent	Only the numeric part of the value is used. Units (px, pt) are not parsed; pixels and points are equivalent.
font-family	fontFamily	A comma-separated list of fonts to use, in descending order of desirability. Any font family name can be used. If you specify a generic font name, it will be converted to an appropriate device font. The following font conversions are available: `mono` is converted to `_typewriter`, `sans-serif` is converted to `_sans`, and `serif` is converted to `_serif`.
color	color	Only hexadecimal color values are supported. Named colors (like `blue`) are not supported.
display	display	Supported values are `inline`, `block`, and `none`.

Creating a style sheet object

CSS style sheets are represented in ActionScript by the `TextField.StyleSheet` class. This class is only available for SWF files that target Flash Player 7 or later. To create a style sheet object, call the TextField.StyleSheet class's constructor function.

```
var newStyle = new TextField.StyleSheet();
```

To add styles to a style sheet object, you can either load an external CSS file into the object, or define the styles in ActionScript. See "Loading external CSS files" on page 345 and "Creating new styles with ActionScript" on page 346.

Loading external CSS files

You can define styles in an external CSS file and then load that file into a style sheet object. The styles defined in the CSS file are added to the style sheet object. To load an external CSS file, you use the load() method of the TextField.StyleSheet class. To determine when the CSS file has finished loading, use the style sheet object's onLoad event handler.

In the following example, you'll create and load an external CSS file and use the TextField.StyleSheet.getStyleNames() method to retrieve the names of the loaded styles.

To load an external style sheet:

1 In your preferred text or XML editor, create a file.

2 Add the following style definitions to the file:

```
// Filename: styles.css
bodyText {
    font-family: Arial,Helvetica,sans-serif;
    font-size: 12px;
}

headline {
    font-family: Arial,Helvetica,sans-serif;
    font-size: 24px;
}
```

3 Save the CSS file as styles.css.

4 In Flash, create a FLA document.

5 In the Timeline (Window > Timeline), select Layer 1.

6 Open the Actions panel (Window > Development Panels > Actions).

7 Add the following code to the Actions panel:

```
var css_styles = new TextField.StyleSheet();
css_styles.load("styles.css");
css_styles.onLoad = function(ok) {
    if(ok) {
        // display style names
        trace(this.getStyleNames());
    } else {
        trace("Error loading CSS file.");
    }
}
```

8 Save the file to the same directory that contains styles.css.

9 Test the movie (Control > Test Movie).

You should see the names of the two styles displayed in the Output panel:

```
body
headLine
```

If you see "Error loading CSS file" displayed in the Output panel, make sure the FLA file and the CSS file are in the same directory and that you typed the name of the CSS file correctly.

As with all other ActionScript methods that load data over the network, the CSS file must reside in the same domain as the SWF file that is loading the file. (See "About allowing cross-domain data loading" on page 394.)

Creating new styles with ActionScript

You can create new text styles with ActionScript by using the `setStyle()` method of the TextField.StyleSheet class. This method takes two parameters: the name of the style and an object that defines that style's properties.

For example, the following code creates a style sheet object named `styles` that defines two styles that are identical to those you imported earlier (see "Loading external CSS files" on page 345).

```
var styles = new TextField.StyleSheet();
styles.setStyle("bodyText",
  {fontFamily: 'Arial,Helvetica,sans-serif',
   fontSize: '12px'}
);
styles.setStyle("headline",
  {fontFamily: 'Arial,Helvetica,sans-serif',
   fontSize: '24px'}
);
```

Applying styles to a TextField object

To apply a style sheet object to a text field, you assign the style sheet object to the text field's `styleSheet` property.

```
textObj_txt.styleSheet = styleSheetObj;
```

Note: Be careful not to confuse the TextField.styleSheet *property* with the TextField.StyleSheet *class*. The capitalization indicates the difference.

When you assign a style sheet object to a TextField object, the following changes occur to the text field's normal behavior:

- The text field's `text` and `htmlText` properties, and any variable associated with the text field, always contain the same value and behave identically.
- The text field becomes read-only and cannot be edited by the user.
- The `setTextFormat()` and `replaceSel()` methods of the TextField class no longer function with the text field. The only way to change the field is by altering the text field's `text` or `htmlText` properties, or by changing the text field's associated variable.
- Any text assigned to the text field's `text` property, `htmlText` property, or associated variable is stored verbatim; anything written to one of these properties can be retrieved in the text's original form.

Combining styles

CSS styles in Flash Player are additive; that is, when styles are nested, each level of nesting can contribute additional style information, which is added together to result in the final formatting.

For example, here is some XML data assigned to a text field:

```
<sectionHeading>This is a section</sectionHeading>
<mainBody>This is some main body text, with one
<emphasized>emphatic</emphasized> word.</mainBody>
```

For the word *emphatic* in the above text, the `emphasized` style is nested within the `mainBody` style. The `mainBody` style contributes color, font-size, and decoration rules. The `emphasized` style adds a font-weight rule to these rules. The word *emphatic* will be formatted using a combination of the rules specified by `mainBody` and `emphasized`.

Using style classes

You can create style "classes" that you can apply to a `<p>` or `<span>` tag using either tag's `class` attribute. When applied to a `<p>` tag, the style affects the entire paragraph. You can also style a span of text that uses a style class by using the `<span>` tag.

For example, the following style sheet defines two styles classes: `mainBody` and `emphasis`.

```
.mainBody {
  font-family: Arial,Helvetica,sans-serif;
  font-size: 24px;
}
.emphasis {
  color: #666666;
  font-style: italic;
}
```

Within HTML text you assign to a text field, you can apply these styles to `<p>` and `<span>` tags, as shown below.

```
<p class="mainBody">This is <span class="emphasis">really exciting!</span></p>
```

Styling built-in HTML tags

Flash Player supports a subset of HTML tags. (For more information, see "Using HTML-formatted text" on page 351.) You can assign a CSS style to every instance of a built-in HTML tag that appears in a text field. For example, the following defines a style for the built-in `<p>` HTML tag. All instances of that tag will be styled in the manner specified by the style rule.

```
p {
  font-family: Arial,Helvetica,sans-serif;
  font-size: 12px;
  display: inline;
}
```

The following table shows which built-in HTML tags can be styled and how each style is applied:

Style name	How the style is applied
p	Affects all `<p>` tags.
body	Affects all `<body>` tags. The p style, if specified, takes precedence over the body style.
li	Affects all `<li>` bullet tags.
a	Affects all `<a>` anchor tags.
a:link	Affects all `<a>` anchor tags. This style is applied after any a style.
a:hover	Applied to an `<a>` anchor tag when the mouse is hovering over the link. This style is applied after any a and a:link style. Once the mouse moves off the link, the a:hover style is removed from the link.
a:active	Applied to an `<a>` anchor tag when the user clicks the link. This style is applied after any a and a:link style. Once the mouse button is released, the a:active style is removed from the link.

An example of using styles with HTML

This section presents an example of using styles with HTML tags. You'll create a style sheet that styles some built-in tags and defines some style classes. You'll then apply that style sheet to a TextField object that contains HTML-formatted text.

To format HTML with a style sheet, do the following:

1 In your preferred text editor, create a file.

2 Add the following style sheet definition to the file:

```
p {
  color: #000000;
  font-family: Arial,Helvetica,sans-serif;
  font-size: 12px;
  display: inline;
}

a:link {
  color: #FF0000;
}

a:hover{
  text-decoration: underline;
}

.headline {
  color: #000000;
  font-family: Arial,Helvetica,sans-serif;
  font-size: 18px;
  font-weight: bold;
  display: block;
}

.byline {
  color: #666600;
  font-style: italic;
  font-weight: bold;
  display: inline;
}
```

This style sheet defines styles for two built-in HTML tags (`<p>` and `<a>`) that will be applied to all instances of those tags. It also defines two style classes (`.headline` and `.byline`) that will be applied to specific paragraphs and text spans.

3 Save the file as html_styles.css.

4 In Flash, create a FLA file.

5 Using the Text tool, create a text field approximately 400 pixels wide and 300 pixels high.

6 Open the Property inspector (Window > Properties) and select the text field.

7 In the Property inspector, select Dynamic Text from the Text Type menu, select Multiline from the Line Type menu, select the Render Text as HTML option, and type `news_txt` in the Instance Name text box.

8 Select the first frame in Layer 1 in the Timeline (Window > Timeline).

9 Open the Actions panel (Window > Development Panels > Actions) and add the following code to the Actions panel:

```
// Create a new style sheet object
var style_sheet = new TextField.StyleSheet();
// Location of CSS file that defines styles
var css_url = "html_styles.css";
// Create some HTML text to display
var storyText:String = "<p class='headline'>Flash Player now supports
    Cascading Style Sheets!</p><p><span class='byline'>San Francisco, CA</
    span>--Macromedia Inc. announced today a new version of Flash Player that
    supports Cascading Style Sheet (CSS) text styles. For more information,
    visit the <a href='http://www.macromedia.com'>Macromedia Flash web site.</
    a></p>";
// Load CSS file and define onLoad handler:
style_sheet.load(css_url);
style_sheet.onLoad = function(ok) {
    if (ok) {
        // If the style sheet loaded without error,
        // then assign it to the text object,
        // and assign the HTML text to the text field.
        news_txt.styleSheet = style_sheet;
        news_txt.text = storyText;
    }
};
```

Note: For simplicity, the HTML text being styled is "hard-coded" into the script; in a real-world application you'll probably want to load the text from an external file. For information on loading external data, see Chapter 10, "Working with External Data," on page 381.

10 Save the file as news_html.fla to the same directory that contains the CSS file you created previously.

11 Run the movie (Control > Test Movie) to see the styles applied to the HTML text automatically.

Using styles to define new tags

If you define a new style in a style sheet, that style can be used as a tag, just as you would use a built-in HTML tag. For example, if a style sheet defines a CSS style named sectionHeading, you can use <sectionHeading> as an element in any text field associated with the style sheet. This feature lets you assign arbitrary XML-formatted text directly to a text field, so that the text will be automatically formatted using the rules in the style sheet.

For example, the following style sheet creates the new styles sectionHeading, mainBody, and emphasized.

```
sectionHeading {
    font-family: Verdana, Arial, Helvetica, sans-serif;
    font-size: 18px; display: block
}
mainBody {
    color: #000099;
    text-decoration: underline;
    font-size: 12px; display: block
}
emphasized {
    font-weight: bold; display: inline
}
```

You could then populate a text field associated with that style sheet with the following XML-formatted text:

```
<sectionHeading>This is a section</sectionHeading>
<mainBody>This is some main body text,
with one <emphasized>emphatic</emphasized> word.
</mainBody>
```

An example of using styles with XML

In this section, you'll create the same FLA file that you created earlier (see "An example of using styles with HTML" on page 348) but with XML-formatted text. In this example, you'll create the style sheet using ActionScript, rather than importing styles from a CSS file.

To format XML with a style sheet:

1 In Flash, create a FLA file.

2 Using the Text tool, create a text field approximately 400 pixels wide and 300 pixels high.

3 Open the Property inspector (Window > Properties) and select the text field.

4 In the Property inspector, select Dynamic Text from the Text Type menu, select Multiline from the Line Type menu, select the Render Text as HTML option, and type news_txt in the Instance Name text box.

5 On Layer 1 in the Timeline (Window > Timeline), select the first frame.

6 To create the style sheet object, open the Actions panel (Window > Development Panels > Actions) and add the following code to the Actions panel:

```
var xml_styles = new TextField.StyleSheet();
xml_styles.setStyle("mainBody", {
   color:'#000000',
   fontFamily:'Arial,Helvetica,sans-serif',
   fontSize:'12',
   display:'block'
});
xml_styles.setStyle("title", {
   color:'#000000',
   fontFamily:'Arial,Helvetica,sans-serif',
   fontSize:'18',
   display:'block',
   fontWeight:'bold'
});
xml_styles.setStyle("byline", {
   color:'#666666',
   fontWeight:'bold',
   fontStyle:'italic',
   display:'inline'
});
xml_styles.setStyle("a:link", {
   color:'#FF0000'
});
xml_styles.setStyle("a:hover", {
   textDecoration:'underline'
});
```

This code creates a new style sheet object named xml_styles that defines styles by using the setStyle() method. The styles exactly match those you created in an external CSS file earlier in this chapter.

7   To create the XML text to assign to the text field, add the following code to the Actions panel:

```
var storyText = "<title>Flash Player now supports CSS</
    title><mainBody><byline>San Francisco, CA</byline>--Macromedia Inc.
    announced today a new version of Flash Player that supports Cascading
    Style Sheets (CSS) text styles. For more information, visit the <a
    href=\"http://www.macromedia.com\">Macromedia Flash website</a></
    mainBody>";
```

8   Last, add the following code to apply the style sheet object to the text field's `styleSheet` property and assign the XML text to the text field.

```
news_txt.styleSheet = xml_styles;
news_txt.text = storyText;
```

9   Save the file as news_xml.fla.

10 Run the movie (Control > Test Movie) to see the styles automatically applied to the text in the field.

Using HTML-formatted text

Flash Player supports a subset of standard HTML tags such as `<p>` and `<li>` that you can use to style text in any dynamic or input text field. Text fields in Flash Player 7 and later also support the `<img>` tag, which lets you embed JPEG files, SWF files, and movie clips in a text field. Flash Player automatically wraps text around images embedded in text fields in much the same way a web browser wraps text around embedded images in an HTML page. For more information, see "Embedding images, SWF files, and movie clips in text fields" on page 356.

Flash Player also supports the `<textformat>` tag, which lets you apply paragraph formatting styles of the TextFormat class to HTML-enabled text fields. For more information, see "Using the TextFormat class" on page 341.

Overview of using HTML-formatted text

To use HTML in a text field, you must enable the text field's HTML formatting either by selecting the Render Text as HTML option in the Property inspector, or by setting the text field's `html` property to `true`. To insert HTML into a text field, use the `TextField.htmlText` property.

For example, the following code enables HTML formatting for a text field named `headline_txt`, and then assigns some HTML to the text field.

```
headline_txt.html = true;
headline_txt.htmlText = "<font face='Times New Roman' size='24'>This is how
    you assign HTML text to a text field.</font>";
```

Attributes of HTML tags must be enclosed in double or single quotation marks. Attribute values without quotation marks may produce unexpected results, such as improper rendering of text. For example, the following HTML snippet will not be rendered properly by Flash Player because the value assigned to the `align` attribute (`left`) is not enclosed in quotation marks:

```
textField.htmlText = "<p align=left>This is left-aligned text</p>";
```

If you enclose attribute values in double quotation marks, you must "escape" the quotation marks (`\"`). For example, either of the following are acceptable:

```
textField.htmlText = "<p align='left'>This uses single quotes</p>";
textField.htmlText = "<p align=\"left\">This uses escaped double quotes</p>";
```

It's not necessary to escape double quotation marks if you're loading text from an external file; it's only necessary if you're assigning a string of text in ActionScript.

Supported HTML tags

This section lists the built-in HTML tags supported by Flash Player. You can also create new styles and tags using Cascading Style Sheets; see "Formatting text with Cascading Style Sheets" on page 343.

Anchor tag (<a>)

The `<a>` tag creates a hyperlink and supports the following attributes:

- `href`   Specifies the URL of the page to load in the browser. The URL can absolute or relative to the location of the SWF file that is loading the page.
- `target`   Specifies the name of the target window to load the page into.

For example, the following HTML snippet creates the link "Go home," which opens www.macromedia.com in a new browser window.

```
<a href="../home.htm" target="_blank">Go home</a>
```

You can also define `a:link`, `a:hover`, and `a:active` styles for anchor tags by using style sheets. See "Styling built-in HTML tags" on page 347.

Bold tag (<b>)

The `<b>` tag renders text as bold. A bold typeface must be available for the font used to display the text.

```
<b>This is bold text.</b>
```

Break tag (<br>)

The `<br>` tag creates a line break in the text field, as shown in this example:

```
One line of text<br>Another line of text<br>
```

Font tag (<font>)

The `<font>` tag specifies a font or list of fonts to display the text.

The font tag supports the following attributes:

- `color`   Only hexadecimal color (#FFFFFF) values are supported. For example, the following HTML code creates red text.
  ```
  <font color="#FF0000">This is red text</font>
  ```
- `face`   Specifies the name of the font to use. You can also specify a list of comma-separated font names, in which case Flash Player chooses the first available font. If the specified font is not installed on the playback system, or isn't embedded in the SWF file, then Flash Player chooses a substitute font.

  Example:
  ```
  <font face="Times, Times New Roman">This is either Times or Times New Roman..</font>
  ```

  For more information on embedding fonts in Flash applications, see `TextField.embedFonts` on page 891 and "Setting dynamic and input text options" in Using Flash Help.
- `size`   Specifies the size of the font, in pixels. You can also use relative point sizes (+2 or -4).
  ```
  <font size="24" color="#0000FF">This is green, 24-point text</font>
  ```

Image tag (`<img>`)

The `<img>` tag lets you embed external JPEG files, SWF files, and movie clips inside text fields. Text automatically flows around images you embed in text fields. This tag is supported only in dynamic and input text fields that are multiline and wrap their text.

To create a multiline text field with word wrapping, do one of the following:

- In the Flash authoring environment, select a text field on the Stage and then, in the Property inspector, select Multiline from the Text Type pop-up menu.
- For a text field created at runtime with `MovieClip.createTextField()`, set the new text field instance's `TextField.multiline` and `TextField.wordWrap` properties to `true`.

The `<img>` tag has one required attribute, `src`, which specifies the path to a JPEG file, a SWF file, or the linkage identifier of a movie clip symbol. All other attributes are optional.

The `<img>` tags supports the following attributes:

- `src` Specifies the URL to a JPEG or SWF file, or the linkage identifier for a movie clip symbol in the library. This attribute is required; all other attributes are optional. External files (JPEG and SWF files) are not displayed until they have downloaded completely.

    Note: Flash Player does not support progressive JPEG files.

- `id` Specifies the name for the movie clip instance (created by Flash Player) that contains the embedded JPEG file, SWF file, or movie clip. This is useful if you want to control the embedded content with ActionScript.
- `width` The width of the image, SWF file, or movie clip, in pixels.
- `height` The height of the image, SWF file, or movie clip being inserted, in pixels.
- `align` Specifies the horizontal alignment of the embedded image within the text field. Valid value are `left` and `right`. The default value is `left`.
- `hspace` Specifies the amount of horizontal space that surrounds the image where no text will appear. The default value is 8.
- `vspace` Specifies the amount of vertical space that surrounds the image where no text will appear. The default value is 8.

For more information and examples of using the `<img>` tag, see "Embedding images, SWF files, and movie clips in text fields" on page 356.

Italic tag (`<i>`)

The `<i>` tag displays the tagged text in italics. An italic typeface must be available for the font used.

```
That is very <i>interesting</i>.
```

The above code would render as follows:

That is very *interesting*.

List item tag (‹li›)

The ‹li› tag places a bullet in front of the text that it encloses.

```
Grocery list:
<li>Apples</li>
<li>Oranges</li>
<li>Lemons</li>
```

The above code would render as follows:

Grocery list:
- Apples
- Oranges
- Lemons

Paragraph tag (‹p›)

The ‹p› tag creates a new paragraph. It supports the following attributes:

- **align**   Specifies alignment of text within the paragraph; valid values are left, right, and center.

- **class**   Specifies a CSS style class defined by an TextField.StyleSheet object. (For more information, see "Using style classes" on page 347.)

  The following example uses the align attribute to align text on the right side of a text field.

  ```
  textField.htmlText = "<p align='right'>This text is aligned on the right
    side of the text field</p>";
  ```

  The following example uses the class attribute to assign a text style class to a ‹p› tag.

  ```
  var myStyleSheet = new TextField.StyleSheet();
  myStyleSheet.secreateTextField("test", 10, 0,0, 300,100);
  createTextField("test", 10, 0,0, 300,100);
  test.styleSheet = myStyleSheet;
  test.htmlText = "<p class='body'>This is some body-styled text.</p>.";
  ```

Span tag (‹span›)

The ‹span› tag is available only for use with CSS text styles. (For more information, see "Formatting text with Cascading Style Sheets" on page 343.) It supports the following attribute:

- **class**   Specifies a CSS style class defined by an TextField.StyleSheet object. For more information on creating text style classes, see "Using style classes" on page 347.

Text format tag (‹textformat›)

The ‹textformat› tag lets you use a subset of paragraph formatting properties of the TextFormat class within HTML text fields, including line leading, indentation, margins, and tab stops. You can combine ‹textformat› tags with the built-in HTML tags.

The ‹textformat› tag has the following attributes:

- **blockindent**   Specifies the block indentation in points; corresponds to TextFormat.blockIndent. (See TextFormat.blockIndent on page 922.)

- **indent**   Specifies the indentation from the left margin to the first character in the paragraph; corresponds to TextFormat.indent. (See TextFormat.indent on page 926.)

- `leading`   Specifies the amount of leading (vertical space) between lines; corresponds to `TextFormat.leading`. (See `TextFormat.leading` on page 926.)
- `leftmargin`   Specifies the left margin of the paragraph, in points; corresponds to `TextFormat.leftMargin`. (See `TextFormat.leftMargin` on page 927.)
- `rightmargin`   Specifies the right margin of the paragraph, in points; corresponds to `TextFormat.rightMargin`. (See `TextFormat.rightMargin` on page 927.)
- `tabstops`   Specifies custom tab stops as an array of non-negative integers; corresponds to `TextFormat.tabStops`. (See `TextFormat.tabStops` on page 927.)

The following code example uses the `tabstops` attribute of the `<textformat>` tag to create a table of data with boldfaced row headers, as shown below:

Name	Age	Department
Tim	32	IMD
Edwin	46	Engineering

To create a formatted table of data using tab stops:

1 Using the Text tool, create a dynamic text field that's approximately 300 pixels wide and 100 pixels high.
2 In the Property inspector, enter `table_txt` in the Instance Name text box, select Multiline from the Line Type menu, and select the Render Text as HTML option.
3 In the Timeline, select the first frame on Layer 1.
4 Open the Actions panel (Window > Development Panels > Actions) and enter the following code in the Actions panel:

```
var rowHeaders = "<b>Name\t</b><b>Age\t</b><b>Department";
var row_1 = "Tim\t31\tIMD";
var row_2 = "Edwin\t42\tQA";
table_txt.htmlText = "<textformat tabstops='[100, 200]'>";
table_txt.htmlText += rowHeaders;
table_txt.htmlText += row_1;
table_txt.htmlText += row_2 ;
table_txt.htmlText += "</textformat>";
```

Note the use of the tab character escape sequence (\t) to add tabs between each "column" in the table.

5 Select Control > Test Movie to test the movie.

Underline tag (<u>)

The `<u>` tag underlines the tagged text.

`This text is <u>underlined</u>.`

The above code would render as follows:

This text is <u>underlined</u>.

Embedding images, SWF files, and movie clips in text fields

In Flash Player 7 and later, you can use the `<img>` tag to embed JPEG files, SWF files, and movie clips inside dynamic and input text fields. (For a full list of attributes for the `<img>` tag, see "Image tag (<img>)" on page 353.)

By default, Flash displays media embedded in a text field at full size. To specify dimensions for embedded media, use the `<img>` tags's `height` and `width` attributes. (See "Specifying height and width values" on page 356.)

In general, an image embedded in a text field appears on the line following the `<img>` tag. However, when the `<img>` tag is the first character in the text field, the image appears on the first line of the text field.

Embedding SWF and JPEG files

To embed a JPEG or SWF file in a text field, specify the absolute or relative path to the JPEG or SWF file in the `<img>` tag's `src` attribute. For example, the following code inserts a JPEG file that's located in the same directory as the SWF file.

```
textField_txt.htmlText = "<p>Here's a picture from my last vacation:<img
    src='beach.jpg'>";
```

Embedding movie clip symbols

To embed a movie clip symbol in a text field, you specify the symbol's linkage identifier for the `<img>` tag's `src` attribute. (For information on defining a linkage identifier, see "Attaching a movie clip symbol to the Stage" on page 331.)

For example, the following code inserts a movie clip symbol with the linkage identifier `symbol_ID`.

```
textField_txt.htmlText = "<p>Here's a movie clip symbol:<img
    src='symbol_ID'>";
```

In order for an embedded movie clip to display properly and completely, the registration point for its symbol should be at point (0,0).

Specifying height and width values

If you specify `width` and `height` attributes for an `<img>` tag, space is reserved in the text field for the JPEG file, SWF file, or movie clip. After a JPEG or SWF file has downloaded completely it is displayed in the reserved space. Flash scales the media up or down according to the `height` and `width` values.

If you don't specify `height` and `width` values, no space is reserved for the embedded media. After a JPEG or SWF file has downloaded completely, Flash inserts it into the text field at full size and rebreaks text around it.

Controlling embedded media with ActionScript

Flash Player creates a new movie clip for each `<img>` tag and embeds that movie clip within the TextField object. The `<img>` tag's `id` attribute lets you assign an instance name to the movie clip that is created. This lets you control that movie clip with ActionScript.

The movie clip created by Flash Player is added as a child movie clip to the text field that contains the image.

For example, the following code embeds a SWF file named animation.swf in the text field named `textField_txt` on level 0 and assigns the instance name `animation_mc` to the movie clip that contains the SWF file.

```
_level0.textField_txt.htmlText = "Here's an interesting animation: <img
    src='animation.swf' id='animation_mc'>
```

In this case, the fully qualified path to the newly create movie clip is `_level0.textField_txt.animation_mc`. For example, you could attach the following code to a button (on the same Timeline as `textField_txt`) that would stop the playhead of the embedded SWF file.

```
on(press) {
    textField_txt.animation_mc.stop();
}
```

Making hyperlinks out of embedded media

To make a hyperlink out of an embedded JPEG file, SWF file, or movie clip, enclose the `<img>` tag in an `<a>` tag:

```
textField.htmlText = "Click the image to return home<a href='home.htm'><img
    src='home.jpg'></a>";
```

When the mouse is over an image, SWF file, or movie clip that is enclosed by `<a>` tags, the mouse pointer turns into a "hand" icon, just like standard hyperlinks. Interactivity, such as mouse clicks and keypresses, do not register in SWF files and movie clips that are enclosed by `<a>` tags.

Creating scrolling text

There are several ways to create scrolling text in Flash. You can make dynamic and input text fields scrollable by selecting the Scrollable Mode option in the Text menu or the context menu, or by Shift-double-clicking the text block handle.

You can use the `scroll` and `maxscroll` properties of the TextField object to control vertical scrolling and the `hscroll` and `maxhscroll` properties to control horizontal scrolling in a text block. The `scroll` and `hscroll` properties specify the current vertical and horizontal scrolling positions, respectively; you can read and write these properties. The `maxscroll` and `maxhscroll` properties specify the maximum vertical and horizontal scrolling positions, respectively; you can only read these properties.

The TextArea component in Flash MX 2004 provides an easy way to create scrolling text fields with a minimum of scripting. For more information, see the "TextArea component entry" in Using Components Help.

To create a scrollable dynamic text block, do one of the following:

- Shift-double-click the handle on the dynamic text block.
- Select the dynamic text block with the Arrow tool, and select Text > Scrollable.
- Select the dynamic text block with the Arrow tool. Right-click (Windows) or Control-click (Macintosh) the dynamic text block, and select Text > Scrollable.

To use the scroll property to create scrolling text:

1 Do one of the following:

- Use the Text tool to drag a text field on the Stage. Assign the text field the instance name textField in the Property inspector.

- Use ActionScript to create a text field dynamically with the MovieClip.createTextField() method. Assign the text field the instance name textField as a parameter of the method.

2 Create an Up button and a Down button, or select Window > Other Panels > Common Libraries > Buttons and drag buttons to the Stage.

   You will use these buttons to scroll the text up and down.

3 Select the Down button on the Stage.

4 In the Actions panel (Window > Development Panels > Actions), enter the following code to scroll the text down in the text field:

```
on(press) {
    textField.scroll += 1;
}
```

5 Select the Up button on the Stage.

6 In the Actions panel, enter the following code to scroll the text up:

```
on(press) {
    textField.scroll += 1;
}
```

Close collapsed procedure

CHAPTER 9
Creating Classes with ActionScript 2.0

ActionScript 2.0 is a restructuring of the ActionScript language that provides several powerful new programming features found in other programming languages, such as Java. ActionScript 2.0 encourages program structures that are reusable, scalable, robust, and maintainable. It also decreases development time by providing users with thorough coding assistance and debugging information. ActionScript 2.0 conforms to existing standards and is based on the ECMAScript 4 proposal (www.mozilla.org/js/language/es4/). ActionScript 2.0 is available in Macromedia Flash MX 2004 and Macromedia Flash MX Professional 2004.

The features of ActionScript 2.0 are described below.

Familiar object-oriented programming (OOP) model   The primary feature of ActionScript 2.0 is a familiar model for creating object-oriented programs. ActionScript 2.0 introduces several new object-oriented concepts and keywords such as *class*, *interface*, and *packages* that will be familiar to you if you've ever programmed with Java.

The OOP model provided by ActionScript 2.0 is a "syntactic formalization" of the prototype chaining method used in previous versions of Macromedia Flash to create objects and establish inheritance.

Strict data typing   ActionScript 2.0 also lets you explicitly specify data types for variables, function parameters, and function return types. For example, the following code declares a variable named userName of type String (a built-in ActionScript data type, or class).

```
var userName:String = "";
```

Compiler warnings and errors   The above two features enable the authoring tool and compiler to provide compiler warnings and error messages that help you find bugs in your applications faster than was previously possible in Flash.

Caution: If you plan to use ActionScript 2.0 syntax, ensure that the Publish settings for the FLA file specify ActionScript 2.0. This is the default for files created in Flash MX 2004. However, if you open an older FLA file that uses ActionScript 1 and begin rewriting it in ActionScript 2.0, change the Publish Settings of the FLA file to ActionScript 2.0. If you don't do so, your FLA file will not compile correctly, but no errors will be generated.

Principles of object-oriented programming

This section provides a brief introduction to principles involved in developing object-oriented programs. These principles are described in more depth in the rest of this chapter, along with details on how they are implemented in Macromedia Flash MX 2004 and Macromedia Flash MX Professional 2004.

Objects

Think of a real-world object—for example, a cat. A cat could be said to have properties (or states) such as name, age, and color; a cat also has behaviors such as sleeping, eating, and purring. In the world of object-oriented programming, objects also have properties and behaviors. Using object-oriented techniques, you can model a real-world object (like a cat) or a more abstract object (like a chemical process).

Classes and class members

Continuing with the real-world analogy, consider that there are cats of different colors, ages, and names, with different ways of eating and purring. But all cats belong to a certain class of object, an object of type "cat." Each individual (real-world) cat is an instance of the cat class type.

Likewise, in object-oriented programming, a *class* defines a blueprint for a type of object. The characteristics and behaviors that belong to a class are referred to as *members* of that class. The characteristics (in the cat example, name, age, and color) are called *properties* of the class, which are represented as variables; the behaviors (eating, sleeping) are called *methods* of the class, and are represented as functions.

For example, you could create a Person class, and then create an individual person that would be an instance of that class, also called a Person object. The Person object would contain all the properties and methods of the Person class.

In ActionScript, you define a class with the class statement (see "Creating and using classes" on page 365). ActionScript includes a number of built-in classes, such as the MovieClip, TextField, and String classes. For more information, see Chapter 6, "Using the Built-In Classes," on page 317.

Inheritance

One of the primary benefits of object-oriented programming is that you can create *subclasses* of a class; the subclass then *inherits* all the properties and methods of the *superclass*. The subclass typically defines additional methods and properties, or *extends* the superclass. Subclasses can also *override* (provide their own definitions for) methods inherited from a superclass.

For example, you might create a Mammal class that defines certain properties and behaviors common to all mammals. You could then create a Cat class that extends the Mammal class. In this way, inheritance can promote code reuse: instead of recreating all the code common to both classes, you can simply extend an existing class. Another subclass, in turn, could extend the Cat class, and so on. In a complex application, determining how to structure the hierarchy of your classes is a large part of the design process.

In ActionScript, you use the extends keyword to establish inheritance between a class and its superclass. For more information, see "Creating subclasses" on page 366.

Interfaces

Interfaces in object-oriented programming can be described as classes whose methods are not implemented (defined). Another class can implement the methods declared by the interface.

An interface can also be thought of as a "programming contract" that can be used to enforce relationships between otherwise unrelated classes. For example, suppose you are working with a team of programmers, each of whom is working on a different part (class) of the same application. While designing the application, you agree on a set of methods that the different classes will use to communicate. So you create an interface that declares these methods, their parameters, and their return types. Any class that implements this interface must provide definitions for those methods; otherwise, a compiler error will result.

You can also use interfaces to provide a limited form of "multiple inheritance," which is not allowed in ActionScript 2.0. In multiple inheritance, a class extends more than one class. For example, in C++ the Cat class could extend the Mammal class, as well as a Playful class, which has methods ChaseTail and EatCatNip. ActionScript 2.0, like Java, does not allow a class to extend multiple classes directly. However, you could create a Playful interface that declares the ChaseTail and EatCatNip methods. A Cat class, or any other class, could then implement this interface and provide definitions for those methods.

For more information, see "Creating an interface" on page 371.

Using classes: a simple example

For those who are new to object-oriented programming, this section provides an overview of the workflow involved in creating and using classes in Flash. At a minimum, this workflow involves the following steps:

1 Defining a class in an external ActionScript class file.
2 Saving the class file to a designated classpath directory (a location where Flash looks for classes).
3 Creating an instance of the class in another script, either in a Flash (FLA) document or an external script file, or creating a subclass based the original class.

Also discussed in this section is a new feature in ActionScript 2.0 called *strict data typing*, which lets you specify the data type for a variable, function parameter, or function return type.

Although this section discusses only classes, the general workflow is the same for using interfaces. For more information, see "Creating and using interfaces" on page 371.

Creating a class file

To create a class, you must first create an external ActionScript (AS) file. Classes (and interfaces) can only be defined in external script files. For example, you can't define a class in a script attached to a frame or button in a Flash document (FLA). To create an external AS file, use the ActionScript editor included with Flash or your preferred code or text editor.

Note: ActionScript code in external files is compiled into a SWF file when you publish, export, test, or debug a FLA file. Therefore, if you make any changes to an external file, you must save the file and recompile any FLA files that use it.

In the steps below you'll create a class called Person that contains two properties (age and name) and a single method (showInfo()) that displays the values of those properties in the Output panel.

To create the class file:

1 Create a new directory on your hard disk and name it PersonFiles. This directory will contain all the files for this project.

2 Do one of the following:

  - Create a new file in your preferred text or code editor.

  - (Flash Professional only) Select File > New to open the New Document dialog box, select ActionScript File from the list of file types, and click OK. The Script window opens with a blank file.

3 Save the file as Person.as in the PersonFiles directory.

4 In the Script window, enter the following code:

```
class Person {
}
```

This is called the class *declaration*. In its most basic form, a class declaration consists of the `class` keyword, followed by the class name (Person, in this case), and then left and right curly braces ({}). Everything between the braces is called the class *body* and is where the class's properties and methods are defined.

Note: The name of the class (Person) matches the name of the AS file that contains it (Person.as). This is very important; if these two names don't match, the class won't compile.

5 To create the properties for the Person class, use the `var` keyword to define two variables named `age` and `name`, as shown below.

```
class Person {

    var age:Number;
    var name:String;

}
```

Tip: By convention, class properties are defined at the top of the class body, which makes the code easier to understand, but this isn't required.

Notice the colon syntax (`var age:Number` and `var name:String`) used in the variable declarations. This is an example of strict data typing. When you type a variable in this way (`var variableName:variableType`), the ActionScript 2.0 compiler ensures that any values assigned to that variable match the specified type. Although this syntax is not required, it is good practice and can make debugging your scripts easier. (For more information, see "Strict data typing" on page 242.)

6 Next you'll create the showInfo() method, which returns a preformatted string containing the values of the age and name properties. Add the showInfo() function definition to the class body, as shown below.

```
class Person {

    var age:Number;
    var name:String;

    // Method to return property values
    function showInfo():String {
        return("Hello, my name is " + name + " and I'm " + age + " years old.");
    }
}
```

Notice the use of data typing (optional but recommended) in the function definition.

```
function showInfo():String {...}
```

In this case, what's being typed is the showInfo() function's return value (a string).

7 The last bit of code you'll add in this section is a special function called a *constructor function*. In object-oriented programming, the constructor function initializes each new instance of a class.

The constructor function always has the same name as the class. To create the class's constructor function, add the following code:

```
class Person {

    var age:Number;
    var name:String;

    // Method to return property values
    function showInfo():String {
        return("Hello, my name is " + name + " and I'm " + age + " years old.");
    }

    // Constructor function
    function Person (myName:String, myAge:Number) {
        name = myName;
        age = myAge;
    }
}
```

The Person() constructor function takes two parameters, myName and myAge, and assigns those parameters to the name and age properties. The two function parameters are strictly typed as String and Number, respectively. For more information about constructor functions, see "Constructor functions" on page 367.

Note: If you don't create a constructor function, an empty one is created automatically during compilation.

8 Save the file as Person.as in the PersonFiles directory that you created in step 1.

If you're using Flash MX 2004 (not Flash Professional), proceed to the next section.

9 (Flash Professional only) Check the syntax of the class file by selecting Tools > Check Syntax, or pressing Control+T (Windows) or Command+T (Macintosh).

If any errors are reported in the Output panel, compare the code in your script to the final code in step 7, above. If you can't fix the code errors, copy the completed code in step 7 from the Help panel.

Creating an instance of the Person class

The next step is to create an instance of the Person class in another script, such as a frame script in a Flash (FLA) document or another AS script, and assign it to a variable. To create an instance of a custom class, you use the new operator, just as you would when creating an instance of a built-in ActionScript class (such as the XML or TextField class).

For example, the following code creates an instance of the Person class and assigns it to the variable newPerson.

```
var newPerson:Person = new Person("Nate", 32);
```

This code invokes the Person class's constructor function, passing as parameters the values "Nate" and 32.

The newPerson variable is typed as a Person object. Typing your objects in this way enables the compiler to ensure that you don't try to access properties or methods that aren't defined in the class. (The exception is if you declare the class to be dynamic using the dynamic keyword. See "Creating dynamic classes" on page 377.)

To create an instance of the Person class in a Flash document:

1 In Flash, select File > New, select Flash Document from the list of document types, and click OK.

2 Save the file as createPerson.fla in the PersonFiles directory you created previously.

3 Select Layer 1 in the Timeline and open the Actions panel (Window > Development Panels > Actions).

4 In the Actions panel, enter the following code:

```
var person_1:Person = new Person("Nate", 32);
var person_2:Person = new Person("Jane", 28);
trace(person_1.showInfo());
trace(person_2.showInfo());
```

The above code creates two instances of the Person class, person_1 and person_2, and then calls the showInfo() method on each instance.

5 Save your work, then select Control > Test Movie. You should see the following in the Output panel:

```
Hello, my name is Nate and I'm 32 years old.
Hello, my name is Jane and I'm 28 years old.
```

When you create an instance of a class by calling its constructor function, Flash looks for an ActionScript file of the same name as the constructor in a set of predetermined directory locations. This group of directory locations is known collectively as the *classpath* (see "Understanding the classpath" on page 373).

You should now have an overall idea of how to create and use classes in your Flash documents. The rest of this chapter explores classes and interfaces in more detail.

Creating and using classes

As discussed previously, a class consists of two parts: the *declaration* and the *body*. The class declaration consists minimally of the `class` statement, followed by an identifier for the class name, then left and right curly braces. Everything inside the braces is the class body.

```
class className {
    // class body
}
```

You can define classes only in ActionScript (AS) files. For example, you can't define a class on a frame script in a FLA file. Also, the specified class name must match the name of the AS file that contains it. For example, if you create a class called Shape, the AS file that contains the class definition must be named Shape.as.

```
// In file Shape.as
class Shape {
    // Shape class body
}
```

All AS class files that you create must be saved in one of the designated classpath directories— directories where Flash looks for class definitions when compiling scripts. (See "Understanding the classpath" on page 373.)

Class names must be identifiers; that is the first character must be a letter, underscore (_), or dollar sign ($), and each subsequent character must be a letter, number, underscore, or dollar sign. Also, the class name must be fully qualified within the file in which it is declared; that is, it must reflect the directory in which it is stored. For example, to create a class named RequiredClass that is stored in the myClasses/education/curriculum directory, you must declare the class in the RequiredClass.as file like this:

```
class myClasses.education.curriculum.RequiredClass {
}
```

For this reason, it's good practice to plan your directory structure before you begin creating classes. Otherwise, if you decide to move class files after you create them, you will have to modify the class declaration statements to reflect their new location.

Creating properties and methods

A class's members consist of properties (variable declarations) and methods (function declarations). You must declare all properties and methods inside the class body (the curly braces); otherwise, an error will occur during compilation.

Any variable declared within a class, but outside a function, is a property of the class. For example, the Person class discussed earlier has two properties, `age` and `name`, of type Number and String, respectively.

```
class Person {
    var age:Number;
    var name:String;
}
```

Similarly, any function declared within a class is considered a method of the class. In the Person class example, you created a single method called showInfo().

```
class Person {
  var age:Number;
  var name:String;
  function showInfo() {
    // showInfo() method definition
  }
}
```

Initializing properties inline

You can initialize properties *inline*—that is, when you declare them—with default values, as shown here:

```
class Person {
  var age:Number = 50;
  var name:String = "John Doe";
}
```

When you initialize properties inline the expression on the right side of an assignment must be a *compile-time constant*. That is, the expression cannot refer to anything that is set or defined at runtime. Compile-time constants include string literals, numbers, Boolean values, null, and undefined, as well as constructor functions for the following built-in classes: Array, Boolean, Number, Object, and String.

For example, the following class definition initializes several properties inline:

```
class CompileTimeTest {
  var foo:String = "my foo"; // OK
  var bar:Number = 5; // OK
  var bool:Boolean = true; // OK
  var name:String = new String("Jane"); // OK
  var who:String = foo; // OK, because 'foo' is a constant

  var whee:String = myFunc(); // error! not compile-time constant expression
  var lala:Number = whee; // error! not compile-time constant expression
  var star:Number = bar + 25; // OK, both 'bar' and '25' are constants

  function myFunc() {
    return "Hello world";
  }
}
```

This rule only applies to instance variables (variables that are copied into each instance of a class), not class variables (variables that belong to the class itself). For more information about these kinds of variables, see "Instance and class members" on page 369.

Creating subclasses

In object-oriented programming, a subclass can inherit the properties and methods of another class, called the superclass. To create this kind of relationship between two classes, you use the class statement's extends clause. To specify a superclass, use the following syntax:

```
class SubClass extends SuperClass {}
```

The class you specify in *SubClass* inherits all the properties and methods defined by the superclass. For example, you might create a Mammal class that defines properties and methods common to all mammals. To create a variation of the Mammal class, such as a Marsupial class, you would extend the Mammal class—that is, create a subclass of the Mammal class.

```
class Marsupial extends Mammal {}
```

The subclass inherits all the properties and methods of the superclass, including any properties or methods that you have declared to be private using the `private` keyword. (For more information on private variables, see "Controlling member access" on page 368.)

You can extend your own custom classes, as well as any of the built-in ActionScript classes, such as the XML, Sound, or MovieClip class. When you extend a built-in ActionScript class, your custom class inherits all the methods and properties of the built-in class.

For example, the following code defines the class JukeBox, which extends the built-in Sound class. It defines an array called `songList` and a method called `playSong()` that plays a song and invokes the `loadSound()` method, which it inherits from the Sound class.

```
class JukeBox extends Sound {
  var songList:Array = new Array("beethoven.mp3", "bach.mp3", "mozart.mp3");
  function playSong(songID:Number) {
    this.loadSound(songList[songID]);
  }
}
```

If you don't place a call to `super()` in the constructor function of a subclass, the compiler automatically generates a call to the constructor of its immediate superclass with no parameters as the first statement of the function. If the superclass doesn't have a constructor, the compiler creates an empty constructor function and then generates a call to it from the subclass. However, if the superclass takes parameters in its definition, you must create a constructor in the subclass and call the superclass with the required parameters.

Multiple inheritance, or inheriting from more than one class, is not allowed. However, classes can effectively inherit from multiple classes if you use individual `extends` statements:

```
// not allowed
class C extends A, B {}
// allowed
class B extends A {}
class C extends B {}
```

You can also use the `extends` keyword to create subclasses of an interface:

```
interface iA extends interface iB {}
```

Constructor functions

A class's *constructor* is a special function that is called automatically when you create an instance of a class using the `new` operator. The constructor function has the same name as the class that contains it. For example, the Person class you created earlier contained the following constructor function:

```
// Person class constructor function
function Person (myName:String, myAge:Number) {
  name = myName;
  age = myAge;
}
```

If no constructor function is explicitly declared—that is, if you don't create a function whose name matches that of the class—the compiler automatically creates an empty constructor function for you.

A class can contain only one constructor function; overloaded constructor functions are not allowed in ActionScript 2.0.

Controlling member access

By default, any property or method of a class can be accessed by any other class: all members of a class are *public* by default. However, in some cases you may want to protect data or methods of a class from access by other classes. You'll need to make those members *private*—available only to the class that declares or defines them.

You specify public or private members using the `public` or `private` member attribute. For example, the following code declares a private variable (a property) and a private method (a function).

For example, the following class (LoginClass) defines a private property named `userName` and a private method named `getUserName()`.

```
class LoginClass {
  private var userName:String;
  private function getUserName() {
    return userName;
  }
  // Constructor:
  function LoginClass(user:String) {
    this.userName = user;
  }
}
```

Private members (properties and methods) are accessible only to the class that defines those members and to subclasses of that original class. Instances of the original class, or instances of subclasses of that class, cannot access privately declared properties and methods; that is, private members are accessible only within class definitions; not at the instance level.

For example, you could create a subclass of LoginClass called NewLoginClass. This subclass can access the private property (`userName`) and method (`getUserName()`) defined by LoginClass.

```
class NewLoginClass extends LoginClass {
  // can access userName and getUserName()
}
```

However, an instance of LoginClass or NewLoginClass cannot access those private members. For example, the following code, added to a frame script in a FLA file, would result in a compiler error indicating that `getUserName()` is private and can't be accessed.

```
var loginObject:LoginClass = new LoginClass("Maxwell");
var user = loginObject.getUserName();
```

Also note that member access control is a compile-time only feature; at runtime, Flash Player does not distinguish between private or public members.

Instance and class members

In object-oriented programming, members (properties or methods) of a class can be either *instance members* or *class members*. Instance members are created for, and copied into, each instance of the class; in contrast, class members are created just once per class. (Class members are also known as *static members*.)

To invoke an instance method or access an instance property, you reference an instance of the class. For example, the following code invokes the `showInfo()` method on an instance of the MovieClip class called `clip_mc`:

```
clip_mc.showInfo();
```

Class (static) members, however, are assigned to the class itself, not to any instance of the class. To invoke a class method or access a class property, you reference the class name itself, rather than a specific instance of the class:

```
ClassName.classMember;
```

For example, the ActionScript Math class consists only of static methods and properties. To call any of its methods, you don't create an instance of the Math class. Instead, you simply call the methods on the Math class itself. The following code calls the `sqrt()` method of the Math class:

```
var square_root:Number = Math.sqrt(4);
```

Instance members can read static members, but cannot write them. Instance members are not enumerable in `for` or `for..in` loops.

Creating class members

To specify that a property of a class is static, you use the `static` modifier, as shown below.

```
static var variableName;
```

You can also declare methods of a class to be static.

```
static function functionName() {
   // function body
}
```

Class (static) methods can access only class (static) properties, not instance properties. For example, the following code will result in a compiler error, because the class method `getName()` references the instance variable `name`.

```
class StaticTest {
  var name="Ted";

  static function getName() {
    var local_name = name;
    // Error! Instance variables cannot be accessed in static functions.
  }
}
```

To solve this problem, you could either make the method an instance method or make the variable a class variable.

Using class members: a simple example

One use of class (static) members is to maintain state information about a class and its instances. For example, suppose you want to keep track of the number of instances that have been created from a particular class. An easy way to do this is to use a class property that's incremented each time a new instance is created.

In the following example, you'll create a class called Widget that defines a single, static instance counter named `widgetCount`. Each time a new instance of the class is created, the value of `widgetCount` is incremented by 1 and the current value of `widgetCount` is displayed in the Output panel.

To create an instance counter using a class variable:

1 Create a new ActionScript (AS) file.

2 Add the following code to the file:

```
class Widget {
    static var widgetCount:Number = 0; // initialize class variable
    function Widget() {
        trace("Creating widget #" + widgetCount);
        widgetCount++;
    }
}
```

The `widgetCount` variable is declared as static, and so initializes to 0 only once. Each time the Widget class's constructor function is called, it adds 1 to `widgetCount`, and then displays the number of the current instance that's being created.

3 Save your file as Widget.as.

4 Create a new Flash (FLA) document and save it as createWidget.fla in the same directory as Widget.as.

In this file, you'll create new instances of the Widget class.

5 In createWidget.fla, select Layer 1 in the Timeline and open the Actions panel (Window > Development Panels > Actions).

6 Add the following code to the Actions panel.

```
// Before you create any instances of the class,
// widgetCount is zero (0)
trace("Widget count at start: " + Widget.widgetCount);
var widget_1 = new Widget();
var widget_2 = new Widget();
var widget_3 = new Widget();
```

7 Save the file, and then test it (Control > Test Movie).

You should see the following in the Output panel:

```
Widget count at start: 0
Creating widget # 0
Creating widget # 1
Creating widget # 2
```

Class members and subclasses

Class members propagate to subclasses of the superclass that defines those members. In the previous example (see "Using class members: a simple example" on page 370), you used a class property to keep track of the number of instances of that class you created. You could create a subclass of the Widget class, as shown below.

```
class SubWidget extends Widget {
  function SubWidget() {
    trace("Creating subwidget # "+Widget.widgetCount);
  }
}
```

Creating and using interfaces

An interface in object-oriented programming is like a class whose methods have been declared, but otherwise don't "do" anything. That is, an interface consists of "empty" methods.

One use of interfaces is to enforce a protocol between otherwise unrelated classes, as discussed next. For example, suppose you're part of a team of programmers, each of whom is working on a different part—that is, a different class—of a large application. Most of these classes are unrelated, but you still need a way for the different classes to communicate. That is, you need to define an interface, or communication protocol, that all the classes must adhere to.

One way to do this would be to create a Communication class that defines all of these methods, and then have each class extend, or inherit from, this superclass. But because the application consists of classes that are unrelated, it doesn't make sense to force them all into a common class hierarchy. A better solution is to create an interface that declares the methods these classes will use to communicate, and then have each class implement (provide its own definitions for) those methods.

You can usually program successfully without using interfaces. When used appropriately, however, interfaces can make the design of your applications more elegant, scalable, and maintainable.

Creating an interface

The process for creating an interface is the same as for creating a class. As with classes, you can only define interfaces in external ActionScript (AS) files. You declare an interface using the `interface` keyword, followed by the interface name, and then left and right curly braces, which define the body of the interface.

```
interface interfaceName {
  // interface method declarations
}
```

An interface can contain only method (function) declarations, including parameters, parameter types, and function return types.

For example, the following code declares an interface named MyInterface that contains two methods, method_1() and method_2(). The first method takes no parameters and has no return type (specified as Void). The second method declaration takes a single parameter of type String, and specifies a return type of Boolean.

```
interface MyInterface {
   function method_1():Void;
   function method_2(param:String):Boolean;
}
```

Interfaces cannot contain any variable declarations or assignments. Functions declared in an interface cannot contain curly braces. For example, the following interface won't compile.

```
interface BadInterface{
   // Compiler error. Variable declarations not allowed in interfaces.
   var illegalVar;

// Compiler error. Function bodies not allowed in interfaces.
   function illegalMethod(){
   }
}
```

The rules for naming interfaces and storing them in packages are the same as those for classes; see "Creating and using classes" on page 365 and "Using packages" on page 375.

Interfaces as data types

Like a class, an interface defines a new data type. Any class that implements an interface can be considered to be of the type defined by the interface. This is useful for determining if a given object implements a given interface. For example, consider the following interface.

```
interface Movable {
   function moveUp();
   function moveDown();
}
```

Now consider the class Box that implements the Movable interface.

```
class Box implements Movable {
   var x_pos, y_pos;

   function moveUp() {
      // method definition
   }
   function moveDown() {
      // method definition
   }
}
```

Then, in another script where you create an instance of the Box class, you could declare a variable to be of the Movable type.

```
var newBox:Movable = new Box();
```

At runtime, in Flash Player 7 and later, you can cast an expression to an interface type. If the expression is an object that implements the interface or has a superclass that implements the interface, the object is returned. Otherwise, null is returned. This is useful if you want to make sure that a particular object implements a certain interface.

For example, the following code first checks if the object name `someObject` implements the Movable interface before calling the `moveUp()` method on the object.

```
if(Movable(someObject) != null) {
   someObject.moveUp();
}
```

Understanding the classpath

In order to use a class or interface that you've defined, Flash must be able to locate the external AS files that contain the class or interface definition. The list of directories in which Flash searches for class and interface definitions is called the *classpath*.

When you create an ActionScript class file, you need to save the file to one of the directories specified in the classpath, or a subdirectory therein. (You can modify the classpath to include the desired directory path; see "Modifying the classpath" on page 374.) Otherwise, Flash won't be able to *resolve*, or locate, the class or interface specified in the script. Subdirectories that you create within a classpath directory are called *packages* and let you organize your classes. (For more information, see "Using packages" on page 375.)

Global and document-level classpaths

Flash has two classpath settings: a global classpath and a document-level classpath. The global classpath applies to external AS and FLA files and is set in the Preferences dialog box (Edit > Preferences). The document-level classpath applies only to FLA files and is set in the Publish Settings dialog (File > Publish Settings) for a particular FLA.

By default, the global classpath contains two directory paths: a relative path that points to the directory that contains the current document, and the Classes directory located in the user configuration directory installed with Flash. The location of this directory is shown here:

- Windows 2000 or Windows XP: C:\Documents and Settings\<user>\Local Settings\ Application Data\Macromedia\Flash MX2004\<language>\Configuration\
- Windows 98: C:\Windows\Application Data\Macromedia\Flash MX 2004\ <language>\Configuration\
- Macintosh OS X: Hard Drive/Users/Library/Application Support/Macromedia/ Flash MX 2004/<language>/Configuration/

The document-level classpath is empty by default.

How the compiler resolves class references

When Flash attempts to resolve class references in a FLA script, it first searches the document-level classpath specified for that FLA. If the class is not found in that classpath, or if that classpath is empty, Flash searches the global classpath. If the class is not found in the global classpath, a compiler error occurs.

When Flash attempts to resolve class references in an AS script, it searches only the global classpath directories, since AS files don't have an associated document class path.

Modifying the classpath

You can modify the global classpath using the Preferences dialog box. To modify the document-level classpath setting, you use the Publish Settings dialog box for the FLA file. You can add absolute directory paths (for example, C:/my_classes) and relative directory paths (for example, ../my_classes or ".").

By default, the global classpath contains one absolute path (the Classes directory in the user configuration directory) and a relative classpath, denoted by a single dot (.), which points to the current document directory. Be aware that relative classpaths can point to different directories, depending on the location of the document being compiled or published. For more information, see "Global and document-level classpaths" on page 373.

To modify the global classpath:

1 Select Edit > Preferences to open the Preferences dialog box.

2 Click the ActionScript tab, then click the ActionScript 2.0 Settings button.

3 Do any of the following:

- To add a directory to the classpath, click the Browse to Path button, browse to the directory you want to add, and click OK.

  Alternatively, click the Add New Path (+) button to add a new line to the Classpath list. Double-click the new line, type a relative or absolute path, and click OK.

- To edit an existing classpath directory, select the path in the Classpath list, click the Browse to Path button, browse to the directory you want to add, and click OK.

  Alternatively, double-click the path in the Classpath list, type the desired path, and click OK.

- To delete a directory from the classpath, select the path in the Classpath list and click the Remove from Path button.

To modify the document-level classpath:

1 Select File > Publish Settings to open the Publish Settings dialog box.

2 Click the Flash tab.

3 Click the Settings button next to the ActionScript Version pop-up menu.

4 Do any of the following:

- To add a directory to the classpath, click the Browse to Path button, browse to the directory you want to add, and click OK.

  Alternatively, click the Add New Path (+) button to add a new line to the Classpath list. Double-click the new line, type a relative or absolute path, and click OK.

- To edit an existing classpath directory, select the path in the Classpath list, click the Browse to Path button, browse to the directory you want to add, and click OK.

  Alternatively, double-click the path in the Classpath list, type the desired path, and click OK.

- To delete a directory from the classpath, select the path in the Classpath list and click the Remove from Path button.

Using packages

You can organize your ActionScript class files in *packages*. A package is a directory that contains one or more class files, and that resides in a designated classpath directory. (See "Understanding the classpath" on page 373.) A package can, in turn, contain other packages, called *subpackages*, each with its own class files.

Package names must be identifiers; that is the first character must be a letter, underscore (_), or dollar sign ($), and each subsequent character must be a letter, number, underscore, or dollar sign.

Packages are commonly used to organize related classes. For example, you might have three related classes, Square, Circle, and Triangle, that are defined in Square.as, Circle.as, and Triangle.as. Assume that you've saved the AS files to a directory specified in the classpath.

```
// In Square.as:
class Square {}

// In Circle.as:
class Circle {}

// In Triangle.as:
class Triangle {}
```

Because these three class files are related, you might decide to put them in a package (directory) called Shapes. In this case, the fully qualified class name would contain the package path, as well as the simple class name. Package paths are denoted with dot syntax, where each dot indicates a subdirectory.

For example, if you placed each AS file that defines a shape in the Shapes directory, you would need to change the name of each class file to reflect the new location, as follows:

```
// In Shapes/Square.as:
class Shapes.Square {}

// In Shapes/Circle.as:
class Shapes.Circle {}

// In Shapes/Triangle.as:
class Shapes.Triangle {}
```

To reference a class that resides in a package directory, you can either specify its fully qualified class name or import the package by using the `import` statement (see below).

Importing classes

To reference a class in another script, you must prefix the class name with the class's package path. The combination of a class's name and its package path is the class's *fully qualified class name*. If a class resides in a top-level classpath directory—not in a subdirectory in the classpath directory—then its fully qualified class name is just its class name.

To specify package paths, use dot notation to separate package directory names. Package paths are hierarchical, where each dot represents a nested directory. For example, suppose you create a class named Data that resides in a com/network/ package in your classpath. To create an instance of that class, you could specify the fully qualified class name, as follows:

```
var dataInstance = new com.network.Data();
```

You can use the fully qualified class name to type your variables, as well:

```
var dataInstance:com.network.Data = new Data();
```

You can use the `import` statement to import packages into a script, which lets you use a class's abbreviated name rather than its fully qualified name. You can also use the wildcard character (*) to import all the classes in a package.

For example, suppose you created a class named UserClass that's included in the package directory path macr/util/users:

```
// In the file macr/util/users/UserClass.as
class macr.util.users.UserClass { ... }
```

Suppose that in another script, you imported that class as follows using the `import` statement:

```
import macr.util.users.UserClass;
```

Later in the same script you could reference that class by its abbreviated name:

```
var myUser:UserClass = new UserClass();
```

You can use the wildcard character (*) to import all the classes in a given package. For example, suppose you have a package named `macr.util` that contains two ActionScript class files, foo.as and bar.as. In another script, you could import both classes in that package using the wildcard character, as shown below.

```
import macr.util.*;
```

In the same script, you can then reference either the foo or bar class directly.

```
var myFoo:foo = new foo();
var myBar:bar = new bar();
```

The `import` statement applies only to the current script (frame or object) in which it's called. If an imported class is not used in a script, the class is not included in the resulting SWF file's bytecode, and the class isn't available to any SWF files that the FLA file containing the `import` statement might call. For more information, see `import` on page 604.

Implicit get/set methods

Object-oriented programming practice discourages direct access to properties within a class. Classes typically define "get" methods that provide read access and "set" methods that provide write access to a given property. For example, imagine a class that contains a property called userName:

```
var userName:String;
```

Instead of allowing instances of the class to directly access this property (`obj.userName = "Jody"`, for example), the class might have two methods, `getUserName` and `setUserName`, that would be implemented as follows:

```
function getUserName:String() {
   return userName;
}

function setUserName(name:String): {
   userName = name;
}
```

As you can see, `getUserName` returns the current value of `userName`, and `setUserName` sets the value of `userName` to the string parameter passed to the method. An instance of the class would then use the following syntax to get or set the `userName` property.

```
// calling "get" method
var name = obj.getUserName();
// calling "set" method
obj.setUserName("Jody");
```

However, if you want to use a more concise syntax, use *implicit* get/set methods. Implicit get/set methods let you access class properties in a direct manner, while maintaining good OOP practice.

To define these methods, use the `get` and `set` method attributes. You create methods that get or set the value of a property, and add the keyword `get` or `set` before the method name.

```
function get user():String {
   return userName;
}

function set user(name:String):Void {
   userName = name;
}
```

A get method must not take any parameters. A set method must take exactly one required parameter. A set method can have the same name as a get method in the same scope. Get/set methods cannot have the same name as other properties. For example, in the example code above that defines get and set methods named `user`, you could not also have a property named `user` in the same class.

Unlike ordinary methods, get/set methods are invoked without any parentheses or arguments. For example, the following syntax could now be used to access or modify the value of `userName` with the get/set methods defined above.

```
var name = obj.user;
obj.user = "Jack";
```

Note: Implicit get/set methods are syntactic shorthand for the `Object.addProperty()` method in ActionScript 1.

Creating dynamic classes

By default, the properties and methods of a class are fixed. That is, an instance of a class can't create or access properties or methods that weren't originally declared or defined by the class. For example, consider a Person class that defines two properties, `name` and `age`:

```
class Person {
   var name:String;
   var age:Number;
}
```

If, in another script, you create an instance of the Person class and try to access a property of the class that doesn't exist, the compiler generates an error. For example, the following code creates a new instance of the Person class (`a_person`) and then tries to assign a value to a property named `hairColor`, which doesn't exist.

```
var a_person:Person = new Person();
a_person.hairColor = "blue"; // compiler error
```

This code causes a compiler error because the Person class doesn't declare a property named `hairColor`. In most cases, this is exactly what you want to happen.

In some cases, however, you might want to add and access properties or methods of a class at runtime that aren't defined in the original class definition. The `dynamic` class modifier lets you do just that. For example, the following code adds the `dynamic` modifier to the Person class discussed previously:

```
dynamic class Person {
  var name:String;
  var age:Number;
}
```

Now, instances of the Person class can add and access properties and methods that aren't defined in the original class.

```
var a_person:Person = new Person();
a_person.hairColor = "blue"; // no compiler error because class is dynamic
```

Subclasses of dynamic classes are also dynamic.

How classes are compiled and exported

By default, classes used by a SWF file are packaged and exported on the SWF's first frame. You can also specify the frame where your classes are packaged and exported. This is useful, for example, if a SWF file uses many classes that require a long time to download. If the classes are exported on the first frame, the user would have to wait until all the class code has downloaded before that frame would appear. By specifying a later frame in the Timeline, you could display a short loading animation in the first few frames of the Timeline while the class code in the later frame downloads.

To specify the export frame for classes for a Flash document:

1 With a FLA file open, select File > Publish Settings.

2 In the Publish Settings dialog box, click the Flash tab.

3 Click the Settings button next to the ActionScript version pop-up menu to open the ActionScript Settings dialog box.

4 In the Export Frame for Classes text box, enter the number of the frame where you want to export your class code.

   If the frame specified does not exist in the Timeline, you will get an error message when you publish your SWF.

5 Click OK to close the ActionScript Settings dialog box, then click OK to close the Publish Settings dialog box.

PART IV
Working with External Data and Media

This part discusses how to incorporate external data and media into your Macromedia Flash applications.

CHAPTER 10
Working with External Data

In Macromedia Flash MX 2004 and Macromedia Flash MX Professional 2004, you can use ActionScript to load data from external sources into a SWF file. You can also send data from a SWF file for processing by an application server (such as Macromedia ColdFusion MX or Macromedia JRun) or another type of server-side script, such as PHP or Perl. Flash Player can send and load data over HTTP or HTTPS or from a local text file. You can also create persistent TCP/IP socket connections for applications that require low latency—for example, chat applications or a stock quote services.

Data that you load into or send from a SWF file can be formatted as XML (Extensible Markup Language) or as name-value pairs.

Flash Player can also send data to and receive data from its host environment—a web browser, for example—or another instance of Flash Player on the same computer.

By default, a SWF file can only access data that resides in the same domain (for example, www.macromedia.com) that the Flash movie originated from. (For more information, see "Flash Player security features" on page 392.)

Sending and loading variables to and from a remote source

A SWF file is a window for capturing and displaying information, much like an HTML page. However, SWF files can stay loaded in the browser and continuously update with new information without having to reload the entire page. Using ActionScript functions and methods, you can send information to and receive information from server-side scripts, text files, and XML files.

In addition, server-side scripts can request specific information from a database and relay it to a SWF file. Server-side scripts can be written in many different languages: some of the most common are CFML, Perl, ASP (Microsoft Active Server Pages), and PHP. By storing information in a database and retrieving it, you can create dynamic and personalized content for your SWF file. For example, you could create a message board, personal profiles for users, or a shopping cart that keeps track of a user's purchases so that it can determine the user's preferences.

Several ActionScript functions and methods let you pass information into and out of a SWF file. Each function or method uses a protocol to transfer information, and requires information to be formatted in a certain way.

- The functions and MovieClip methods that use the HTTP or HTTPS protocol to send information in URL-encoded format are getURL(), loadVariables(), loadVariablesNum(), loadMovie(), and loadMovieNum().

- The LoadVars methods that use the HTTP or HTTPS protocol to send and load information in URL-encoded format are load(), send(), and sendAndLoad().

- The methods that use HTTP or HTTPS protocol to send and load information as XML are XML.send(), XML.load(), and XML.sendAndLoad().

- The methods that create and use a TCP/IP socket connection to send and load information as XML are XMLSocket.connect() and XMLSocket.send().

Checking for loaded data

Each function or method that loads data into a SWF file (except XMLSocket.send()) is *asynchronous*: the results of the action are returned at an indeterminate time.

Before you can use loaded data in a SWF file, you must check to see if it has been loaded. For example, you can't load variables and manipulate their values in the same script. In the following script, you can't use the variable lastFrameVisited until you're sure the variable has loaded from the file myData.txt:

```
loadVariables("myData.txt", 0);
gotoAndPlay(lastFrameVisited);
```

Each function or method has a specific technique you can use to check data it has loaded. If you use loadVariables() or loadMovie(), you can load information into a movie clip target and use the data event of the onClipEvent() handler to execute a script. If you use loadVariables() to load the data, the onClipEvent(data) handler executes when the last variable is loaded. If you use loadMovie() to load the data, the onClipEvent(data) handler executes each time a fragment of the SWF file is streamed into Flash Player.

For example, the following button action loads the variables from the file myData.txt into the movie clip loadTargetMC:

```
on(release){
   loadVariables("myData.txt", _root.loadTargetMC);
}
```

An onClipEvent() handler assigned to the loadTargetMC instance uses the variable lastFrameVisited, which is loaded from the file myData.txt. The following will execute only after all the variables, including lastFrameVisited, are loaded:

```
onClipEvent(data) {
   goToAndPlay(lastFrameVisited);
}
```

If you use the XML.load(), XML.sendAndLoad(), and XMLSocket.connect() methods, you should define a handler that will process the data when it arrives. This handler is a property of an XML or XMLSocket object to which you assign a function you have defined. The handlers are called automatically when the information is received. For the XML object, use XML.onLoad() or XML.onData(). For the XMLSocket object, use XMLSocket.onConnect().

For more information, see "Using the XML class" on page 385 and "Using the XMLSocket class" on page 388.

Using HTTP to connect to server-side scripts

The loadVariables(), loadVariablesNum(), getURL(), loadMovie(), and loadMovieNum() functions and the MovieClip.loadVariables(), MovieClip.loadMovie(), and MovieClip.getURL() methods can all communicate with server-side scripts over HTTP or HTTPS protocols. These functions send all the variables from the Timeline to which the function is attached. When used as methods of the MovieClip object, loadVariables(), getURL(), and loadMovie() send all the variables of the specified movie clip; each function (or method) handles its response as follows:

- getURL() returns any information to a browser window, not to Flash Player.
- loadVariables() loads variables into a specified Timeline or level in Flash Player.
- loadMovie() loads a SWF file into a specified level or movie clip in Flash Player.

When you use loadVariables(), getURL(), or loadMovie(), you can specify several parameters:

- *URL* is the file in which the remote variables reside.
- *Location* is the level or target in the SWF file that receives the variables. (The getURL() function does not take this parameter.)

  For more information about levels and targets, see "About multiple Timelines and levels" in Using Flash Help.

- *Variables* sets the HTTP method, either GET or POST, by which the variables will be sent. When omitted, Flash Player defaults to GET, but no variables are sent.

For example, if you wanted to track the high scores for a game, you could store the scores on a server and use loadVariables() to load them into the SWF file each time someone played the game. The function call might look like this:

```
loadVariables("http://www.mySite.com/scripts/high_score.php", _root.scoreClip,
  GET);
```

This loads variables from the PHP script called high_score.php into the movie clip instance scoreClip using the GET HTTP method.

Any variables loaded with the loadVariables() function must be in the standard MIME format *application/x-www-form-urlencoded* (a standard format used by CGI scripts). The file you specify in the *URL* parameter of loadVariables() must write out the variable and value pairs in this format so that Flash can read them. This file can specify any number of variables; variable and value pairs must be separated with an ampersand (&), and words within a value must be separated with a plus (+). For example, this phrase defines several variables:

```
highScore1=54000&playerName1=rockin+good&highScore2=53455&playerName2=
  bonehelmet&highScore3=42885&playerName3=soda+pop
```

For more information, see loadVariables() on page 626, getURL() on page 598, loadMovie() on page 624, and the LoadVars class entry in Chapter 12, "ActionScript Dictionary," on page 409.

Using the LoadVars class

You can use the LoadVars class instead of `loadVariables()` to transfer variables between a SWF file and a server. The LoadVars class lets you send all the variables in an object to a specified URL and load all the variables at a specified URL into an object. The response from the server triggers the `LoadVars.onLoad()` method and sets variables in the target. You can use LoadVars to obtain error information and progress indications and to stream the data while it downloads.

The LoadVars class is similar to the XML class; it uses the methods `load()`, `send()`, and `sendAndLoad()` to initiate communication with the server. The main difference between the LoadVars and XML classes is that the LoadVars data is a property of the LoadVars object, rather than an XML DOM (Document Object Model) tree stored in the XML object.

You must create a LoadVars object to call its methods. This object is a container to hold the loaded data.

The following procedure shows how to use a LoadVars object to load variables from a text file and display those variables in a text field.

To load data with the LoadVars object:

1 In a text editor such as Notepad or SimpleText, create a text file and add the following text to the text file:

    day=11&month=July&year=2003

2 Save the file as date.txt.

3 In Flash, create a document.

4 Create a dynamic text field on the Stage and give it the instance name `date_txt`.

5 Select Frame 1 in the Timeline and open the Actions panel (Window > Development Panels > Actions) if it isn't already open.

6 Enter the following code in the Actions panel:

```
var dateVars = new LoadVars();
dateVars.onLoad = function(ok) {
   if (ok) {
      date_txt.text = dateVars.day+"/"+dateVars.month+"/"+dateVars.year;
   }
};
dateVars.load("date.txt");
```

This code loads the variables in data.txt (`day`, `month`, `year`), then formats and displays them in the text field `date_txt`.

7 Save the document as dateReader.fla to the same directory that contains date.txt (the text file you saved in step 3).

8 Select Control > Test Movie to test the document.

For more information, see the LoadVars class entry in Chapter 12, "ActionScript Dictionary," on page 409.

About XML

XML (*Extensible Markup Language*) is becoming the standard for the interchange of structured data in Internet applications. You can integrate data in Flash with servers that use XML technology to build sophisticated applications, such as chat systems or brokerage systems.

In XML, as with HTML, you use tags to *mark up*, or specify, a body of text. In HTML, you use predefined tags to indicate how text should appear in a web browser (for example, the `<b>` tag indicates that text should be bold). In XML, you define tags that identify the type of a piece of data (for example, `<password>VerySecret</password>`). XML separates the structure of the information from the way it's displayed, so the same XML document can be used and reused in different environments.

Every XML tag is called a *node*, or an element. Each node has a type (1, which indicates an XML element, or 3, which indicates a text node), and elements may also have attributes. A node nested in a node is called a *child node*. This hierarchical tree structure of nodes is called the XML Document Object Model (DOM)—much like the JavaScript DOM, which is the structure of elements in a web browser.

In the following example, `<PORTFOLIO>` is the parent node; it has no attributes and contains the child node `<HOLDING>`, which has the attributes `SYMBOL`, `QTY`, `PRICE`, and `VALUE`:

```
<PORTFOLIO>
    <HOLDING SYMBOL="RICH"
        QTY="75"
        PRICE="245.50"
        VALUE="18412.50" />
</PORTFOLIO>
```

Using the XML class

The methods of the ActionScript XML class (for example, `appendChild()`, `removeNode()`, and `insertBefore()`) let you structure XML data in Flash to send to a server and manipulate and interpret downloaded XML data.

The following XML class methods send and load XML data to a server by using the HTTP `POST` method:

- The `load()` method downloads XML from a URL and places it in an ActionScript XML object.
- The `send()` method passes an XML object to a URL. Any returned information is sent to another browser window.
- The `sendAndLoad()` method sends an XML object to a URL. Any returned information is placed in an ActionScript XML object.

For example, you could create a brokerage system that stores all its information (user names, passwords, session IDs, portfolio holdings, and transaction information) in a database.

The server-side script that passes information between Flash and the database reads and writes the data in XML format. You can use ActionScript to convert information collected in the SWF file (for example, a user name and password) to an XML object and then send the data to the server-side script as an XML document. You can also use ActionScript to load the XML document that the server returns into an XML object to be used in the SWF file.

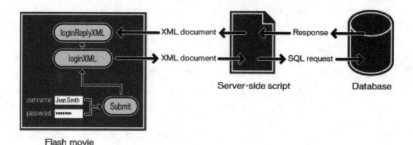

The flow and conversion of data between a Flash movie, a server-side script, and a database

The password validation for the brokerage system requires two scripts: a function defined on Frame 1, and a script that creates and sends the XML objects attached to the Submit button in the form.

When users enter their information into text fields in the SWF file with the variables `username` and `password`, the variables must be converted to XML before being passed to the server. The first section of the script loads the variables into a newly created XML object called `loginXML`. When a user clicks the Submit button, the `loginXML` object is converted to a string of XML and sent to the server.

The following script is attached to the Submit button. To understand this script, read the commented lines (indicated by the characters / /):

```
on (release) {
    // A. Construct an XML document with a LOGIN element
    loginXML = new XML();
    loginElement = loginXML.createElement("LOGIN");
    loginElement.attributes.username = username;
    loginElement.attributes.password = password;
    loginXML.appendChild(loginElement);

    // B. Construct an XML object to hold the server's reply
    loginReplyXML = new XML();
    loginReplyXML.onLoad = onLoginReply;

    // C. Send the LOGIN element to the server,
    //     place the reply in loginReplyXML
    loginXML.sendAndLoad("https://www.imexstocks.com/main.cgi",
                loginReplyXML);
}
```

The first section of the script generates the following XML when the user clicks the Submit button:

```
<LOGIN USERNAME="JeanSmith" PASSWORD="VerySecret" />
```

The server receives the XML, generates an XML response, and sends it back to the SWF file. If the password is accepted, the server responds with the following:

```
<LOGINREPLY STATUS="OK" SESSION="rnr6f7vkj2oe14m7jkkycilb" />
```

This XML includes a SESSION attribute that contains a unique, randomly generated session ID, which will be used in all communications between the client and server for the rest of the session. If the password is rejected, the server responds with the following message:

```
<LOGINREPLY STATUS="FAILED" />
```

The LOGINREPLY XML node must load into a blank XML object in the SWF file. The following statement creates the XML object loginreplyXML to receive the XML node:

```
// B. Construct an XML object to hold the server's reply
loginReplyXML = new XML();
loginReplyXML.onLoad = onLoginReply;
```

The second statement assigns the onLoginReply() function to the loginReplyXML.onLoad handler.

The LOGINREPLY XML element arrives asynchronously, much like the data from a loadVariables() function, and loads into the loginReplyXML object. When the data arrives, the onLoad handler of the loginReplyXML object is called. You must define the onLoginReply() function and assign it to the loginReplyXML.onLoad handler so that it can process the LOGINREPLY element. You must also assign the onLoginReply() function to the frame that contains the Submit button.

The onLoginReply() function is defined in the first frame of the SWF file. (To understand this script, read the commented lines.)

```
function onLoginReply() {
    // Get the first XML element
    var e = this.firstChild;
    // If the first XML element is a LOGINREPLY element with
    // status OK, go to the portfolio screen. Otherwise,
    // go to the login failure screen and let the user try again.
    if (e.nodeName == "LOGINREPLY" && e.attributes.status == "OK") {
    // Save the session ID for future communications with server
    sessionID = e.attributes.session;
    // Go to the portfolio viewing screen
        gotoAndStop("portfolioView");
    } else {
        // Login failed!  Go to the login failure screen.
        gotoAndStop("loginFailed");
    }
}
```

The first line of this function, var e = this.firstChild, uses the keyword this to refer to the XML object loginReplyXML that has just been loaded with XML from the server. You can use this because onLoginReply() has been invoked as loginReplyXML.onLoad, so even though onLoginReply() appears to be a normal function, it actually behaves as a method of loginReplyXML.

To send the user name and password as XML to the server and to load an XML response back into the SWF file, you can use the sendAndLoad() method, as shown here:

```
// C. Send the LOGIN element to the server,
//    place the reply in loginReplyXML
    loginXML.sendAndLoad("https://www.imexstocks.com/main.cgi", loginReplyXML);
```

Note: This design is only an example, and Macromedia can make no claims about the level of security it provides. If you are implementing a secure password-protected system, make sure you have a good understanding of network security.

For more information, see "Integrating XML and Flash in a Web Application" at www.macromedia.com/support/flash/interactivity/xml/ and the XML class entry in Chapter 12, "ActionScript Dictionary," on page 409.

Using the XMLSocket class

ActionScript provides a built-in XMLSocket class that allows you to open a continuous connection with a server. A socket connection allows the server to publish (or "push") information to the client as soon as that information is available. Without a continuous connection, the server must wait for an HTTP request. This open connection removes latency issues and is commonly used for real-time applications such as chats. The data is sent over the socket connection as one string and should be in XML format. You can use the XML class to structure the data.

To create a socket connection, you must create a server-side application to wait for the socket connection request and send a response to the SWF file. This type of server-side application can be written in a programming language such as Java.

You can use the `connect()` and `send()` methods of the XMLSocket class to transfer XML to and from a server over a socket connection. The `connect()` method establishes a socket connection with a web server port. The `send()` method passes an XML object to the server specified in the socket connection.

When you invoke the `connect()` method, Flash Player opens a TCP/IP connection to the server and keeps that connection open until one of the following happens:

- The `close()` method of the XMLSocket class is called.
- No more references to the XMLSocket object exist.
- Flash Player exits.
- The connection is broken (for example, the modem disconnects).

The following example creates an XML socket connection and sends data from the XML object `myXML`. To understand the script, read the commented lines (indicated by the characters `//`):

```
// Create a new XMLSocket object
sock = new XMLSocket();
// Call its connect() method to establish a connection with port 1024
// of the server at the URL
sock.connect("http://www.myserver.com", 1024);
// Define a function to assign to the sock object that handles
// the server's response. If the connection succeeds, send the
// myXML object. If it fails, provide an error message in a text
// field.
function onSockConnect(success){
  if (success){
    sock.send(myXML);
  } else {
    msg="There has been an error connecting to "+serverName;
  }
}
// Assign the onSockConnect() function to the onConnect property
sock.onConnect = onSockConnect;
```

For more information, see the XMLSocket class entry in Chapter 12, "ActionScript Dictionary," on page 409.

Sending messages to and from Flash Player

To send messages from a SWF file to its host environment (for example, a web browser, a Macromedia Director movie, or the stand-alone Flash Player), you can use the `fscommand()` function. This function lets you extend your SWF file by using the capabilities of the host. For example, you could pass an `fscommand()` function to a JavaScript function in an HTML page that opens a new browser window with specific properties.

To control a SWF in Flash Player from web browser scripting languages such as JavaScript, VBScript, and Microsoft JScript, you can use Flash Player methods—functions that send messages from a host environment to the SWF. For example, you could have a link in an HTML page that sends your SWF file to a specific frame.

Using fscommand()

Use the `fscommand()` function to send a message to whichever program is hosting Flash Player. The `fscommand()` function has two parameters: *command* and *arguments*. To send a message to the stand-alone version of Flash Player, you must use predefined commands and arguments. For example, the following action sets the stand-alone player to scale the SWF file to the full monitor screen size when the button is released:

```
on(release){
    fscommand("fullscreen", "true");
}
```

The following table shows the values you can specify for the *command* and *arguments* parameters of `fscommand()` to control a SWF file playing in the stand-alone player (including projectors):

Command	Arguments	Purpose
quit	None	Closes the projector.
fullscreen	true or false	Specifying true sets Flash Player to full-screen mode. Specifying false returns the player to normal menu view.
allowscale	true or false	Specifying false sets the player so that the SWF file is always drawn at its original size and never scaled. Specifying true forces the SWF file to scale to 100% of the player.
showmenu	true or false	Specifying true enables the full set of context menu items. Specifying false dims all the context menu items except Settings and About Flash Player.
exec	Path to application	Executes an application from within the projector.

To use `fscommand()` to send a message to a scripting language such as JavaScript in a web browser, you can pass any two parameters in the *command* and *arguments* parameters. These parameters can be strings or expressions and will be used in a JavaScript function that "catches," or handles, the `fscommand()` function.

An `fscommand()` function invokes the JavaScript function *moviename*_DoFSCommand in the HTML page that embeds the SWF file, where *moviename* is the name of Flash Player as assigned by the NAME attribute of the EMBED tag or the ID attribute of the OBJECT tag. If Flash Player is assigned the name myMovie, the JavaScript function invoked is myMovie_DoFSCommand.

To use `fscommand()` **to open a message box from a SWF file in the HTML page through JavaScript:**

1 In the HTML page that embeds the SWF file, add the following JavaScript code:

```
function theMovie_DoFSCommand(command, args) {
  if (command == "messagebox") {
    alert(args);
  }
}
```

If you publish your SWF file using the Flash with FSCommand template in the HTML Publish Settings dialog box, this code is inserted automatically. The SWF file's `NAME` and `ID` attributes will be the filename. For example, for the file myMovie.fla, the attributes would be set to `myMovie`. (For more information about publishing, see "Publishing" in Using Flash Help.)

Alternatively, for Microsoft Internet Explorer applications, you can attach an event handler directly in the `<SCRIPT>` tag, as shown in this example:

```
<Script Language = "JavaScript" event="FSCommand (command, args)" for=
  "theMovie">
...
</Script>
```

2 In the Flash document, add the `fscommand()` function to a button, as shown in this example:

```
on(press) {
  fscommand("messagebox", "This is a message box invoked from within
  Flash.");
}
```

You can also use expressions for `fscommand()` and parameters, as in this example:

```
fscommand("messagebox", "Hello, " + name + ", welcome to our website!")
```

3 Select File > Publish Preview > HTML to test the document.

The `fscommand()` function can send messages to Macromedia Director that are interpreted by Lingo as strings, events, or executable Lingo code. If the message is a string or an event, you must write the Lingo code to receive it from the `fscommand()` function and carry out an action in Director. For more information, see the Director Support Center at www.macromedia.com/support/director.

In Visual Basic, Visual C++, and other programs that can host ActiveX controls, `fscommand()` sends a VB event with two strings that can be handled in the environment's programming language. For more information, use the keywords *Flash method* to search the Flash Support Center at www.macromedia.com/support/flash.

About Flash Player methods

You can use Flash Player methods to control a SWF file in Flash Player from web browser scripting languages such as JavaScript and VBScript. As with other methods, you can use Flash Player methods to send calls to SWF files from a scripting environment other than ActionScript. Each method has a name, and most methods take parameters. A parameter specifies a value that the method operates upon. The calculation performed by some methods returns a value that can be used by the scripting environment.

There are two different technologies that enable communication between the browser and Flash Player: LiveConnect (Netscape Navigator 3.0 or later on Windows 95/98/2000/NT or Power Macintosh) and ActiveX (Internet Explorer 3.0 and later on Windows 95/98/2000/NT). Although the techniques for scripting are similar for all browsers and languages, there are additional properties and events available for use with ActiveX controls.

For more information, including a complete list of Flash Player scripting methods, use the keywords *Flash method* to search the Flash Support Center at www.macromedia.com/support/flash.

About using Flash JavaScript methods with Flash Player

Flash Player 6 version 40 and later supports Flash JavaScript methods and FSCommand in Netscape 6.2 and later. Earlier versions do not support Flash JavaScript methods and FSCommand in Netscape 6.2 or later.

For Netscape 6.2 and later, you do not need to set swLiveConnect to true. However, setting swLiveConnect to true has no adverse effects.

Flash Player security features

By default, Flash Player 7 and later prevents a SWF file served from one domain from accessing data, objects, or variables from SWF files that are served from different domains cannot access each other's objects and variables. In addition, content that is loaded through nonsecure (non-HTTPS) protocols cannot access content loaded through a secure (HTTPS) protocol, even when both are in exactly the same domain. For example, a SWF file located at http://www.macromedia.com/main.swf cannot load data from https://www.macromedia.com/data.txt without explicit permission. Nor can a SWF file served from one domain load data (using loadVariables(), for example) from another domain.

Identical numeric IP addresses are compatible. However, a domain name is not compatible with an IP address, even if the domain name resolves to the same IP address.

The following table shows examples of compatible domains:

www.macromedia.com	www.macromedia.com
data.macromedia.com	data.macromedia.com
65.57.83.12	65.57.83.12

The following table shows examples of incompatible domains:

www.macromedia.com	data.macromedia.com
macromedia.com	www.macromedia.com
www.macromedia.com	macromedia.com
65.57.83.12	www.macromedia.com (even if this domain resolves to 65.57.83.12)
www.macromedia.com	65.57.83.12 (even if www.macromedia.com resolves to this IP)

For information on how to permit a SWF file served from one domain to access data, objects, or variables from SWF files that are served from another domain, see "About allowing data access between cross-domain SWF files" on page 393. For information on how to permit a SWF file served from a secure (HTTPS) protocol to access data, objects, or variables from SWF files that are served from insecure protocols, see "About allowing HTTP to HTTPS protocol access between SWF files" on page 394. For information on how to permit a SWF file served from one domain to load data (using loadVariables(), for example) from another domain, see "About allowing cross-domain data loading" on page 394.

For information about how these security changes affect content authored in Flash MX and earlier, see "About compatibility with previous Flash Player security models" on page 395.

About allowing data access between cross-domain SWF files

One SWF file can load another SWF file from any location on the Internet. However, in order for the two SWF files to be able to access each other's data (variables and objects), the two files must originate from the same domain. By default, in Flash Player 7 and later, the two domains must match exactly in order for the two files to share data. However, a SWF file may grant access to SWF files served from specific domains by calling LocalConnection.allowDomain or System.security.allowDomain().

For example, suppose main.swf is served from www.macromedia.com. That SWF file then loads another SWF file (data.swf) from data.macromedia.com into a movie clip instance (target_mc).

```
// In macromedia.swf
target_mc.loadMovie("http://data.macromedia.com/data.swf");
```

Furthermore, suppose that data.swf defines a method named getData() on its main Timeline. By default, main.swf cannot call the getData() method defined in data.swf once that file has loaded. This is because the two SWF files don't reside in the same domain. For example, the following method call in main.swf, once data.swf has loaded, will fail.

```
// In macromedia.swf, after data.swf has loaded:
target_mc.getData(); // This method call will fail
```

However, data.swf may grant access to SWF files served from www.macromedia.com by using the LocalConnection.allowDomain handler or the System.security.allowDomain() method, depending on the type of access required. The following code, added to data.swf, allows a SWF file served from www.macromedia.com to access its variables and methods:

```
// Within data.swf
System.security.allowDomain("www.macromedia.com");
my_lc.allowDomain = function(sendingDomain) {
   return(sendingDomain=="www.macromedia.com");
}
```

Notice that allowDomain permits any SWF file in the allowed domain to script any other SWF file in the domain permitting the access, unless the SWF file being accessed is hosted on a site using a secure protocol (HTTPS). In this case, you must use allowInsecureDomain instead of allowDomain; see "About allowing HTTP to HTTPS protocol access between SWF files" below.

For more information on domain-name matching, see "Flash Player security features" on page 392.

About allowing HTTP to HTTPS protocol access between SWF files

As discussed in the previous section, you must use an allowDomain handler or method to permit a SWF file in one domain to be accessed by a SWF file in another domain. However, if the SWF being accessed is hosted at a site that uses a secure protocol (HTTPS), the allowDomain handler or method doesn't permit access from a SWF file hosted at a site that uses an insecure protocol. To permit such access, you must use the LocalConnection.allowInsecure Domain() or System.security.allowInsecureDomain() statements.

For example, if the SWF file at https://www.someSite.com/data.swf must allow access by a SWF file at http://www.someSite.com, the following code added to data.swf allows such access:

```
// Within data.swf
System.security.allowInsecureDomain("www.someSite.com");
my_lc.allowInsecureDomain = function(sendingDomain) {
   return(sendingDomain=="www.someSite.com");
}
```

About allowing cross-domain data loading

A Flash document can load data from an external source by using one of the following data loading calls: XML.load(), XML.sendAndLoad(), LoadVars.load(), LoadVars.sendAndLoad(), loadVariables(), loadVariablesNum(). Also, a SWF file can import runtime shared libraries, or assets defined in another SWF file, at runtime. By default, the data or SWF media, in the case of runtime shared libraries, must reside in the same domain as the SWF that is loading that external data or media.

To make data and assets in runtime shared libraries available to SWF files in different domains, use a *cross-domain policy file*. A cross-domain policy file is an XML file that provides a way for the server to indicate that its data and documents are available to SWF files served from certain domains, or from all domains. Any SWF file that is served from a domain specified by the server's policy file will be permitted to access data or assets from that server.

When a Flash document attempts to access data from another domain, Flash Player automatically attempts to load a policy file from that domain. If the domain of the Flash document that is attempting to access the data is included in the policy file, the data is automatically accessible.

Policy files must be named crossdomain.xml and reside at the root directory of the server that is serving the data. Policy files function only on servers that communicate over HTTP, HTTPS, or FTP. The policy file is specific to the port and protocol of the server where it resides.

For example, a policy file located at https://www.macromedia.com:8080/crossdomain.xml will apply only to data loading calls made to www.macromedia.com over HTTPS at port 8080.

An exception to this rule is the use of an XMLSocket object to connect to a socket server in another domain. In that case, an HTTP server running on port 80 in the same domain as the socket server must provide the policy file for the method call.

An XML policy file contains a single `<cross-domain-policy>` tag, which in turn contains zero or more `<allow-access-from>` tags. Each `<allow-access-from>` tag contains one attribute, `domain`, which specifies either an exact IP address, an exact domain, or a wildcard domain (any domain). Wildcard domains are indicated by either a single asterisk (*), which matches all domains and all IP addresses, or an asterisk followed by a suffix, which matches only those domains that end with the specified suffix. Suffixes must begin with a dot. However, wildcard domains with suffixes can match domains that consist of only the suffix without the leading dot. For example, foo.com is considered to be part of *.foo.com. Wildcards are not allowed in IP domain specifications.

If you specify an IP address, access will be granted only to SWF files loaded from that IP address using IP syntax (for example, http://65.57.83.12/flashmovie.swf), not those loaded using domain-name syntax. Flash Player does not perform DNS resolution.

Here is an example policy file that permits access to Flash documents that originate from foo.com, friendOfFoo.com, *.foo.com, and 105.216.0.40, from a Flash document on foo.com:

```
<?xml version="1.0"?>
<!-- http://www.foo.com/crossdomain.xml -->
<cross-domain-policy>
  <allow-access-from domain="www.friendOfFoo.com" />
  <allow-access-from domain="*.foo.com" />
  <allow-access-from domain="105.216.0.40" />
</cross-domain-policy>
```

A policy file that contains no `<allow-access-from>` tags has the same effect as not having a policy on a server.

About compatibility with previous Flash Player security models

As a result of the security feature changes in Flash Player (see "Flash Player security features" on page 392), content that runs properly in Flash Player 6 or earlier may not run properly in Flash Player 7 or later.

For example, in Flash Player 6, a SWF file that resides in www.macromedia.com could access data on a server located at data.macromedia.com. That is, Flash Player 6 allowed a SWF file from one domain to load data from a "similar" domain.

In Flash Player 7 and later, if a version 6 (or earlier) SWF file attempts to load data from a server that resides in another domain, and that server doesn't provide a policy file that allows access from that SWF file's domain, then the Macromedia Flash Player Settings dialog box appears. The dialog box asks the user to allow or deny the cross-domain data access.

If the user clicks Allow, the SWF file is permitted to access the requested data; if the user clicks Deny, the SWF file is not allowed to access the requested data.

To prevent this dialog box from appearing, create a security policy file on the server providing the data. For more information, see "About allowing cross-domain data loading" on page 394.

CHAPTER 11
Working with External Media

If you import an image or a sound while you author a document in Macromedia Flash MX 2004 or Macromedia Flash MX Professional 2004, the image and sound are packaged and stored in the SWF file when you publish it. In addition to importing media while authoring, you can load external media at runtime. There are several reasons you might want to keep media outside a Flash document.

Reduce file size   By keeping large media files outside your Flash document and loading them at runtime, you can reduce the initial download time for your applications and presentations, especially over slow Internet connections.

Modularize large presentations   You can break up a large presentation or application into separate SWF files and then load those separate files as needed at runtime. Not only does this reduce initial download time, but it also makes maintaining and updating the contents of the presentation easier.

Separate content from presentation   This a common theme in application development, especially data-driven applications. For example, a shopping cart application might display a JPEG image of each product. By loading the JPEG files for each image at runtime, you can easily update a product's image without modifying the original FLA file.

Take advantage of runtime-only features   Some features, such as streaming FLV and MP3 playback, are only available at runtime through ActionScript.

Overview of loading external media

There are four types of media files that you can load into a Flash application at runtime: SWF, MP3, JPEG, and FLV files. Flash Player can load external media from any HTTP or FTP address, from a local disk using a relative path, or by using the `file://` protocol.

To load external SWF and JPEG files, you can use either the `loadMovie()` or `loadMovieNum()` function, or the `MovieClip.loadMovie()` method. When you load a SWF or JPEG file, you specify a movie clip or movie level as the target for that media. For more information on loading SWF and JPEG files, see "Loading external SWF and JPEG files" on page 398.

To play back an external MP3 (MPEG Layer 3) file, use the `loadSound()` method of the Sound class. This method lets you specify whether the MP3 file should stream or download completely before it starts to play. You can also read the ID3 information embedded in MP3 files, if they're available. For more information, see "Reading ID3 tags in MP3 files" on page 400.

Flash Video (FLV) is the native video format used by Flash Player. You can play back FLV files over HTTP, or from the local file system. Playing external FLV files provides several advantages over embedding video in a Flash document, such as better performance and memory management, and independent video and Flash frame rates. For more information, see "Playing back external FLV files dynamically" on page 401.

You can also preload, or track the download progress, of external media. Flash Player 7 introduces the MovieClipLoader class, which you can use to track the download progress of SWF or JPEG files. To preload MP3 and FLV files, you can use the `getBytesLoaded()` method of the Sound class and the `bytesLoaded` property of the NetStream class. For more information, see "Preloading external media" on page 402.

Loading external SWF and JPEG files

To load a SWF or JPEG file, use the `loadMovie()` or `loadMovieNum()` global function, or the `loadMovie()` method of the MovieClip class. To load a SWF or JPEG file into a level in Flash Player, use `loadMovieNum()`. To load a SWF or JPEG file into a movie clip target, use the `loadMovie()` function or method. In either case, the loaded content replaces the content of the specified level or target movie clip.

When you load a SWF or JPEG file into a movie clip target, the upper left corner of the SWF file or JPEG image is placed on the registration point of the movie clip. Because this registration point is often the center of the movie clip, the loaded content may not appear centered. Also, when you load a SWF file or JPEG image to a root Timeline, the upper left corner of the image is placed on the upper left corner of the Stage. The loaded content inherits rotation and scaling from the movie clip, but the original content of the movie clip is removed.

You can optionally send ActionScript variables with a `loadMovie()` or `loadMovieNum()` call. This is useful, for example, if the URL you're specifying in the method call is a server-side script that returns a JPEG or SWF file according to data passed from the Flash application.

For image files, Flash supports only the standard JPEG image file type, not progressive JPEG files.

When you use the global `loadMovie()` or `loadMovieNum()` function, specify the target level or clip as a parameter. For example, the following code loads the Flash application contents.swf into the movie clip instance named `target_mc`:

```
loadMovieNum("contents.swf", target_mc);
```

Equivalently, you can use `MovieClip.loadMovie()` to achieve the same result:

```
target_mc.loadMovie("contents.swf");
```

The following code loads the JPEG image flowers.jpg into the movie clip instance `image_clip`:

```
image_clip.loadMovie("flowers.jpg");
```

For more information about `loadMovie()`, `loadMovieNum()`, and `MovieClip.loadMovie()`, see their entries in Chapter 12, "ActionScript Dictionary," on page 409.

About loaded SWF files and the root Timeline

The ActionScript property `_root` specifies or returns a reference to the root Timeline of a SWF file. If you load a SWF file into a movie clip in another SWF file, any references to `_root` in the loaded SWF file resolve to the root Timeline in the host SWF file, not that of the loaded SWF file. This can sometimes lead to unexpected behavior at runtime, for example, if the host SWF file and the loaded SWF file both use `_root` to specify a variable.

In Flash Player 7 and later, you can use the `MovieClip._lockroot` property to force references to `_root` made by a movie clip to resolve to its own Timeline, rather than to the Timeline of the SWF file that contains that movie clip. For more information, see "Specifying a root Timeline for loaded SWF files" on page 327.

About accessing data in loaded SWF files

One SWF file can load another SWF file from any location on the Internet. However, for one SWF file to access data (variables, methods, and so forth) defined in the other SWF file, the two files must originate from the same domain. In Flash Player 7 and later, cross-domain scripting is prohibited unless the loaded SWF file specifies otherwise by calling `System.security.allowDomain()`.

For more information, see "Flash Player security features" on page 392 and `System.security.allowDomain()` in Chapter 12, "ActionScript Dictionary," on page 409.

Loading external MP3 files

To load MP3 files at runtime, use the `loadSound()` method of the Sound class. First, create a Sound object:

```
var song_1_sound = new Sound();
```

You then use the new object to call `loadSound()` to load an event or a streaming sound. Event sounds are loaded completely before being played; streaming sounds are played as they are downloaded. You can set the *isStreaming* parameter of `loadSound()` to specify a sound as an event sound or a streaming sound. After you load an event sound, you must call the `start()` method of the Sound class to make the sound play. Streaming sounds begin playing when sufficient data is loaded into the SWF file; you don't need to use `start()`.

For example, the following code creates a Sound object named `classical` and then loads an MP3 file named beethoven.mp3:

```
var classical:Sound = new Sound();
classical.loadSound("http://server.com/mp3s/beethoven.mp3", true);
```

In most cases, set the *isStreaming* parameter to `true`, especially if you're loading large sound files that should start playing as soon as possible—for example, when creating an MP3 "jukebox" application. However, if you're downloading shorter sound clips and need to play them at a specified time (for example, when a user clicks a button), set *isStreaming* to `false`.

To determine when a sound has completely downloaded, use the `Sound.onLoad` event handler. This event handler automatically receives a Boolean (`true` or `false`) value that indicates whether the file downloaded successfully.

For example, suppose you're creating an online game that uses different sounds depending on what level the user has reached in the game. The following code loads an MP3 file (blastoff.mp3) into a Sound object named gameSound, and then plays the sound when it has completely downloaded:

```
var gameSound = new Sound();
gameSound.onLoad = function (loadedOK) {
  if(loadedOK) {
    gameSound.start();
  }
}
gameSound.loadSound("http://server.com/sounds/blastoff.mp3", false);
```

For sound files, Flash Player supports only the MP3 sound file type.

For more information, see Sound.loadSound(), Sound.start(), and Sound.onLoad in Chapter 12, "ActionScript Dictionary," on page 409.

Reading ID3 tags in MP3 files

ID3 tags are data fields added to an MP3 file that contain information about the file, such as the song name, album name, and artist name.

To read ID3 tags from an MP3 file, use the Sound.ID3 property, whose properties correspond to the names of ID3 tags included in the MP3 file being loaded. To determine when ID3 tags for a downloading MP3 file are available, use the Sound.onID3 event handler. Flash Player 7 supports version 1.0, 1.1, 2.3, and 2.4 tags; version 2.2 tags are not supported.

For example, the following code loads an MP3 file named favoriteSong.mp3 into the Sound object named song. When the ID3 tags for the file are available, a text field named display_txt displays the artist name and song name.

```
var song = new Sound();
song.onID3 = function () {
  display_txt.text = "Artist: " + song.id3.TCOM + newline;
  display_txt.text += "Song: " + song.id3.TIT2);
}
song.loadSound("mp3s/favoriteSong.mp3, true");
```

Because ID3 2.0 tags are located at the beginning of an MP3 file (before the sound data), they are available as soon as the file starts downloading. ID3 1.0 tags, however, are located at the end of the file (after the sound data) and thus aren't available until the entire MP3 file has finished downloading.

The onID3 event handler is called each time new ID3 data is available. This means that if an MP3 file contains ID3 2.0 tags and ID3 1.0 tags, the onID3 handler will be called twice, because the tags are located in different parts of the file.

For a list of supported ID3 tags, see Sound.ID3 on page 833.

Playing back external FLV files dynamically

As an alternative to importing video into the Flash authoring environment, you can use ActionScript to dynamically play back external FLV files in Flash Player. You can play back FLV files from an HTTP address or from the local file system. To play back FLV files, you use the NetConnection and NetStream classes and the `attachVideo()` method of the Video class. (For complete information, see the NetConnection class, NetStream class, and `Video.attachVideo()` entries in Chapter 12, "ActionScript Dictionary," on page 409.)

You can create FLV files by importing video into the Flash authoring tool and exporting it as an FLV file. (See "Macromedia Flash Video" in Using Flash Help.) If you have Flash Professional, you can use the FLV Export plug-in to export FLV files from supported video-editing applications. (See "Exporting FLV files from video-editing applications (Flash Professional only)" in Using Flash Help.)

Using external FLV files provides certain capabilities that are not available when you use imported video:

- You can use longer video clips in your Flash documents without slowing down playback. External FLV files are played using *cached memory*. This means that large files are stored in small pieces and accessed dynamically, and do not require as much memory as embedded video files.

- An external FLV file can have a different frame rate than the Flash document in which it plays. For example, you can set the Flash document frame rate to 30 fps and the video frame rate to 21 fps. This gives you greater control in ensuring smooth video playback.

- With external FLV files, Flash document playback does not have to be interrupted while the video file is loading. Imported video files may sometimes interrupt document playback to perform certain functions; for example, accessing a CD-ROM drive. FLV files can perform functions independently of the Flash document, and thus do not interrupt playback.

- Captioning of video content is easier with external FLV files, because you can use event handlers to access metadata for the video.

The following procedure shows how you would play back a file named videoFile.flv that is stored in the same location as your SWF file.

To play back an external FLV file in a Flash document:

1 With the document open in the Flash authoring tool, in the Library panel (Window > Library) select New Video from the Library options menu to create a video object.

2 Drag a video object from the Library panel onto the Stage. This creates a video object instance.

3 With the video object selected on the Stage, in the Property inspector (Window > Properties) enter `my_video` in the Instance Name text box.

4 Open the Components panel (Window > Development Panels > Components) and drag a TextArea component to the Stage.

5 With the TextArea object selected on the Stage, enter `status` in the Instance Name text box in the Property inspector.

6 Select Frame 1 in the Timeline, and open the Actions panel (Window > Development Panels > Actions).

7 Add the following code to the Actions panel:

```
// Create a NetConnection object:
var netConn:NetConnection = new NetConnection();
// Create a local streaming connection:
netConn.connect(null);
// Create a NetStream object and define an onStatus() function:
var netStream:NetStream = new NetStream(netConn);
netStream.onStatus = function(infoObject) {
    status.text += "Status (NetStream)" + newline;
    status.text += "Level: "+infoObject.level + newline;
    status.text += "Code: "+infoObject.code + newline;
};
// Attach the NetStream video feed to the Video object:
my_video.attachVideo(netStream);
// Set the buffer time:
netStream.setBufferTime(5);
// Being playing the FLV file:
netStream.play("videoFile.flv");
```

Preloading external media

ActionScript provides several ways to preload or track the download progress of external media. To preload SWF and JPEG files, use the MovieClipLoader class, which provides an event listener mechanism for checking download progress. This class is new in Flash Player 7. For more information, see "Preloading SWF and JPEG files" on page 403.

To track the download progress of MP3 files, use the `Sound.getBytesLoaded()` and `Sound.getBytesTotal()` methods; to track the download progress of FLV files, use the `NetStream.bytesLoaded` and `NetStream.bytesTotal` properties. For more information, see "Preloading MP3 and FLV files" on page 405.

Preloading SWF and JPEG files

To preload SWF and JPEG files into movie clip instances, you can use the MovieClipLoader class. This class provides an event listener mechanism to give notification about the status of file downloads into movie clips. Using a MovieClipLoader object to preload SWF and JPEG files involves the following steps:

Create a new MovieClipLoader object   You can use a single MovieClipLoader object to track the download progress of multiple files, or create a separate object for each file's progress.

```
var loader:MovieClipLoader = new MovieClipLoader();
```

Create a listener object and create event handlers   The listener object can be any ActionScript object, such as a generic Object object, a movie clip, or a custom component.

For example, the following code creates a generic listener object named loadListener, and defines for itself onLoadStart, onLoadProgress, and onLoadComplete functions.

```
// Create listener object:
var loadListener:Object = new Object();
loadListener.onLoadStart = function (loadTarget) {
  trace("Loading into " + loadTarget + " has started.");
}
loadListener.onLoadProgress = function(loadTarget, bytesLoaded, bytesTotal) {
  var percentLoaded = bytesLoaded/bytesTotal * 100;
  trace("%" + percentLoaded + " into target " + loadTarget);
}
loadListener.onLoadComplete = function(loadTarget) {
  trace("Load completed into: " + loadTarget);
}
```

Register the listener object with the MovieClipLoader object   In order for the listener object to receive the loading events, you must register it with the MovieClipLoader object.

```
loader.addListener(loadListener);
```

Begin loading the file (JPEG or SWF) into a target clip   To start the download of the JPEG or SWF file, you use the MovieClipLoader.loadClip() method.

```
loader.loadClip("scene_2.swf");
```

Note: You can use only MovieClipLoader methods to track the download progress of files loaded with the MovieClipLoader.loadClip() method. You cannot use the loadMovie() function or MovieClip.loadMovie() method.

The following example uses the setProgress() method of the ProgressBar component to display the download progress of a SWF file. (See "ProgressBar component" in Using Components Help.)

To display download progress using the ProgressBar component:

1 In a new Flash document, create a movie clip on the Stage and name it `target_mc`.

2 Open the Components panel (Window > Development Panels > Components).

3 Drag a ProgressBar component from the Components panel to the Stage.

4 In the Property inspector, give the ProgressBar component the name `pBar` and, on the Parameters tab, select Manual from the Mode pop-up menu.

5 Select Frame 1 in the Timeline and then open the Actions panel (Window > Development Panels > Actions).

6 Add the following code to the Actions panel:

```
// create both a MovieClipLoader object and a listener object
myLoader = new MovieClipLoader();
myListener = new Object();
// add the MovieClipLoader callbacks to your listener object
myListener.onLoadStart = function(clip) {
  // this event is triggered once, when the load starts
  pBar.label = "Now loading: " + clip;
};
myListener.onLoadProgress = function(clip, bytesLoaded, bytesTotal) {
  var percentLoaded = int (100*(bytesLoaded/bytesTotal));
  pBar.setProgress(bytesLoaded, bytesTotal);
};myLoader.addListener(myListener);
myLoader.loadClip("veryLargeFile.swf", target_mc);
```

7 Test the document by selecting Control > Test Movie.

For more information, see the MovieClipLoader class entry in Chapter 12, "ActionScript Dictionary," on page 409.

Preloading MP3 and FLV files

To preload MP3 and FLV files, you can use the `setInterval()` function to create a "polling" mechanism that checks the bytes loaded for a Sound or NetStream object at predetermined intervals. To track the download progress of MP3 files, use the `Sound.getBytesLoaded()` and `Sound.getBytesTotal()` methods; to track the download progress of FLV files, use the `NetStream.bytesLoaded` and `NetStream.bytesTotal` properties.

The following code uses `setInterval()` to check the bytes loaded for a Sound or NetStream object at predetermined intervals.

```
// Create a new Sound object to play the sound.
var songTrack = new Sound();
// Create the polling function that tracks download progress.
// This is the function that is "polled." It checks
// the download progress of the Sound object passed as a reference.
checkProgress = function (soundObj) {
    var bytesLoaded = soundObj.getBytesLoaded();
    var bytesTotal = soundObj.getBytesTotal();
    var percentLoaded = Math.floor(bytesLoaded/bytesTotal * 100);
    trace("%" + percentLoaded + " loaded.");
}
// When the file has finished loading, clear the interval polling.
songTrack.onLoad = function () {
    clearInterval(poll);
}
// Load streaming MP3 file and start calling checkProgress()
songTrack.loadSound("beethoven.mp3", true);
var poll = setInterval(checkProgress, 1000, songTrack);
```

You can use this same kind of polling technique to preload external FLV files. To get the total bytes and current number of bytes loaded for an FLV file, use the `NetStream.bytesLoaded` and `NetStream.bytesTotal` properties.

Another way to preload FLV files is to use the `NetStream.setBufferTime()` method. This method takes a single parameter that indicates the number of seconds of the FLV stream to download before playback begins.

For more information, see `MovieClip.getBytesLoaded()`, `MovieClip.getBytesTotal()`, `NetStream.bytesLoaded`, `NetStream.bytesTotal`, `NetStream.setBufferTime()`, `setInterval()`, `Sound.getBytesLoaded()`, and `Sound.getBytesTotal()` in Chapter 12, "ActionScript Dictionary," on page 409.

This part contains the ActionScript Dictionary, which provides syntax and usage information for every element in the ActionScript language. It also contains appendixes that provide reference material you may want to review as you write your scripts.

CHAPTER 12
ActionScript Dictionary

This dictionary describes the syntax and use of ActionScript elements in Macromedia Flash MX 2004 and Macromedia Flash MX Professional 2004. To use examples in a script, copy the example code from this dictionary and paste it in the Script pane or into an external script file. The dictionary lists all ActionScript elements—operators, keywords, statements, actions, properties, functions, classes, and methods. For an overview of all dictionary entries, see "Contents of the dictionary" on page 411; the tables in this section are a good starting point for looking up symbolic operators or methods whose class you don't know. For information on components, see *Using Components*.

There are two types of entries in this dictionary:

- Individual entries for operators, keywords, functions, variables, properties, methods, and statements
- Class entries, which provide general information about built-in classes

Use the information in the sample entries to interpret the structure and conventions used in these types of entries.

Sample entry for most ActionScript elements

The following sample dictionary entry explains the conventions used for all ActionScript elements that are not classes.

Entry title

All entries are listed alphabetically. The alphabetization ignores capitalization, leading underscores, and so on.

Availability

Unless otherwise noted, the Availability section tells which versions of Flash Player support the element. This is not the same as the version of Flash used to author the content. For example, if you use Macromedia Flash MX 2004 or Macromedia Flash MX Professional 2004 to create content for Flash Player 6, you can use only ActionScript elements that are available to Flash Player 6.

In a few cases, this section also indicates which version of the authoring tool supports an element. For an example, see System.setClipboard().

Finally, if an element is supported only in ActionScript 2.0, that information is also noted in this section.

Usage

This section provides correct syntax for using the ActionScript element in your code. The required portion of the syntax is in `code font`, and the code that you provide is in *`italicized code font`*. Brackets ([ ]) indicate optional parameters.

Parameters

This section describes any parameters listed in the syntax.

Returns

This section identifies what, if any, values the element returns.

Description

This section identifies the type of element (for example, operator, method, function, and so on) and then describes how to use the element.

Example

This section provides a code sample demonstrating how to use the element.

See also

This section lists related ActionScript dictionary entries.

Sample entry for classes

The following sample dictionary entry explains the conventions used for built-in ActionScript classes. Classes are listed alphabetically with all other elements in the dictionary.

Entry title

The entry title provides the name of the class. The class name is followed by general descriptive information.

Method and property summary tables

Each class entry contains a table listing all of the associated methods. If the class has properties (often constants), event handlers, or event listeners, these elements are summarized in additional tables. All of the elements listed in these tables also have their own dictionary entries, which follow the class entry.

Constructor

If a class requires that you use a constructor to access its methods and properties, the constructor is described in each class entry. This description has all of the standard elements (syntax, description, and so on) of other dictionary entries.

Method and property listings

The methods and properties of a class are listed alphabetically after the class entry.

Contents of the dictionary

All dictionary entries are listed alphabetically. However, some operators are symbols and are presented in ASCII order. In addition, methods that are associated with a class are listed along with the class name—for example, the `abs()` method of the Math class is listed as `Math.abs()`.

The following two tables help you locate these elements. The first table lists the symbolic operators in the order in which they occur in the dictionary. The second table lists all other ActionScript elements.

Symbolic operators	See entry
`--`	`-- (decrement)`
`++`	`++ (increment)`
`!`	`! (logical NOT)`
`!=`	`!= (inequality)`
`!==`	`!== (strict inequality)`
`%`	`% (modulo)`
`%=`	`%= (modulo assignment)`
`&`	`& (bitwise AND operator)`
`&&`	`&& (logical AND)`

Symbolic operators	See entry
&=	&= (bitwise AND assignment)
()	() (parentheses)
-	- (minus)
*	* (multiplication)
*=	*= (multiplication assignment)
,	, (comma)
.	. (dot)
:	: (type)
?:	?: (conditional)
/	/ (division)
//	// (comment delimiter)
/*	/* (comment delimiter)
/=	/= (division assignment)
[]	[] (array access)
^	^ (bitwise XOR)
^=	^= (bitwise XOR assignment)
{}	{} (object initializer)
|	| (bitwise OR)
||	|| (logical OR)
|=	|= (bitwise OR assignment)
~	~ (bitwise NOT)
+	+ (addition)
+=	+= (addition assignment)
<	< (less than)
<<	<< (bitwise left shift)
<<=	<<= (bitwise left shift and assignment)
<=	<= (less than or equal to)
<>	<> (inequality)
=	= (assignment)
-=	-= (subtraction assignment)
==	== (equality)
===	=== (strict equality)
>	> (greater than)

Symbolic operators	See entry
>=	>= (greater than or equal to)
>>	>> (bitwise right shift)
>>=	>>= (bitwise right shift and assignment)
>>>	>>> (bitwise unsigned right shift)
>>>=	>>>= (bitwise unsigned right shift and assignment)

The following table lists all ActionScript elements that are not symbolic operators.

ActionScript element	See entry
#endinitclip	#endinitclip
#include	#include
#initclip	#initclip
__proto__	Object.__proto__
_accProps	_accProps
_alpha	MovieClip._alpha, Button._alpha, TextField._alpha
_currentframe	MovieClip._currentframe
_droptarget	MovieClip._droptarget
_focusrect	_focusrect, Button._focusrect, MovieClip._focusrect
_framesloaded	MovieClip._framesloaded
_global	_global object
_height	Button._height, MovieClip._height, TextField._height
_highquality	_highquality, Button._highquality, MovieClip._highquality, TextField._highquality
_lockroot	MovieClip._lockroot
_name	Button._name, MovieClip._name, TextField._name
_parent	_parent, Button._parent, MovieClip._parent, TextField._parent
_quality	_quality, Button._quality, TextField._quality
_root	_root
_rotation	Button._rotation, MovieClip._rotation, TextField._rotation
_soundbuftime	_soundbuftime, Button._soundbuftime, MovieClip._soundbuftime, TextField._soundbuftime
_target	Button._target, MovieClip._target, TextField._target
_totalframes	MovieClip._totalframes
_url	Button._url, MovieClip._url, TextField._url
_visible	Button._visible, MovieClip._visible, TextField._visible

ActionScript element	See entry
_width	Button._width, MovieClip._width, TextField._width
_x	Button._x, MovieClip._x, TextField._x
_xmouse	Button._xmouse, MovieClip._xmouse, TextField._xmouse
_xscale	Button._xscale, MovieClip._xscale, TextField._xscale
_y	Button._y, MovieClip._y, TextField._y
_ymouse	Button._ymouse, MovieClip._ymouse, TextField._ymouse
_yscale	Button._yscale, MovieClip._yscale, TextField._yscale
abs	Math.abs()
Accessibility	**Accessibility class**
acos	Math.acos()
activityLevel	Camera.activityLevel, Microphone.activityLevel
add	add
addListener	**Key.addListener()**, Mouse.addListener(), **MovieClipLoader.addListener()**, Selection.addListener(), Stage.addListener(), TextField.addListener()
addPage	PrintJob.addPage()
addProperty	Object.addProperty()
addRequestHeader	LoadVars.addRequestHeader(), XML.addRequestHeader()
align	Stage.align, TextFormat.align
allowDomain	LocalConnection.allowDomain, System.security.allowDomain()
allowInsecureDomain	**LocalConnection.allowInsecureDomain, System.security.allowInsecureDomain()**
and	and
appendChild	XML.appendChild()
apply	Function.apply()
Arguments	**Arguments class**
Array	**Array class, Array()**
asfunction	asfunction
asin	Math.asin()
atan	Math.atan()
atan2	Math.atan2()
attachAudio	MovieClip.attachAudio()
attachMovie	MovieClip.attachMovie()

ActionScript element	See entry
ceil	Math.ceil()
charAt	String.charAt()
charCodeAt	String.charCodeAt()
childNodes	XML.childNodes
chr	chr
class	class
clear	MovieClip.clear(), SharedObject.clear(), Video.clear()
clearInterval	clearInterval()
cloneNode	XML.cloneNode()
close	LocalConnection.close(), NetStream.close(), XMLSocket.close()
Color	Color class, TextFormat.color
concat	Array.concat(), String.concat()
connect	LocalConnection.connect(), NetConnection.connect(), XMLSocket.connect()
condenseWhite	TextField.condenseWhite
constructor	Array class, Boolean class, Camera class, Color class, ContextMenu class, ContextMenuItem class, Date class, Error class, LoadVars class, LocalConnection class, Microphone class, NetConnection class, NetStream class, Number class, Object class, PrintJob class, SharedObject class, Sound class, String class, TextField.StyleSheet class, TextFormat class, XML class, XMLSocket class
contentType	LoadVars.contentType, XML.contentType
ContextMenu	ContextMenu class
ContextMenuItem	ContextMenuItem class
continue	continue
CONTROL	Key.CONTROL
copy	ContextMenu.copy(), ContextMenuItem.copy()
cos	Math.cos()
createElement	XML.createElement()
createEmptyMovieClip	MovieClip.createEmptyMovieClip()
createTextField	MovieClip.createTextField()
createTextNode	XML.createTextNode()
currentFps	Camera.currentFps, NetStream.currentFps
curveTo	MovieClip.curveTo()
CustomActions	CustomActions class

ActionScript element	See entry
customItems	ContextMenu.customItems
data	SharedObject.data
Date	**Date class**
deblocking	Video.deblocking
default	default
delete	delete
DELETEKEY	Key.DELETEKEY
do while	do while
docTypeDecl	XML.docTypeDecl
domain	LocalConnection.domain()
DOWN	Key.DOWN
duplicateMovieClip	duplicateMovieClip(), MovieClip.duplicateMovieClip()
duration	Sound.duration
dynamic	dynamic
E	Math.E
else	else
else if	else if
embedFonts	TextField.embedFonts
enabled	Button.enabled, ContextMenuItem.enabled, MovieClip.enabled
END	Key.END
endFill	MovieClip.endFill()
ENTER	Key.ENTER
eq	eq (equal — string specific)
Error	**Error class**
ESCAPE (constant)	Key.ESCAPE
escape (function)	escape
eval	eval()
exactSettings	System.exactSettings
exp	Math.exp()
extends	extends
false	false
finally	try..catch..finally
findText	**TextSnapshot.findText()**

ActionScript element	See entry
firstChild	XML.firstChild
floor	Math.floor()
flush	SharedObject.flush()
focusEnabled	MovieClip.focusEnabled
font	TextFormat.font
for	for
for..in	for..in
fps	**Camera.fps**
fromCharCode	String.fromCharCode()
fscommand	fscommand()
function	function, Function class
gain	Microphone.gain
ge	ge (greater than or equal to — string specific)
get	Camera.get(), CustomActions.get(), get, Microphone.get()
getAscii	Key.getAscii()
getBeginIndex	Selection.getBeginIndex()
getBounds	MovieClip.getBounds()
getBytesLoaded	LoadVars.getBytesLoaded(), MovieClip.getBytesLoaded(), Sound.getBytesLoaded(), XML.getBytesLoaded()
getBytesTotal	LoadVars.getBytesTotal(), MovieClip.getBytesTotal(), Sound.getBytesTotal(), XML.getBytesTotal()
getCaretIndex	Selection.getCaretIndex()
getCode	Key.getCode()
getCount	TextSnapshot.getCount()
getDate	Date.getDate()
getDay	Date.getDay()
getDepth	Button.getDepth(), MovieClip.getDepth(), TextField.getDepth()
getEndIndex	Selection.getEndIndex()
getFocus	Selection.getFocus()
getFontList	TextField.getFontList()
getFullYear	Date.getFullYear()
getHours	Date.getHours()
getInstanceAtDepth	MovieClip.getInstanceAtDepth()
getLocal	SharedObject.getLocal()

ActionScript element	See entry
getMilliseconds	Date.getMilliseconds()
getMinutes	Date.getMinutes()
getMonth	Date.getMonth()
getNewTextFormat	TextField.getNewTextFormat()
getNextHighestDepth	MovieClip.getNextHighestDepth()
getPan	Sound.getPan()
getProgress	**MovieClipLoader.getProgress()**
getProperty	getProperty
getRGB	Color.getRGB()
getSeconds	Date.getSeconds()
getSelected	TextSnapshot.getSelected()
getSelectedText	TextSnapshot.getSelectedText()
getSize	SharedObject.getSize()
getStyle	TextField.StyleSheet.getStyle()
getStyleNames	TextField.StyleSheet.getStyleNames()
getSWFVersion	MovieClip.getSWFVersion()
getText	TextSnapshot.getText()
getTextExtent	TextFormat.getTextExtent()
getTextFormat	TextField.getTextFormat()
getTextSnapshot	**MovieClip.getTextSnapshot()**
getTime	Date.getTime()
getTimer	getTimer
getTimezoneOffset	Date.getTimezoneOffset()
getTransform	Color.getTransform(), Sound.getTransform()
getURL	getURL(), MovieClip.getURL()
getUTCDate	Date.getUTCDate()
getUTCDay	Date.getUTCDay()
getUTCFullYear	Date.getUTCFullYear()
getUTCHours	Date.getUTCHours()
getUTCMilliseconds	Date.getUTCMilliseconds()
getUTCMinutes	Date.getUTCMinutes()
getUTCMonth	Date.getUTCMonth()
getUTCSeconds	Date.getUTCSeconds()

ActionScript element	See entry
getVersion	getVersion
getVolume	Sound.getVolume()
getYear	Date.getYear()
globalToLocal	MovieClip.globalToLocal()
goto	gotoAndPlay(), gotoAndStop()
gotoAndPlay	gotoAndPlay(), MovieClip.gotoAndPlay()
gotoAndStop	gotoAndStop(), MovieClip.gotoAndStop()
gt	gt (greater than — string specific)
hasAccessibility	System.capabilities.hasAccessibility
hasAudio	System.capabilities.hasAudio
hasAudioEncoder	System.capabilities.hasAudioEncoder
hasChildNodes	XML.hasChildNodes()
hasEmbeddedVideo	System.capabilities.hasEmbeddedVideo
hasMP3	System.capabilities.hasMP3
hasPrinting	System.capabilities.hasPrinting
hasScreenBroadcast	System.capabilities.hasScreenBroadcast
hasScreenPlayback	System.capabilities.hasScreenPlayback
hasStreamingAudio	System.capabilities.hasStreamingAudio
hasStreamingVideo	System.capabilities.hasStreamingVideo
hasVideoEncoder	System.capabilities.hasVideoEncoder
height	Camera.height, Stage.height, Video.height
hide	Mouse.hide()
hideBuiltInItems	ContextMenu.hideBuiltInItems()
hitArea	MovieClip.hitArea
hitTest	MovieClip.hitTest()
hitTestTextNearPos	TextSnapshot.hitTestTextNearPos()
HOME	Key.HOME
hscroll	TextField.hscroll
html	TextField.html
htmlText	TextField.htmlText
ID3	Sound.ID3
if	if
ifFrameLoaded	ifFrameLoaded

ActionScript element	See entry
ignoreWhite	XML.ignoreWhite
implements	implements
import	import
indent	TextFormat.indent
index	Camera.index, Microphone.index
indexOf	String.indexOf()
Infinity	Infinity
-Infinity	-Infinity
INSERT	Key.INSERT
insertBefore	XML.insertBefore()
install	CustomActions.install()
instanceof	instanceof
int	int
interface	interface
isActive	Accessibility.isActive()
isDebugger	System.capabilities.isDebugger
isDown	Key.isDown()
isFinite	isFinite
isNaN	isNaN()
isToggled	Key.isToggled()
italic	TextFormat.italic
join	Array.join()
Key	**Key class**
language	System.capabilities.language
lastChild	XML.lastChild
lastIndexOf	String.lastIndexOf()
le	le (less than or equal to — string specific)
leading	TextFormat.leading
LEFT	Key.LEFT
leftMargin	TextFormat.leftMargin
length	length, arguments.length, Array.length, String.length, TextField.length
level	_level

ActionScript element	See entry
lineStyle	MovieClip.lineStyle()
lineTo	MovieClip.lineTo()
list	CustomActions.list()
LN10	Math.LN10
LN2	Math.LN2
load	LoadVars.load(), TextField.StyleSheet.load(), XML.load(),
loadClip	MovieClipLoader.loadClip()
loaded	LoadVars.loaded, XML.loaded
loadMovie	loadMovie(), MovieClip.loadMovie()
loadMovieNum	loadMovieNum()
loadSound	Sound.loadSound()
loadVariables	loadVariables(), MovieClip.loadVariables()
loadVariablesNum	loadVariablesNum()
LoadVars	LoadVars class
LocalConnection	LocalConnection class
localFileReadDisable	System.capabilities.localFileReadDisable
localToGlobal	MovieClip.localToGlobal()
log	Math.log()
LOG10E	Math.LOG10E
LOG2E	Math.LOG2E
lt	lt (less than — string specific)
manufacturer	System.capabilities.manufacturer
Math	Math class
max	Math.max()
MAX_VALUE	Number.MAX_VALUE
maxChars	TextField.maxChars
maxhscroll	TextField.maxhscroll
maxscroll	maxscroll, TextField.maxscroll
mbchr	mbchr
mblength	mblength
mbord	mbord
mbsubstring	mbsubstring
menu	Button.menu, MovieClip.menu, TextField.menu

ActionScript element	See entry
message	Error.message
Microphone	**Microphone class**
min	Math.min()
MIN_VALUE	Number.MIN_VALUE
MMExecute	MMExecute()
motionLevel	Camera.motionLevel
motionTimeOut	Camera.motionTimeOut
Mouse	**Mouse class**
mouseWheelEnabled	TextField.mouseWheelEnabled
moveTo	MovieClip.moveTo()
MovieClip	MovieClip class
MovieClipLoader	MovieClipLoader class
multiline	TextField.multiline
muted	Camera.muted, Microphone.muted
name	Error.name, Microphone.name
names	Camera.names, Microphone.names
NaN	NaN, Number.NaN
ne	ne (not equal — string specific)
NEGATIVE_INFINITY	Number.NEGATIVE_INFINITY
NetConnection	**NetConnection class**
NetStream	**NetStream class**
new (operator)	new
newline	newline
nextFrame	nextFrame(), MovieClip.nextFrame()
nextScene	nextScene()
nextSibling	XML.nextSibling
nodeName	XML.nodeName
nodeType	XML.nodeType
nodeValue	XML.nodeValue
not	not
null	null
Number	Number(), **Number class**
Object	**Object class**, Object()

ActionScript element	See entry
on	on()
onActivity	Camera.onActivity, Microphone.onActivity
onChanged	TextField.onChanged
onClipEvent	onClipEvent()
onClose	XMLSocket.onClose()
onConnect	XMLSocket.onConnect()
onData	LoadVars.onData, MovieClip.onData, XML.onData, XMLSocket.onData()
onDragOut	Button.onDragOut, MovieClip.onDragOut
onDragOver	Button.onDragOver, MovieClip.onDragOver
onEnterFrame	MovieClip.onEnterFrame
onID3	Sound.onID3
onKeyDown	Button.onKeyDown, Key.onKeyDown, MovieClip.onKeyDown
onKeyUp	Button.onKeyUp, Key.onKeyUp, MovieClip.onKeyUp
onKillFocus	Button.onKillFocus, MovieClip.onKillFocus, TextField.onKillFocus
onLoad	LoadVars.onLoad, MovieClip.onLoad, Sound.onLoad, TextField.StyleSheet.onLoad, XML.onLoad()
onLoadComplete	MovieClipLoader.onLoadComplete()
onLoadError	MovieClipLoader.onLoadError()
onLoadInit	MovieClipLoader.onLoadInit()
onLoadProgress	MovieClipLoader.onLoadProgress()
onLoadStart	MovieClipLoader.onLoadStart()
onMouseDown	Mouse.onMouseDown, MovieClip.onMouseDown
onMouseMove	Mouse.onMouseMove, MovieClip.onMouseMove
onMouseUp	Mouse.onMouseUp, MovieClip.onMouseUp
onMouseWheel	Mouse.onMouseWheel
onPress	Button.onPress, MovieClip.onPress
onRelease	Button.onRelease, MovieClip.onRelease
onReleaseOutisde	Button.onReleaseOutside, MovieClip.onReleaseOutside
onResize	Stage.onResize
onRollOut	Button.onRollOut, MovieClip.onRollOut
onRollOver	Button.onRollOver, MovieClip.onRollOver
onScroller	TextField.onScroller
onSelect	ContextMenu.onSelect, ContextMenuItem.onSelect

ActionScript element	See entry
onSetFocus	`Button.onSetFocus`, `MovieClip.onSetFocus`, `Selection.onSetFocus`, `TextField.onSetFocus`
onSoundComplete	`Sound.onSoundComplete`
onStatus	`Camera.onStatus`, `LocalConnection.onStatus`, `Microphone.onStatus`, `NetStream.onStatus`, `SharedObject.onStatus`, `System.onStatus`
onUnload	`MovieClip.onUnload`
onUpdate	`onUpdate`
onXML	`XMLSocket.onXML()`
or (logical OR)	`or`
ord	`ord`
os	`System.capabilities.os`
parentNode	`XML.parentNode`
parseCSS	`TextField.StyleSheet.parseCSS()`
parseFloat	`parseFloat()`
parseInt	`parseInt`
parseXML	`XML.parseXML()`
password	`TextField.password`
pause	`NetStream.pause()`
PGDN	`Key.PGDN`
PGUP	`Key.PGUP`
PI	`Math.PI`
pixelAspectRatio	`System.capabilities.pixelAspectRatio`
play	`play()`, `MovieClip.play()`, `NetStream.play()`
playerType	`System.capabilities.playerType`
pop	`Array.pop()`
position	`Sound.position`
POSITIVE_INFINITY	`Number.POSITIVE_INFINITY`
pow	`Math.pow()`
prevFrame	`prevFrame()`, `MovieClip.prevFrame()`
previousSibling	`XML.previousSibling`
prevScene	`prevScene()`
print	`print()`
printAsBitmap	`printAsBitmap()`
printAsBitmapNum	`printAsBitmapNum()`

ActionScript element	See entry
PrintJob	PrintJob class
printNum	printNum()
private	private
prototype	Function.prototype
public	public
push	Array.push()
quality	Camera.quality
random	random, Math.random()
rate	Microphone.rate
registerClass	Object.registerClass()
removeListener	Key.removeListener(), Mouse.removeListener(), MovieClipLoader.removeListener(), Selection.removeListener(), Stage.removeListener(), TextField.removeListener()
removeMovieClip	removeMovieClip(), MovieClip.removeMovieClip()
removeNode	XML.removeNode()
removeTextField	TextField.removeTextField()
replaceSel	TextField.replaceSel()
replaceText	**TextField.replaceText()**
resolutionX	System.capabilities.screenResolutionX
resolutionY	System.capabilities.screenResolutionY
restrict	TextField.restrict
return	return
reverse	Array.reverse()
RIGHT	Key.RIGHT
rightMargin	TextFormat.rightMargin
round	Math.round()
scaleMode	Stage.scaleMode
screenColor	System.capabilities.screenColor
screenDPI	System.capabilities.screenDPI
screenResolutionX	System.capabilities.screenResolutionX
screenResolutionY	System.capabilities.screenResolutionY
scroll	scroll, TextField.scroll
seek	NetStream.seek()
selectable	TextField.selectable

ActionScript element	See entry
Selection	Selection class
send	LoadVars.send(), LocalConnection.send(), PrintJob.send(), XML.send(), XMLSocket.send()
sendAndLoad	LoadVars.sendAndLoad(), XML.sendAndLoad()
separatorBefore	ContextMenuItem.separatorBefore
serverString	System.capabilities.serverString
set	set
set variable	set variable
setBufferTime	NetStream.setBufferTime()
setClipboard	**System.setClipboard()**
setDate	Date.setDate()
setFocus	Selection.setFocus()
setFullYear	Date.setFullYear()
setGain	Microphone.setGain()
setHours	Date.setHours()
setInterval	setInterval()
setMask	MovieClip.setMask()
setMilliseconds	Date.setMilliseconds()
setMinutes	Date.setMinutes()
setMode	Camera.setMode()
setMonth	Date.setMonth()
setMotionLevel	Camera.setMotionLevel()
setNewTextFormat	TextField.setNewTextFormat()
setPan	Sound.setPan()
setProperty	setProperty()
setQuality	Camera.setQuality()
setRate	Microphone.setRate()
setRGB	Color.setRGB()
setSeconds	Date.setSeconds()
setSelectColor	TextSnapshot.setSelectColor()
setSelected	**TextSnapshot.setSelected()**
setSelection	Selection.setSelection()
setSilenceLevel	Microphone.setSilenceLevel()

ActionScript element	See entry
setStyle	TextField.StyleSheet.setStyle()
setTextFormat	TextField.setTextFormat()
setTime	Date.setTime()
setTransform	Color.setTransform(), Sound.setTransform()
setUseEchoSuppression	Microphone.setUseEchoSuppression()
setUTCDate	Date.setUTCDate()
setUTCFullYear	Date.setUTCFullYear()
setUTCHours	Date.setUTCHours()
setUTCMilliseconds	Date.setUTCMilliseconds()
setUTCMinutes	Date.setUTCMinutes()
setUTCMonth	Date.setUTCMonth()
setUTCSeconds	Date.setUTCSeconds()
setVolume	Sound.setVolume()
setYear	Date.setYear()
SharedObject	SharedObject class
SHIFT (constant)	Key.SHIFT
shift (method)	Array.shift()
show	Mouse.show()
showMenu	Stage.showMenu
showSettings	System.showSettings()
silenceLevel	Microphone.silenceLevel()
silenceTimeout	Microphone.silenceTimeout()
sin	Math.sin()
size	TextFormat.size
slice	Array.slice(), String.slice()
smoothing	Video.smoothing
sort	Array.sort()
sortOn	Array.sortOn()
Sound	Sound class
SPACE	Key.SPACE
splice	Array.splice()
split	String.split()
sqrt	Math.sqrt()

ActionScript element	See entry
SQRT1_2	Math.SQRT1_2
SQRT2	Math.SQRT2
Stage	Stage class
start	PrintJob.start(), Sound.start()
startDrag	startDrag(), MovieClip.startDrag()
static	static
status	XML.status
stop	stop(), MovieClip.stop(), Sound.stop()
stopAllSounds	stopAllSounds()
stopDrag	stopDrag(), MovieClip.stopDrag()
String	String class, String()
StyleSheet (class)	TextField.StyleSheet class
styleSheet (property)	TextField.styleSheet
substr	String.substr()
substring	substring, String.substring()
super	super
swapDepths	MovieClip.swapDepths()
switch	switch
System	System class
TAB	Key.TAB
tabChildren	MovieClip.tabChildren
tabEnabled	Button.tabEnabled, MovieClip.tabEnabled, TextField.tabEnabled
tabIndex	Button.tabIndex, MovieClip.tabIndex, TextField.tabIndex
tabStops	TextFormat.tabStops
tan	Math.tan()
target	TextFormat.target
targetPath	targetPath
tellTarget	tellTarget
text	TextField.text
textColor	TextField.textColor
TextField	TextField class
TextFormat	TextFormat class
textHeight	TextField.textHeight

ActionScript element	See entry
TextSnapshot	TextSnapshot object
textWidth	TextField.textWidth
this	this
throw	throw
time	NetStream.time
toggleHighQuality	toggleHighQuality()
toLowerCase	String.toLowerCase()
toString	Array.toString(), Boolean.toString(), Date.toString(), Error.toString(), LoadVars.toString(), Number.toString(), Object.toString(), XML.toString()
toUpperCase	String.toUpperCase()
trace	trace()
trackAsMenu	Button.trackAsMenu, MovieClip.trackAsMenu
true	true
try	try..catch..finally
type	TextField.type
typeof	typeof
undefined	undefined
underline	TextFormat.underline
unescape	unescape
uninstall	CustomActions.uninstall()
unloadClip	**MovieClipLoader.unloadClip()**
unloadMovie	unloadMovie(), MovieClip.unloadMovie()
unLoadMovieNum	unloadMovieNum()
unshift	Array.unshift()
unwatch	Object.unwatch()
UP	Key.UP
updateAfterEvent	updateAfterEvent()
updateProperties	**Accessibility.updateProperties()**
url	TextFormat.url
useCodePage	System.useCodepage
useEchoSuppression	Microphone.useEchoSuppression()
useHandCursor	Button.useHandCursor, MovieClip.useHandCursor
UTC	Date.UTC()

ActionScript element	See entry
valueOf	Boolean.valueOf(), Number.valueOf(), Object.valueOf()
var	var
variable	TextField.variable
version	System.capabilities.version
Video	Video class
visible	ContextMenuItem.visible
void	void
watch	Object.watch()
while	while
width	Camera.width, Stage.width, Video.width
with	with
wordwrap	TextField.wordWrap
XML	XML class
xmlDecl	XML.xmlDecl
XMLNode	XMLNode class
XMLSocket	XMLSocket class

-- (decrement)

Availability

Flash Player 4.

Usage

```
--expression
expression--
```

Parameters

None.

Returns

A number.

Description

Operator (arithmetic); a pre-decrement and post-decrement unary operator that subtracts 1 from the *expression*. The pre-decrement form of the operator (*--expression*) subtracts 1 from *expression* and returns the result. The post-decrement form of the operator (*expression--*) subtracts 1 from the *expression* and returns the initial value of *expression* (the value prior to the subtraction).

Example

The pre-decrement form of the operator decrements x to 2 (x - 1 = 2), and returns the result as y:

```
x = 3;
y = --x;
//y is equal to 2
```

The post-decrement form of the operator decrements x to 2 (x - 1 = 2), and returns the original value of x as the result y:

```
x = 3;
y = x--
//y is equal to 3
```

++ (increment)

Availability

Flash Player 4.

Usage

```
++expression
expression++
```

Parameters

None.

Returns

A number.

Description

Operator (arithmetic); a pre-increment and post-increment unary operator that adds 1 to *expression*. The *expression* can be a variable, element in an array, or property of an object. The pre-increment form of the operator (++*expression*) adds 1 to *expression* and returns the result. The post-increment form of the operator (*expression*++) adds 1 to *expression* and returns the initial value of *expression* (the value prior to the addition).

The pre-increment form of the operator increments x to 2 (x + 1 = 2), and returns the result as y:

```
x = 1;
y = ++x
//y is equal to 2
```

The post-increment form of the operator increments x to 2 (x + 1 = 2), and returns the original value of x as the result y:

```
x = 1;
y = x++;
//y is equal to 1
```

Example

The following example uses ++ as a post-increment operator to make a `while` loop run five times.

```
i = 0;
while(i++ < 5){
trace("this is execution " + i);
}
```

This example uses ++ as a pre-increment operator.

```
var a = [];
var i = 0;
while (i < 10) {
   a.push(++i);
}
trace(a.join());
```

This script displays the following result in the Output panel:

```
1,2,3,4,5,6,7,8,9,10
```

The following example uses ++ as a post-increment operator.

```
var a = [];
var i = 0;
while (i < 10) {
a.push(i++);
   }
trace(a.join());
```

This script displays the following result in the Output panel:

```
0,1,2,3,4,5,6,7,8,9
```

! (logical NOT)

Availability

Flash Player 4.

Usage

!expression

Parameters

None.

Returns

A Boolean value.

Description

Operator (logical); inverts the Boolean value of a variable or expression. If *expression* is a variable with the absolute or converted value `true`, the value of `!expression` is `false`. If the expression `x && y` evaluates to `false`, the expression `!(x && y)` evaluates to `true`.

The following expressions illustrate the result of using the ! operator:

`!true` returns `false`

`!false` returns `true`

Example

In the following example, the variable `happy` is set to `false`. The `if` condition evaluates the condition `!happy`, and if the condition is `true`, the `trace()` action sends a string to the Output panel.

```
happy = false;
if (!happy) {
    trace("don't worry, be happy");
}
```

!= (inequality)

Availability

Flash Player 5.

Usage

expression1 != expression2

Parameters

None.

Returns

A Boolean value.

Description

Operator (inequality); tests for the exact opposite of the `==` operator. If *expression1* is equal to *expression2*, the result is `false`. As with the `==` operator, the definition of *equal* depends on the data types being compared.

- Numbers, strings, and Boolean values are compared by value.
- Variables, objects, arrays, and functions are compared by reference.

Example

The following example illustrates the result of the `!=` operator:

`5 != 8 returns true`

`5 != 5 returns false`

This example illustrates the use of the `!=` operator in an `if` statement.

```
a = "David";
b = "Fool"
if (a != b){
    trace("David is not a fool");
}
```

See also

`!==` (strict inequality), `==` (equality), `===` (strict equality)

!== (strict inequality)

Availability

Flash Player 6.

Usage

```
expression1 !== expression2
```

Description

Operator; tests for the exact opposite of the === operator. The strict inequality operator performs the same as the inequality operator except that data types are not converted. If *expression1* is equal to *expression2*, and their data types are equal, the result is false. As with the === operator, the definition of *equal* depends on the data types being compared.

- Numbers, strings, and Boolean values are compared by value.
- Variables, objects, arrays, and functions are compared by reference.

Example

The following code displays the returned value of operations that use the equality, strict equality, and strict inequality operators.

```
s1 = new String("5");
s2 = new String("5");
s3 = new String("Hello");
n  = new Number(5);
b = new Boolean(true);

s1 == s2; // true
s1 == s3; // false
s1 == n; // true
s1 == b; // false

s1 === s2;  // true
s1 === s3; // false
s1 === n; // false
s1 === b; // false

s1 !== s2; // false
s1 !== s3; // true
s1 !== n; // true
s1 !== b; // true
```

See also

!= (inequality), == (equality), === (strict equality)

% (modulo)

Flash Player 4. In Flash 4 files, the `%` operator is expanded in the SWF file as `x - int(x/y) * y`, and may not be as fast or as accurate in later versions of Flash Player.

Usage

```
expression1 % expression2
```

Parameters

None.

Returns

Nothing.

Description

Operator (arithmetic); calculates the remainder of *expression1* divided by *expression2*. If either of the *expression* parameters are non-numeric, the modulo operator attempts to convert them to numbers. The *expression* can be a number or string that converts to a numeric value.

Example

The following is a numeric example that uses the modulo (`%`) operator.

```
trace (12 % 5);
// returns 2
trace (4.3 % 2.1);
// returns approximately 0.1
```

%= (modulo assignment)

Availability

Flash Player 4.

Usage

```
expression1 %= expression2
```

Parameters

None.

Returns

Nothing.

Description

Operator (arithmetic compound assignment); assigns *expression1* the value of *expression1* `%` *expression2*. For example, the following two expressions are the same:

```
x %= y
x = x % y
```

Example

The following example assigns the value 4 to the variable x.

```
x = 14;
y = 5;
trace(x %= y);
// returns 4
```

See also

`% (modulo)`

& (bitwise AND operator)

Availability

Flash Player 5. In Flash 4, the & operator was used for concatenating strings. In Flash 5 and later, the & operator is a bitwise AND, and you must use the add and + operators to concatenate strings. Flash 4 files that use the & operator are automatically updated to use add when brought into the Flash 5 or later authoring environment.

Usage

expression1 & *expression2*

Parameters

None.

Returns

Nothing.

Description

Operator (bitwise); converts *expression1* and *expression2* to 32-bit unsigned integers, and performs a Boolean AND operation on each bit of the integer parameters. The result is a new 32-bit unsigned integer.

&& (logical AND)

Availability

Flash Player 4.

Usage

expression1 && *expression2*

Parameters

None.

Returns

A Boolean value.

Description

Operator (logical); performs a Boolean operation on the values of one or both of the expressions. Evaluates *expression1* (the expression on the left side of the operator) and returns false if the expression evaluates to false. If *expression1* evaluates to true, *expression2* (the expression on the right side of the operator) is evaluated. If *expression2* evaluates to true, the final result is true; otherwise, it is false.

Example

This example uses the && operator to perform a test to determine if a player has won the game. The turns variable and the score variable are updated when a player takes a turn or scores points during the game. The following script displays "You Win the Game!" in the Output panel when the player's score reaches 75 or higher in 3 turns or less.

```
turns=2;
score=77;
winner = (turns <= 3) && (score >= 75);
if (winner) {
   trace("You Win the Game!");
} else {
   trace("Try Again!");
}
```

&= (bitwise AND assignment)

Availability

Flash Player 5.

Usage

```
expression1 &= expression2
```

Parameters

None.

Returns

Nothing.

Description

Operator; assigns *expression1* the value of *expression1* & *expression2*. For example, the following two expressions are the same.

```
x &= y;
x = x & y;
```

Example

The following example assigns the value 9 to x.

```
x = 15;
y = 9;
trace(x &= y);
// returns 9
```

See also

```
& (bitwise AND operator)
```

() (parentheses)

Availability

Flash Player 4.

Usage

```
(expression1, expression2)
function(parameter1,..., parameterN)
```

Parameters

expression1, expression2 Numbers, strings, variables, or text.

function The function to be performed on the contents of the parentheses.

parameter1...parameterN A series of parameters to execute before the results are passed as parameters to the function outside the parentheses.

Returns

Nothing.

Description

Operator; performs a grouping operation on one or more parameters, or surrounds one or more parameters and passes them as parameters to a function outside the parentheses.

Usage 1: Controls the order in which the operators are executed in the expression. Parentheses override the normal precedence order and cause the expressions within the parentheses to be evaluated first. When parentheses are nested, the contents of the innermost parentheses are evaluated before the contents of the outer ones.

Usage 2: Surrounds one or more parameters and passes them as parameters to the function outside the parentheses.

Example

Usage 1: The following statements illustrate the use of parentheses to control the order in which expressions are executed. The value of each expression is displayed below each line, as follows:

```
trace((2 + 3) * (4 + 5));
// displays 45

trace(2 + (3 * (4 + 5)));
// displays 29

trace(2 + (3 * 4) + 5);
// displays 19
```

Usage 2: The following examples illustrate the use of parentheses with functions.

```
getDate();

invoice(item, amount);

function traceParameter(param){
  trace(param);
}
traceParameter(2*2);
```

- (minus)

Availability

Flash Player 4.

Usage

(Negation) `-expression`

(Subtraction) *expression1 - expression2*

Parameters

None.

Returns

Nothing.

Description

Operator (arithmetic); used for negating or subtracting.

Usage 1: When used for negating, it reverses the sign of the numerical *expression*.

Usage 2: When used for subtracting, it performs an arithmetic subtraction on two numerical expressions, subtracting *expression2* from *expression1*. When both expressions are integers, the difference is an integer. When either or both expressions are floating-point numbers, the difference is a floating-point number.

Example

Usage 1: The following statement reverses the sign of the expression 2 + 3.

`-(2 + 3)`

The result is `-5`.

Usage 2: The following statement subtracts the integer 2 from the integer 5.

`5 - 2`

The result is 3, which is an integer.

Usage 2: The following statement subtracts the floating-point number 1.5 from the floating-point number 3.25.

`3.25 - 1.5`

The result is `1.75`, which is a floating-point number.

* (multiplication)

Availability

Flash Player 4.

Usage

```
expression1 * expression2
```

Parameters

None.

Returns

Nothing.

Description

Operator (arithmetic); multiplies two numerical expressions. If both expressions are integers, the product is an integer. If either or both expressions are floating-point numbers, the product is a floating-point number.

Example

Usage 1: The following statement multiplies the integers 2 and 3.

```
2 * 3
```

The result is 6, which is an integer.

Usage 2: This statement multiplies the floating-point numbers 2.0 and 3.1416.

```
2.0 * 3.1416
```

The result is 6.2832, which is a floating-point number.

*= (multiplication assignment)

Availability

Flash Player 4.

Usage

```
expression1 *= expression2
```

Parameters

None.

Returns

Nothing.

Description

Operator (arithmetic compound assignment); assigns *expression1* the value of *expression1* * *expression2*. For example, the following two expressions are the same:

```
x *= y
x = x * y
```

Example

Usage 1: The following example assigns the value 50 to the variable x.

```
x = 5;
y = 10;
trace (x *= y);
// returns 50
```

Usage 2: The second and third lines of the following example calculate the expressions on the right-hand side of the equals sign and assign the results to x and y.

```
i = 5;
x = 4 - 6;
y = i + 2;
trace(x *= y);
// returns -14
```

See also

```
* (multiplication)
```

, (comma)

Availability

Flash Player 4.

Usage

expression1, expression2

Parameters

None.

Returns

Nothing.

Description

Operator; evaluates *expression1*, then *expression2*, and returns the value of *expression2*. This operator is primarily used with the for loop statement.

Example

The following code sample uses the comma operator:

```
var a=1, b=2, c=3;
```

This is equivalent to writing the following code:

```
var a=1;
var b=2;
var c=3;
```

. (dot)

Availability

Flash Player 4.

Usage

```
object.property_or_method
instancename.variable
instancename.childinstance.variable
```

Parameters

object   An instance of a class. The object can be an instance of any of the built-in ActionScript classes or a custom class. This parameter is always to the left of the dot (.) operator.

property_or_method   The name of a property or method associated with an object. All of the valid method and properties for the built-in classes are listed in the method and property summary tables for that class. This parameter is always to the right of the dot (.) operator.

instancename   The instance name of a movie clip.

childinstance   A movie clip instance that is a child of, or nested in, another movie clip.

variable   A variable on the Timeline of the movie clip instance name to the left of the dot (.) operator.

Returns

Nothing.

Description

Operator; used to navigate movie clip hierarchies in order to access nested (child) movie clips, variables, or properties. The dot operator is also used to test or set the properties of an object, execute a method of an object, or create a data structure.

Example

The following statement identifies the current value of the variable `hairColor` in the movie clip `person_mc`.

```
person_mc.hairColor
```

This is equivalent to the following Flash 4 syntax:

```
/person_mc:hairColor
```

: (type)

Availability

Flash Player 6.

Usage

```
[modifiers] [var] variableName:[type]
function functionName():[type] { ... }
function functionName(parameter1[:type], ... , parameterN[:type]) { ... }
```

Parameters

variableName   An identifier for a variable.

type   A native data type, class name that you have defined, or interface name.

functionName   An identifier for a function.

parameter   An identifier for a function parameter.

Description

Operator; specifies the variable type, function return type, or function parameter type. When used in a variable declaration or assignment, this operator specifies the variable's type; when used in a function declaration or definition, this operator specifies the function's return type; when used with a function parameter in a function definition, this operator specifies the variable type expected for that parameter.

Types are a compile-time-only feature. All types are checked at compile time, and errors are generated when there is a mismatch. (For more information, see Appendix A, "Error Messages," on page 987.) Mismatches can occur during assignment operations, function calls, and class member dereferencing using the dot (.) operator. To avoid type mismatch errors, use explicit typing (see "Strict data typing" on page 242).

Types that you can use include all native object types, classes and interfaces that you define, and Void and Function (which exist only as types, not as objects). The recognized native types are Array, Boolean, Button, Color, CustomActions, Date, Function, LoadVars, LocalConnection, Microphone, MovieClip, NetConnection, NetStream, Number, Object, SharedObject, Sound, String, TextField, TextFormat, Video, Void, XML, XMLNode, and XMLSocket.

Example

Usage 1: The following example declares a public variable named userName whose type is String and assigns an empty string to it.

```
public var userName:String = "";
```

Usage 2: This example demonstrates how to specify a function's parameter type. The following code defines a function named setDate() that takes a parameter named currentDate of type Date.

```
function setDate(currentDate:Date) {
    this.date = currentDate;
}
```

Usage 3: The following code defines a function named squareRoot() that takes a parameter named val of the Number type and returns the square root of val, also a Number type.

```
function squareRoot(val:Number):Number {
  return Math.sqrt(val);
}
```

?: (conditional)

Availability

Flash Player 4.

Usage

```
expression1 ? expression2 : expression3
```

Parameters

expression1   An expression that evaluates to a Boolean value, usually a comparison expression, such as x < 5.

expression2, expression3   Values of any type.

Returns

Nothing.

Description

Operator; instructs Flash to evaluate *expression1*, and if the value of *expression1* is true, it returns the value of *expression2*; otherwise it returns the value of *expression3*.

Example

The following statement assigns the value of variable x to variable z because expression1 evaluates to true:

```
x = 5;
y = 10;
z = (x < 6) ? x: y;
trace (z);
// returns 5
```

/ (division)

Availability

Flash Player 4.

Usage

```
expression1 / expression2
```

Parameters

expression   A number or a variable that evaluates to a number.

Returns

Nothing.

Description

Operator (arithmetic); divides *expression1* by *expression2*. The result of the division operation is a double-precision floating-point number.

Example

The following statement divides the floating-point number 22.0 by 7.0 and then displays the result in the Output panel.

```
trace(22.0 / 7.0);
```

The result is 3.1429, which is a floating-point number.

// (comment delimiter)

Availability

Flash 1.

Usage

```
// comment
```

Parameters

comment   Any characters.

Returns

Nothing.

Description

Comment; indicates the beginning of a script comment. Any characters that appear between the comment delimiter // and the end-of-line character are interpreted as a comment and ignored by the ActionScript interpreter.

Example

This script uses comment delimiters to identify the first, third, fifth, and seventh lines as comments.

```
// record the X position of the ball movie clip
ballX = ball._x;
// record the Y position of the ball movie clip
ballY = ball._y;
// record the X position of the bat movie clip
batX = bat._x;
// record the Y position of the bat movie clip
batY = bat._y;
```

See also

/* (comment delimiter)

/* (comment delimiter)

Availability

Flash Player 5.

Usage

```
/* comment */

/*
comment
comment
*/
```

Parameters

comment   Any characters.

Returns

Nothing.

Description

Comment; indicates one or more lines of script comments. Any characters that appear between the opening comment tag /* and the closing comment tag */, are interpreted as a comment and ignored by the ActionScript interpreter. Use the first type of syntax to identify single-line comments. Use the second type of syntax to identify comments on multiple successive lines. Leaving off the closing tag */ when using this form of comment delimiter returns an error message.

Example

This script uses comment delimiters at the beginning of the script.

```
/* records the X and Y positions of the
ball and bat movie clips
*/

ballX = ball._x;
ballY = ball._y;
batX = bat._x;
batY = bat._y;
```

See also

```
// (comment delimiter)
```

/= (division assignment)

Availability

Flash Player 4.

Usage

```
expression1 /= expression2
```

Parameters

expression1,expression2   A number or a variable that evaluates to a number.

Returns

Nothing.

Description

Operator (arithmetic compound assignment); assigns *expression1* the value of *expression1 / expression2*. For example, the following two statements are the same:

```
x /= y
x = x / y
```

Example

The following code illustrates using the /= operator with variables and numbers.

```
x = 10;
y = 2;
x /= y;
// x now contains the value 5
```

[] (array access)

Availability

Flash Player 4.

Usage

```
my_array = ["a0", a1,...aN]
myMultiDimensional_array = [["a0",...aN],...["a0",...aN]]
my_array[E] = value
myMultiDimensional_array[E][E] = value
object["value"]
```

Parameters

my_array   The name of an array.

a0, a1,...aN   Elements in an array.

myMultiDimensional_array   The name of a simulated multidimensional array.

E   The number (or index) of an element in an array.

object   The name of an object.

value   A string or an expression that evaluates to a string that names a property of the object.

Returns

Nothing.

Description

Operator; initializes a new array or multidimensional array with the specified elements (*a0*, and so on), or accesses elements in an array. The array access operator lets you dynamically set and retrieve instance, variable, and object names. It also lets you access object properties.

Usage 1: An array is an object whose properties are called *elements*, which are each identified by a number called an *index*. When you create an array, you surround the elements with the array access operator (or *brackets*). An array can contain elements of various types. For example, the following array, called `employee`, has three elements; the first is a number and the second two are strings (inside quotation marks).

```
employee = [15, "Barbara", "Erick"];
```

Usage 2: You can nest brackets to simulate multidimensional arrays. The following code creates an array called `ticTacToe` with three elements; each element is also an array with three elements.

```
ticTacToe = [[1,2,3],[4,5,6],[7,8,9]];

// choose Debug > List Variables in test movie mode
// to see a list of the array elements
```

Usage 3: Surround the index of each element with brackets to access it directly; you can add a new element to an array, change or retrieve the value of an existing element. The first element in an array is always 0:

```
my_array[0] = 15;
my_array[1] = "Hello";
my_array[2] = true;
```

You can use brackets to add a fourth element, as in the following:

```
my_array[3] = "George";
```

Usage 4: You can use brackets to access an element in a multidimensional array. The first set of brackets identifies the element in the original array, and the second set identifies the element in the nested array. The following line of code sends the number 6 to the Output panel.

```
ticTacToe = [[1,2,3],[4,5,6],[7,8,9]];
trace(ticTacToe[1][2]);

// returns 6
```

Usage 5: You can use the array access operator instead of the `eval` function to dynamically set and retrieve values for movie clip names or any property of an object:

```
name["mc" + i] = "left_corner";
```

Example

Usage 1: The following code samples show two different ways of creating a new empty Array object; the first line uses brackets.

```
my_array =[];
my_array = new Array();
```

Usage 1 and 2: The following example creates an array called `employee_array` and uses the `trace()` action to send the elements to the Output panel. In the fourth line, an element in the array is changed and the fifth line sends the newly modified array to the Output panel:

```
employee_array = ["Barbara", "George", "Mary"];
trace(employee_array);
// Barbara, George, Mary
employee_array[2]="Sam";
trace(employee_array);
// Barbara, George, Sam
```

Usage 3: In the following example, the expression inside the brackets (`"piece"` + i) is evaluated and the result is used as the name of the variable to be retrieved from the `my_mc` movie clip. In this example, the variable i must live on the same Timeline as the button. If the variable i is equal to 5, for example, the value of the variable `piece5` in the `my_mc` movie clip will be displayed in the Output panel:

```
on(release){
    x = my_mc["piece"+i];
    trace(x);
}
```

Usage 3: In the following code, the expression inside the brackets is evaluated and the result is used as the name of the variable to be retrieved from movie clip `name_mc`:

```
name_mc["A" + i];
```

If you are familiar with the Flash 4 ActionScript slash syntax, you can use the `eval` function to accomplish the same result:

```
eval("name.A" & i);
```

Usage 3: You can also use the array access operator on the left side of an assignment statement to dynamically set instance, variable, and object names:

```
name[index] = "Gary";
```

See also

Array class, Object class, `eval()`

^ (bitwise XOR)

Availability

Flash Player 5.

Usage

expression1 ^ *expression2*

Parameters

expression1,expression2   A number.

Returns

None.

Description

Operator (bitwise); converts *expression1* and *expression2* to 32-bit unsigned integers, and returns a 1 in each bit position where the corresponding bits in *expression1* or *expression1*, but not both, are 1.

Example

The following example uses the bitwise XOR operator on the decimals 15 and 9 and assigns the result to the variable x.

```
// 15 decimal = 1111 binary
// 9 decimal = 1001 binary
x = 15 ^ 9
trace(x)
// 1111 ^ 1001 = 0110
// returns 6 decimal( = 0110 binary)
```

^= (bitwise XOR assignment)

Availability

Flash Player 5.

Usage

expression1 ^= *expression2*

Parameters

expression1,expression2   Integers and variables.

Returns

None.

Description

Operator (bitwise compound assignment); assigns *expression1* the value of *expression1* ^ *expression2*. For example, the following two statements are the same:

```
x ^= y
x = x ^ y
```

Example

The following is an example of a ^= operation.

```
// 15 decimal = 1111 binary
x = 15;
// 9 decimal = 1001 binary
y = 9;
trace(x ^= y);
//returns 6 decimal ( = 0110 binary)
```

See also

```
^ (bitwise XOR)
```

{} (object initializer)

Availability

Flash Player 5.

Usage

```
object = {name1: value1, name2: value2,...nameN: valueN}
```

Parameters

object   The object to create.

name1,2,...N   The names of the properties.

value1,2,...N   The corresponding values for each *name* property.

Returns

None.

Description

Operator; creates a new object and initializes it with the specified *name* and *value* property pairs. Using this operator is the same as using the `new Object` syntax and populating the property pairs using the assignment operator. The prototype of the newly created object is generically named the *Object* object.

Example

The first line of the following code creates an empty object using the object initializer operator; the second line creates a new object using a constructor function.

```
object = {};
object = new Object();
```

The following example creates an object `account` and initializes the properties `name`, `address`, `city`, `state`, `zip`, and `balance` with accompanying values.

```
account = { name: "Betty Skate",
  address: "123 Main Street",
  city: "Blossomville",
  state: "California",
  zip: "12345",
  balance: "1000" };
```

The following example shows how array and object initializers can be nested within each other.

```
person = { name: "Gina Vechio",
  children: [ "Ruby", "Chickie", "Puppa"] };
```

The following example uses the information in the previous example and produces the same result using constructor functions.

```
person = new Object();
person.name = 'Gina Vechio';
person.children = new Array();
person.children[0] = 'Ruby';
person.children[1] = 'Chickie';
person.children[2] = 'Puppa';
```

| (bitwise OR)

Availability

Flash Player 5.

Usage

```
expression1 | expression2
```

Parameters

expression1, *expression2*   A number.

Returns

None.

Description

Operator (bitwise); converts *expression1* and *expression2* to 32-bit unsigned integers, and returns a 1 in each bit position where the corresponding bits of either *expression1* or *expression2* are 1.

Example

The following is an example of a bitwise OR operation.

```
// 15 decimal = 1111 binary
x = 15;
// 9 decimal = 1001 binary
y = 9;
trace(x | y);
// 1111 | 0011 = 1111
//returns 15 decimal (= 1111 binary)
```

|| (logical OR)

Availability

Flash Player 4.

Usage

```
expression1 || expression2
```

Parameters

expression1, *expression2*   A Boolean value or an expression that converts to a Boolean value.

Returns

A Boolean value.

Description

Operator (logical); evaluates *expression1* and *expression2*. The result is `true` if either or both expressions evaluate to `true`; the result is `false` only if both expressions evaluate to `false`. You can use the logical OR operator with any number of operands; if any operand evaluates to `true`, the result is `true`.

With non-Boolean expressions, the logical OR operator causes Flash to evaluate the expression on the left; if it can be converted to `true`, the result is `true`. Otherwise, it evaluates the expression on the right and the result is the value of that expression.

Example

Usage 1: The following example uses the `||` operator in an `if` statement. The second expression evaluates to `true` so the final result is `true`:

```
x = 10
y = 250
start = false
if(x > 25 || y > 200 || start){
    trace('the logical OR test passed');
}
```

Usage 2: This example demonstrates how a non-Boolean expression can produce an unexpected result. If the expression on the left converts to `true`, that result is returned without converting the expression on the right.

```
function fx1(){
    trace ("fx1 called");
    returns true;
}
function fx2(){
    trace ("fx2 called");
    return true;
}
if (fx1() || fx2()){
    trace ("IF statement entered");
}
// The following is sent to the Output panel:
// fx1 called
// IF statement entered
```

|= (bitwise OR assignment)

Availability

Flash Player 5.

Usage

expression1 `|=` *expression2*

Parameters

expression1,expression2   A number or variable.

Returns

None.

Description

Operator (bitwise compound assignment); assigns *expression1* the value of *expression1* | *expression2*. For example, the following two statements are the same:

```
x |= y;
x = x | y;
```

Example

The following example uses the |= operator:

```
// 15 decimal = 1111 binary
x = 15;
// 9 decimal = 1001 binary
y = 9;
trace(x |= y);
// 1111 |= 1001
//returns 15 decimal (= 1111 binary)
```

See also

| (bitwise OR)

~ (bitwise NOT)

Availability

Flash Player 5.

Usage

```
~ expression
```

Parameters

expression   A number.

Returns

None.

Description

Operator (bitwise); converts the *expression* to a 32-bit unsigned integer, then inverts the bits. A bitwise NOT operation changes the sign of a number and subtracts 1.

Example

The following example shows a bitwise NOT operation performed on a variable.

```
a = 0;
trace ("when a = 0, ~a = "+~a);
// when a = 0, ~a = -1
a = 1;
trace ("when a = 1, ~a = "+~a);
// when a = 0, ~a = -2
// therefore, ~0=-1 and ~1=-2
```

+ (addition)

Availability

Flash Player 4; Flash Player 5. In Flash 5 and later, + is either a numeric operator or string concatenator depending on the data type of the parameter. In Flash 4, + is only a numeric operator. Flash 4 files brought into the Flash 5 or later authoring environment undergo a conversion process to maintain data type integrity. The following example illustrates the conversion of a Flash 4 file containing a numeric quality comparison:

Flash 4 file:

```
x + y
```

Converted Flash 5 or later file:

```
Number(x) + Number(y)
```

Usage

```
expression1 + expression2
```

Parameters

expression1,expression2   A number or string.

Returns

None.

Description

Operator; adds numeric expressions or concatenates (combines) strings. If one expression is a string, all other expressions are converted to strings and concatenated.

If both expressions are integers, the sum is an integer; if either or both expressions are floating-point numbers, the sum is a floating-point number.

Example

Usage 1: The following example concatenates two strings and displays the result in the Output panel.

```
name = "Cola";
instrument = "Drums";
trace (name + " plays " + instrument);
```

Usage 2: Variables associated with dynamic and input text fields have the data type String. In the following example, the variable deposit is an input text field on the Stage. After a user enters a deposit amount, the script attempts to add deposit to oldBalance. However, because deposit is a String data type, the script concatenates (combines to form one string) the variable values rather than summing them.

```
oldBalance = 1345.23;
currentBalance = deposit + oldBalance;
trace (currentBalance);
```

For example, if a user enters 475 in the deposit text field, the trace() action sends the value 4751345.23 to the Output panel.

To correct this, use the Number() function to convert the string to a number, as in the following:

```
currentBalance = Number(deposit) + oldBalance;
```

Usage 3: This statement adds the integers 2 and 3 and displays the resulting integer, 5, in the Output panel:

```
trace (2 + 3);
```

This statement adds the floating-point numbers 2.5 and 3.25 and displays the result, 5.75, a floating-point number, in the Output panel:

```
trace (2.5 + 3.25);
```

See also

```
_accProps
```

+= (addition assignment)

Availability

Flash Player 4.

Usage

```
expression1 += expression2
```

Parameters

expression1,expression2   A number or string.

Returns

Nothing.

Description

Operator (arithmetic compound assignment); assigns *expression1* the value of *expression1 + expression2*. For example, the following two statements have the same result:

```
x += y;
x = x + y;
```

This operator also performs string concatenation. All the rules of the addition operator (+) apply to the addition assignment (+=) operator.

Example

The following example shows a numeric use of the += operator.

```
x = 5;
y = 10;
x += y;
trace(x);
//x returns 15
```

This example uses the += operator with a string expression and sends "My name is Gilbert" to the Output panel.

```
x = "My name is "
x += "Gilbert"
trace (x)
// returns "My name is Gilbert"
```

See also

```
+ (addition)
```

‹ (less than)

Availability

Flash Player 4; Flash Player 5. In Flash 5 and later, the ‹ (less than) operator is a comparison operator capable of handling various data types. In Flash 4, ‹ is an numeric operator. Flash 4 files brought into the Flash 5 or later authoring environment undergo a conversion process to maintain data type integrity. The following illustrates the conversion of a Flash 4 file containing a numeric quality comparison.

Flash 4 file:

```
x < y
```

Converted Flash 5 or later file:

```
Number(x) < Number(y)
```

Usage

```
expression1 < expression2
```

Parameters

expression1,expression2   A number or string.

Description

Operator (comparison); compares two expressions and determines whether *expression1* is less than *expression2*; if so, the operator returns `true`. If *expression1* is greater than or equal to *expression2*, the operator returns `false`. String expressions are evaluated using alphabetical order; all capital letters come before lowercase letters.

Example

The following examples illustrate `true` and `false` returns for both numeric and string comparisons.

```
3 < 10;
// true

10 < 3;
// false

"Allen" < "Jack";
// true

"Jack" < "Allen";
// false

"11" < "3";
//true

"11" < 3;
// numeric comparison
// false

"C" < "abc";
// false

"A" < "a";
// true
```

<< (bitwise left shift)

Availability

Flash Player 5.

Usage

```
expression1 << expression2
```

Parameters

expression1   A number or expression to be shifted left.

expression2   A number or expression that converts to an integer from 0 to 31.

Returns

Nothing.

Description

Operator (bitwise); converts *expression1* and *expression2* to 32-bit integers, and shifts all of the bits in *expression1* to the left by the number of places specified by the integer resulting from the conversion of *expression2*. The bit positions that are emptied as a result of this operation are filled in with 0. Shifting a value left by one position is the equivalent of multiplying it by 2.

Example

In the following example, the integer 1 is shifted 10 bits to the left.

```
x = 1 << 10
```

The result of this operation is x = 1024. This is because 1 decimal equals 1 binary, 1 binary shifted left by 10 is 10000000000 binary, and 10000000000 binary is 1024 decimal.

In the following example, the integer 7 is shifted 8 bits to the left.

```
x = 7 << 8
```

The result of this operation is x = 1792. This is because 7 decimal equals 111 binary, 111 binary shifted left by 8 bits is 11100000000 binary, and 11100000000 binary is 1792 decimal.

See also

```
>>= (bitwise right shift and assignment), >> (bitwise right shift), <<= (bitwise
left shift and assignment)
```

<<= (bitwise left shift and assignment)

Availability

Flash Player 5.

Usage

```
expression1 <<= expression2
```

Parameters

expression1   A number or expression to be shifted left.

expression2   A number or expression that converts to an integer from 0 to 31.

Returns

Nothing.

Description

Operator (bitwise compound assignment); this operator performs a bitwise left shift operation and stores the contents as a result in *expression1*. The following two expressions are equivalent.

```
A <<= B
A = (A << B)
```

See also

`<<` (bitwise left shift), `>>=` (bitwise right shift and assignment), `>>` (bitwise right shift)

<= (less than or equal to)

Availability

Flash Player 4.

Flash 4 file:

```
x <= y
```

Converted Flash 5 or later file:

```
Number(x) <= Number(y)
```

Usage

expression1 `<=` *expression2*

Parameters

expression1, expression2   A number or string.

Returns

A Boolean value.

Description

Operator (comparison); compares two expressions and determines whether *expression1* is less than or equal to *expression2*; if it is, the operator returns `true`. If *expression1* is greater than *expression2*, the operator returns `false`. String expressions are evaluated using alphabetical order; all capital letters come before lowercase letters.

In Flash 5 or later, the less than or equal to (`<=`) operator is a comparison operator capable of handling various data types. In Flash 4, `<=` is a numeric operator. Flash 4 files brought into the Flash 5 or later authoring environment undergo a conversion process to maintain data type integrity. The following illustrates the conversion of a Flash 4 file containing a numeric quality comparison.

Example

The following examples illustrate `true` and `false` results for both numeric and string comparisons:

```
5 <= 10;
```

```
// true

2 <= 2;
// true

10 <= 3;
// false

"Allen" <= "Jack";
// true

"Jack" <= "Allen";
// false

"11" <= "3";
//true

"11" <= 3;
// numeric comparison
// false

"C" <= "abc";
// false

"A" <= "a";
// true
```

<> (inequality)

Availability

Flash 2.

Usage

expression1 <> *expression2*

Parameters

expression1,expression2   A number, string, Boolean value, variable, object, array, or function.

Returns

A Boolean value.

Description

Operator (inequality); tests for the exact opposite of the == operator. If *expression1* is equal to *expression2*, the result is false. As with the == operator, the definition of *equal* depends on the data types being compared:

- Numbers, strings, and Boolean values are compared by value.
- Variables, objects, arrays, and functions are compared by reference.

This operator was deprecated in Flash 5, and Macromedia recommends that you use the != operator.

See also

!= (inequality)

= (assignment)

Availability

Flash Player 4.

Flash 4 file:

```
x = y
```

Converted Flash 5 or later file:

```
Number(x) == Number(y)
```

Usage

```
expression1 = expression2
```

Parameters

expression1   A variable, element of an array, or property of an object.

expression2   A value of any type.

Returns

Nothing.

Description

Operator; assigns the type of *expression2* (the parameter on the right) to the variable, array element, or property in *expression1*.

In Flash 5 or later, = is an assignment operator, and the == operator is used to evaluate equality. In Flash 4, = is a numeric equality operator. Flash 4 files brought into the Flash 5 or later authoring environment undergo a conversion process to maintain data type integrity.

Example

The following example uses the assignment operator to assign the Number data type to the variable x.

```
x = 5
```

The following example uses the assignment operator to assign the String data type to the variable x.

```
x = "hello"
```

See also

```
== (equality)
```

-= (subtraction assignment)

Availability

Flash Player 4.

Usage

```
expression1 -= expression2
```

Parameters

expression1, expression2   A number or expression that evaluates to a number.

Returns

Nothing.

Description

Operator (arithmetic compound assignment); assigns *expression1* the value of *expression1* -
expression2. For example, the following two statements are the same:

```
x -= y;
x = x - y;
```

String expressions must be converted to numbers; otherwise, NaN is returned.

Example

Usage 1: The following example uses the -= operator to subtract 10 from 5 and assign the result
to the variable x.

```
x = 5;
y = 10;
x -= y
trace(x);
//returns -5
```

Usage 2: The following example shows how strings are converted to numbers.

```
x = "5";
y = "10";
x -= y;
trace(x);
// returns -5
```

== (equality)

Usage

```
expression1 == expression2
```

Parameters

expression1,expression2   A number, string, Boolean value, variable, object, array, or function.

Returns

A Boolean value.

Description

Operator (equality); tests two expressions for equality. The result is `true` if the expressions are equal.

The definition of *equal* depends on the data type of the parameter:

- Numbers and Boolean values are compared by value, and are considered equal if they have the same value.
- String expressions are equal if they have the same number of characters and the characters are identical.
- Variables, objects, arrays, and functions are compared by reference. Two variables are equal if they refer to the same object, array, or function. Two separate arrays are never considered equal, even if they have the same number of elements.

Example

Usage 1: The following example uses the `==` operator with an `if` statement:

```
a = "David" , b = "David";
if (a == b){
   trace("David is David");
}
```

Usage 2: These examples show the results of operations that compare mixed types.

```
x = "5"; y = "5";
trace(x == y);
// true

x = "5"; y = "66";
trace(x ==y);
// false

x = "chris"; y = "steve";
trace (x == y);
//false
```

See also

`!= (inequality)`, `=== (strict equality)`, `!== (strict inequality)`

=== (strict equality)

Availability

Flash Player 6.

Usage

```
expression1 === expression2
```

Returns

A Boolean value.

Description

Operator; tests two expressions for equality; the strict equality operator performs just like the equality operator except that data types are not converted. The result is true if both expressions, including their data types, are equal.

The definition of *equal* depends on the data type of the parameter:

- Numbers and Boolean values are compared by value, and are considered equal if they have the same value.
- String expressions are equal if they have the same number of characters and the characters are identical.
- Variables, objects, arrays, and functions are compared by reference. Two variables are equal if they refer to the same object, array, or function. Two separate arrays are never considered equal, even if they have the same number of elements.

Example

The following code displays the returned value of operations that use the equality, strict equality, and strict inequality operators.

```
s1 = new String("5");
s2 = new String("5");
s3 = new String("Hello");
n  = new Number(5);
b = new Boolean(true);

s1 == s2; // true
s1 == s3; // false
s1 == n; // true
s1 == b; // false

s1 === s2;  // true
s1 === s3; // false
s1 === n; // false
s1 === b; // false

s1 !== s2; // false
s1 !== s3; // true
s1 !== n; // true
s1 !== b; // true
```

See also

== (equality), != (inequality), === (strict equality)

> (greater than)

Availability

Flash Player 4.

Flash 4 file:

```
x > y
```

Converted Flash 5 or later file:

```
Number(x) > Number(y)
```

Usage

```
expression1 >expression2
```

Parameters

expression1,expression2   A number or string.

Returns

A Boolean value.

Description

Operator (comparison); compares two expressions and determines whether *expression1* is greater than *expression2*; if it is, the operator returns true. If *expression1* is less than or equal to *expression2*, the operator returns false. String expressions are evaluated using alphabetical order; all capital letters come before lowercase letters.

In Flash 5 or later, the less than or equal to (<=) operator is a comparison operator capable of handling various data types. In Flash 4, <= is a numeric operator. Flash 4 files brought into the Flash 5 or later authoring environment undergo a conversion process to maintain data type integrity.

>= (greater than or equal to)

Availability

Flash Player 4.

Flash 4 file:

```
x > y
```

Converted Flash 5 or later file:

```
Number(x) > Number(y)
```

Usage

```
expression1 >= expression2
```

Parameters

expression1, expression2   A string, integer, or floating-point number.

Returns

A Boolean value.

Description

Operator (comparison); compares two expressions and determines whether *expression1* is greater than or equal to *expression2* (true), or whether *expression1* is less than *expression2* (false).

In Flash 5 or later, greater than or equal to (>) is a comparison operator capable of handling various data types. In Flash 4, > is an numeric operator. Flash 4 files brought into the Flash 5 or later authoring environment undergo a conversion process to maintain data type integrity.

» (bitwise right shift)

Availability

Flash Player 5.

Usage

```
expression1 >> expression2
```

Parameters

expression1   A number or expression to be shifted right.

expression2   A number or expression that converts to an integer from 0 to 31.

Returns

Nothing.

Description

Operator (bitwise); converts *expression1* and *expression2* to 32-bit integers, and shifts all of the bits in *expression1* to the right by the number of places specified by the integer resulting from the conversion of *expression2*. Bits that are shifted to the right are discarded. To preserve the sign of the original *expression*, the bits on the left are filled in with 0 if the most significant bit (the bit farthest to the left) of *expression1* is 0, and filled in with 1 if the most significant bit is 1. Shifting a value right by one position is the equivalent of dividing by 2 and discarding the remainder.

Example

The following example converts 65535 to a 32-bit integer, and shifts it 8 bits to the right.

```
x = 65535 >> 8
```

The result of the above operation is as follows:

```
x = 255
```

This is because 65535 decimal equals 1111111111111111 binary (sixteen 1's), 1111111111111111 binary shifted right by 8 bits is 11111111 binary, and 11111111 binary is 255 decimal. The most significant bit is 0 because the integers are 32-bit, so the fill bit is 0.

The following example converts -1 to a 32-bit integer and shifts it 1 bit to the right.

```
x = -1 >> 1
```

The result of the above operation is as follows:

```
x = -1
```

This is because -1 decimal equals 11111111111111111111111111111111 binary (thirty-two 1's), shifting right by one bit causes the least significant (bit farthest to the right) to be discarded and the most significant bit to be filled in with 1. The result is 11111111111111111111111111111111 (thirty-two 1's) binary, which represents the 32-bit integer -1.

See also

>>= (bitwise right shift and assignment)

>>= (bitwise right shift and assignment)

Availability

Flash Player 5.

Usage

expression1 =>>*expression2*

Parameters

expression1   A number or expression to be shifted left.

expression2   A number or expression that converts to an integer from 0 to 31.

Returns

Nothing.

Description

Operator (bitwise compound assignment); this operator performs a bitwise right-shift operation and stores the contents as a result in *expression1*.

Example

The following two expressions are equivalent.

```
A >>= B
A = (A >> B)
```

The following commented code uses the bitwise (>>=) operator. It is also an example of using all bitwise operators.

```
function convertToBinary(number){
  var result = "";
  for (var i=0; i<32; i++) {
    // Extract least significant bit using bitwise AND
    var lsb = number & 1;
    // Add this bit to our result string
    result = (lsb ? "1" : "0") + result;
    // Shift number right by one bit, to see next bit
    number >>= 1;}
  return result;
}
trace(convertToBinary(479));
// Returns the string 00000000000000000000000111011111
// The above string is the binary representation of the decimal
// number 479
```

```
<< (bitwise left shift)
```

>>> (bitwise unsigned right shift)

Availability

Flash Player 5.

Usage

```
expression1 >>> expression2
```

Parameters

expression1   A number or expression to be shifted right.

expression2   A number or expression that converts to an integer between 0 and 31.

Returns

Nothing.

Description

Operator (bitwise); the same as the bitwise right shift (>>) operator except that it does not preserve the sign of the original *expression* because the bits on the left are always filled with 0.

Example

The following example converts -1 to a 32-bit integer and shifts it 1 bit to the right.

```
x = -1 >>> 1
```

The result of the above operation is as follows:

```
x = 2147483647
```

This is because -1 decimal is 11111111111111111111111111111111 binary (thirty-two 1's), and when you shift right (unsigned) by 1 bit, the least significant (rightmost) bit is discarded, and the most significant (leftmost) bit is filled with a 0. The result is 01111111111111111111111111111111 binary, which represents the 32-bit integer 2147483647.

See also

```
>>= (bitwise right shift and assignment)
```

»>= (bitwise unsigned right shift and assignment)

Availability

Flash Player 5.

Usage

expression1 >>>= expression2

Parameters

expression1   A number or expression to be shifted left.

expression2   A number or expression that converts to an integer from 0 to 31.

Returns

Nothing.

Description

Operator (bitwise compound assignment); performs an unsigned bitwise right-shift operation and stores the contents as a result in *expression1*. The following two expressions are equivalent:

```
A >>>= B
A = (A >>> B)
```

See also

>>> (bitwise unsigned right shift), >>= (bitwise right shift and assignment)

Accessibility class

Availability

Flash Player 6 version 65.

Description

The Accessibility class manages communication with screen readers. The methods of the Accessibility class are static—that is, you don't have to create an instance of the class to use its methods.

To get and set accessible properties for a specific object, such as a button, movie clip, or text field, use the _accProps property. To determine whether the player is running in an environment that supports accessibility aids, use System.capabilities.hasAccessibility.

Method summary for the Accessibility class

Method	Description
Accessibility.isActive()	Indicates whether a screen reader program is active.
Accessibility.updateProperties()	Updates the description of objects on the screen for screen readers.

Accessibility.isActive()

Availability

Flash Player 6 version 65.

Usage

```
Accessibility.isActive()
```

Parameters

None.

Returns

A Boolean value of `true` if there are active Microsoft Active Accessibility (MSAA) clients and the player is running in an environment that supports communication between Flash Player and accessibility aids, `false` otherwise.

Description

Method; indicates whether an MSAA screen reader program is currently active and the player is running in an environment that supports communication between Flash Player and accessibility aids. Use this method when you want your application to behave differently in the presence of a screen reader.

To determine whether the player is running in an environment that supports accessibility aids, use `System.capabilities.hasAccessibility`.

Note: If you call this method within about one or two seconds of the first appearance of the Flash window in which your document is playing, you might get a return value of `false` even if there is an active MSAA client. This is because of an asynchronous communication mechanism between Flash and MSAA clients. You can work around this limitation by ensuring a delay of one to two seconds after loading your document before calling this method.

See also

Accessibility.updateProperties(), _accProps, `System.capabilities.hasAccessibility`

Accessibility.updateProperties()

Availability

Flash Player 6 version 65.

Usage

```
Accessibility.updateProperties()
```

Parameters

None.

Returns

Nothing.

Description

Method; causes Flash Player to reexamine all accessibility properties, update its description of objects for screen readers, and, if necessary, send events to screen readers to indicate that changes have occurred. For information on setting accessibility properties, see _accProps.

To determine whether the player is running in an environment that supports accessibility aids, use System.capabilities.hasAccessibility.

If you modify the accessibility properties for multiple objects, only one call to Accessibility.updateProperties() is necessary; multiple calls can result in reduced performance and unintelligible screen reader results.

Example

The following ActionScript code takes advantage of dynamic accessibility properties. This example is from a nontextual button that can change which icon it displays.

```
function setIcon( newIconNum, newTextEquivalent )
{
   this.iconImage = this.iconImages[ newIconNum ];
   if ( newTextEquivalent != undefined )
   {
      if ( this._accProps == undefined )
         this._accProps = new Object();
      this._accProps.name = newTextEquivalent;
      Accessibility.updateProperties();
   }
}
```

See also

Accessibility.isActive(), _accProps, System.capabilities.hasAccessibility

_accProps

Availability

Flash Player 6 version 65.

Usage

_accProps.propertyName

instanceName._accProps.propertyName

Parameters

propertyName   An accessibility property name (see the following description for valid names).

instanceName   The instance name assigned to an instance of a movie clip, button, dynamic text field, or input text field.

Description

Property; lets you control screen reader accessibility options for SWF files, movie clips, buttons, dynamic text fields, and input text fields at runtime. These properties override the corresponding settings available in the Accessibility panel during authoring. For changes to these properties to take effect, you must call Accessibility.updateProperties(). For information on the Accessibility panel, see "Introducing the Flash Accessibility panel" in Using Flash Help.

To determine whether the player is running in an environment that supports accessibility aids, use `System.capabilities.hasAccessibility`.

The following table lists the name and data type of each `_accProps` property, its equivalent setting in the Accessibility panel, and the kinds of objects to which the property can be applied. The term *inverse logic* means that the property setting is the inverse of the corresponding setting in the Accessibility panel. For example, setting the `silent` property to `true` is equivalent to deselecting the Make Movie Accessible or Make Object Accessible option.

Property	Data type	Equivalent in Accessibility panel	Applies to
silent	Boolean	Make Movie Accessible/ Make Object Accessible *(inverse logic)*	Whole movies Movie clips Buttons Dynamic text Input text
forceSimple	Boolean	Make Child Objects Accessible *(inverse logic)*	Whole movies Movie clips
name	String	Name	Whole movies Movie clips Buttons Input text
description	String	Description	Whole movies Movie clips Buttons Dynamic text Input text
shortcut	String	Shortcut*	Movie clips Buttons Input text

* For information on assigning a keyboard shortcut to an accessible object, see Key.addListener().

To specify settings that correspond to the Tab index setting in the Accessibility panel, use the `Button.tabIndex`, `MovieClip.tabIndex`, or `TextField.tabIndex` property.

There is no way to specify an Auto Label setting at runtime.

When used without the *instanceName* parameter, changes made to `_accProps` properties apply to the whole movie. For example, the following code sets the Accessibility `name` property for the whole movie to the string `"Pet Store"`, and then calls `Accessibility.updateProperties()` to effect that change.

```
_accprops.name = "Pet Store";
Accessbility.updateProperties();
```

In contrast, the following code sets the `name` property for a movie clip with the instance name `price_mc` to the string `"Price"`:

```
price_mc._accProps.name = "Price";
Accessbility.updateProperties();
```

If you are specifying several accessibility properties, make as many changes as you can before calling `Accessibility.updateProperties()`, instead of calling it after each property statement:

```
_accprops.name = "Pet Store";
animal_mc._accProps.name = "Animal";
animal_mc._accProps.description = "Cat, dog, fish, etc.";
price_mc._accProps.name = "Price";
price_mc._accProps.description = "Cost of a single item";
Accessbility.updateProperties();
```

If you don't specify an accessibility property for a movie or an object, any values set in the Accessibility panel are implemented.

After you specify an accessibility property, you can't revert its value to a value set in the Accessibility panel. However, you can set the property to its default value (false for Boolean values, empty strings for string values) by deleting the _accProps object:

```
my_mc._accProps.silent = true; // set a property
// other code here
delete my_mc._accProps.silent; // revert to default value
```

To revert all accessibility values for an object to default values, you can delete the *instanceName*._accProps object:

```
delete my_btn._accProps;
```

To revert accessibility values for all objects to default values, you can delete the global _accProps object:

```
delete _accProps;
```

If you specify a property for an object type that doesn't support that property, the property assignment is ignored and no error is thrown. For example, the forceSimple property isn't supported for buttons, so a line like the following is ignored:

```
my_btn._accProps.forceSimple = false; //ignored
```

Example

Here is some example ActionScript code that takes advantage of dynamic accessibility properties. You would assign this code to a nontextual icon button component that can change which icon it displays.

```
function setIcon( newIconNum, newTextEquivalent )
{
   this.iconImage = this.iconImages[ newIconNum ];
   if ( newTextEquivalent != undefined )
   {
      if ( this._accProps == undefined )
         this._accProps = new Object();
      this._accProps.name = newTextEquivalent;
      Accessibility.updateProperties();
   }
}
```

See also

`Accessibility.isActive()`, **Accessibility.updateProperties()**, `System.capabilities.hasAccessibility`

add

Availability

Flash Player 4.

Usage

string1 add *string2*

Parameters

string1, string2   A string.

Returns

Nothing.

Description

Operator; concatenates (combines) two or more strings. The add operator replaces the Flash 4 add (&) operator; Flash Player 4 files that use the & operator are automatically converted to use the add operator for string concatenation when brought into the Flash 5 or later authoring environment. However, the add operator was deprecated in Flash Player 5, and Macromedia recommends that you use the + operator when creating content for Flash Player 5 or later. Use the add operator to concatenate strings if you are creating content for Flash Player 4 or earlier versions of the player.

See also

+ (addition)

and

Availability

Flash Player 4.

Usage

condition1 and *condition2*

Parameters

condition1,condition2   Conditions or expressions that evaluate to true or false.

Returns

Nothing.

Description

Operator; performs a logical AND operation in Flash Player 4. If both expressions evaluate to true, then the entire expression is true. This operator was deprecated in Flash 5, and Macromedia recommends that you use the && operator.

See also

&& (logical AND)

Arguments class

Availability

Flash Player 5; property added in Flash Player 6.

Description

The Arguments class is an array that contains the values that were passed as parameters to any function. Each time a function is called in ActionScript, an Arguments object is automatically created for that function. A local variable, `arguments`, is also created and lets you refer to the Arguments object.

Property summary for the Arguments class

Property	Description
arguments.callee	Refers to the function being called.
arguments.caller	Refers to the calling function.
arguments.length	The number of parameters passed to a function.

arguments.callee

Availability

Flash Player 5.

Usage

`arguments.callee`

Description

Property; refers to the function that is currently being called.

Example

You can use the `arguments.callee` property to make an anonymous function that is recursive, as in the following:

```
factorial = function (x) {
  if (x <= 1) {
    return 1;
  } else {
    return x * arguments.callee(x-1);
  }
};
```

The following is a named recursive function:

```
function factorial (x) {
  if (x <= 1) {
    return 1;
  } else {
    return x * factorial(x-1);
  }
}
```

arguments.caller

Availability

Flash Player 6.

Usage

```
arguments.caller
```

Description

Property; refers to the calling function.

arguments.length

Availability

Flash Player 5.

Usage

```
arguments.length
```

Description

Property; the number of parameters actually passed to a function.

Array class

Availability

Flash Player 5 (became a native object in Flash Player 6, which improved performance significantly).

Description

The Array class lets you access and manipulate arrays. An array is an object whose properties are identified by a number representing their position in the array. This number is referred to as the *index*. All arrays are zero-based, which means that the first element in the array is [0], the second element is [1], and so on. In the following example, my_array contains the months of the year.

```
my_array[0] = "January"
my_array[1] = "February"
my_array[2] = "March"
my_array[3] = "April"
```

To create an Array object, use the constructor new Array() or the array access operator ([]). To access the elements of an array, use the array access operator ([]).

Method summary for the Array class

Method	Description
`Array.concat()`	Concatenates the parameters and returns them as a new array.
`Array.join()`	Joins all elements of an array into a string.
`Array.pop()`	Removes the last element of an array and returns its value.
`Array.push()`	Adds one or more elements to the end of an array and returns the array's new length.
`Array.reverse()`	Reverses the direction of an array.
`Array.shift()`	Removes the first element from an array and returns its value.
`Array.slice()`	Extracts a section of an array and returns it as a new array.
`Array.sort()`	Sorts an array in place.
`Array.sortOn()`	Sorts an array based on a field in the array.
`Array.splice()`	Adds and removes elements from an array.
`Array.toString()`	Returns a string value representing the elements in the Array object.
`Array.unshift()`	Adds one or more elements to the beginning of an array and returns the array's new length.

Property summary for the Array class

Property	Description
`Array.length`	A nonzero-based integer specifying the number of elements in the array.

Constructor for the Array class

Availability

Flash Player 5.

Usage

```
new Array()
new Array(length)
new Array(element0, element1, element2,...elementN)
```

Parameters

length   An integer specifying the number of elements in the array. In the case of noncontiguous elements, the *length* parameter specifies the index number of the last element in the array plus 1.

element0...elementN   A list of two or more arbitrary values. The values can be numbers, strings, objects, or other arrays. The first element in an array always has an index or position of 0.

Returns

Nothing.

Description

Constructor; lets you create an array. You can use the constructor to create different types of arrays: an empty array, an array with a specific length but whose elements have no values, or an array whose elements have specific values.

Usage 1: If you don't specify any parameters, an array with a length of 0 is created.

Usage 2: If you specify only a length, an array is created with *length* number of elements with no values.

Usage 3: If you use the *element* parameters to specify values, an array is created with specific values.

Example

Usage 1: The following example creates a new Array object with an initial length of 0.

```
my_array = new Array();
trace(my_array.length); // returns 0
```

Usage 2: The following example creates a new Array object with an initial length of 4.

```
my_array = new Array(4);
trace(my_array.length); // returns 4
```

Usage 3: The following example creates the new Array object go_gos_array, with an initial length of 5.

```
go_gos_array = new Array("Belinda", "Gina", "Kathy", "Charlotte", "Jane");
trace(my_array.length); // returns 5
trace(go_gos_array.join(", ")); // displays elements
```

The initial elements of the go_gos array are identified as follows:

```
go_gos_array[0] = "Belinda";
go_gos_array[1] = "Gina";
go_gos_array[2] = "Kathy";
go_gos_array[3] = "Charlotte";
go_gos_array[4] = "Jane";
```

The following code adds a sixth element to the go_gos_array array and changes the second element:

```
go_gos_array[5] = "Donna";
go_gos_array[1] = "Nina"
trace(go_gos_array.join(" + "));
```

See also

Array.length, [] (array access)

Array.concat()

Availability

Flash Player 5.

Usage

```
my_array.concat( [ value0, value1,...valueN ])
```

Parameters

value0,...valueN   Numbers, elements, or strings to be concatenated in a new array. If you don't pass any values, a duplicate of *my_array* is created.

Returns

Nothing.

Description

Method; concatenates the elements specified in the parameters with the elements in *my_array*, and creates a new array. If the *value* parameters specify an array, the elements of that array are concatenated, rather than the array itself. The array *my_array* is left unchanged.

Example

The following code concatenates two arrays.

```
alpha_array = new Array("a","b","c");
numeric_array = new Array(1,2,3);
alphaNumeric_array=alpha_array.concat(numeric_array);
trace(alphaNumeric_array);
// creates array ["a","b","c",1,2,3]
```

The following code concatenates three arrays.

```
num1_array = [1,3,5];
num2_array = [2,4,6];
num3_array = [7,8,9];
nums_array=num1_array.concat(num2_array,num3_array)
trace(nums_array);
// creates array [1,3,5,2,4,6,7,8,9]
```

Nested arrays are not flattened in the same way normal arrays are. The elements in a nested array are not broken into separate elements in array x_array, as in the following example.

```
a_array = new Array ("a","b","c");

// 2 and 3 are elements in a nested array
n_array = new Array(1, [2, 3], 4);

x_array = a_array.concat(n_array);
trace(x_array[0]); // "a"
trace(x_array[1]); // "b"
trace(x_array[2]); // "c"
trace(x_array[3]); // 1
trace(x_array[4]); // 2, 3
trace(x_array[5]); // 4
```

Array.join()

Availability

Flash Player 5.

Usage

```
my_array.join([separator])
```

Parameters

separator   A character or string that separates array elements in the returned string. If you omit this parameter, a comma is used as the default separator.

Returns

String.

Description

Method; converts the elements in an array to strings, inserts the specified separator between the elements, concatenates them, and returns the resulting string. A nested array is always separated by a comma, not by the separator passed to the join() method.

Example

The following example creates an array with three elements: Earth, Moon, and Sun. It then joins the array three times—first using the default separator (a comma and a space), then using a dash, and then using a plus sign (+)—and displays them in the Output panel:

```
a_array = new Array("Earth","Moon","Sun")
trace(a_array.join());
// returns Earth, Moon, Sun
trace(a_array.join(" - "));
// returns Earth - Moon - Sun
trace(a_array.join(" + "));
// returns Earth + Moon + Sun
```

Array.length

Availability

Flash Player 5.

Usage

my_array.length

Description

Property; a nonzero-based integer specifying the number of elements in the array. This property is automatically updated when new elements are added to the array. When you assign a value to an array element (for example, *my_array[index]* = *value*), if *index* is a number, and *index*+1 is greater than the length property, the length property is updated to *index*+1.

Example

The following code explains how the length property is updated.

```
my_array = new Array();
trace(my_array.length); // initial length is 0
my_array[0] = 'a';
trace(my_array.length); // my_array.length is updated to 1
my_array[1] = 'b';
trace(my_array.length); // my_array.length is updated to 2
my_array[9] = 'c';
trace(my_array.length); // my_array.length is updated to 10
```

Array.pop()

Availability

Flash Player 5.

Usage

my_array.pop()

Parameters

None.

Returns

The value of the last element in the specified array.

Description

Method; removes the last element from an array and returns the value of that element.

Example

The following code creates the myPets array containing four elements, then removes its last element.

```
myPets = ["cat", "dog", "bird", "fish"];
popped = myPets.pop();
trace(popped);
// returns fish
```

Array.push()

Availability

Flash Player 5.

Usage

my_array.push(*value,...*)

Parameters

value   One or more values to append to the array.

Returns

The length of the new array.

Description

Method; adds one or more elements to the end of an array and returns the array's new length.

Example

The following example creates the array myPets with two elements, cat and dog. The second line adds two elements to the array. After the push() method is called, the variable pushed contains four elements. Because the push() method returns the new length of the array, the trace() action in the last line sends the new length of myPets (4) to the Output panel:

```
myPets = ["cat", "dog"];
pushed = myPets.push("bird", "fish");
trace(pushed);
```

Array.reverse()

Availability

Flash Player 5.

Usage

my_array.reverse()

Parameters

None.

Returns

Nothing.

Description

Method; reverses the array in place.

Example

The following is an example of using this method.

```
var numbers_array = [1, 2, 3, 4, 5, 6];
trace(numbers_array.join()); //1,2,3,4,5,6
numbers_array.reverse();
trace(numbers_array.join()); // 6,5,4,3,2,1
```

Array.shift()

Availability

Flash Player 5.

Usage

my_array.shift()

Parameters

None.

Returns

The first element in an array.

Description

Method; removes the first element from an array and returns that element.

Example

The following code creates the array myPets and then removes the first element from the array and assigns it to the variable shifted.

```
var myPets_array = ["cat", "dog", "bird", "fish"];
shifted = myPets_array.shift();
trace(shifted); // returns "cat"
```

See also

Array.pop()

Array.slice()

Availability

Flash Player 5.

Usage

my_array.slice([*start* [, *end*]])

Parameters

start   A number specifying the index of the starting point for the slice. If *start* is a negative number, the starting point begins at the end of the array, where -1 is the last element.

end   A number specifying the index of the ending point for the slice. If you omit this parameter, the slice includes all elements from the start to the end of the array. If *end* is a negative number, the ending point is specified from the end of the array, where -1 is the last element.

Returns

An array.

Description

Method; extracts a slice or a substring of the array and returns it as a new array without modifying the original array. The returned array includes the *start* element and all elements up to, but not including, the *end* element.

If you don't pass any parameters, a duplicate of *my_array* is created.

Array.sort()

Availability

Flash Player 5; additional capabilities added in Flash Player 7.

Usage

```
my_array.sort()
my_array.sort(compareFunction)
my_array.sort(option | option |... )
my_array.sort(compareFunction, option | option |... )
```

Parameters

compareFunction An optional comparison function used to determine the sorting order of elements in an array. Given the elements A and B, the result of *compareFunction* can have one of the following three values:

- -1 if A should appear before B in the sorted sequence
- 0 if A = B
- 1 if A should appear after B in the sorted sequence

option One or more numbers or strings, separated by the | (bitwise OR) operator, that change the behavior of the sort from the default. The following values are acceptable for *option*:

- 1 or Array.CASEINSENSITIVE
- 2 or Array.DESCENDING
- 4 or Array.UNIQUE
- 8 or Array.RETURNINDEXEDARRAY
- 16 or Array.NUMERIC

For information on this parameter, see Array.sortOn().

Returns

The return value depends on whether you pass any parameters:

- If you specify a value of 4 or Array.UNIQUE for *option* and two or more elements being sorted have identical sort fields, Flash returns a value of 0 and does not modify the array.
- If you specify a value of 8 or Array.RETURNINDEXEDARRAY for *option*, Flash returns an array that reflects the results of the sort and does not modify the array.
- Otherwise, Flash returns nothing and modifies the array to reflect the sort order.

Description

Method; sorts the elements in an array. Flash sorts according to ASCII (Unicode) values. If either of the elements being compared does not contain the field specified in the *fieldName* parameter, the field is assumed to be undefined, and the elements are placed consecutively in the sorted array in no particular order.

By default, Array.sort() works as follows:

- Sorting is case sensitive (*Z* precedes *a*).
- Sorting is ascending (*a* precedes *b*).
- The array is modified to reflect the sort order; multiple elements that have identical sort fields are placed consecutively in the sorted array in no particular order.
- Numeric fields are sorted as if they were strings, so 100 precedes 99, because "1" is a lower string value than "9".
- Nothing is returned.

If you want to sort in another way, create a function to do the sorting and pass its name as the *compareFunction* parameter. You might do this, for example, if you want to sort alphabetically by last name, ascending, and then by ZIP code, descending.

If you want to specify one or more fields on which to sort, using either the default sort or the *options* parameter, use Array.sortOn().

Example

Usage 1: The following example shows the use of Array.sort() with and without a value passed for *option*:

```
var fruits_array = ["oranges", "apples", "strawberries", "pineapples",
    "cherries"];
trace(fruits_array.join());
fruits_array.sort();
trace(fruits_array.join());
fruits_array.sort(Array.DESCENDING);
trace(fruits_array.join());
```

The Output panel displays the following results:

```
oranges,apples,strawberries,pineapples,cherries// original array
apples,cherries,oranges,pineapples,strawberries// default sort
strawberries,pineapples,oranges,cherries,apples// descending sort
```

Usage 2: The following example uses Array.sort() with a compare function.

```
var passwords = ["mom:glam","ana:ring","jay:mag","anne:home","regina:silly"];
function order (a,b){
  //Entries to be sorted are in form name:password
  //Sort using only the name part of the entry as a key.
  var name1 =a.split(":")[0 ];
  var name2 =b.split(":")[0 ];
  if (name1 <name2){
    return -1;
  }
  else if (name1 >name2){
    return 1;
  }
  else {
    return 0;
```

```
  }
}
trace ("Unsorted:");
trace (passwords.join());

passwords.sort(order);
trace ("Sorted:");
trace (passwords.join());
```

The Output panel displays the following results:

```
Unsorted:
mom:glam,ana:ring,jay:mag,anne:home,regina:silly
Sorted:
ana:ring,anne:home,jay:mag,mom:glam,regina:silly
```

See also

| (bitwise OR), Array.sortOn()

Array.sortOn()

Availability

Flash Player 6; additional capabilities added in Flash Player 7.

Usage

```
my_array.sortOn("fieldName" )
my_array.sortOn("fieldName", option | option |... )
my_array.sortOn( [ "fieldName" , "fieldName" , ... ] )
my_array.sortOn( [ "fieldName" , "fieldName" , ... ] , option | option |... )
```

Note: Where brackets ([]) are shown, you must include them in the code; that is, the brackets don't represent optional parameters.

Parameters

fieldName   A string that identifies a field (in an element of the Array) to be used as the sort value.

option   One or more numbers or strings, separated by the | (bitwise OR) operator, that change the behavior of the sort from the default. The following values are acceptable for *option*:

- 1 or Array.CASEINSENSITIVE
- 2 or Array.DESCENDING
- 4 or Array.UNIQUE
- 8 or Array.RETURNINDEXEDARRAY
- 16 or Array.NUMERIC

Each of these options in discussed in more detail in "Description," below.

Returns

The return value depends on whether you pass any parameters:

- If you specify a value of 4 or Array.UNIQUE for *option*, and two or more elements being sorted have identical sort fields, Flash returns a value of 0 and does not modify the array.
- If you specify a value of 8 or Array.RETURNINDEXEDARRAY for *option*, Flash returns an array that reflects the results of the sort and does not modify the array.
- Otherwise, Flash returns nothing and modifies the array to reflect the sort order.

Description

Method; sorts the elements in an array according to one or more fields in the array. If you pass multiple *fieldName* parameters, the first field represents the primary sort field, the second represents the next sort field, and so on. Flash sorts according to ASCII (Unicode) values. If either of the elements being compared does not contain the field specified in the *fieldName* parameter, the field is assumed to be undefined, and the elements are placed consecutively in the sorted array in no particular order.

By default, Array.sortOn() works as follows:

- Sorting is case sensitive (*Z* precedes *a*).
- Sorting is ascending (*a* precedes *b*).
- The array is modified to reflect the sort order; multiple elements that have identical sort fields are placed consecutively in the sorted array in no particular order.
- Numeric fields are sorted as if they were strings, so 100 precedes 99, because "1" is a lower string value than "9".
- Nothing is returned.

You can use the *option* flags to override these defaults. The following examples use different forms of the *option* flag for illustration purposes. If you want to sort a simple array (for example, an array with only one field), or if you want to specify a sort order that the *options* parameter doesn't support, use Array.sort().

To pass multiple flags in numeric format, separate them with the | (bitwise OR) operator or add the values of the flags together. The following code shows three different ways to specify a numeric descending sort:

```
my_Array.sortOn(someFieldName, 2 | 16);
my_Array.sortOn(someFieldName, 18);
my_Array.sortOn(someFieldName, Array.DESCENDING | Array.NUMERIC);
```

Code hinting (see "Using code hints" on page 267) is enabled if you use the string form of the flag (for example, DESCENDING) rather than the numeric form (2).

Consider the following array:

```
var my_array:Array = new Array();
my_array.push({password: "Bob", age:29});
my_array.push({password: "abcd", age:3});
my_array.push({password: "barb", age:35});
my_array.push({password: "catchy", age:4});
```

Performing a default sort on the password field produces the following results:

```
my_array.sortOn("password")
// Bob
// abcd
// barb
// catchy
```

Performing a case-insensitive sort on the password field produces the following results:

```
my_array.sortOn("password", Array.CASEINSENSITIVE)
// abcd
// barb
// Bob
// catchy
```

Performing a case-insensitive, descending sort on the password field produces the following results:

```
my_array.sortOn("password", 1|2)
// catchy
// Bob
// barb
// abcd
```

Performing a default sort on the age field produces the following results:

```
my_array.sortOn("age")
// 29
// 3
// 35
// 4
```

Performing a numeric sort on the age field produces the following results:

```
my_array.sortOn("age", 16)
// 3
// 4
// 29
// 35
```

Performing a descending numeric sort on the age field produces the following results:

```
my_array.sortOn("age", 18)
// 35
// 29
// 4
// 3
```

Performing a sort changes the elements in the array as follows:

```
// Before sorting
// my_array[0].age = 29;
// my_array[1].age = 3;
// my_array[2].age = 35;
// my_array[3].age = 4;

// After any sort that doesn't pass a value of 8 for option
my_array.sortOn("age", Array.NUMERIC);
// my_array[0].age = 3;
// my_array[1].age = 4;
// my_array[2].age = 29;
// my_array[3].age = 35;
```

Performing a sort that returns an index array doesn't change the elements in the array:

```
// Before sorting
// my_array[0].age = 29;
// my_array[1].age = 3;
// my_array[2].age = 35;
// my_array[3].age = 4;

// After a sort that returns an array containing index values
// Note that the original array is unchanged.
// You can then use the returned array to display sorted information
// without modifying the original array.
var indexArray:Array = my_array.sortOn("age", Array.RETURNINDEXEDARRAY);
// my_array[0].age = 29;
// my_array[1].age = 3;
// my_array[2].age = 35;
// my_array[3].age = 4;
```

Example

This example creates a new array and sorts it according to the fields name and city: The first sort uses name as the first sort value and city as the second. The second sort uses city as the first sort value and name as the second.

```
var rec_array = new Array();
rec_array.push( { name: "john", city: "omaha", zip: 68144 } );
rec_array.push( { name: "john", city: "kansas city", zip: 72345 } );
rec_array.push( { name: "bob", city: "omaha", zip: 94010 } );
for(i=0; i<rec_array.length; i++) {
 trace(rec_array[i].name + ", " + rec_array[i].city);
}
// results in
// john, omaha
// john, kansas city
// bob, omaha

rec_array.sortOn( [ "name", "city" ]);
for(i=0; i<rec_array.length; i++) {
 trace(rec_array[i].name + ", " + rec_array[i].city);
}
// results in
// bob, omaha
// john, kansas city
// john, omaha

rec_array.sortOn( ["city", "name" ]);
for(i=0; i<rec_array.length; i++) {
 trace(rec_array[i].name + ", " + rec_array[i].city);
}
// results in
// john, kansas city
// bob, omaha
// john, omaha
```

See also

| (bitwise OR), Array.sort()

Array.splice()

Flash Player 5.

Usage

`my_array.splice(start, deleteCount [, value0, value1...valueN])`

Parameters

`start`   The index of the element in the array where the insertion or deletion begins.

`deleteCount`   The number of elements to be deleted. This number includes the element specified in the `start` parameter. If no value is specified for `deleteCount`, the method deletes all of the values from the `start` element to the last element in the array. If the value is 0, no elements are deleted.

`value`   An optional parameter specifying the values to insert into the array at the insertion point specified in the `start` parameter.

Returns

Nothing.

Description

Method; adds and removes elements from an array. This method modifies the array without making a copy.

Array.toString()

Availability

Flash Player 5.

Usage

`my_array.toString()`

Parameters

None.

Returns

A string.

Description

Method; returns a string value representing the elements in the specified Array object. Every element in the array, starting with index 0 and ending with index `my_array.length-1`, is converted to a concatenated string and separated by commas.

Example

The following example creates my_array, converts it to a string, and displays 1,2,3,4,5 in the Output panel.

```
my_array = new Array();
my_array[0] = 1;
my_array[1] = 2;
my_array[2] = 3;
my_array[3] = 4;
my_array[4] = 5;
trace(my_array.toString());
```

Array.unshift()

Availability

Flash Player 5.

Usage

my_array.unshift(*value1,value2,...valueN*)

Parameters

value1,...valueN   One or more numbers, elements, or variables to be inserted at the beginning of the array.

Returns

The new length of the array.

Description

Method; adds one or more elements to the beginning of an array and returns the array's new length.

Array()

Availability

Flash Player 6 .

Usage

Array()

Array([*element0* [, *element1* , *element2,...elementN*]])

Parameters

element   One or more elements to place in the array.

Returns

An array.

Description

Conversion function; creates a new, empty array or converts specified elements to an array. Using this function is similar to creating an array using the Array constructor (see "Constructor for the Array class" on page 478).

---

asfunction

Availability

Flash Player 5.

Usage

```
asfunction:function,"parameter"
```

Parameters

function   An identifier for a function.

parameter   A string that is passed to the function named in the *function* parameter.

Returns

Nothing.

Description

Protocol; a special protocol for URLs in HTML text fields. In HTML text fields, text may be hyperlinked using the HTML A tag. The HREF attribute of the A tag contains a URL that may be for a standard protocol like HTTP, HTTPS, or FTP. The asfunction protocol is an additional protocol specific to Flash, which causes the link to invoke an ActionScript function.

Example

In this example, the MyFunc() function is defined in the first three lines of code. The TextField object myTextField is associated with an HTML text field. The text "Click Me!" is a hyperlink inside the text field. The MyFunc() function is called when the user clicks on the hyperlink:

```
function MyFunc(arg){
   trace ("You clicked me! Argument was "+arg);
}
myTextField.htmlText ="<A HREF=\"asfunction:MyFunc,Foo \">Click Me!</A>";
```

When the hyperlink is clicked, the following results are displayed in the Output panel:

```
You clicked me!  Parameter was Foo
```

Boolean class

Availability

Flash Player 5 (became a native object in Flash Player 6, which improved performance significantly).

Description

The Boolean class is a wrapper object with the same functionality as the standard JavaScript Boolean object. Use the Boolean class to retrieve the primitive data type or string representation of a Boolean object.

You must use the constructor new Boolean() to create a Boolean object before calling its methods.

Method summary for the Boolean class

Method	Description
Boolean.toString()	Returns the string representation ("true" or "false") of the Boolean object.
Boolean.valueOf()	Returns the primitive value type of the specified Boolean object.

Constructor for the Boolean class

Availability

Flash Player 5.

Usage

```
new Boolean([x])
```

Parameters

x   Any expression. This parameter is optional.

Returns

Nothing.

Description

Constructor; creates a Boolean object. If you omit the *x* parameter, the Boolean object is initialized with a value of false. If you specify a value for the *x* parameter, the method evaluates it and returns the result as a Boolean value according to the rules in the Boolean() function.

Example

The following code creates a new empty Boolean object called myBoolean.

```
myBoolean = new Boolean();
```

Boolean.toString()

Availability

Flash Player 5.

Usage

```
myBoolean.toString()
```

Parameters

None.

Returns

A Boolean value.

Description

Method; returns the string representation ("true" or "false") of the Boolean object.

Boolean.valueOf()

Availability

Flash Player 5.

Usage

`myBoolean.valueOf()`

Parameters

None.

Returns

A Boolean value.

Description

Method; returns `true` if the primitive value type of the specified Boolean object is true, `false` if it is false.

Example

```
var x:Boolean = new Boolean();
trace(x.valueOf());   // false
x = (6==3+3);
trace(x.valueOf());   // true
```

Boolean()

Availability

Flash Player 5; behavior changed in Flash Player 7.

Usage

`Boolean(expression)`

Parameters

`expression`   An expression to convert to a Boolean value.

Returns

A Boolean value or the value `expression`, as described below.

Description

Function; converts the parameter `expression` to a Boolean value and returns a value as follows:

If `expression` is a Boolean value, the return value is `expression`.

If `expression` is a number, the return value is `true` if the number is not zero, otherwise the return value is `false`.

If `expression` is a string, the return value is as follows:

- In files published for Flash Player 6 or earlier, the string is first converted to a number; the value is `true` if the number is nonzero, `false` otherwise.
- In files published for Flash Player 7 or later, the result is `true` if the string has a length greater than zero; the value is `false` for an empty string.

If *expression* is undefined, the return value is `false`.

If *expression* is a movie clip or an object, the return value is `true`.

See also

Boolean class

break

Availability

Flash Player 4.

Usage

```
break
```

Parameters

None.

Returns

Nothing.

Description

Statement; appears within a loop (`for`, `for..in`, `do while` or `while`) or within a block of statements associated with a particular case within a `switch` action. The `break` action instructs Flash to skip the rest of the loop body, stop the looping action, and execute the statement following the loop statement. When using the `break` action, the Flash interpreter skips the rest of the statements in that `case` block and jumps to the first statement following the enclosing `switch` action. Use the `break` action to break out of a series of nested loops.

Example

The following example uses the `break` action to exit an otherwise infinite loop.

```
i = 0;
while (true) {
   if (i >= 100) {
     break;
   }
   i++;
}
```

See also

`break`, `for`, `for..in`, `do while`, `while`, **switch**, `case`

Button class

Availability

Flash Player 6.

Description

All button symbols in a SWF file are instances of the Button object. You can give a button an instance name in the Property inspector, and use the methods and properties of the Button class to manipulate buttons with ActionScript. Button instance names are displayed in the Movie Explorer and in the Insert Target Path dialog box in the Actions panel.

The Button class inherits from the Object class.

Method summary for the Button class

Method	Description
Button.getDepth()	Returns the depth of a button instance.

Property summary for the Button class

Property	Description
Button._alpha	The transparency value of a button instance.
Button.enabled	Indicates whether a button is active.
Button._focusrect	Indicates whether a button with focus has a yellow rectangle around it.
Button._height	The height of a button instance, in pixels.
Button._highquality	The level of anti-aliasing applied to the current SWF file.
Button.menu	Associates a ContextMenu object with the button object.
Button._name	The instance name of a button instance.
Button._parent	A reference to the movie clip or object that contains the current movie clip or object.
Button._quality	Indicates the rendering quality of the SWF file.
Button._rotation	The degree of rotation of a button instance.
Button._soundbuftime	Number of seconds for a sound to preload.
Button.tabEnabled	Indicates whether a button is included in automatic tab ordering.
Button.tabIndex	Indicates the tab order of an object.
Button._target	The target path of a button instance.
Button.trackAsMenu	Indicates whether other buttons can receive mouse release events.
Button._url	The URL of the SWF file that created the button instance.
Button.useHandCursor	Indicates whether the pointing hand is displayed when the mouse passes over a button.

Property	Description
Button._visible	A Boolean value that indicates whether a button instance is hidden or visible.
Button._width	The width of a button instance, in pixels.
Button._x	The x coordinate of a button instance.
Button._xmouse	The x coordinate of the mouse pointer relative to a button instance.
Button._xscale	The value specifying the percentage for horizontally scaling a button instance.
Button._y	The y coordinate of a button instance.
Button._ymouse	The y coordinate of the mouse pointer relative to a button instance.
Button._yscale	The value specifying the percentage for vertically scaling a button instance.

Event handler summary for the Button class

Event handler	Description
Button.onDragOut	Invoked when the mouse button is pressed over the button and the pointer then rolls outside the button.
Button.onDragOver	Invoked when the user presses and drags the mouse button outside and then over the button.
Button.onKeyUp	Invoked when a key is released.
Button.onKillFocus	Invoked when focus is removed from a button.
Button.onPress	Invoked when the mouse is pressed while the pointer is over a button.
Button.onRelease	Invoked when the mouse is released while the pointer is over a button.
Button.onReleaseOutside	Invoked when the mouse is released while the pointer is outside the button after the button is pressed while the pointer is inside the button.
Button.onRollOut	Invoked when the pointer rolls outside of a button area.
Button.onRollOver	Invoked when the mouse pointer rolls over a button.
Button.onSetFocus	Invoked when a button has input focus and a key is released.

Button._alpha

Availability

Flash Player 6.

Usage

my_btn._alpha

Description

Property; the alpha transparency value of the button specified by *my_btn*. Valid values are 0 (fully transparent) to 100 (fully opaque). The default value is 100. Objects in a button with _alpha set to 0 are active, even though they are invisible.

Example

The following code sets the _alpha property of a button named star_btn to 30% when the button is clicked:

```
on(release) {
    star_btn._alpha = 30;
}
```

See also

MovieClip._alpha, TextField._alpha

Button.enabled

Availability

Flash Player 6.

Usage

my_btn.enabled

Description

Property; a Boolean value that specifies whether a button is enabled. The default value is true.

Button._focusrect

Availability

Flash Player 6.

Usage

my_btn._focusrect

Description

Property; a Boolean value that specifies whether a button has a yellow rectangle around it when it has keyboard focus. This property can override the global _focusrect property.

Button.getDepth()

Availability

Flash Player 6.

Usage

```
my_btn.getDepth()
```

Returns

An integer.

Description

Method; returns the depth of a button instance.

Button._height

Availability

Flash Player 6.

Usage

```
my_btn._height
```

Description

Property; the height of the button, in pixels.

Example

The following code example sets the height and width of a button when the user clicks the mouse:

```
my_btn._width = 200;
my_btn._height = 200;
```

Button._highquality

Availability

Flash Player 6.

Usage

```
my_btn._highquality
```

Description

Property (global); specifies the level of anti-aliasing applied to the current SWF file. Specify 2 (best quality) to apply high quality with bitmap smoothing always on. Specify 1 (high quality) to apply anti-aliasing; this will smooth bitmaps if the SWF file does not contain animation. Specify 0 (low quality) to prevent anti-aliasing.

See also

```
_quality
```

Button.menu

Availability

Flash Player 7.

Usage

```
my_button.menu = contextMenu
```

Parameters

contextMenu   A ContextMenu object.

Description

Property; associates the ContextMenu object *contextMenu* with the button object *my_button*. The ContextMenu class lets you modify the context menu that appears when the user right-clicks (Windows) or Control-clicks (Macintosh) in Flash Player.

Example

The following example assigns a ContextMenu object to a Button object named save_btn. The ContextMenu object contains a single menu item (labeled "Save...") with an associated callback handler function named doSave (not shown).

```
var menu_cm = new ContextMenu();
menu_cm.customItems.push(new ContextMenuItem("Save...", doSave));
function doSave(menu, obj) {
    // "Save" code here
}
save_btn.menu = menu_cm;
```

See also

ContextMenu class, ContextMenuItem class, MovieClip.menu, TextField.menu

Button._name

Availability

Flash Player 6.

Usage

```
my_btn._name
```

Description

Property; instance name of the button specified by *my_btn*.

Button.onDragOut

Availability

Flash Player 6.

Usage

```
my_btn.onDragOut = function() {
    // your statements here
}
```

Parameters

None.

Returns

Nothing.

Description

Event handler; invoked when the mouse button is pressed over the button and the pointer then rolls outside the button.

You must define a function that executes when the event handler is invoked.

Button.onDragOver

Availability

Flash Player 6.

Usage

```
my_btn.onDragOver = function() {
    // your statements here
}
```

Parameters

None.

Returns

Nothing.

Description

Event handler; invoked when the user presses and drags the mouse button outside and then over the button.

You must define a function that executes when the event handler is invoked.

Example

The following example defines a function for the onKeyDown handler that sends a trace() action to the Output panel:

```
my_btn.onDragOver = function () {
    trace ("onDragOver called");
};
```

See also

Button.onKeyUp

Button.onKeyDown

Availability

Flash Player 6.

Usage

```
my_btn.onKeyDown = function() {
    // your statements here
}
```

Parameters

None.

Returns

Nothing.

Description

Event handler; invoked when a button has keyboard focus and a key is pressed. The onKeyDown event handler is invoked with no parameters. You can use Key.getAscii() and Key.getCode() to determine which key was pressed.

You must define a function that executes when the event handler is invoked.

Example

In the following example, a function that sends a trace() action to the Output panel is defined for the onKeyDown handler.

```
my_btn.onKeyDown = function () {
    trace ("onKeyDown called");
};
```

See also

Button.onKeyUp

Button.onKeyUp

Availability

Flash Player 6.

Usage

```
my_btn.onKeyUp = function() {
    // your statements here
}
```

Parameters

None.

Returns

Nothing.

Description

Event handler; invoked when a button has input focus and a key is released. The `onKeyUp` event handler is invoked with no parameters. You can use `Key.getAscii()` and `Key.getCode()` to determine which key was pressed.

You must define a function that executes when the event handler is invoked.

Example

In the following example, a function that sends a `trace()` action to the Output panel is defined for the `onKeyPress` handler.

```
my_btn.onKeyUp = function () {
  trace ("onKeyUp called");
};
```

Button.onKillFocus

Availability

Flash Player 6.

Usage

```
my_btn.onKillFocus = function (newFocus) {
  // your statements here
}
```

Parameters

newFocus   The object that is receiving the focus.

Returns

Nothing.

Description

Event handler; invoked when a button loses keyboard focus. The `onKillFocus` method receives one parameter, *newFocus*, which is an object representing the new object receiving the focus. If no object receives the focus, *newFocus* contains the value `null`.

Button.onPress

Availability

Flash Player 6.

Usage

```
my_btn.onPress = function() {
  // your statements here
}
```

Parameters

None.

Returns

Nothing.

Description

Event handler; invoked when a button is pressed. You must define a function that executes when the event handler is invoked.

Example

In the following example, a function that sends a trace() action to the Output panel is defined for the onPress handler.

```
my_btn.onPress = function () {
  trace ("onPress called");
};
```

Button.onRelease

Availability

Flash Player 6.

Usage

```
my_btn.onRelease = function() {
  // your statements here
}
```

Parameters

None.

Returns

Nothing.

Description

Event handler; invoked when a button is released. You must define a function that executes when the event handler is invoked.

Example

In the following example, a function that sends a trace() action to the Output panel is defined for the onRelease handler.

```
my_btn.onRelease = function () {
  trace ("onRelease called");
};
```

Button.onReleaseOutside

Availability

Flash Player 6.

Usage

```
my_btn.onReleaseOutside = function() {
    // your statements here
}
```

Parameters

None.

Returns

Nothing.

Description

Event handler; invoked when the mouse is released while the pointer is outside the button after the button is pressed while the pointer is inside the button.

You must define a function that executes when the event handler is invoked.

Example

In the following example, a function that sends a trace() action to the Output panel is defined for the onReleaseOutside handler.

```
my_btn.onReleaseOutside = function () {
    trace ("onReleaseOutside called");
};
```

Button.onRollOut

Availability

Flash Player 6.

Usage

```
my_btn.onRollOut = function() {
    // your statements here
}
```

Parameters

None.

Returns

Nothing.

Description

Event handler; invoked when the pointer moves outside a button area. You must define a function that executes when the event handler is invoked.

Example

In the following example, a function that sends a trace() action to the Output panel is defined for the onRollOut handler.

```
my_btn.onRollOut = function () {
    trace ("onRollOut called");
};
```

Button.onRollOver

Availability

Flash Player 6.

Usage

```
my_btn.onRollOver = function() {
    // your statements here
}
```

Parameters

None.

Returns

Nothing.

Description

Event handler; invoked when the pointer moves over a button area. You must define a function that executes when the event handler is invoked.

Example

In the following example, a function that sends a trace() action to the Output panel is defined for the onRollOver handler.

```
my_btn.onRollOver = function () {
    trace ("onRollOver called");
};
```

Button.onSetFocus

Availability

Flash Player 6.

Usage

```
my_btn.onSetFocus = function(oldFocus){
    // your statements here
}
```

Parameters

oldFocus   The object to lose keyboard focus.

Returns

Nothing.

Description

Event handler; invoked when a button receives keyboard focus. The *oldFocus* parameter is the object that loses the focus. For example, if the user presses the Tab key to move the input focus from a text field to a button, *oldFocus* contains the text field instance.

If there is no previously focused object, *oldFocus* contains a `null` value.

Button._parent

Availability

Flash Player 6.

Usage

```
my_btn._parent.property
_parent.property
```

Description

Property; a reference to the movie clip or object that contains the current movie clip or object. The current object is the one containing the ActionScript code that references `_parent`.

Use `_parent` to specify a relative path to movie clips or objects that are above the current movie clip or object. You can use `_parent` to climb up multiple levels in the display list as in the following:

```
_parent._parent._alpha = 20;
```

See also

`MovieClip._parent`, `_root`, `targetPath`

Button._quality

Availability

Flash Player 6.

Usage

```
my_btn._quality
```

Description

Property (global); sets or retrieves the rendering quality used for a SWF file. Device fonts are always aliased and therefore are unaffected by the `_quality` property.

Note: Although you can specify this property for a Button object, it is actually a global property, and you can specify its value simply as `_quality`. For more information, see `_quality`.

Button._rotation

Availability

Flash Player 6.

Usage

*my_btn._*rotation

Description

Property; the rotation of the button, in degrees, from its original orientation. Values from 0 to 180 represent clockwise rotation; values from 0 to -180 represent counterclockwise rotation. Values outside this range are added to or subtracted from 360 to obtain a value within the range. For example, the statement my_btn._rotation = 450 is the same as my_btn._rotation = 90.

See also

MovieClip._rotation, TextField._rotation

Button._soundbuftime

Availability

Flash Player 6.

Usage

*myButton.*_soundbuftime

Description

Property (global); an integer that specifies the number of seconds a sound prebuffers before it starts to stream.

Note: Although you can specify this property for a Button object, it is actually a global property, and you can specify its value simply as _soundbuftime. For more information, see _soundbuftime.

Button.tabEnabled

Availability

Flash Player 6.

Usage

my_btn.tabEnabled

Description

Property; specifies whether *my_btn* is included in automatic tab ordering. It is undefined by default.

If the tabEnabled property is undefined or true, the object is included in automatic tab ordering. If the tabIndex property is also set to a value, the object is included in custom tab ordering as well. If tabEnabled is false, the object is not included in automatic or custom tab ordering, even if the tabIndex property is set.

See also

Button.tabIndex, MovieClip.tabEnabled, TextField.tabEnabled

Button.tabIndex

Availability

Flash Player 6.

Usage

`my_btn.tabIndex`

Description

Property; lets you customize the tab ordering of objects in a SWF file. You can set the `tabIndex` property on a button, movie clip, or text field instance; it is `undefined` by default.

If any currently displayed object in the SWF file contains a `tabIndex` property, automatic tab ordering is disabled, and the tab ordering is calculated from the `tabIndex` properties of objects in the SWF file. The custom tab ordering only includes objects that have `tabIndex` properties.

The `tabIndex` property may be an non-negative integer. The objects are ordered according to their `tabIndex` properties, in ascending order. An object with a `tabIndex` value of 1 precedes an object with a `tabIndex` value of 2. If two objects have the same `tabIndex` value, the one that precedes the other in the tab ordering is `undefined`.

The custom tab ordering defined by the `tabIndex` property is *flat*. This means that no attention is paid to the hierarchical relationships of objects in the SWF file. All objects in the SWF file with `tabIndex` properties are placed in the tab order, and the tab order is determined by the order of the `tabIndex` values. If two objects have the same `tabIndex` value, the one that goes first is undefined. You shouldn't use the same `tabIndex` value for multiple objects.

See also

`Button.tabEnabled, MovieClip.tabChildren, MovieClip.tabEnabled, MovieClip.tabIndex, TextField.tabIndex`

Button._target

Availability

Flash Player 6.

Usage

`myButton._target`

Description

Property (read-only); returns the target path of the button instance specified by `my_btn`.

See also

`targetPath`

Button.trackAsMenu

Availability

Flash Player 6.

Usage

`my_btn.trackAsMenu`

Description

Property; a Boolean value that indicates whether other buttons or movie clips can receive mouse release events. This allows you to create menus. You can set the `trackAsMenu` property on any button or movie clip object. If the `trackAsMenu` property has not been defined, the default behavior is `false`.

You can change the `trackAsMenu` property at any time; the modified button immediately takes on the new behavior.

See also

`MovieClip.trackAsMenu`

Button._url

Availability

Flash Player 6.

Usage

`my_btn._url`

Description

Property (read only); retrieves the URL of the SWF file that created the button.

Button.useHandCursor

Availability

Flash Player 6.

Usage

`my_btn.useHandCursor`

Description

Property; a Boolean value that, when set to `true` (the default), indicates whether a hand cursor (pointing hand) is displayed when the mouse rolls over a button. If this property is set to `false`, the arrow cursor is used instead.

You can change the `useHandCursor` property at any time; the modified button immediately takes on the new cursor behavior. The `useHandCursor` property can be read out of a prototype object.

Button._visible

Availability

Flash Player 6.

Usage

`my_btn._visible`

Description

Property; a Boolean value that indicates whether the button specified by *my_btn* is visible. Buttons that are not visible (`_visible` property set to `false`) are disabled.

See also

`MovieClip._visible, TextField._visible`

Button._width

Availability

Flash Player 6.

Usage

`my_btn._width`

Description

Property; the width of the button, in pixels.

Example

The following example sets the height and width properties of a button.

```
my_btn._width=200;
my_btn._height=200;
```

See also

`MovieClip._width`

Button._x

Availability

Flash Player 6.

Usage

`my_btn._x`

Description

Property; an integer that sets the *x* coordinate of a button relative to the local coordinates of the parent movie clip. If a button is on the main Timeline, then its coordinate system refers to the upper left corner of the Stage as (0, 0). If the button is inside a movie clip that has transformations, the button is in the local coordinate system of the enclosing movie clip. Thus, for a movie clip rotated 90 degrees counterclockwise, the enclosed button inherits a coordinate system that is rotated 90 degrees counterclockwise. The button's coordinates refer to the registration point position.

See also

Button._xscale, Button._y, Button._yscale

Button._xmouse

Availability

Flash Player 6.

Usage

`my_btn._xmouse`

Description

Property (read-only); returns the *x* coordinate of the mouse position relative to the button.

See also

Button._ymouse

Button._xscale

Availability

Flash Player 6.

Usage

`my_btn._xscale`

Description

Property; the horizontal scale of the button as applied from the registration point of the button, expressed as a percentage. The default registration point is (0,0).

Scaling the local coordinate system affects the _x and _y property settings, which are defined in pixels. For example, if the parent movie clip is scaled to 50%, setting the _x property moves an object in the button by half the number of pixels as it would if the SWF file were at 100%.

See also

Button._x, Button._y, Button._yscale

Button._y

Availability

Flash Player 6.

Usage

`my_btn._y`

Description

Property; the *y* coordinate of the button relative to the local coordinates of the parent movie clip. If a button is in the main Timeline, its coordinate system refers to the upper left corner of the Stage as (0, 0). If the button is inside another movie clip that has transformations, the button is in the local coordinate system of the enclosing movie clip. Thus, for a movie clip rotated 90 degrees counterclockwise, the enclosed button inherits a coordinate system that is rotated 90 degrees counterclockwise. The button's coordinates refer to the registration point position.

See also

Button._x, Button._xscale, Button._yscale

Button._ymouse

Availability

Flash Player 6.

Usage

```
my_btn._ymouse
```

Description

Property (read-only); indicates the *y* coordinate of the mouse position relative to the button.

See also

Button._xmouse

Button._yscale

Availability

Flash Player 6.

Usage

```
my_btn._yscale
```

Description

Property; the vertical scale of the button as applied from the registration point of the button, expressed as a percentage. The default registration point is (0,0).

See also

Button._y, Button._x, Button._xscale

call()

Availability

Flash Player 4. This action was deprecated in Flash 5, and Macromedia recommends that you use the `function` action instead.

Usage

```
call(frame)
```

Parameters

frame   The label or number of a frame in the Timeline.

Returns

Nothing.

Description

Deprecated action; executes the script in the called frame without moving the playhead to that frame. Local variables do not exist after the script executes.

function, Function.call()

Camera class

Availability

Flash Player 6.

Description

The Camera class is primarily for use with Macromedia Flash Communication Server, but can be used in a limited fashion without the server.

The Camera class lets you capture video from a video camera attached to the computer that is running the Macromedia Flash Player—for example, to monitor a video feed from a web camera attached to your local system. (Flash provides similar audio capabilities; for more information, see the Microphone class entry.)

To create or reference a Camera object, use Camera.get().

Method summary for the Camera class

Method	Description
Camera.get()	Returns a default or specified Camera object, or null if the camera is not available.
Camera.setMode()	Sets aspects of the camera capture mode, including height, width, and frames per second.
Camera.setMotionLevel()	Specifies how much motion is required to invoke Camera.onActivity(true) and how much time should elapse without motion before Camera.onActivity(false) is invoked.
Camera.setQuality()	An integer that specifies the maximum amount of bandwidth that the current outgoing video feed can use, in bytes per second.

Property summary for the Camera class

Property (read-only)	Description
Camera.activityLevel	The amount of motion the camera is detecting.
Camera.bandwidth	The maximum amount of bandwidth the current outgoing video feed can use, in bytes.
Camera.currentFps	The rate at which the camera is capturing data, in frames per second.
Camera.fps	The rate at which you would like the camera to capture data, in frames per second.
Camera.height	The current capture height, in pixels.
Camera.index	The index of the camera, as reflected in the array returned by Camera.names.
Camera.motionLevel	The amount of motion required to invoke Camera.onActivity(true).

Property (read-only)	Description
Camera.motionTimeOut	The number of milliseconds between the time when the camera stops detecting motion and the time Camera.onActivity(false) is invoked.
Camera.muted	A Boolean value that specifies whether the user has allowed or denied access to the camera.
Camera.name	The name of the camera as specified by the camera hardware.
Camera.names	Class property; an array of strings reflecting the names of all available video capture devices, including video cards and cameras.
Camera.quality	An integer specifying the required level of picture quality, as determined by the amount of compression being applied to each video frame.
Camera.width	The current capture width, in pixels.

Event handler summary for the Camera class

Event handler	Description
Camera.onActivity	Invoked when the camera starts or stops detecting motion.
Camera.onStatus	Invoked when the user allows or denies access to the camera.

Constructor for the Camera class

See Camera.get().

Camera.activityLevel

Availability

Flash Player 6.

Usage

active_cam.activityLevel

Description

Read-only property; a numeric value that specifies the amount of motion the camera is detecting. Values range from 0 (no motion is being detected) to 100 (a large amount of motion is being detected). The value of this property can help you determine if you need to pass a setting to Camera.setMotionLevel().

If the camera is available but is not yet being used because Video.attachVideo() has not been called, this property is set to -1.

If you are streaming only uncompressed local video, this property is set only if you have assigned a function to the Camera.onActivity event handler. Otherwise, it is undefined.

See also

Camera.motionLevel, Camera.setMotionLevel()

Camera.bandwidth

Availability

Flash Player 6.

Usage

active_cam.bandwidth

Description

Read-only property; an integer that specifies the maximum amount of bandwidth the current outgoing video feed can use, in bytes. A value of 0 means that Flash video can use as much bandwidth as needed to maintain the desired frame quality.

To set this property, use `Camera.setQuality()`.

Example

The following example loads another SWF file if the camera's bandwidth is 32 kilobytes or greater.

```
if(myCam.bandwidth >= 32768){
    loadMovie("splat.swf",_root.hiddenvar);
}
```

See also

Camera.setQuality()

Camera.currentFps

Availability

Flash Player 6.

Usage

active_cam.currentFps

Description

Read-only property; the rate at which the camera is capturing data, in frames per second. This property cannot be set; however, you can use the `Camera.setMode()` method to set a related property—`Camera.fps`—which specifies the maximum frame rate at which you would like the camera to capture data.

See also

Camera.fps, Camera.setMode()

Camera.fps

Availability

Flash Player 6.

Usage

```
active_cam.fps
```

Description

Read-only property; the maximum rate at which you want the camera to capture data, in frames per second. The maximum rate possible depends on the capabilities of the camera; that is, if the camera doesn't support the value you set here, this frame rate will not be achieved.

- To set a desired value for this property, use `Camera.setMode()`.
- To determine the rate at which the camera is currently capturing data, use the `Camera.currentFps` property.

Example

The following example sets the fps rate of the active camera, `myCam.fps`, to the value provided by the user's text box, `this.config.txt_fps`.

```
if (this.config.txt_fps != undefined) {
    myCam.setMode(myCam.width, myCam.height, this.config.txt_fps, false);
}
```

Note: The setMode function does not guarantee the requested fps setting; it sets the fps you requested or the fastest fps available.

See also

`Camera.currentFps, Camera.setMode()`

Camera.get()

Availability

Flash Player 6.

Usage

```
Camera.get([index])
```

Note: The correct syntax is Camera.get(). To assign the Camera object to a variable, use syntax like `active_cam = Camera.get()`.

Parameters

index   An optional zero-based integer that specifies which camera to get, as determined from the array returned by the `Camera.names` property. To get the default camera (which is recommended for most applications), omit this parameter.

Returns

- If *index* is not specified, this method returns a reference to the default camera or, if it is in use by another application, to the first available camera. (If there is more than one camera installed, the user may specify the default camera in the Flash Player Camera Settings panel.) If no cameras are available or installed, the method returns `null`.

- If *index* is specified, this method returns a reference to the requested camera, or `null` if it is not available.

Description

Method; returns a reference to a Camera object for capturing video. To actually begin capturing the video, you must attach the Camera object to a Video object (see `Video.attachVideo()`).

Unlike objects that you create using the `new` constructor, multiple calls to `Camera.get()` reference the same camera. Thus, if your script contains the lines `first_cam = Camera.get()` and `second_cam = Camera.get()`, both `first_cam` and `second_cam` reference the same (default) camera.

In general, you shouldn't pass a value for *index*; simply use `Camera.get()` to return a reference to the default camera. By means of the Camera settings panel (discussed later in this section), the user can specify the default camera Flash should use. If you pass a value for *index*, you might be trying to reference a camera other than the one the user prefers. You might use *index* in rare cases—for example, if your application is capturing video from two cameras at the same time.

When a SWF file tries to access the camera returned by `Camera.get()`, Flash Player displays a Privacy dialog box that lets the user choose whether to allow or deny access to the camera. (Make sure your Stage size is at least 215 x 138 pixels; this is the minimum size Flash requires to display the dialog box.)

When the user responds to this dialog box, the `Camera.onStatus` event handler returns an information object that indicates the user's response. To determine whether the user has denied or allowed access to the camera without processing this event handler, use the `Camera.muted` property.

The user can also specify permanent privacy settings for a particular domain by right-clicking (Windows) or Control-clicking (Macintosh) while a SWF file is playing, choosing Settings, opening the Privacy panel, and selecting Remember.

You can't use ActionScript to set the Allow or Deny value for a user, but you can display the Privacy panel for the user by using `System.showSettings(0)`. If the user selects Remember, Flash Player no longer displays the Privacy dialog box for movies from this domain.

If `Camera.get` returns `null`, either the camera is in use by another application, or there are no cameras installed on the system. To determine whether any cameras are installed, use `Camera.names.length`. To display the Flash Player Camera Settings panel, which lets the user choose the camera to be referenced by `Camera.get()`, use `System.showSettings(3)`.

Scanning the hardware for cameras takes time. When Flash finds at least one camera, the hardware is not scanned again for the lifetime of the player instance. However, if Flash doesn't find any cameras, it will scan each time `Camera.get` is called. This is helpful if a user has forgotten to connect the camera; if your SWF file provides a Try Again button that calls `Camera.get`, Flash can find the camera without the user having to restart the SWF file.

Example

The following example captures and displays video locally within a Video object named `my_video` on the Stage.

```
var my_cam = Camera.get();
my_video.attachVideo(myCam);
```

See also

`Camera.index`, `Camera.muted`, `Camera.names`, `Camera.onStatus`, `Camera.setMode()`, System.showSettings(), `Video.attachVideo()`

Camera.height

Availability

Flash Player 6.

Usage

active_cam.height

Description

Read-only property; the current capture height, in pixels. To set a value for this property, use `Camera.setMode()`.

Example

The following line of code updates a text box in the user interface with the current height value.

```
my_txt._height = myCam.height;
```

See also the example for `Camera.setMode()`.

See also

`Camera.setMode()`, `Camera.width`

Camera.index

Availability

Flash Player 6.

Usage

active_cam.index

Description

Read-only property; a zero-based integer that specifies the index of the camera, as reflected in the array returned by `Camera.names`.

Example

The following example gets the camera that has the value of `index`.

```
my_cam = Camera.get(index);
```

See also

`Camera.get()`, `Camera.names`

Camera.motionLevel

Availability

Flash Player 6.

Usage

active_cam.motionLevel

Description

Read-only property; a numeric value that specifies the amount of motion required to invoke Camera.onActivity(true). Acceptable values range from 0 to 100. The default value is 50.

Video can be displayed regardless of the value of the motionLevel property. For more information, see Camera.setMotionLevel().

See also

Camera.activityLevel, Camera.onActivity, Camera.onStatus, Camera.setMotionLevel()

Camera.motionTimeOut

Availability

Flash Player 6.

Usage

active_cam.motionTimeOut

Description

Read-only property; the number of milliseconds between the time the camera stops detecting motion and the time Camera.onActivity(false) is invoked. The default value is 2000 (2 seconds).

To set this value, use Camera.setMotionLevel().

Example

The following example sets the number of milliseconds between the time the camera stops detecting motion and the time Camera.onActivity(false) is invoked to 1000 milliseconds, or one second.

```
if(my_cam.motionTimeOut >= 1000){
  my_cam.setMotionLevel(myCam.motionLevel, 1000);
}
```

See also

Camera.onActivity, Camera.setMotionLevel()

Camera.muted

Availability

Flash Player 6.

Usage

```
active_cam.muted
```

Description

Read-only property; a Boolean value that specifies whether the user has denied access to the camera (true) or allowed access (false) in the Flash Player Privacy Settings panel. When this value changes, Camera.onStatus is invoked. For more information, see Camera.get().

See also

Camera.get(), Camera.onStatus

Camera.name

Availability

Flash Player 6.

Usage

```
active_cam.name
```

Description

Read-only property; a string that specifies the name of the current camera, as returned by the camera hardware.

Example

The following example displays the name of the default camera in the Output panel. In Windows, this name is the same as the device name listed in the Scanners and Cameras properties sheet.

```
my_cam = Camera.get();
trace("The camera name is: " + my_cam.name);
```

See also

Camera.get(), Camera.names

Camera.names

Availability

Flash Player 6.

Usage

```
Camera.names
```

Note: The correct syntax is `Camera.names`. To assign the return value to a variable, use syntax like `cam_array = Camera.names`. To determine the name of the current camera, use `active_cam.name`.

Description

Read-only class property; retrieves an array of strings reflecting the names of all available cameras without displaying the Flash Player Privacy Settings panel. This array behaves the same as any other ActionScript array, implicitly providing the zero-based index of each camera and the number of cameras on the system (by means of `Camera.names.length`). For more information, see the Array class entry.

Calling the `Camera.names` property requires an extensive examination of the hardware, and it may take several seconds to build the array. In most cases, you can just use the default camera.

Example

The following example uses the default camera unless more than one camera is available, in which case the user can choose which camera to set as the default camera.

```
cam_array = Camera.names;
if (cam_array.length == 1){
  my_cam = Camera.get();
}
else {
  System.showSettings(3);
  my_cam = Camera.get();
}
```

See also

`Camera.get()`, `Camera.index`, `Camera.name`

Camera.onActivity

Availability

Flash Player 6.

Usage

```
active_cam.onActivity = function(activity) {
  // your statements here
}
```

Parameters

`activity`   A Boolean value set to `true` when the camera starts detecting motion, `false` when it stops.

Returns

Nothing.

Description

Event handler; invoked when the camera starts or stops detecting motion. If you want to respond to this event handler, you must create a function to process its *activity* value.

To specify the amount of motion required to invoke `Camera.onActivity(true)` and the amount of time that must elapse without activity before invoking `Camera.onActivity(false)`, use `Camera.setMotionLevel()`.

Example

The following example displays `true` or `false` in the Output panel when the camera starts or stops detecting motion.

```
// Assumes a Video object named "myVideoObject" is on the Stage
my_cam = Camera.get();
myVideoObject.attachVideo(my_cam);
my_cam.setMotionLevel(10, 500);
my_cam.onActivity = function(mode)
{
    trace(mode);
}
```

See also

`Camera.onActivity`, `Camera.setMotionLevel()`

Camera.onStatus

Availability

Flash Player 6.

Usage

```
active_cam.onStatus = function(infoObject) {
    // your statements here
}
```

Parameters

infoObject   A parameter defined according to the status message.

Returns

Nothing.

Description

Event handler; invoked when the user allows or denies access to the camera. If you want to respond to this event handler, you must create a function to process the information object generated by the camera.

When a SWF file tries to access the camera, Flash Player displays a Privacy dialog box that lets the user choose whether to allow or deny access.

- If the user allows access, the `Camera.muted` property is set to `false`, and this handler is invoked with an information object whose `code` property is `"Camera.Unmuted"` and whose `level` property is `"Status"`.

- If the user denies access, the `Camera.muted` property is set to `true`, and this handler is invoked with an information object whose `code` property is `"Camera.Muted"` and whose `level` property is `"Status"`.

To determine whether the user has denied or allowed access to the camera without processing this event handler, use the `Camera.muted` property.

Note: If the user chooses to permanently allow or deny access for all SWF files from a specified domain, this handler is not invoked for SWF files from that domain unless the user later changes the privacy setting. For more information, see `Camera.get()`.

Example

The following event handler displays a message whenever the user allows or denies access to the camera.

```
myCam = Camera.get();
myVideoObject.attachVideo(myCam);
myCam.onStatus = function(infoMsg) {

    if(infoMsg.code == "Camera.Muted"){
      trace("User denies access to the camera");
    }
    else
      trace("User allows access to the camera");
}
// Change the Allow or Deny value to invoke the function
System.showSettings(0);
```

See also

`Camera.get()`, `Camera.muted`

Camera.quality

Availability

Flash Player 6.

Usage

active_cam.quality

Description

Read-only property; an integer specifying the required level of picture quality, as determined by the amount of compression being applied to each video frame. Acceptable quality values range from 1 (lowest quality, maximum compression) to 100 (highest quality, no compression). The default value is 0, which means that picture quality can vary as needed to avoid exceeding available bandwidth.

See also

Camera.setQuality()

Camera.setMode()

Availability

Flash Player 6.

Usage

```
active_cam.setMode(width, height, fps [,favorSize])
```

Parameters

width   The requested capture width, in pixels. The default value is 160.

height   The requested capture height, in pixels. The default value is 120.

fps   The requested rate at which the camera should capture data, in frames per second. The default value is 15.

favorSize   Optional: a Boolean value that specifies how to manipulate the width, height, and frame rate if the camera does not have a native mode that meets the specified requirements. The default value is true, which means that maintaining capture size is favored; using this parameter selects the mode that most closely matches *width* and *height* values, even if doing so adversely affects performance by reducing the frame rate. To maximize frame rate at the expense of camera height and width, pass false for the *favorSize* parameter.

Returns

Nothing.

Description

Method; sets the camera capture mode to the native mode that best meets the specified requirements. If the camera does not have a native mode that matches all the parameters you pass, Flash selects a capture mode that most closely synthesizes the requested mode. This manipulation may involve cropping the image and dropping frames.

By default, Flash drops frames as needed to maintain image size. To minimize the number of dropped frames, even if this means reducing the size of the image, pass false for the *favorSize* parameter.

When choosing a native mode, Flash tries to maintain the requested aspect ratio whenever possible. For example, if you issue the command *active_cam*.setMode(400, 400, 30), and the maximum width and height values available on the camera are 320 and 288, Flash sets both the width and height at 288; by setting these properties to the same value, Flash maintains the 1:1 aspect ratio you requested.

To determine the values assigned to these properties after Flash selects the mode that most closely matches your requested values, use Camera.width, Camera.height, and Camera.fps.

Example

The following example sets the width, height, and fps based on the user's input if the user clicks the button. The optional parameter, *favorSize* is not included, because the default value, true, will provide the settings closest to the user's preference without sacrificing the picture quality, although the fps may then be sacrificed. The user interface is then updated with the new settings.

```
on (press)
{
    // Sets width, height, and fps to user's input.
    _root.myCam.setMode(txt_width, my_txt._height, txt_fps);

    // Update the user's text fields with the new settings.
    _root.txt_width = myCam.width;
    _root.txt_height = myCam.height;
    _root.txt_fps = myCam.fps;
}
```

See also

Camera.currentFps, **Camera.fps,** Camera.height, Camera.width

Camera.setMotionLevel()

Availability

Flash Player 6.

Usage

active_cam.setMotionLevel(*sensitivity* [, *timeout*])

Parameters

sensitivity   A numeric value that specifies the amount of motion required to invoke Camera.onActivity(true). Acceptable values range from 0 to 100. The default value is 50.

timeout   An optional numeric parameter that specifies how many milliseconds must elapse without activity before Flash considers activity to have stopped and invokes the Camera.onActivity(false) event handler. The default value is 2000 (2 seconds).

Returns

Nothing.

Description

Method; specifies how much motion is required to invoke Camera.onActivity(true). Optionally sets the number of milliseconds that must elapse without activity before Flash considers motion to have stopped and invokes Camera.onActivity(false).

Note: Video can be displayed regardless of the value of the *sensitivity* parameter. This parameter only determines when and under what circumstances Camera.onActivity is invoked, not whether video is actually being captured or displayed.

- To prevent the camera from detecting motion at all, pass a value of 100 for *sensitivity*; Camera.onActivity is never invoked. (You would probably use this value only for testing purposes—for example, to temporarily disable any actions set to occur when Camera.onActivity is invoked.)

- To determine the amount of motion the camera is currently detecting, use the Camera.activityLevel property.

Motion sensitivity values correspond directly to activity values. Complete lack of motion is an activity value of 0. Constant motion is an activity value of 100. Your activity value is less than your motion sensitivity value when you're not moving; when you are moving, activity values frequently exceed your motion sensitivity value.

This method is similar in purpose to `Microphone.setSilenceLevel()`; both methods are used to specify when the `onActivity` event handler should be invoked. However, these methods have a significantly different impact on publishing streams:

- `Microphone.setSilenceLevel()` is designed to optimize bandwidth. When an audio stream is considered silent, no audio data is sent. Instead, a single message is sent, indicating that silence has started.

- `Camera.setMotionLevel()` is designed to detect motion and does not affect bandwidth usage. Even if a video stream does not detect motion, video is still sent.

Example

The following example sends messages to the Output panel when video activity starts or stops. Change the motion sensitivity value of 30 to a higher or lower number to see how different values affect motion detection.

```
// Assumes a Video object named "myVideoObject" is on the Stage
c = Camera.get();
x = 0;
function motion(mode)
{
   trace(x + ": " + mode);
   x++;
}
c.onActivity = function(mode) {motion(mode);};
c.setMotionLevel(30, 500);
myVideoObject.attachVideo(c);
```

See also

`Camera.activityLevel`, `Camera.motionLevel`, `Camera.motionTimeOut`, `Camera.onActivity`

Camera.setQuality()

Availability

Flash Player 6.

Usage

active_cam.setQuality(*bandwidth*, *frameQuality*)

Parameters

bandwidth   An integer that specifies the maximum amount of bandwidth that the current outgoing video feed can use, in bytes per second. To specify that Flash video can use as much bandwidth as needed to maintain the value of *frameQuality*, pass 0 for *bandwidth*. The default value is 16384.

frameQuality   An integer that specifies the required level of picture quality, as determined by the amount of compression being applied to each video frame. Acceptable values range from 1 (lowest quality, maximum compression) to 100 (highest quality, no compression). To specify that picture quality can vary as needed to avoid exceeding bandwidth, pass 0 for *frameQuality*. The default value is 0.

Returns

Nothing.

Description

Method; sets the maximum amount of bandwidth per second or the required picture quality of the current outgoing video feed. This method is generally applicable only if you are transmitting video using Flash Communication Server.

Use this method to specify which element of the outgoing video feed is more important to your application—bandwidth use or picture quality.

- To indicate that bandwidth use takes precedence, pass a value for *bandwidth* and 0 for *frameQuality*. Flash will transmit video at the highest quality possible within the specified bandwidth. If necessary, Flash will reduce picture quality to avoid exceeding the specified bandwidth. In general, as motion increases, quality decreases.

- To indicate that quality takes precedence, pass 0 for *bandwidth* and a numeric value for *frameQuality*. Flash will use as much bandwidth as required to maintain the specified quality. If necessary, Flash will reduce the frame rate to maintain picture quality. In general, as motion increases, bandwidth use also increases.

- To specify that both bandwidth and quality are equally important, pass numeric values for both parameters. Flash will transmit video that achieves the specified quality and that doesn't exceed the specified bandwidth. If necessary, Flash will reduce the frame rate to maintain picture quality without exceeding the specified bandwidth.

Example

The following examples illustrate how to use this method to control bandwidth use and picture quality.

```
// Ensure that no more than 8192 (8K/second) is used to send video
active_cam.setQuality(8192,0);

// Ensure that no more than 8192 (8K/second) is used to send video
// with a minimum quality of 50
active_cam.setQuality(8192,50);

// Ensure a minimum quality of 50, no matter how much bandwidth it takes
active_cam.setQuality(0,50);
```

See also

Camera.bandwidth, Camera.quality

Camera.width

Availability

Flash Player 6.

Usage

`active_cam.width`

Description

Read-only property; the current capture width, in pixels. To set a desired value for this property, use `Camera.setMode()`.

Example

The following line of code updates a text box in the user interface with the current width value.

`myTextField.text=myCam.width;`

See also the example for `Camera.setMode()`.

See also

`Camera.height`

case

Availability

Flash Player 4.

Usage

`case expression: statements`

Parameters

`expression`   Any expression.

`statements`   Any statements.

Returns

Nothing.

Description

Statement; defines a condition for the `switch` action. The statements in the `statements` parameter execute if the `expression` parameter that follows the `case` keyword equals the `expression` parameter of the `switch` action using strict equality (`===`)

If you use the `case` action outside of a `switch` statement, it produces an error and the script doesn't compile.

See also

`break`, `default`, `===` (strict equality), `switch`

chr

Availability

Flash Player 4. This function was deprecated in Flash 5 in favor of `String.fromCharCode()`.

Usage

`chr(number)`

Parameters

number   An ASCII code number.

Returns

Nothing.

Description

String function; converts ASCII code numbers to characters.

Example

The following example converts the number 65 to the letter *A* and assigns it to the variable `myVar`.

`myVar = chr(65);`

See also

`String.fromCharCode()`

class

Availability

Flash Player 6.

Usage

```
[dynamic] class className [ extends superClass ]
                [ implements interfaceName [, interfaceName... ] ]
{
    // class definition here
}
```

Note: To use this keyword, you must specify ActionScript 2.0 and Flash Player 6 or later in the Flash tab of your FLA file's Publish Settings dialog box. This keyword is supported only when used in external script files, not in scripts written in the Actions panel.

Parameters

className   The fully qualified name of the class.

superClass   Optional; the name of the class that *className* extends (inherits from).

interfaceName   Optional; the name of the interface whose methods *className* must implement.

Description

Statement; defines a custom class, which lets you instantiate objects that share methods and properties that you define. For example, if you are developing an invoice-tracking system, you could create an invoice class that defines all the methods and properties that each invoice should have. You would then use the `new invoice()` command to create invoice objects.

The name of the class must be the same as the name of the external file that contains the class. For example, if you name a class *Student*, the file that defines the class must be named *Student.as*.

The class name must be fully qualified within the file in which it is declared; that is, it must reflect the directory in which it is stored. For example, to create a class named RequiredClass that is stored in the myClasses/education/curriculum directory, you must declare the class in the RequiredClass.as file like this:

```
class myClasses.education.curriculum.RequiredClass {
}
```

For this reason, it's good practice to plan your directory structure before you begin creating classes. Otherwise, if you decide to move class files after you create them, you will have to modify the class declaration statements to reflect their new location.

You cannot nest class definitions; that is, you cannot define additional classes within a class definition.

To indicate that objects can add and access dynamic properties at runtime, precede the class statement with the `dynamic` keyword. To create classes based on interfaces, use the `implements` keyword. To create subclasses of a class, use the `extends` keyword. (A class can extend only one class, but can implement several interfaces.) You can use `implements` and `extends` in a single statement.

```
class C implements Interface_i, Interface_j    // OK
class C extends Class_d implements Interface_i, Interface_j    // OK
class C extends Class_d, Class_e    // not OK
```

For more information, see "Creating and using classes" on page 365.

Example

The following example creates a class called Plant. Its constructor takes two parameters.

```
// Filename Plant.as
class Plant {
  // Define property names and types
  var leafType:String;
  var bloomSeason:String;
  // Following line is constructor
  // because it has the same name as the class
  function Plant (param_leafType:String, param_bloomSeason:String) {
    // Assign passed values to properties when new Plant object is created
    leafType = param_leafType;
    bloomSeason = param_bloomSeason;
  }
  // Create methods to return property values, because best practice
  // recommends against directly referencing a property of a class
  function getLeafType():String {return leafType};
  function getBloomSeason():String {return bloomSeason};
}
```

In an external script file or in the Actions panel, use the new operator to create a Plant object.

```
var pineTree:Plant = new Plant("Evergreen","N/A");
// Confirm parameters were passed correctly
trace(pineTree.getLeafType());
trace(pineTree.getBloomSeason());
```

See also

dynamic, extends, implements, interface, new

clearInterval()

Availability

Flash Player 6.

Usage

```
clearInterval( intervalID )
```

Parameters

intervalID   An object returned from a call to setInterval().

Returns

Nothing.

Description

Function; clears a call to setInterval().

Example

The following example first sets and then clears an interval call:

```
function callback() {
        trace("interval called");
}
var intervalID;
intervalID = setInterval( callback, 1000 );

// sometime later
clearInterval( intervalID );
```

See also

setInterval()

Color class

Availability

Flash Player 5.

Description

The Color class lets you set the RGB color value and color transform of movie clips and retrieve those values once they have been set.

You must use the constructor new Color() to create a Color object before calling its methods.

Method summary for the Color class

Method	Description
Color.getRGB()	Returns the numeric RGB value set by the last setRGB() call.
Color.getTransform()	Returns the transform information set by the last setTransform() call.
Color.setRGB()	Sets the hexadecimal representation of the RGB value for a Color object.
Color.setTransform()	Sets the color transform for a Color object.

Constructor for the Color class

Availability

Flash Player 5.

Usage

```
new Color(target)
```

Parameters

target   The instance name of a movie clip.

Returns

Nothing.

Description

Constructor; creates a Color object for the movie clip specified by the *target* parameter. You can then use the methods of that Color object to change the color of the entire target movie clip.

Example

The following example creates a Color object called my_color for the movie clip my_mc and sets its RGB value:

```
my_color = new Color(my_mc);
my_color.setRGB(0xff9933);
```

Color.getRGB()

Availability

Flash Player 5.

Usage

```
my_color.getRGB()
```

Parameters

None.

Returns

A number that represents the RGB numeric value for the color specified.

Description

Method; returns the numeric values set by the last `setRGB()` call.

Example

The following code retrieves the RGB value for the Color object `my_color`, converts it to a hexadecimal string, and assigns it to the `value` variable.

```
value = my_color.getRGB().toString(16);
```

See also

`Color.setRGB()`

Color.getTransform()

Availability

Flash Player 5.

Usage

`my_color.getTransform()`

Parameters

None.

Returns

An object whose properties contain the current offset and percentage values for the specified color.

Description

Method; returns the transform value set by the last `Color.setTransform()` call.

See also

`Color.setTransform()`

Color.setRGB()

Availability

Flash Player 5.

Usage

`my_color.setRGB(0xRRGGBB)`

Parameters

`0xRRGGBB`   The hexadecimal or RGB color to be set. `RR`, `GG`, and `BB` each consist of two hexadecimal digits specifying the offset of each color component. The `0x` tells the ActionScript compiler that the number is a hexadecimal value.

Description

Method; specifies an RGB color for a Color object. Calling this method overrides any previous `Color.setTransform()` settings.

Returns

Nothing.

Example

This example sets the RGB color value for the movie clip my_mc. To see this code work, place a movie clip on the Stage with the instance name my_mc. Then place the following code on Frame 1 in the main Timeline and choose Control > Test Movie.

```
my_color = new Color(my_mc);
my_color.setRGB(0x993366);
```

See also

Color.setTransform()

Color.setTransform()

Availability

Flash Player 5.

Usage

my_color.setTransform(*colorTransformObject*)

Parameters

colorTransformObject   An object created with the new Object constructor. This instance of the Object class must have the following properties that specify color transform values: ra, rb, ga, gb, ba, bb, aa, ab. These properties are explained below.

Returns

Nothing.

Description

Method; sets color transform information for a Color object. The *colorTransformObject* parameter is a generic object that you create from the new Object constructor. It has parameters specifying the percentage and offset values for the red, green, blue, and alpha (transparency) components of a color, entered in the format *0xRRGGBBAA*.

The parameters for a color transform object correspond to the settings in the Advanced Effect dialog box and are defined as follows:

- *ra* is the percentage for the red component (-100 to 100).
- *rb* is the offset for the red component (-255 to 255).
- *ga* is the percentage for the green component (-100 to 100).
- *gb* is the offset for the green component (-255 to 255).
- *ba* is the percentage for the blue component (-100 to 100).
- *bb* is the offset for the blue component (-255 to 255).
- *aa* is the percentage for alpha (-100 to 100).
- *ab* is the offset for alpha (-255 to 255).

You create a *colorTransformObject* parameter as follows:

```
myColorTransform = new Object();
myColorTransform.ra = 50;
myColorTransform.rb = 244;
myColorTransform.ga = 40;
myColorTransform.gb = 112;
myColorTransform.ba = 12;
myColorTransform.bb = 90;
myColorTransform.aa = 40;
myColorTransform.ab = 70;
```

You can also use the following syntax to create a *colorTransformObject* parameter:

```
myColorTransform = { ra: '50', rb: '244', ga: '40', gb: '112', ba: '12', bb:
    '90', aa: '40', ab: '70'}
```

Example

This example creates a new Color object for a target SWF file, creates a generic object called myColorTransform with the properties defined above, and uses the setTransform() method to pass the *colorTransformObject* to a Color object. To use this code in a Flash (FLA) document, place it on Frame 1 on the main Timeline and place a movie clip on the Stage with the instance name my_mc, as in the following code:

```
// Create a color object called my_color for the target my_mc
my_color = new Color(my_mc);
// Create a color transform object called myColorTransform using
// the generic Object object
myColorTransform = new Object();
// Set the values for myColorTransform
myColorTransform = { ra: '50', rb: '244', ga: '40', gb: '112', ba: '12', bb:
    '90', aa: '40', ab: '70'};
// Associate the color transform object with the Color object
// created for my_mc
my_color.setTransform(myColorTransform);
```

ContextMenu class

Availability

Flash Player 7.

Description

The ContextMenu class provides runtime control over the items in the Flash Player context menu, which appears when a user right-clicks (Windows) or Control-clicks (Macintosh) on Flash Player. You can use the methods and properties of the ContextMenu class to add custom menu items, control the display of the built-in context menu items (for example, Zoom In and Print), or create copies of menus.

You can attach a ContextMenu object to a specific button, movie clip, or text field object, or to an entire movie level. You use the menu property of the Button, MovieClip, or TextField classes to do this. For more information about the menu property, see Button.menu, MovieClip.menu, and TextField.menu.

To add new items to a ContextMenu object, you create a ContextMenuItem object, and then add that object to the ContextMenu.customItems array. For more information about creating context menu items, see the ContextMenuItem class entry.

Flash Player has three types of context menus: the standard menu (which appears when you right-click in Flash Player), the edit menu (which appears when you right-click over a selectable or editable text field), and an error menu (which appears when a SWF file has failed to load into Flash Player.) Only the standard and edit menus can be modified with the ContextMenu class.

Custom menu items always appear at the top of the Flash Player context menu, above any visible built-in menu items; a separator bar distinguishes built-in and custom menu items. A context menu can contain no more than 15 custom menu items.

You must use the constructor `new ContextMenu()` to create a ContextMenu object before calling its methods.

Method summary for the ContextMenu class

Method	Description
`ContextMenu.copy()`	Returns a copy of the specified ContextMenu object.
`ContextMenu.hideBuiltInItems()`	Hides most built-in items in the Flash Player context menu.

Property summary for the ContextMenu class

Property	Description
`ContextMenu.builtInItems`	An object whose members correspond to built-in context menu items.
`ContextMenu.customItems`	An array, undefined by default, that contains ContextMenuItem objects.

Event handler summary for the ContextMenu class

Property	Description
`ContextMenu.onSelect`	Invoked before the menu is displayed.

Constructor for the ContextMenu class

Availability

Flash Player 7.

Usage

`new ContextMenu ([callBackFunction])`

Parameters

callBackFunction   A reference to a function that is called when the user right-clicks or Control-clicks, before the menu is displayed. This parameter is optional.

Returns

Nothing.

Description

Constructor; creates a new ContextMenu object. You can optionally specify an identifier for an event handler when you create the object. The specified function is called when the user invokes the context menu, but *before* the menu is actually displayed. This is useful for customizing menu contents based on application state or based on the type of object (movie clip, text field, or button) that the user right-clicks or Control-clicks. (For an example of creating an event handler, see `ContextMenu.onSelect`.)

Example

The following example hides all the built-in objects in the Context menu. (However, the Settings and About items still appear, because they cannot be disabled.)

```
var newMenu = new ContextMenu();
newMenu.hideBuiltInItems();
_root.menu = newMenu;
```

In this example, the specified event handler, `menuHandler`, enables or disables a custom menu item (using the `ContextMenu.customItems` array) based on the value of a Boolean variable named `showItem`. If `false`, the custom menu item is disabled; otherwise, it's enabled.

```
var showItem = false; // Change this to true to see its effect
my_cm = new ContextMenu(menuHandler);
my_cm.customItems.push(new ContextMenuItem("Hello", itemHandler));
function menuHandler(obj, menuObj) {
   if (showItem == false) {
      menuObj.customItems[0].enabled = false;
   } else {
      menuObj.customItems[0].enabled = true;
   }
}
function itemHandler(obj, item) {
}
_root.menu = my_cm;
```

See also

`Button.menu`, `ContextMenu.onSelect`, `ContextMenu.customItems`, `ContextMenu.hideBuiltInItems()`, **MovieClip.menu**, `TextField.menu`

ContextMenu.builtInItems

Availability

Flash Player 7.

Usage

my_cm.builtInItems

Description

Property; an object that has the following Boolean properties: `save`, `zoom`, `quality`, `play`, `loop`, `rewind`, `forward_back`, and `print`. Setting these variables to `false` removes the corresponding menu items from the specified ContextMenu object. These properties are enumerable and are set to `true` by default.

Example

In this example, the built-in Quality and Print menu items are disabled for the ContextMenu object my_cm, which is attached to the root Timeline of the SWF file.

```
var my_cm = new ContextMenu ();
my_cm.builtInItems.quality=false;
my_cm.builtInItems.print=false;
_root.menu = my_cm;
```

In the next example, a `for..in` loop enumerates through all names and values of the built-in menu items of the ContextMenu object, my_cm.

```
my_cm = new ContextMenu();
for(eachProp in my_cm.builtInItems) {
   var propName = eachProp;
   var propValue = my_cm.builtInItems[propName];
   trace(propName + ": " + propValue;
}
```

ContextMenu.copy()

Availability

Flash Player 7.

Usage

```
my_cm.copy()
```

Parameters

None.

Returns

A ContextMenu object.

Description

Method; creates a copy of the specified ContextMenu object. The copy inherits all the properties of the original menu object.

Example

This example creates a copy of the ContextMenu object named my_cm whose built-in menu items are hidden, and adds a menu item with the text "Save...". It then creates a copy of my_cm and assigns it to the variable clone_cm, which inherits all the properties of the original menu.

```
my_cm = new ContextMenu();
my_cm.hideBuiltInItems();
my_cm.customItems.push(new ContextMenuItem("Save...", saveHandler);
function saveHandler (obj, menuItem) {
   saveDocument(); // custom function (not shown)
}
clone_cm = my_cm.copy();
```

ContextMenu.customItems

Availability

Flash Player 7.

Usage

my_cm.customItems

Description

Property; an array of ContextMenuItem objects. Each object in the array represents a context menu item that you have defined. Use this property to add, remove, or modify these custom menu items.

To add new menu items, you first create a new ContextMenuItem object, and then add it to the *menu_mc*.customItems array (using Array.push(), for example). For more information about creating new menu items, see the ContextMenuItem class entry.

Example

The following example creates a new custom menu item called menuItem_cm with a caption of "Send e-mail" and a callback handler named emailHandler (not shown). The new menu item is then added to the ContextMenu object, my_cm, using the customItems array. Lastly, the new menu is attached to a movie clip named email_mc.

```
var my_cm = new ContextMenu();
var menuItem_cm = new ContextMenuItem("Send e-mail", emailHandler);
my_cm.customItems.push(menuItem_cm);
email_mc.menu = my_cm;
```

See also

Button.menu, ContextMenu class, MovieClip.menu, TextField.menu

ContextMenu.hideBuiltInItems()

Availability

Flash Player 7.

Usage

my_cm.hideBuiltInItems()

Parameters

None.

Returns

Nothing.

Description

Method; hides all built-in menu items (except Settings) in the specified ContextMenu object. If the Flash Debug Player is running, the Debugging menu item shows, although it is dimmed for SWF files that don't have remote debugging enabled.

This method hides only menu items that appear in the standard context menu; it does not affect items that appear in the edit or error menus. For more information about the different menu types, see the ContextMenu class entry.

This method works by setting all the Boolean members of `my_cm.builtInItems` to `false`. You can selectively make a built-in item visible by setting its corresponding member in `my_cm.builtInItems` to `true` (as demonstrated in the following example).

Example

The following example creates a new ContextMenu object named `my_cm` whose built-in menu items are hidden, except for Print. The menu object is attached to the root Timeline.

```
my_cm = new ContextMenu();
my_cm.hideBuiltInItems();
my_cm.builtInItems.print = true;
_root.menu = my_cm;
```

ContextMenu.onSelect

Availability

Flash Player 7.

Usage

```
my_cm.onSelect = function (item:Object, item_menu:ContextMenu) {
    // your code here
}
```

Parameters

item   A reference to the object (movie clip, button, or selectable text field) that was under the mouse pointer when the Flash Player context menu was invoked and whose menu property is set to a valid ContextMenu object.

item_menu   A reference to the ContextMenu object assigned to the menu property of *object*.

Returns

Nothing.

Description

Event handler; called when a user invokes the Flash Player context menu, but before the menu is actually displayed. This lets you customize the contents of the context menu based on the current application state.

You can also specify the callback handler for a ContextMenu object when you construct a new ContextMenu object. For more information, see the ContextMenu class entry.

Example

The following example determines over what type of object the context menu was invoked.

```
my_cm = new ContextMenu();
menuHandler = function (obj:Object, menu:ContextMenu) {
  if(obj instanceof MovieClip) {
    trace("Movie clip: " + obj);
  }
  if(obj instanceof TextField) {
    trace("Text field: " + obj);
  }
  if(obj instanceof Button) {
    trace("Button: " + obj);
  }
}
my_cm.onSelect = menuHandler;
```

ContextMenuItem class

Availability

Flash Player 7.

Description

You use the ContextMenuItem class to create custom menu items to display in the Flash Player context menu. Each ContextMenuItem object has a caption (text) that's displayed in the context menu and a callback handler (a function) that's invoked when the menu item is selected. To add a new context menu item to a context menu, you add it to the customItems array of a ContextMenu object.

You can enable or disable specific menu items, make items visible or invisible, or change the caption or callback handler associated with a menu item.

Custom menu items appear at the top of the context menu, above any built-in items. A separator bar always divides custom menu items from built-in items. You can add no more than 15 custom items to the Flash Player context menu. Each item must contain at least one visible character—control characters, newlines, and other white space characters are ignored. No item can be more than 100 characters long. Items that are identical to any built-in menu item, or to another custom item, are ignored, whether the matching item is visible or not. Menu items are compared without regard to case, punctuation, or white space.

None of the following words can appear in a custom item: *Macromedia, Flash Player,* or *Settings.*

Method summary for the ContextMenuItem class

Method	Description
ContextMenuItem.copy()	Returns a copy of the specified ContextMenuItem object.

Property summary for the ContextMenuItem class

Property	Description
ContextMenuItem.caption	Specifies the text displayed in the menu item.
ContextMenuItem.enabled	Specifies whether the menu item is enabled or disabled.
ContextMenuItem.separatorBefore	Specifies whether a separator bar should appear above the menu item.
ContextMenuItem.visible	Specifies whether the menu item is visible or not.

Event handler summary for the ContextMenuItem class

Event handler	Description
ContextMenuItem.onSelect	Invoked when the menu item is selected.

Constructor for the ContextMenuItem class

Availability

Flash Player 7.

Usage

```
new ContextMenuItem(caption, callbackFunction, [ separatorBefore, [ enabled,
    [ visible ] ] ] )
```

Parameters

caption   A string that specifies the text associated with the menu item.

callbackFunction   A function that you define, which is called when the menu item is selected.

separatorBefore   A Boolean value that indicates whether a separator bar should appear above the menu item in the context menu. This parameter is optional; its default value is false.

enabled   A Boolean value that indicates whether the menu item is enabled or disabled in the context menu. This parameter is optional; its default value is true.

visible   A Boolean value that indicates whether the menu item is visible or invisible. This parameter is optional; its default value is true.

Returns

Nothing.

Description

Constructor; creates a new ContextMenuItem object that can be added to the ContextMenu.customItems array.

Example

This example adds Start and Stop menu items, separated by a bar, to the ContextMenu object my_cm. The startHandler() function is called when Start is selected from the context menu; stopHandler() is called when Stop is selected. The ContextMenu object is applied to the root Timeline.

```
my_cm = new ContextMenu();
my_cm.customItems.push(new ContextMenuItem("Start", startHandler));
my_cm.customItems.push(new ContextMenuItem("Stop", stopHandler, true));
function stopHandler(obj, item) {
  trace("Stopping...");
}
function startHandler(obj, item) {
  trace("Starting...");
}
_root.menu = my_cm;
```

ContextMenuItem.caption

Availability

Flash Player 7.

Usage

menuItem_cmi.caption

Description

Property; a string that specifies the menu item caption (text) displayed in the context menu.

Example

This example displays the caption for the selected menu item (Pause Game) in the Output panel.

```
my_cm = new ContextMenu();
menuItem_cmi = new ContextMenuItem("Pause Game", onPause);
my_cm.customItems.
function onPause(obj, menuItem) {
  trace("You chose: " + menuItem.caption);
}
```

ContextMenuItem.copy()

Availability

Flash Player 7.

Usage

menuItem_cmi.copy();

Returns

A ContextMenuItem object.

Description

Method; creates and returns a copy of the specified ContextMenuItem object. The copy includes all properties of the original object.

Example

This example creates a new ContextMenuItem object named `original_cmi` with the caption text Pause and a callback handler set to the function `onPause`. The example then creates a copy of the ContextMenuItem object and assigns it to the variable `copy_cmi`.

```
original_cmi = new ContextMenuItem("Pause", onPause);
function onPause(obj, menu) {
    _root.stop();
}
original_cmi.visible = false;
copy_cmi = orig_cmi.copy();
```

ContextMenuItem.enabled

Availability

Flash Player 7.

Usage

menuItem_cmi.enabled

Description

Property; a Boolean value that indicates whether the specified menu item is enabled or disabled. By default, this property is `true`.

Example

The following example creates a new context menu item and then disables that menu item.

```
var saveMenuItem = new ContextMenuItem("Save...", doSave);
saveMenuItem.enabled = false;
```

ContextMenuItem.onSelect

Availability

Flash Player 7.

Usage

```
menuItem_cmi.onSelect = function (obj, menuItem) {
    // your statements here
}
```

Parameters

obj   A reference to the movie clip (or Timeline), button, or selectable (editable) text field that the user right-clicked or Control-clicked.

menuItem   A reference to the selected ContextMenuItem object.

Returns

Nothing.

Description

Event handler; invoked when the specified menu item is selected from the Flash Player context menu. The specified callback handler receives two parameters: *obj*, a reference to the object under the mouse when the user invoked the Flash Player context menu, and *menuItem*, a reference to the ContextMenuItem object that represents the selected menu item.

Example

The following example assigns a function to the `onSelect` handler for a ContextMenuItem object named `start_cmi`. The function displays the caption of the selected menu item.

```
start_cmi.onSelect = function (obj, item) {
    trace("You choose: " + item.caption);
}
```

See also

`ContextMenu.onSelect`

ContextMenuItem.separatorBefore

Availability

Flash Player 7.

Usage

menuItem_cmi.separatorBefore

Description

Property; a Boolean value that indicates whether a separator bar should appear above the specified menu item. By default, this property is `false`.

Note: A separator bar always appears between any custom menu items and the built-in menu items.

Example

This example creates three menu items labeled Open, Save, and Print. A separator bar divides the Save and Print items. The menu items are then added to the ContextMenu object's `customItems` array. Lastly, the menu is attached to the root Timeline of the SWF file.

```
my_cm = new ContextMenu();
open_cmi = new ContextMenuItem("Open", itemHandler);
save_cmi = new ContextMenuItem("Save", itemHandler);
print_cmi = new ContextMenuItem("Print", itemHandler);
print_cmi.separatorBefore = true;
my_cm.customItems.push(open_cmi, save_cmi, print_cmi);
function itemHandler(obj, menuItem) {
    trace("You chose: " + menuItem.caption);
};
_root.menu = my_cm;
```

See also

`ContextMenu.onSelect`

ContextMenuItem.visible

Availability

Flash Player 7.

Usage

`menuItem_cmi.visible`

Description

Property; a Boolean value that indicates whether the specified menu item is visible when the Flash Player context menu is displayed. By default, this property is `true`.

continue

Availability

Flash Player 4.

Usage

`continue`

Parameters

None.

Returns

Nothing.

Description

Statement; appears within several types of loop statements; it behaves differently in each type of loop.

In a `while` loop, `continue` causes the Flash interpreter to skip the rest of the loop body and jump to the top of the loop, where the condition is tested.

In a `do while` loop, `continue` causes the Flash interpreter to skip the rest of the loop body and jump to the bottom of the loop, where the condition is tested.

In a `for` loop, `continue` causes the Flash interpreter to skip the rest of the loop body and jump to the evaluation of the `for` loop's post-expression.

In a `for..in` loop, `continue` causes the Flash interpreter to skip the rest of the loop body and jump back to the top of the loop, where the next value in the enumeration is processed.

See also

`do while`, `for`, `for..in`, `while`

CustomActions class

Availability

Flash Player 6.

Description

The methods of the CustomActions class allow a SWF file playing in the Flash authoring tool to manage any custom actions that are registered with the authoring tool. A SWF file can install and uninstall custom actions, retrieve the XML definition of a custom action, and retrieve the list of registered custom actions.

You can use these methods to build SWF files that are extensions of the Flash authoring tool. Such an extension could, for example, use the Flash Application Protocol to navigate a UDDI repository and download web services into the Actions toolbox.

Method summary for the CustomActions class

Method	Description
CustomActions.get()	Reads the contents of a custom action XML definition file.
CustomActions.install()	Installs a new custom action XML definition file.
CustomActions.list()	Returns a list of all registered custom actions.
CustomActions.uninstall()	Removes a custom action XML definition file.

CustomActions.get()

Availability

Flash Player 6.

Usage

CustomActions.get(*customActionsName*)

Parameters

customActionsName   The name of the custom action definition to retrieve.

Returns

If the custom action XML definition is located, returns a string; otherwise, returns undefined.

Description

Method; reads the contents of the custom action XML definition file named *customActionsName*.

The name of the definition file must be a simple filename, without the .xml file extension, and without any directory separators (':', '/' or '\').

If the definition file specified by the *customActionsName* cannot be found, a value of undefined is returned. If the custom action XML definition specified by the *customActionsName* parameter is located, it is read in its entirety and returned as a string.

CustomActions.install()

Availability

Flash Player 6.

Usage

```
CustomActions.install(customActionsName, customXMLDefinition)
```

Parameters

customActionsName   The name of the custom action definition to install.

customXMLDefinition   The text of the XML definition to install.

Returns

A Boolean value of false if an error occurs during installation; otherwise, a value of true is returned to indicate that the custom action has been successfully installed.

Description

Method; installs a new custom action XML definition file indicated by the *customActionsName* parameter. The contents of the file is specified by the string *customXMLDefinition*.

The name of the definition file must be a simple filename, without the .xml file extension, and without any directory separators (':', '/' or '\').

If a custom actions file already exists with the name *customActionsName*, it is overwritten.

If the Configuration/ActionsPanel/CustomActions directory does not exist when this method is invoked, the directory is created.

CustomActions.list()

Availability

Flash Player 6.

Usage

```
CustomActions.list()
```

Parameters

None.

Returns

An array.

Description

Method; returns an Array object containing the names of all the custom actions that are registered with the Flash authoring tool. The elements of the array are simple names, without the .xml file extension, and without any directory separators (for example, ":", "/", or "\"). If there are no registered custom actions, list() returns a zero-length array. If an error occurs, list() returns the value undefined.

CustomActions.uninstall()

Availability

Flash Player 6.

Usage

```
CustomActions.uninstall(customActionsName)
```

Parameters

customActionsName   The name of the custom action definition to uninstall.

Returns

A Boolean value of `false` if no custom actions are found with the name *customActionsName*. If the custom actions were successfully removed, a value of `true` is returned.

Description

Method; removes the Custom Actions XML definition file named *customActionsName*.

The name of the definition file must be a simple filename, without the .xml file extension, and without any directory separators (':', '/' or '\').

Date class

Availability

Flash Player 5.

Description

The Date class lets you retrieve date and time values relative to universal time (Greenwich Mean Time, now called universal time or UTC) or relative to the operating system on which Flash Player is running. The methods of the Date class are not static, but apply only to the individual Date object specified when the method is called. The `Date.UTC()` method is an exception; it is a static method.

The Date class handles daylight saving time differently depending on the operating system and Flash Player version. Flash Player 6 and later versions handle daylight saving time on the following operating systems in these ways:

- Windows—the Date object automatically adjusts its output for daylight saving time. The Date object detects whether daylight saving time is employed in the current locale, and if so, it detects what the standard-to-daylight-saving-time transition date and times are. However, the transition dates currently in effect are applied to dates in the past and the future, so the daylight saving time bias may be calculated incorrectly for dates in the past when the locale had different transition dates.

- Mac OS X—the Date object automatically adjusts its output for daylight saving time. The time zone information database in Mac OS X is used to determine whether any date or time in the present or past should have a daylight-saving-time bias applied.

Flash Player 5 handles daylight saving time on the following operating systems as follows:

- Windows—the U.S. rules for daylight saving time are always applied, which leads to incorrect transitions in Europe and other areas that employ daylight saving time but have different transition times than the U.S. Flash correctly detects whether DST is employed in the current locale.

To call the methods of the Date class, you must first create a Date object using the constructor for the Date class, described later in this section.

Method summary for the Date class

Method	Description
Date.getDate()	Returns the day of the month according to local time.
Date.getDay()	Returns the day of the week according to local time.
Date.getFullYear()	Returns the four-digit year according to local time.
Date.getHours()	Returns the hour according to local time.
Date.getMilliseconds()	Returns the milliseconds according to local time.
Date.getMinutes()	Returns the minutes according to local time.
Date.getMonth()	Returns the month according to local time.
Date.getSeconds()	Returns the seconds according to local time.
Date.getTime()	Returns the number of milliseconds since midnight January 1, 1970, universal time.
Date.getTimezoneOffset()	Returns the difference, in minutes, between the computer's local time and the universal time.
Date.getUTCDate()	Returns the day (date) of the month according to universal time.
Date.getUTCDay()	Returns the day of the week according to universal time.
Date.getUTCFullYear()	Returns the four-digit year according to universal time.
Date.getUTCHours()	Returns the hour according to universal time.
Date.getUTCMilliseconds()	Returns the milliseconds according to universal time.
Date.getUTCMinutes()	Returns the minutes according to universal time.
Date.getUTCMonth()	Returns the month according to universal time.
Date.getUTCSeconds()	Returns the seconds according to universal time.
Date.getYear()	Returns the year according to local time.
Date.setDate()	Sets the day of the month according to local time. Returns the new time in milliseconds.
Date.setFullYear()	Sets the full year according to local time. Returns the new time in milliseconds.
Date.setHours()	Sets the hour according to local time. Returns the new time in milliseconds.

Method	Description
`Date.setMilliseconds()`	Sets the milliseconds according to local time. Returns the new time in milliseconds.
`Date.setMinutes()`	Sets the minutes according to local time. Returns the new time in milliseconds.
`Date.setMonth()`	Sets the month according to local time. Returns the new time in milliseconds.
`Date.setSeconds()`	Sets the seconds according to local time. Returns the new time in milliseconds.
`Date.setTime()`	Sets the date in milliseconds. Returns the new time in milliseconds.
`Date.setUTCDate()`	Sets the date according to universal time. Returns the new time in milliseconds.
`Date.setUTCFullYear()`	Sets the year according to universal time. Returns the new time in milliseconds.
`Date.setUTCHours()`	Sets the hour according to universal time. Returns the new time in milliseconds.
`Date.setUTCMilliseconds()`	Sets the milliseconds according to universal time. Returns the new time in milliseconds.
`Date.setUTCMinutes()`	Sets the minutes according to universal time. Returns the new time in milliseconds.
`Date.setUTCMonth()`	Sets the month according to universal time. Returns the new time in milliseconds.
`Date.setUTCSeconds()`	Sets the seconds according to universal time. Returns the new time in milliseconds.
`Date.setYear()`	Sets the year according to local time.
`Date.toString()`	Returns a string value representing the date and time stored in the specified Date object.
`Date.UTC()`	Returns the number of milliseconds between midnight on January 1, 1970, universal time, and the specified time.

Constructor for the Date class

Availability

Flash Player 5.

Usage

```
new Date()
new Date(year, month [, date [, hour [, minute [, second [, millisecond ]]]]])
```

Parameters

year A value of 0 to 99 indicates 1900 though 1999; otherwise all four digits of the year must be specified.

month   An integer from 0 (January) to 11 (December).

date   An integer from 1 to 31. This parameter is optional.

hour   An integer from 0 (midnight) to 23 (11 p.m.).

minute   An integer from 0 to 59. This parameter is optional.

second   An integer from 0 to 59. This parameter is optional.

millisecond   An integer from 0 to 999. This parameter is optional.

Returns

Nothing.

Description

Object; constructs a new Date object that holds the current date and time, or the date specified.

Example

The following example retrieves the current date and time.

```
now_date = new Date();
```

The following example creates a new Date object for Gary's birthday, August 12, 1974. (Because the month parameter is zero-based, the example uses 7 for the month, not 8.)

```
garyBirthday_date = new Date (74, 7, 12);
```

The following example creates a new Date object, concatenates the returned values of Date.getMonth(), Date.getDate(), and Date.getFullYear(), and displays them in the text field specified by the variable date_str.

```
today_date = new Date();
date_str = ((today_date.getMonth() + 1) + "/" + today_date.getDate() + "/" +
    today_date.getFullYear());
```

Date.getDate()

Availability

Flash Player 5.

Usage

```
my_date.getDate()
```

Parameters

None.

Returns

An integer.

Description

Method; returns the day of the month (an integer from 1 to 31) of the specified Date object according to local time. Local time is determined by the operating system on which Flash Player is running.

Date.getDay()

Availability

Flash Player 5.

Usage

my_date.getDay()

Parameters

None.

Returns

An integer.

Description

Method; returns the day of the week (0 for Sunday, 1 for Monday, and so on) of the specified Date object according to local time. Local time is determined by the operating system on which Flash Player is running.

Date.getFullYear()

Availability

Flash Player 5.

Usage

my_date.getFullYear()

Parameters

None.

Returns

An integer.

Description

Method; returns the full year (a four-digit number, for example, 2000) of the specified Date object, according to local time. Local time is determined by the operating system on which Flash Player is running.

Example

The following example uses the constructor to create a new Date object and send the value returned by the getFullYear() method to the Output panel:

```
my_date = new Date();
trace(my_date.getFullYear());
```

Date.getHours()

Availability

Flash Player 5.

Usage

my_date.getHours()

Parameters

None.

Returns

An integer.

Description

Method; returns the hour (an integer from 0 to 23) of the specified Date object, according to local time. Local time is determined by the operating system on which Flash Player is running.

Date.getMilliseconds()

Availability

Flash Player 5.

Usage

my_date.getMilliseconds()

Parameters

None.

Returns

An integer.

Description

Method; returns the milliseconds (an integer from 0 to 999) of the specified Date object, according to local time. Local time is determined by the operating system on which Flash Player is running.

Date.getMinutes()

Availability

Flash Player 5.

Usage

my_date.getMinutes()

Parameters

None.

Returns

An integer.

Description

Method; returns the minutes (an integer from 0 to 59) of the specified Date object, according to local time. Local time is determined by the operating system on which Flash Player is running.

Date.getMonth()

Availability

Flash Player 5.

Usage

my_date.getMonth()

Parameters

None.

Returns

An integer.

Description

Method; returns the month (0 for January, 1 for February, and so on) of the specified Date object, according to local time. Local time is determined by the operating system on which Flash Player is running.

Date.getSeconds()

Availability

Flash Player 5.

Usage

my_date.getSeconds()

Parameters

None.

Returns

An integer.

Description

Method; returns the seconds (an integer from 0 to 59) of the specified Date object, according to local time. Local time is determined by the operating system on which Flash Player is running.

Date.getTime()

Availability

Flash Player 5.

Usage

```
my_date.getTime()
```

Parameters

None.

Returns

An integer.

Description

Method; returns the number of milliseconds since midnight January 1, 1970, universal time, for the specified Date object. Use this method to represent a specific instant in time when comparing two or more Date objects.

Date.getTimezoneOffset()

Availability

Flash Player 5.

Usage

```
my_date.getTimezoneOffset()
```

Parameters

None.

Returns

An integer.

Description

Method; returns the difference, in minutes, between the computer's local time and universal time.

Example

The following example returns the difference between the local daylight saving time for San Francisco and universal time. Daylight saving time is factored into the returned result only if the date defined in the Date object occurs during daylight saving time.

```
trace(new Date().getTimezoneOffset());

// 420 is displayed in the Output panel
// (7 hours * 60 minutes/hour = 420 minutes)
// This example is Pacific Daylight Time (PDT, GMT-0700).
// Result will vary depending on locale and time of year.
```

Date.getUTCDate()

Availability

Flash Player 5.

Usage

my_date.getUTCDate()

Parameters

None.

Returns

An integer.

Description

Method; returns the day of the month (an integer from 1 to 31) in the specified Date object, according to universal time.

Date.getUTCDay()

Availability

Flash Player 5.

Usage

my_date.getUTCDay()

Parameters

None.

Returns

An integer.

Description

Method; returns the day of the week (0 for Sunday, 1 for Monday, and so on) of the specified Date object, according to universal time.

Date.getUTCFullYear()

Availability

Flash Player 5.

Usage

my_date.getUTCFullYear()

Parameters

None.

Returns

An integer.

Description

Method; returns the four-digit year of the specified Date object, according to universal time.

Date.getUTCHours()

Availability

Flash Player 5.

Usage

my_date.getUTCHours()

Parameters

None.

Returns

An integer.

Description

Method; returns the hours of the specified Date object, according to universal time.

Date.getUTCMilliseconds()

Availability

Flash Player 5.

Usage

my_date.getUTCMilliseconds()

Parameters

None.

Returns

An integer.

Description

Method; returns the milliseconds of the specified Date object, according to universal time.

Date.getUTCMinutes()

Availability

Flash Player 5.

Usage

my_date.getUTCMinutes()

Parameters

None.

Returns

An integer.

Description

Method; returns the minutes of the specified Date object, according to universal time.

Date.getUTCMonth()

Availability

Flash Player 5.

Usage

my_date.getUTCMonth()

Parameters

None.

Returns

An integer.

Description

Method; returns the month (0 for January, 1 for February, and so on) of the specified Date object, according to universal time.

Date.getUTCSeconds()

Availability

Flash Player 5.

Usage

my_date.getUTCSeconds()

Parameters

None.

Returns

An integer.

Description

Method; returns the seconds in the specified Date object, according to universal time.

Date.getYear()

Availability

Flash Player 5.

Usage

my_date.getYear()

Parameters

None.

Returns

An integer.

Description

Method; returns the year of the specified Date object, according to local time. Local time is determined by the operating system on which Flash Player is running. The year is the full year minus 1900. For example, the year 2000 is represented as 100.

See also

`Date.getFullYear()`

Date.setDate()

Availability

Flash Player 5.

Usage

`my_date.setDate(date)`

Parameters

date   An integer from 1 to 31.

Returns

An integer.

Description

Method; sets the day of the month for the specified Date object, according to local time, and returns the new time in milliseconds. Local time is determined by the operating system on which Flash Player is running.

Date.setFullYear()

Availability

Flash Player 5.

Usage

`my_date.setFullYear(year [, month [, date]] )`

Parameters

year   A four-digit number specifying a year. Two-digit numbers do not represent years; for example, 99 is not the year 1999, but the year 99.

month   An integer from 0 (January) to 11 (December). This parameter is optional.

date   A number from 1 to 31. This parameter is optional.

Returns

An integer.

Description

Method; sets the year of the specified Date object, according to local time, and returns the new time in milliseconds. If the *month* and *date* parameters are specified, they are also set to local time. Local time is determined by the operating system on which Flash Player is running.

Calling this method does not modify the other fields of the specified Date object but `Date.getUTCDay()` and `Date.getDay()` may report a new value if the day of the week changes as a result of calling this method.

Date.setHours()

Availability

Flash Player 5.

Usage

`my_date.setHours(hour)`

Parameters

hour   An integer from 0 (midnight) to 23 (11 p.m.).

Returns

An integer.

Description

Method; sets the hours for the specified Date object according to local time, and returns the new time in milliseconds. Local time is determined by the operating system on which Flash Player is running.

Date.setMilliseconds()

Availability

Flash Player 5.

Usage

`my_date.setMilliseconds(millisecond)`

Parameters

millisecond   An integer from 0 to 999.

Returns

An integer.

Description

Method; sets the milliseconds for the specified Date object according to local time, and returns the new time in milliseconds. Local time is determined by the operating system on which Flash Player is running.

Date.setMinutes()

Availability

Flash Player 5.

Usage

`my_date.setMinutes(minute)`

Parameters

`minute`   An integer from 0 to 59.

Returns

An integer.

Description

Method; sets the minutes for a specified Date object according to local time, and returns the new time in milliseconds. Local time is determined by the operating system on which Flash Player is running.

Date.setMonth()

Availability

Flash Player 5.

Usage

`my_date.setMonth(month [, date ])`

Parameters

`month`   An integer from 0 (January) to 11 (December).

`date`   An integer from 1 to 31. This parameter is optional.

Returns

An integer.

Description

Method; sets the month for the specified Date object in local time, and returns the new time in milliseconds. Local time is determined by the operating system on which Flash Player is running.

Date.setSeconds()

Availability

Flash Player 5.

Usage

my_date.setSeconds(*second*)

Parameters

second   An integer from 0 to 59.

Returns

An integer.

Description

Method; sets the seconds for the specified Date object in local time, and returns the new time in milliseconds. Local time is determined by the operating system on which Flash Player is running.

Date.setTime()

Availability

Flash Player 5.

Usage

my_date.setTime(*milliseconds*)

Parameters

milliseconds   An integer value where 0 is 0:00 GMT 1970 Jan 1.

Returns

An integer.

Description

Method; sets the date for the specified Date object in milliseconds since midnight on January 1, 1970, and returns the new time in milliseconds.

Date.setUTCDate()

Availability

Flash Player 5.

Usage

my_date.setUTCDate(*date*)

Parameters

date   An integer from 1 to 31.

Returns

An integer.

Description

Method; sets the date for the specified Date object in universal time, and returns the new time in milliseconds. Calling this method does not modify the other fields of the specified Date object, but Date.getUTCDay() and Date.getDay() may report a new value if the day of the week changes as a result of calling this method.

Date.setUTCFullYear()

Availability

Flash Player 5.

Usage

my_date.setUTCFullYear(*year* [, *month* [, *date*]])

Parameters

year   The year specified as a full four-digit year, for example, 2000.

month   An integer from 0 (January) to 11 (December). This parameter is optional.

date   An integer from 1 to 31. This parameter is optional.

Returns

An integer.

Description

Method; sets the year for the specified Date object (*my_date*) in universal time, and returns the new time in milliseconds.

Optionally, this method can also set the month and date represented by the specified Date object. Calling this method does not modify the other fields of the specified Date object, but Date.getUTCDay() and Date.getDay() may report a new value if the day of the week changes as a result of calling this method.

Date.setUTCHours()

Availability

Flash Player 5.

Usage

my_date.setUTCHours(*hour* [, *minute* [, *second* [, *millisecond*]]])

Parameters

hour An integer from 0 (midnight) to 23 (11 p.m.).

minute An integer from 0 to 59. This parameter is optional.

second An integer from 0 to 59. This parameter is optional.

millisecond An integer from 0 to 999. This parameter is optional.

Returns

An integer.

Description

Method; sets the hour for the specified Date object in universal time, and returns the new time in milliseconds.

Date.setUTCMilliseconds()

Availability

Flash Player 5.

Usage

my_date.setUTCMilliseconds(*millisecond*)

Parameters

millisecond An integer from 0 to 999.

Returns

An integer.

Description

Method; sets the milliseconds for the specified Date object in universal time, and returns the new time in milliseconds.

Date.setUTCMinutes()

Availability

Flash Player 5.

Usage

```
my_date.setUTCMinutes(minute [, second [, millisecond]])
```

Parameters

minute   An integer from 0 to 59.

second   An integer from 0 to 59. This parameter is optional.

millisecond   An integer from 0 to 999. This parameter is optional.

Returns

An integer.

Description

Method; sets the minute for the specified Date object in universal time, and returns the new time in milliseconds.

Date.setUTCMonth()

Availability

Flash Player 5.

Usage

```
my_date.setUTCMonth(month [, date])
```

Parameters

month   An integer from 0 (January) to 11 (December).

date   An integer from 1 to 31. This parameter is optional.

Returns

An integer.

Description

Method; sets the month, and optionally the day (*date*), for the specified Date object in universal time, and returns the new time in milliseconds. Calling this method does not modify the other fields of the specified Date object, but `Date.getUTCDay()` and `Date.getDay()` may report a new value if the day of the week changes as a result of specifying a value for the *date* parameter.

Date.setUTCSeconds()

Availability

Flash Player 5.

Usage

```
my_date.setUTCSeconds(second [, millisecond]))
```

Parameters

second   An integer from 0 to 59.

millisecond   An integer from 0 to 999. This parameter is optional.

Returns

An integer.

Description

Method; sets the seconds for the specified Date object in universal time, and returns the new time in milliseconds.

Date.setYear()

Availability

Flash Player 5.

Usage

```
my_date.setYear(year)
```

Parameters

year   If *year* is an integer between 0–99, setYear sets the year at 1900 + *year*; otherwise, the year is the value of the *year* parameter.

Returns

An integer.

Description

Method; sets the year for the specified Date object in local time, and returns the new time in milliseconds. Local time is determined by the operating system on which Flash Player is running.

Date.toString()

Flash Player 5.

Usage

```
my_date.toString()
```

Parameters

None.

Returns

A string.

Description

Method; returns a string value for the specified date object in a readable format, and returns the new time in milliseconds.

Example

The following example returns the information in the dateOfBirth_date Date object as a string.

```
var dateOfBirth_date = new Date(74, 7, 12, 18, 15);
trace (dateOfBirth_date.toString());
```

Output (for Pacific Standard Time):

```
Mon Aug 12 18:15:00 GMT-0700 1974
```

Date.UTC()

Availability

Flash Player 5.

Usage

```
Date.UTC(year, month [, date [, hour [, minute [, second [, millisecond ]]]]])
```

Parameters

year A four-digit number, for example, 2000.

month An integer from 0 (January) to 11 (December).

date An integer from 1 to 31. This parameter is optional.

hour An integer from 0 (midnight) to 23 (11 p.m.).

minute An integer from 0 to 59. This parameter is optional.

second An integer from 0 to 59. This parameter is optional.

millisecond An integer from 0 to 999. This parameter is optional.

Returns

An integer.

Description

Method; returns the number of milliseconds between midnight on January 1, 1970, universal time, and the time specified in the parameters. This is a static method that is invoked through the Date object constructor, not through a specific Date object. This method lets you create a Date object that assumes universal time, whereas the Date constructor assumes local time.

Example

The following example creates a new `garyBirthday_date` Date object defined in universal time. This is the universal time variation of the example used for the `new Date` constructor method:

```
garyBirthday_date = new Date(Date.UTC(1974, 7, 12));
```

default

Availability

Flash Player 6.

Usage

```
default: statements
```

Parameters

statements   Any statements.

Returns

Nothing.

Description

Statement; defines the default case for a `switch` action. The statements execute if the *expression* parameter of the `switch` action doesn't equal (using strict equality) any of the *expression* parameters that follow the `case` keywords for a given `switch` action.

A `switch` is not required to have a `default` case. A `default` case does not have to be last in the list. Using a `default` action outside a `switch` action is an error and the script doesn't compile.

Example

In the following example, the expression A does not equal the expressions B or D so the statement following the default keyword is run and the `trace()` action is sent to the Output panel.

```
switch ( A ) {
  case B:
    C;
    break;
  case D:
    E;
    break;
  default:
    trace ("no specific case was encountered");
}
```

See also

switch, case, break

delete

Availability

Flash Player 5.

Usage

```
delete reference
```

Parameters

reference   The name of the variable or object to eliminate.

Returns

A Boolean value.

Description

Operator; destroys the object or variable specified by the *reference* parameter, and returns `true` if the object was successfully deleted; otherwise returns a value of `false`. This operator is useful for freeing up memory used by scripts. Although `delete` is an operator, it is typically used as a statement, as in the following:

```
delete x;
```

The `delete` operator may fail and return `false` if the *reference* parameter does not exist, or may not be deleted. Predefined objects and properties, and variables declared with `var`, may not be deleted. You cannot use the `delete` operator to remove movie clips.

Example

Usage 1: The following example creates an object, uses it, and then deletes it after it is no longer needed.

```
account = new Object();
account.name = 'Jon';
account.balance = 10000;

delete account;
```

Usage 2: The following example deletes a property of an object.

```
// create the new object "account"
account = new Object();
// assign property name to the account
account.name = 'Jon';
// delete the property
delete account.name;
```

Usage 3: The following is another example of deleting an object property.

```
// create an Array object with length 0
my_array = new Array();
// add an element to the array. Array.length is now 1
my_array[0] = "abc";
// add another element to the array. Array.length is now 2
my_array[1] = "def";
// add another element to the array. Array.length is now 3
my_array[2] = "ghi";
// my_array[2] is deleted, but Array.length is not changed
```

```
delete array[2];
trace(my_array.length);
```

Usage 4: The following example illustrates the behavior of delete on object references.

```
// create a new object, and assign the variable ref1
// to refer to the object
ref1 = new Object();
ref1.name = "Jody";
// copy the reference variable into a new variable
// and delete ref1
ref2 = ref1;
delete ref1;
```

If ref1 had not been copied into ref2, the object would have been deleted when ref1 was deleted, because there would be no references to it. If you delete ref2, there will no longer be any references to the object; it will be destroyed, and the memory it was using will be made available.

See also

var

do while

Availability

Flash Player 4.

Usage

```
do {
    statement(s)
} while (condition)
```

Parameters

condition   The condition to evaluate.

statement(s)   The statement(s) to execute as long as the condition parameter evaluates to true.

Returns

Nothing.

Description

Statement; executes the statements, and then evaluates the condition in a loop for as long as the condition is true.

See also

break, continue

duplicateMovieClip()

Availability

Flash Player 4.

Usage

```
duplicateMovieClip(target, newname, depth)
```

Parameters

target   The target path of the movie clip to duplicate.

newname   A unique identifier for the duplicated movie clip.

depth   A unique depth level for the duplicated movie clip. The depth level is a stacking order for duplicated movie clips. This stacking order is much like the stacking order of layers in the Timeline; movie clips with a lower depth level are hidden under clips with a higher stacking order. You must assign each duplicated movie clip a unique depth level to prevent it from replacing SWF files on occupied depths.

Returns

A reference to the duplicated movie clip.

Description

Function; creates an instance of a movie clip while the SWF file is playing. The playhead in duplicate movie clips always starts at Frame 1, regardless of where the playhead is in the original (or "parent") movie clip. Variables in the parent movie clip are not copied into the duplicate movie clip. If the parent movie clip is deleted the duplicate movie clip is also deleted. Use the removeMovieClip() action or method to delete a movie clip instance created with duplicateMovieClip().

See also

MovieClip.duplicateMovieClip(), removeMovieClip(), MovieClip.removeMovieClip()

dynamic

Availability

Flash Player 6.

Usage

```
dynamic class className [ extends superClass ]
              [ implements interfaceName [, interfaceName... ] ]
{
   // class definition here
}
```

Note: To use this keyword, you must specify ActionScript 2.0 and Flash Player 6 or later in the Flash tab of your FLA file's Publish Settings dialog box. This keyword is supported only when used in external script files, not in scripts written in the Actions panel.

Description

Keyword; specifies that objects based on the specified class can add and access dynamic properties at runtime.

Type checking on dynamic classes is less strict than type-checking on nondynamic classes, because members accessed inside the class definition and on class instances are not compared to those defined in the class scope. Class member functions, however, can still be type checked for return type and parameter types. This behavior is especially useful when you work with MovieClip objects, because there are many different ways of adding properties and objects to a movie clip dynamically, such as `MovieClip.createEmptyMovieClip()` and `MovieClip.createTextField()`.

Subclasses of dynamic classes are also dynamic.

For more information, see "Creating dynamic classes" on page 377.

Example

In the following example, class B has been marked as dynamic, so calling an undeclared function on it will not throw an error at compile time.

```
// in B.as
dynamic class B extends class_A {
  function B() {
    /*this is the constructor*/
  }
  function m():Number {return 25;}
  function o(s:String):Void {trace(s);}
}

// in C.as
class C extends class_A {
  function C() {
    /*this is the constructor*/
  }
  function m():Number {return 25;}
  function o(s:String):Void {trace(s);}
}
// in another script
var var1 = B.n();    // no error
var var2 = C.n()     // error, as there is no function n in C.as
```

See also

`class, extends`

else

Availability

Flash Player 4.

Usage

```
if (condition){
   statement(s);
} else (condition){
   statement(s);
}
```

Parameters

condition   An expression that evaluates to `true` or `false`.

statement(s)   An alternative series of statements to run if the condition specified in the `if` statement is `false`.

Returns

Nothing.

Description

Statement; specifies the statements to run if the condition in the `if` statement returns `false`.

See also

`if`

else if

Availability

Flash Player 4.

Usage

```
if (condition){
   statement(s);
} else if (condition){
   statement(s);
}
```

Parameters

condition   An expression that evaluates to `true` or `false`.

statement(s)   An alternative series of statements to run if the condition specified in the `if` statement is `false`.

Returns

Nothing.

Description

Statement; evaluates a condition and specifies the statements to run if the condition in the initial `if` statement returns `false`. If the `else if` condition returns `true`, the Flash interpreter runs the statements that follow the condition inside curly braces (`{ }`). If the `else if` condition is `false`, Flash skips the statements inside the curly braces and runs the statements following the curly braces. Use the `else if` action to create branching logic in your scripts.

Example

The following example uses `else if` actions to check whether each side of an object is within a specific boundary:

```
// if the object goes off bounds,
// send it back and reverse its travel speed
    if (this._x>rightBound) {
       this._x = rightBound;
       xInc = -xInc;
    } else if (this._x<leftBound) {
       this._x = leftBound;
       xInc = -xInc;
    } else if (this._y>bottomBound) {
       this._y = bottomBound;
       yInc = -yInc;
    } else if (this._y<topBound) {
       this._y = topBound;
       yInc = -yInc;
    }
```

See also

`if`

#endinitclip

Availability

Flash Player 6.

Usage

```
#endinitclip
```

Parameters

None.

Returns

Nothing.

Description

Compiler directive; indicates the end of a block of initialization actions.

Example

```
#initclip
...initialization actions go here...
#endinitclip
```

    #initclip

eq (equal – string specific)

Availability

Flash Player 4. This operator was deprecated in Flash 5 in favor of the == (equality) operator.

Usage

    expression1 eq expression2

Parameters

expression1, expression2   Numbers, strings, or variables.

Returns

Nothing.

Description

Comparison operator; compares two expressions for equality and returns a value of true if the string representation of *expression1* is equal to the string representation of *expression2*; otherwise, the operation returns a value of false.

See also

    == (equality)

Error class

Availability

Flash Player 7.

Description

Contains information about an error that occurred in a script. You create an Error object using the Error constructor function. Typically, you "throw" a new Error object from within a try code block that is then "caught" by a catch or finally code block.

You can also create a subclass of the Error class and throw instances of that subclass.

Method summary for the Error class

Method	Description
Error.toString()	Returns the string representation of an Error object.

Property summary for the Error class

Property	Description
Error.message	A string that contains an error message associated with an error.
Error.name	A string that contains the name of the Error object.

Constructor for the Error class

Availability

Flash Player 7.

Usage

```
new Error([message])
```

Parameters

message   A string associated with the Error object; this parameter is optional.

Returns

Nothing.

Description

Constructor; creates a new Error object. If *message* is specified, its value is assigned to the object's
Error.message property.

Example

In the following example, a function throws an error (with a specified message) if the two strings
that are passed to it are not identical.

```
function compareStrings(string_1, string_2) {
    if(string_1 != string_2) {
        throw new Error("Strings do not match.");
    }
}
try {
    compareStrings("Dog","dog");
} catch (e) {
    trace(e.toString());
}
```

See also

throw, try..catch..finally

Error.message

Availability

Flash Player 7.

Usage

```
myError.message
```

Description

Property; contains the message associated with the Error object. By default, the value of this
property is "Error". You can specify a message property when you create a new Error object by
passing the error string to the Error constructor function.

See also

throw, try..catch..finally

Error.name

Availability

Flash Player 7.

Usage

myError.name

Description

Property; contains the name of the Error object. By default, the value of this property is "Error".

See also

throw, try..catch..finally

Error.toString()

Availability

Flash Player 7.

Usage

my_err.toString()

Returns

A string.

Description

Method; returns the string "Error" by default, or the value contained in Error.message, if defined.

See also

Error.message, throw, try..catch..finally

escape

Availability

Flash Player 5.

Usage

escape(*expression*)

Parameters

expression   The expression to convert into a string and encode in a URL-encoded format.

Returns

Nothing.

Description

Function; converts the parameter to a string and encodes it in a URL-encoded format, where all nonalphanumeric characters are escaped with % hexadecimal sequences.

Example

Running the following code gives the result, `Hello%7B%5BWorld%5D%7D`.

```
escape("Hello{[World]}");
```

See also

```
unescape
```

eval()

Availability

Flash Player 5 or later for full functionality. You can use the `eval()` function when exporting to Flash Player 4, but you must use slash notation, and can only access variables, not properties or objects.

Usage

```
eval(expression)
```

Parameters

expression   A string containing the name of a variable, property, object, or movie clip to retrieve.

Returns

A value, reference to an object or movie clip, or `undefined`.

Description

Function; accesses variables, properties, objects, or movie clips by name. If *expression* is a variable or a property, the value of the variable or property is returned. If *expression* is an object or movie clip, a reference to the object or movie clip is returned. If the element named in *expression* cannot be found, `undefined` is returned.

In Flash 4, `eval()` was used to simulate arrays; in Flash 5 or later, it is recommended that you use the Array class to simulate arrays.

In Flash 4, you can also use `eval()` to dynamically set and retrieve the value of a variable or instance name. However, you can also do this with the array access operator (`[]`).

In Flash 5 or later, you cannot use `eval()` to dynamically set and retrieve the value of a variable or instance name, because you cannot use `eval()` on the left side of an equation. For example, replace the code

```
eval ("var" + i) = "first";
```

with this:

```
this["var"+i] = "first"
```

or this:

```
set ("var" + i, "first");
```

Example

The following example uses eval() to determine the value of the expression "piece" + x. Because the result is a variable name, piece3, eval() returns the value of the variable and assigns it to y:

```
piece3 = "dangerous";
x = 3;

y = eval("piece" + x);
trace(y);

// Output: dangerous
```

See also

Array class

extends

Availability

Flash Player 6.

Usage

```
class className extends otherClassName {}

interface interfaceName extends otherInterfaceName {}
```

Note: To use this keyword, you must specify ActionScript 2.0 and Flash Player 6 or later in the Flash tab of your FLA file's Publish Settings dialog box. This keyword is supported only when used in external script files, not in scripts written in the Actions panel.

Parameters

className   The name of the class you are defining.

otherClassName   The name of the class on which *className* is based.

interfaceName   The name of the interface you are defining.

otherInterfaceName   The name of the interface on which *interfaceName* is based.

Description

Keyword; defines a class or interface that is a subclass of another class or interface; the latter is the superclass. The subclass inherits all the methods, properties, functions, and so on that are defined in the superclass.

For more information, see "Creating subclasses" on page 366.

Example

In class B as defined below, a call to class A's constructor will automatically be inserted as the first statement of B's constructor function, because a call does not already exist there. (That is, it is commented out in the example.)

```
class B extends class A
{
  function B() { // this is the constructor
//  super(); // optional; inserted during compilation if omitted
  }
  function m():Number {return 25;}
  function o(s:String):Void {trace(s);}
}
```

See also

class, implements, interface

false

Availability

Flash Player 5.

Usage

false

Description

Constant; a unique Boolean value that represents the opposite of true.

See also

true

_focusrect

Availability

Flash Player 4.

Usage

_focusrect = Boolean;

Description

Property (global); specifies whether a yellow rectangle appears around the button or movie clip that has keyboard focus. The default value, true, displays a yellow rectangle around the currently focused button or movie clip as the user presses the Tab key to navigate through objects in a SWF file. Specify false if you do not want to display the yellow rectangle. This is a global property that can be overridden for specific instances.

See also

Button._focusrect, MovieClip._focusrect

for

Availability

Flash Player 5.

Usage

```
for(init; condition; next) {
   statement(s);
}
```

Parameters

init An expression to evaluate before beginning the looping sequence, typically an assignment expression. A `var` statement is also permitted for this parameter.

condition An expression that evaluates to `true` or `false`. The condition is evaluated before each loop iteration; the loop exits when the condition evaluates to `false`.

next An expression to evaluate after each loop iteration; usually an assignment expression using the ++ (increment) or -- (decrement) operators.

statement(s) An instruction or instructions to execute within the body of the loop.

Description

Statement; a loop construct that evaluates the `init` (initialize) expression once, and then begins a looping sequence by which, as long as the *condition* evaluates to `true`, *statement* is executed and the next expression is evaluated.

Some properties cannot be enumerated by the `for` or `for..in` actions. For example, the built-in methods of the Array class (such as `Array.sort()` and `Array.reverse()`) are not included in the enumeration of an Array object, and movie clip properties, such as _x and _y, are not enumerated. In external class files, instance members are not enumerable; only dynamic and static members are enumerable.

Example

The following example uses `for` to add the elements in an array:

```
my_array=new Array();
for(i=0; i<10; i++) {
   my_array [i] = (i + 5)*10;
   trace(my_array[i]);
}
```

The following results are displayed in the Output panel:

```
50
60
70
80
90
100
110
120
130
140
```

The following is an example of using `for` to perform the same action repeatedly. In the following code, the `for` loop adds the numbers from 1 to 100:

```
var sum = 0;
  for (var i=1; i<=100; i++) {
    sum = sum + i;
  }
```

See also

`++` (increment), `--` (decrement), `for..in`, `var`

for..in

Availability

Flash Player 5.

Usage

```
for(variableIterant in object){
  statement(s);
}
```

Parameters

variableIterant   The name of a variable to act as the iterant, referencing each property of an object or element in an array.

object   The name of an object to be repeated.

statement(s)   An instruction to execute for each iteration.

Returns

Nothing.

Description

Statement; loops through the properties of an object or element in an array, and executes the *statement* for each property of an object.

Some properties cannot be enumerated by the `for` or `for..in` actions. For example, the built-in methods of the Array class (such as `Array.sort()` and `Array.reverse()`) are not included in the enumeration of an Array object, and movie clip properties, such as `_x` and `_y`, are not enumerated. In external class files, instance members are not enumerable; only dynamic and static members are enumerable.

The `for..in` statement iterates over properties of objects in the iterated object's prototype chain. If the child's prototype is `parent`, iterating over the properties of the child with `for..in`, will also iterate over the properties of `parent`.

The `for..in` action enumerates all objects in the prototype chain of an object. Properties of the object are enumerated first, then properties of its immediate prototype, then properties of the prototype's prototype, and so on. The `for..in` action does not enumerate the same property name twice. If the object `child` has prototype `parent` and both contain the property `prop`, the `for..in` action called on `child` enumerates `prop` from `child` but ignores the one in `parent`.

Example

The following is an example of using `for..in` to iterate over the properties of an object:

```
myObject = { name:'Tara', age:27, city:'San Francisco' };
for (name in myObject) {
   trace ("myObject." + name + " = " + myObject[name]);
}
```

The output of this example is as follows:

```
myObject.name = Tara
myObject.age = 27
myObject.city = San Francisco
```

The following is an example of using the `typeof` operator with `for..in` to iterate over a particular type of child:

```
for (name in my_mc) {
   if (typeof (my_mc[name]) = "movieclip") {
      trace ("I have a movie clip child named " + name);
   }
}
```

The following example enumerates the children of a movie clip and sends each to Frame 2 in their respective Timelines. The `RadioButtonGroup` movie clip is a parent with several children, `_RedRadioButton_`, `_GreenRadioButton_` and `_BlueRadioButton`.

```
for (var name in RadioButtonGroup) {
   RadioButtonGroup[name].gotoAndStop(2);
}
```

fscommand()

Availability

Flash Player 3.

Usage

```
fscommand("command", "parameters")
```

Parameters

command   A string passed to the host application for any use or a command passed to Flash Player.

parameters   A string passed to the host application for any use or a value passed to Flash Player.

Returns

Nothing.

Description

Function; allows the SWF file to communicate with either Flash Player or the program hosting Flash Player, such as a web browser. You can also use the `fscommand` action to pass messages to Macromedia Director, or to Visual Basic, Visual C++, and other programs that can host ActiveX controls.

Usage 1: To send a message to Flash Player, you must use predefined commands and parameters. The following table shows the values you can specify for the *command* and *parameters* parameters of the fscommand action to control a SWF file playing in Flash Player (including projectors):

Command	Parameters	Purpose
quit	None	Closes the projector.
fullscreen	true or false	Specifying true sets Flash Player to full-screen mode. Specifying false returns the player to normal menu view.
allowscale	true or false	Specifying false sets the player so that the SWF file is always drawn at its original size and never scaled. Specifying true forces the SWF file to scale to 100% of the player.
showmenu	true or false	Specifying true enables the full set of context menu items. Specifying false dims all the context menu items except About Flash Player.
exec	Path to application	Executes an application from within the projector.
trapallkeys	true or false	Specifying true sends all key events, including accelerator keys, to the onClipEvent(keyDown/keyUp) handler in Flash Player.

The exec command can contain only the characters A–Z, a–z, 0–9, period ()., and underscore (_). The exec command runs in the subdirectory fscommand only. In other words, if you use the fscommand exec command to call an application, the application must reside in a subdirectory named fscommand.

Usage 2: To use the fscommand action to send a message to a scripting language such as JavaScript in a web browser, you can pass any two parameters in the *command* and *parameters* parameters. These parameters can be strings or expressions and are used in a JavaScript function that "catches," or handles, the fscommand action.

In a web browser, the fscommand action calls the JavaScript function moviename_DoFScommand in the HTML page containing the SWF file. The moviename is the name of the Flash Player as assigned by the NAME attribute of the EMBED tag or the ID property of the OBJECT tag. If you assign the Flash Player the name myDocument, the JavaScript function called is myDocument_DoFScommand.

Usage 3: The fscommand action can send messages to Macromedia Director that are interpreted by Lingo as strings, events, or executable Lingo code. If the message is a string or an event, you must write the Lingo code to receive the message from the fscommand action and carry out an action in Director. For more information, see the Director Support Center at www.macromedia.com/support/director.

Usage 4: In Visual Basic, Visual C++, and other programs that can host ActiveX controls, fscommand sends a VB event with two strings that can be handled in the environment's programming language. For more information, use the keywords *Flash method* to search the Flash Support Center at www.macromedia.com/support/flash.

Example

Usage 1: In the following example, the `fscommand` action sets the Flash Player to scale the SWF file to the full monitor screen size when the button is released.

```
on(release){
   fscommand("fullscreen", true);
}
```

Usage 2: The following example uses the `fscommand` action applied to a button in Flash to open a JavaScript message box in an HTML page. The message itself is sent to JavaScript as the `fscommand` parameter.

You must add a function to the HTML page that contains the SWF file. This function, *myDocument*_DoFSCommand sits in the HTML page and waits for an `fscommand` action in Flash. When an `fscommand` is triggered in Flash (for example, when a user presses the button), the `command` and `parameter` strings are passed to the *myDocument*_DoFSCommand function. You can use the passed strings in your JavaScript or VBScript code in any way you like. In this example, the function contains a conditional `if` statement that checks to see if the command string is `"messagebox"`. If it is, a JavaScript alert box (or "message box") opens and displays the contents of the `parameters` string.

```
function myDocument_DoFSCommand(command, args) {
   if (command == "messagebox") {
      alert(args);
   }
}
```

In the Flash document, add the `fscommand` action to a button:

```
fscommand("messagebox", "This is a message box called from within Flash.")
```

You can also use expressions for the `fscommand` action and parameters, as in the following example:

```
fscommand("messagebox", "Hello, " + name + ", welcome to our website!")
```

To test the movie, choose File > Publish Preview > HTML.

Note: If you publish your SWF file using the Flash with FSCommand template in the HTML Publish Settings, the `myDocument_DoFSCommand` function is inserted automatically. The SWF file's `NAME` and `ID` attributes will be the filename. For example, for the file myDocument.fla, the attributes would be set to `myDocument`.

function

Availability

Flash Player 5.

Usage

```
function functionname ([parameter0, parameter1,...parameterN]){
   statement(s)
}
function ([parameter0, parameter1,...parameterN]){
   statement(s)
}
```

Parameters

functionname   The name of the new function.

parameter   An identifier that represents a parameter to pass to the function. These parameters are optional.

statement(s)   Any ActionScript instruction you have defined for the body of the `function`.

Returns

Nothing.

Description

Statement; comprises a set of statements that you define to perform a certain task. You can *declare*, or define, a function in one location and call, or invoke, it from different scripts in a SWF file. When you define a function, you can also specify parameters for the function. Parameters are placeholders for values on which the function operates. You can pass different parameters to a function each time you call it. This lets you reuse one function in many different situations.

Use the `return` action in a function's *statement(s)* to cause a function to return, or generate, a value.

Usage 1: Declares a `function` with the specified *functionname*, *parameters*, and *statement(s)*. When a function is called, the function declaration is invoked. Forward referencing is permitted; within the same Action list, a function may be declared after it is called. A function declaration replaces any prior declaration of the same function. You can use this syntax wherever a statement is permitted.

Usage 2: Creates an anonymous function and returns it. This syntax is used in expressions, and is particularly useful for installing methods in objects.

Example

Usage 1: The following example defines the function `sqr`, which accepts one parameter and returns the `square(x*x)` of the parameter. If the function is declared and used in the same script, the function declaration may appear after using the function.

```
y=sqr(3);

function sqr(x) {
   return x*x;
}
```

Usage 2: The following function defines a Circle object:

```
function Circle(radius) {
  this.radius = radius;
}
```

The following statement defines an anonymous function that calculates the area of a circle and attaches it to the object `Circle` as a method:

```
Circle.prototype.area = function () {return Math.PI * this.radius *
  this.radius}
```

Function class

Availability

Flash Player 6.

Method summary for the Function class

Method	Description
Function.apply()	Enables ActionScript code to call a function.
Function.call()	Invokes the function represented by a Function object.

Property summary for the Function class

Property	Description
Function.prototype	Refers to an object that is the prototype for a class.

Function.apply()

Availability

Flash Player 6.

Usage

myFunction.apply(*thisObject*, *argumentsObject*)

Parameters

thisObject   The object that *myFunction* is applied to.

argumentsObject   An array whose elements are passed to *myFunction* as parameters.

Returns

Any value that the called function specifies.

Description

Method; specifies the value of `this` to be used within any function that ActionScript calls. This method also specifies the parameters to be passed to any called function. Because `apply()` is a method of the Function class, it is also a method of every function object in ActionScript.

The parameters are specified as an Array object. This is often useful when the number of parameters to be passed is not known until the script actually executes.

Example

The following function invocations are equivalent:

```
Math.atan2(1, 0)
Math.atan2.apply(null, [1, 0])
```

You could construct a SWF file that contains input entry fields that permit the user to enter the name of a function to invoke, and zero or more parameters to pass to the function. Pressing a "Call" button would then use the `apply` method to call the function, specifying the parameters.

In this example, the user specifies a function name in an input text field called `functionName`. The number of parameters is specified in an input text field called `numParameters`. Up to 10 parameters are specified in text fields called `parameter1`, `parameter2`, up to `parameter10`.

```
on (release) {
  callTheFunction();
}
...
function callTheFunction()
{
    var theFunction = eval(functionName.text);
    var n = Number(numParameters);
    var parameters = [];
    for (var i = 0; i < n; i++) {
       parameters.push(eval("parameter" + i));
    }
    theFunction.apply(null, parameters);
}
```

Function.call()

Availability

Flash Player 6.

Usage

```
myFunction.call(thisObject, parameter1, ..., parameterN)
```

Parameters

thisObject   Specifies the value of `this` within the function body.

parameter1   A parameter to be passed to the *myFunction*. You can specify zero or more parameters.

parameterN

Returns

Nothing.

Description

Method; invokes the function represented by a Function object. Every function in ActionScript is represented by a Function object, so all functions support this method.

In almost all cases, the function call operator (( )) can be used instead of this method. The function call operator produces code that is concise and readable. This method is primarily useful when the this parameter of the function invocation needs to be explicitly controlled. Normally, if a function is invoked as a method of an object, within the body of the function, this is set to myObject as in the following:

```
myObject.myMethod(1, 2, 3);
```

In some situations, you may want this to point somewhere else; for example, if a function must be invoked as a method of an object, but is not actually stored as a method of that object.

```
myObject.myMethod.call(myOtherObject, 1, 2, 3);
```

You can pass the value null for the *thisObject* parameter to invoke a function as a regular function and not as a method of an object. For example, the following function invocations are equivalent:

```
Math.sin(Math.PI / 4)
Math.sin.call(null, Math.PI / 4)
```

Example

This example uses Function.call() to make a function behave as a method of another object, without storing the function in the object.

```
function MyObject() {
}
function MyMethod(obj) {
  trace("this == obj? " + (this == obj));
}
var obj = new MyObject();
MyMethod.call(obj, obj);
```

The trace() action sends the following code to the Output panel:

```
this == obj? true
```

Function.prototype

Availability

Flash Player 5. If you are using ActionScript 2.0, you don't need to use this property; it reflects the implementation of inheritance in ActionScript 1.

Usage

myFunction.prototype

Description

Property; in an ActionScript 1 constructor function, the prototype property refers to an object that is the prototype of the constructed class. Each instance of the class that is created by the constructor function inherits all the properties and methods of the prototype object.

ge (greater than or equal to – string specific)

Availability

Flash Player 4. This operator was deprecated in Flash 5 in favor of the >= (greater than or equal to) operator.

Usage

expression1 ge *expression2*

Parameters

expression1, *expression2*   Numbers, strings, or variables.

Returns

Nothing.

Description

Operator (comparison); compares the string representation of *expression1* to the string representation of *expression2* and returns true if *expression1* is greater than or equal to *expression2*; otherwise, returns false.

See also

>= (greater than or equal to)

get

Availability

Flash Player 6.

Usage

```
function get property() {
   // your statements here
}
```

Note: To use this keyword, you must specify ActionScript 2.0 and Flash Player 6 or later in the Flash tab of your FLA file's Publish Settings dialog box. This keyword is supported only when used in external script files, not in scripts written in the Actions panel.

Parameters

property   The word you want to use to refer to the property that get accesses; this value must be the same as the value used in the corresponding set command.

Returns

The value of the property specified by *propertyName*.

Description

Keyword; permits implicit "getting" of properties associated with objects based on classes you have defined in external class files. Using implicit get methods lets you access properties of objects without accessing them directly. Implicit get/set methods are syntactic shorthand for the Object.addProperty() method in ActionScript 1.

For more information, see "Implicit get/set methods" on page 376.

Object.addProperty(), set

getProperty

Availability

Flash Player 4.

Usage

```
getProperty(my_mc, property)
```

Parameters

my_mc   The instance name of a movie clip for which the property is being retrieved.

property   A property of a movie clip.

Returns

The value of the specified property.

Description

Function; returns the value of the specified property for the movie clip *my_mc*.

Example

The following example retrieves the horizontal axis coordinate (_x) for the movie clip my_mc and assigns it to the variable my_mc_x:

```
my_mc_x = getProperty(_root.my_mc, _x);
```

getTimer

Availability

Flash Player 4.

Usage

```
getTimer()
```

Parameters

None.

Returns

The number of milliseconds that have elapsed since the SWF file started playing.

Description

Function; returns the number of milliseconds that have elapsed since the SWF file started playing.

getURL()

Availability

Flash 2. The GET and POST options are only available to Flash Player 4 and later versions of the player.

Usage

```
getURL(url [, window [, "variables"]])
```

Parameters

url   The URL from which to obtain the document.

window   An optional parameter specifying the window or HTML frame that the document should load into. You can enter the name of a specific window or choose from the following reserved target names:

- _self specifies the current frame in the current window.
- _blank specifies a new window.
- _parent specifies the parent of the current frame.
- _top specifies the top-level frame in the current window.

variables   A GET or POST method for sending variables. If there are no variables, omit this parameter. The GET method appends the variables to the end of the URL, and is used for small numbers of variables. The POST method sends the variables in a separate HTTP header and is used for sending long strings of variables.

Returns

Nothing.

Description

Function; loads a document from a specific URL into a window or passes variables to another application at a defined URL. To test this action, make sure the file to be loaded is at the specified location. To use an absolute URL (for example, *http://www.myserver.com*), you need a network connection.

Example

This example loads a new URL into a blank browser window. The getURL() action targets the variable incomingAd as the *url* parameter so that you can change the loaded URL without having to edit the SWF file. The incomingAd variable's value is passed into Flash earlier in the SWF file using a loadVariables() action.

```
on(release) {
  getURL(incomingAd, "_blank");
}
```

See also

loadVariables(), XML.send(), XML.sendAndLoad(), XMLSocket.send()

getVersion

Availability

Flash Player 5.

Usage

```
getVersion()
```

Parameters

None.

Returns

A string containing Flash Player version and platform information.

Description

Function; returns a string containing Flash Player version and platform information.

The `getVersion` function only returns information for Flash Player 5 or later versions of the Player.

Example

The following is an example of a string returned by the `getVersion` function.

```
WIN 5,0,17,0
```

This indicates that the platform is Microsoft Windows, and the version number of Flash Player is major version 5, minor version 17 (5.0r17).

See also

`System.capabilities.os, System.capabilities.version`

_global object

Availability

Flash Player 6.

Usage

```
_global.identifier
```

Parameters

None.

Returns

A reference to the global object that holds the core ActionScript classes, such as String, Object, Math, and Array.

Description

Identifier; creates global variables, objects, or classes. For example, you could create a library that is exposed as a global ActionScript object, much like the Math or Date object. Unlike Timeline-declared or locally declared variables and functions, global variables and functions are visible to every Timeline and scope in the SWF file, provided they are not obscured by identifiers with the same names in inner scopes.

Example

The following example creates a top-level function `factorial()` that is available to every Timeline and scope in a SWF file:

```
_global.factorial = function (n) {
  if (n <= 1) {
    return 1;
  } else {
    return n * factorial(n-1);
  }
}
```

See also

`var, set variable`

gotoAndPlay()

Availability

Flash 2.

Usage

`gotoAndPlay([scene,] frame)`

Parameters

`scene`   An optional string specifying the name of the scene to which the playhead is sent.

`frame`   A number representing the frame number, or a string representing the label of the frame, to which the playhead is sent.

Returns

Nothing.

Description

Function; sends the playhead to the specified frame in a scene and plays from that frame. If no scene is specified, the playhead goes to the specified frame in the current scene.

Example

When the user clicks a button to which `gotoAndPlay()` is assigned, the playhead is sent to Frame 16 in the current scene and starts to play.

```
on(release) {
  gotoAndPlay(16);
}
```

See also

`MovieClip.gotoAndPlay()`

gotoAndStop()

Availability

Flash 2.

Usage

```
gotoAndStop([scene,] frame)
```

Parameters

scene   An optional string specifying the name of the scene to which the playhead is sent.

frame   A number representing the frame number, or a string representing the label of the frame, to which the playhead is sent.

Returns

Nothing.

Description

Function; sends the playhead to the specified frame in a scene and stops it. If no scene is specified, the playhead is sent to the frame in the current scene.

Example

When the user clicks a button that `gotoAndStop()` is assigned to, the playhead is sent to Frame 5 in the current scene and the SWF file stops playing.

```
on(release) {
   gotoAndStop(5);
}
```

See also

```
stop()
```

gt (greater than – string specific)

Availability

Flash Player 4. This operator was deprecated in Flash 5 in favor of the new > (greater than) operator.

Usage

```
expression1 gt expression2
```

Parameters

expression1, expression2   Numbers, strings, or variables.

Description

Operator (comparison); compares the string representation of *expression1* to the string representation of *expression2* and returns `true` if *expression1* is greater than *expression2*; otherwise, returns `false`.

See also

```
> (greater than)
```

_highquality

Availability

Flash Player 4; deprecated in favor of _quality.

Usage

_highquality

Description

Deprecated property (global); specifies the level of anti-aliasing applied to the current SWF file. Specify 2 (best quality) to apply high quality with bitmap smoothing always on. Specify 1 (high quality) to apply anti-aliasing; this will smooth bitmaps if the SWF file does not contain animation. Specify 0 (low quality) to prevent anti-aliasing.

Example

_highquality = 1;

See also

_quality, toggleHighQuality()

if

Availability

Flash Player 4.

Usage

```
if(condition) {
    statement(s);
}
```

Parameters

condition   An expression that evaluates to true or false.

statement(s)   The instructions to execute if or when the condition evaluates to true.

Returns

Nothing.

Description

Statement; evaluates a condition to determine the next action in a SWF file. If the condition is true, Flash runs the statements that follow the condition inside curly braces ({ }). If the condition is false, Flash skips the statements inside the curly braces and runs the statements following the curly braces. Use the if action to create branching logic in your scripts.

Example

In the following example, the condition inside the parentheses evaluates the variable name to see if it has the literal value "Erica". If it does, the play() action inside the curly braces runs.

```
if(name == "Erica"){
    play();
}
```

The following example uses an if action to evaluate when a draggable object in the SWF file is released by the user. If the object was released less than 300 milliseconds after dragging it, the condition evaluates to true and the statements inside the curly braces run. Those statements set variables to store the new location of the object, how hard it was thrown, and the speed at which it was thrown. The timePressed variable is also reset. If the object was released more than 300 milliseconds after it was dragged, the condition evaluates to false and none of the statements run.

```
if (getTimer()<timePressed+300) {
    // if the condition is true,
    // the object was thrown.
    // what is the new location of this object?
    xNewLoc = this._x;
    yNewLoc = this._y;
    // how hard did they throw it?
    xTravel = xNewLoc-xLoc;
    yTravel = yNewLoc-yLoc;
    // setting the speed of the object depending on
    // how far they travelled with it
    xInc = xTravel/2;
    yInc = yTravel/2;
    timePressed = 0;
}
```

See also

else

ifFrameLoaded

Availability

Flash Player 3. The ifFrameLoaded action was deprecated in Flash 5; Macromedia recommends using the MovieClip._framesloaded property.

Usage

```
ifFrameLoaded([scene,] frame) {
    statement(s);
}
```

Parameters

scene   An optional string specifying the name of the scene that must be loaded.

frame   The frame number or frame label that must be loaded before the next statement is executed.

statement(s)   The instructions to execute if the specified scene, or scene and frame, are loaded.

Returns

Nothing.

Description

Deprecated action; checks whether the contents of a specific frame are available locally. Use ifFrameLoaded to start playing a simple animation while the rest of the SWF file downloads to the local computer. The difference between using _framesloaded and ifFrameLoaded is that _framesloaded allows you to add your own if or else statements.

See also

MovieClip._framesloaded

implements

Availability

Flash Player 6.

Usage

myClass implements *interface01* [, *interface02*, ...]

Note: To use this keyword, you must specify ActionScript 2.0 and Flash Player 6 or later in the Flash tab of your FLA file's Publish Settings dialog box. This keyword is supported only when used in external script files, not in scripts written in the Actions panel.

Description

Keyword; defines a class that must supply implementations for all the methods defined in the interface (or interfaces) being implemented. For more information, see "Interfaces as data types" on page 372.

Example

See interface.

See also

class, extends, interface

import

Availability

Flash Player 6.

Usage

import *className*

import *packageName*.*

Note: To use this keyword, you must specify ActionScript 2.0 and Flash Player 6 or later in the Flash tab of your FLA file's Publish Settings dialog box. This statement is supported in the Actions panel as well as in external class files.

Parameters

className   The fully qualified name of a class you have defined in an external class file.

packageName   A directory in which you have stored related class files.

Description

Keyword; lets you access classes without specifying their fully qualified names. For example, if you want to use the class macr.util.users.UserClass.as in a script, you must either refer to it by its fully qualified name or import it; if you import it, you can then refer to it by the class name:

```
// before importing
var myUser:UserClass = new macr.util.users.UserClass();
// after importing
import macr.util.users.UserClass;
var myUser:UserClass = new UserClass();
```

If there are several class files in the directory that you want to access, you can import them all in a single statement:

```
import macr.util.users.*;
```

You must issue the import statement before you try to access the imported class without fully specifying its name.

If you import a class but then don't use it in your script, the class isn't exported as part of the SWF file. This means you can import large packages without worrying about the size of your SWF file; the bytecode associated with a class is included in a SWF file only if that class is actually used.

The import statement applies only to the current script (frame or object) in which it's called. For example, suppose on Frame 1 of a Flash document you import all the classes in the macr.util package. On that frame, you can reference classes in that package by their simple names.

```
// On Frame 1 of a FLA:
import macr.util.*;

var myFoo:foo = new foo();
```

On another frame script, however, you would need to reference classes in that package by their fully qualified names (var myFoo:foo = new macr.util.foo();) or add an import statement to the other frame, as well, that imports the classes in that package.

For more information on importing, see "Importing classes" on page 375 and "Using packages" on page 375.

#include

Availability

Flash Player 4.

Usage

```
#include "[path] filename.as"
```

Note: Do not place a semicolon (;) at the end of the line that contains the #include statement.

Parameters

[path] filename.as   The filename and optional path for the script to add to the Actions panel; *.as* is the recommended file extension.

Returns

Nothing.

Description

Compiler directive: includes the contents of the specified file, as if the commands in the file were part of the calling script itself. The #include directive is invoked at compile time. Therefore, if you make any changes to an external file, you must save the file and recompile any FLA files that use it.

If you use the Check Syntax button for a script that contains #include statements, the syntax of the included files is also checked.

You can use #include in FLA files and in external script files, but not in ActionScript 2.0 class files.

You can specify no path, a relative path, or an absolute path for the file to be included.

- If you don't specify a path, the AS file must be in the same directory as the FLA file or the script containing the #include statement.
- To specify a path for the AS file relative to the FLA file or script, use a single dot (.) to indicate the current directory, two dots (..) to indicate a parent directory, and forward slashes (/). See the following examples.
- To specify an absolute path for the AS file, use the format supported by your platform (Macintosh or Windows). See the following examples. However, this usage is not recommended, because it requires that the directory structure be the same on any machine you use to compile the script.

Example

The following examples show various ways of specifying a path for a file to be included in your script.

```
// Note that #include statements do not end with a semicolon (;)
// AS file is in same directory as FLA file or script
#include "init_script.as"

// AS file is in a subdirectory of the directory
//   containing the FLA file or script
// The subdirectory is named "FLA_includes"
#include "FLA_includes/init_script.as"

// AS file is in a directory at the same level as the FLA file or script
// The directory is named "ALL_includes"
#include "../ALL_includes/init_script.as"

// AS file is specified by an absolute path in Windows
// Note use of forward slashes, not backslashes
#include "C:/Flash_scripts/init_script.as"

// AS file is specified by an absolute path on Macintosh
#include "Mac HD:Flash_scripts:init_script.as"
```

See also

import

Infinity

Availability

Flash Player 5.

Usage

```
Infinity
```

Description

Constant; specifies the IEEE-754 value representing positive infinity. The value of this constant is the same as `Number.POSITIVE_INFINITY`.

-Infinity

Availability

Flash Player 5.

Usage

```
-Infinity
```

Description

Constant; specifies the IEEE-754 value representing negative infinity. The value of this constant is the same as `Number.NEGATIVE_INFINITY`.

#initclip

Availability

Flash Player 6.

Usage

```
#initclip order
```

Parameters

`order`   An integer that specifies the execution order of blocks of `#initclip` code. This is an optional parameter.

Description

Compiler directive; indicates the beginning of a block of initialization actions. When multiple clips are initialized at the same time, you can use the `order` parameter to specify which initialization occurs first. Initialization actions execute when a movie clip symbol is defined. If the movie clip is an exported symbol, the initialization actions execute before the actions on Frame 1 of the SWF file. Otherwise, they execute immediately before the frame actions of the frame that contains the first instance of the associated movie clip symbol.

Initialization actions execute only once during the playback of a SWF file; use them for one-time initializations, such as class definition and registration.

See also

```
#endinitclip
```

instanceof

Availability

Flash Player 6.

Usage

```
object instanceof class
```

Parameters

`object`   An ActionScript object.

`class`   A reference to an ActionScript constructor function, such as String or Date.

Returns

If `object` is an instance of `class`, `instanceof` returns `true`; otherwise, `instanceof` returns `false`. Also, `_global instanceof Object` returns `false`.

Description

Operator; determines whether an object belongs to a specified class. Tests whether `object` is an instance of `class`.

The `instanceof` operator does not convert primitive types to wrapper objects. For example, the following code returns `true`:

```
new String("Hello") instanceof String;
```

Whereas the following code returns `false`:

```
"Hello" instanceof String;
```

See also

`typeof`

int

Availability

Flash Player 4. This function was deprecated in Flash 5 in favor of `Math.round()`.

Usage

```
int(value)
```

Parameters

`value`   A number to be rounded to an integer.

Returns

Nothing.

Description

Function; converts a decimal number to the closest integer value.

Math.floor()

interface

Availability

Flash Player 6.

Usage

```
interface InterfaceName {}
interface InterfaceName [extends InterfaceName [, InterfaceName ...] {}
```

Note: To use this keyword, you must specify ActionScript 2.0 and Flash Player 6 or later in the Flash tab of your FLA file's Publish Settings dialog box. This keyword is supported only when used in external script files, not in scripts written in the Actions panel.

Description

Keyword; defines an interface. An interface is similar to a class, with the following important differences:

- Interfaces contain only declarations of methods, not their implementation. That is, every class that implements an interface must provide an implementation for each method declared in the interface.

- Only public members are allowed in an interface definition. In addition, instance and class members are not permitted.

- The get and set statements are not allowed in interface definitions.

For more information, see "Creating and using interfaces" on page 371.

Example

The following example shows several ways to define and implement interfaces.

```
(in top-level package .as files Ia, B, C, Ib, D, Ic, E)

// filename Ia.as
interface Ia
{
  function k():Number;        // method declaration only
  function n(x:Number):Number; // without implementation
}
// filename B.as
class B implements Ia
{
  function k():Number {return 25;}
  function n(x:Number):Number {return x+5;}
}
// external script or Actions panel
mvar = new B();
trace(B.k());   // 25
trace(B.n(7)); // 12

// filename c.as
class C implements Ia
{
  function k():Number {return 25;}
```

```
} // error: class must implement all interface methods

// filename Ib.as
interface Ib
{
   function o():Void;
}
class D implements Ia, Ib
{
   function k():Number {return 15;}
   function n(x:Number):Number {return x*x;}
   function o():Void {trace("o");}
}

// external script or Actions panel
mvar = new D();
trace(D.k());   // 15
trace(D.n(7));  // 49
trace(D.o());   // "o"

interface Ic extends Ia
{
   function p():Void;
}
class E implements Ib, Ic
{
   function k():Number {return 25;}
   function n(x:Number):Number {return x+5;}
   function o():Void {trace("o");}
   function p():Void {trace("p");}
}
```

See also

class, extends, implements

isFinite

Availability

Flash Player 5.

Usage

isFinite(*expression*)

Parameters

expression   A Boolean value, variable, or other expression to be evaluated.

Returns

A Boolean value.

Description

Function; evaluates *expression* and returns true if it is a finite number or false if it is infinity or negative infinity. The presence of infinity or negative infinity indicates a mathematical error condition such as division by 0.

Example

The following are examples of return values for isFinite:

```
isFinite(56)
// returns true

isFinite(Number.POSITIVE_INFINITY)
// returns false
```

isNaN()

Availability

Flash Player 5.

Usage

```
isNaN(expression)
```

Parameters

expression   A Boolean, variable, or other expression to be evaluated.

Returns

A Boolean value.

Description

Function; evaluates the parameter and returns true if the value is not a number (NaN), indicating the presence of mathematical errors.

Example

The following code illustrates return values for the isNaN function.

```
isNaN("Tree")
// returns true

isNaN(56)
// returns false

isNaN(Number.POSITIVE_INFINITY)
// returns false
```

See also

NaN, Number.NaN

Key class

Availability

Flash Player 6.

Description

The Key class is a top-level class whose methods and properties you can use without using a constructor. Use the methods of the Key class to build an interface that can be controlled by a user with a standard keyboard. The properties of the Key class are constants representing the keys most commonly used to control games. For a complete list of key code values, see Appendix C, "Keyboard Keys and Key Code Values," on page 993.

Method summary for the Key class

Method	Description
Key.addListener()	Registers an object to receive notification when the onKeyDown and onKeyUp methods are invoked.
Key.getAscii()	Returns the ASCII value of the last key pressed.
Key.getCode()	Returns the virtual key code of the last key pressed.
Key.isDown()	Returns true if the key specified in the parameter is pressed.
Key.isToggled()	Returns true if the Num Lock or Caps Lock key is activated.
Key.removeListener()	Removes an object that was previously registered with Key.addListener().

Property summary for the Key class

All of the properties for the Key class are constants.

Property	Description
Key.BACKSPACE	Constant associated with the key code value for the Backspace key (8).
Key.CAPSLOCK	Constant associated with the key code value for the Caps Lock key (20).
Key.CONTROL	Constant associated with the key code value for the Control key (17).
Key.DELETEKEY	Constant associated with the key code value for the Delete key (46).
Key.DOWN	Constant associated with the key code value for the Down Arrow key (40).
Key.END	Constant associated with the key code value for the End key (35).
Key.ENTER	Constant associated with the key code value for the Enter key (13).
Key.ESCAPE	Constant associated with the key code value for the Escape key (27).
Key.HOME	Constant associated with the key code value for the Home key (36).
Key.INSERT	Constant associated with the key code value for the Insert key (45).
Key.LEFT	Constant associated with the key code value for the Left Arrow key (37).
Key.PGDN	Constant associated with the key code value for the Page Down key (34).
Key.PGUP	Constant associated with the key code value for the Page Up key (33).

Property	Description
Key.RIGHT	Constant associated with the key code value for the Right Arrow key (39).
Key.SHIFT	Constant associated with the key code value for the Shift key (16).
Key.SPACE	Constant associated with the key code value for the Spacebar (32).
Key.TAB	Constant associated with the key code value for the Tab key (9).
Key.UP	Constant associated with the key code value for the Up Arrow key (38).

Listener summary for the Key class

Method	Description
Key.onKeyDown	Notified when a key is pressed.
Key.onKeyUp	Notified when a key is released.

Key.addListener()

Availability

Flash Player 6.

Usage

```
Key.addListener (newListener)
```

Parameters

newListener   An object with methods onKeyDown and onKeyUp.

Returns

Nothing.

Description

Method; registers an object to receive onKeyDown and onKeyUp notification. When a key is pressed or released, regardless of the input focus, all listening objects registered with addListener() have either their onKeyDown method or onKeyUp method invoked. Multiple objects can listen for keyboard notifications. If the listener newListener is already registered, no change occurs.

Example

The following example creates a new listener object and defines a function for onKeyDown and onKeyUp. The last line uses addListener() to register the listener with the Key object so that it can receive notification from the key down and key up events.

```
myListener = new Object();
myListener.onKeyDown = function () {
  trace ("You pressed a key.");
}
myListener.onKeyUp = function () {
  trace ("You released a key.");
}
Key.addListener(myListener);
```

The following example assigns the keyboard shortcut Control+7 to a button with an instance name of myButton, and makes information about the shortcut available to screen readers (see _accProps). In this example, when you press Control+7 the `myOnPress` function displays the text "hello" in the Output panel; in your file, you would create a function that does something more meaningful.

```
function myOnPress() {
    trace( "hello" );
}

function myOnKeyDown() {
    if (Key.isDown(Key.CONTROL) && Key.getCode() == 55) // 55 is key code for 7
    {
        Selection.setFocus( myButton );
        myButton.onPress();
    }
}

var myListener = new Object();
myListener.onKeyDown = myOnKeyDown;
Key.addListener( myListener );

myButton.onPress = myOnPress;
myButton._accProps.shortcut = "Ctrl+F"
Accessibility.updateProperties();
```

See also

Key.getCode(), Key.isDown(), Key.onKeyDown, Key.onKeyUp, Key.removeListener()

Key.BACKSPACE

Availability

Flash Player 5.

Usage

Key.BACKSPACE

Description

Property; constant associated with the key code value for the Backspace key (8).

Key.CAPSLOCK

Availability

Flash Player 5.

Usage

Key.CAPSLOCK

Description

Property; constant associated with the key code value for the Caps Lock key (20).

Key.CONTROL

Availability

Flash Player 5.

Usage

```
Key.CONTROL
```

Description

Property; constant associated with the key code value for the Control key (17).

Key.DELETEKEY

Availability

Flash Player 5.

Usage

```
Key.DELETEKEY
```

Description

Property; constant associated with the key code value for the Delete key (46).

Key.DOWN

Availability

Flash Player 5.

Usage

```
Key.DOWN
```

Description

Property; constant associated with the key code value for the Down Arrow key (40).

Key.END

Availability

Flash Player 5.

Usage

```
Key.END
```

Description

Property; constant associated with the key code value for the End key (35).

Key.ENTER

Availability

Flash Player 5.

Usage

`Key.ENTER`

Description

Property; constant associated with the key code value for the Enter key (13).

Key.ESCAPE

Availability

Flash Player 5.

Usage

`Key.ESCAPE`

Description

Property; constant associated with the key code value for the Escape key (27).

Key.getAscii()

Availability

Flash Player 5.

Usage

`Key.getAscii();`

Parameters

None.

Returns

An integer that represents the ASCII value of the last key pressed.

Description

Method; returns the ASCII code of the last key pressed or released. The ASCII values returned are English keyboard values. For example, if you press Shift+2, `Key.getAscii()` returns @ on a Japanese keyboard, just as it does on an English keyboard.

Key.getCode()

Availability

Flash Player 5.

Usage

```
Key.getCode();
```

Parameters

None.

Returns

An integer that represents the key code of the last key pressed.

Description

Method; returns the key code value of the last key pressed. To match the returned key code value with the key on a standard keyboard, see Appendix C, "Keyboard Keys and Key Code Values," on page 993.

Key.HOME

Availability

Flash Player 5.

Usage

```
Key.HOME
```

Description

Property; constant associated with the key code value for the Home key (36).

Key.INSERT

Availability

Flash Player 5.

Usage

```
Key.INSERT
```

Description

Property; constant associated with the key code value for the Insert key (45).

Key.isDown()

Availability

Flash Player 5.

Usage

`Key.isDown(keycode)`

Parameters

keycode   The key code value assigned to a specific key, or a Key class property associated with a specific key. To match the returned key code value with the key on a standard keyboard, see Appendix C, "Keyboard Keys and Key Code Values," on page 993.

Returns

A Boolean value.

Description

Method; returns `true` if the key specified in *keycode* is pressed, `false` if it is not. On the Macintosh, the key code values for the Caps Lock and Num Lock keys are identical.

Example

The following script lets the user control a movie clip's location.

```
onClipEvent (enterFrame) {
  if(Key.isDown(Key.RIGHT)) {
    this._x=_x+10;
  } else if (Key.isDown(Key.DOWN)) {
    this._y=_y+10;
  }
}
```

Key.isToggled()

Availability

Flash Player 5.

Usage

`Key.isToggled(keycode)`

Parameters

keycode   The key code for Caps Lock (20) or Num Lock (144).

Returns

A Boolean value.

Description

Method; returns `true` if the Caps Lock or Num Lock key is activated (toggled), `false` if it is not. On the Macintosh, the key code values for the Caps Lock and Num Lock keys are identical.

Key.LEFT

Availability

Flash Player 5.

Usage

`Key.LEFT`

Description

Property; constant associated with the key code value for the Left Arrow key (37).

Key.onKeyDown

Availability

Flash Player 6.

Usage

`someListener.onKeyDown`

Description

Listener; notified when a key is pressed. To use `onKeyDown` you must create a listener object. You can then define a function for `onKeyDown` and use `addListener()` to register the listener with the Key object, as in the following:

```
someListener = new Object();
someListener.onKeyDown = function () { ... };
Key.addListener(someListener);
```

Listeners enable different pieces of code to cooperate because multiple listeners can receive notification about a single event.

See also

`Key.addListener()`

Key.onKeyUp

Availability

Flash Player 6.

Usage

`someListener.onKeyUp`

Description

Listener; notified when a key is released. To use `onKeyUp` you must create a listener object. You can then define a function for `onKeyUp` and use `addListener()` to register the listener with the Key object, as in the following:

```
someListener = new Object();
someListener.onKeyUp = function () { ... };
Key.addListener(someListener);
```

Listeners enable different pieces of code to cooperate because multiple listeners can receive notification about a single event.

See also

Key.addListener()

Key.PGDN

Availability

Flash Player 5.

Usage

Key.PGDN

Description

Property; constant associated with the key code value for the Page Down key (34).

Key.PGUP

Availability

Flash Player 5.

Usage

Key.PGUP

Description

Property; constant associated with the key code value for the Page Up key (33).

Key.removeListener()

Availability

Flash Player 6.

Usage

Key.removeListener (*listener*)

Parameters

listener   An object.

Returns

If the *listener* was successfully removed, the method returns true. If the *listener* was not successfully removed, for example if the *listener* was not on the Key object's listener list, the method returns false.

Description

Method; removes an object previously registered with Key.addListener().

Key.RIGHT

Availability

Flash Player 5.

Usage

```
Key.RIGHT
```

Description

Property; constant associated with the key code value for the Right Arrow key (39).

Key.SHIFT

Availability

Flash Player 5.

Usage

```
Key.SHIFT
```

Description

Property; constant associated with the key code value for the Shift key (16).

Key.SPACE

Availability

Flash Player 5.

Usage

```
Key.SPACE
```

Description

Property; constant associated with the key code value for the Spacebar (32).

Key.TAB

Availability

Flash Player 5.

Usage

```
Key.TAB
```

Description

Property; constant associated with the key code value for the Tab key (9).

Key.UP

Availability

Flash Player 5.

Usage

`Key.UP`

Description

Property; constant associated with the key code value for the Up Arrow key (38).

le (less than or equal to – string specific)

Availability

Flash Player 4. This operator was deprecated in Flash 5 in favor of the `<=` (less than or equal to) operator.

Usage

expression1 `le` *expression2*

Parameters

expression1,expression2   Numbers, strings, or variables.

Returns

Nothing.

Description

Operator (comparison); compares *expression1* to *expression2* and returns a value of `true` if *expression1* is less than or equal to *expression2*; otherwise, it returns a `false` value.

See also

`<=` (less than or equal to)

length

Availability

Flash Player 4. This function, along with all of the string functions, was deprecated in Flash 5. Macromedia recommends using the methods of the String class and the `String.length` property to perform the same operations.

Usage

`length(`*expression*`)`
`length(`*variable*`)`

Parameters

expression   A string.

variable   The name of a variable.

Returns

The length of the specified string or variable name.

Description

String function; returns the length of the specified string or variable name.

Example

The following example returns the value of the string `"Hello"`.

```
length("Hello");
```

The result is 5.

See also

`" "` (string delimiter), **String class**, `String.length`

_level

Availability

Flash Player 4.

Usage

`_level`*N*

Description

Identifier; a reference to the root Timeline of `_level`*N*. You must use `loadMovieNum()` to load SWF files into the Flash Player before you use the `_level` property to target them. You can also use `_level`*N* to target a loaded SWF file at the level assigned by *N*.

The initial SWF file loaded into an instance of the Flash Player is automatically loaded into `_level0`. The SWF file in `_level0` sets the frame rate, background color, and frame size for all subsequently loaded SWF files. SWF files are then stacked in higher-numbered levels above the SWF file in `_level0`.

You must assign a level to each SWF file that you load into the Flash Player using `loadMovieNum()`. You can assign levels in any order. If you assign a level that already contains a SWF file (including `_level0`), the SWF file at that level is unloaded and replaced by the new SWF file.

Example

The following example stops the playhead in the main Timeline of the SWF file in `_level9`.

```
_level9.stop();
```

The following example sends the playhead in the main Timeline of the SWF file in `_level4` to Frame 5. The SWF file in `_level4` must have previously been loaded with a `loadMovieNum()` action.

```
_level4.gotoAndStop(5);
```

See also

`loadMovie()`, `MovieClip.swapDepths()`

loadMovie()

Availability

Flash Player 3.

Usage

```
loadMovie("url",target [, method])
```

Parameters

url   The absolute or relative URL of the SWF file or JPEG file to be loaded. A relative path must be relative to the SWF file at level 0. Absolute URLs must include the protocol reference, such as http:// or file:///.

target   A path to a target movie clip. The target movie clip will be replaced by the loaded SWF file or image.

method   An optional parameter specifying an HTTP method for sending variables. The parameter must be the string GET or POST. If there are no variables to be sent, omit this parameter. The GET method appends the variables to the end of the URL, and is used for small numbers of variables. The POST method sends the variables in a separate HTTP header and is used for long strings of variables.

Returns

Nothing.

Description

Function; loads a SWF or JPEG file into Flash Player while the original SWF file is playing.

Tip: If you want to monitor the progress of the download, use MovieClipLoader.loadClip() instead of this function.

The loadMovie() function lets you display several SWF files at once and switch between SWF files without loading another HTML document. Without the loadMovie() function, Flash Player displays a single SWF file and then closes.

If you want to load a SWF or JPEG file into a specific level, use loadMovieNum() instead of loadMovie().

When a SWF file is loaded into a target movie clip, you can use the target path of that movie clip to target the loaded SWF file. A SWF file or image loaded into a target inherits the position, rotation, and scale properties of the targeted movie clip. The upper left corner of the loaded image or SWF file aligns with the registration point of the targeted movie clip. Alternatively, if the target is the _root Timeline, the upper left corner of the image or SWF file aligns with the upper left corner of the Stage.

Use unloadMovie() to remove SWF files that were loaded with loadMovie().

Example

The following `loadMovie()` statement is attached to a navigation button labeled Products. There is an invisible movie clip on the Stage with the instance name `dropZone`. The `loadMovie()` function uses this movie clip as the target parameter to load the products in the SWF file into the correct position on the Stage.

```
on(release) {
   loadMovie("products.swf",_root.dropZone);
}
```

The following example loads a JPEG image from the same directory as the SWF file that calls the `loadMovie()` function:

```
loadMovie("image45.jpeg", "ourMovieClip");
```

See also

`_level`, `loadMovieNum()`, MovieClipLoader.loadClip(), `unloadMovie()`

loadMovieNum()

Availability

Flash Player 4. Flash 4 files opened in Flash 5 or later are converted to use the correct syntax.

Usage

```
loadMovieNum("url",level [, variables])
```

Parameters

url   The absolute or relative URL of the SWF or JPEG file to be loaded. A relative path must be relative to the SWF file at level 0. For use in the stand-alone Flash Player or for testing in test-movie mode in the Flash authoring application, all SWF files must be stored in the same folder; and the filenames cannot include folder or disk drive specifications.

level   An integer specifying the level in Flash Player into which the SWF file will be loaded.

variables   An optional parameter specifying an HTTP method for sending variables. The parameter must be the string `GET` or `POST`. If there are no variables to be sent, omit this parameter. The `GET` method appends the variables to the end of the URL and is used for small numbers of variables. The `POST` method sends the variables in a separate HTTP header and is used for long strings of variables.

Returns

Nothing.

Description

Function; loads a SWF or JPEG file into a level in Flash Player while the originally loaded SWF file is playing.

Tip: If you want to monitor the progress of the download, use MovieClipLoader.loadClip() instead of this function.

Normally, Flash Player displays a single SWF file and then closes. The `loadMovieNum()` action lets you display several SWF files at once and switch between SWF files without loading another HTML document.

If you want to specify a target instead of a level, use loadMovie() instead of loadMovieNum().

Flash Player has a stacking order of levels starting with level 0. These levels are like layers of acetate; they are transparent except for the objects on each level. When you use loadMovieNum(), you must specify a level in Flash Player into which the SWF file will load. When a SWF file is loaded into a level, you can use the syntax, _levelN, where N is the level number, to target the SWF file.

When you load a SWF file, you can specify any level number and you can load SWF files into a level that already has a SWF file loaded into it. If you do, the new SWF file will replace the existing SWF file. If you load a SWF file into level 0, every level in Flash Player is unloaded, and level 0 is replaced with the new file. The SWF file in level 0 sets the frame rate, background color, and frame size for all other loaded SWF files.

The loadMovieNum() action also allows you to load JPEG files into a SWF file while it plays. For both images and SWF files, the upper left corner of the image aligns with the upper left corner of the Stage when the file loads. Also in both cases, the loaded file inherits rotation and scaling, and the original content is overwritten.

Use unloadMovieNum() to remove SWF files or images that were loaded with loadMovieNum().

Example

This example loads the JPEG image image45.jpg into level 2 of Flash Player.

```
loadMovieNum("http://www.blag.com/image45.jpg", 2);
```

See also

loadMovie(), unloadMovieNum(), _level

loadVariables()

Availability

Flash Player 4; behavior changed in Flash Player 7.

Usage

```
loadVariables ("url" , target [, variables])
```

Parameters

url An absolute or relative URL where the variables are located. If the SWF file issuing this call is running in a web browser, *url* must be in the same domain as the SWF file; for details, see "Description," below.

target The target path to a movie clip that receives the loaded variables.

variables An optional parameter specifying an HTTP method for sending variables. The parameter must be the string GET or POST. If there are no variables to be sent, omit this parameter. The GET method appends the variables to the end of the URL and is used for small numbers of variables. The POST method sends the variables in a separate HTTP header and is used for long strings of variables.

Returns

Nothing.

Description

Function; reads data from an external file, such as a text file or text generated by a CGI script, Active Server Pages (ASP), or PHP, or Perl script, and sets the values for variables in a target movie clip. This action can also be used to update variables in the active SWF file with new values.

The text at the specified URL must be in the standard MIME format *application/x-www-form-urlencoded* (a standard format used by CGI scripts). Any number of variables can be specified. For example, the following phrase defines several variables:

```
company=Macromedia&address=600+Townsend&city=San+Francisco&zip=94103
```

In SWF files running in a version of the player earlier than Flash Player 7, *url* must be in the same superdomain as the SWF file that is issuing this call. For example, a SWF file at www.someDomain.com can load variables from a SWF file at store.someDomain.com, because both files are in the same superdomain of someDomain.com.

In SWF files of any version running in Flash Player 7 or later, *url* must be in exactly the same domain (see "Flash Player security features" on page 392). For example, a SWF file at www.someDomain.com can load variables only from SWF files that are also at www.someDomain.com. If you want to load variables from a different domain, you can place a *cross-domain policy file* on the server hosting the SWF file that is being accessed. For more information, see "About allowing cross-domain data loading" on page 394.

If you want to load variables into a specific level, use loadVariablesNum() instead of loadVariables().

Example

This example loads information from a text file into text fields into the varTarget movie clip on the main Timeline. The variable names of the text fields must match the variable names in the data.txt file.

```
on(release) {
   loadVariables("data.txt", "_root.varTarget");
}
```

See also

loadVariablesNum(), loadMovie(), loadMovieNum(), getURL(), MovieClip.loadMovie(), MovieClip.loadVariables()

loadVariablesNum()

Availability

Flash Player 4. Flash 4 files opened in Flash 5 or later will be converted to use the correct syntax. Behavior changed in Flash Player 7.

Usage

```
loadVariablesNum ("url" ,level [, variables])
```

Parameters

url An absolute or relative URL where the variables are located. If the SWF file issuing this call is running in a web browser, *url* must be in the same domain as the SWF file; for details, see "Description," below.

level   An integer specifying the level in Flash Player to receive the variables.

variables   An optional parameter specifying an HTTP method for sending variables. The parameter must be the string GET or POST. If there are no variables to be sent, omit this parameter. The GET method appends the variables to the end of the URL, and is used for small numbers of variables. The POST method sends the variables in a separate HTTP header and is used for long strings of variables.

Returns

Nothing.

Description

Function; reads data from an external file, such as a text file or text generated by a CGI script, Active Server Pages (ASP), PHP, or Perl script, and sets the values for variables in a Flash Player level. You can also use this function to update variables in the active SWF file with new values.

The text at the specified URL must be in the standard MIME format *application/x-www-form-urlencoded* (a standard format used by CGI scripts). Any number of variables can be specified. For example, the following phrase defines several variables:

```
company=Macromedia&address=600+Townsend&city=San+Francisco&zip=94103
```

In SWF files running in a version of the player earlier than Flash Player 7, *url* must be in the same superdomain as the SWF file that is issuing this call. For example, a SWF file at www.someDomain.com can load variables from a SWF file at store.someDomain.com, because both files are in the same superdomain of someDomain.com.

In SWF files of any version running in Flash Player 7 or later, *url* must be in exactly the same domain (see "Flash Player security features" on page 392). For example, a SWF file at www.someDomain.com can load variables only from SWF files that are also at www.someDomain.com. If you want to load variables from a different domain, you can place a *cross-domain policy file* on the server hosting the SWF file that is being accessed. For more information, see "About allowing cross-domain data loading" on page 394.

If you want to load variables into a target MovieClip, use loadVariables() instead of loadVariablesNum().

Example

This example loads information from a text file into text fields in the main Timeline of the SWF at level 0 in Flash Player. The variable names of the text fields must match the variable names in the data.txt file.

```
on(release) {
   loadVariablesNum("data.txt", 0);
}
```

See also

getURL(), loadMovie(), loadMovieNum(), loadVariables(), MovieClip.loadMovie(), MovieClip.loadVariables()

LoadVars class

Availability

Flash Player 6.

Description

The LoadVars class is an alternative to the `loadVariables()` function for transferring variables between a Flash application and a server.

You can use the LoadVars class to obtain verification of successful data loading, progress indications, and stream data while it downloads. The LoadVars class works much like the XML class; it uses the methods `load()`, `send()`, and `sendAndLoad()` to communicate with a server. The main difference between the LoadVars class and the XML class is that LoadVars transfers ActionScript name and value pairs, rather than an XML DOM tree stored in the XML object.

The LoadVars class follows the same security restrictions as the XML class.

Method summary for the LoadVars class

Method	Description
`LoadVars.addRequestHeader()`	Adds or changes HTTP headers for `POST` operations.
`LoadVars.getBytesLoaded()`	Returns the number of bytes downloaded by `LoadVars.load()` or `LoadVars.sendAndLoad()`.
`LoadVars.getBytesTotal()`	Returns the total number of bytes that will be downloaded by a `load` or `sendAndLoad` method.
`LoadVars.load()`	Downloads variables from a specified URL.
`LoadVars.send()`	Posts variables from a LoadVars object to a URL.
`LoadVars.sendAndLoad()`	Posts variables from a LoadVars object to a URL and downloads the server's response to a target object.
`LoadVars.toString()`	Returns a URL-encoded string that contains all the enumerable variables in the LoadVars object.

Property summary for the LoadVars class

Property	Description
`LoadVars.contentType`	Indicates the MIME type of the data.
`LoadVars.loaded`	A Boolean value that indicates whether a `load` or `sendAndLoad` operation has completed.

Event handler summary for the LoadVars class

Event handler	Description
`LoadVars.onData`	Invoked when data has been completely downloaded from the server, or when an error occurs while data is downloading from a server.
`LoadVars.onLoad`	Invoked when a `load` or `sendAndLoad` operation has completed.

Constructor for the LoadVars class

Availability

Flash Player 6.

Usage

```
new LoadVars()
```

Parameters

None.

Returns

Nothing.

Description

Constructor; creates a LoadVars object. You can then use the methods of that LoadVars object to send and load data.

Example

The following example creates a LoadVars object called `my_lv`:

```
var my_lv = new LoadVars();
```

LoadVars.addRequestHeader()

Availability

Flash Player 6.

Usage

```
my_lv.addRequestHeader(headerName, headerValue)
my_lv.addRequestHeader(["headerName_1", "headerValue_1" ... "headerName_n",
    "headerValue_n"])
```

Parameters

headerName   An HTTP request header name.

headerValue   The value associated with *headerName*.

Returns

Nothing.

Description

Method; adds or changes HTTP request headers (such as `Content-Type` or `SOAPAction`) sent with `POST` actions. In the first usage, you pass two strings to the method: *headerName* and *headerValue*. In the second usage, you pass an array of strings, alternating header names and header values.

If multiple calls are made to set the same header name, each successive value will replace the value set in the previous call.

The following standard HTTP headers *cannot* be added or changed with this method: `Accept-Ranges`, `Age`, `Allow`, `Allowed`, `Connection`, `Content-Length`, `Content-Location`, `Content-Range`, `ETag`, `Host`, `Last-Modified`, `Locations`, `Max-Forwards`, `Proxy-Authenticate`, `Proxy-Authorization`, `Public`, `Range`, `Retry-After`, `Server`, `TE`, `Trailer`, `Transfer-Encoding`, `Upgrade`, `URI`, `Vary`, `Via`, `Warning`, and `WWW-Authenticate`.

Example

This example adds a custom HTTP header named `SOAPAction` with a value of `Foo` to the `my_lv` object.

```
my_lv.addRequestHeader("SOAPAction", "'Foo'");
```

This next example creates an array named `headers` that contains two alternating HTTP headers and their associated values. The array is passed as an argument to `addRequestHeader()`.

```
var headers = ["Content-Type", "text/plain", "X-ClientAppVersion", "2.0"];
my_lv.addRequestHeader(headers);
```

See also

`XML.addRequestHeader()`

LoadVars.contentType

Availability

Flash Player 6.

Usage

`my_lv.contentType`

Description

Property; the MIME type that is sent to the server when you call `LoadVars.send()` or `LoadVars.sendAndLoad()`. The default is `application/x-www-form-urlencoded`.

See also

`LoadVars.send()`, `LoadVars.sendAndLoad()`

LoadVars.getBytesLoaded()

Availability

Flash Player 6.

Usage

my_lv.getBytesLoaded()

Parameters

None.

Returns

An integer.

Description

Method; returns the number of bytes downloaded by LoadVars.load() or LoadVars.sendAndLoad(). This method returns undefined if no load operation is in progress, or if a load operation has not yet begun.

LoadVars.getBytesTotal()

Availability

Flash Player 6.

Usage

my_lv.getBytesTotal()

Parameters

None.

Returns

An integer.

Description

Method; returns the total number of bytes downloaded by LoadVars.load() or LoadVars.sendAndLoad(). This method returns undefined if no load operation is in progress or if a load operation has not yet begun. This method also returns undefined if the number of total bytes can't be determined; for example, if the download was initiated but the server did not transmit an HTTP content-length.

LoadVars.load()

Availability

Flash Player 6; behavior changed in Flash Player 7.

Usage

my_1v.load(*url*)

Parameters

url The URL from which to download the variables. If the SWF file issuing this call is running in a web browser, *url* must be in the same domain as the SWF file; for details, see "Description," below.

Returns

A string.

Description

Method; downloads variables from the specified URL, parses the variable data, and places the resulting variables into *my_1v*. Any properties in *my_1v* with the same names as downloaded variables are overwritten. Any properties in *my_1v* with different names than downloaded variables are not deleted. This is an asynchronous action.

The downloaded data must be in the MIME content type *application/x-www-form-urlencoded*. This is the same format used by loadVariables().

In SWF files running in a version of the player earlier than Flash Player 7, *url* must be in the same superdomain as the SWF file that is issuing this call. For example, a SWF file at www.someDomain.com can load variables from a SWF file at store.someDomain.com, because both files are in the same superdomain of someDomain.com.

In SWF files of any version running in Flash Player 7 or later, *url* must be in exactly the same domain (see "Flash Player security features" on page 392). For example, a SWF file at www.someDomain.com can load variables only from SWF files that are also at www.someDomain.com. If you want to load variables from a different domain, you can place a *cross-domain policy file* on the server hosting the SWF file that is being accessed. For more information, see "About allowing cross-domain data loading" on page 394.

Also, in files published for Flash Player 7, case sensitivity (see "Case sensitivity" on page 233) is supported for external variables loaded with LoadVars.load().

This method is similar to XML.load().

LoadVars.loaded

Availability

Flash Player 6.

Usage

`my_lv.loaded`

Description

Property; undefined by default. When a `LoadVars.load()` or `LoadVars.sendAndLoad()` operation is started, the `loaded` property is set to `false`; when the operation completes, the `loaded` property is set to `true`. If the operation has not yet completed or has failed with an error, the `loaded` property remains set to `false`.

This property is similar to the `XML.loaded` property.

LoadVars.onData

Availability

Flash Player 6.

Usage

```
my_lv.onData = function(src) {
    // your statements here
}
```

Parameters

`src`   The raw (unparsed) data from a `LoadVars.load()` or `LoadVars.sendAndLoad()` method call.

Returns

Nothing.

Description

Event handler; invoked when data has been completely downloaded from the server, or when an error occurs while data is downloading from a server. This handler is invoked before the data is parsed and therefore can be used to call a custom parsing routine instead of the one built in to Flash Player. The value of the `src` parameter passed to the function assigned to `LoadVars.onData` can either be `undefined`, or a string that contains the URL-encoded name-value pairs downloaded from the server. If the returned value is `undefined`, an error occurred while downloading the data from the server.

The default implementation of `LoadVars.onData` invokes `LoadVars.onLoad`. You can override this default implementation by assigning a custom function to `LoadVars.onData`, but LoadVars.onLoad will no longer be called unless you call it in your implementation of `LoadVars.onData`.

LoadVars.onLoad

Availability

Flash Player 6.

Usage

```
my_lv.onLoad = function(success) {
    // your statements here
}
```

Parameters

success   The parameter indicates whether the load operation ended in success (true) or failure (false).

Returns

A Boolean value.

Description

Event handler; invoked when a LoadVars.load() or LoadVars.sendAndLoad() operation has ended. If the operation was successful, *my_lv* is populated with variables downloaded by the operation, and these variables are available when this handler is invoked.

This handler is undefined by default.

This method is similar to XML.onLoad().

LoadVars.send()

Availability

Flash Player 6.

Usage

`my_lv.send(url [,target, method])`

Parameters

url   The URL to upload variables to.

target   The browser frame window in which any response will be displayed.

method   The GET or POST method of the HTTP protocol.

Returns

A string.

Description

Method; sends the variables in the *my_lv* object to the specified URL. All enumerable variables in *my_lv* are concatenated into a string in the *application/x-www-form-urlencoded* format by default, and the string is posted to the URL using the HTTP POST method. This is the same format used by the loadVariables() action. The MIME content type sent in the HTTP request headers is the value of my_lv.contentType, or the default *application/x-www-form-urlencoded*. The POST method is used unless GET is specified.

If the *target* parameter is specified, the server's response is displayed in the browser frame window named target. If the *target* parameter is omitted, the server's response is discarded.

This method is similar to XML.send().

LoadVars.sendAndLoad()

Availability

Flash Player 6; behavior changed in Flash Player 7.

Usage

`my_lv.sendAndLoad(url, targetObject[, method])`

Parameters

url   The URL to upload variables to. If the SWF file issuing this call is running in a web browser, *url* must be in the same domain as the SWF file; for details, see "Description," below.

targetObject   The LoadVars object that receives the downloaded variables.

method   The GET or POST method of the HTTP protocol.

Returns

A string.

Description

Method; posts variables in the *my_lv* object to the specified URL. The server response is downloaded, parsed as variable data, and the resulting variables are placed in the *targetObject* object.

Variables are posted in the same manner as `LoadVars.send()`. Variables are downloaded into *targetObject* in the same manner as `LoadVars.load()`.

In SWF files running in a version of the player earlier than Flash Player 7, *url* must be in the same superdomain as the SWF file that is issuing this call. For example, a SWF file at www.someDomain.com can load variables from a SWF file at store.someDomain.com, because both files are in the same superdomain of someDomain.com.

In SWF files of any version running in Flash Player 7 or later, *url* must be in exactly the same domain (see "Flash Player security features" on page 392). For example, a SWF file at www.someDomain.com can load variables only from SWF files that are also at www.someDomain.com. If you want to load variables from a different domain, you can place a *cross-domain policy file* on the server hosting the SWF file that is being accessed. For more information, see "About allowing cross-domain data loading" on page 394.

This method is similar to `XML.sendAndLoad()`.

LoadVars.toString()

Availability

Flash Player 6.

Usage

my_lv.toString()

Parameters

None.

Returns

A string.

Description

Method; returns a string containing all enumerable variables in *my_lv*, in the MIME content encoding *application/x-www-form-urlencoded*.

Example

```
var myVars = new LoadVars();
myVars.name = "Gary";
myVars.age = 26;
trace (myVars.toString());
//would output
//name=Gary&age=26
```

LocalConnection class

Availability

Flash Player 6.

Description

The LocalConnection class lets you develop SWF files that can send instructions to each other without the use of `fscommand()` or JavaScript. LocalConnection objects can communicate only between SWF files that are running on the same client machine, but they can be running in two different applications—for example, a SWF file running in a browser and a SWF file running in a projector. You can use LocalConnection objects to send and receive data within a single SWF file, but this is not a standard implementation; all the examples in this section illustrate communication between different SWF files.

The primary methods used to send and receive data are `LocalConnection.send()` and `LocalConnection.connect()`. At its most basic, your code will implement the following commands; notice that both the `LocalConnection.send()` and `LocalConnection.connect()` commands specify the same connection name, `lc_name`:

```
// Code in the receiving movie
receiving_lc = new LocalConnection();
receiving_lc.methodToExecute = function(param1, param2)
{
  // Code to be executed
}
receiving_lc.connect("lc_name");
// Code in the sending movie
sending_lc = new LocalConnection();
sending_lc.send("lc_name", "methodToExecute", dataItem1, dataItem2)
```

The simplest way to use a LocalConnection object is to allow communication only between LocalConnection objects located in the same domain, since you won't have to address issues related to security. However, if you need to allow communication between domains, you have a number of ways to implement security measures. For more information, see the discussion of the *connectionName* parameter in `LocalConnection.send()`, and also the `LocalConnection.allowDomain` and `LocalConnection.domain()` entries.

Method summary for the LocalConnection class

Method	Description
LocalConnection.close()	Closes (disconnects) the LocalConnection object.
LocalConnection.connect()	Prepares the LocalConnection object to receive commands from a `LocalConnection.send()` command.
LocalConnection.domain()	Returns a string representing the superdomain of the location of the current SWF file.
LocalConnection.send()	Invokes a method on a specified LocalConnection object.

Event handler summary for the LocalConnection class

Event handler	Description
LocalConnection.allowDomain	Invoked whenever the current (receiving) LocalConnection object receives a request to invoke a method from a sending LocalConnection object.
LocalConnection.allowInsecureDomain	Invoked whenever the current (receiving) LocalConnection object, which is in a SWF file hosted at a domain using a secure protocol (HTTPS), receives a request to invoke a method from a sending LocalConnection object that is in a SWF file that is hosted at a nonsecure protocol.
LocalConnection.onStatus	Invoked after a sending LocalConnection object tries to send a command to a receiving LocalConnection object.

Constructor for the LocalConnection class

Availability

Flash Player 6.

Usage

```
new LocalConnection()
```

Parameters

None.

Returns

Nothing.

Description

Constructor; creates a LocalConnection object.

Example

The following example shows how receiving and sending SWF files create LocalConnnection objects. Notice that the two SWF files can use the same name or different names for their respective LocalConnection objects. In this example, they use the same name—my_lc.

```
// Code in the receiving SWF
my_lc = new LocalConnection();
my_lc.someMethod = function() {
   // Your statements here
}
my_lc.connect("connectionName");

// Code in the sending SWF
my_lc = new LocalConnection();
my_lc.send("connectionName", "someMethod");
```

See also

LocalConnection.connect(), LocalConnection.send()

LocalConnection.allowDomain

Availability

Flash Player 6; behavior changed in Flash Player 7.

Usage

```
receiving_lc.allowDomain = function([sendingDomain]) {
   // Your statements here return true or false
}
```

Parameters

sendingDomain   An optional parameter specifying the domain of the SWF file containing the sending LocalConnection object.

Returns

Nothing.

Description

Event handler; invoked whenever *receiving_lc* receives a request to invoke a method from a sending LocalConnection object. Flash expects the code you implement in this handler to return a Boolean value of true or false. If the handler doesn't return true, the request from the sending object is ignored, and the method is not invoked.

Use this command to explicitly permit LocalConnection objects from specified domains, or from any domain, to execute methods of the receiving LocalConnection object. If you don't declare the *sendingDomain* parameter, you probably want to accept commands from any domain, and the code in your handler would be simply return true. If you do declare *sendingDomain*, you probably want to compare the value of *sendingDomain* with domains from which you want to accept commands. The following examples illustrate both of these implementations.

In files running in Flash Player 6, the *sendingDomain* parameter contains the superdomain of the caller. In files running in Flash Player 7 or later, the *sendingDomain* parameter contains the exact domain of the caller. In the latter case, to allow access by SWF files hosted at either www.domain.com or store.domain.com, you must explicitly allow access from both domains.

```
// For Flash Player 6
receiving_lc.allowDomain = function(sendingDomain) {
   return(sendingDomain=="domain.com");
}
// Corresponding commands to allow access by SWF files
// that are running in Flash Player 7 or later
receiving_lc.allowDomain = function(sendingDomain) {
   return(sendingDomain=="www.domain.com" ||
     sendingDomain=="store.domain.com");
}
```

Also, for files running in Flash Player 7 or later, you can't use this method to allow SWF files hosted using a secure protocol (HTTPS) to permit access from SWF files hosted in nonsecure protocols; you must use the LocalConnection.allowInsecureDomain event handler instead.

Example

The following example shows how a LocalConnection object in a receiving SWF file can permit SWF files from any domain to invoke its methods. Compare this to the example in LocalConnection.connect(), in which only SWF files from the same domain can invoke the Trace method in the receiving SWF file. For a discussion of the use of the underscore (_) in the connection name, see LocalConnection.send().

```
var aLocalConnection = new LocalConnection();
aLocalConnection.Trace = function(aString)
{
   aTextField = aTextField + aString + newline;
}

aLocalConnection.allowDomain = function() {
   // Any domain can invoke methods on this LocalConnection object
   return true;
}

aLocalConnection.connect("_trace");
```

In the following example, the receiving SWF file accepts commands only from SWF files located in thisDomain.com or thatDomain.com.

```
var aLocalConnection = new LocalConnection();
aLocalConnection.Trace = function(aString)
{
   aTextField = aTextField + aString + newline;
}

aLocalConnection.allowDomain = function(sendingDomain)
{
   return(sendingDomain=="thisDomain.com" || sendingDomain=="thatDomain.com");
}

aLocalConnection.connect("_trace");
```

See also

LocalConnection.connect(), LocalConnection.domain(), LocalConnection.send()

LocalConnection.allowInsecureDomain

Availability

Flash Player 7.

Usage

```
receiving_lc.allowInsecureDomain = function([sendingDomain]) {
   // Your statements here return true or false
}
```

Parameters

sendingDomain An optional parameter specifying the domain of the SWF file containing the sending LocalConnection object.

Returns

Nothing.

Description

Event handler; invoked whenever *receiving_lc*, which is in a SWF file hosted at a domain using a secure protocol (HTTPS), receives a request to invoke a method from a sending LocalConnection object that is in a SWF file that is hosted at a nonsecure protocol. Flash expects the code you implement in this handler to return a Boolean value of `true` or `false`. If the handler doesn't return `true`, the request from the sending object is ignored, and the method is not invoked.

By default, SWF files hosted using the HTTPS protocol can be accessed only by other SWF files hosted using the HTTPS protocol. This implementation maintains the integrity provided by the HTTPS protocol.

Using this method to override the default behavior is not recommended, as it compromises HTTPS security. However, you may need to do so, for example, if you need to permit access to HTTPS files published for Flash Player 7 or later from HTTP files published for Flash Player 6.

A SWF file published for Flash Player 6 can use the `LocalConnection.allowDomain` event handler to permit HTTP to HTTPS access. However, because security is implemented differently in Flash Player 7, you must use the `LocalConnection.allowInsecureDomain()` method to permit such access in SWF files published for Flash Player 7 or later.

See also

`LocalConnection.allowDomain`, `LocalConnection.connect()`

LocalConnection.close()

Availability

Flash Player 6.

Usage

receiving_lc.close

Parameters

None.

Returns

Nothing.

Description

Method; closes (disconnects) a LocalConnection object. Issue this command when you no longer want the object to accept commands—for example, when you want to issue a `LocalConnection.connect()` command using the same *connectionName* parameter in another SWF file.

See also

`LocalConnection.connect()`

LocalConnection.connect()

Availability

Flash Player 6.

Usage

```
receiving_lc.connect(connectionName)
```

Parameters

connectionName   A string that corresponds to the connection name specified in the `LocalConnection.send()` command that wants to communicate with *receiving_lc*.

Returns

A Boolean value of `true` if no other process running on the same client machine has already issued this command using the same value for the *connectionName* parameter, `false` otherwise.

Description

Method; prepares a LocalConnection object to receive commands from a `LocalConnection.send()` command (called the "sending LocalConnection object"). The object used with this command is called the "receiving LocalConnection object." The receiving and sending objects must be running on the same client machine.

Be sure to define the methods attached to *receiving_lc* before calling this method, as shown in all the examples in this section.

By default, the Flash Player resolves *connectionName* into a value of "*superdomain*:connectionName", where *superdomain* is the superdomain of the SWF file containing the `LocalConnection.connect()` command. For example, if the SWF file containing the receiving LocalConnection object is located at www.someDomain.com, *connectionName* resolves to "`someDomain.com:connectionName`". (If a SWF file is located on the client machine, the value assigned to `superdomain` is "`localhost`".)

Also by default, the Flash Player lets the receiving LocalConnection object accept commands only from sending LocalConnection objects whose connection name also resolves into a value of "*superdomain*:connectionName". In this way, Flash makes it very simple for SWF files located in the same domain to communicate with each other.

If you are implementing communication only between SWF files in the same domain, specify a string for *connectionName* that does not begin with an underscore (_) and that does not specify a domain name (for example, "`myDomain:connectionName`"). Use the same string in the `LocalConnection.connect(connectionName)` command.

If you are implementing communication between SWF files located in different domains, see the discussion of *connectionName* in `LocalConnection.send()`, and also the `LocalConnection.allowDomain` and `LocalConnection.domain()` entries.

Example

The following example shows how a SWF file in a particular domain can invoke a method named Trace in a receiving SWF file in the same domain. The receiving SWF file functions as a trace window for the sending SWF file; it contains two methods that other SWF files can call— Trace and Clear. Buttons pressed in the sending SWF files call these methods with specified parameters.

```
// Receiving SWF
var aLocalConnection = new LocalConnection();
aLocalConnection.Trace = function(aString)
{
    aTextField = aTextField + aString + newline;
}
aLocalConnection.Clear = function()
{
    aTextField = "";
}
aLocalConnection.connect("trace");
stop();
```

SWF 1 contains the following code attached to a button labeled PushMe. When you push the button, you see the sentence "The button was pushed." in the receiving SWF file.

```
on (press)
{
    var lc = new LocalConnection();
    lc.send("trace", "Trace", "The button was pushed.");
    delete lc;
}
```

SWF 2 contains an input text box with a var name of myText, and the following code attached to a button labeled Copy. When you type some text and then push the button, you see the text you typed in the receiving SWF file.

```
on (press)
{
    _parent.lc.send("trace", "Trace", _parent.myText);
    _parent.myText = "";
}
```

SWF 3 contains the following code attached to a button labeled Clear. When you push the button, the contents of the trace window in the receiving SWF file are cleared (erased).

```
on (press)
{
    var lc = new LocalConnection();
    lc.send("trace", "Clear");
    delete lc;
}
```

See also

LocalConnection.send()

LocalConnection.domain()

Availability

Flash Player 6; behavior changed in Flash Player 7.

Usage

```
my_lc.domain()
```

Parameters

None.

Returns

A string representing the domain of the location of the current SWF file; for details, see "Description," below.

Description

Method; returns a string representing the domain of the location of the current SWF file.

In SWF files published for Flash Player 6, the returned string is the superdomain of the current SWF file. For example, if the SWF file is located at www.macromedia.com, this command returns `"macromedia.com"`.

In SWF files published for Flash Player 7 or later, the returned string is the exact domain of the current SWF file. For example, if the SWF file is located at www.macromedia.com, this command returns `"www.macromedia.com"`.

If the current SWF file is a local file residing on the client machine, this command returns `"localhost"`.

The most common way to use this command is to include the domain name of the sending LocalConnection object as a parameter to the method you plan to invoke in the receiving LocalConnection object, or in conjunction with `LocalConnection.allowDomain` to accept commands from a specified domain. If you are enabling communication only between LocalConnection objects that are located in the same domain, you probably don't need to use this command.

Example

In the following example, a receiving SWF file accepts commands only from SWF files located in the same domain or at macromedia.com.

```
my_lc = new LocalConnection();
my_lc.allowDomain = function(sendingDomain)
{
    return (sendingDomain==this.domain() || sendingDomain=="macromedia.com");
}
```

In the following example, a sending SWF file located at yourdomain.com invokes a method in a receiving SWF file located at mydomain.com. The sending SWF file includes its domain name as a parameter to the method it invokes, so the receiving SWF file can return a reply value to a LocalConnection object in the correct domain. The sending SWF file also specifies that it will accept commands only from SWF files at mydomain.com.

Line numbers are included for reference purposes. The sequence of events is as follows:

- The receiving SWF file prepares to receive commands on a connection named "sum" (line 11). The Flash Player resolves the name of this connection to "mydomain.com:sum" (see LocalConnection.connect()).

- The sending SWF file prepares to receive a reply on the LocalConnection object named "result" (line 58). It also specifies that it will accept commands only from SWF files at mydomain.com (lines 51 to 53).

- The sending SWF file invokes the aSum method of a connection named "mydomain.com:sum" (line 59), and passes the following parameters: its domain (lc.domain()), the name of the connection to receive the reply ("result"), and the values to be used by aSum (123 and 456).

- The aSum method (line 6) is invoked with the following values: sender = "mydomain.com:result", replyMethod = "aResult", n1 = 123, and n2 = 456. It therefore executes the following line of code:

  ```
  this.send("mydomain.com:result", "aResult", (123 + 456));
  ```

- The aResult method (line 54) displays the value returned by aSum (579).

  ```
  // The receiving SWF at http://www.mydomain.com/folder/movie.swf
  // contains the following code

  1    var aLocalConnection = new LocalConnection();
  2    aLocalConnection.allowDomain = function()
  3    {
       // Allow connections from any domain
  4      return true;
  5    }
  6    aLocalConnection.aSum = function(sender, replyMethod, n1, n2)
  7    {
  8      this.send(sender, replyMethod, (n1 + n2));
  9    }
  10
  11   aLocalConnection.connect("sum");

  // The sending SWF at http://www.yourdomain.com/folder/movie.swf
  // contains the following code

  50   var lc = new LocalConnection();
  51   lc.allowDomain = function(aDomain) {
       // Allow connections only from mydomain.com
  52     return (aDomain == "mydomain.com");
  53   }
  54   lc.aResult = function(aParam) {
  55     trace("The sum is " + aParam);
  56   }
  57
  58   lc.connect("result");
  59   lc.send("mydomain.com:sum", "aSum", lc.domain() + ':' + "result",
         "aResult", 123, 456);
  ```

See also

LocalConnection.allowDomain

LocalConnection.onStatus

Availability

Flash Player 6.

Usage

```
sending_lc.onStatus = function(infoObject) {
   // your statements here
}
```

Parameters

infoObject   A parameter defined according to the status message. For details about this parameter, see "Description," below.

Returns

Nothing.

Description

Event handler; invoked after a sending LocalConnection object tries to send a command to a receiving LocalConnection object. If you want to respond to this event handler, you must create a function to process the information object sent by the LocalConnection object.

If the information object returned by this event handler contains a `level` value of `"Status"`, Flash successfully sent the command to a receiving LocalConnection object. This does not mean that Flash successfully invoked the specified method of the receiving LocalConnection object, only that Flash was able to send the command. For example, the method is not invoked if the receiving LocalConnection object doesn't allow connections from the sending domain, or if the method does not exist. The only way to know for sure if the method was invoked is to have the receiving object send a reply to the sending object.

If the information object returned by this event handler contains a `level` value of `"Error"`, Flash was unable to send the command to a receiving LocalConnection object, most likely because there is no receiving LocalConnection object connected whose name corresponds to the name specified in the *sending_lc*.send() command that invoked this handler.

In addition to this `onStatus` handler, Flash also provides a "super" function called System.onStatus. If `onStatus` is invoked for a particular object and there is no function assigned to respond to it, Flash processes a function assigned to `System.onStatus` if it exists.

In most cases, you will implement this handler only to respond to error conditions, as shown in the following example.

Example

The following example displays information about a failed connection in the Output panel:

```
sending_lc = new LocalConnection();
sending_lc.onStatus = function(infoObject)
{
   if (infoObject.level == "Error")
   {
      trace("Connection failed.");
   }
}
sending_lc.send("receiving_lc", "methodName");
```

See also

LocalConnection.send(), System.onStatus

LocalConnection.send()

Availability

Flash Player 6.

Usage

```
sending_lc.send (connectionName, method [, p1,...,pN])
```

Parameters

connectionName   A string that corresponds to the connection name specified in the LocalConnection.connect() command that wants to communicate with *sending_lc*.

method   A string specifying the name of the method to be invoked in the receiving LocalConnection object. The following method names cause the command to fail: send, connect, close, domain, onStatus, and allowDomain.

p1,...pN   Optional parameters to be passed to the specified method.

Returns

A Boolean value of true if Flash can carry out the request, false otherwise.

Note: A return value of true does not necessarily mean that Flash successfully connected to a receiving LocalConnection object, only that the command is syntactically correct. To determine whether the connection succeeded, see LocalConnection.onStatus.

Description

Method; invokes the method named *method* on a connection opened with the LocalConnection.connect(*connectionName*) command (called the "receiving LocalConnection object"). The object used with this command is called the "sending LocalConnection object". The SWF files that contain the sending and receiving objects must be running on the same client machine.

There is a limit to the amount of data you can pass as parameters to this command. If the command returns false but your syntax is correct, try breaking up the LocalConnection.send() requests into multiple commands.

As discussed in the entry LocalConnection.connect(), Flash adds the current superdomain to *connectionName* by default. If you are implementing communication between different domains, you need to define *connectionName* in both the sending and receiving LocalConnection objects in such a way that Flash does not add the current superdomain to *connectionName*. There are two ways you can do so:

- Use an underscore (_) at the beginning of *connectionName* in both the sending and receiving LocalConnection objects. In the SWF file containing the receiving object, use LocalConnection.allowDomain to specify that connections from any domain will be accepted. This implementation lets you store your sending and receiving SWF files in any domain.

- Include the superdomain in *connectionName* in the sending LocalConnection object—for example, myDomain.com:myConnectionName. In the receiving object, use LocalConnection.allowDomain to specify that connections from the specified superdomain will be accepted (in this case, myDomain.com), or that connections from any domain will be accepted.

Note: You cannot specify a superdomain in *connectionName* in the receiving LocalConnection object, only in the sending LocalConnection object.

Example

For an example of communicating between LocalConnection objects located in the same domain, see LocalConnection.connect(). For an example of communicating between LocalConnection objects located in any domain, see LocalConnection.allowDomain. For an example of communicating between LocalConnection objects located in specified domains, see LocalConnection.allowDomain and LocalConnection.domain().

See also

LocalConnection.allowDomain, LocalConnection.connect(), LocalConnection.domain(), LocalConnection.onStatus

lt (less than – string specific)

Availability

Flash Player 4. This operator was deprecated in Flash 5 in favor of the new < (less than) operator.

Usage

expression1 lt *expression2*

Parameters

expression1, *expression2* Numbers, strings, or variables.

Description

Operator (comparison); compares *expression1* to *expression2* and returns true if *expression1* is less than *expression2*; otherwise, it returns false.

See also

< (less than)

Math class

Availability

Flash Player 5. In Flash Player 4, the methods and properties of the Math class are emulated using approximations and may not be as accurate as the non-emulated math functions supported by Flash Player 5.

Description

The Math class is a top-level class whose methods and properties you can use without using a constructor.

Use the methods and properties of this class to access and manipulate mathematical constants and functions. All of the properties and methods of the Math class are static, and must be called using the syntax `Math.method(parameter)` or `Math.constant`. In ActionScript, constants are defined with the maximum precision of double-precision IEEE-754 floating-point numbers.

Several of the Math class methods take the radian of an angle as an parameter. You can use the equation below to calculate radian values, or simply pass the equation (entering a value for degrees) for the radian parameter.

To calculate a radian value, use this formula:

```
radian = Math.PI/180 * degree
```

The following is an example of passing the equation as an parameter to calculate the sine of a 45-degree angle:

`Math.SIN(Math.PI/180 * 45)` is the same as `Math.SIN(.7854)`

The Math class is fully supported in Flash Player 5. In Flash Player 4, you can use methods of the Math class, but they are emulated using approximations and may not be as accurate as the non-emulated math functions supported by Flash Player 5.

Method summary for the Math class

Method	Description
Math.abs()	Computes an absolute value.
Math.acos()	Computes an arc cosine.
Math.asin()	Computes an arc sine.
Math.atan()	Computes an arc tangent.
Math.atan2()	Computes an angle from the x-axis to the point.
Math.ceil()	Rounds a number up to the nearest integer.
Math.cos()	Computes a cosine.
Math.exp()	Computes an exponential value.
Math.floor()	Rounds a number down to the nearest integer.
Math.log()	Computes a natural logarithm.
Math.max()	Returns the larger of the two integers.
Math.min()	Returns the smaller of the two integers.
Math.pow()	Computes x raised to the power of the y.
Math.random()	Returns a pseudo-random number between 0.0 and 1.0.
Math.round()	Rounds to the nearest integer.
Math.sin()	Computes a sine.
Math.sqrt()	Computes a square root.
Math.tan()	Computes a tangent.

Property summary for the Math class

All of the properties for the Math class are constants.

Property	Description
Math.E	Euler's constant and the base of natural logarithms (approximately 2.718).
Math.LN2	The natural logarithm of 2 (approximately 0.693).
Math.LOG2E	The base 2 logarithm of e (approximately 1.442).
Math.LN2	The natural logarithm of 10 (approximately 2.302).
Math.LOG10E	The base 10 logarithm of e (approximately 0.434).
Math.PI	The ratio of the circumference of a circle to its diameter (approximately 3.14159).
Math.SQRT1_2	The reciprocal of the square root of 1/2 (approximately 0.707).
Math.SQRT2	The square root of 2 (approximately 1.414).

Math.abs()

Availability

Flash Player 5. In Flash Player 4, the methods and properties of the Math class are emulated using approximations and may not be as accurate as the non-emulated math functions supported by Flash Player 5.

Usage

```
Math.abs(x)
```

Parameters

x   A number.

Returns

A number.

Description

Method; computes and returns an absolute value for the number specified by the parameter *x*.

Math.acos()

Availability

Flash Player 5. In Flash Player 4, the methods and properties of the Math class are emulated using approximations and may not be as accurate as the non-emulated math functions supported by Flash Player 5.

Usage

```
Math.acos(x)
```

Parameters

x   A number from -1.0 to 1.0.

Returns

Nothing.

Description

Method; computes and returns the arc cosine of the number specified in the parameter x, in radians.

Math.asin()

Availability

Flash Player 5. In Flash Player 4, the methods and properties of the Math class are emulated using approximations and may not be as accurate as the non-emulated math functions supported by Flash Player 5.

Usage

```
Math.asin(x);
```

Parameters

x A number from -1.0 to 1.0.

Returns

A number.

Description

Method; computes and returns the arc sine for the number specified in the parameter x, in radians.

Math.atan()

Availability

Flash Player 5. In Flash Player 4, the methods and properties of the Math class are emulated using approximations and may not be as accurate as the non-emulated math functions supported by Flash Player 5.

Usage

```
Math.atan(x)
```

Parameters

x A number.

Returns

A number.

Description

Method; computes and returns the arc tangent for the number specified in the parameter x. The return value is between negative pi divided by 2, and positive pi divided by 2.

Math.atan2()

Availability

Flash Player 5. In Flash Player 4, the methods and properties of the Math class are emulated using approximations and may not be as accurate as the non-emulated math functions supported by Flash Player 5.

Usage

```
Math.atan2(y, x)
```

Parameters

x   A number specifying the *x* coordinate of the point.

y   A number specifying the *y* coordinate of the point.

Returns

A number.

Description

Method; computes and returns the arc tangent of *y* / *x* in radians. The return value represents the angle opposite the opposite angle of a right triangle, where *x* is the adjacent side length and *y* is the opposite side length.

Math.ceil()

Availability

Flash Player 5. In Flash Player 4, the methods and properties of the Math class are emulated using approximations and may not be as accurate as the non-emulated math functions supported by Flash Player 5.

Usage

```
Math.ceil(x)
```

Parameters

x   A number or expression.

Returns

A number.

Description

Method; returns the ceiling of the specified number or expression. The ceiling of a number is the closest integer that is greater than or equal to the number.

Math.cos()

Availability

Flash Player 5. In Flash Player 4, the methods and properties of the Math class are emulated using approximations and may not be as accurate as the non-emulated math functions supported by Flash Player 5.

Usage

`Math.cos(x)`

Parameters

x   An angle measured in radians.

Returns

A number.

Description

Method; returns the cosine (a value from -1.0 to 1.0) of the angle specified by the parameter *x*. The angle *x* must be specified in radians. Use the information outlined in the Math class entry to calculate a radian.

Math.E

Availability

Flash Player 5. In Flash Player 4, the methods and properties of the Math class are emulated using approximations and may not be as accurate as the non-emulated math functions supported by Flash Player 5.

Usage

`Math.E`

Parameters

None.

Returns

Nothing.

Description

Constant; a mathematical constant for the base of natural logarithms, expressed as *e*. The approximate value of *e* is 2.71828.

Math.exp()

Flash Player 5. In Flash Player 4, the methods and properties of the Math class are emulated using approximations and may not be as accurate as the non-emulated math functions supported by Flash Player 5.

Usage

```
Math.exp(x)
```

Parameters

x   The exponent; a number or expression.

Returns

A number.

Description

Method; returns the value of the base of the natural logarithm (*e*), to the power of the exponent specified in the parameter *x*. The constant `Math.E` can provide the value of *e*.

Math.floor()

Availability

Flash Player 5. In Flash Player 4, the methods and properties of the Math class are emulated using approximations and may not be as accurate as the non-emulated math functions supported by Flash Player 5.

Usage

```
Math.floor(x)
```

Parameters

x   A number or expression.

Returns

A number.

Description

Method; returns the floor of the number or expression specified in the parameter *x*. The floor is the closest integer that is less than or equal to the specified number or expression.

Example

The following code returns a value of 12:

```
Math.floor(12.5);
```

Math.log()

Availability

Flash Player 5. In Flash Player 4, the methods and properties of the Math class are emulated using approximations and may not be as accurate as the non-emulated math functions supported by Flash Player 5.

Usage

```
Math.log(x)
```

Parameters

x   A number or expression with a value greater than 0.

Returns

A number.

Description

Method; returns the logarithm of parameter *x*.

Math.LN2

Availability

Flash Player 5. In Flash Player 4, the methods and properties of the Math class are emulated using approximations and may not be as accurate as the non-emulated math functions supported by Flash Player 5.

Usage

```
Math.LN2
```

Parameters

None.

Returns

Nothing.

Description

Constant; a mathematical constant for the natural logarithm of 2, expressed as $\log_e 2$, with an approximate value of 0.69314718055994528623.

Math.LN10

Availability

Flash Player 5. In Flash Player 4, the methods and properties of the Math class are emulated using approximations and may not be as accurate as the non-emulated math functions supported by Flash Player 5.

Usage

```
Math.LN10
```

Parameters

None.

Returns

Nothing.

Description

Constant; a mathematical constant for the natural logarithm of 10, expressed as $\log_e 10$, with an approximate value of 2.30258509299404590011.

Math.LOG2E

Availability

Flash Player 5. In Flash Player 4, the methods and properties of the Math class are emulated using approximations and may not be as accurate as the non-emulated math functions supported by Flash Player 5.

Usage

```
Math.LOG2E
```

Parameters

None.

Returns

Nothing.

Description

Constant; a mathematical constant for the base-2 logarithm of the constant e (Math.E), expressed as $\log 2_e$, with an approximate value of 1.442695040888963387.

Math.LOG10E

Availability

Flash Player 5. In Flash Player 4, the methods and properties of the Math class are emulated using approximations and may not be as accurate as the non-emulated math functions supported by Flash Player 5.

Usage

```
Math.LOG10E
```

Parameters

None.

Returns

Nothing.

Description

Constant; a mathematical constant for the base-10 logarithm of the constant e (Math.E), expressed as $\log_{10}e$, with an approximate value of 0.43429448190325181667.

Math.max()

Availability

Flash Player 5. In Flash Player 4, the methods and properties of the Math class are emulated using approximations and may not be as accurate as the non-emulated math functions supported by Flash Player 5.

Usage

```
Math.max(x , y)
```

Parameters

x A number or expression.

y A number or expression.

Returns

A number.

Description

Method; evaluates x and y and returns the larger value.

Math.min()

Availability

Flash Player 5. In Flash Player 4, the methods and properties of the Math class are emulated using approximations and may not be as accurate as the non-emulated math functions supported by Flash Player 5.

Usage

```
Math.min(x , y)
```

Parameters

x   A number or expression.

y   A number or expression.

Returns

A number.

Description

Method; evaluates *x* and *y* and returns the smaller value.

Math.PI

Availability

Flash Player 5. In Flash Player 4, the methods and properties of the Math class are emulated using approximations and may not be as accurate as the non-emulated math functions supported by Flash Player 5.

Usage

```
Math.PI
```

Parameters

None.

Returns

Nothing.

Description

Constant; a mathematical constant for the ratio of the circumference of a circle to its diameter, expressed as pi, with a value of 3.14159265358979.

Math.pow()

Availability

Flash Player 5. In Flash Player 4, the methods and properties of the Math class are emulated using approximations and may not be as accurate as the non-emulated math functions supported by Flash Player 5.

Usage

```
Math.pow(x , y)
```

Parameters

x A number to be raised to a power.

y A number specifying a power the parameter *x* is raised to.

Returns

A number.

Description

Method; computes and returns *x* to the power of *y*: xy.

Math.random()

Availability

Flash Player 5. In Flash Player 4, the methods and properties of the Math class are emulated using approximations and may not be as accurate as the non-emulated math functions supported by Flash Player 5.

Usage

```
Math.random()
```

Parameters

None.

Returns

A number.

Description

Method; returns n, where 0 <= n < 1.

See also

```
random
```

Math.round()

Availability

Flash Player 5. In Flash Player 4, the methods and properties of the Math class are emulated using approximations and may not be as accurate as the non-emulated math functions supported by Flash Player 5.

Usage

```
Math.round(x)
```

Parameters

x   A number.

Returns

A number.

Description

Method; rounds the value of the parameter *x* up or down to the nearest integer and returns the value.

Math.sin()

Availability

Flash Player 5. In Flash Player 4, the methods and properties of the Math class are emulated using approximations and may not be as accurate as the non-emulated math functions supported by Flash Player 5.

Usage

```
Math.sin(x)
```

Parameters

x   An angle measured in radians.

Returns

Number; the sine of the specified angle (between -1.0 and 1.0).

Description

Method; computes and returns the sine of the specified angle in radians. Use the information outlined in the Math class entry to calculate a radian.

Math.sqrt()

Availability

Flash Player 5. In Flash Player 4, the methods and properties of the Math class are emulated using approximations and may not be as accurate as the non-emulated math functions supported by Flash Player 5.

Usage

```
Math.sqrt(x)
```

Parameters

x A number or expression greater than or equal to 0.

Returns

A number.

Description

Method; computes and returns the square root of the specified number.

Math.SQRT1_2

Availability

Flash Player 5. In Flash Player 4, the methods and properties of the Math class are emulated using approximations and may not be as accurate as the non-emulated math functions supported by Flash Player 5.

Usage

```
Math.SQRT1_2
```

Parameters

None.

Returns

Nothing.

Description

Constant; a mathematical constant for the square root of one-half.

Math.SQRT2

Availability

Flash Player 5. In Flash Player 4, the methods and properties of the Math class are emulated using approximations and may not be as accurate as the non-emulated math functions supported by Flash Player 5.

Usage

```
Math.SQRT2
```

Parameters

None.

Returns

Nothing.

Description

Constant; a mathematical constant for the square root of 2, with an approximate value of 1.414213562373.

Math.tan()

Availability

Flash Player 5. In Flash Player 4, the methods and properties of the Math class are emulated using approximations and may not be as accurate as the non-emulated math functions supported by Flash Player 5.

Usage

`Math.tan(x)`

Parameters

x   An angle measured in radians.

Returns

A number.

Description

Method; computes and returns the tangent of the specified angle. To calculate a radian, use the information outlined in the introduction to the Math class.

maxscroll

Availability

Flash Player 4. This function has been deprecated in favor of the `TextField.maxscroll` property.

Usage

`variable_name.maxscroll`

Description

Property (read-only); a deprecated property that indicates the line number of the topmost visible line of text in a text field when the bottommost line in the field is also visible. The `maxscroll` property works with the `scroll` property to control the display of information in a text field. This property can be retrieved, but not modified.

See also

`TextField.maxscroll`, `TextField.scroll`

mbchr

Availability

Flash Player 4. This function has been deprecated in favor of the `String.fromCharCode()` method.

Usage

`mbchr(number)`

Parameters

number   The number to convert to a multibyte character.

Returns

A string.

Description

String function; converts an ASCII code number to a multibyte character.

See also

`String.fromCharCode()`

mblength

Availability

Flash Player 4. This function has been deprecated in favor of the String class.

Usage

`mblength(string)`

Parameters

string   A string.

Returns

A number.

Description

String function; returns the length of the multibyte character string.

mbord

Availability

Flash Player 4. This function was deprecated in Flash 5 in favor of `String.charCodeAt()`.

Usage

`mbord(character)`

Parameters

character   The character to convert to a multibyte number.

Returns

A number.

Description

String function; converts the specified character to a multibyte number.

See also

`String.fromCharCode()`

mbsubstring

Availability

Flash Player 4. This function was deprecated in Flash 5 in favor of `String.substr()`.

Usage

```
mbsubstring(value, index, count)
```

Parameters

value   The multibyte string from which to extract a new multibyte string.

index   The number of the first character to extract.

count   The number of characters to include in the extracted string, not including the index character.

Returns

A string.

Description

String function; extracts a new multibyte character string from a multibyte character string.

See also

```
String.substr()
```

Microphone class

Availability

Flash Player 6.

Description

The Microphone class lets you capture audio from a microphone attached to the computer that is running Flash Player.

The Microphone class is primarily for use with Flash Communication Server, but can be used in a limited fashion without the server—for example, to transmit sound from your microphone through the speakers on your local system.

To create or reference a Microphone object, use the `Microphone.get()` method.

Method summary for the Microphone class

Method	Description
`Microphone.get()`	Returns a default or specified Microphone object, or `null` if the microphone is not available.
`Microphone.setGain()`	Specifies the amount by which the microphone should boost the signal.
`Microphone.setRate()`	Specifies the rate at which the microphone should capture sound, in kHz.

Method	Description
Microphone.setSilenceLevel()	Specifies the amount of sound required to activate the microphone.
Microphone.setUseEchoSuppression()	Specifies whether to use the echo suppression feature of the audio codec.

Property summary for the Microphone class

Property (read-only)	Description
Microphone.activityLevel	The amount of sound the microphone is detecting.
Microphone.gain	The amount by which the microphone boosts the signal before transmitting it.
Microphone.index	The index of the current microphone.
Microphone.muted	A Boolean value that specifies whether the user has allowed or denied access to the microphone.
Microphone.name	The name of the current sound capture device, as returned by the sound capture hardware.
Microphone.names	Class property: an array of strings reflecting the names of all available sound capture devices, including sound cards and microphones.
Microphone.rate	The sound capture rate, in kHz.
Microphone.silenceLevel()	The amount of sound required to activate the microphone.
Microphone.silenceTimeout()	The number of milliseconds between the time the microphone stops detecting sound and the time Microphone.onActivity(false) is called.
Microphone.useEchoSuppression()	A Boolean value that specifies whether echo suppression is being used.

Event handler summary for the Microphone class

Event handler	Description
Microphone.onActivity	Invoked when the microphone starts or stops detecting sound.
Microphone.onStatus	Invoked when the user allows or denies access to the microphone.

Constructor for the Microphone class

See Microphone.get().

Microphone.activityLevel

Availability

Flash Player 6.

Usage

activeMicrophone.activityLevel

Description

Read-only property; a numeric value that specifies the amount of sound the microphone is detecting. Values range from 0 (no sound is being detected) to 100 (very loud sound is being detected). The value of this property can help you determine a good value to pass to Microphone.setSilenceLevel() method.

If the microphone is available but is not yet being used because Microphone.get() has not been called, this property is set to -1.

Example

The following example sets the variable level to the activity level of the current microphone, myMic.activityLevel.

```
var level = myMic.activityLevel;
```

See also

Microphone.setGain()

Microphone.gain

Availability

Flash Player 6.

Usage

activeMicrophone.gain

Description

Read-only property; the amount by which the microphone boosts the signal. Valid values are 0 to 100. The default value is 50.

Example

The following example is attached to the nib of a slide bar. When this clip is loaded, Flash checks for the value myMic.gain and provides a default value if this value is undefined. The _x position is then used to set the gain on the microphone to the user's preference.

```
onClipEvent (load) {
  if (_root.myMic.gain == undefined) {
    _root.myMic.setGain = 75;
  }

  this._x = _root.myMic.gain;
  _root.txt_micgain = this._x;

  left = this._x;
  right = left+50;
```

```
      top = this._y;
      bottom = top;
  }

  on (press) {
      startDrag(this, false, left, top, right, bottom);
      this._xscale = 100;
      this._yscale = 100;
  }

  on (release, releaseOutside) {
      stopDrag();
      g = (this._x-50)*2;
      _root.myMic.setGain(g);
      _root.txt_micgain = g;
      this._xscale = 100;
      this._yscale = 100;
  }
```

See also

Microphone.setGain()

Microphone.get()

Availability

Flash Player 6.

Usage

Microphone.get([*index*])

Note: The correct syntax is Microphone.get(). To assign the Microphone object to a variable, use syntax like active_mic = Microphone.get().

Parameters

index   An optional zero-based integer that specifies which microphone to get, as determined from the array that Microphone.names contains. To get the default microphone (which is recommended for most applications), omit this parameter.

Returns

- If *index* is not specified, this method returns a reference to the default microphone or, if it is not available, to the first available microphone. If no microphones are available or installed, the method returns null.

- If *index* is specified, this method returns a reference to the requested microphone, or null if it is not available.

Description

Method; returns a reference to a Microphone object for capturing audio. To actually begin capturing the audio, you must attach the Microphone object to a MovieClip object (see MovieClip.attachAudio()).

Unlike objects that you create using the new constructor, multiple calls to Microphone.get() reference the same microphone. Thus, if your script contains the lines mic1 = Microphone.get() and mic2 = Microphone.get(), both mic1 and mic2 reference the same (default) microphone.

In general, you shouldn't pass a value for *index*; simply use the `Microphone.get()` method to return a reference to the default microphone. By means of the Microphone settings panel (discussed later in this section), the user can specify the default microphone Flash should use. If you pass a value for *index*, you might be trying to reference a microphone other than the one the user prefers. You might use *index* in rare cases—for example, if your application is capturing audio from two microphones at the same time.

When a SWF file tries to access the microphone returned by the `Microphone.get()` method— for example, when you issue `MovieClip.attachAudio()`— Flash Player displays a Privacy dialog box that lets the user choose whether to allow or deny access to the microphone. (Make sure your Stage size is at least 215 x 138 pixels; this is the minimum size Flash requires to display the dialog box.)

When the user responds to this dialog box, the `Microphone.onStatus` event handler returns an information object that indicates the user's response. To determine whether the user has denied or allowed access to the camera without processing this event handler, use `Microphone.muted`.

The user can also specify permanent privacy settings for a particular domain by right-clicking (Windows) or Control-clicking (Macintosh) while a SWF file is playing, choosing Settings, opening the Privacy panel, and selecting Remember.

If `Microphone.get()` returns `null`, either the microphone is in use by another application, or there are no microphones installed on the system. To determine whether any microphones are installed, use `Microphones.names.length`. To display the Flash Player Microphone Settings panel, which lets the user choose the microphone to be referenced by `Microphone.get()`, use `System.showSettings(2)`.

Example

The following example lets the user specify the default microphone, then captures audio and plays it back locally. To avoid feedback, you may want to test this code while wearing headphones.

```
System.showSettings(2);
myMic = Microphone.get();
_root.attachAudio(myMic);
```

See also

Microphone.index, Microphone.muted, Microphone.names, Microphone.onStatus, MovieClip.attachAudio()

Microphone.index

Availability

Flash Player 6.

Usage

activeMicrophone.index

Description

Read-only property; a zero-based integer that specifies the index of the microphone, as reflected in the array returned by Microphone.names.

See also

Microphone.get(), Microphone.names

Microphone.muted

Availability

Flash Player 6.

Usage

activeMicrophone.muted

Description

Read-only property; a Boolean value that specifies whether the user has denied access to the microphone (true) or allowed access (false). When this value changes, Microphone.onStatus is invoked. For more information, see Microphone.get().

Example

In the following example, when the user clicks the button, Flash publishes and plays a live stream if the microphone is not muted.

```
on (press)
{
   // If the user mutes microphone, display offline notice.
   // Else, publish and play live stream from microphone.
   if(myMic.muted) {
      _root.debugWindow+="Microphone offline." + newline;
   } else {
```

```
    // Publish the microphone data by calling
    // the root function pubLive().
    _root.pubLive();

    // Play what is being published by calling
    // the root function playLive().
    _root.playLive();
  }
}
```

See also

Microphone.get( ), Microphone.onStatus

Microphone.name

Availability

Flash Player 6.

Usage

activeMicrophone.name

Description

Read-only property; a string that specifies the name of the current sound capture device, as returned by the sound capture hardware.

Example

The following example displays the name of the default microphone in the Output panel.

```
myMic = Microphone.get( );
trace("The microphone name is: " + myMic.name);
```

See also

Microphone.get( ), Microphone.names

Microphone.names

Availability

Flash Player 6.

Usage

Microphone.names

Note: The correct syntax is Microphone.names. To assign the return value to a variable, use syntax like *mic_array* = Microphone.names. To determine the name of the current microphone, use *activeMicrophone*.name.

Description

Read-only class property; retrieves an array of strings reflecting the names of all available sound capture devices without displaying the Flash Player Privacy Settings panel. This array behaves the same as any other ActionScript array, implicitly providing the zero-based index of each sound capture device and the number of sound capture devices on the system (by means of Microphone.names.length). For more information, see the Array class entry.

Calling `Microphone.names` requires an extensive examination of the hardware, and it may take several seconds to build the array. In most cases, you can just use the default microphone.

Example

The following code returns information on the array of audio devices.

```
allMicNames_array = Microphone.names;
_root.debugWindow += "Microphone.names located these device(s):" + newline;
for(i=0; i < allMicNames_array.length; i++){
   debugWindow += "[" + i + "]: " + allMicNames[i] + newline;
}
```

For example, the following information could be displayed.

```
Microphone.names located these device(s):
[0]: Crystal SoundFusion(tm)
[1]: USB Audio Device
```

See also

Array class, `Microphone.name`

Microphone.onActivity

Availability

Flash Player 6.

Usage

```
activeMicrophone.onActivity = function(activity) {
   // your statements here
}
```

Parameters

activity   A Boolean value set to `true` when the microphone starts detecting sound, `false` when it stops.

Returns

Nothing.

Description

Event handler; invoked when the microphone starts or stops detecting sound. If you want to respond to this event handler, you must create a function to process its *activity* value.

To specify the amount of sound required to invoke `Microphone.onActivity(true)`, and the amount of time that must elapse without sound before `Microphone.onActivity(false)` is invoked, use `Microphone.setSilenceLevel()`.

Example

The following example displays `true` or `false` in the Output panel when the microphone starts or stops detecting sound.

```
m = Microphone.get();
_root.attachAudio(m);
m.onActivity = function(mode)
{
```

```
    trace(mode);
};
```

See also

`Microphone.onActivity, Microphone.setSilenceLevel()`

Microphone.onStatus

Availability

Flash Player 6.

Usage

```
activeMicrophone.onStatus = function(infoObject) {
    // your statements here
}
```

Parameters

infoObject   A parameter defined according to the status message.

Returns

Nothing.

Description

Event handler; invoked when the user allows or denies access to the microphone. If you want to respond to this event handler, you must create a function to process the information object generated by the microphone.

When a SWF file tries to access the microphone, Flash Player displays a Privacy dialog box that lets the user choose whether to allow or deny access.

- If the user allows access, the `Microphone.muted` property is set to `false`, and this event handler is invoked with an information object whose `code` property is `"Microphone.Unmuted"` and whose `level` property is `"Status"`.

- If the user denies access, the `Microphone.muted` property is set to `true`, and this event handler is invoked with an information object whose `code` property is `"Microphone.Muted"` and whose `level` property is `"Status"`.

To determine whether the user has denied or allowed access to the microphone without processing this event handler, use `Microphone.muted`.

Note: If the user chooses to permanently allow or deny access for all SWF files from a specified domain, this method is not invoked for SWF files from that domain unless the user later changes the privacy setting. For more information, see `Microphone.get()`.

Example

See the example for `Camera.onStatus`.

See also

`Microphone.get(), Microphone.muted`

Microphone.rate

Availability

Flash Player 6.

Usage

activeMicrophone.rate

Description

Read-only property; the rate at which the microphone is capturing sound, in kHz. The default value is 8 kHz if your sound capture device supports this value. Otherwise, the default value is the next available capture level above 8 kHz that your sound capture device supports, usually 11 kHz.

To set this value, use Microphone.setRate().

Example

The following example saves the current rate to the variable original.

original = myMic.rate;

See also

Microphone.setRate()

Microphone.setGain()

Availability

Flash Player 6.

Usage

activeMicrophone.setGain(*gain*)

Parameters

gain An integer that specifies the amount by which the microphone should boost the signal. Valid values are 0 to 100. The default value is 50; however, the user may change this value in the Flash Player Microphone Settings panel.

Returns

Nothing.

Description

Method; sets the microphone gain—that is, the amount by which the microphone should multiply the signal before transmitting it. A value of 0 tells Flash to multiply by 0; that is, the microphone transmits no sound.

You can think of this setting like a volume knob on a stereo: 0 is no volume and 50 is normal volume; numbers below 50 specify lower than normal volume, while numbers above 50 specify higher than normal volume.

Example

The following example ensures that the microphone gain setting is less than or equal to 55.

```
var myMic = Microphone.get();
if (myMic.gain > 55){
  myMic.setGain(55);
}
```

See also

Microphone.gain, Microphone.setUseEchoSuppression()

Microphone.setRate()

Availability

Flash Player 6.

Usage

activeMicrophone.setRate(*kHz*)

Parameters

kHz   The rate at which the microphone should capture sound, in kHz. Acceptable values are 5, 8, 11, 22, and 44. The default value is 8 kHz if your sound capture device supports this value. Otherwise, the default value is the next available capture level above 8 kHz that your sound capture device supports, usually 11 kHz.

Returns

Nothing.

Description

Method; sets the rate, in kHz, at which the microphone should capture sound.

Example

The following example sets the microphone rate to the user's preference (which you have assigned to the userRate variable) if it is one of the following values: 5, 8, 11, 22, or 44. If it is not, the value is rounded to the nearest acceptable value that the sound capture device supports.

myMic.setRate(userRate);

See also

Microphone.rate

Microphone.setSilenceLevel()

Availability

Flash Player 6.

Usage

activeMicrophone.setSilenceLevel(*level* [, *timeout*])

Parameters

level   An integer that specifies the amount of sound required to activate the microphone and invoke Microphone.onActivity(true). Acceptable values range from 0 to 100. The default value is 10.

timeout   An optional integer parameter that specifies how many milliseconds must elapse without activity before Flash considers sound to have stopped and invokes Microphone.onActivity(false). The default value is 2000 (2 seconds).

Returns

Nothing.

Description

Method; sets the minimum input level that should be considered sound and (optionally) the amount of silent time signifying that silence has actually begun.

- To prevent the microphone from detecting sound at all, pass a value of 100 for *level*; Microphone.onActivity is never invoked.

- To determine the amount of sound the microphone is currently detecting, use Microphone.activityLevel.

Activity detection is the ability to detect when audio levels suggest that a person is talking. When someone is not talking, bandwidth can be saved because there is no need to send the associated audio stream. This information can also be used for visual feedback so that users know they (or others) are silent.

Silence values correspond directly to activity values. Complete silence is an activity value of 0. Constant loud noise (as loud as can be registered based on the current gain setting) is an activity value of 100. After gain is appropriately adjusted, your activity value is less than your silence value when you're not talking; when you are talking, the activity value exceeds your silence value.

This method is similar in purpose to Camera.setMotionLevel(); both methods are used to specify when the onActivity event handler should be invoked. However, these methods have a significantly different impact on publishing streams:

- Camera.setMotionLevel() is designed to detect motion and does not affect bandwidth usage. Even if a video stream does not detect motion, video is still sent.

- Microphone.setSilenceLevel() is designed to optimize bandwidth. When an audio stream is considered silent, no audio data is sent. Instead, a single message is sent, indicating that silence has started.

Example

The following example changes the silence level based on the user's input. The button has the following code attached:

```
on (press)
{
    this.makeSilenceLevel(this.silenceLevel);
}
```

The `makeSilenceLevel()` function called by the button continues:

```
function makeSilenceLevel(s)
{
    this.obj.setSilenceLevel(s);
    this.SyncMode();
    this.silenceLevel= s;
}
```

For more information, see the example for `Camera.setMotionLevel()`.

See also

`Microphone.activityLevel`, `Microphone.onActivity`, `Microphone.setGain()`, `Microphone.silenceLevel()`, `Microphone.silenceTimeout()`

Microphone.setUseEchoSuppression()

Availability

Flash Player 6.

Usage

activeMicrophone.setUseEchoSuppression(*suppress*)

Parameters

suppress   A Boolean value indicating whether echo suppression should be used (`true`) or not (`false`).

Returns

Nothing.

Description

Method; specifies whether to use the echo suppression feature of the audio codec. The default value is `false` unless the user has selected Reduce Echo in the Flash Player Microphone Settings panel.

Echo suppression is an effort to reduce the effects of audio feedback, which is caused when sound going out the speaker is picked up by the microphone on the same computer. (This is different from echo cancellation, which completely removes the feedback.)

Generally, echo suppression is advisable when the sound being captured is played through speakers—instead of a headset—on the same computer. If your SWF file allows users to specify the sound output device, you may want to call `Microphone.setUseEchoSuppression(true)` if they indicate they are using speakers and will be using the microphone as well.

Users can also adjust these settings in the Flash Player Microphone Settings panel.

Example

The following example turns on echo suppression.

```
my_mic.setUseEchoSuppression(true);
```

See also

```
Microphone.setGain(), Microphone.useEchoSuppression()
```

Microphone.silenceLevel()

Availability

Flash Player 6.

Usage

activeMicrophone.silenceLevel

Description

Read-only property; an integer that specifies the amount of sound required to activate the microphone and invoke Microphone.onActivity(true). The default value is 10.

Example

See the example for Microphone.silenceTimeout().

See also

```
Microphone.gain, Microphone.setSilenceLevel()
```

Microphone.silenceTimeout()

Availability

Flash Player 6.

Usage

activeMicrophone.silenceTimeout

Description

Read-only property; a numeric value representing the number of milliseconds between the time the microphone stops detecting sound and the time Microphone.onActivity(false) is invoked. The default value is 2000 (2 seconds).

To set this value, use Microphone.setSilenceLevel().

Example

The following example sets the timeout to two times its current value.

```
myMic.setSilenceLevel(myMic.silenceLevel, myMic.silenceTimeOut * 2);
```

See also

```
Microphone.setSilenceLevel()
```

Microphone.useEchoSuppression()

Availability

Flash Player 6.

Usage

activeMicrophone.useEchoSuppression

Description

Read-only property; a Boolean value of true if echo suppression is enabled, false otherwise. The default value is false unless the user has selected Reduce Echo in the Flash Player Microphone Settings panel.

Example

The following example checks for echo suppression and turns it on if it is off.

```
_root.myMic.onActivity = function(active) {
  if (active == true) {
    if (_root.myMic.useEchoSuppression == false) {
      _root.myMic.setUseEchoSuppression(true);
    }
  }
}
```

See also

Microphone.setUseEchoSuppression()

MMExecute()

Availability

Flash Player 7.

Usage

MMExecute("*Flash JavaScript API command;*")

Parameters

Flash JavaScript API command Any command that you can use in a Flash JavaScript (JSFL) file.

Returns

The result, if any, sent by the JavaScript statement.

Description

Function; lets you issue Flash JavaScript API commands from ActionScript.

The Flash JavaScript API (JSAPI) provides several objects, methods, and properties to duplicate or emulate commands that a user can enter in the authoring environment. Using the JSAPI, you can write scripts that extend Flash in several ways: adding commands to menus, manipulating objects on the Stage, repeating sequences of commands, and so on.

In general, a user runs a JSAPI script by selecting Commands > Run Command. However, you can use this function in an ActionScript script to call a JSAPI command directly. If you use MMExecute() in a script on Frame 1 of your file, the command executes when the SWF file is loaded.

For more information on the JSAPI, see www.macromedia.com/go/jsapi_info_en.

Example

The following command returns an array of objects in the library:

```
var libe:Array = MMExecute("fl.getDocumentDOM().library.items;");
trace(libe.length + " items in library");
```

Mouse class

Availability

Flash Player 5.

Description

The Mouse class is a top-level class whose properties and methods you can access without using a constructor. You can use the methods of the Mouse class to hide and show the mouse pointer (cursor) in the SWF file. The mouse pointer is visible by default, but you can hide it and implement a custom pointer that you create using a movie clip (see "Creating a custom mouse pointer" on page 298).

Method summary for the Mouse class

Method	Description
Mouse.addListener()	Registers an object to receive onMouseDown, onMouseMove, and onMouseUp notification.
Mouse.hide()	Hides the mouse pointer in the SWF file.
Mouse.removeListener()	Removes an object that was registered with addListener().
Mouse.show()	Displays the mouse pointer in the SWF file.

Listener summary for the Mouse class

Method	Description
Mouse.onMouseDown	Notified when the mouse button is pressed down.
Mouse.onMouseMove	Notified when the mouse button is moved.
Mouse.onMouseUp	Notified when the mouse button is released.
Mouse.onMouseWheel	Notified when the user rolls the mouse wheel.

Mouse.addListener()

Availability

Flash Player 6.

Usage

`Mouse.addListener (`*`newListener`*`)`

Parameters

`newListener`   An object.

Returns

Nothing.

Description

Method; registers an object to receive notifications of the `onMouseDown`, `onMouseMove`, and `onMouseUp` listeners.

The *`newListener`* parameter should contain an object with defined methods for the `onMouseDown`, `onMouseMove`, and `onMouseUp` listeners.

When the mouse is pressed, moved, or released, regardless of the input focus, all listening objects that are registered with this method have their `onMouseDown`, `onMouseMove`, or `onMouseUp` method invoked. Multiple objects can listen for mouse notifications. If the listener *`newListener`* is already registered, no change occurs.

See also

`Mouse.onMouseDown`, `Mouse.onMouseMove`, `Mouse.onMouseUp`

Mouse.hide()

Availability

Flash Player 5.

Usage

`Mouse.hide()`

Parameters

None.

Returns

A Boolean value: `true` if the pointer is visible, and `false` if the pointer is invisible.

Description

Method; hides the pointer in a SWF file. The pointer is visible by default.

Example

The following code, attached to a movie clip on the main Timeline, hides the standard pointer, and sets the *x* and *y* positions of the customPointer_mc movie clip instance to the *x* and *y* mouse positions in the main Timeline.

```
onClipEvent(enterFrame){
  Mouse.hide();
  customPointer_mc._x = _root._xmouse;
  customPointer_mc._y = _root._ymouse;
}
```

See also

Mouse.show(), MovieClip._xmouse, MovieClip._ymouse

Mouse.onMouseDown

Availability

Flash Player 6.

Usage

someListener.onMouseDown

Parameters

None.

Returns

Nothing.

Description

Listener; notified when the mouse is pressed. To use the onMouseDown listener, you must create a listener object. You can then define a function for onMouseDown and use addListener() to register the listener with the Mouse object, as in the following code:

```
someListener = new Object();
someListener.onMouseDown = function () { ... };
Mouse.addListener(someListener);
```

Listeners enable different pieces of code to cooperate because multiple listeners can receive notification about a single event.

See also

Mouse.addListener()

Mouse.onMouseMove

Availability

Flash Player 6.

Usage

someListener.onMouseMove

Parameters

None.

Returns

Nothing.

Description

Listener; notified when the mouse moves. To use the onMouseMove listener, you must create a listener object. You can then define a function for onMouseMove and use addListener() to register the listener with the Mouse object, as in the following code:

```
someListener = new Object();
someListener.onMouseMove = function () { ... };
Mouse.addListener(someListener);
```

Listeners enable different pieces of code to cooperate because multiple listeners can receive notification about a single event.

See also

Mouse.addListener()

Mouse.onMouseUp

Availability

Flash Player 6.

Usage

someListener.onMouseUp

Parameters

None.

Returns

Nothing.

Description

Listener; notified when the mouse is released. To use the onMouseUp listener, you must create a listener object. You can then define a function for onMouseUp and use addListener() to register the listener with the Mouse object, as in the following code:

```
someListener = new Object();
someListener.onMouseUp = function () { ... };
Mouse.addListener(someListener);
```

Listeners enable different pieces of code to cooperate because multiple listeners can receive notification about a single event.

See also

```
Mouse.addListener()
```

Mouse.onMouseWheel

Availability

Flash Player 7 (Windows only).

Usage

```
someListener.onMouseWheel = function ( [ delta , scrollTarget ]) {
    // your statements here
}
```

Parameters

delta   An optional number indicating how many lines should be scrolled for each notch the user rolls the mouse wheel. A positive *delta* value indicates an upward scroll; a negative value indicates a downward scroll. Typical values are from 1 to 3, whereas faster scrolling may produce larger values.

If you don't want to specify a value for *delta* but want to specify a value for *scrollTarget*, pass null for *delta*.

scrollTarget   The topmost movie clip instance under the mouse when the mouse wheel was scrolled.

Returns

Nothing.

Description

Listener; notified when the user rolls the mouse wheel. To use the onMouseWheel listener, you must create a listener object. You can then define a function for onMouseWheel and use addListener() to register the listener with the Mouse object.

Note: Mouse wheel event listeners are available only on Windows versions of Flash Player.

Example

The following example shows how to create a listener object that responds to mouse wheel events. In this example, the *x* coordinate of a movie clip object named clip_mc (not shown) is changed each time the user rolls the mouse wheel.

```
mouseListener = new Object();
mouseListener.onMouseWheel = function(delta) {
    clip_mc._x += delta;
}
Mouse.addListener(mouseListener);
```

See also

```
Mouse.addListener(), TextField.mouseWheelEnabled
```

Mouse.removeListener()

Availability

Flash Player 6.

Usage

```
Mouse.removeListener (listener)
```

Parameters

listener   An object.

Returns

If the *listener* object was successfully removed, the method returns true; if the *listener* was not successfully removed (for example, if the *listener* was not on the Mouse object's listener list), the method returns false.

Description

Method; removes an object that was previously registered with addListener().

Mouse.show()

Availability

Flash Player 5.

Usage

```
Mouse.show()
```

Parameters

None.

Returns

Nothing.

Description

Method; displays the mouse pointer in a SWF file. The pointer is visible by default.

See also

```
Mouse.show(), MovieClip._xmouse, MovieClip._ymouse
```

MovieClip class

Availability

Flash Player 3.

Description

The methods for the MovieClip class provide the same functionality as actions that target movie clips. There are also additional methods that do not have equivalent actions in the Actions toolbox in the Actions panel.

You do not need to use a constructor method to call the methods of the MovieClip class; instead, you reference movie clip instances by name, using the following syntax:

```
my_mc.play();
my_mc.gotoAndPlay(3);
```

Method summary for the MovieClip class

Method	Description
MovieClip.attachAudio()	Captures and plays local audio from the microphone hardware.
MovieClip.attachMovie()	Attaches a SWF file in the library.
MovieClip.createEmptyMovieClip()	Creates an empty movie clip.
MovieClip.createTextField()	Creates an empty text field.
MovieClip.duplicateMovieClip()	Duplicates the specified movie clip.
MovieClip.getBounds()	Returns the minimum and maximum x and y coordinates of a SWF file in a specified coordinate space.
MovieClip.getBytesLoaded()	Returns the number of bytes loaded for the specified movie clip.
MovieClip.getBytesTotal()	Returns the size of the movie clip, in bytes.
MovieClip.getDepth()	Returns the depth of a movie clip.
MovieClip.getInstanceAtDepth()	Specifies whether a particular depth is already occupied by a movie clip.
MovieClip.getNextHighestDepth()	Specifies a depth value that you can pass to other methods to to ensure that Flash renders the movie clip in front of all other objects in the current movie clip.
MovieClip.getSWFVersion()	Returns an integer that indicates the Flash Player version for which the movie clip was published
MovieClip.getTextSnapshot()	Returns a TextSnapshot object that contains the text in the static text fields in the specified movie clip.
MovieClip.getURL()	Retrieves a document from a URL.
MovieClip.globalToLocal()	Converts the point object from Stage coordinates to the local coordinates of the specified movie clip.
MovieClip.gotoAndPlay()	Sends the playhead to a specific frame in the movie clip and plays the SWF file.
MovieClip.gotoAndStop()	Sends the playhead to a specific frame in the movie clip and stops the SWF file.

Method	Description
MovieClip.hitTest()	Returns true if bounding box of the specified movie clip intersects the bounding box of the target movie clip.
MovieClip.loadMovie()	Loads the specified SWF file into the movie clip.
MovieClip.loadVariables()	Loads variables from a URL or other location into the movie clip.
MovieClip.localToGlobal()	Converts a point object from the local coordinates of the movie clip to the global Stage coordinates.
MovieClip.nextFrame()	Sends the playhead to the next frame of the movie clip.
MovieClip.play()	Plays the specified movie clip.
MovieClip.prevFrame()	Sends the playhead to the previous frame of the movie clip.
MovieClip.removeMovieClip()	Removes the movie clip from the Timeline if it was created with duplicateMovieClip(), MovieClip.duplicateMovieClip(), or MovieClip.attachMovie().
MovieClip.setMask()	Specifies a movie clip as a mask for another movie clip.
MovieClip.startDrag()	Specifies a movie clip as draggable and begins dragging the movie clip.
MovieClip.stop()	Stops the currently playing SWF file.
MovieClip.stopDrag()	Stops the dragging of any movie clip that is being dragged.
MovieClip.swapDepths()	Swaps the depth level of two SWF files.
MovieClip.unloadMovie()	Removes a SWF file that was loaded with loadMovie().

Drawing method summary for the MovieClip class

Method	Description
MovieClip.beginFill()	Begins drawing a fill on the Stage.
MovieClip.beginGradientFill()	Begins drawing a gradient fill on the Stage.
MovieClip.clear()	Removes all the drawing commands associated with a movie clip instance.
MovieClip.curveTo()	Draws a curve using the latest line style.
MovieClip.endFill()	Ends the fill specified by beginFill() or beginGradientFill().
MovieClip.lineStyle()	Defines the stroke of lines created with the lineTo() and curveTo() methods.
MovieClip.lineTo()	Draws a line using the current line style.
MovieClip.moveTo()	Moves the current drawing position to specified coordinates.

Property summary for the MovieClip class

Property	Description
MovieClip._alpha	The transparency value of a movie clip instance.
MovieClip._currentframe	The frame number in which the playhead is currently located.
MovieClip._droptarget	The absolute path in slash syntax notation of the movie clip instance on which a draggable movie clip was dropped.
MovieClip.enabled	Indicates whether a button movie clip is enabled.
MovieClip.focusEnabled	Enables a movie clip to receive focus.
MovieClip._focusrect	Indicates whether a focused movie clip has a yellow rectangle around it.
MovieClip._framesloaded	The number of frames that have been loaded from a streaming SWF file.
MovieClip._height	The height of a movie clip instance, in pixels.
MovieClip.hitArea	Designates another movie clip to serve as the hit area for a button movie clip.
MovieClip._highquality	Sets the rendering quality of a SWF file.
MovieClip.menu	Associates a ContextMenu object with a movie clip.
MovieClip._name	The instance name of a movie clip instance.
MovieClip._parent	A reference to the movie clip that encloses the movie clip.
MovieClip._rotation	The degree of rotation of a movie clip instance.
MovieClip._soundbuftime	The number of seconds before a sound starts to stream.
MovieClip.tabChildren	Indicates whether the children of a movie clip are included in automatic tab ordering.

Property	Description
MovieClip.tabEnabled	Indicates whether a movie clip is included in tab ordering.
MovieClip.tabIndex	Indicates the tab order of an object.
MovieClip._target	The target path of a movie clip instance.
MovieClip._totalframes	The total number of frames in a movie clip instance.
MovieClip.trackAsMenu	Indicates whether other buttons can receive mouse release events.
MovieClip._url	The URL of the SWF file from which a movie clip was downloaded.
MovieClip.useHandCursor	Determines whether the hand is displayed when a user rolls over a button movie clip.
MovieClip._visible	A Boolean value that determines whether a movie clip instance is hidden or visible.
MovieClip._width	The width of a movie clip instance, in pixels.
MovieClip._x	The x coordinate of a movie clip instance
MovieClip._xmouse	The x coordinate of the mouse pointer within a movie clip instance.
MovieClip._xscale	The value specifying the percentage for horizontally scaling a movie clip.
MovieClip._y	The y coordinate of a movie clip instance.
MovieClip._ymouse	The y coordinate of the mouse pointer within a movie clip instance.
MovieClip._yscale	The value specifying the percentage for vertically scaling a movie clip.

Event handler summary for the MovieClip class

Event handler	Description
MovieClip.onData	Invoked when all the data is loaded into a movie clip.
MovieClip.onDragOut	Invoked while the pointer is outside the button; the mouse button is pressed inside, and then rolls outside the button area.
MovieClip.onDragOver	Invoked while the pointer is over the button; the mouse button has been pressed then rolled outside the button, and then rolled back over the button.
MovieClip.onEnterFrame	Invoked continually at the frame rate of the SWF file. The actions associated with the enterFrame clip event are processed before any frame actions that are attached to the affected frames.
MovieClip.onKeyDown	Invoked when a key is pressed. Use the `Key.getCode()` and `Key.getAscii()` methods to retrieve information about the last key pressed.
MovieClip.onKeyUp	Invoked when a key is released.
MovieClip.onKillFocus	Invoked when focus is removed from a button.
MovieClip.onLoad	Invoked when the movie clip is instantiated and appears in the Timeline.
MovieClip.onMouseDown	Invoked when the left mouse button is pressed.
MovieClip.onMouseMove	Invoked every time the mouse is moved.
MovieClip.onMouseUp	Invoked when the left mouse button is released.
MovieClip.onPress	Invoked when the mouse is pressed while the pointer is over a button.
MovieClip.onRelease	Invoked when the mouse is released while the pointer is over a button.
MovieClip.onReleaseOutside	Invoked when the mouse is released while the pointer is outside the button after the button is pressed while the pointer is inside the button.
MovieClip.onRollOut	Invoked when the pointer rolls outside of a button area.
MovieClip.onRollOver	Invoked when the mouse pointer rolls over a button.
MovieClip.onSetFocus	Invoked when a button has input focus and a key is released.
MovieClip.onUnload	Invokes in the first frame after the movie clip is removed from the Timeline. The actions associated with the Unload movie clip event are processed before any actions are attached to the affected frame.

MovieClip._alpha

Availability

Flash Player 4.

Usage

my_mc._alpha

Description

Property; the alpha transparency value of the movie clip specified by *my_mc*. Valid values are 0 (fully transparent) to 100 (fully opaque). The default value is 100. Objects in a movie clip with _alpha set to 0 are active, even though they are invisible. For example, you can still click a button in a movie clip whose _alpha property is set to 0.

Example

The following code sets the _alpha property of a movie clip named star_mc to 30% when the button is clicked:

```
on(release) {
   star_mc._alpha = 30;
}
```

See also

Button._alpha, TextField._alpha

MovieClip.attachAudio()

Availability

Flash Player 6; the ability to attach audio from Flash Video (FLV) files was added in Flash Player 7.

Usage

my_mc.attachAudio(*source*)

Parameters

source   The object containing the audio to play. Valid values are a Microphone object, a NetStream object that is playing an FLV file, and false (stops playing the audio).

Returns

Nothing.

Description

Method; specifies the audio source to be played. To stop playing the audio source, pass false for *source*.

Example

The following code attaches a microphone to a movie clip.

```
my_mic = Microphone.get();
this.attachAudio(my_mic);
```

The following example shows how you can use a Sound object to control the sound associated with an FLV file.

```
// Clip is the instance name of the movie clip
// that contains the video object "my_video".
_root.Clip.my_video.attachVideo(_root.myNetStream);
_root.Clip.attachAudio(_root.myNetStream);
var snd = new Sound("_root.Clip");
//To adjust the audio:
_root.snd.setVolume(100);
```

See also

Microphone class, NetStream.play(), Sound class, Video.attachVideo()

MovieClip.attachMovie()

Availability

Flash Player 5.

Usage

```
my_mc.attachMovie(idName, newName, depth [, initObject])
```

Parameters

idName   The linkage name of the movie clip symbol in the library to attach to a movie clip on the Stage. This is the name entered in the Identifier field in the Linkage Properties dialog box.

newname   A unique instance name for the movie clip being attached to the movie clip.

depth   An integer specifying the depth level where the SWF file is placed.

initObject   (Supported for Flash Player 6 and later) An object containing properties with which to populate the newly attached movie clip. This parameter allows dynamically created movie clips to receive clip parameters. If *initObject* is not an object, it is ignored. All properties of *initObject* are copied into the new instance. The properties specified with *initObject* are available to the constructor function. This parameter is optional.

Returns

A reference to the newly created instance.

Description

Method; takes a symbol from the library and attaches it to the SWF file on the Stage specified by *my_mc*. Use removeMovieClip() or unloadMovie() to remove a SWF file attached with attachMovie().

Example

The following example attaches the symbol with the linkage identifier "circle" to the movie clip instance, which is on the Stage in the SWF file.

```
on (release) {
    thing.attachMovie( "circle", "circle1", 2 );
}
```

See also

`MovieClip.removeMovieClip()`, `MovieClip.unloadMovie()`, Object.registerClass(), `removeMovieClip()`

MovieClip.beginFill()

Availability

Flash Player 6.

Usage

`my_mc.beginFill([rgb[, alpha]])`

Parameter

`rgb`   A hex color value (for example, red is 0xFF0000, blue is 0x0000FF, and so on). If this value is not provided or is undefined, a fill is not created.

`alpha`   An integer between 0–100 that specifies the alpha value of the fill. If this value is not provided, 100 (solid) is used. If the value is less than 0, Flash uses 0. If the value is greater than 100, Flash uses 100.

Returns

Nothing.

Description

Method; indicates the beginning of a new drawing path. If an open path exists (that is, if the current drawing position does not equal the previous position specified in a `moveTo()` method) and it has a fill associated with it, that path is closed with a line and then filled. This is similar to what happens when `endFill()` is called. If no fill is currently associated with the path, `endFill()` must be called in order to apply the fill.

See also

`MovieClip.beginGradientFill()`, `MovieClip.endFill()`

MovieClip.beginGradientFill()

Availability

Flash Player 6.

Usage

```
my_mc.beginGradientFill(fillType, colors, alphas, ratios, matrix)
```

Parameter

fillType   Either the string "linear" or the string "radial".

colors   An array of RGB hex color values to be used in the gradient (for example, red is 0xFF0000, blue is 0x0000FF, and so on).

alphas   An array of alpha values for the corresponding colors in the *colors* array; valid values are 0–100. If the value is less than 0, Flash uses 0. If the value is greater than 100, Flash uses 100.

ratios   An array of color distribution ratios; valid values are 0–255. This value defines the percentage of the width where the color is sampled at 100 percent.

matrix   A transformation matrix that is an object with either of the following two sets of properties.

- *a*, *b*, *c*, *d*, *e*, *f*, *g*, *h*, *i*, which can be used to describe a 3 x 3 matrix of the following form:

  ```
  a b c
  d e f
  g h i
  ```

  The following example uses a beginGradientFill() method with a *matrix* parameter that is an object with these properties.

  ```
  _root.createEmptyMovieClip( "grad", 1 );
    with ( _root.grad )

    {

    colors = [ 0xFF0000, 0x0000FF ];
    alphas = [ 100, 100 ];
    ratios = [ 0, 0xFF ];
    matrix = { a:200, b:0, c:0, d:0, e:200, f:0, g:200, h:200, i:1 };
    beginGradientFill( "linear", colors, alphas, ratios, matrix );
    moveto(100,100);
    lineto(100,300);
    lineto(300,300);
    lineto(300,100);
    lineto(100,100);
    endFill();

    }
  ```

If a *matrixType* property does not exist then the remaining parameters are all required; the function fails if any of them are missing. This matrix scales, translates, rotates, and skews the unit gradient, which is defined at (-1,-1) and (1,1).

- *matrixType, x, y, w, h, r.*

The properties indicate the following: *matrixType* is the string "box", *x* is the horizontal position relative to the registration point of the parent clip for the upper left corner of the gradient, *y* is the vertical position relative to the registration point of the parent clip for the upper left corner of the gradient, *w* is the width of the gradient, *h* is the height of the gradient, and *r* is the rotation in radians of the gradient.

The following example uses a beginGradientFill() method with a *matrix* parameter that is an object with these properties.

```
_root.createEmptyMovieClip( "grad", 1 );
            with ( _root.grad )

            {

            colors = [ 0xFF0000, 0x0000FF ];
            alphas = [ 100, 100 ];
            ratios = [ 0, 0xFF ];
            matrix = { matrixType:"box", x:100, y:100, w:200, h:200, r:(45/
180)*Math.PI };
            beginGradientFill( "linear", colors, alphas, ratios, matrix );
            moveto(100,100);
            lineto(100,300);
            lineto(300,300);
            lineto(300,100);
            lineto(100,100);
            endFill();
            }
```

If a *matrixType* property exists then it must equal "box" and the remaining parameters are all required. The function fails if any of these conditions are not met.

Returns

Nothing.

Description

Method; indicates the beginning of a new drawing path. If the first parameter is undefined, or if no parameters are passed, the path has no fill. If an open path exists (that is if the current drawing position does not equal the previous position specified in a moveTo() method), and it has a fill associated with it, that path is closed with a line and then filled. This is similar to what happens when you call endFill().

This method fails if any of the following conditions exist:

- The number of items in the *colors*, *alphas*, and *ratios* parameters are not equal.
- The *fillType* parameter is not "linear" or "radial".
- Any of the fields in the object for the *matrix* parameter are missing or invalid.

Example

The following code uses both methods to draw two stacked rectangles with a red-blue gradient fill and a 5-pt. solid green stroke.

```
_root.createEmptyMovieClip("goober",1);
with ( _root.goober )
{
   colors = [ 0xFF0000, 0x0000FF ];
   alphas = [ 100, 100 ];
   ratios = [ 0, 0xFF ];
   lineStyle( 5, 0x00ff00 );
   matrix = { a:500,b:0,c:0,d:0,e:200,f:0,g:350,h:200,i:1};
   beginGradientFill( "linear", colors, alphas, ratios, matrix );
   moveto(100,100);
   lineto(100,300);
   lineto(600,300);
   lineto(600,100);
   lineto(100,100);
   endFill();
   matrix = { matrixType:"box", x:100, y:310, w:500, h:200, r:(0/180)*Math.PI
   };
   beginGradientFill( "linear", colors, alphas, ratios, matrix );
   moveto(100,310);
   lineto(100,510);
   lineto(600,510);
   lineto(600,310);
   lineto(100,310);
   endFill();
}
```

See also

MovieClip.beginFill(), MovieClip.endFill(), MovieClip.lineStyle(),
MovieClip.lineTo(), MovieClip.moveTo()

MovieClip.clear()

Availability

Flash Player 6.

Usage

my_mc.clear()

Parameters

None.

Returns

Nothing.

Description

Method; removes all the graphics created during runtime using the movie clip draw methods, including line styles specified with MovieClip.lineStyle(). Shapes and lines that are manually drawn during authoring time (with the Flash drawing tools) are unaffected.

See also

MovieClip.lineStyle()

MovieClip.createEmptyMovieClip()

Availability

Flash Player 6.

Usage

`my_mc.createEmptyMovieClip(instanceName, depth)`

Parameters

instanceName   A string that identifies the instance name of the new movie clip.

depth   An integer that specifies the depth of the new movie clip.

Returns

A reference to the newly created movie clip.

Description

Method; creates an empty movie clip as a child of an existing movie clip. This method behaves similarly to the `attachMovie()` method, but you don't need to provide an external linkage name for the new movie clip. The registration point for a newly created empty movie clip is the upper left corner. This method fails if any of the parameters are missing.

See also

`MovieClip.attachMovie()`

MovieClip.createTextField()

Availability

Flash Player 6.

Usage

`my_mc.createTextField(instanceName, depth, x, y, width, height)`

Parameters

instanceName   A string that identifies the instance name of the new text field.

depth   A positive integer that specifies the depth of the new text field.

x   An integer that specifies the *x* coordinate of the new text field.

y   An integer that specifies the *y* coordinate of the new text field.

width   A positive integer that specifies the width of the new text field.

height   A positive integer that specifies the height of the new text field.

Returns

Nothing.

Description

Method; creates a new, empty text field as a child of the movie clip specified by *my_mc*. You can use createTextField() to create text fields while a SWF file plays. The text field is positioned at (*x, y*) with dimensions *width* by *height*. The x and y parameters are relative to the container movie clip; these parameters correspond to the _x and _y properties of the text field. The *width* and *height* parameters correspond to the _width and _height properties of the text field.

The default properties of a text field are as follows:

```
type = "dynamic"
border = false
background = false
password = false
multiline = false
html = false
embedFonts = false
variable = null
maxChars = null
```

A text field created with createTextField() receives the following default TextFormat object:

```
font = "Times New Roman"
size = 12
textColor = 0x000000
bold = false
italic = false
underline = false
url = ""
target = ""
align = "left"
leftMargin = 0
rightMargin = 0
indent = 0
leading = 0
bullet = false
tabStops = [] (empty array)
```

Example

The following example creates a text field with a width of 300, a height of 100, an *x* coordinate of 100, a *y* coordinate of 100, no border, red, and underlined text.

```
_root.createTextField("mytext",1,100,100,300,100);
mytext.multiline = true;
mytext.wordWrap = true;
mytext.border = false;

myformat = new TextFormat();
myformat.color = 0xff0000;
myformat.bullet = false;
myformat.underline = true;

mytext.text = "this is my first test field object text";
mytext.setTextFormat(myformat);
```

See also

TextFormat class

MovieClip._currentframe

Availability

Flash Player 4.

Usage

```
my_mc._currentframe
```

Description

Property (read-only); returns the number of the frame in which the playhead is located in the Timeline specified by *my_mc*.

Example

The following example uses the _currentframe property to direct the playhead of the movie clip actionClip_mc to advance five frames ahead of its current location.

```
actionClip_mc.gotoAndStop(_currentframe + 5);
```

MovieClip.curveTo()

Availability

Flash Player 6.

Usage

```
my_mc.curveTo(controlX, controlY, anchorX, anchorY)
```

Parameters

controlX   An integer that specifies a horizontal position relative to the registration point of the parent movie clip of the control point.

controlY   An integer that specifies a vertical position relative to the registration point of the parent movie clip of the control point.

anchorX   An integer that specifies a horizontal position relative to the registration point of the parent movie clip of the next anchor point.

anchorY   An integer that specifies a vertical position relative to the registration point of the parent movie clip of the next anchor point.

Returns

Nothing.

Description

Method; draws a curve using the current line style from the current drawing position to (*anchorX*, *anchorY*) using the control point specified by (*controlX*, *controlY*). The current drawing position is then set to (*anchorX*, *anchorY*). If the movie clip you are drawing in contains content created with the Flash drawing tools, calls to curveTo() are drawn underneath this content. If you call curveTo() before any calls to moveTo(), the current drawing position defaults to (0, 0). If any of the parameters are missing, this method fails and the current drawing position is not changed.

Example

The following example draws a circle with a hairline point, solid blue line, and a solid red fill.

```
_root.createEmptyMovieClip( "circle", 1 );
with ( _root.circle )
{
  lineStyle( 0, 0x0000FF, 100 );
  beginFill( 0xFF0000 );
  moveTo( 500, 500 );
  curveTo( 600, 500, 600, 400 );
  curveTo( 600, 300, 500, 300 );
  curveTo( 400, 300, 400, 400 );
  curveTo( 400, 500, 500, 500 );
  endFill();
}
```

See also

MovieClip.beginFill(), MovieClip.createEmptyMovieClip(), MovieClip.endFill(), MovieClip.lineStyle(), MovieClip.lineTo(), MovieClip.moveTo()

MovieClip._droptarget

Availability

Flash Player 4.

Usage

*my_mc.*_droptarget

Description

Property (read-only); returns the absolute path in slash syntax notation of the movie clip instance on which *my_mc* was dropped. The _droptarget property always returns a path that starts with a slash (/). To compare the _droptarget property of an instance to a reference, use the eval() function to convert the returned value from slash syntax to a dot syntax reference.

Note: You must perform this conversion if you are using ActionScript 2.0, which does not support slash syntax.

Example

The following example evaluates the _droptarget property of the garbage movie clip instance and uses eval() to convert it from slash syntax to a dot syntax reference. The garbage reference is then compared to the reference to the trash movie clip instance. If the two references are equivalent, the visibility of garbage is set to false. If they are not equivalent, the garbage instance is reset to its original position.

```
if (eval(garbage._droptarget) == _root.trash) {
  garbage._visible = false;
} else {
  garbage._x = x_pos;
  garbage._y = y_pos;
}
```

The variables x_pos and y_pos are set on Frame 1 of the SWF file with the following script:

```
x_pos = garbage._x;
y_pos = garbage._y;
```

startDrag()

MovieClip.duplicateMovieClip()

Availability

Flash Player 5.

Usage

my_mc.duplicateMovieClip(*newname, depth* [,*initObject*])

Parameters

newname   A unique identifier for the duplicate movie clip.

depth   A unique number specifying the depth at which the SWF file specified is to be placed.

initObject   (Supported for Flash Player 6 and later.) An object containing properties with which to populate the duplicated movie clip. This parameter allows dynamically created movie clips to receive clip parameters. If initObject is not an object, it is ignored. All properties of initObject are copied into the new instance. The properties specified with initObject are available to the constructor function. This parameter is optional.

Returns

A reference to the duplicated movie clip.

Description

Method; creates an instance of the specified movie clip while the SWF file is playing. Duplicated movie clips always start playing at Frame 1, no matter what frame the original movie clip is on when the duplicateMovieClip() method is called. Variables in the parent movie clip are not copied into the duplicate movie clip. Movie clips that have been created using duplicateMovieClip() are not duplicated if you call duplicateMovieClip() on their parent. If the parent movie clip is deleted, the duplicate movie clip is also deleted. .

See also

duplicateMovieClip(), MovieClip.removeMovieClip()

MovieClip.enabled

Availability

Flash Player 6.

Usage

my_mc.enabled

Description

Property; a Boolean value that indicates whether a button movie clip is enabled. The default value of enabled is true. If enabled is set to false, the button movie clip's callback methods and on *action* event handlers are no longer invoked, and the Over, Down, and Up frames are disabled. The enabled property does not affect the Timeline of the button movie clip; if a movie clip is playing, it continues to play. The movie clip continues to receive movie clip events (for example, mouseDown, mouseUp, keyDown, and keyUp).

The enabled property only governs the button-like properties of a button movie clip. You can change the enabled property at any time; the modified button movie clip is immediately enabled or disabled. The enabled property can be read out of a prototype object. If enabled is set to false, the object is not included in automatic tab ordering.

MovieClip.endFill()

Availability

Flash Player 6.

Usage

my_mc.endFill()

Parameters

None.

Returns

Nothing.

Description

Method; applies a fill to the lines and curves added since the last call to beginFill() or beginGradientFill(). Flash uses the fill that was specified in the previous call to beginFill() or beginGradientFill(). If the current drawing position does not equal the previous position specified in a moveTo() method and a fill is defined, the path is closed with a line and then filled.

MovieClip.focusEnabled

Availability

Flash Player 6.

Usage

`my_mc.focusEnabled`

Description

Property; if the value is `undefined` or `false`, a movie clip cannot receive input focus unless it is a button movie clip. If the `focusEnabled` property value is `true`, a movie clip can receive input focus even if it is not a button movie clip.

MovieClip._focusrect

Availability

Flash Player 6.

Usage

`my_mc._focusrect`

Description

Property; a Boolean value that specifies whether a movie clip has a yellow rectangle around it when it has keyboard focus. This property can override the global `_focusrect` property.

MovieClip._framesloaded

Availability

Flash Player 4.

Usage

`my_mc._framesloaded`

Description

Property (read-only); the number of frames that have been loaded from a streaming SWF file. This property is useful for determining whether the contents of a specific frame, and all the frames before it, have loaded and are available locally in the browser. This property is useful for monitoring the downloading of large SWF files. For example, you might want to display a message to users indicating that the SWF file is loading until a specified frame in the SWF file has finished loading.

Example

The following example uses the `_framesloaded` property to start a SWF file when all the frames are loaded. If all the frames aren't loaded, the `_xscale` property of the movie clip instance `loader` is increased proportionally to create a progress bar.

```
if (_framesloaded >= _totalframes) {
  gotoAndPlay ("Scene 1", "start");
} else {
  _root.loader._xscale = (_framesloaded/_totalframes)*100;
}
```

See also

MovieClipLoader class

MovieClip.getBounds()

Availability

Flash Player 5.

Usage

`my_mc.getBounds(targetCoordinateSpace)`

Parameters

`targetCoordinateSpace`   The target path of the Timeline whose coordinate system you want to use as a reference point.

Returns

An object with the properties `xMin`, `xMax`, `yMin`, and `yMax`.

Description

Method; returns properties that are the minimum and maximum *x* and *y* coordinate values of the instance specified by *my_mc* for the `targetCoordinateSpace` parameter.

Note: Use `MovieClip.localToGlobal()` and `MovieClip.globalToLocal()` to convert the movie clip's local coordinates to Stage coordinates, or Stage coordinates to local coordinates, respectively.

Example

In the following example, the object that `getBounds()` returns is assigned to the identifier `clipBounds`. You can then access the values of each property and use them in a script. In this script, another movie clip instance, `clip2`, is placed alongside `clip`.

```
clipBounds = clip.getBounds(_root);
clip2._x = clipBounds.xMax;
```

See also

`MovieClip.globalToLocal()`, `MovieClip.localToGlobal()`

MovieClip.getBytesLoaded()

Availability

Flash Player 5.

Usage

`my_mc.getBytesLoaded()`

Parameters

None.

Returns

An integer indicating the number of bytes loaded.

Description

Method; returns the number of bytes that have already loaded (streamed) for the movie clip specified by *my_mc*. You can compare this value with the value returned by `MovieClip.getBytesTotal()` to determine what percentage of a movie clip has loaded.

See also

`MovieClip.getBytesTotal()`

MovieClip.getBytesTotal()

Availability

Flash Player 5.

Usage

`my_mc.getBytesTotal()`

Parameters

None.

Returns

An integer indicating the total size, in bytes, of *my_mc*.

Description

Method; returns the size, in bytes, of the movie clip specified by *my_mc*. For movie clips that are external (the root SWF file or a movie clip that is being loaded into a target or a level), the return value is the size of the SWF file.

See also

`MovieClip.getBytesLoaded()`

MovieClip.getDepth()

Availability

Flash Player 6.

Usage

my_mc.getDepth()

Parameters

None.

Returns

An integer.

Description

Method; returns the depth of a movie clip instance. For more information, see "Managing movie clip depths" on page 333.

See also

MovieClip.getInstanceAtDepth(), MovieClip.getNextHighestDepth(), MovieClip.swapDepths()

MovieClip.getInstanceAtDepth()

Availability

Flash Player 7.

Usage

my_mc.getInstanceAtDepth(*depth*)

Parameters

depth An integer that specifies the depth level to query.

Returns

A string representing the name of the movie clip located at the specified depth, or undefined if there is no movie clip at that depth.

Description

Method; lets you determine if a particular depth is already occupied by a movie clip. You can use this method before using MovieClip.attachMovie(), MovieClip.duplicateMovieClip(), or MovieClip.createEmptyMovieClip() to determine if the depth parameter you want to pass to any of these methods already contains a movie clip. For more information, see "Managing movie clip depths" on page 333.

See also

MovieClip.getDepth(), MovieClip.getNextHighestDepth(), MovieClip.swapDepths()

MovieClip.getNextHighestDepth()

Availability

Flash Player 7.

Usage

```
my_mc.getNextHighestDepth()
```

Parameters

None.

Returns

An integer that reflects the next available depth index that would render above all other objects on the same level and layer within *my_mc*.

Description

Method; lets you determine a depth value that you can pass to `MovieClip.attachMovie()`, `MovieClip.duplicateMovieClip()`, or `MovieClip.createEmptyMovieClip()` to ensure that Flash renders the movie clip in front of all other objects on the same level and layer in the current movie clip. The value returned is 0 or higher (that is, negative numbers are not returned).

For more information, see "Managing movie clip depths" on page 333.

See also

`MovieClip.getDepth()`, `MovieClip.getInstanceAtDepth()`, `MovieClip.swapDepths()`

MovieClip.getSWFVersion()

Availability

Flash Player 7.

Usage

```
my_mc.getSWFVersion()
```

Parameters

None.

Returns

An integer that specifies the Flash Player version that was targeted when the SWF file loaded into *my_mc* was published.

Description

Method; returns an integer that indicates the Flash Player version for which *my_mc* was published. If *my_mc* is a JPEG file, or if an error occurs and Flash can't determine the SWF version of *my_mc*, -1 is returned.

MovieClip.getTextSnapshot()

Availability

Authoring: Flash MX 2004.

Playback: SWF files published for Flash Player 6 or later, playing in Flash Player 7 or later.

Usage

```
my_mc.getTextSnapshot();
```

Parameters

None.

Returns

A TextSnapshot object that contains the static text from `my_mc`, or an empty string if `my_mc` contains no static text.

Description

Method; returns a TextSnapshot object that contains the text in all the static text fields in the specified movie clip; text in child movie clips is not included.

Flash concatenates text and places it in the TextSnapshot object in an order that reflects the tab index order of the static text fields in the movie clip. Text fields that don't have tab index values are placed in a random order in the object, and precede any text from fields that do have tab index values. No line breaks or formatting indicates where one field ends and the next begins.

Note: You can't specify a tab index value for static text in Flash. However, other products may do so; for example, Macromedia FlashPaper.

The contents of the TextSnapshot object aren't dynamic; that is, if the movie clip moves to a different frame, or is altered in some way (for example, objects in the movie clip are added or removed), the TextSnapshot object might not represent the current text in the movie clip. To ensure that the object's contents are current, reissue this command as needed.

See also

TextSnapshot object

MovieClip.getURL()

Availability

Flash Player 5.

Usage

```
my_mc.getURL(URL [,window, variables])
```

Parameters

URL   The URL from which to obtain the document.

window   An optional parameter specifying the name, frame, or expression that specifies the window or HTML frame that the document is loaded into. You can also use one of the following reserved target names: _self specifies the current frame in the current window, _blank specifies a new window, _parent specifies the parent of the current frame, and _top specifies the top-level frame in the current window.

variables   An optional parameter specifying a method for sending variables associated with the SWF file to load. If there are no variables, omit this parameter; otherwise, specify whether to load variables using a GET or POST method. GET appends the variables to the end of the URL and is used for a small numbers of variables. POST sends the variables in a separate HTTP header and is used for long strings of variables.

Returns

Nothing.

Description

Method; loads a document from the specified URL into the specified window. The getURL method can also be used to pass variables to another application defined at the URL using a GET or POST method.

See also

```
getURL()
```

MovieClip.globalToLocal()

Availability

Flash Player 5.

Usage

```
my_mc.globalToLocal(point)
```

Parameters

point   The name or identifier of an object created with the generic Object class. The object specifies the *x* and *y* coordinates as properties.

Returns

Nothing.

Description

Method; converts the *point* object from Stage (global) coordinates to the movie clip's (local) coordinates.

Example

The following example converts the global *x* and *y* coordinates of the *point* object to the local coordinates of the movie clip.

```
onClipEvent(mouseMove) {
   point = new object();
   point.x = _root._xmouse;
   point.y = _root._ymouse;
   globalToLocal(point);
   trace(_root._xmouse + " " + _root._ymouse);
   trace(point.x + " " + point.y);
   updateAfterEvent();
}
```

See also

`MovieClip.getBounds()`, `MovieClip.localToGlobal()`

MovieClip.gotoAndPlay()

Availability

Flash Player 5.

Usage

`my_mc.gotoAndPlay(frame)`

Parameters

frame   A number representing the frame number, or a string representing the label of the frame, to which the playhead is sent.

Returns

Nothing.

Description

Method; starts playing the SWF file at the specified frame. If you want to specify a scene as well as a frame, use `gotoAndPlay()`.

MovieClip.gotoAndStop()

Availability

Flash Player 5.

Usage

`my_mc.gotoAndStop(frame)`

Parameters

frame   The frame number to which the playhead is sent.

Returns

Nothing.

Description

Method; brings the playhead to the specified frame of this movie clip and stops it there.

See also

`gotoAndStop()`

MovieClip._height

Availability

Flash Player 4.

Usage

`my_mc._height`

Description

Property; the height of the movie clip, in pixels.

Example

The following code example sets the height and width of a movie clip when the user clicks the mouse button.

```
onClipEvent(mouseDown) {
  _width=200;
  _height=200;
}
```

MovieClip._highquality

Availability

Flash Player 6.

Usage

`my_mc._highquality`

Description

Property (global); specifies the level of anti-aliasing applied to the current SWF file. Specify 2 (best quality) to apply high quality with bitmap smoothing always on. Specify 1 (high quality) to apply anti-aliasing; this will smooth bitmaps if the SWF file does not contain animation. Specify 0 (low quality) to prevent anti-aliasing. This property can overwrite the global `_highquality` property.

Example

`my_mc._highquality = 2;`

See also

`_quality`

MovieClip.hitArea

Availability

Flash Player 6.

Usage

my_mc.hitArea

Returns

A reference to a movie clip.

Description

Property; designates another movie clip to serve as the hit area for a button movie clip. If the hitArea property does not exist or is null or undefined, the button movie clip itself is used as the hit area. The value of the hitArea property may be a reference to a movie clip object.

You can change the hitArea property at any time; the modified button movie clip immediately takes on the new hit area behavior. The movie clip designated as the hit area does not need to be visible; its graphical shape, although not visible, is hit-tested. The hitArea property can be read out of a prototype object.

MovieClip.hitTest()

Availability

Flash Player 5.

Usage

my_mc.hitTest(*x, y, shapeFlag*)
my_mc.hitTest(*target*)

Parameters

x   The *x* coordinate of the hit area on the Stage.

y   The *y* coordinate of the hit area on the Stage.

The *x* and *y* coordinates are defined in the global coordinate space.

target   The target path of the hit area that may intersect or overlap with the instance specified by *my_mc*. The *target* parameter usually represents a button or text-entry field.

shapeFlag   A Boolean value specifying whether to evaluate the entire shape of the specified instance (*true*), or just the bounding box (*false*). This parameter can be specified only if the hit area is identified using *x* and *y* coordinate parameters.

Returns

A Boolean value of true if *my_mc* overlaps with the specified hit area, false otherwise.

Description

Method; evaluates the instance specified by *my_mc* to see if it overlaps or intersects with the hit area identified by the *target* or *x* and *y* coordinate parameters.

Usage 1: Compares the *x* and *y* coordinates to the shape or bounding box of the specified instance, according to the *shapeFlag* setting. If *shapeFlag* is set to `true`, only the area actually occupied by the instance on the Stage is evaluated, and if *x* and *y* overlap at any point, a value of `true` is returned. This is useful for determining if the movie clip is within a specified hit or hotspot area.

Usage 2: Evaluates the bounding boxes of the *target* and specified instance, and returns `true` if they overlap or intersect at any point.

Example

The following example uses `hitTest()` with the _xmouse and _ymouse properties to determine whether the mouse pointer is over the target's bounding box:

```
if (hitTest( _root._xmouse, _root._ymouse, false));
```

The following example uses `hitTest()` to determine if the movie clip `ball` overlaps or intersects the movie clip `square`:

```
if(_root.ball.hitTest(_root.square)){
   trace("ball intersects square");
}
```

See also

MovieClip.getBounds(), MovieClip.globalToLocal(), MovieClip.localToGlobal()

MovieClip.lineStyle()

Availability

Flash Player 6.

Usage

my_mc.lineStyle([*thickness*[, *rgb*[, *alpha*]]])

Parameters

thickness   An integer that indicates the thickness of the line in points; valid values are 0 to 255. If a number is not specified, or if the parameter is `undefined`, a line is not drawn. If a value of less than 0 is passed, Flash uses 0. The value 0 indicates hairline thickness; the maximum thickness is 255. If a value greater than 255 is passed, the Flash interpreter uses 255.

rgb   A hex color value (for example, red is 0xFF0000, blue is 0x0000FF, and so on) of the line. If a value isn't indicated, Flash uses 0x000000 (black).

alpha   An integer that indicates the alpha value of the line's color; valid values are 0–100. If a value isn't indicated, Flash uses 100 (solid). If the value is less than 0, Flash uses 0; if the value is greater than 100, Flash uses 100.

Returns

Nothing.

Description

Method; specifies a line style that Flash uses for subsequent calls to `lineTo()` and `curveTo()` until you call `lineStyle()` with different parameters. You can call `lineStyle()` in the middle of drawing a path to specify different styles for different line segments within a path.

Note: Calls to `clear` reset `lineStyle()` back to `undefined`.

Example

The following code draws a triangle with a 5-point, solid magenta line and no fill.

```
_root.createEmptyMovieClip( "triangle", 1 );
with ( _root.triangle )
{
lineStyle( 5, 0xff00ff, 100 );
moveTo( 200, 200 );
lineTo( 300,300 );
lineTo( 100, 300 );
lineTo( 200, 200 );
}
```

See also

`MovieClip.beginFill()`, `MovieClip.beginGradientFill()`, `MovieClip.clear()`, `MovieClip.curveTo()`, `MovieClip.lineTo()`, `MovieClip.moveTo()`

MovieClip.lineTo()

Availability

Flash Player 6.

Usage

my_mc.lineTo(*x*, *y*)

Parameters

x   An integer indicating the horizontal position relative to the registration point of the parent movie clip.

y   An integer indicating the vertical position relative to the registration point of the parent movie clip.

Returns

Nothing.

Description

Method; draws a line using the current line style from the current drawing position to (*x*, *y*); the current drawing position is then set to (*x*, *y*). If the movie clip that you are drawing in contains content that was created with the Flash drawing tools, calls to `lineTo()` are drawn underneath the content. If you call `lineTo()` before any calls to the `moveTo()` method, the current drawing position defaults to (0, 0). If any of the parameters are missing, this method fails and the current drawing position is not changed.

Example

The following example draws a triangle with no lines and a partially transparent blue fill.

```
_root.createEmptyMovieClip ("triangle", 1);
   with (_root.triangle){
      beginFill (0x0000FF, 50);
      lineStyle (5, 0xFF00FF, 100);
      moveTo (200, 200);
      lineTo (300, 300);
      lineTo (100, 300);
      lineTo (200, 200);
      endFill();
   }
```

See also

MovieClip.beginFill(), MovieClip.createEmptyMovieClip(), MovieClip.endFill(), MovieClip.lineStyle(), MovieClip.moveTo()

MovieClip.loadMovie()

Availability

Flash Player 5.

Usage

my_mc.loadMovie("*url*" [,*variables*])

Parameters

url   The absolute or relative URL of the SWF file or JPEG file to be loaded. A relative path must be relative to the SWF file at level 0. Absolute URLs must include the protocol reference, such as http:// or file:///.

variables   An optional parameter specifying an HTTP method for sending or loading variables. The parameter must be the string GET or POST. If there are no variables to be sent, omit this parameter. The GET method appends the variables to the end of the URL and is used for small numbers of variables. The POST method sends the variables in a separate HTTP header and is used for long strings of variables.

Returns

Nothing.

Description

Method; loads SWF or JPEG files into a movie clip in Flash Player while the original SWF file is playing.

Tip: If you want to monitor the progress of the download, use MovieClipLoader.loadClip() instead of this function.

Without the loadMovie() method, Flash Player displays a single SWF file and then closes. The loadMovie() method lets you display several SWF files at once and switch between SWF files without loading another HTML document.

A SWF file or image loaded into a movie clip inherits the position, rotation, and scale properties of the movie clip. You can use the target path of the movie clip to target the loaded SWF file.

Use the `unloadMovie()` method to remove SWF files or images loaded with the `loadMovie()` method. Use the `loadVariables()` method to keep the active SWF file, and update the variables with new values.

See also

`loadMovie()`, `loadMovieNum()`, `MovieClip.loadVariables()`, `MovieClip.unloadMovie()`, `unloadMovie()`, `unloadMovieNum()`

MovieClip.loadVariables()

Availability

Flash Player 5; behavior changed in Flash Player 7.

Usage

`my_mc.loadVariables("url", variables)`

Parameters

`url`   The absolute or relative URL for the external file that contains the variables to be loaded. If the SWF file issuing this call is running in a web browser, `url` must be in the same domain as the SWF file; for details, see "Description," below.

`variables`   An optional parameter specifying an HTTP method for sending variables. The parameter must be the string `GET` or `POST`. If there are no variables to be sent, omit this parameter. The `GET` method appends the variables to the end of the URL and is used for small numbers of variables. The `POST` method sends the variables in a separate HTTP header and is used for long strings of variables.

Returns

Nothing.

Description

Method; reads data from an external file and sets the values for variables in `my_mc`. The external file can be a text file generated by a CGI script, Active Server Page (ASP), or PHP script and can contain any number of variables.

This method can also be used to update variables in the active movie clip with new values.

This method requires that the text of the URL be in the standard MIME format: *application/x-www-form-urlencoded* (CGI script format).

In SWF files running in a version of the player earlier than Flash Player 7, `url` must be in the same superdomain as the SWF file that is issuing this call. For example, a SWF file at www.someDomain.com can load variables from a SWF file at store.someDomain.com, because both files are in the same superdomain of someDomain.com.

In SWF files of any version running in Flash Player 7 or later, `url` must be in exactly the same domain (see "Flash Player security features" on page 392). For example, a SWF file at www.someDomain.com can load variables only from SWF files that are also at www.someDomain.com. If you want to load variables from a different domain, you can place a *cross-domain policy file* on the server hosting the SWF file that is being accessed. For more information, see "About allowing cross-domain data loading" on page 394.

MovieClip.localToGlobal()

Availability

Flash Player 5.

Usage

my_mc.localToGlobal(*point*)

Parameters

point   The name or identifier of an object created with the Object class, specifying the *x* and *y* coordinates as properties.

Returns

Nothing.

Description

Method; converts the *point* object from the movie clip's (local) coordinates to the Stage (global) coordinates.

Example

The following example converts *x* and *y* coordinates of the *point* object, from the movie clip's (local) coordinates to the Stage (global) coordinates. The local *x* and *y* coordinates are specified using the _xmouse and _ymouse properties to retrieve the *x* and *y* coordinates of the mouse pointer position.

```
onClipEvent(mouseMove) {
    point = new object();
    point.x = _xmouse;
    point.y = _ymouse;
    _root.out3 = point.x + " === " + point.y;
    _root.out = _root._xmouse + " === " + _root._ymouse;
    localToGlobal(point);
    _root.out2 = point.x + " === " + point.y;
    updateAfterEvent();
}
```

See also

MovieClip.globalToLocal()

MovieClip._lockroot

Availability

Flash Player 7.

Usage

my_mc._lockroot

Description

Property; specifies what _root refers to when a SWF file is loaded into a movie clip. The _lockroot property is undefined by default. You can set this property within the SWF file that is being loaded or in the handler that is loading the movie clip.

For example, suppose you have a document called Games.fla that lets a user choose a game to play, and loads the game (for example, Chess.swf) into the game_mc movie clip. You want to make sure that, if _root is used in Chess.swf, it still refers to _root in Chess.swf after being loaded into Games.swf. If you have access to Chess.fla and publish it to Flash Player 7 or later, you can add this statement to it:

this._lockroot = true;

If you don't have access to Chess.fla (for example, if you are loading Chess.swf from someone else's site), you can set its _lockroot property when you load it, as shown below. In this case, Chess.swf can be published for any version of Flash Player, as long as Games.swf is published for Flash Player 7 or later.

```
onClipEvent (load)
{
    this._lockroot = true;
}
game_mc.loadMovie ("Chess.swf");
```

If you didn't use the this._lockroot = true statement in either of the SWF files, _root in Chess.swf would refer to _root in Games.swf after Chess.swf is loaded into Games.swf.

See also

_root, MovieClip.attachMovie(), MovieClip.loadMovie()

MovieClip.menu

Availability

Flash Player 7.

Usage

```
my_mc.menu = contextMenu
```

Parameters

contextMenu   A ContextMenu object.

Description

Property; associates the specified ContextMenu object with the movie clip *my_mc*. The ContextMenu class lets you modify the context menu that appears when the user right-clicks (Windows) or Control-clicks (Macintosh) in Flash Player.

Example

The following example assigns the ContextMenu object menu_cm to the movie clip content_mc. The ContextMenu object contains a custom menu item labeled "Print..." that has an associated callback handler named doPrint().

```
var menu_cm = new ContextMenu();
menu_cm.customItems.push(new ContextMenuItem("Print...", doPrint));
function doPrint(menu, obj) {
  // "Print" code here
}
content_mc.menu = menu_cm;
```

See also

Button.menu, ContextMenu class, ContextMenuItem class, TextField.menu

MovieClip.moveTo()

Availability

Flash Player 6.

Usage

```
my_mc.moveTo(x, y)
```

Parameters

x   An integer indicating the horizontal position relative to the registration point of the parent movie clip.

y   An integer indicating the vertical position relative to the registration point of the parent movie clip.

Returns

Nothing.

Description

Method; moves the current drawing position to (*x*, *y*). If any of the parameters are missing, this method fails and the current drawing position is not changed.

Example

This example draws a triangle with 5-point, solid magenta lines and no fill. The first line creates an empty movie clip to draw with. Inside the `with` statement, a line type is defined; then the starting drawing position is indicated by the `moveTo()` method.

```
_root.createEmptyMovieClip( "triangle", 1 );
with ( _root.triangle )
{
lineStyle( 5, 0xff00ff, 100 );
moveTo( 200, 200 );
lineTo( 300,300 );
lineTo( 100, 300 );
lineTo( 200, 200 );
}
```

See also

`MovieClip.createEmptyMovieClip()`, `MovieClip.lineStyle()`, `MovieClip.lineTo()`

MovieClip._name

Availability

Flash Player 4.

Usage

my_mc._name

Description

Property; the instance name of the movie clip specified by *my_mc*.

MovieClip.nextFrame()

Availability

Flash Player 5.

Usage

my_mc.nextFrame()

Parameters

None.

Returns

Nothing.

Description

Method; sends the playhead to the next frame and stops it.

See also

`nextFrame()`

MovieClip.onData

Availability

Flash Player 6.

Usage

```
my_mc.onData = function() {
    // your statements here
}
```

Parameters

None.

Returns

Nothing.

Description

Event handler; invoked when a movie clip receives data from a `loadVariables()` or `loadMovie()` call. You must define a function that executes when the event handler is invoked.

This handler can be used only with movie clips for which you have a symbol in the library that is associated with a class. If you want an event handler to be invoked when a specific movie clip receives data, you must use `onClipEvent(data)` instead of this handler. The latter handler is invoked when any movie clip receives data.

Example

The following example illustrates the correct use of `MovieClip.onData()` and `onClipEvent(data)`.

```
// symbol_mc is a movie clip symbol in the library.
// It is linked to the MovieClip class.
// The following function is triggered for each instance of symbol_mc
//   when it receives data.
symbol_mc.onData = function() {
    trace("The movie clip has received data");
}

// dynamic_mc is a movie clip that is being loaded with MovieClip.loadMovie().
//   This code attempts to call a function when the clip is loaded,
//   but it will not work, because the loaded SWF is not a symbol
//   in the library associated with the MovieClip class.
function output()
{
    trace("Will never be called.");
}
dynamic_mc.onData = output;
dynamic_mc.loadMovie("replacement.swf");

// The following function is invoked for any movie clip that
// receives data, whether it is in the library or not.
// Therefore, this function is invoked when symbol_mc is instantiated
//   and also when replacement.swf is loaded.
OnClipEvent( data ) {
    trace("The movie clip has received data");
}
```

onClipEvent()

MovieClip.onDragOut

Availability

Flash Player 6.

Usage

```
my_mc.onDragOut = function() {
    // your statements here
}
```

Parameters

None.

Returns

Nothing.

Description

Event handler; invoked when the mouse button is pressed and the pointer rolls outside the object. You must define a function that executes when the event handler is invoked.

Example

The following example defines a function for the onDragOut method that sends a trace() action to the Output panel.

```
my_mc.onDragOut = function () {
    trace ("onDragOut called");
};
```

See also

MovieClip.onDragOver

MovieClip.onDragOver

Availability

Flash Player 6.

Usage

```
my_mc.onDragOver = function() {
    // your statements here
}
```

Parameters

None.

Returns

Nothing.

Description

Event handler; invoked when the pointer is dragged outside and then over the movie clip. You must define a function that executes when the event handler is invoked.

Example

The following example defines a function for the onDragOver method that sends a trace() action to the Output panel.

```
my_mc.onDragOver = function () {
  trace ("onDragOver called");
};
```

See also

MovieClip.onDragOut

MovieClip.onEnterFrame

Availability

Flash Player 6.

Usage

```
my_mc.onEnterFrame = function() {
  // your statements here
}
```

Parameters

None.

Returns

Nothing.

Description

Event handler; invoked continually at the frame rate of the SWF file. The actions associated with the enterFrame clip event are processed before any frame actions that are attached to the affected frames.

You must define a function that executes when the event handler is invoked.

Example

The following example defines a function for the onEnterFrame method that sends a trace() action to the Output panel.

```
my_mc.onEnterFrame = function () {
  trace ("onEnterFrame called");
};
```

MovieClip.onKeyDown

Availability

Flash Player 6.

Usage

```
my_mc.onKeyDown = function() {
    // your statements here
}
```

Parameters

None.

Returns

Nothing.

Description

Event handler; invoked when a movie clip has input focus and a key is pressed. The `onKeyDown` event handler is invoked with no parameters. You can use the `Key.getAscii()` and `Key.getCode()` methods to determine which key was pressed. You must define a function that executes when the event handler is invoked.

The `onKeyDown` event handler works only if the movie clip has input focus enabled and set. First, the `focusEnabled` property must be set to `true` for the movie clip. Then, the clip must be given focus. This can be done either by using `Selection.setFocus()` or by setting the tab key to navigate to the clip.

If `Selection.setFocus()` is used, the path for the movie clip must be passed to `Selection.setFocus()`. It is very easy for other elements to take the focus back once the mouse is moved.

Example

The following example defines a function for the `onKeyDown()` method that sends a `trace()` action to the Output panel.

```
my_mc.onKeyDown = function () {
    trace ("onKeyDown called");
};
```

The following example sets input focus.

```
MovieClip.focusEnabled = true;
Selection.setFocus(MovieClip);
```

See also

`MovieClip.onKeyUp`

MovieClip.onKeyUp

Availability

Flash Player 6.

Usage

```
my_mc.onKeyUp = function() {
  // your statements here
}
```

Parameters

None.

Returns

Nothing.

Description

Event handler; invoked when a key is released. The onKeyUp event handler is invoked with no parameters. You can use the Key.getAscii() and Key.getCode() methods to determine which key was pressed. You must define a function that executes when the event handler is invoked.

The onKeyUp event handler works only if the movie clip has input focus enabled and set. First, the focusEnabled property must be set to true for the movie clip. Then, the clip must be given focus. This can be done either by using Selection.setFocus() or by setting the tab key to navigate to the clip.

If Selection.setFocus() is used, the path for the movie clip must be passed to Selection.setFocus(). It is very easy for other elements to take the focus back once the mouse is moved.

Example

The following example defines a function for the onKeyUp method that sends a trace() action to the Output panel.

```
my_mc.onKeyUp = function () {
  trace ("onKeyUp called");
};
```

The following example sets input focus:

```
MovieClip.focusEnabled = true;
Selection.setFocus(MovieClip);
```

MovieClip.onKillFocus

Availability

Flash Player 6.

Usage

```
my_mc.onKillFocus = function (newFocus) {
    // your statements here
}
```

Parameters

newFocus   The object that is receiving the keyboard focus.

Returns

Nothing.

Description

Event handler; invoked when a movie clip loses keyboard focus. The onKillFocus method receives one parameter, *newFocus*, which is an object representing the new object receiving the focus. If no object receives the focus, *newFocus* contains the value null.

MovieClip.onLoad

Availability

Flash Player 6.

Usage

```
my_mc.onLoad = function() {
    // your statements here
}
```

Parameters

None.

Returns

Nothing.

Description

Event handler; invoked when the movie clip is instantiated and appears in the Timeline. You must define a function that executes when the event handler is invoked.

This handler can be used only with movie clips for which you have a symbol in the library that is associated with a class. If you want an event handler to be invoked when a specific movie clip loads, for example when you use MovieClip.loadMovie() to load a SWF file dynamically, you must use onClipEvent(load) instead of this handler. The latter handler is invoked when any movie clip loads.

Example

The following example illustrates the correct use of MovieClip.onLoad() and
onClipEvent(load).

```
// symbol_mc is a movie clip symbol in the library.
// It is linked to the MovieClip class.
// The following function is triggered for each instance of symbol_mc
//   as it is instantiated and appears on the Timeline.
symbol_mc.onLoad = function() {
   trace("The movie clip is loaded");
}

// dynamic_mc is a movie clip that is being loaded with MovieClip.loadMovie().
//   This code attempts to call a function when the clip is loaded,
//   but it will not work, because the loaded SWF is not a symbol
//   in the library associated with the MovieClip class.
function output()
{
    trace("Will never be called.");
}
dynamic_mc.onLoad = output;
dynamic_mc.loadMovie("replacement.swf");

// The following function is invoked for any movie clip that
// appears on the Timeline, whether it is in the library or not.
// Therefore, this function is invoked when symbol_mc is instantiated
//    and also when replacement.swf is loaded.
OnClipEvent( load ) {
   trace("The movie clip is loaded");
}
```

See also

onClipEvent()

MovieClip.onMouseDown

Availability

Flash Player 6.

Usage

```
my_mc.onMouseDown = function() {
   // your statements here
}
```

Parameters

None.

Returns

Nothing.

Description

Event handler; invoked when the mouse button is pressed. You must define a function that
executes when the event handler is invoked.

Example

The following example defines a function for the onMouseDown method that sends a trace()
action to the Output panel.

```
my_mc.onMouseDown = function () {
  trace ("onMouseDown called");
}
```

MovieClip.onMouseMove

Availability

Flash Player 6.

Usage

```
my_mc.onMouseMove = function() {
  // your statements here
}
```

Parameters

None.

Returns

Nothing.

Description

Event handler; invoked when the mouse moves. You must define a function that executes when
the event handler is invoked.

Example

The following example defines a function for the onMouseMove method that sends a trace()
action to the Output panel.

```
my_mc.onMouseMove = function () {
  trace ("onMouseMove called");
};
```

MovieClip.onMouseUp

Availability

Flash Player 6.

Usage

```
my_mc.onMouseUp = function() {
    // your statements here
}
```

Parameters

None.

Returns

Nothing.

Description

Event handler; invoked when the mouse button is released. You must define a function that executes when the event handler is invoked.

Example

The following example defines a function for the onMouseUp method that sends a trace() action to the Output panel.

```
my_mc.onMouseUp = function () {
    trace ("onMouseUp called");
};
```

MovieClip.onPress

Availability

Flash Player 6.

Usage

```
my_mc.onPress = function() {
    // your statements here
}
```

Parameters

None.

Returns

Nothing.

Description

Event handler; invoked when the user clicks the mouse while the pointer is over a movie clip. You must define a function that executes when the event handler is invoked.

Example

The following example defines a function for the `onPress` method that sends a `trace()` action to the Output panel.

```
my_mc.onPress = function () {
  trace ("onPress called");
};
```

MovieClip.onRelease

Availability

Flash Player 6.

Usage

```
my_mc.onRelease = function() {
  // your statements here
}
```

Parameters

None.

Returns

Nothing.

Description

Event handler; invoked when a button movie clip is released. You must define a function that executes when the event handler is invoked.

Example

The following example defines a function for the `onPress` method that sends a `trace()` action to the Output panel.

```
my_mc.onRelease = function () {
  trace ("onRelease called");
};
```

MovieClip.onReleaseOutside

Availability

Flash Player 6.

Usage

```
my_mc.onReleaseOutside = function() {
  // your statements here
}
```

Parameters

None.

Returns

Nothing.

Description

Event handler; invoked when the mouse is released while the pointer is outside the movie clip after the mouse button is pressed inside the movie clip.

You must define a function that executes when the event handler is invoked.

Example

The following example defines a function for the `onReleaseOutside` method that sends a `trace()` action to the Output panel.

```
my_mc.onReleaseOutside = function () {
  trace ("onReleaseOutside called");
};
```

MovieClip.onRollOut

Availability

Flash Player 6.

Usage

```
my_mc.onRollOut = function() {
  // your statements here
}
```

Parameters

None.

Returns

Nothing.

Description

Event handler; invoked when the pointer moves outside a movie clip area. You must define a function that executes when the event handler is invoked.

Example

The following example defines a function for the `onRollOut` method that sends a `trace()` action to the Output panel.

```
my_mc.onRollOut = function () {
  trace ("onRollOut called");
};
```

MovieClip.onRollOver

Availability

Flash Player 6.

Usage

```
my_mc.onRollOver = function() {
    // your statements here
}
```

Parameters

None.

Returns

Nothing.

Description

Event handler; invoked when the pointer moves over a movie clip area. You must define a function that executes when the event handler is invoked.

Example

The following example defines a function for the onRollOver method that sends a trace() to the Output panel.

```
my_mc.onRollOver = function () {
    trace ("onRollOver called");
};
```

MovieClip.onSetFocus

Availability

Flash Player 6.

Usage

```
my_mc.onSetFocus = function(oldFocus){
    // your statements here
}
```

Parameters

oldFocus   The object to lose focus.

Returns

Nothing.

Description

Event handler; invoked when a movie clip receives keyboard focus. The *oldFocus* parameter is the object that loses the focus. For example, if the user presses the Tab key to move the input focus from a movie clip to a text field, *oldFocus* contains the movie clip instance.

If there is no previously focused object, *oldFocus* contains a null value.

MovieClip.onUnload

Availability

Flash Player 6.

Usage

```
my_mc.onUnload = function() {
    // your statements here
}
```

Parameters

None.

Returns

Nothing.

Description

Event handler; invoked in the first frame after the movie clip is removed from the Timeline. Flash processes the actions associated with the onUnload event handler before attaching any actions to the affected frame. You must define a function that executes when the event handler is invoked.

Example

The following example defines a function for the MovieClip.onUnload method that sends a trace() action to the Output panel.

```
my_mc.onUnload = function () {
    trace ("onUnload called");
};
```

MovieClip._parent

Availability

Flash Player 5.

Usage

```
my_mc._parent.property
```
```
_parent.property
```

Description

Property; a reference to the movie clip or object that contains the current movie clip or object. The current object is the object containing the ActionScript code that references _parent. Use the _parent property to specify a relative path to movie clips or objects that are above the current movie clip or object.

You can use _parent to climb up multiple levels in the display list as in the following:

```
_parent._parent._alpha = 20;
```

See also

Button._parent, _root, targetPath, TextField._parent

MovieClip.play()

Availability

Flash Player 5.

Usage

`my_mc.play()`

Parameters

None.

Returns

Nothing.

Description

Method; moves the playhead in the Timeline of the movie clip.

See also

`play()`

MovieClip.prevFrame()

Availability

Flash Player 5.

Usage

`my_mc.prevFrame()`

Parameters

None.

Returns

Nothing.

Description

Method; sends the playhead to the previous frame and stops it.

See also

`prevFrame()`

MovieClip.removeMovieClip()

Availability

Flash Player 5.

Usage

`my_mc.removeMovieClip()`

Parameters

None.

Returns

Nothing.

Description

Method; removes a movie clip instance created with `duplicateMovieClip()`, `MovieClip.duplicateMovieClip()`, or `MovieClip.attachMovie()`.

MovieClip._rotation

Availability

Flash Player 4.

Usage

`my_mc._rotation`

Description

Property; the rotation of the movie clip, in degrees, from its original orientation. Values from 0 to 180 represent clockwise rotation; values from 0 to -180 represent counterclockwise rotation. Values outside this range are added to or subtracted from 360 to obtain a value within the range. For example, the statement `my_mc._rotation = 450` is the same as `my_mc._rotation = 90`.

See also

Button._rotation, `TextField._rotation`

MovieClip.setMask()

Availability

Flash Player 6.

Usage

```
my_mc.setMask(mask_mc)
```

Parameters

my_mc   The instance name of a movie clip to be masked.

mask_mc   The instance name of a movie clip to be a mask.

Returns

Nothing.

Description

Method; makes the movie clip in the parameter *mask_mc* a mask that reveals the movie clip specified by the *my_mc* parameter.

This method allows multiple-frame movie clips with complex, multilayered content to act as masks. You can shut masks on and off at runtime. However, you can't use the same mask for multiple masks (which is possible by using mask layers). If you have device fonts in a masked movie clip, they are drawn but not masked. You can't set a movie clip to be its own mask—for example, `my_mc.setMask(my_mc)`.

If you create a mask layer that contains a movie clip, and then apply the `setMask()` method to it, the `setMask()` call takes priority and this is not reversible. For example, you could have a movie clip in a mask layer called `UIMask` that masks another layer containing another movie clip called `UIMaskee`. If, as the SWF file plays, you call `UIMask.setMask(UIMaskee)`, from that point on, `UIMask` is masked by `UIMaskee`.

To cancel a mask created with ActionScript, pass the value `null` to the `setMask()` method. The following code cancels the mask without affecting the mask layer in the Timeline.

```
UIMask.setMask(null);
```

Example

The following code uses the movie clip `circleMask_mc` to mask the movie clip `theMaskee_mc`.

```
theMaskee_mc.setMask(circleMask_mc);
```

MovieClip._soundbuftime

Availability

Flash Player 6.

Usage

```
my_mc._soundbuftime
```

Description

Property (global); an integer that specifies the number of seconds a sound prebuffers before it starts to stream.

MovieClip.startDrag()

Availability

Flash Player 5.

Usage

`my_mc.startDrag([lock, [left, top, right, bottom]])`

Parameters

lock A Boolean value specifying whether the draggable movie clip is locked to the center of the mouse position (`true`), or locked to the point where the user first clicked on the movie clip (`false`). This parameter is optional.

left, top, right, bottom Values relative to the coordinates of the movie clip's parent that specify a constraint rectangle for the movie clip. These parameters are optional.

Returns

Nothing.

Description

Method; lets the user drag the specified movie clip. The movie clip remains draggable until explicitly stopped through a call to `MovieClip.stopDrag()`, or until another movie clip is made draggable. Only one movie clip is draggable at a time.

See also

`MovieClip._droptarget, startDrag(), MovieClip.stopDrag()`

MovieClip.stop()

Availability

Flash Player 5.

Usage

`my_mc.stop()`

Parameters

None.

Returns

Nothing.

Description

Method; stops the movie clip currently playing.

See also

`stop()`

MovieClip.stopDrag()

Availability

Flash Player 5.

Usage

`my_mc.stopDrag()`

Parameters

None.

Returns

Nothing.

Description

Method; ends a `MovieClip.startDrag()` method. A movie clip that was made draggable with that method remains draggable until a `stopDrag()` method is added, or until another movie clip becomes draggable. Only one movie clip is draggable at a time.

See also

`MovieClip._droptarget, MovieClip.startDrag(), stopDrag()`

MovieClip.swapDepths()

Availability

Flash Player 5.

Usage

`my_mc.swapDepths(depth)`

`my_mc.swapDepths(target)`

Parameters

`depth`   A number specifying the depth level where *my_mc* is to be placed.

`target`   A string specifying the movie clip instance whose depth is swapped by the instance specified by *my_mc*. Both instances must have the same parent movie clip.

Returns

Nothing.

Description

Method; swaps the stacking, or *z*-order (depth level), of the specified instance (*my_mc*) with the movie clip specified by the `target` parameter, or with the movie clip that currently occupies the depth level specified in the `depth` parameter. Both movie clips must have the same parent movie clip. Swapping the depth level of movie clips has the effect of moving one movie clip in front of or behind the other. If a movie clip is tweening when this method is called, the tweening is stopped. For more information, see "Managing movie clip depths" on page 333.

```
_level, MovieClip.getDepth( ), MovieClip.getInstanceAtDepth( ),
MovieClip.getNextHighestDepth( )
```

MovieClip.tabChildren

Availability

Flash Player 6.

Usage

my_mc.tabChildren

Description

Property; undefined by default. If tabChildren is undefined or true, the children of a movie clip are included in automatic tab ordering. If the value of tabChildren is false, the children of a movie clip are not included in automatic tab ordering.

Example

A list box UI widget built as a movie clip contains several items. The user can click each item to select it, so each item is a button. However, only the list box itself should be a tab stop. The items inside the list box should be excluded from tab ordering. To do this, the tabChildren property of the list box should be set to false.

The tabChildren property has no effect if the tabIndex property is used; the tabChildren property affects only automatic tab ordering.

See also

Button.tabIndex, MovieClip.tabEnabled, MovieClip.tabIndex, TextField.tabIndex

MovieClip.tabEnabled

Availability

Flash Player 6.

Usage

my_mc.tabEnabled

Description

Property; specifies whether *my_mc* is included in automatic tab ordering. It is undefined by default.

If tabEnabled is undefined, the object is included in automatic tab ordering only if it defines at least one button handler, such as MovieClip.onRelease. If tabEnabled is true, the object is included in automatic tab ordering. If the tabIndex property is also set to a value, the object is included in custom tab ordering as well.

If tabEnabled is false, the object is not included in automatic or custom tab ordering, even if the tabIndex property is set. However, if MovieClip.tabChildren is true, the movie clip's children can still be included in automatic tab ordering, even if tabEnabled is false.

MovieClip.tabIndex

Availability

Flash Player 6.

Usage

`my_mc.tabIndex`

Description

Property; lets you customize the tab ordering of objects in a movie. The tabIndex property is undefined by default. You can set tabIndex on a button, movie clip, or text field instance.

If an object in a SWF file contains a tabIndex property, automatic tab ordering is disabled, and the tab ordering is calculated from the tabIndex properties of objects in the SWF file. The custom tab ordering includes only objects that have tabIndex properties.

The tabIndex property must be a positive integer. The objects are ordered according to their tabIndex properties, in ascending order. An object with a tabIndex value of 1 precedes an object with a tabIndex value of 2. The custom tab ordering disregards the hierarchical relationships of objects in a SWF file. All objects in the SWF file with tabIndex properties are placed in the tab order. You shouldn't use the same tabIndex value for multiple objects.

See also

`Button.tabIndex, TextField.tabIndex`

MovieClip._target

Availability

Flash Player 4.

Usage

`my_mc._target`

Description

Property (read-only); returns the target path of the movie clip instance specified by *my_mc*.

MovieClip._totalframes

Availability

Flash Player 4.

Usage

`my_mc._totalframes`

Description

Property (read-only); returns the total number of frames in the movie clip instance specified in the `MovieClip` parameter.

MovieClip.trackAsMenu

Availability

Flash Player 6.

Usage

`my_mc.trackAsMenu`

Description

Property; a Boolean property that indicates whether or not other buttons or movie clips can receive mouse release events. This allows you to create menus. You can set the `trackAsMenu` property on any button or movie clip object. If the `trackAsMenu` property does not exist, the default behavior is `false`.

You can change the `trackAsMenu` property at any time; the modified button movie clip immediately takes on the new behavior.

See also

`Button.trackAsMenu`

MovieClip.unloadMovie()

Availability

Flash Player 5.

Usage

`my_mc.unloadMovie()`

Parameters

None.

Returns

Nothing.

Description

Method; removes the contents of a movie clip instance. The instance properties and clip handlers remain.

To remove the instance, including its properties and clip handlers, use `MovieClip.removeMovieClip()`.

See also

`MovieClip.attachMovie()`, `MovieClip.loadMovie()`, `unloadMovie()`, `unloadMovieNum()`

MovieClip._url

Availability

Flash Player 4.

Usage

`my_mc._url`

Description

Property (read only); retrieves the URL of the SWF file from which the movie clip was downloaded.

MovieClip.useHandCursor

Availability

Flash Player 6.

Usage

`my_mc.useHandCursor`

Description

Property; a Boolean value that indicates whether the hand cursor (pointing hand) appears when the mouse rolls over a button movie clip. The default value of `useHandCursor` is `true`. If `useHandCursor` is set to `true`, the pointing hand used for buttons is displayed when the mouse rolls over a button movie clip. If `useHandCursor` is `false`, the arrow cursor is used instead.

You can change the `useHandCursor` property at any time; the modified button movie clip immediately takes on the new cursor behavior. The `useHandCursor` property can be read out of a prototype object.

MovieClip._visible

Availability

Flash Player 4.

Usage

*my_mc.*_visible

Description

Property; a Boolean value that indicates whether the movie clip specified by *my_mc* is visible. Movie clips that are not visible (_visible property set to false) are disabled. For example, a button in a movie clip with _visible set to false cannot be clicked.

See also

Button._visible, TextField._visible

MovieClip._width

Availability

Flash Player 4 as a read-only property.

Usage

*my_mc.*_width

Description

Property; the width of the movie clip, in pixels.

Example

The following example sets the height and width properties of a movie clip when the user clicks the mouse.

```
onclipEvent(mouseDown) {
  _width=200;
  _height=200;
}
```

See also

MovieClip._height

MovieClip._x

Availability

Flash Player 3.

Usage

`my_mc._x`

Description

Property; an integer that sets the *x* coordinate of a movie clip relative to the local coordinates of the parent movie clip. If a movie clip is in the main Timeline, then its coordinate system refers to the upper left corner of the Stage as (0, 0). If the move clip is inside another movie clip that has transformations, the movie clip is in the local coordinate system of the enclosing movie clip. Thus, for a movie clip rotated 90 degrees counterclockwise, the movie clip's children inherit a coordinate system that is rotated 90 degrees counterclockwise. The movie clip's coordinates refer to the registration point position.

See also

`MovieClip._xscale, MovieClip._y, MovieClip._yscale`

MovieClip._xmouse

Availability

Flash Player 5.

Usage

`my_mc._xmouse`

Description

Property (read-only); returns the *x* coordinate of the mouse position.

See also

Mouse class, `MovieClip._ymouse`

MovieClip._xscale

Flash Player 4.

Usage

`my_mc._xscale`

Description

Property; determines the horizontal scale (`percentage`) of the movie clip as applied from the registration point of the movie clip. The default registration point is (0,0).

Scaling the local coordinate system affects the _x and _y property settings, which are defined in whole pixels. For example, if the parent movie clip is scaled to 50%, setting the _x property moves an object in the movie clip by half the number of pixels as it would if the movie were set at 100%.

See also

`MovieClip._x, MovieClip._y, MovieClip._yscale`

MovieClip._y

Availability

Flash Player 3.

Usage

`my_mc._y`

Description

Property; sets the *y* coordinate of a movie clip relative to the local coordinates of the parent movie clip. If a movie clip is in the main Timeline, then its coordinate system refers to the upper left corner of the Stage as (0, 0). If the move clip is inside another movie clip that has transformations, the movie clip is in the local coordinate system of the enclosing movie clip. Thus, for a movie clip rotated 90 degrees counterclockwise, the movie clip's children inherit a coordinate system that is rotated 90 degrees counterclockwise. The movie clip's coordinates refer to the registration point position.

See also

`MovieClip._x, MovieClip._xscale, MovieClip._yscale`

MovieClip._ymouse

Availability

Flash Player 5.

Usage

*my_mc.*_ymouse

Description

Property (read-only); indicates the *y* coordinate of the mouse position.

See also

Mouse class, MovieClip._xmouse

MovieClip._yscale

Availability

Flash Player 4.

Usage

*my_mc.*_yscale

Description

Property; sets the vertical scale (*percentage*) of the movie clip as applied from the registration point of the movie clip. The default registration point is (0,0).

Scaling the local coordinate system affects the _x and _y property settings, which are defined in whole pixels. For example, if the parent movie clip is scaled to 50%, setting the _x property moves an object in the movie clip by half the number of pixels as it would if the movie were at 100%.

See also

MovieClip._x, MovieClip._xscale, MovieClip._y

MovieClipLoader class

Availability

Flash Player 7.

Description

This class lets you implement listener callbacks that provide status information while SWF or JPEG files are being loaded (downloaded) into movie clips. To use MovieClipLoader features, use MovieClipLoader.loadClip() instead of `loadMovie()` or `MovieClip.loadMovie()` to load SWF files.

After you issue the `MovieClipLoader.loadClip()` command, the following events take place in the order listed:

- When the first bytes of the downloaded file have been written to disk, the MovieClipLoader.onLoadStart() listener is invoked.
- If you have implemented the MovieClipLoader.onLoadProgress() listener, it is invoked during the loading process.

  Note: You can call MovieClipLoader.getProgress() at any time during the load process.

- When the entire downloaded file has been written to disk, the MovieClipLoader.onLoadComplete() listener is invoked.
- After the downloaded file's first frame actions have been executed, the MovieClipLoader.onLoadInit() listener is invoked.

After `MovieClipLoader.onLoadInit()`has been invoked, you can set properties, use methods, and otherwise interact with the loaded movie.

If the file fails to load completely, the MovieClipLoader.onLoadError() listener is invoked.

Method summary for the MovieClipLoader class

Method	Description
MovieClipLoader.addListener()	Registers an object to receive notification when a MovieClipLoader event handler is invoked.
MovieClipLoader.getProgress()	Returns the number of bytes loaded and total number of bytes for a file that is being loaded using `MovieClipLoader.loadClip()`.
MovieClipLoader.loadClip()	Loads a SWF or JPEG file into a movie clip in Flash Player while the original movie is playing.
MovieClipLoader.removeListener()	Deletes an object that was registered using `MovieClipLoader.addListener()`.
MovieClipLoader.unloadClip()	Removes a movie clip that was loaded by means of `MovieClipLoader.loadClip()`.

Listener summary for the MovieClipLoader class

Listener	Description
`MovieClipLoader.onLoadComplete()`	Invoked when a file loaded with `MovieClipLoader.loadClip()` has completely downloaded.
`MovieClipLoader.onLoadError()`	Invoked when a file loaded with `MovieClipLoader.loadClip()` has failed to load.
`MovieClipLoader.onLoadInit()`	Invoked when the actions on the first frame of the loaded clip have been executed.
`MovieClipLoader.onLoadProgress()`	Invoked every time the loading content is written to disk during the loading process.
`MovieClipLoader.onLoadStart()`	Invoked when a call to `MovieClipLoader.loadClip()` has successfully begun to download a file.

Constructor for the MovieClipLoader class

Availability

Flash Player 7.

Usage

```
new MovieClipLoader()
```

Parameters

None.

Returns

Nothing.

Description

Constructor; creates a MovieClipLoader object that you can use to implement a number of listeners to respond to events while a SWF or JPEG file is downloading.

Example

See MovieClipLoader.loadClip().

See also

MovieClipLoader.addListener()

MovieClipLoader.addListener()

Availability

Flash Player 7.

Usage

my_mcl.addListener(*listenerObject*)

Parameters

listenerObject An object that listens for a callback notification from the MovieClipLoader event handlers.

Returns

Nothing.

Description

Method; registers an object to receive notification when a MovieClipLoader event handler is invoked.

Example

See MovieClipLoader.loadClip().

See also

MovieClipLoader.onLoadComplete(), MovieClipLoader.onLoadError(), MovieClipLoader.onLoadInit(), MovieClipLoader.onLoadProgress(), MovieClipLoader.onLoadStart(), MovieClipLoader.removeListener()

MovieClipLoader.getProgress()

Availability

Flash Player 7.

Usage

my_mcl.getProgress(*target_mc*)

Parameters

target_mc A SWF or JPEG file that is loaded using MovieClipLoader.loadClip().

Returns

An object that has two integer properties: bytesLoaded and bytesTotal.

Description

Method; returns the number of bytes loaded and total number of bytes for a file that is being loaded using MovieClipLoader.loadClip(); for compressed movies, it reflects the number of compressed bytes. This method lets you explicitly request this information, instead of (or in addition to) writing a MovieClipLoader.onLoadProgress() listener function.

Example

See MovieClipLoader.loadClip().

See also

MovieClipLoader.onLoadProgress()

MovieClipLoader.loadClip()

Availability

Flash Player 7.

Usage

```
my_mcl.loadMovie("url", target )
```

Parameters

url   The absolute or relative URL of the SWF file or JPEG file to be loaded. A relative path must be relative to the SWF file at level 0. Absolute URLs must include the protocol reference, such as http:// or file:///. Filenames cannot include disk drive specifications.

target   The target path of a movie clip, or an integer specifying the level in Flash Player into which the movie will be loaded. The target movie clip will be replaced by the loaded movie or image.

Returns

Nothing.

Description

Method; loads a SWF or JPEG file into a movie clip in Flash Player while the original movie is playing. Using this method lets you display several movies at once and switch between movies without loading another HTML document.

Using this method instead of `loadMovie()` or `MovieClip.loadMovie()` has a number of advantages:

* The MovieClipLoader.onLoadStart() handler is invoked when loading begins.
* The MovieClipLoader.onLoadError() handler is invoked if the clip cannot be loaded.
* The MovieClipLoader.onLoadProgress() handler is invoked as the loading process progresses.
* The MovieClipLoader.onLoadInit() handler is invoked after the actions in the first frame of the clip have executed, so you can being manipulating the loaded clip.

A movie or image loaded into a movie clip inherits the position, rotation, and scale properties of the movie clip. You can use the target path of the movie clip to target the loaded movie.

You can use this method to load one or more files into a single movie clip or level; MovieClipLoader listener objects are passed the loading target movie clip instance as a parameter. Alternately, you can create a different MovieClipLoader object for each file you load.

Use `MovieClipLoader.unloadClip()` to remove movies or images loaded with this method or to cancel a load operation that is in progress.

Example

The following example illustrates the use of many of the MovieClipLoader methods and listeners.

```
// first set of listeners
var my_mcl = new MovieClipLoader();
myListener = new Object();
myListener.onLoadStart = function (target_mc)
{
myTrace ("*********First my_mcl instance*********");
myTrace ("Your load has begun on movie clip . = " + target_mc);
var loadProgress = my_mcl.getProgress(target_mc);
myTrace(loadProgress.bytesLoaded + " = bytes loaded at start");
myTrace(loadProgress.bytesTotal + " = bytes total at start");
}
myListener.onLoadProgress = function (target_mc, loadedBytes, totalBytes)
{
myTrace ("*********First my_mcl instance Progress*********");
myTrace ("onLoadProgress() called back on movie clip " + target_mc);
myTrace(loadedBytes + " = bytes loaded at progress callback " );
myTrace(totalBytes + " = bytes total at progress callback \n");
}
myListener.onLoadComplete = function (target_mc)
{
myTrace ("*********First my_mcl instance*********");
myTrace ("Your load is done on movie clip = " + target_mc);
var loadProgress = my_mcl.getProgress(target_mc);
myTrace(loadProgress.bytesLoaded + " = bytes loaded at end" );
myTrace(loadProgress.bytesTotal + " = bytes total at end=");
}
myListener.onLoadInit = function (target_mc)
{
myTrace ("*********First my_mcl instance*********");
myTrace ("Movie clip = " + target_mc + " is now initialized");
// you can now do any setup required, for example:
target_mc._width = 100;
target_mc._width = 100;
}
myListener.onLoadError = function (target_mc, errorCode)
{
myTrace ("*********First my_mcl instance*********");
myTrace ("ERROR CODE = " + errorCode);
myTrace ("Your load failed on movie clip = " + target_mc + "\n");
}
my_mcl.addListener(myListener);
//Now load the files into their targets.
// loads into movie clips - strings used as target
my_mcl.loadClip("http://www.somedomain.somewhere.com/
  someFile.swf","_root.myMC");
my_mcl.loadClip("http://www.somedomain.somewhere.com/someOtherFile.swf",
  "_level0.myMC2");
//failed load
my_mcl.loadClip("http://www.somedomain.somewhere.com/someFile.jpg",
  _root.myMC5);

// loads into movie clips - movie clip instances used as target.
my_mcl.loadClip("http://www.somedomain.somewhere.com/someOtherFile.jpg",
  _level0.myMC3);

// loads into _level1
my_mcl.loadClip("file:///C:/media/images/somePicture.jpg", 1);
```

```
//Second set of listeners
var another_mcl = new MovieClipLoader();
myListener2 = new Object();
myListener2.onLoadStart = function (target_mc)
{
myTrace("*********Second my_mcl instance*********");
myTrace ("Your load has begun on movie clip22 . = " + target_mc);
var loadProgress = my_mcl.getProgress(target_mc);
myTrace(loadProgress.bytesLoaded + " = bytes loaded at start" );
myTrace(loadProgress.bytesTotal + " = bytes total at start");
}
myListener2.onLoadComplete = function (target_mc)
{
myTrace ("*********Second my_mcl instance*********");
myTrace ("Your load is done on movie clip = " + target_mc);
var loadProgress = my_mcl.getProgress(target_mc);
myTrace(loadProgress.bytesLoaded + " = bytes loaded at end");
myTrace(loadProgress.bytesTotal + " = bytes total at end" );
}
myListener2.onLoadError = function (target_mc, errorCode)
{
myTrace ("*********Second my_mcl instance*********");
myTrace ("ERROR CODE = " + errorCode);
myTrace ("Your load failed on movie clip = " + target_mc + "\n");
 }
another_mcl.addListener(myListener2);
//Now load the files into their targets (using the second instance of
  MovieClipLoader)
another_mcl.loadClip("http://www.somedomain.somewhere.com/
  yetAnotherFile.jpg", _root.myMC4);
// Issue the following statements after the download is complete,
// and after my_mcl.onLoadInit has been called.
// my_mcl.removeListener(myListener)
// my_mcl.removeListener(myListener2)
```

See also

MovieClipLoader.unloadClip()

MovieClipLoader.onLoadComplete()

Availability

Flash Player 7.

Usage

```
listenerObject.onLoadComplete() = function(target_mc) {
    // your statements here
}
```

Parameters

listenerObject   A listener object that was added using MovieClipLoader.addListener().

target_mc   The movie clip loaded by a MovieClipLoader.loadClip() method.

Returns

Nothing.

Description

Listener; invoked when a file loaded with MovieClipLoader.loadClip() has completely downloaded.

Example

See MovieClipLoader.loadClip().

See also

MovieClipLoader.addListener(), MovieClipLoader.onLoadStart(), MovieClipLoader.onLoadError()

MovieClipLoader.onLoadError()

Availability

Flash Player 7.

Usage

```
listenerObject.onLoadError() = function(target_mc, errorCode) {
    // your statements here
}
```

Parameters

listenerObject   A listener object that was added using MovieClipLoader.addListener().

target_mc   The movie clip loaded by a MovieClipLoader.loadClip() method.

errorCode   A string that explains the reason for the failure.

Returns

One of two strings: "URLNotFound" or "LoadNeverCompleted".

Description

Listener; invoked when a file loaded with MovieClipLoader.loadClip() has failed to load.

The string "URLNotFound" is returned if neither the MovieClipLoader.onLoadStart() or MovieClipLoader.onLoadComplete() listener has been called. For example, if a server is down or the file is not found, these listeners are not called.

The string "LoadNeverCompleted" is returned if `MovieClipLoader.onLoadStart()` was called but `MovieClipLoader.onLoadComplete()` was not called. For example, if `MovieClipLoader.onLoadStart()` is called but the download is interrupted due to server overload, server crash, and so on, `MovieClipLoader.onLoadComplete()` will not be called.

Example

See MovieClipLoader.loadClip().

MovieClipLoader.onLoadInit()

Availability

Flash Player 7.

Usage

```
listenerObject.onLoadInit() = function(target_mc) {
    // your statements here
}
```

Parameters

listenerObject   A listener object that was added using MovieClipLoader.addListener().

target_mc   The movie clip loaded by a MovieClipLoader.loadClip() method.

Returns

Nothing.

Description

Listener; invoked when the actions on the first frame of the loaded clip have been executed. After this listener has been invoked, you can set properties, use methods, and otherwise interact with the loaded movie.

Example

See MovieClipLoader.loadClip().

See also

MovieClipLoader.onLoadStart()

MovieClipLoader.onLoadProgress()

Availability

Flash Player 7.

Usage

```
listenerObject.onLoadProgress() =
    function(target_mc [, loadedBytes [, totalBytes ] ] ) {
    // your statements here
}
```

Parameters

listenerObject   A listener object that was added using MovieClipLoader.addListener().

target_mc   The movie clip loaded by a MovieClipLoader.loadClip() method.

loadedBytes   The number of bytes that had been loaded when the listener was invoked.

totalBytes   The total number of bytes in the file being loaded.

Returns

Nothing.

Description

Listener; invoked every time the loading content is written to disk during the loading process (that is, between `MovieClipLoader.onLoadStart()` and `MovieClipLoader.onLoadComplete()`). You can use this method to display information about the progress of the download, using the `loadedBytes` and `totalBytes` parameters.

Example

See MovieClipLoader.loadClip().

See also

MovieClipLoader.getProgress()

MovieClipLoader.onLoadStart()

Availability

Flash Player 7.

Usage

```
listenerObject.onLoadStart() = function(target_mc) {
    // your statements here
}
```

Parameters

listenerObject   A listener object that was added using MovieClipLoader.addListener().

target_mc   The movie clip loaded by a MovieClipLoader.loadClip() method.

Returns

Nothing.

Description

Listener; invoked when a call to MovieClipLoader.loadClip() has successfully begun to download a file.

Example

See MovieClipLoader.loadClip().

See also

MovieClipLoader.onLoadError(), MovieClipLoader.onLoadInit(), MovieClipLoader.onLoadComplete()

MovieClipLoader.removeListener()

Availability

Flash Player 7.

Usage

my_mcl.removeListener(*listenerObject*)

Parameters

listenerObject   A listener object that was added using MovieClipLoader.addListener().

Returns

Nothing.

Description

Method; deletes an object that was used to receive notification when a MovieClipLoader event handler was invoked.

Example

See MovieClipLoader.loadClip().

MovieClipLoader.unloadClip()

Availability

Flash Player 7.

Usage

my_mcl.unloadClip(*target*)

Parameters

target   The string or integer passed to the corresponding call to *my_mcl*.loadClip().

Returns

Nothing.

Description

Method; removes a movie clip that was loaded by means of MovieClipLoader.loadClip(). If you issue this command while a movie is loading, MovieClipLoader.onLoadError() is invoked.

See also

MovieClipLoader.loadClip()

NaN

Availability

Flash Player 5.

Usage

```
NaN
```

Description

Variable; a predefined variable with the IEEE-754 value for NaN (Not a Number). To determine if a number is NaN, use isNaN().

See also

isNaN(), Number.NaN

ne (not equal – string specific)

Availability

Flash Player 4. This operator has been deprecated in favor of the != (inequality) operator.

Usage

```
expression1 ne expression2
```

Parameters

expression1, expression2   Numbers, strings, or variables.

Returns

A Boolean value.

Description

Operator (comparison); compares *expression1* to *expression2* and returns true if *expression1* is not equal to *expression2*; otherwise, returns false.

See also

!= (inequality)

NetConnection class

Availability

Flash Player 7.

Note: This class is also supported in Flash Player 6 when used with Flash Communication Server. For more information, see your Flash Communication Server documentation.

Description

The NetConnection class provides the means to play back streaming FLV files from a local drive or HTTP address. For more information on video playback, see "Playing back external FLV files dynamically" on page 401.

Method summary for the NetConnection class

Method	Description
NetConnection.connect()	Opens a local connection through which you can play back video (FLV) files from an HTTP address or from the local file system.

Constructor for the NetConnection class

Availability

Flash Player 7.

Note: This class is also supported in Flash Player 6 when used with Flash Communication Server. For more information, see your Flash Communication Server documentation.

Usage

```
new NetConnection()
```

Parameters

None.

Returns

Nothing.

Description

Constructor; creates a NetConnection object that you can use in conjunction with a NetStream object to play back local streaming video (FLV) files. After creating the NetConnection object, use NetConnection.connect() to make the actual connection.

Playing external FLV files provides several advantages over embedding video in a Flash document, such as better performance and memory management, and independent video and Flash frame rates. For more information, see "Playing back external FLV files dynamically" on page 401.

See also

NetStream class, Video.attachVideo()

NetConnection.connect()

Flash Player 7.

Note: This method is also supported in Flash Player 6 when used with Flash Communication Server. For more information, see your Flash Communication Server documentation.

Usage

`my_nc.connect(null);`

Parameters

None (you must pass `null`).

Returns

Nothing.

Description

Constructor; opens a local connection through which you can play back video (FLV) files from an HTTP address or from the local file system.

See also

NetStream class

NetStream class

Availability

Flash Player 7.

Note: This class is also supported in Flash Player 6 when used with Flash Communication Server. For more information, see your Flash Communication Server documentation.

Description

The NetStream class provides methods and properties for playing Flash Video (FLV) files from the local file system or an HTTP address. You use a NetStream object to stream video through a NetConnection object. Playing external FLV files provides several advantages over embedding video in a Flash document, such as better performance and memory management, and independent video and Flash frame rates. This class provides a number of methods and properties you can use to track the progress of the file as it loads and plays, and to give the user control over playback (stopping, pausing, and so on).

For more information on video playback, see "Playing back external FLV files dynamically" on page 401.

Method summary for the NetStream class

The following methods and properties of the NetConnection and NetStream classes are used to control FLV playback.

Method	Purpose
NetStream.close()	Closes the stream but does not clear the video object.
NetStream.pause()	Pauses or resumes playback of a stream.
NetStream.play()	Begins playback of an external video (FLV) file.
NetStream.seek()	Seeks a specific position in the FLV file.
NetStream.setBufferTime()	Specifies how long to buffer data before starting to display the stream.

Property summary for the NetStream class

Property	Description
NetStream.bufferLength	The number of seconds of data currently in the buffer.
NetStream.bufferTime	Read-only: the number of seconds assigned to the buffer by NetStream.setBufferTime().
NetStream.bytesLoaded	Read-only; the number of bytes of data that have been loaded into the player.
NetStream.bytesTotal	Read-only; the total size in bytes of the file being loaded into the player.
NetStream.currentFps	The number of frames per second being displayed.
NetStream.time	Read-only; the position of the playhead, in seconds.

Event handler summary for the NetStream class

Event handler	Description
NetStream.onStatus	Invoked every time a status change or error is posted for the NetStream object.

Constructor for the NetStream class

Availability

Flash Player 7.

Note: This class is also supported in Flash Player 6 when used with Flash Communication Server. For more information, see your Flash Communication Server documentation.

Usage

```
new NetStream(my_nc)
```

Parameters

my_nc   A NetConnection object.

Returns

Nothing.

Description

Constructor; creates a stream that can be used for playing FLV files through the specified NetConnection object.

Example

The following code first constructs a new NetConnection object, my_nc, and uses it to construct a new NetStream object called videoStream_ns.

```
my_nc = new NetConnection();
my_nc.connect(null);
videoStream_ns = new NetStream(my_nc);
```

See also

NetConnection class, NetStream class, Video.attachVideo()

NetStream.bufferLength

Availability

Flash Player 7.

Note: This property is also supported in Flash Player 6 when used with Flash Communication Server. For more information, see your Flash Communication Server documentation.

Usage

```
my_ns.bufferLength
```

Description

Read-only property; the number of seconds of data currently in the buffer. You can use this property in conjunction with NetStream.bufferTime to estimate how close the buffer is to being full—for example, to display feedback to a user who is waiting for data to be loaded into the buffer.

See also

NetStream.bytesLoaded

NetStream.bufferTime

Availability

Flash Player 7.

Note: This property is also supported in Flash Player 6 when used with Flash Communication Server. For more information, see your Flash Communication Server documentation.

Usage

`myStream.bufferTime`

Description

Read-only property; the number of seconds assigned to the buffer by `NetStream.setBufferTime()`. The default value is .1(one-tenth of a second). To determine the number of seconds currently in the buffer, use NetStream.bufferLength.

See also

NetStream.time

NetStream.bytesLoaded

Availability

Flash Player 7.

Usage

`my_ns.bytesLoaded`

Description

Read-only property; the number of bytes of data that have been loaded into the player. You can use this method in conjunction with NetStream.bytesTotal to estimate how close the buffer is to being full—for example, to display feedback to a user who is waiting for data to be loaded into the buffer

See also

NetStream.bufferLength

NetStream.bytesTotal

Availability

Flash Player 7.

Usage

`my_ns.bytesLoaded`

Description

Read-only property; the total size in bytes of the file being loaded into the player.

See also

NetStream.bytesLoaded, NetStream.bufferTime

NetStream.close()

Availability

Flash Player 7.

Note: This method is also supported in Flash Player 6 when used with Flash Communication Server. For more information, see your Flash Communication Server documentation.

Usage

`my_ns.close()`

Parameters

None.

Returns

Nothing.

Description

Method; stops playing all data on the stream, sets the `NetStream.time` property to 0, and makes the stream available for another use. This command also deletes the local copy of an FLV file that was downloaded using HTTP.

Example

The following `onDisconnect()` function closes a connection and deletes the temporary copy of someFile.flv that was stored on the local disk.

```
my_nc = new NetConnection();
my_nc.connect(null);
my_ns = new NetStream(my_nc);
my_ns.play("http://www.someDomain.com/videos/someFile.flv");

function onDisconnect() {
  my_ns.close();
}
```

See also

`NetStream.pause()`, NetStream.play()

NetStream.currentFps

Availability

Flash Player 7.

Note: This property is also supported in Flash Player 6 when used with Flash Communication Server. For more information, see your Flash Communication Server documentation.

Usage

`my_ns.currentFps`

Description

Read-only property; the number of frames per second being displayed. If you are exporting FLV files to be played back on a number of systems, you can check this value during testing to help you determine how much compression to apply when exporting the file.

NetStream.onStatus

Availability

Flash Player 7.

Note: This handler is also supported in Flash Player 6 when used with Flash Communication Server. For more information, see your Flash Communication Server documentation.

Usage

```
my_ns.onStatus = function(infoObject) {
  // Your code here
}
```

Parameters

infoObject   A parameter defined according to the status or error message. For more information about this parameter, see "Description," below.

Returns

Nothing.

Description

Event handler; invoked every time a status change or error is posted for the NetStream object. If you want to respond to this event handler, you must create a function to process the information object.

The information object has a `code` property containing a string that describes the result of the `onStatus` handler, and a `level` property containing a string that is either `"Status"` or `"Error"`.

In addition to this `onStatus` handler, Flash also provides a "super" function called `System.onStatus`. If `onStatus` is invoked for a particular object and there is no function assigned to respond to it, Flash processes a function assigned to `System.onStatus` if it exists.

The following events notify you when certain NetStream activities occur.

Code property	Level property	Meaning
NetStream.Buffer.Empty	Status	Data is not being received quickly enough to fill the buffer. Data flow will be interrupted until the buffer refills, at which time a `NetStream.Buffer.Full` message will be sent and the stream will begin playing again.
NetStream.Buffer.Full	Status	The buffer is full and the stream will begin playing.
NetStream.Play.Start	Status	Playback has started.
NetStream.Play.Stop	Status	Playback has stopped.
NetStream.Play.StreamNotFound	Error	The FLV passed to the `play()` method can't be found.

Example

The following example writes data about the stream to a log file.

```
my_ns.onStatus = function(info)
{
   _root.log_stream += "Stream status.\n";
   _root.log_stream += "Event: " + info.code + "\n";
   _root.log_stream += "Type: " + info.level + "\n";
}
```

See also

System.onStatus

NetStream.pause()

Availability

Flash Player 7.

Note: This method is also supported in Flash Player 6 when used with Flash Communication Server. For more information, see your Flash Communication Server documentation.

Usage

my_ns.pause([*pauseResume*])

Parameters

pauseResume   Optional: a Boolean value specifying whether to pause play (true) or resume play (false). If you omit this parameter, NetStream.pause() acts as a toggle: the first time it is called on a specified stream, it pauses play, and the next time it is called, it resumes play.

Returns

Nothing.

Description

Method; pauses or resumes playback of a stream.

The first time you call this method (without sending a parameter), it pauses play; the next time, it resumes play. You might want to attach this method to a button that the user presses to pause or resume playback.

Example

The following examples illustrate some uses of this method.

```
my_ns.pause(); // pauses play first time issued
my_ns.pause(); // resumes play
my_ns.pause(false); // no effect, play continues
my_ns.pause(); // pauses play
```

See also

NetStream.close(), NetStream.play()

NetStream.play()

Availability

Flash Player 7.

Note: This method is also supported in Flash Player 6 when used with Flash Communication Server. For more information, see your Flash Communication Server documentation.

Usage

```
my_ns.play("fileName");
```

Parameters

`fileName` The name of an FLV file to play, in quotation marks. Both http:// and file:// formats are supported; the file:// location is always relative to the location of the SWF file.

Returns

Nothing.

Description

Method; begins playback of an external video (FLV) file. To view video data, you must call a `Video.attachVideo()` method; audio being streamed with the video, or an FLV file that contains only audio, is played automatically.

If you want to control the audio associated with an FLV file, you can use `MovieClip.attachAudio()` to route the audio to a movie clip; you can then create a Sound object to control some aspects of the audio. For more information, see `MovieClip.attachAudio()`.

If the FLV file can't be found, the NetStream.onStatus event handler is invoked. If you want to stop a stream that is currently playing, use NetStream.close().

You can play local FLV files that are stored in the same directory as the SWF file or in a subdirectory; you can't navigate to a higher-level directory. For example, if the SWF file is located in a directory named /training, and you want to play a video stored in the /training/videos directory, you would use the following syntax:

```
my_ns.play("file://videos/videoName.flv");
```

To play a video stored in the /training directory, you would use the following syntax:

my_ns.play("file://videoName.flv");

Example

The following example illustrates some ways to use the `NetStream.play()` command.

```
// Play a file that is on the user's computer
// The joe_user directory is a subdirectory of the directory
//   in which the SWF is stored
my_ns.play("file://joe_user/flash/videos/lectureJune26.flv");

// Play a file on a server
my_ns.play("http://someServer.someDomain.com/flash/video/orientation.flv");
```

See also

`MovieClip.attachAudio()`, NetStream.close(), NetStream.pause(), `Video.attachVideo()`

NetStream.seek()

Availability

Flash Player 7.

Note: This method is also supported in Flash Player 6 when used with Flash Communication Server. For more information, see your Flash Communication Server documentation.

Usage

```
my_ns.seek(numberOfSeconds)
```

Parameters

numberOfSeconds　The approximate time value, in seconds, to move to in an FLV file. The playhead moves to the keyframe closest to *numberOfSeconds*.

- To return to the beginning of the stream, pass 0 for *numberOfSeconds*.
- To seek forward from the beginning of the stream, pass the number of seconds you want to advance. For example, to position the playhead at 15 seconds from the beginning, use *myStream*.seek(15).
- To seek relative to the current position, pass *mystream*.time + *n* or *mystream*.time - *n* to seek *n* seconds forward or backward, respectively, from the current position. For example, to rewind 20 seconds from the current position, use my_ns.seek(my_ns.time - 20).

Returns

Nothing.

Description

Method; seeks the keyframe closest to the specified number of seconds from the beginning of the stream. The stream resumes playing when it reaches the specified location in the stream.

Example

The following example illustrates some ways to use the NetStream.seek() command.

```
// Return to the beginning of the stream
my_ns.seek(0);

// Move to a location 30 seconds from the beginning of the stream
my_ns.seek(30);

//Move backwards three minutes from current location
my_ns.seek(my_ns.time - 180);
```

See also

NetStream.play(), NetStream.time

NetStream.setBufferTime()

Availability

Flash Player 7.

Note: This method is also supported in Flash Player 6 when used with Flash Communication Server. For more information, see your Flash Communication Server documentation.

Usage

my_ns.setBufferTime(*numberOfSeconds*)

Parameters

numberOfSeconds   The number of seconds of data to be buffered before Flash begins displaying data. The default value is .1 (one-tenth of a second).

Description

Method; specifies how long to buffer messages before starting to display the stream. For example, if you want to make sure that the first 15 seconds of the stream play without interruption, set *numberOfSeconds* to 15; Flash begins playing the stream only after 15 seconds of data are buffered.

See also

NetStream.bufferTime

NetStream.time

Availability

Flash Player 7.

Note: This property is also supported in Flash Player 6 when used with Flash Communication Server. For more information, see your Flash Communication Server documentation.

Usage

my_ns.time

Description

Read-only property; the position of the playhead, in seconds.

See also

NetStream.bufferLength, NetStream.bytesLoaded

new

Availability

Flash Player 5.

Usage

```
new constructor()
```

Parameters

constructor   A function followed by any optional parameters in parentheses. The function is usually the name of the object type (for example, Array, Number, or Object) to be constructed.

Returns

Nothing.

Description

Operator; creates a new, initially anonymous, object and calls the function identified by the *constructor* parameter. The new operator passes to the function any optional parameters in parentheses, as well as the newly created object, which is referenced using the keyword this. The constructor function can then use this to set the variables of the object.

Example

The following example creates the Book() function and then uses the new operator to create the objects book1 and book2.

```
function Book(name, price){
   this.name = name;
   this.price = price;
}

book1 = new Book("Confederacy of Dunces", 19.95);
book2 = new Book("The Floating Opera", 10.95);
```

Example

The following example uses the new operator to create an Array object with 18 elements:

```
golfCourse_array = new Array(18);
```

See also

[] (array access), {} (object initializer)

newline

Availability

Flash Player 4.

Usage

```
newline
```

Parameters

None.

Returns

Nothing.

Description

Constant; inserts a carriage return character (\n) that generates a blank line in text output generated by your code. Use newline to make space for information that is retrieved by a function or action in your code.

Example

The following example shows how newline displays output from the trace() action on multiple lines.

```
var myName:String = "Lisa", myAge:Number = 30;
trace(myName + myAge);
trace(myName + newline + myAge);
```

nextFrame()

Availability

Flash 2.

Usage

```
nextFrame()
```

Parameters

None.

Returns

Nothing.

Description

Function; sends the playhead to the next frame and stops it.

Example

In this example, when the user clicks the button, the playhead goes to the next frame and stops.

```
on (release) {
  nextFrame();
}
```

nextScene()

Availability

Flash 2.

Usage

```
nextScene()
```

Parameters

None.

Returns

Nothing.

Description

Function; sends the playhead to Frame 1 of the next scene and stops it.

Example

In this example, when a user releases the button, the playhead is sent to Frame 1 of the next scene.

```
on(release) {
   nextScene();
}
```

See also

```
prevScene()
```

not

Availability

Flash Player 4. This operator has been deprecated in favor of the ! (logical NOT) operator.

Usage

```
not expression
```

Parameters

expression   A variable or other expression that converts to a Boolean value.

Description

Operator; performs a logical NOT operation in Flash Player 4.

See also

```
! (logical NOT)
```

null

Availability

Flash Player 5.

Usage

```
null
```

Parameters

None.

Returns

Nothing.

Description

Constant; a special value that can be assigned to variables, or returned by a function if no data was provided. You can use `null` to represent values that are missing or do not have a defined data type.

Example

In a numeric context, `null` evaluates to 0. Equality tests can be performed with `null`. In this statement, a binary tree node has no left child, so the field for its left child could be set to `null`.

```
if (tree.left == null) {
  tree.left = new TreeNode();
}
```

Number class

Availability

Flash Player 5 (became a native object in Flash Player 6, which improved performance significantly).

Description

The Number class is a simple wrapper object for the Number data type. You can manipulate primitive numeric values by using the methods and properties associated with the Number class. This class is identical to the JavaScript Number class.

You must use a constructor when calling the methods of a Number object, but you do not need to use the constructor when calling the properties of a Number object. The following examples specify the syntax for calling the methods and properties of a Number object.

The following example calls the `toString()` method of a Number object, which returns the string "1234".

```
myNumber = new Number(1234);
myNumber.toString();
```

This example calls the `MIN_VALUE` property (also called a constant) of a Number object:

```
smallest = Number.MIN_VALUE
```

Method summary for the Number class

Method	Description
Number.toString()	Returns the string representation of a Number object.
Number.valueOf()	Returns the primitive value of a Number object.

Property summary for the Number class

Property	Description
Number.MAX_VALUE	Constant representing the largest representable number (double-precision IEEE-754). This number is approximately 1.79E+308.
Number.MIN_VALUE	Constant representing the smallest representable number (double-precision IEEE-754). This number is approximately 5e-324.
Number.NaN	Constant representing the value for Not a Number (NaN).
Number.NEGATIVE_INFINITY	Constant representing the value for negative infinity.
Number.POSITIVE_INFINITY	Constant representing the value for positive infinity. This value is the same as the global variable Infinity.

Constructor for the Number class

Availability

Flash Player 5.

Usage

```
new Number(value)
```

Parameters

value   The numeric value of the Number object being created, or a value to be converted to a number.

Returns

Nothing.

Description

Constructor; creates a new Number object. You must use the Number constructor when using Number.toString() and Number.valueOf(). You do not use a constructor when using the properties of a Number object. The new Number constructor is primarily used as a placeholder. A Number object is not the same as the Number() function that converts a parameter to a primitive value.

Example

The following code constructs new Number objects.

```
n1 = new Number(3.4);
n2 = new Number(-10);
```

See also

Number()

Number.MAX_VALUE

Availability

Flash Player 5.

Usage

```
Number.MAX_VALUE
```

Description

Property; the largest representable number (double-precision IEEE-754). This number is approximately 1.79E+308.

Number.MIN_VALUE

Availability

Flash Player 5.

Usage

```
Number.MIN_VALUE
```

Description

Property; the smallest representable number (double-precision IEEE-754). This number is approximately 5e-324.

Number.NaN

Availability

Flash Player 5.

Usage

```
Number.NaN
```

Description

Property; the IEEE-754 value representing Not A Number (NaN).

See also

```
isNaN(), NaN
```

Number.NEGATIVE_INFINITY

Availability

Flash Player 5.

Usage

```
Number.NEGATIVE_INFINITY
```

Description

Property; specifies the IEEE-754 value representing negative infinity. The value of this property is the same as that of the constant `-Infinity`.

Negative infinity is a special numeric value that is returned when a mathematical operation or function returns a negative value larger than can be represented.

Number.POSITIVE_INFINITY

Availability

Flash Player 5.

Usage

```
Number.POSITIVE_INFINITY
```

Description

Property; specifies the IEEE-754 value representing positive infinity. The value of this property is the same as that of the constant `Infinity`.

Positive infinity is a special numeric value that is returned when a mathematical operation or function returns a value larger than can be represented.

Number.toString()

Availability

Flash Player 5; behavior changed in Flash Player 7.

Usage

```
myNumber.toString(radix)
```

Parameters

`radix`   Specifies the numeric base (from 2 to 36) to use for the number-to-string conversion. If you do not specify the `radix` parameter, the default value is 10.

Returns

A string.

Description

Method; returns the string representation of the specified Number object (*myNumber*).

If *myNumber* is undefined, the return value is as follows:

- In files published for Flash Player 6 or earlier, the result is 0.
- In files published for Flash Player 7 or later, the result is NaN.

Example

The following example uses 2 and 8 for the *radix* parameter and returns a string that contains the corresponding representation of the number 9.

```
myNumber = new Number (9);
trace(myNumber.toString(2)); / 1001
trace(myNumber.toString(8)); / 11
```

See also

NaN

Number.valueOf()

Availability

Flash Player 5.

Usage

myNumber.valueOf()

Parameters

None.

Returns

A number.

Description

Method; returns the primitive value type of the specified Number object.

Number()

Availability

Flash Player 4; behavior changed in Flash Player 7.

Usage

Number(*expression*)

Parameters

expression   An expression to convert to a number.

Returns

A number or NaN.

Description

Function; converts the parameter *expression* to a number and returns a value as follows:

- If *expression* is a number, the return value is *expression*.
- If *expression* is a Boolean value, the return value is 1 if *expression* is true, 0 if *expression* is false.
- If *expression* is a string, the function attempts to parse *expression* as a decimal number with an optional trailing exponent, that is, 1.57505e-3.
- If *expression* is undefined, the return value is as follows:
  - In files published for Flash Player 6 or earlier, the result is 0.
  - In files published for Flash Player 7 or later, the result is NaN.

This function is used to convert Flash 4 files containing deprecated operators that are imported into the Flash 5 or later authoring environment. For more information, see & (bitwise AND operator).

See also

NaN, Number class

Object class

Availability

Flash Player 5 (became a native object in Flash Player 6, which improved performance significantly).

Description

The Object class is at the root of the ActionScript class hierarchy. This class contains a small subset of the features provided by the JavaScript Object class.

Method summary for the Object class

Method	Description
Object.addProperty()	Creates a getter/setter property on an object.
Object.registerClass()	Associates a movie clip symbol with an ActionScript object class.
Object.toString()	Converts the specified object to a string and returns it.
Object.unwatch()	Removes the watchpoint that Object.watch() created.
Object.valueOf()	Returns the primitive value of an object.
Object.watch()	Registers an event handler to be invoked when a specified property of an ActionScript object changes.

Property summary for the Object class

Property	Description
Object.__proto__	A reference to the prototype property of the object's constructor function.

Constructor for the Object class

Availability

Flash Player 5.

Usage

```
new Object([value])
```

Parameters

value   A number, Boolean value, or string to be converted to an object. This parameter is optional. If you do not specify *value*, the constructor creates a new object with no defined properties.

Returns

Nothing.

Description

Constructor; creates a new Object object.

Object.addProperty()

Availability

Flash Player 6. In external class files, you can use get or set instead of this method.

Usage

```
myObject.addProperty(prop, getFunc, setFunc)
```

Parameters

prop   The name of the object property to create.

getFunc   The function that is invoked to retrieve the value of the property; this parameter is a function object.

setFunc   The function that is invoked to set the value of the property; this parameter is a function object. If you pass the value null for this parameter, the property is read-only.

Returns

Returns a value of true if the property is successfully created; otherwise, returns false.

Description

Method; creates a getter/setter property. When Flash reads a getter/setter property, it invokes the get function and the function's return value becomes a value of *prop*. When Flash writes a getter/setter property, it invokes the set function and passes it the new value as a parameter. If a property with the given name already exists, the new property overwrites it.

A "get" function is a function with no parameters. Its return value can be of any type. Its type can change between invocations. The return value is treated as the current value of the property.

A "set" function is a function that takes one parameter, which is the new value of the property. For example, if property x is assigned by the statement x = 1, the set function is passed the parameter 1 of type number. The return value of the set function is ignored.

You can add getter/setter properties to prototype objects. If you add a getter/setter property to a prototype object, all object instances that inherit the prototype object inherit the getter/setter property. This makes it possible to add a getter/setter property in one location, the prototype object, and have it propagate to all instances of a class (much like adding methods to prototype objects). If a get/set function is invoked for a getter/setter property in an inherited prototype object, the reference passed to the get/set function will be the originally referenced object, not the prototype object.

If invoked incorrectly, Object.addProperty() may fail with an error. The following table describes errors that may occur:

Error condition	What happens
prop is not a valid property name; for instance, an empty string.	Returns false and the property is not added.
getFunc is not a valid function object.	Returns false and the property is not added.
setFunc is not a valid function object.	Returns false and the property is not added.

Example

Usage 1: An object has two internal methods, setQuantity() and getQuantity(). A property, bookcount, can be used to invoke these methods when it is either set or retrieved. A third internal method, getTitle(), returns a read-only value that is associated with the property bookname:

```
function Book() {
  this.setQuantity = function(numBooks) {
    this.books = numBooks;
  }
  this.getQuantity = function() {
    return this.books;
  }
  this.getTitle = function() {
    return "Catcher in the Rye";
  }
  this.addProperty("bookcount", this.getQuantity, this.setQuantity);
  this.addProperty("bookname", this.getTitle, null);
}
myBook = new Book();
myBook.bookcount = 5;
order = "You ordered " + myBook.bookcount + " copies of " + myBook.bookname;
```

When a script retrieves the value of myBook.bookcount, the ActionScript interpreter automatically invokes myBook.getQuantity(). When a script modifies the value of myBook.bookcount, the interpreter invokes myObject.setQuantity(). The bookname property does not specify a set function, so attempts to modify bookname are ignored.

Usage 2: The above example of bookcount and bookname works, but the properties bookcount and bookname are added to every instance of the Book object. That means that the cost of having the properties is two property slots for every instance of the object. If there are many properties like bookcount and bookname in a class, they could consume a great deal of memory. Instead, you can add the properties to Book.prototype:

```
function Book () {}
Book.prototype.setQuantity = function(numBooks) {
    this.books = numBooks;
}
Book.prototype.getQuantity = function() {
    return this.books;
}
Book.prototype.getTitle = function() {
    return "Catcher in the Rye";
}
Book.prototype.addProperty("bookcount", Book.prototype.getQuantity,
    Book.prototype.setQuantity);
Book.prototype.addProperty("bookname", Book.prototype.getTitle, null);
myBook = new Book();
myBook.bookcount = 5;
order = "You ordered "+myBook.bookcount+" copies of "+myBook.bookname;
```

Now, the bookcount and bookname properties exist only in one place: the Book.prototype object. The effect, however, is the same as that of the code in Usage 1, which added bookcount and bookname directly to every instance. If bookcount or bookname is accessed in a Book instance, the prototype chain is ascended and the getter/setter property in Book.prototype is found.

Usage 3: The built-in properties TextField.scroll and TextField.maxscroll are getter/setter properties. The TextField object has internal methods getScroll(), setScroll(), and getMaxScroll(). The TextField constructor creates the getter/setter properties and points them to the internal get/set methods, as in the following:

```
this.addProperty("scroll", this.getScroll, this.setScroll);
this.addProperty("maxscroll", this.getMaxScroll, null);
```

When a script retrieves the value of myTextField.scroll, the ActionScript interpreter automatically invokes myTextField.getScroll(). When a script modifies the value of myTextField.scroll, the interpreter invokes myTextField.setScroll(). The maxscroll property does not specify a set function, so attempts to modify maxscroll are ignored.

Usage 4: Although the built-in TextField.scroll and TextField.maxscroll properties work in the Usage 3 example, the properties scroll and maxscroll are added to every instance of the TextField object. That means the cost of having the properties is two property slots for every instance of the object. If there are many properties like scroll and maxscroll in a class, they could consume a great deal of memory. Instead, you can add the scroll and maxscroll properties to TextField.prototype:

```
TextField.prototype.addProperty("scroll", this.getScroll, this.setScroll);
TextField.prototype.addProperty("maxscroll", this.getMaxScroll, null);
```

Now, the scroll and maxscroll properties only exist in one place: the TextField.prototype object. The effect, however, is the same as the above code that added scroll and maxscroll directly to every instance. If scroll or maxscroll is accessed in a TextField instance, the prototype chain is ascended and the getter/setter property in TextField.prototype is found.

Object.__proto__

Availability

Flash Player 5.

Usage

```
myObject.__proto__
```

Parameters

None.

Description

Property; refers to the `prototype` property of the constructor function that created `myObject`. The `__proto__` property is automatically assigned to all objects when they are created. The ActionScript interpreter uses the `__proto__` property to access the `prototype` property of the object's constructor function to find out what properties and methods the object inherits from its class.

Object.registerClass()

Availability

Flash Player 6. If you are using external class files, you can use the ActionScript 2.0 Class field in the Linkage Properties or Symbol Properties dialog box to associate an object with a class instead of using this method.

Usage

```
Object.registerClass(symbolID, theClass)
```

Parameters

symbolID The linkage identifier of the movie clip symbol, or the string identifier for the ActionScript class.

theClass A reference to the constructor function of the ActionScript class, or `null` to unregister the symbol.

Returns

If the class registration succeeds, a value of `true` is returned; otherwise, `false` is returned.

Description

Method; associates a movie clip symbol with an ActionScript object class. If a symbol doesn't exist, Flash creates an association between a string identifier and an object class.

When an instance of the specified movie clip symbol is placed by the Timeline, it is registered to the class specified by the *theClass* parameter rather than to class MovieClip.

When an instance of the specified movie clip symbol is created by means of `MovieClip.attachMovie()` or `MovieClip.duplicateMovieClip()`, it is registered to the class specified by *theClass* rather than to the MovieClip class. If *theClass* is `null`, this method removes any ActionScript class definition associated with the specified movie clip symbol or class identifier. For movie clip symbols, any existing instances of the movie clip remain unchanged, but new instances of the symbol are associated with the default class MovieClip.

If a symbol is already registered to a class, this method replaces it with the new registration.

When a movie clip instance is placed by the Timeline or created using `attachMovie()` or `duplicateMovieClip()`, ActionScript invokes the constructor for the appropriate class with the keyword `this` pointing to the object. The constructor function is invoked with no parameters.

If you use this method to register a movie clip with an ActionScript class other than MovieClip, the movie clip symbol doesn't inherit the methods, properties, and events of the built-in MovieClip class unless you include the MovieClip class in the prototype chain of the new class. The following code creates a new ActionScript class called `theClass` that inherits the properties of the MovieClip class:

```
theClass.prototype = new MovieClip();
```

See also

`MovieClip.attachMovie()`, `MovieClip.duplicateMovieClip()`

Object.toString()

Availability

Flash Player 5.

Usage

```
myObject.toString()
```

Parameters

None.

Returns

A string.

Description

Method; converts the specified object to a string and returns it.

Object.unwatch()

Availability

Flash Player 6.

Usage

myObject.unwatch (*prop*)

Parameters

prop   The name of the object property that should no longer be watched, as a string.

Returns

A Boolean value.

Description

Method; removes a watchpoint that Object.watch() created. This method returns a value of true if the watchpoint was successfully removed; otherwise, it returns a false value.

Object.valueOf()

Availability

Flash Player 5.

Usage

myObject.valueOf()

Parameters

None.

Returns

The primitive value of the specified object, or the object itself.

Description

Method; returns the primitive value of the specified object. If the object does not have a primitive value, the object itself is returned.

Object.watch()

Availability

Flash Player 6.

Usage

```
myObject.watch( prop, callback [, userData] )
```

Parameters

prop   A string indicating the name of the object property to watch.

callback   The function to invoke when the watched property changes. This parameter is a function object, not a function name as a string. The form of callback is callback(prop, oldval, newval, userData).

userData   An arbitrary piece of ActionScript data that is passed to the *callback* method. If the *userData* parameter is omitted, undefined is passed to the callback method. This parameter is optional.

Returns

A value of true if the watchpoint is created successfully; otherwise, returns a false value.

Description

Method; registers an event handler to be invoked when a specified property of an ActionScript object changes. When the property changes, the event handler is invoked with myObject as the containing object. You must return the new value from the Object.watch() method, or the watched object property is assigned a value of undefined.

A watchpoint can filter (or nullify) the value assignment, by returning a modified newval (or oldval). If you delete a property for which a watchpoint has been set, that watchpoint does not disappear. If you later recreate the property, the watchpoint is still in effect. To remove a watchpoint, use the Object.unwatch method.

Only a single watchpoint may be registered on a property. Subsequent calls to Object.watch() on the same property replace the original watchpoint.

The Object.watch() method behaves similarly to the Object.watch() function in Netscape JavaScript 1.2 and later. The primary difference is the *userData* parameter, which is a Flash addition to Object.watch() that Netscape Navigator does not support. You can pass the *userData* parameter to the event handler and use it in the event handler.

The Object.watch() method cannot watch getter/setter properties. Getter/setter properties operate through "lazy evaluation"— the value of the property is not determined until the property is actually queried. "Lazy evaluation" is often efficient because the property is not constantly updated; it is, rather, evaluated when needed. However, Object.watch() needs to evaluate a property in order to fire watchpoints on it. To work with a getter/setter property, Object.watch() needs to evaluate the property constantly, which is inefficient.

Generally, ActionScript predefined properties, such as _x, _y, _width and _height, are getter/setter properties, and thus cannot be watched with Object.watch().

Example

This example shows a CheckBox component with methods that set the label or value of each check box instance:

```
myCheckBox1.setValue(true);
myCheckBox1.setLabel("new label");
...
```

It's convenient to think of the value and label of a check box as properties. It's possible to use `Object.watch()` to make accessing the value and label look like property access rather than method invocation, as in the following:

```
// Define constructor for (and thus define) CheckBox class
function CheckBox() {
   ...
   this.watch('value', function (id, oldval, newval){
      ...
   });
   this.watch('label', function(id, oldval, newval){
      ...
   });
}
```

When the value or label property is modified, the function specified by the component is invoked to perform any tasks needed to update the appearance and state of the component. The following example invokes an `Object.watch()` method to notify the component that the variable has changed, causing the component to update its graphical representation.

```
myCheckBox1.value = false;
```

This syntax is more concise than the former syntax:

```
myCheckBox1.setValue(false);
```

See also

Object.addProperty(), `Object.unwatch()`

Object()

Availability

Flash Player 5 .

Usage

```
Object( [ value ] )
```

Parameters

value   A number, string, or Boolean value.

Returns

An object.

Description

Conversion function; creates a new, empty object or converts the specified number, string, or Boolean value to an object. This command is equivalent to creating an object using the Object constructor (see "Constructor for the Object class" on page 779).

on()

Availability

Flash 2. Not all events are supported in Flash 2.

Usage

```
on(mouseEvent) {
    // your statements here
}
```

Parameters

statement(s) The instructions to execute when the *mouseEvent* takes place.

A *mouseEvent* is a trigger called an "event." When the event takes place, the statements following it within curly braces execute. Any of the following values can be specified for the *mouseEvent* parameter:

- press The mouse button is pressed while the pointer is over the button.
- release The mouse button is released while the pointer is over the button.
- releaseOutside The mouse button is released while the pointer is outside the button after the button is pressed while the pointer is inside the button.
- rollOut The pointer rolls outside of the button area.
- rollOver The mouse pointer rolls over the button.
- dragOut While the pointer is over the button, the mouse button is pressed and then rolls outside the button area.
- dragOver While the pointer is over the button, the mouse button has been pressed then rolled outside the button and then rolled back over the button.
- keyPress ("*key*") The specified key is pressed. For the key portion of the parameter, specify a key code or key constant. For a list of key codes associated with the keys on a standard keyboard, see Appendix C, "Keyboard Keys and Key Code Values," on page 993; for a list of key constants, see "Property summary for the Key class" on page 612.

Description

Event handler; specifies the mouse event or keypress that triggers an action.

Example

In the following script, the startDrag() action executes when the mouse is pressed and the conditional script is executed when the mouse is released and the object is dropped.

```
on(press) {
    startDrag("rabbit");
}
on(release) {
    trace(_root.rabbit._y);
    trace(_root.rabbit._x);
    stopDrag();
}
```

See also

onClipEvent()

onClipEvent()

Availability

Flash Player 5.

Usage

```
onClipEvent(movieEvent){
  // your statements here
}
```

Parameters

A *movieEvent* is a trigger called an *event*. When the event takes place, the statements following it within curly braces are executed. Any of the following values can be specified for the *movieEvent* parameter:

- `load`   The action is initiated as soon as the movie clip is instantiated and appears in the Timeline.

- `unload`   The action is initiated in the first frame after the movie clip is removed from the Timeline. The actions associated with the `Unload` movie clip event are processed before any actions are attached to the affected frame.

- `enterFrame`   The action is triggered continually at the frame rate of the movie clip. The actions associated with the `enterFrame` clip event are processed before any frame actions that are attached to the affected frames.

- `mouseMove`   The action is initiated every time the mouse is moved. Use the `_xmouse` and `_ymouse` properties to determine the current mouse position.

- `mouseDown`   The action is initiated when the left mouse button is pressed.

- `mouseUp`   The action is initiated when the left mouse button is released.

- `keyDown`   The action is initiated when a key is pressed. Use `Key.getCode()` to retrieve information about the last key pressed.

- `keyUp`   The action is initiated when a key is released. Use the `Key.getCode()` method to retrieve information about the last key pressed.

- `data`   The action is initiated when data is received in a `loadVariables()` or `loadMovie()` action. When specified with a `loadVariables()` action, the `data` event occurs only once, when the last variable is loaded. When specified with a `loadMovie()` action, the `data` event occurs repeatedly, as each section of data is retrieved.

Description

Event handler; triggers actions defined for a specific instance of a movie clip.

Example

The following statement includes the script from an external file when the SWF file is exported; the actions in the included script are run when the movie clip they are attached to loads:

```
onClipEvent(load) {
  #include "myScript.as"
}
```

The following example uses onClipEvent() with the keyDown movie event. The keyDown movie event is usually used in conjunction with one or more methods and properties of the Key object. The following script uses Key.getCode() to find out which key the user has pressed; if the pressed key matches the Key.RIGHT property, the movie is sent to the next frame; if the pressed key matches the Key.LEFT property, the movie is sent to the previous frame.

```
onClipEvent(keyDown) {
    if (Key.getCode() == Key.RIGHT) {
        _parent.nextFrame();
    } else if (Key.getCode() == Key.LEFT){
        _parent.prevFrame();
    }
}
```

The following example uses onClipEvent() with the mouseMove movie event. The _xmouse and _ymouse properties track the position of the mouse each time the mouse moves.

```
onClipEvent(mouseMove) {
    stageX=_root._xmouse;
    stageY=_root._ymouse;
}
```

See also

Key class, MovieClip._xmouse, MovieClip._ymouse, on(), updateAfterEvent()

onUpdate

Availability

Flash Player 6.

Usage

```
function onUpdate() {
    ...statements...;
}
```

Parameters

None.

Returns

Nothing.

Description

Event handler; onUpdate is defined for a Live Preview movie used with a component. When an instance of a component on the Stage has a Live Preview movie, the authoring tool invokes the Live Preview movie's onUpdate function whenever the component parameters of the component instance change. The onUpdate function is invoked by the authoring tool with no parameters, and its return value is ignored. The onUpdate function should be declared on the main Timeline of the Live Preview movie.

Defining an onUpdate function in a Live Preview movie is optional.

For more information on Live Preview movies, see *Using Components*.

Example

The onUpdate function gives the Live Preview movie an opportunity to update its visual appearance to match the new values of the component parameters. When the user changes a parameter value in the components Property inspector or Component Parameters panel, onUpdate is invoked. The onUpdate function will do something to update itself. For instance, if the component includes a color parameter, the onUpdate function might alter the color of a movie clip inside the Live Preview to reflect the new parameter value. In addition, it might store the new color in an internal variable.

Here is an example of using the onUpdate function to pass parameter values through an empty movie clip in the Live Preview movie. Suppose you have a labeled button component with a variable labelColor, which specifies the color of the text label color. The following code is in the first frame of the main Timeline of the component movie:

```
//Define the textColor parameter variable to specify the color of the button
    label text.
buttonLabel.textColor = labelColor;
```

In the Live Preview movie, place an empty movie clip named "xch" in the Live Preview movie. Then place the following code in the first frame of the Live Preview movie. Add "xch" to the labelColor variable path, to pass the variable through the my_mc movie clip:

```
//Write an onUpdate function, adding "my_mc." to the parameter variable names:
function onUpdate (){
    buttonLabel.textColor = my_mc.labelColor;
}
```

or

Availability

Flash 4. This operator has been deprecated in favor of the || (logical OR) operator.

Usage

condition1 or *condition2*

Parameters

condition1,2   An expression that evaluates to true or false.

Returns

Nothing.

Description

Operator; evaluates *condition1* and *condition2*, and if either expression is true, then the whole expression is true.

See also

|| (logical OR), | (bitwise OR)

ord

Availability

Flash Player 4. This function has been deprecated in favor of the methods and properties of the String class.

Usage

```
ord(character)
```

Parameters

`character`   The character to convert to an ASCII code number.

Returns

Nothing.

Description

String function; converts characters to ASCII code numbers.

See also

String class

_parent

Availability

Flash Player 5.

Usage

```
_parent.property
_parent._parent.property
```

Description

Identifier; specifies or returns a reference to the movie clip or object that contains the current movie clip or object. The current object is the object containing the ActionScript code that references _parent. Use _parent to specify a relative path to movie clips or objects that are above the current movie clip or object.

Example

In the following example, the movie clip desk is a child of the movie clip classroom. When the following script executes inside the movie clip desk, the playhead will jump to Frame 10 in the Timeline of the movie clip classroom.

```
_parent.gotoAndStop(10);
```

See also

`_root, targetPath`

parseFloat()

Availability

Flash Player 5.

Usage

```
parseFloat(string)
```

Parameters

string   The string to read and convert to a floating-point number.

Returns

A number or Nan.

Description

Function; converts a string to a floating-point number. The function reads, or "parses," and returns the numbers in a string until it reaches a character that is not a part of the initial number. If the string does not begin with a number that can be parsed, parseFloat returns NaN. White space preceding valid integers is ignored, as are trailing nonnumeric characters.

Example

The following examples use the parseFloat function to evaluate various types of numbers.

parseFloat("-2") returns -2

parseFloat("2.5") returns 2.5

parseFloat("3.5e6") returns 3.5e6, or 3500000

parseFloat("foobar") returns NaN

parseFloat(" 5.1") returns 5.1

parseFloat("3.75math") returns 3.75

parseFloat("0garbage") returns 0

See also

NaN

parseInt

Availability

Flash Player 5.

Usage

```
parseInt(expression [, radix])
```

Parameters

expression   A string to convert to a integer.

radix   Optional; an integer representing the radix (base) of the number to parse. Legal values are from 2 to 36.

Returns

A number or `NaN`.

Description

Function; converts a string to an integer. If the specified string in the parameters cannot be converted to a number, the function returns `NaN`. Strings beginning with 0x are interpreted as hexadecimal numbers. Integers beginning with 0 or specifying a radix of 8 are interpreted as octal numbers. White space preceding valid integers is ignored, as are trailing nonnumeric characters.

Example

The following examples use the `parseInt` function to evaluate various types of numbers.

```
parseInt("3.5")
// returns 3

parseInt("bar")
// returns NaN

parseInt("4foo")
// returns 4
```

The following are examples of hexadecimal conversions:

```
parseInt("0x3F8")
// returns 1016

parseInt("3E8", 16)
// returns 1000
```

The following is an example of a binary conversion:

```
parseInt("1010", 2)
// returns 10 (the decimal representation of the binary 1010)
```

The following are examples of octal number parsing:

```
parseInt("0777")
parseInt("777", 8)
// returns 511 (the decimal representation of the octal 777)
```

play()

Availability

Flash 2.

Usage

```
play()
```

Parameters

None.

Returns

Nothing.

Description

Function; moves the playhead forward in the Timeline.

Example

The following code uses an `if` statement to check the value of a name the user enters. If the user enters `Steve`, the `play()` action is called and the playhead moves forward in the Timeline. If the user enters anything other than `Steve`, the SWF file does not play and a text field with the variable name `alert` is displayed.

```
stop();
if (name == "Steve") {
  play();
} else {
  alert="You are not Steve!";
}
```

prevFrame()

Availability

Flash 2.

Usage

```
prevFrame()
```

Parameters

None.

Returns

Nothing.

Description

Function; sends the playhead to the previous frame and stops it. If the current frame is Frame 1, the playhead does not move.

Example

When the user clicks a button that has the following handler attached to it, the playhead is sent to the previous frame.

```
on(release) {
    prevFrame();
}
```

See also

```
MovieClip.prevFrame()
```

prevScene()

Availability

Flash 2.

Usage

```
prevScene()
```

Parameters

None.

Returns

Nothing.

Description

Function; sends the playhead to Frame 1 of the previous scene and stops it.

See also

```
nextScene()
```

print()

Availability

Flash Player 4.20.

Note: If you are authoring for Flash Player 7 or later, you can create a PrintJob object, which gives you (and the user) more control over the printing process. For more information, see the PrintJob class entry.

Usage

```
print(target, "Bounding box")
```

Parameters

target   The instance name of a movie clip to print. By default, all of the frames in the target instance print. If you want to print specific frames in the movie clip, assign a #p frame label to those frames.

Bounding box   A modifier that sets the print area of the movie clip. Enclose this parameter in quotation marks, and specify one of the following values:

- bmovie   Designates the bounding box of a specific frame in a movie as the print area for all printable frames in the movie. Assign a #b frame label to the frame whose bounding box you want to use as the print area.

- bmax   Designates a composite of all of the bounding boxes of all the printable frames as the print area. Specify bmax when the printable frames in your movie vary in size.

- bframe   Indicates that the bounding box of each printable frame should be used as the print area for that frame. This changes the print area for each frame and scales the objects to fit the print area. Use bframe if you have objects of different sizes in each frame and want each object to fill the printed page.

Returns

None.

Description

Function; prints the *target* movie clip according to the boundaries specified in the parameter (bmovie, bmax, or bframe). If you want to print specific frames in the target movie clip, attach a #p frame label to those frames. Although print() results in higher quality prints than printAsBitmap(), it cannot be used to print movie clips that use alpha transparencies or special color effects.

If you use bmovie for the *Bounding box* parameter but do not assign a #b label to a frame, the print area is determined by the Stage size of the loaded movie. (The loaded movie does not inherit the main movie's Stage size.)

All of the printable elements in a movie must be fully loaded before printing can begin.

The Flash Player printing feature supports PostScript and non-PostScript printers. Non-PostScript printers convert vectors to bitmaps.

Example

The following example prints all of the printable frames in the movie clip my_mc with the print area defined by the bounding box of the frame with the #b frame label attached:

```
print(my_mc,"bmovie");
```

The following example prints all of the printable frames in my_mc with a print area defined by the bounding box of each frame:

```
print(my_mc,"bframe");
```

See also

printAsBitmap(), printAsBitmapNum(), **PrintJob class**, printNum()

printAsBitmap()

Availability

Flash Player 4.20.

Note: If you are authoring for Flash Player 7 or later, you can create a PrintJob object, which gives you (and the user) more control over the printing process. For more information, see the PrintJob class entry.

Usage

```
printAsBitmap(target, "Bounding box")
```

Parameters

target   The instance name of movie clip to print. By default, all of the frames in the movie are printed. If you want to print specific frames in the movie, attach a #p frame label to those frames.

Bounding box   A modifier that sets the print area of the movie. Enclose this parameter in quotation marks, and specify one of the following values:

- bmovie   Designates the bounding box of a specific frame in a movie as the print area for all printable frames in the movie. Assign a #b frame label to the frame whose bounding box you want to use as the print area.
- bmax   Designates a composite of all of the bounding boxes of all the printable frames as the print area. Specify the bmax parameter when the printable frames in your movie vary in size.
- bframe   Indicates that the bounding box of each printable frame should be used as the print area for that frame. This changes the print area for each frame and scales the objects to fit the print area. Use bframe if you have objects of different sizes in each frame and want each object to fill the printed page.

Returns

Nothing.

Description

Function; prints the *target* movie clip as a bitmap according to the boundaries specified in the parameter (bmovie, bmax, or bframe). Use printAsBitmap() to print movies that contain frames with objects that use transparency or color effects. The printAsBitmap() action prints at the highest available resolution of the printer in order to maintain as much definition and quality as possible.

If your movie does not contain alpha transparencies or color effects, Macromedia recommends that you use print() for better quality results.

If you use bmovie for the *Bounding box* parameter but do not assign a #b label to a frame, the print area is determined by the Stage size of the loaded movie. (The loaded movie does not inherit the main movie's Stage size.)

All of the printable elements in a movie must be fully loaded before printing can begin.

The Flash Player printing feature supports PostScript and non-PostScript printers. Non-PostScript printers convert vectors to bitmaps.

See also

print(), printAsBitmapNum(), **PrintJob class**, printNum()

printAsBitmapNum()

Availability

Flash Player 5.

Note: If you are authoring for Flash Player 7 or later, you can create a PrintJob object, which gives you (and the user) more control over the printing process. For more information, see the PrintJob class entry.

Usage

```
printAsBitmapNum( level, "Bounding box")
```

Parameters

level   The level in Flash Player to print. By default, all of the frames in the level print. If you want to print specific frames in the level, assign a #p frame label to those frames.

Bounding box   A modifier that sets the print area of the movie. Enclose this parameter in quotation marks, and specify one of the following values:

- bmovie   Designates the bounding box of a specific frame in a movie as the print area for all printable frames in the movie. Assign a #b frame label to the frame whose bounding box you want to use as the print area.

- bmax   Designates a composite of all of the bounding boxes of all the printable frames as the print area. Specify the bmax parameter when the printable frames in your movie vary in size.

- bframe   Indicates that the bounding box of each printable frame should be used as the print area for that frame. This changes the print area for each frame and scales the objects to fit the print area. Use bframe if you have objects of different sizes in each frame and want each object to fill the printed page.

Returns

None.

Description

Function; prints a level in Flash Player as a bitmap according to the boundaries specified in the parameter (bmovie, bmax, or bframe). Use printAsBitmapNum() to print movies that contain frames with objects that use transparency or color effects. The printAsBitmapNum() action prints at the highest available resolution of the printer in order to maintain the highest possible definition and quality. To calculate the printable file size of a frame designated to print as a bitmap, multiply pixel width by pixel height by printer resolution.

If your movie does not contain alpha transparencies or color effects, it is recommended that you use printNum() for better quality results.

If you use bmovie for the *Bounding box* parameter but do not assign a #b label to a frame, the print area is determined by the Stage size of the loaded movie. (The loaded movie does not inherit the main movie's Stage size.)

All of the printable elements in a movie must be fully loaded before printing can begin.

The Flash Player printing feature supports PostScript and non-PostScript printers. Non-PostScript printers convert vectors to bitmaps.

See also

print(), printAsBitmap(), **PrintJob class**, printNum()

PrintJob class

Flash Player 7.

Description

The PrintJob class lets you create content and print it to one or more pages. This class, in addition to offering improvements to print functionality provided by the `print()` method, lets you render dynamic content offscreen, prompt users with a single print dialog box, and print an unscaled document with proportions that map to the proportions of the content. This capability is especially useful for rendering and printing external dynamic content, such as database content and dynamic text.

Additionally, with properties populated by `PrintJob.start()`, your document can access your user's printer settings, such as page height, width, and orientation, and you can configure your document to dynamically format Flash content that's appropriate for the printer settings.

Method summary for the PrintJob class

You must use the methods for PrintJob class in the order listed in the following table.

Method	Description
`PrintJob.start()`	Displays the operating system's print dialog boxes and starts spooling.
`PrintJob.addPage()`	Adds one page to the print spooler.
`PrintJob.send()`	Sends spooled pages to the printer.

Constructor for the PrintJob class

Availability

Flash Player 7.

Usage

```
my_pj = new PrintJob()
```

Parameters

None.

Returns

Nothing.

Description

Constructor; creates a PrintJob object that you can use to print one or more pages.

To implement a print job, use these methods in the sequence shown:

```
// create PrintJob object
my_pj = new PrintJob();                       // instantiate object

// display print dialog box
my_pj.start();                                // initiate print job

// add specified area to print job
// repeat once for each page to be printed
my_pj.addPage([params]);                      // send page(s) to spooler
my_pj.addPage([params]);
my_pj.addPage([params]);
my_pj.addPage([params]);

// send pages from the spooler to the printer
my_pj.send();                                 // print page(s)

// clean up
delete my_pj;                                 // delete object
```

In your own implementation of PrintJob objects, you should check for return values from `PrintJob.start()` and `PrintJob.addPage()` before continuing to print. See the examples for `PrintJob.addPage()`.

You cannot create a PrintJob object until any PrintJob object that you already created is no longer active (that is, it either completed successfully or failed). If you try to create a second PrintJob object (by calling `new PrintJob()`) while the first PrintJob object is still active, the second PrintJob object will not be created.

Example

See `PrintJob.addPage()`.

See also

`PrintJob.addPage()`, `PrintJob.send()`, `PrintJob.start()`

PrintJob.addPage()

Availability

Flash Player 7.

Usage

```
my_pj.addPage(target [, printArea] [, options ] [, frameNumber])
```

Parameters

target   The level or instance name of the movie clip to print. Pass a number to specify a level (for example, 0 is the _root movie), or a string (in quotation marks) to specify the instance name of a movie clip.

printArea   An optional object that specifies the area to print, in the following format:

{xMin:*topLeft*, xMax:*topRight*, yMin:*bottomLeft*, yMax:*bottomRight*}

The coordinates you specify for *printArea* represent screen pixels relative to the registration point of the _root movie (if `target` = 0) or of the level or movie clip specified by `target`. You must provide all four coordinates. The width (xMax-xMin) and height (yMax-yMin) must each be greater than 0.

Points are print units of measurement, and pixels are screen units of measurement; one point is equal in size to one pixel. You can use the following equivalencies to convert inches or centimeters to twips, pixels or points (a twip is 1/20 of a pixel):

- 1 pixel = 1 point = 1/72 inch = 20 twips
- 1 inch = 72 pixels = 72 points = 1440 twips
- 1 cm = 567 twips

Note: If you have previously used `print()`, `printAsBitmap()`, `printAsBitmapNum()`, or `printNum()` to print from Flash, you used a #b frame label to specify the area to print. When using the `addPage()` method, you must use the *printArea* parameter to specify the print area; #b frame labels are ignored.

If you omit the *printArea* parameter, or if it is passed incorrectly, the full Stage area of `target` is printed. If you don't want to specify a value for *printArea* but want to specify a value for *options* or *frameNumber*, pass `null` for *printArea*.

options   An optional parameter that specifies whether to print as vector or bitmap, in the following format:

`{printAsBitmap:Boolean}`

By default, pages are printed in vector format. To print `target` as a bitmap, pass `true` for printAsBitmap. The default value is `false`, which represents a request for vector printing. Keep in mind the following suggestions when determining which value to use:

- If the content that you're printing includes a bitmap image, use `{printAsBitmap:true}` to include any transparency and color effects.
- If the content does not include bitmap images, omit this parameter or use `{printAsBitmap:false}` to print the content in higher quality vector format.

If *options* is omitted or passed incorrectly, vector printing is implemented. If you don't want to specify a value for *options* but want to specify a value for *frameNumber*, pass `null` for *options*.

frameNumber   An optional number that lets you specify which frame to print; notice that any ActionScript on the frame is not invoked. If you omit this parameter, the current frame in `target` is printed.

Note: If you previously used `print()`, `printAsBitmap()`, `printAsBitmapNum()`, or `printNum()` to print from Flash, you may have used a #p frame label on multiple frames to specify which pages to print. To use `PrintJob.addPage()` to print multiple frames, you must issue a PrintJob.addPage() command for each frame; #p frame labels are ignored. For one way to do this programmatically, see the example later in this entry.

Returns

A Boolean value of `true` if the page was successfully sent to the print spooler, `false` otherwise.

Description

Method; sends the specified level or movie clip as a single page to the print spooler. Before using this method, you must use `PrintJob.start()`; after calling `PrintJob.addPage()` one or more times for a print job, you must use `PrintJob.send()` to send the spooled pages to the printer.

If this method returns `false` (for example, if you haven't called `PrintJob.start()` or the user canceled the print job), any subsequent calls to `PrintJob.addPage()` will fail. However, if prior calls to `PrintJob.addPage()` were successful, the concluding `PrintJob.send()` command sends the successfully spooled pages to the printer.

If you passed a value for *printArea*, the `xMin` and `yMin` coordinates map to the upper left corner (0,0 coordinates) of the printable area on the page; the printable area is determined by the `pageHeight` and `pageWidth` properties set by `PrintJob.start()`. Because the printout aligns with the upper left corner of the printable area on the page, the printout is clipped to the right and/or bottom if the area defined in *printArea* is bigger than the printable area on the page. If you haven't passed a value for *printArea* and the Stage is larger than the printable area, the same type of clipping takes place.

If you want to scale a movie clip before you print it, set its `MovieClip._xscale` and `MovieClip._yscale` properties before calling this method, then set them back to their original values afterward. The scale of a movie clip has no relation to *printArea*. That is, if you specify that you print an area that is 50 x 50 pixels in size, 2500 pixels are printed. If you have scaled the movie clip, the same 2500 pixels are printed, but at the scaled size.

The Flash Player printing feature supports PostScript and non-PostScript printers. Non-PostScript printers convert vectors to bitmaps.

Example

The following example illustrates several ways to issue the `addPage()` command.

```
my_btn.onRelease = function()
{
   var pageCount = 0;

   var my_pj = new PrintJob();

   if (my_pj.start())
   {
     // Print entire current frame of the _root movie in vector format
     if (my_pj.addPage(0))
     {
       pageCount++;

       // Starting at 0,0, print an area 400 pixels wide and 500 pixels high
       // of the current frame of the _root movie in vector format
       if (my_pj.addPage(0, {xMin:0,xMax:400,yMin:0,yMax:500}))
       {
         pageCount++;

         // Starting at 0,0, print an area 400 pixels wide and 500 pixels high
         // of frame 1 of the _root movie in bitmap format
         if (my_pj.addPage(0, {xMin:0,xMax:400,yMin:0,yMax:500},
             {printAsBitmap:true}, 1))
         {
           pageCount++;

           // Starting 50 pixels to the right of 0,0 and 70 pixels down,
           // print an area 500 pixels wide and 600 pixels high
           // of frame 4 of level 5 in vector format
           if (my_pj.addPage(5, {xMin:50,xMax:550,yMin:70,yMax:670},null, 4))
           {
             pageCount++;
```

```
            // Starting at 0,0, print an area 400 pixels wide
            // and 400 pixels high of frame 3 of the "dance_mc" movie clip
            // in bitmap format
            if (my_pj.addPage("dance_mc",
                {xMin:0,xMax:400,yMin:0,yMax:400},{printAsBitmap:true}, 3))
            {
              pageCount++;

              // Starting at 0,0, print an area 400 pixels wide
              // and 600 pixels high of frame 3 of the "dance_mc" movie clip
              // in vector format at 50% of its actual size
              var x = dance_mc._xscale;
              var y = dance_mc._yscale;
              dance_mc._xscale = 50;
              dance_mc._yscale = 50;

              if (my_pj.addPage("dance_mc",
                  {xMin:0,xMax:400,yMin:0,yMax:600},null, 3))
              {
                pageCount++;
              }

              dance_mc._xscale = x;
              dance_mc._yscale = y;
            }
          }
        }
      }
    }
  }

  if (pageCount)
  {
    my_pj.send();
  }
  delete my_pj;
}
```

See also

```
PrintJob.send(), PrintJob.start()
```

PrintJob.send()

Availability

Flash Player 7.

Usage

```
my_pj.send()
```

Parameters

None.

Returns

Nothing.

Description

Method; is used following `PrintJob.start()` and `PrintJob.addPage()` to send spooled pages to the printer.

Example

See `PrintJob.addPage()`.

See also

`PrintJob.addPage()`, `PrintJob.start()`

PrintJob.start()

Availability

Flash Player 7.

Usage

`my_pj.start()`

Parameters

None.

Returns

A Boolean value of `true` if the user clicks OK when the print dialog boxes appear, or `false` if the user clicks Cancel or if an error occurs.

Description

Method; displays the operating system's print dialog boxes and starts spooling. The print dialog boxes give the user an opportunity to change print settings, and then populate the following read-only properties (notice that 1 point equals 1 onscreen pixel):

Property	Type	Units	Notes
`PrintJob.paperHeight`	Number	Points	Overall paper height
`PrintJob.paperWidth`	Number	Points	Overall paper width
`PrintJob.pageHeight`	Number	Points	Height of actual printable area on the page; any user-set margins are ignored
`PrintJob.pageWidth`	Number	Points	Width of actual printable area on the page; any user-set margins are ignored
`PrintJob.orientation`	String	n/a	"Portrait" or "landscape"

After the user clicks OK in the print dialog box, the player begins spooling a print job to the operating system. You should issue any ActionScript commands that affect the printout, and then you can begin using `PrintJob.addPage()` commands to begin sending pages to the spooler. If you wish, use the height, width, and orientation properties this method returns to determine how to format the printout.

Because the user sees information such as "Printing page 1" immediately after clicking OK, you should call the `PrintJob.addPage()` and `PrintJob.send()` commands as soon as possible.

If this method returns `false` (for example, if the user clicks Cancel instead of OK), any subsequent calls to `PrintJob.addPage()` and `PrintJob.send()` will fail. However, if you test for this return value and don't send `PrintJob.addPage()` commands as a result, you should still delete the PrintJob object to make sure the print spooler is cleared, as shown below.

```
var my_pj = new PrintJob();
var myResult = my_pj.start();
    if(myResult) {
        // addPage() and send() statements here
    }
delete my_pj;
```

Example

See `PrintJob.addPage()`.

See also

`PrintJob.addPage()`, `PrintJob.send()`

printNum()

Availability

Flash Player 5.

Note: If you are authoring for Flash Player 7 or later, you can create a PrintJob object, which gives you (and the user) more control over the printing process. For more information, see the PrintJob class entry.

Usage

```
printNum (level, "Bounding box")
```

Parameters

level   The level in Flash Player to print. By default, all of the frames in the level print. If you want to print specific frames in the level, assign a #p frame label to those frames.

Bounding box   A modifier that sets the print area of the movie. Enclose this parameter in quotation marks, and specify one of the following values:

- bmovie   Designates the bounding box of a specific frame in a movie as the print area for all printable frames in the movie. Assign a #b frame label to the frame whose bounding box you want to use as the print area.

- bmax   Designates a composite of all of the bounding boxes of all the printable frames as the print area. Specify the bmax parameter when the printable frames in your movie vary in size.

- bframe   Indicates that the bounding box of each printable frame should be used as the print area for that frame. This changes the print area for each frame and scales the objects to fit the print area. Use bframe if you have objects of different sizes in each frame and want each object to fill the printed page.

Returns

Nothing.

Description

Function; prints the level in Flash Player according to the boundaries specified in the *Bounding box* parameter ("bmovie", "bmax", "bframe"). If you want to print specific frames in the target movie, attach a #p frame label to those frames. Although using printNum() results in higher quality prints than using printAsBitmapNum(), you cannot use printNum() to print movies with alpha transparencies or special color effects.

If you use bmovie for the *Bounding box* parameter but do not assign a #b label to a frame, the print area is determined by the Stage size of the loaded movie. (The loaded movie does not inherit the main movie's Stage size.)

All of the printable elements in a movie must be fully loaded before printing can begin.

The Flash Player printing feature supports PostScript and non-PostScript printers. Non-PostScript printers convert vectors to bitmaps.

See also

print(), printAsBitmap(), printAsBitmapNum(), PrintJob class

private

Availability

Flash Player 6.

Usage

```
class someClassName{
   private var name;
   private function name() {
      // your statements here
   }
}
```

Note: To use this keyword, you must specify ActionScript 2.0 and Flash Player 6 or later in the Flash tab of your FLA file's Publish Settings dialog box. This keyword is supported only when used in external script files, not in scripts written in the Actions panel.

Parameters

name   The name of the variable or function that you want to specify as private.

Description

Keyword; specifies that a variable or function is available only to the class that declares or defines it, or to subclasses of that class. By default, a variable or function is available to any class that calls it. Use this keyword if you want to restrict access to a variable or function. For more information, see "Controlling member access" on page 368.

You can use this keyword only in class definitions, not in interface definitions.

See also

public, static

public

Flash Player 6.

Usage

```
class someClassName{
  public var name;
  public function name() {
    // your statements here
  }
}
```

Note: To use this keyword, you must specify ActionScript 2.0 and Flash Player 6 or later in the Flash tab of your FLA file's Publish Settings dialog box. This keyword is supported only when used in external script files, not in scripts written in the Actions panel.

Parameters

name   The name of the variable or function that you want to specify as public.

Description

Keyword; specifies that a variable or function is available to any class that calls it. Because variables and functions are public by default, this keyword is used primarily for stylistic reasons. For example, you might want to use it for reasons of consistency in a block of code that also contains private or static variables.

Example

The following two blocks of code are functionally identical.

```
private var age:Number;
public var name:String;
static var birth:Date;
```

```
private var age:Number;
var name:String;
static var birth:Date;
```

For more information, see "Controlling member access" on page 368.

See also

`private, static`

_quality

Availability

Flash Player 5.

Usage

`_quality`

Description

Property (global); sets or retrieves the rendering quality used for a movie. Device fonts are always aliased and therefore are unaffected by the `_quality` property.

The _quality property can be set to the following values:

- "LOW"   Low rendering quality. Graphics are not anti-aliased, bitmaps are not smoothed.
- "MEDIUM"   Medium rendering quality. Graphics are anti-aliased using a 2 x 2 grid, in pixels, but bitmaps are not smoothed. Suitable for movies that do not contain text.
- "HIGH"   High rendering quality. Graphics are anti-aliased using a 4 x 4 grid, in pixels, and bitmaps are smoothed if the movie is static. This is the default rendering quality setting used by Flash.
- "BEST"   Very high rendering quality. Graphics are anti-aliased using a 4 x 4 grid, in pixels, and bitmaps are always smoothed.

Example

The following example sets the rendering quality to LOW:

```
_quality = "LOW";
```

See also

```
_highquality, toggleHighQuality()
```

random

Availability

Flash Player 4. This function was deprecated in Flash 5 in favor of Math.random().

Usage

```
random(value)
```

Parameters

value   An integer.

Returns

An integer.

Description

Function; returns a random integer between 0 and one less than the integer specified in the *value* parameter.

Example

The following use of random() returns a value of 0, 1, 2, 3, or 4:

```
random(5);
```

See also

```
Math.random()
```

removeMovieClip()

Availability

Flash Player 4.

Usage

```
removeMovieClip(target)
```

Parameters

target   The target path of a movie clip instance created with `duplicateMovieClip()`, or the instance name of a movie clip created with `MovieClip.attachMovie()` or `MovieClip.duplicateMovieClip()`.

Returns

None.

Description

Function; deletes the specified movie clip.

See also

`duplicateMovieClip()`, `MovieClip.duplicateMovieClip()`, `MovieClip.attachMovie()`, `MovieClip.removeMovieClip()`

return

Availability

Flash Player 5.

Usage

```
return[expression]
```

Parameters

expression   A string, number, array, or object to evaluate and return as a value of the function. This parameter is optional.

Returns

The evaluated *expression* parameter, if provided.

Description

Statement; specifies the value returned by a function. The `return` action evaluates *expression* and returns the result as a value of the function in which it executes. The `return` action causes the function to stop running and replaces the function with the returned value. If the `return` statement is used alone, it returns `null`.

You can't return multiple values. If you try to do so, only the last value is returned. In the following example, c is returned:

```
return a, b, c ;
```

Example

The following example uses the `return` action inside the body of the `sum()` function to return the added value of the three parameters. The next line of code calls `sum()` and assigns the returned value to the variable `newValue`.

```
function sum(a, b, c){
   return a + b + c;
}
newValue = sum(4, 32, 78);
trace(newValue);
// sends 114 to the Output panel
```

See also

`function`

_root

Availability

Flash Player 5.

Usage

```
_root.movieClip
_root.action
_root.property
```

Parameters

movieClip   The instance name of a movie clip.

action   An action or method.

property   A property of the MovieClip object.

Description

Property; specifies or returns a reference to the root movie Timeline. If a movie has multiple levels, the root movie Timeline is on the level containing the currently executing script. For example, if a script in level 1 evaluates `_root`, `_level1` is returned.

Specifying `_root` is the same as using the slash notation (/) to specify an absolute path within the current level.

Note: If a movie that contains `_root` is loaded into another movie, `_root` refers to the Timeline of the loading movie, not to the Timeline that contains `_root`. If you want to ensure that `_root` refers to the Timeline of the loaded movie even if it is loaded into another movie, use `MovieClip._lockroot`.

Example

The following example stops the Timeline of the level containing the currently executing script:

`_root.stop();`

The following example sends the Timeline in the current level to Frame 3:

`_root.gotoAndStop(3);`

See also

`MovieClip._lockroot, _parent, targetPath`

scroll

Availability

Flash Player 4.

Usage

```
textFieldVariableName.scroll = x
```

Description

Property; a deprecated property that controls the display of information in a text field associated with a variable. The `scroll` property defines where the text field begins displaying content; after you set it, Flash Player updates it as the user scrolls through the text field. The `scroll` property is useful for directing users to a specific paragraph in a long passage, or creating scrolling text fields. This property can be retrieved and modified.

Example

The following code is attached to an Up button that scrolls the text field `myText`:

```
on (release) {
   myText.scroll = myText.scroll + 1;
}
```

See also

`TextField.maxscroll`, `TextField.scroll`

Selection class

Availability

Flash Player 5.

Description

The Selection class lets you set and control the text field in which the insertion point is located; that is, the field that has focus. Selection-span indexes are zero-based (for example, the first position is 0, the second position is 1, and so on).

There is no constructor function for the Selection class, because there can only be one currently focused field at a time.

Method summary for the Selection class

Method	Description
Selection.addListener()	Registers an object to receive notification when onSetFocus is invoked.
Selection.getBeginIndex()	Returns the index at the beginning of the selection span. Returns -1 if there is no index or currently selected field.
Selection.getCaretIndex()	Returns the current caret (insertion point) position in the currently focused selection span. Returns -1 if there is no caret position or currently focused selection span.
Selection.getEndIndex()	Returns the index at the end of the selection span. Returns -1 if there is no index or currently selected field.
Selection.getFocus()	Returns the name of the variable for the currently focused text field. Returns null if there is no currently focused text field.
Selection.removeListener()	Removes an object that was registered with addListener().
Selection.setFocus()	Focuses the text field associated with the specified variable.
Selection.setSelection()	Sets the beginning and ending indexes of the selection span.

Listener summary for the Selection class

Listener	Description
Selection.onSetFocus	Notified when the input focus changes.

Selection.addListener()

Availability

Flash Player 6.

Usage

Selection.addListener(*newListener*)

Parameters

newListener   An object with an onSetFocus method.

Returns

None.

Description

Method; registers an object to receive keyboard focus change notifications. When the focus changes (for example, whenever Selection.setFocus() is invoked), all listening objects registered with addListener() have their onSetFocus method invoked. Multiple objects may listen for focus change notifications. If the listener *newListener* is already registered, no change occurs.

Selection.getBeginIndex()

Availability

Flash Player 5.

Usage

```
Selection.getBeginIndex()
```

Parameters

None.

Returns

An integer.

Description

Method; returns the index at the beginning of the selection span. If no index exists or no text field currently has focus, the method returns -1. Selection span indexes are zero-based (for example, the first position is 0, the second position is 1, and so on).

Selection.getCaretIndex()

Availability

Flash Player 5.

Usage

```
Selection.getCaretIndex()
```

Parameters

None.

Returns

An integer.

Description

Method; returns the index of the blinking insertion point (caret) position. If there is no blinking insertion point displayed, the method returns -1. Selection span indexes are zero-based (for example, the first position is 0, the second position is 1, and so on).

Selection.getEndIndex()

Availability

Flash Player 5.

Usage

```
Selection.getEndIndex()
```

Parameters

None.

Returns

An integer.

Description

Method; returns the ending index of the currently focused selection span. If no index exists, or if there is no currently focused selection span, the method returns -1. Selection span indexes are zero-based (for example, the first position is 0, the second position is 1, and so on).

Selection.getFocus()

Availability

Flash Player 5. Instance names for buttons and text fields work in Flash Player 6 and later.

Usage

```
Selection.getFocus()
```

Parameters

None.

Returns

A string or `null`.

Description

Method; returns the variable name of the text field that has focus. If no text field has focus, the method returns `null`. If the current focus is a button, and the button is a Button object, `getFocus()` returns the target path as a string. If the current focus is a text field, and the text field is a TextField object, `getFocus()` returns the target path as a string.

If a button movie clip is the currently focused button, `Selection.getFocus()` returns the target path of the button movie clip. If a Text Field with an instance name is currently focused, `Selection.getFocus()` returns the target path of the TextField object. Otherwise, it returns the Text Field's variable name.

Selection.onSetFocus

Availability

Flash Player 6.

Usage

```
someListener.onSetFocus = function(oldFocus, newFocus){
statements;
}
```

Description

Listener; notified when the input focus changes. To use onSetFocus, you must create a listener object. You can then define a function for onSetFocus and use addListener() to register the listener with the Selection object, as in the following:

```
someListener = new Object();
someListener.onSetFocus = function () { ... };
Selection.addListener(someListener);
```

Listeners enable different pieces of code to cooperate because multiple listeners can receive notification about a single event.

See also

Selection.addListener()

Selection.removeListener()

Availability

Flash Player 6.

Usage

Selection.removeListener(*listener*)

Parameters

listener   The object that will no longer receive focus notifications.

Returns

If the *listener* was successfully removed, the method returns a true value. If the *listener* was not successfully removed, for example if the *listener* was not on the Selection object's listener list, the method returns a value of false.

Description

Method; removes an object previously registered with addListener().

Selection.setFocus()

Availability

Flash Player 5. Instance names for buttons and movie clips work only in Flash Player 6 and later.

Usage

```
Selection.setFocus("instanceName")
```

Parameters

instanceName   A string specifying the path to the instance name of a button, movie clip, or text field.

Returns

An event.

Description

Method; gives focus to the selectable (editable) text field, button, or movie clip specified by *instanceName*. The *instanceName* parameter must be a string literal of the path to the instance. You can use dot or slash notation to specify the path. You can also use a relative or absolute path. If you are using ActionScript 2.0, you must use dot notation.

If null is passed, the current focus is removed.

Example

The following example gives focus to a text field associated with myVar, on the main Timeline. Because the *instanceName* parameter is an absolute path, you can call the action from any Timeline.

```
Selection.setFocus("_root.myVar");
```

In the following example, the text field associated with myVar is in a movie clip called myClip on the main Timeline. You can use either of the following two paths to set focus; the first is relative and the second is absolute.

```
Selection.setFocus("myClip.myVar");
Selection.setFocus("_root.myClip.myVar");
```

Selection.setSelection()

Availability

Flash Player 5.

Usage

```
Selection.setSelection(start, end)
```

Parameters

start   The beginning index of the selection span.

end   The ending index of the selection span.

Returns

Nothing.

Description

Method; sets the selection span of the currently focused text field. The new selection span will begin at the index specified in the *start* parameter, and end at the index specified in the *end* parameter. Selection span indexes are zero-based (for example, the first position is 0, the second position is 1, and so on). This method has no effect if there is no currently focused text field.

set

Availability

Flash Player 6.

Usage

```
function set property(varName) {
  // your statements here
}
```

Note: To use this keyword, you must specify ActionScript 2.0 and Flash Player 6 or later in the Flash tab of your FLA file's Publish Settings dialog box. This keyword is supported only when used in external script files, not in scripts written in the Actions panel.

Parameters

property   Word you want to use to refer to the property that set will access; this value must be the same as the value used in the corresponding get command.

varName   The local variable that sets the value you're assigning.

Returns

Nothing.

Description

Keyword; permits implicit "setting" of properties associated with objects based on classes you have defined in external class files. Using implicit set methods lets you access properties of objects without accessing them directly. Implicit get/set methods are syntactic shorthand for the Object.addProperty() method in ActionScript 1.

For more information, see "Implicit get/set methods" on page 376.

See also

get, Object.addProperty()

set variable

Availability

Flash Player 4.

Usage

```
set(variable, expression)
```

Parameters

variable   An identifier to hold the value of the *expression* parameter.

expression   A value assigned to the variable.

Returns

Nothing.

Description

Statement; assigns a value to a variable. A *variable* is a container that holds data. The container itself is always the same, but the contents can change. By changing the value of a variable as the SWF file plays, you can record and save information about what the user has done, record values that change as the SWF file plays, or evaluate whether a condition is `true` or `false`.

Variables can hold any data type (for example, String, Number, Boolean, Object, or MovieClip). The Timeline of each SWF file and movie clip has its own set of variables, and each variable has its own value independent of variables on other Timelines.

Strict data typing is not supported inside a `set` statement. If you use this statement to set a variable to a value whose data type is different from the data type associated with the variable in a class file, no compiler error is thrown.

Example

This example sets a variable called `orig_x_pos`, which stores the original *x* axis position of the `ship` movie clip in order to reset the ship to its starting location later in the SWF file.

```
on(release) {
  set("orig_x_pos", getProperty ("ship", _x ));
}
```

The previous code gives the same result as the following code:

```
on(release) {
  orig_x_pos = ship._x;
}
```

See also

var, call()

setInterval()

Availability

Flash Player 6.

Usage

```
setInterval(functionName, interval [, param1, param2, ..., paramN])
```

Parameters

functionName   A function name or a reference to an anonymous function.

interval   The time in milliseconds between calls to the *functionName* parameter.

param1, param2, ..., paramN   Optional parameters passed to the *function* or *methodName* parameter.

Returns

An interval identifier that you can pass to `clearInterval()` to cancel the interval.

Description

Function; calls a function or a method or an object at periodic intervals while a SWF file plays. You can use an interval function to update variables from a database or update a time display.

If *interval* is less than the SWF file's frame rate (for example, 10 frames per second [fps] is equal to 100 milliseconds), the interval function is called as close to *interval* as possible. You must use the `updateAfterEvent()` function to make sure that the screen refreshes often enough. If *interval* is greater than the SWF file's frame rate, the interval function is only called each time the playhead enters a frame; this minimizes the impact each time the screen is refreshed.

Example

Usage 1: The following example calls an anonymous function every 1000 milliseconds (every 1 second).

```
setInterval( function(){ trace("interval called"); }, 1000 );
```

Usage 2: The following example defines two event handlers and calls each of them. Both calls to `setInterval()` send the string `"interval called"` to the Output panel every 1000 milliseconds. The first call to `setInterval()` calls the `callback1()` function, which contains a `trace()` action. The second call to `setInterval()` passes the `"interval called"` string to the function `callback2()` as a parameter.

```
function callback1() {
   trace("interval called");
}

function callback2(arg) {
   trace(arg);
}

setInterval( callback1, 1000 );
setInterval( callback2, 1000, "interval called" );
```

Usage 3: This example uses a method of an object. You must use this syntax when you want to call a method that is defined for an object.

```
obj = new Object();
obj.interval = function() {
  trace("interval function called");
}

setInterval( obj, "interval", 1000 );

obj2 = new Object();
obj2.interval = function(s) {
  trace(s);
}
setInterval( obj2, "interval", 1000, "interval function called" );
```

You must use the second form of the setInterval() syntax to call a method of an object, as follows:

```
setInterval( obj2, "interval", 1000, "interval function called" );
```

See also

clearInterval(), updateAfterEvent()

setProperty()

Availability

Flash Player 4.

Usage

```
setProperty(target, property, value/expression)
```

Parameters

target   The path to the instance name of the movie clip whose property is to be set.

property   The property to be set.

value   The new literal value of the property.

expression   An equation that evaluates to the new value of the property.

Returns

Nothing.

Description

Function; changes a property value of a movie clip as the movie plays.

Example

This statement sets the _alpha property of a movie clip named star to 30% when the button is clicked:

```
on(release) {
  setProperty("star", _alpha, "30");
}
```

See also

getProperty

SharedObject class

Availability

Flash Player 6.

Description

Shared objects are quite powerful: they offer real-time data sharing between objects that are persistent on the user's computer. You can think of local shared objects as "cookies."

You can use local shared objects to maintain local persistence. This is the simplest way to use a shared object. For example, you can call `SharedObject.getLocal()` to create a shared object, such as a calculator with memory, in the player. Because the shared object is locally persistent, Flash saves its data attributes on the user's machine when the SWF file ends. The next time the SWF file runs, the calculator contains the values it had when the SWF file ended. Alternatively, if you set the shared object's properties to `null` before the SWF ends, the calculator opens without any prior values the next time the SWF file runs.

To create a local shared object, use the following syntax:

```
// Create a local shared object
so = SharedObject.getLocal("foo");
```

Local disk space considerations

Local shared objects are always persistent on the client, up to available memory and disk space.

By default, Flash can save locally persistent remote shared objects up to 100K in size. When you try to save a larger object, Flash Player displays the Local Storage dialog box, which lets the user allow or deny local storage for the domain that is requesting access. Make sure your Stage size is at least 215 x 138 pixels; this is the minimum size Flash requires to display the dialog box.

If the user clicks Allow, the object is saved and `SharedObject.onStatus` is invoked with a `code` property of `SharedObject.Flush.Success`; if the user clicks Deny, the object is not saved and `SharedObject.onStatus` is invoked with a `code` property of `SharedObject.Flush.Failed`.

The user can also specify permanent local storage settings for a particular domain by right-clicking (Windows) or Control-clicking (Macintosh) while a SWF file is playing, choosing Settings, and then opening the Local Storage panel.

The following list summarizes how the user's disk space choices interact with shared objects:

- If the user selects Never, objects are never saved locally, and all `SharedObject.flush()` commands issued for the object return `false`.

- If the user selects Unlimited (moves the slider all the way to the right), objects are saved locally up to available disk space.

- If the user selects None (moves the slider all the way to the left), all `SharedObject.flush()` commands issued for the object return `"pending"` and cause the player to ask the user if additional disk space can be allotted to make room for the object, as explained above.

- If the user selects 10 KB, 100 KB, 1 MB, or 10 MB, objects are saved locally and `SharedObject.flush()` returns `true` if the object fits within the specified amount of space. If more space is needed, `SharedObject.flush()` returns `"pending"`, and the player asks the user if additional disk space can be allotted to make room for the object, as explained above.

Additionally, if the user selects a value that is less than the amount of disk space currently being used for locally persistent data, the player warns the user that any locally saved shared objects will be deleted.

Note: There is no size limit in Flash Player that runs from the authoring environment.

Method summary for the SharedObject class

Method	Description
`SharedObject.clear()`	Purges all of the data from the shared object and deletes the shared object from the disk.
`SharedObject.flush()`	Immediately writes a locally persistent shared object to a local file.
`SharedObject.getLocal()`	Returns a reference to a locally persistent shared object that is available only to the current client.
`SharedObject.getSize()`	Gets the current size of the shared object, in bytes.

Property summary for the SharedObject class

Property (read-only)	Description
`SharedObject.data`	The collection of attributes assigned to the data property of the object; these attributes can be shared and/or stored.

Event handler summary for the SharedObject class

Event handler	Description
`SharedObject.onStatus`	Invoked every time an error, warning, or informational note is posted for a shared object.

Constructor for the SharedObject class

For information on creating local shared objects, see `SharedObject.getLocal()`.

SharedObject.clear()

Availability

Flash Player 7.

Usage

`my_so.clear()`

Parameters

None.

Returns

Nothing.

Description

Method; purges all of the data from the shared object and deletes the shared object from the disk. The reference to *my_so* is still active, and *my_so* is now empty.

SharedObject.data

Availability

Flash Player 6.

Usage

`myLocalSharedObject.data`

Description

Read-only property; the collection of attributes assigned to the `data` property of the object; these attributes can be shared and/or stored. Each attribute can be an object of any of the basic ActionScript or JavaScript types—Array, Number, Boolean, and so on. For example, the following lines assign values to various aspects of a shared object:

```
itemsArray = new Array(101,346,483);
currentUserIsAdmin = true;
currentUserName = "Ramona";
so.data.itemNumbers = itemsArray;
so.data.adminPrivileges = currentUserIsAdmin;
so.data.userName = currentUserName;
```

All attributes of a shared object's `data` property are saved if the object is persistent.

Note: Do not assign values directly to the `data` property of a shared object, as in `so.data = someValue;` Flash ignores these assignments.

To delete attributes for local shared objects, use code like `delete so.data.attributeName;` setting an attribute to `null` or `undefined` for a local shared object does not delete the attribute.

To create "private" values for a shared object—values that are available only to the client instance while the object is in use and are not stored with the object when it is closed—create properties that are not named data to store them, as shown in the following example.

```
so.favoriteColor = "blue";
so.favoriteNightClub = "The Bluenote Tavern";
so.favoriteSong = "My World is Blue";
```

Example

The following example sets the current stream to the user's selection.

```
curStream = _root.so.data.msgList[selected].streamName;
```

See also

Sound class

SharedObject.flush()

Availability

Flash Player 6.

Usage

```
myLocalSharedObject.flush([minimumDiskSpace])
```

Parameters

minimumDiskSpace   An optional integer specifying the number of bytes that must be allotted for this object. The default value is 0.

Returns

A Boolean value of true or false, or a string value of "pending".

- If the user has permitted local information storage for objects from this domain, and the amount of space allotted is sufficient to store the object, this method returns true. (If you have passed a value for *minimumDiskSpace*, the amount of space allotted must be at least equal to that value for true to be returned).

- If the user has permitted local information storage for objects from this domain, but the amount of space allotted is not sufficient to store the object, this method returns "pending".

- If the user has permanently denied local information storage for objects from this domain, or if Flash is unable to save the object for any reason, this method returns false.

Description

Method; immediately writes a locally persistent shared object to a local file. If you don't use this method, Flash writes the shared object to a file when the shared object session ends—that is, when the SWF file is closed, when the shared object is garbage-collected because it no longer has any references to it, or when you call SharedObject.data.

If this method returns "pending", the Flash Player displays a dialog box asking the user to increase the amount of disk space available to objects from this domain. To allow space for the shared object to "grow" when it is saved in the future, thus avoiding return values of "pending", pass a value for *minimumDiskSpace*. When Flash tries to write the file, it looks for the number of bytes passed to *minimumDiskSpace*, instead of looking for just enough space to save the shared object at its current size.

For example, if you expect a shared object to grow to a maximum size of 500 bytes, even though it may start out much smaller, pass 500 for *minimumDiskSpace*. If Flash asks the user to allot disk space for the shared object, it will ask for 500 bytes. After the user allots the requested amount of space, Flash won't have to ask for more space on future attempts to flush the object (as long as its size doesn't exceed 500 bytes).

After the user responds to the dialog box, this method is called again and returns either true or false; also, SharedObject.onStatus is invoked with a code property of SharedObject.Flush.Success or SharedObject.Flush.Failed.

For more information, see "Local disk space considerations" on page 821.

Example

The following function gets a shared object, SO, and fills writable properties with user-provided settings. Finally, flush() is called to save the settings and allot a minimum of 1000 bytes of disk space.

```
this.SyncSettingsCore=function(soname, override, settings)
{
   var SO=SharedObject.getLocal(soname, "http://www.mydomain.com/app/sys");

   // settings list index
   var i;

   // For each specified value in settings:
   // If override is true, set the persistent setting to the provided value.
   // If override is false, fetch the persistent setting, unless there
   // isn't one, in which case, set it to the provided value.
   for (i in settings) {
      if (override || (SO.data[i] == null)) {
         SO.data[i]= settings[i];
      } else {
         settings[i]= SO.data[i];
      }
   }
   SO.flush(1000);
}
```

SharedObject.getLocal()

Availability

Flash Player 6.

Usage

```
SharedObject.getLocal(objectName [, localPath])
```

Note: The correct syntax is `SharedObject.getLocal`. To assign the object to a variable, use syntax like `myLocalSO = SharedObject.getLocal`.

Parameters

objectName   The name of the object. The name can include forward slashes (/); for example, `work/addresses` is a legal name. Spaces are not allowed in a shared object name, nor are the following characters:

~ % & \ ; : " ' , < > ? #

localPath   An optional string parameter that specifies the full or partial path to the SWF file that created the shared object, and that determines where the shared object will be stored locally. The default value is the full path.

Returns

A reference to a shared object that is persistent locally and is available only to the current client. If Flash can't create or find the shared object (for example, if *localPath* was specified but no such directory exists), this method returns `null`.

Description

Method; returns a reference to a locally persistent shared object that is available only to the current client.

To avoid name collisions, Flash looks at the location of the SWF file that is creating the shared object. For example, if a SWF file at www.myCompany.com/apps/stockwatcher.swf creates a shared object named `portfolio`, that shared object will not conflict with another object named `portfolio` that was created by a SWF file at www.yourCompany.com/photoshoot.swf, because the SWF files originate from two different directories.

Example

The following example saves the last frame a user entered to a local shared object `kookie`.

```
// Get the kookie
so = sharedobject.getlocal("kookie");

// Get the user of the kookie and go to the frame number saved for this user.
if (so.data.user != undefined) {
  this.user = so.data.user;
  this.gotoAndStop(so.data.frame);
}
```

The following code block is placed on each SWF frame.

```
// On each frame, call the rememberme function to save the frame number.
function rememberme() {
  so.data.frame=this._currentFrame;
  so.data.user="John";
}
```

SharedObject.getSize()

Availability

Flash Player 6.

Usage

```
myLocalSharedObject.getSize()
```

Parameters

None.

Returns

A numeric value specifying the size of the shared object, in bytes.

Description

Method; gets the current size of the shared object, in bytes.

Flash calculates the size of a shared object by stepping through each of its data properties; the more data properties the object has, the longer it takes to estimate its size. For this reason, estimating object size can have significant processing cost. Therefore, you may want to avoid using this method unless you have a specific need for it.

Example

The following example gets the size of the shared object so.

```
var soSize= this.so.getSize();
```

SharedObject.onStatus

Availability

Flash Player 6.

Usage

```
myLocalSharedObject.onStatus = function(infoObject) {
    // your statements here
}
```

Parameters

infoObject   A parameter defined according to the status message.

Returns

Nothing.

Description

Event handler; invoked every time an error, warning, or informational note is posted for a shared object. If you want to respond to this event handler, you must create a function to process the information object generated by the shared object.

The information object has a `code` property containing a string that describes the result of the `onStatus` handler, and a `level` property containing a string that is either `"Status"` or `"Error"`.

In addition to this onStatus handler, Flash also provides a "super" function called System.onStatus. If onStatus is invoked for a particular object and there is no function assigned to respond to it, Flash processes a function assigned to System.onStatus if it exists.

The following events notify you when certain SharedObject activities occur.

Code property	Level property	Meaning
SharedObject.Flush.Failed	Error	A SharedObject.flush() command that returned "pending" has failed (the user did not allot additional disk space for the shared object when Flash Player displayed the Local Storage Settings dialog box).
SharedObject.Flush.Success	Status	A SharedObject.flush() command that returned "pending" has been successfully completed (the user allotted additional disk space for the shared object).

See also

SharedObject.getLocal(), System.onStatus

Sound class

Availability

Flash Player 5.

Description

The Sound class lets you control sound in a movie. You can add sounds to a movie clip from the library while the movie is playing and control those sounds. If you do not specify a target when you create a new Sound object, you can use the methods to control sound for the whole movie.

You must use the constructor new Sound to create a Sound object before calling the methods of the Sound class.

Method summary for the Sound class

Method	Description
Sound.attachSound()	Attaches the sound specified in the parameter.
Sound.getBytesLoaded()	Returns the number of bytes loaded for the specified sound.
Sound.getBytesTotal()	Returns the size of the sound in bytes.
Sound.getPan()	Returns the value of the previous setPan() call.
Sound.getTransform()	Returns the value of the previous setTransform() call.
Sound.getVolume()	Returns the value of the previous setVolume() call.
Sound.loadSound()	Loads an MP3 file into Flash Player.
Sound.setPan()	Sets the left/right balance of the sound.

Method	Description
Sound.setTransform()	Sets the amount of each channel, left and right, to be played in each speaker.
Sound.setVolume()	Sets the volume level for a sound.
Sound.start()	Starts playing a sound from the beginning or, optionally, from an offset point set in the parameter.
Sound.stop()	Stops the specified sound or all sounds currently playing.

Property summary for the Sound class

Property	Description
Sound.duration	Length of a sound, in milliseconds.
Sound.ID3	Provides access to the metadata that is part of an MP3 file.
Sound.position	Number of milliseconds a sound has been playing.

Event handler summary for the Sound class

Event handler	Description
Sound.onID3	Invoked each time new ID3 data is available.
Sound.onLoad	Invoked when a sound loads.
Sound.onSoundComplete	Invoked when a sound stops playing.

Constructor for the Sound class

Availability

Flash Player 5.

Usage

```
new Sound([target])
```

Parameters

target   The movie clip instance on which the Sound object operates. This parameter is optional.

Returns

Nothing.

Description

Constructor; creates a new Sound object for a specified movie clip. If you do not specify a target instance, the Sound object controls all of the sounds in the movie.

Example

The following example creates a new Sound object called `global_sound`. The second line calls `setVolume()` and adjusts the volume on all sounds in the movie to 50%.

```
global_sound = new Sound();
global_sound.setVolume(50);
```

The following example creates a new Sound object, passes it the target movie clip *my_mc*, and calls the *start* method, which starts any sound in *my_mc*.

```
movie_sound = new Sound(my_mc);
movie_sound.start();
```

Sound.attachSound()

Availability

Flash Player 5.

Usage

my_sound.attachSound("*idName*")

Parameters

idName   The identifier of an exported sound in the library. The identifier is located in the Linkage Properties dialog box.

Returns

Nothing.

Description

Method; attaches the sound specified in the *idName* parameter to the specified Sound object. The sound must be in the library of the current SWF file and specified for export in the Linkage Properties dialog box. You must call `Sound.start()` to start playing the sound.

To make sure that the sound can be controlled from any scene in the SWF file, place the sound on the main Timeline of the SWF file.

Sound.duration

Availability

Flash Player 6.

Usage

my_sound.duration

Description

Property (read-only); the duration of a sound, in milliseconds.

Sound.getBytesLoaded()

Availability

Flash Player 6.

Usage

`my_sound.getBytesLoaded()`

Parameters

None.

Returns

An integer indicating the number of bytes loaded.

Description

Method; returns the number of bytes loaded (streamed) for the specified Sound object. You can compare the value of `getBytesLoaded()` with the value of `getBytesTotal()` to determine what percentage of a sound has loaded.

See also

`Sound.getBytesTotal()`

Sound.getBytesTotal()

Availability

Flash Player 6.

Usage

`my_sound.getBytesTotal()`

Parameters

None.

Returns

An integer indicating the total size, in bytes, of the specified Sound object.

Description

Method; returns the size, in bytes, of the specified Sound object.

See also

`Sound.getBytesLoaded()`

Sound.getPan()

Availability

Flash Player 5.

Usage

`my_sound.getPan();`

Parameters

None.

Returns

An integer.

Description

Method; returns the pan level set in the last `setPan()` call as an integer from -100 (left) to 100 (right). (0 sets the left and right channels equally.) The pan setting controls the left-right balance of the current and future sounds in a SWF file.

This method is cumulative with `setVolume()` or `setTransform()`.

See also

`Sound.setPan()`

Sound.getTransform()

Availability

Flash Player 5.

Usage

`my_sound.getTransform();`

Parameters

None.

Returns

An object with properties that contain the channel percentage values for the specified sound object.

Description

Method; returns the sound transform information for the specified Sound object set with the last `Sound.setTransform()` call.

Sound.getVolume()

Availability

Flash Player 5.

Usage

my_sound.getVolume()

Parameters

None.

Returns

An integer.

Description

Method; returns the sound volume level as an integer from 0 to 100, where 0 is off and 100 is full volume. The default setting is 100.

See also

Sound.setVolume()

Sound.ID3

Availability

Flash Player 6; behavior updated in Flash Player 7.

Usage

my_sound.ID3

Description

Property (read-only); provides access to the metadata that is part of an MP3 file.

MP3 sound files can contain ID3 tags, which provide metadata about the file. If an MP3 sound that you load using Sound.attachSound() or Sound.loadSound() contains ID3 tags, you can query these properties. Only ID3 tags that use the UTF-8 character set are supported.

Flash Player 6 release 40 and later use the Sound.id3 property to support ID3 1.0 and ID3 1.1 tags. Flash Player 7 adds support for ID3 2.0 tags, specifically 2.3 and 2.4. For backward compatibility, both Sound.id3 and Sound.ID3 are supported. Code hints are supported only for the lowercase use of id3 (see "Using code hints" on page 267).

The following table lists the standard ID3 2.0 tags and the type of content the tags represent; you query them in the format *my_sound*.ID3.COMM, *my_sound*.ID3.TIME, and so on. MP3 files can contain tags other than those in this table; Sound.ID3 provides access to those tags as well.

Property	Description
COMM	Comment
TALB	Album/movie/show title
TBPM	Beats per minute

Property	Description
TCOM	Composer
TCON	Content type
TCOP	Copyright message
TDAT	Date
TDLY	Playlist delay
TENC	Encoded by
TEXT	Lyricist/text writer
TFLT	File type
TIME	Time
TIT1	Content group description
TIT2	Title/song name/content description
TIT3	Subtitle/description refinement
TKEY	Initial key
TLAN	Languages
TLEN	Length
TMED	Media type
TOAL	Original album/movie/show title
TOFN	Original filename
TOLY	Original lyricists/text writers
TOPE	Original artists/performers
TORY	Original release year
TOWN	File owner/licensee
TPE1	Lead performers/soloists
TPE2	Band/orchestra/accompaniment
TPE3	Conductor/performer refinement
TPE4	Interpreted, remixed, or otherwise modified by
TPOS	Part of a set
TPUB	Publisher
TRCK	Track number/position in set
TRDA	Recording dates
TRSN	Internet radio station name
TRSO	Internet radio station owner

Property	Description
TSIZ	Size
TSRC	ISRC (international standard recording code)
TSSE	Software/hardware and settings used for encoding
TYER	Year
WXXX	URL link frame

Flash Player 6 supported several ID31.0 tags. If these tags are in not in the MP3 file, but corresponding ID3 2.0 tags are, the ID3 2.0 tags are copied into the ID3 1.0 properties, as shown in the following table. This process provides backward compatibility with scripts that you may have written already that read ID3 1.0 properties.

ID3 2.0 tag	Corresponding ID3 1.0 property
COMM	Sound.id3.comment
TALB	Sound.id3.album
TCON	Sound.id3.genre
TIT2	Sound.id3.songname
TPE1	Sound.id3.artist
TRCK	Sound.id3.track
TYER	Sound.id3.year

Example

See Sound.onID3 for an example of the use of this property.

See also

Sound.attachSound(), Sound.loadSound()

Sound.loadSound()

Availability

Flash Player 6.

Usage

my_sound.loadSound("*url*", *isStreaming*)

Parameters

url   The location on a server of an MP3 sound file.

isStreaming   A Boolean value that indicates whether the sound is a streaming sound (true) or an event sound (false).

Returns

Nothing.

Description

Method; loads an MP3 file into a Sound object. You can use the *isStreaming* parameter to indicate whether the sound is an event or a streaming sound.

Event sounds are completely loaded before they play. They are managed by the ActionScript Sound class and respond to all methods and properties of this class.

Streaming sounds play while they are downloading. Playback begins when sufficient data has been received to start the decompressor.

All MP3s (event or streaming) loaded with this method are saved in the browser's file cache on the user's system.

Example

The following example loads an event sound:

```
my_sound.loadSound( "http://serverpath:port/mp3filename", false);
```

The following example loads a streaming sound:

```
my_sound.loadSound( "http://serverpath:port/mp3filename", true);
```

See also

```
Sound.onLoad
```

Sound.onID3

Availability

Flash Player 7.

Usage

```
my_sound.onID3 = function(){
    // your statements here
}
```

Parameters

None.

Returns

Nothing.

Description

Event handler; invoked each time new ID3 data is available for an MP3 file that you load using `Sound.attachSound()` or `Sound.loadSound()`. This handler provides access to ID3 data without polling. If both ID3 1.0 and ID3 2.0 tags are present in a file, this handler is called twice.

Example

The following example traces the ID3 properties of song.mp3 to the Output panel.

```
my_sound = new Sound();
my_sound.onID3 = function(){
  for( var prop in my_sound.ID3 ){
    trace( prop + " : "+ my_sound.ID3[prop] );
  }
}
my_sound.loadSound("song.mp3", false);
```

See also

```
Sound.attachSound(), Sound.ID3, Sound.loadSound()
```

Sound.onLoad

Availability

Flash Player 6.

Usage

```
my_sound.onLoad = function(success){
  // your statements here
}
```

Parameters

success A Boolean value of `true` if *my_sound* has been loaded successfully, false otherwise.

Returns

Nothing.

Description

Event handler; invoked automatically when a sound loads. You must create a function that executes when the this handler is invoked. You can use either an anonymous function or a named function (for an example of each, see `Sound.onSoundComplete`). You should define this handler before you call *my_sound*.`loadSound()`.

See also

```
Sound.loadSound()
```

Sound.onSoundComplete

Availability

Flash Player 6.

Usage

```
my_sound.onSoundComplete = function(){
    // your statements here
}
```

Parameters

None.

Returns

Nothing.

Description

Event handler; invoked automatically when a sound finishes playing. You can use this handler to trigger events in a SWF file when a sound finishes playing.

You must create a function that executes when this handler is invoked. You can use either an anonymous function or a named function.

Example

Usage 1: The following example uses an anonymous function:

```
my_sound = new Sound();
my_sound.attachSound("mySoundID");
my_sound.onSoundComplete = function() {
    trace("mySoundID completed");
}
my_sound.start();
```

Usage 2: The following example uses a named function:

```
function callback1() {
    trace("mySoundID completed");
}

my_sound = new Sound();
my_sound.attachSound("mySoundID");
my_sound.onSoundComplete = callback1;
my_sound.start();
```

See also

Sound.onLoad

Sound.position

Availability

Flash Player 6.

Usage

my_sound.position

Description

Property (read-only); the number of milliseconds a sound has been playing. If the sound is looped, the position will be reset to 0 at the beginning of each loop.

Sound.setPan()

Availability

Flash Player 5.

Usage

my_sound.setPan(*pan*);

Parameters

pan   An integer specifying the left-right balance for a sound. The range of valid values is -100 to 100, where -100 uses only the left channel, 100 uses only the right channel, and 0 balances the sound evenly between the two channels.

Returns

An integer.

Description

Method; determines how the sound is played in the left and right channels (speakers). For mono sounds, *pan* determines which speaker (left or right) the sound plays through.

Example

The following example creates a Sound object called my_sound and attaches a sound with the identifier L7 from the library. It also calls setVolume() and setPan() to control the L7 sound.

```
onClipEvent(mouseDown) {
// create a sound object
  my_sound = new Sound(this);
// attach a sound from the library
  my_sound.attachSound("L7");
//set volume to 50%
  my_sound.setVolume(50);
//turn off the sound in the right channel
  my_sound.setPan(-100);
//start 30 seconds into the sound and play it 5 times
  my_sound.start(30, 5);
```

See also

Sound.attachSound(), Sound.setPan(), Sound.setTransform(), Sound.setVolume(), Sound.start()

Sound.setTransform()

Availability

Flash Player 5.

Usage

my_sound.setTransform(*soundTransformObject*)

Parameters

soundTransformObject   An object created with the constructor for the generic Object class.

Returns

Nothing.

Description

Method; sets the sound transform (or balance) information, for a Sound object.

The *soundTransformObject* parameter is an object that you create using the constructor method of the generic Object class with parameters specifying how the sound is distributed to the left and right channels (speakers).

Sounds use a considerable amount of disk space and memory. Because stereo sounds use twice as much data as mono sounds, it is generally best to use 22-KHz 6-bit mono sounds. You can use setTransform() to play mono sounds as stereo, play stereo sounds as mono, and to add interesting effects to sounds.

The properties for the *soundTransformObject* are as follows:

ll   A percentage value specifying how much of the left input to play in the left speaker (0-100).

lr   A percentage value specifying how much of the right input to play in the left speaker (0-100).

rr   A percentage value specifying how much of the right input to play in the right speaker (0-100).

rl   A percentage value specifying how much of the left input to play in the right speaker (0-100).

The net result of the parameters is represented by the following formula:

```
leftOutput = left_input * ll + right_input * lr
rightOutput = right_input * rr + left_input * rl
```

The values for left_input or right_input are determined by the type (stereo or mono) of sound in your SWF file.

Stereo sounds divide the sound input evenly between the left and right speakers and have the following transform settings by default:

```
ll = 100
lr = 0
rr = 100
rl = 0
```

Mono sounds play all sound input in the left speaker and have the following transform settings by default:

```
ll = 100
lr = 100
rr = 0
rl = 0
```

Example

The following example illustrates a setting that can be achieved by using setTransform(), but cannot be achieved by using setVolume() or setPan(), even if they are combined.

The following code creates a new soundTransformObject object and sets its properties so that sound from both channels will play only in the left channel.

```
mySoundTransformObject = new Object;
mySoundTransformObject.ll = 100;
mySoundTransformObject.lr = 100;
mySoundTransformObject.rr = 0;
mySoundTransformObject.rl = 0;
```

To apply the soundTransformObject object to a Sound object, you then need to pass the object to the Sound object using setTransform() as follows:

```
my_sound.setTransform(mySoundTransformObject);
```

The following example plays a stereo sound as mono; the soundTransformObjectMono object has the following parameters:

```
mySoundTransformObjectMono = new Object;
mySoundTransformObjectMono.ll = 50;
mySoundTransformObjectMono.lr = 50;
mySoundTransformObjectMono.rr = 50;
mySoundTransformObjectMono.rl = 50;
my_sound.setTransform(soundTransformObjectMono);
```

This example plays the left channel at half capacity and adds the rest of the left channel to the right channel; the soundTransformObjectHalf object has the following parameters:

```
mySoundTransformObjectHalf = new Object;
mySoundTransformObjectHalf.ll = 50;
mySoundTransformObjectHalf.lr = 0;
mySoundTransformObjectHalf.rr = 100;
mySoundTransformObjectHalf.rl = 50;
my_sound.setTransform(soundTransformObjectHalf);
```

See also

Object class

Sound.setVolume()

Availability

Flash Player 5.

Usage

```
my_sound.setVolume(volume)
```

Parameters

volume   A number from 0 to 100 representing a volume level. 100 is full volume and 0 is no volume. The default setting is 100.

Returns

Nothing.

Description

Method; sets the volume for the Sound object.

Example

The following example sets volume to 50% and transfers the sound over time from the left speaker to the right speaker:

```
onClipEvent (load) {
   i = -100;
   my_sound = new Sound();
   my_sound.setVolume(50);
}
onClipEvent (enterFrame) {
   if (i <= 100) {
      my_sound.setPan(i++);
   }
}
```

See also

```
Sound.setPan(), Sound.setTransform()
```

Sound.start()

Availability

Flash Player 5.

Usage

```
my_sound.start([secondOffset, loop])
```

Parameters

secondOffset   An optional parameter that lets you start playing the sound at a specific point. For example, if you have a 30-second sound and want the sound to start playing in the middle, specify 15 for the *secondOffset* parameter. The sound is not delayed 15 seconds, but rather starts playing at the 15-second mark.

loop   An optional parameter allowing you to specify the number of times the sound should play consecutively.

Returns

Nothing.

Description

Method; starts playing the last attached sound from the beginning if no parameter is specified, or starting at the point in the sound specified by the *secondOffset* parameter.

See also

Sound.stop()

Sound.stop()

Availability

Flash Player 5.

Usage

my_sound.stop(["*idName*"])

Parameters

idName   An optional parameter specifying a specific sound to stop playing. The *idName* parameter must be enclosed in quotation marks (" ").

Returns

Nothing.

Description

Method; stops all sounds currently playing if no parameter is specified, or just the sound specified in the *idName* parameter.

See also

Sound.start()

_soundbuftime

Availability

Flash Player 4.

Usage

_soundbuftime = *integer*

Parameters

integer   The number of seconds before the SWF file starts to stream.

Description

Property (global); establishes the number of seconds of streaming sound to prebuffer. The default value is 5 seconds.

Stage class

Availability

Flash Player 6.

Description

The Stage class is a top-level class whose methods, properties, and handlers you can access without using a constructor.

Use the methods and properties of this class to access and manipulate information about the boundaries of a SWF file.

Method summary for the Stage class

Method	Description
Stage.addListener()	Adds a listener object that detects when a SWF file is resized.
Stage.removeListener()	Removes a listener object from the Stage object.

Property summary for the Stage class

Property	Description
Stage.align	Alignment of the SWF file in the player or browser.
Stage.height	Height of the Stage, in pixels.
Stage.scaleMode	The current scaling of the SWF file.
Stage.showMenu	Shows or hides the default items in the Flash Player context menu.
Stage.width	Width of the Stage, in pixels.

Event handler summary for the Stage class

Event handler	Description
Stage.onResize	Invoked when Stage.scaleMode is set to "noScale" and the SWF file is resized.

Stage.addListener()

Availability

Flash Player 6.

Usage

```
Stage.addListener(myListener)
```

Parameters

myListener   An object that listens for a callback notification from the `Stage.onResize` event.

Returns

Nothing.

Description

Method; detects when a SWF file is resized (but only if `Stage.scaleMode = "noScale"`). The `addListener()` method doesn't work with the default movie scaling setting (`"showAll"`) or other scaling settings (`"exactFit"` and `"noBorder"`).

To use `addListener()`, you must first create a *listener object*. Stage listener objects receive notification from `Stage.onResize`.

Example

This example creates a new listener object called `myListener`. It then uses `myListener` to call `onResize` and define a function that will be called when `onResize` is triggered. Finally, the code adds the `myListener` object to the callback list of the Stage object. Listener objects allow multiple objects to listen for resize notifications.

```
myListener = new Object();
myListener.onResize = function () { ... }
Stage.scaleMode = "noScale"
Stage.addListener(myListener);
```

See also

`Stage.onResize`, `Stage.removeListener()`

Stage.align

Availability

Flash Player 6.

Usage

```
Stage.align
```

Description

Property; indicates the current alignment of the SWF file in the player or browser.

The following table lists the values for the `align` property. Any value not listed here centers the SWF file in the player or browser area.

Value	Vertical	Horizontal
"T"	top	center
"B"	bottom	center
"L"	center	left
"R"	center	right
"TL"	top	left
"TR"	top	right
"BL"	bottom	left
"BR"	bottom	right

Stage.height

Availability

Flash Player 6.

Usage

`Stage.height`

Description

Property (read-only); indicates the current height, in pixels, of the Stage. When the value of `Stage.scaleMode` is "noScale", the `height` property represents the height of the player. When the value of `Stage.scaleMode` is not "noScale", `height` represents the height of the SWF file.

See also

`Stage.align`, `Stage.scaleMode`, `Stage.width`

Stage.onResize

Availability

Flash Player 6.

Usage

```
myListener.onResize = function(){
   // your statements here
}
```

Parameters

None.

Parameters

None.

Returns

Nothing.

Description

Event handler; invoked when `Stage.scaleMode` is set to `"noScale"` and the SWF file is resized. You can use this event handler to write a function that lays out the objects on the Stage when a SWF file is resized.

Example

The following example displays a message in the Output panel when the Stage is resized.

```
Stage.scaleMode = "noScale"
myListener = new Object();
myListener.onResize = function () {
    trace("Stage size is now " + Stage.width + " by " + Stage.height);
}
Stage.addListener(myListener);
// later, call Stage.removeListener(myListener)
```

See also

`Stage.addListener()`, `Stage.removeListener()`

Stage.removeListener()

Availability

Flash Player 6.

Usage

`Stage.removeListener(myListener)`

Parameters

`myListener` An object added to an object's callback list with `addListener()`.

Returns

A Boolean value.

Description

Method; removes a listener object created with `addListener()`.

See also

`Stage.addListener()`

Stage.scaleMode

Availability

Flash Player 6.

Usage

```
Stage.scaleMode = "value"
```

Description

Property; indicates the current scaling of the SWF file within the Stage. The `scaleMode` property forces the SWF file into a specific scaling mode. By default, the SWF file uses the HTML parameters set in the Publish Settings dialog box.

The `scaleMode` property can use the values `"exactFit"`, `"showAll"`, `"noBorder"`, and `"noScale"`. Any other value sets the `scaleMode` property to the default `"showAll"`.

Stage.showMenu

Availability

Flash Player 6.

Usage

```
Stage.showMenu
```

Description

Property (read-write); specifies whether to show or hide the default items in the Flash Player context menu. If `showMenu` is set to `true` (the default), all context menu items appear. If `showMenu` is set to `false`, only the Settings item appears.

See also

ContextMenu class, ContextMenuItem class

Stage.width

Availability

Flash Player 6.

Usage

```
Stage.width
```

Description

Property (read-only); indicates the current width, in pixels, of the Stage. When the value of `Stage.scaleMode` is `"noScale"`, the `width` property represents the width of the player. When the value of `Stage.scaleMode` is not `"noScale"`, `width` represents the width of the SWF file.

See also

`Stage.align`, `Stage.height`, `Stage.scaleMode`

startDrag()

Availability

Flash Player 4.

Usage

```
startDrag(target,[lock, left, top, right, bottom])
```

Parameters

target   The target path of the movie clip to drag.

lock   A Boolean value specifying whether the draggable movie clip is locked to the center of the mouse position (*true*), or locked to the point where the user first clicked on the movie clip (*false*). This parameter is optional.

left, *top*, *right*, *bottom*   Values relative to the coordinates of the movie clip's parent that specify a constraint rectangle for the movie clip. These parameters are optional.

Returns

Nothing.

Description

Function; makes the *target* movie clip draggable while the movie is playing. Only one movie clip can be dragged at a time. Once a startDrag() operation is executed, the movie clip remains draggable until explicitly stopped by stopDrag(), or until a startDrag() action for another movie clip is called.

Example

To create a movie clip that users can position in any location, attach the startDrag() and stopDrag() actions to a button inside the movie clip.

```
on(press) {
    startDrag(this,true);
}
on(release) {
    stopDrag();
}
```

See also

MovieClip._droptarget, MovieClip.startDrag(), stopDrag()

static

Availability

Flash Player 6.

Usage

```
class someClassName{
   static var name;
   static function name() {
      // your statements here
   }
}
```

Note: To use this keyword, you must specify ActionScript 2.0 and Flash Player 6 or later in the Flash tab of your FLA file's Publish Settings dialog box. This keyword is supported only when used in external script files, not in scripts written in the Actions panel.

Parameters

name   The name of the variable or function that you want to specify as static.

Description

Keyword; specifies that a variable or function is created only once per class rather than being created in every object based on that class. For more information, see "Instance and class members" on page 369.

You can use this keyword in class definitions only, not in interface definitions.

See also

`private`, `public`

stop()

Availability

Flash 2.

Usage

`stop()`

Parameters

None.

Returns

Nothing.

Description

Function; stops the SWF file that is currently playing. The most common use of this action is to control movie clips with buttons.

stopAllSounds()

Availability

Flash Player 3.

Usage

```
stopAllSounds()
```

Parameters

None.

Returns

Nothing.

Description

Function; stops all sounds currently playing in a SWF file without stopping the playhead. Sounds set to stream will resume playing as the playhead moves over the frames they are in.

Example

The following code could be applied to a button that, when clicked, stops all sounds in the SWF file.

```
on(release) {
   stopAllSounds();
}
```

See also

Sound class

stopDrag()

Availability

Flash Player 4.

Usage

```
stopDrag()
```

Parameters

None.

Returns

Nothing.

Description

Function; stops the current drag operation.

Example

This code stops the drag action on the instance `my_mc` when the user releases the mouse button:

```
on(press) {
    startDrag("my_mc");
}
on(release) {
    stopdrag();
}
```

See also

`MovieClip._droptarget`, `MovieClip.stopDrag()`, `startDrag()`

" " (string delimiter)

Availability

Flash Player 4.

Usage

`"text"`

Parameters

text   A character.

Returns

Nothing.

Description

String delimiter; when used before and after characters, quotation marks indicate that the characters have a literal value and are considered a *string*—not a variable, numerical value, or other ActionScript element.

Example

This example uses quotation marks to indicate that the value of the variable *yourGuess* is the literal string "Prince Edward Island" and not the name of a variable. The value of `province` is a variable, not a literal; to determine the value of `province`, the value of *yourGuess* must be located.

```
yourGuess = "Prince Edward Island";

on(release){
    province = yourGuess;
    trace(province);
}

// displays Prince Edward Island in the Output panel
```

See also

String class, `String()`

String class

Availability

Flash Player 5 (became a native object in Flash Player 6, which improved performance significantly).

Description

The String class is a wrapper for the string primitive data type, and provides methods and properties that let you manipulate primitive string value types. You can convert the value of any object into a string using the `String()` function.

All of the methods of the String class, except for `concat()`, `fromCharCode()`, `slice()`, and `substr()`, are generic. This means the methods themselves call `this.toString()` before performing their operations, and you can use these methods with other non-String objects.

Because all string indexes are zero-based, the index of the last character for any string x is `x.length - 1`.

You can call any of the methods of the String class using the constructor method `new String` or using a string literal value. If you specify a string literal, the ActionScript interpreter automatically converts it to a temporary String object, calls the method, and then discards the temporary String object. You can also use the `String.length` property with a string literal.

Do not confuse a string literal with a String object. In the following example, the first line of code creates the string literal `s1`, and the second line of code creates the String object `s2`.

```
s1 = "foo"
s2 = new String("foo")
```

Use string literals unless you specifically need to use a String object.

Method summary for the String class

Method	Description
String.charAt()	Returns the character at a specific location in a string.
String.charCodeAt()	Returns the value of the character at the specified index as a 16-bit integer between 0 and 65535.
String.concat()	Combines the text of two strings and returns a new string.
String.fromCharCode()	Returns a string made up of the characters specified in the parameters.
String.indexOf()	Returns the position of the first occurrence of a specified substring.
String.lastIndexOf()	Returns the position of the last occurrence of a specified substring.
String.slice()	Extracts a section of a string and returns a new string.
String.split()	Splits a String object into an array of strings by separating the string into substrings.
String.substr()	Returns a specified number of characters in a string, beginning at a specified location.
String.substring()	Returns the characters between two indexes in a string.

Method	Description
`String.toLowerCase()`	Converts the string to lowercase and returns the result; does not change the contents of the original object.
`String.toUpperCase()`	Converts the string to uppercase and returns the result; does not change the contents of the original object.

Property summary for the String class

Property	Description
`String.length`	A nonzero-based integer specifying the number of characters in the specified String object.

Constructor for the String class

Availability

Flash Player 5.

Usage

```
new String(value)
```

Parameters

value   The initial value of the new String object.

Returns

Nothing.

Description

Constructor; creates a new String object.

See also

`String()`, `" "` (string delimiter)

String.charAt()

Availability

Flash Player 5.

Usage

```
my_str.charAt(index)
```

Parameters

index   An integer that specifies the position of a character in the string. The first character is indicated by 0, and the last character is indicated by `my_str.length-1`.

Returns

A character.

Description

Method; returns the character in the position specified by the parameter *index*. If *index* is not a number from 0 to `string.length` - 1, an empty string is returned.

This method is similar to `String.charCodeAt()` except that the returned value is a character, not a 16-bit integer character code.

Example

In the following example, this method is called on the first letter of the string `"Chris"`.

```
my_str = new String("Chris");
i = my_str.charCodeAt(0); // i = "C"
```

String.charCodeAt()

Availability

Flash Player 5.

Usage

```
my_str.charCodeAt(index)
```

Parameters

index   An integer that specifies the position of a character in the string. The first character is indicated by 0, and the last character is indicated by `my_str.length` - 1.

Returns

An integer.

Description

Method; returns a 16-bit integer from 0 to 65535 that represents the character specified by *index*. If *index* is not a number from 0 to `string.length` - 1, `NaN` is returned.

This method is similar to `String.charAt()` except that the returned value is a 16-bit integer character code, not a character.

Example

In the following example, this method is called on the first letter of the string `"Chris"`.

```
my_str = new String("Chris");
i = my_str.charCodeAt(0); // i = 67
```

String.concat()

Availability

Flash Player 5.

Usage

my_str.concat(*value1*,...*valueN*)

Parameters

value1,...*valueN*   Zero or more values to be concatenated.

Returns

A string.

Description

Method; combines the value of the String object with the parameters and returns the newly formed string; the original value, *my_str*, is unchanged.

String.fromCharCode()

Availability

Flash Player 5.

Usage

String.fromCharCode(*c1*,*c2*,...*cN*)

Parameters

c1,*c2*,...*cN*   Decimal integers that represent ASCII values.

Returns

A string.

Description

Method; returns a string made up of the characters represented by the ASCII values in the parameters.

Example

This example uses fromCharCode() to insert an @ character in the e-mail address.

```
address_str = "dog" + String.fromCharCode(64) + "house.net";
trace(address_str); // dog@house.net
```

String.indexOf()

Availability

Flash Player 5.

Usage

`my_str.indexOf(substring, [startIndex])`

Parameters

`substring`   An integer or string specifying the substring to be searched for within `my_str`.

`startIndex`   An optional integer specifying the starting point in `my_str` to search for the substring.

Returns

The position of the first occurrence of the specified substring, or -1.

Description

Method; searches the string and returns the position of the first occurrence of `substring` found at or after `startIndex` within the calling string. If `substring` is not found, the method returns -1.

See also

`String.lastIndexOf()`

String.lastIndexOf()

Availability

Flash Player 5.

Usage

`my_str.lastIndexOf(substring, [startIndex])`

Parameters

`substring`   An integer or string specifying the string to be searched for.

`startIndex`   An optional integer specifying the starting point to search for `substring`.

Returns

The position of the last occurrence of the specified substring, or -1.

Description

Method; searches the string from right to left and returns the index of the last occurrence of `substring` found before `startIndex` within the calling string. If `substring` is not found, the method returns -1.

See also

`String.indexOf()`

String.length

Availability

Flash Player 5.

Usage

```
my_str.length
```

Description

Property; a nonzero-based integer specifying the number of characters in the specified String object.

Because all string indexes are zero-based, the index of the last character for any string x is `x.length - 1`.

String.slice()

Availability

Flash Player 5.

Usage

```
my_str.slice(start, [end])
```

Parameters

start   A number specifying the index of the starting point for the slice. If *start* is a negative number, the starting point is determined from the end of the string, where -1 is the last character.

end   An integer that is 1+ the index of the ending point for the slice. The character indexed by the *end* parameter is not included in the extracted string. If this parameter is omitted, `String.length` is used. If *end* is a negative number, the ending point is determined by counting back from the end of the string, where -1 is the last character.

Returns

A substring of the specified string.

Description

Method; returns a string that includes the *start* character and all characters up to (but not including) the *end* character. The original String object is not modified. If the *end* parameter is not specified, the end of the substring is the end of the string. If the value of *start* is greater than or equal to the value of *end*, the method returns an empty string.

Example

The following example sets a variable, text, creates a String object, my_str, and passes it the text variable. The slice() method extracts a section of the string contained in the variable, and trace() sends it to the Output panel. The example shows using both a positive and negative value for the end parameter.

```
text = "Lexington";
my_str = new String( text );
trace(my_str.slice( 1, 3 )); // "ex"
trace(my_str.slice( 1, -6 )); // "ex"
```

See also

```
String.substr(), String.substring()
```

String.split()

Availability

Flash Player 5.

Usage

```
my_str.split("delimiter", [limit])
```

Parameters

delimiter The character or string at which *my_str* splits.

limit The number of items to place into the array. This parameter is optional.

Returns

An array containing the substrings of *my_str*.

Description

Method; splits a String object into substrings by breaking it wherever the specified *delimiter* parameter occurs, and returns the substrings in an array. If you use an empty string ("") as a delimiter, each character in the string is placed as an element in the array, as in the following code.

```
my_str = "Joe";
i = my_str.split("");
trace (i);
```

The Output panel displays the following:

```
J,o,e
```

If the *delimiter* parameter is undefined, the entire string is placed into the first element of the returned array.

Example

The following example returns an array with five elements.

```
my_str = "P, A, T, S, Y";
my_str.split(",");
```

This example returns an array with two elements, "P" and "A".

```
my_str.split(",", 2);
```

String.substr()

Availability

Flash Player 5.

Usage

`my_str.substr(start, [length])`

Parameters

start   An integer that indicates the position of the first character in *my_str* to be used to create the substring. If *start* is a negative number, the starting position is determined from the end of the string, where the -1 is the last character.

length   The number of characters in the substring being created. If *length* is not specified, the substring includes all of the characters from the start to the end of the string.

Returns

A substring of the specified string.

Description

Method; returns the characters in a string from the index specified in the *start* parameter through the number of characters specified in the *length* parameter. The substr method does not change the string specified by *my_str*; it returns a new string.

String.substring()

Availability

Flash Player 5.

Usage

`my_str.substring(start, [end])`

Parameters

start   An integer that indicates the position of the first character of *my_str* used to create the substring. Valid values for *start* are 0 through String.length - 1. If *start* is a negative value, 0 is used.

end   An integer that is 1+ the index of the last character in *my_str* to be extracted. Valid values for *end* are 1 through String.length. The character indexed by the *end* parameter is not included in the extracted string. If this parameter is omitted, String.length is used. If this parameter is a negative value, 0 is used.

Returns

A string.

Description

Method; returns a string consisting of the characters between the points specified by the *start* and *end* parameters. If the *end* parameter is not specified, the end of the substring is the end of the string. If the value of *start* equals the value of *end*, the method returns an empty string. If the value of *start* is greater than the value of *end*, the parameters are automatically swapped before the function executes and the original value is unchanged.

String.toLowerCase()

Availability

Flash Player 5.

Usage

```
my_str.toLowerCase()
```

Parameters

None.

Returns

A string.

Description

Method; returns a copy of the String object, with all of the uppercase characters converted to lowercase. The original value is unchanged.

String.toUpperCase()

Availability

Flash Player 5.

Usage

```
my_str.toUpperCase()
```

Parameters

None.

Returns

A string.

Description

Method; returns a copy of the String object, with all of the lowercase characters converted to uppercase. The original value is unchanged.

String()

Availability

Flash Player 4; behavior changed in Flash Player 7.

Usage

```
String(expression)
```

Parameters

expression   An expression to convert to a string.

Returns

A string.

Description

Function; returns a string representation of the specified parameter as follows:

If *expression* is a number, the return string is a text representation of the number.

If *expression* is a string, the return string is *expression*.

If *expression* is an object, the return value is a string representation of the object generated by calling the string property for the object, or by calling `Object.toString()` if no such property exists.

If *expression* is `undefined`, the return values are as follows:

- In files published for Flash Player 6 or earlier, the result is an empty string ("").
- In files published for Flash Player 7 or later, the result is `undefined`.

If *expression* is a Boolean value, the return string is `"true"` or `"false"`.

If *expression* is a movie clip, the return value is the target path of the movie clip in slash (/) notation.

Note: Slash notation is not supported by ActionScript 2.0.

See also

`Number.toString()`, `Object.toString()`, String class, `" "` `(string delimiter)`

substring

Availability

Flash Player 4. This function has been deprecated in favor of `String.substr()`.

Usage

`substring("`*string*`", `*index*`, `*count*`)`

Parameters

string   The string from which to extract the new string.

index   The number of the first character to extract.

count   The number of characters to include in the extracted string, not including the index character.

Returns

Nothing.

Description

String function; extracts part of a string. This function is one-based, whereas the String object methods are zero-based.

See also

`String.substr()`

super

Availability

Flash Player 6.

Usage

```
super.method([arg1, ..., argN])
super([arg1, ..., argN])
```

Parameters

method   The method to invoke in the superclass.

arg1   Optional parameters that are passed to the superclass version of the method (syntax 1) or to the constructor function of the superclass (syntax 2).

Returns

Both forms invoke a function. The function may return any value.

Description

Operator: the first syntax style may be used within the body of an object method to invoke the superclass version of a method, and can optionally pass parameters (*arg1* ... *argN*) to the superclass method. This is useful for creating subclass methods that add additional behavior to superclass methods, but also invoke the superclass methods to perform their original behavior.

The second syntax style may be used within the body of a constructor function to invoke the superclass version of the constructor function and may optionally pass it parameters. This is useful for creating a subclass that performs additional initialization, but also invokes the superclass constructor to perform superclass initialization.

switch

Availability

Flash Player 4.

Usage

```
switch (expression){
   caseClause:
   [defaultClause:]
}
```

Parameters

expression   Any expression.

caseClause   A case keyword followed by an expression, a colon, and a group of statements to execute if the expression matches the switch *expression* parameter using strict equality (===).

defaultClause   A default keyword followed by statements to execute if none of the case expressions match the switch *expression* parameter strict equality (===).

Returns

Nothing.

Description

Statement; creates a branching structure for ActionScript statements. Like the `if` action, the `switch` action tests a condition and executes statements if the condition returns a value of `true`.

Example

In the following example, if the `number` parameter evaluates to 1, the `trace()` action that follows `case 1` executes, if the `number` parameter evaluates to 2, the `trace()` action that follows `case 2` executes, and so on. If no `case` expression matches the `number` parameter, the `trace()` action that follows the `default` keyword executes.

```
switch (number) {
  case 1:
    trace ("case 1 tested true");
    break;
  case 2:
    trace ("case 2 tested true");
    break;
  case 3:
    trace ("case 3 tested true");
    break;
  default:
    trace ("no case tested true")
}
```

In the following example, there isn't a break in the first case group so if the number is 1, both A and B are sent to the Output panel:

```
switch (number) {
  case 1:
    trace ("A");
  case 2:
    trace ("B");
    break;
  default:
    trace ("D")
}
```

See also

`===` (strict equality), `break`, `case`, `default`, `if`

System class

Availability

Flash Player 6.

Description

This is a top-level class that contains the capabilities object (see System.capabilities object), the security object (see System.security object), and the methods, properties, and event handlers listed below.

Method summary for the System class

Method	Description
System.setClipboard()	Replaces the contents of the system clipboard with a text string.
System.showSettings()	Displays a Flash Player Settings panel.

Property summary for the System class

Method	Description
System.exactSettings	Specifies whether to use superdomain or exact-domain matching rules when accessing local settings.
System.useCodepage	Tells Flash Player whether to use Unicode or the traditional code page of the operating system running the player to interpret external text files.

Event handler summary for the System class

Method	Description
System.onStatus	Provides a super event handler for certain objects

System.exactSettings

Availability

Authoring: Flash MX 2004.

Playback: SWF files published for Flash Player 6 or later, playing in Flash Player 7 or later.

Usage

```
System.exactSettings
```

Description

Property; specifies whether to use superdomain or exact-domain matching rules when accessing local settings (such as camera or microphone access permissions) or locally persistent data (shared objects). The default value is `true` for files published for Flash Player 7 or later, and `false` for files published for Flash Player 6.

If this value is `true`, the settings and data for a SWF file hosted at here.xyz.com are stored at here.xyz.com, the settings and data for a SWF file hosted at there.xyz.com are stored at there.xyz.com, and so on. If this value is `false`, the settings and data for SWF files hosted at here.xyz.com, there.xyz.com, and xyz.com are shared, and are all stored at xyz.com.

If some of your files set this property to `false` and others set it to `true`, you might find that Swf files in different subdomains share settings and data. For example, if this property is `false` in a SWF file hosted at here.xyz.com and `true` in a SWF file hosted at xyz.com, both files will use the same settings and data—namely, those at xyz.com. If this isn't the behavior you want, make sure that you set this property in each file to correctly represent where you want to store settings and data.

If you want to change this property from its default value, issue the `System.exactSettings = false` command in the first frame of your document. The property can't be changed after any activity that requires access to local settings, such as `System.ShowSettings()` or `SharedObject.getLocal()`.

If you use `loadMovie()`, `MovieClip.loadMovie()`, or MovieClipLoader.loadClip() to load one SWF file into another, all of the files published for Flash Player 7 share a single value for `System.exactSettings`, and all of the files published for Flash Player 6 share a single value for `System.exactSettings`. Therefore, if you specify a value for this property in one file published for a particular Player version, you should do so in all files that you plan to load. If you load multiple files, the setting specified in the last file loaded overwrites any previously specified setting.

For more information on how domain matching is implemented in Flash, see "Flash Player security features" on page 392.

See also

`SharedObject.getLocal()`, System.showSettings()

System.onStatus

Availability

Flash Player 6.

Description

Event handler: provides a "super" event handler for certain objects.

The LocalConnection, NetStream, and SharedObject objects provide an onStatus event handler that uses an information object for providing information, status, or error messages. To respond to this event handler, you must create a function to process the information object, and you must know the format and contents of the information object returned.

In addition to the specific onStatus methods provided for the objects listed above, Flash also provides a "super" function called System.onStatus. If onStatus is invoked for a particular object with a level property of "error" and there is no function assigned to respond to it, Flash processes a function assigned to System.onStatus if it exists.

Note: The Camera and Microphone classes also have onStatus handlers, but do not pass information objects with a level property of "error". Therefore, System.onStatus is not called if you don't specify a function for these handlers.

The following example illustrates how you can create generic and specific functions to process information objects sent by the onStatus method.

```
// Create generic function
System.onStatus = function(genericError)
{
  // Your script would do something more meaningful here
  trace("An error has occurred. Please try again.");
}

// Create function for NetStream object
// If the NetStream object returns a different information object
// from the one listed below, with a level property of "error",
// System.onStatus will be invoked

videoStream_ns.onStatus = function(infoObject) {
  if (infoObject.code == "NetStream.Play.StreamNotFound") {
    trace("Could not find video file.");
  }
}
```

See also

Camera.onStatus, LocalConnection.onStatus, Microphone.onStatus, NetStream.onStatus, SharedObject.onStatus

System.setClipboard()

Availability

Authoring: Flash MX 2004.

Playback: SWF files published for Flash Player 6 or later, playing in Flash Player 7 or later.

Usage

```
System.setClipboard(string)
```

Parameters

string A plain-text string of characters to place on the system clipboard, replacing its current contents (if any). If you pass a string literal, as opposed to a variable of type string, enclose the literal in quotation marks.

Returns

A Boolean value of `true` if the text was successfully placed on the clipboard, `false` otherwise.

Description

Method; replaces the contents of the system clipboard with a specified text string.

System.showSettings()

Availability

Flash Player 6.

Usage

```
System.showSettings([panel])
```

Parameters

panel An optional number that specifies which Flash Player Settings panel to display, as shown in the following table:

Value passed for *panel*	Settings panel displayed
None (parameter is omitted) or an unsupported value	Whichever panel was open the last time the user closed the Player Settings panel
0	Privacy
1	Local Storage
2	Microphone
3	Camera

Returns

Nothing.

Description

Method; displays the specified Flash Player Settings panel, which lets users do any of the following:

- Allow or deny access to the camera and microphone
- Specify the local disk space available for shared objects
- Select a default camera and microphone
- Specify microphone gain and echo suppression settings

For example, if your application requires the use of a camera, you can tell the user to select Allow in the Privacy Settings panel, and then issue a `System.showSettings(0)` command. (Make sure your Stage size is at least 215 x 138 pixels; this is the minimum size Flash requires to display the panel.)

See also

`Camera.get()`, `Microphone.get()`, `SharedObject.getLocal()`

System.useCodepage

Availability

Flash Player 6.

Usage

`System.useCodepage`

Description

Property; a Boolean value that tells Flash Player whether to use Unicode or the traditional code page of the operating system running the player to interpret external text files. The default value of `system.useCodepage` is `false`.

- When the property is set to `false`, Flash Player interprets external text files as Unicode. (These files must be encoded as Unicode when you save them.)
- When the property is set to `true`, Flash Player interprets external text files using the traditional code page of the operating system running the player.

Text that you include or load as an external file (using the `#include` command, the `loadVariables()` or `getURL` actions, or the LoadVars or XML objects) must be encoded as Unicode when you save the text file, in order for Flash Player to recognize it as Unicode. To encode external files as Unicode, save the files in an application that supports Unicode, such as Notepad on Windows 2000.

If you include or load external text files that are not Unicode-encoded, you should set `system.useCodepage` to `true`. Add the following code as the first line of code in the first frame of the SWF file that is loading the data:

`system.useCodepage = true;`

When this code is present, Flash Player interprets external text using the traditional code page of the operating system running Flash Player. This is generally CP1252 for an English Windows operating system and Shift-JIS for a Japanese operating system. If you set `system.useCodepage` to `true`, Flash Player 6 and later treat text as Flash Player 5 does. (Flash Player 5 treated all text as if it were in the traditional code page of the operating system running the player.)

If you set `system.useCodepage` to `true`, keep in mind that the traditional code page of the operating system running the player must include the characters used in your external text file in order for the text to display. For example, if you load an external text file that contains Chinese characters, those characters will not display on a system that uses the CP1252 code page, because that code page does not include Chinese characters.

To ensure that users on all platforms can view external text files used in your SWF files, you should encode all external text files as Unicode and leave `System.useCodepage` set to `false` by default. This way Flash Player 6 and later will interpret the text as Unicode.

System.capabilities object

Availability

Flash Player 6.

Description

You can use the System.capabilities object to determine the abilities of the system and player hosting a SWF file. This allows you to tailor content for different formats. For example, the screen of a cell phone (black and white, 100 square pixels) is different than the 1000-square-pixel color PC screen. To provide appropriate content to as many users as possible, you can use the System.capabilities object to determine the type of device a user has. You can then either specify to the server to send different SWF files based on the device capabilities, or tell the SWF file to alter its presentation based on the capabilities of the device.

You can send capabilities information using a `GET` or `POST` HTTP method. The following is an example of a server string for a device that does not have MP3 support and has a 400 x 200 pixel, 8 x 4 centimeter screen:

```
"A=t&SA=t&SV=t&EV=t&MP3=t&AE=t&VE=t&ACC=f&PR=t&SP=t&SB=f&DEB=t&V=WIN%207%2C0%
2C0%2C226&M=Macromedia%20Windows&R=1152x864&DP=72&COL=color&AR=1.0&OS=Windo
ws%20XP&L=en&PT=External&AVD=f&LFD=f"
```

Property summary for the System.capabilities object

Property	Description	Server string
System.capabilities.avHardwareDisable	Read-only; specifies whether the user's camera and microphone are enabled or disabled.	AVD
System.capabilities.hasAccessibility	Indicates whether the player is running on a system that supports communication between Flash Player and accessibility aids.	ACC
System.capabilities.hasAudio	Indicates whether the player is running on a system that has audio capabilities.	A
System.capabilities.hasAudioEncoder	Indicates whether the player is running on a system that can encode an audio stream, such as that coming from a microphone.	AE
System.capabilities.hasEmbeddedVideo	Indicates whether the player is running on a system that supports embedded video.	EV

Property	Description	Server string
`System.capabilities.hasMP3`	Indicates whether the player is running on a system that has an MP3 decoder.	MP3
`System.capabilities.hasPrinting`	Indicates whether the player is running on a system that supports printing.	PR
`System.capabilities.hasScreenBroadcast`	Indicates whether the player supports the development of screen broadcast applications to be run through the Flash Communication Server.	SB
`System.capabilities.hasScreenPlayback`	Indicates whether the player supports the playback of screen broadcast applications that are being run through the Flash Communication Server.	SP
`System.capabilities.hasStreamingAudio`	Indicates whether the player can play streaming audio.	SA
`System.capabilities.hasStreamingVideo`	Indicates whether the player can play streaming video.	SV
`System.capabilities.hasVideoEncoder`	Indicates whether the player can encode a video stream, such as that coming from a web camera.	VE
`System.capabilities.isDebugger`	Indicates whether the player is an officially released version or a special debugging version.	DEB
`System.capabilities.language`	Indicates the language of the system on which the player is running.	L
`System.capabilities.localFileReadDisable`	Read-only; specifies whether the player will attempt to read anything (including the first SWF file the player launches with) from the user's hard disk.	LFD
`System.capabilities.manufacturer`	Indicates the manufacturer of Flash Player.	M
`System.capabilities.os`	Indicates the operating system hosting Flash Player.	OS
`System.capabilities.pixelAspectRatio`	Indicates the pixel aspect ratio of the screen.	AR
`System.capabilities.playerType`	Indicates the type of player: stand-alone, external, plug-in, or ActiveX.	PT
`System.capabilities.screenColor`	Indicates whether the screen is color, grayscale, or black and white.	COL
`System.capabilities.screenDPI`	Indicates the dots-per-inch screen resolution, in pixels.	DP
`System.capabilities.screenResolutionX`	Indicates the horizontal size of the screen.	R
`System.capabilities.screenResolutionY`	Indicates the vertical size of the screen.	R

Property	Description	Server string
System.capabilities.serverString	A URL-encoded string that specifies values for each System.capabilities property.	n/a
System.capabilities.version	A string containing Flash Player version and platform information.	V

System.capabilities.avHardwareDisable

Availability

Flash Player 7.

Usage

System.capabilities.avHardwareDisable

Description

Read-only property; a Boolean value that specifies whether the user's camera and microphone are enabled or disabled.

See also

Camera.get(), Microphone.get(), System.showSettings()

System.capabilities.hasAccessibility

Availability

Flash Player 6 version 65.

Usage

System.capabilities.hasAccessibility

Description

Property; a Boolean value that indicates whether the player is running in an environment that supports communication between Flash Player and accessibility aids. The server string is ACC.

See also

Accessibility.isActive(), Accessibility.updateProperties(), _accProps

System.capabilities.hasAudio

Availability

Flash Player 6.

Usage

System.capabilities.hasAudio

Description

Property; a Boolean value that indicates whether the player is running on a system that has audio capabilities. The server string is A.

System.capabilities.hasAudioEncoder

Availability

Flash Player 6.

Usage

```
System.capabilities.hasAudioEncoder
```

Description

Property; a Boolean value that indicates whether the player can encode an audio stream, such as that coming from a microphone. The server string is AE.

System.capabilities.hasEmbeddedVideo

Availability

Flash Player 6.

Usage

```
System.capabilities.hasEmbeddedVideo
```

Description

Property; a Boolean value that indicates whether the player is running on a system that supports embedded video. The server string is EV.

System.capabilities.hasMP3

Availability

Flash Player 6.

Usage

```
System.capabilities.hasMP3
```

Description

Property; a Boolean value that indicates whether the player is running on a system that has an MP3 decoder. The server string is MP3.

System.capabilities.hasPrinting

Availability

Flash Player 6.

Usage

```
System.capabilities.hasPrinting
```

Description

Property; a Boolean value that indicates whether the player is running on a system that supports printing. The server string is PR.

System.capabilities.hasScreenBroadcast

Availability

Flash Player 6.

Usage

```
System.capabilities.hasScreenBroadcast
```

Description

Property; a Boolean value that indicates whether the player supports the development of screen broadcast applications to be run through the Flash Communication Server. The server string is SB.

System.capabilities.hasScreenPlayback

Availability

Flash Player 6.

Usage

```
System.capabilities.hasScreenPlayback
```

Description

Property; a Boolean value that indicates whether the player supports the playback of screen broadcast applications that are being run through the Flash Communication Server. The server string is SP.

System.capabilities.hasStreamingAudio

Availability

Flash Player 6.

Usage

```
System.capabilities.hasStreamingAudio
```

Description

Property; a Boolean value that indicates whether the player can play streaming audio. The server string is SA.

System.capabilities.hasStreamingVideo

Availability

Flash Player 6.

Usage

```
System.capabilities.hasStreamingVideo
```

Description

Property; a Boolean value that indicates whether the player can play streaming video. The server string is SV.

System.capabilities.hasVideoEncoder

Availability

Flash Player 6.

Usage

```
System.capabilities.hasVideoEncoder
```

Description

Property; a Boolean value that indicates whether the player can encode a video stream, such as that coming from a web camera. The server string is VE.

System.capabilities.isDebugger

Availability

Flash Player 6.

Usage

```
System.capabilities.isDebugger
```

Description

Property; a Boolean value that indicates whether the player is an officially released version (false) or a special debugging version (true). The server string is DEB.

System.capabilities.language

Availability

Flash Player 6.

Usage

```
System.capabilities.language
```

Description

Property; indicates the language of the system on which the player is running. This property is specified as a lowercase two-letter language code from ISO 639-1 and an optional uppercase two-letter country code subtag from ISO 3166. The codes represent the language of the system on which the player is running. The languages themselves are named with the English tags. For example, "fr" specifies French.

Language	Tag	Supported countries and tags
Czech	cs	
Danish	da	
Dutch	nl	
English	en	
Finnish	fi	
French	fr	

Language	Tag	Supported countries and tags
German	de	
Hungarian	hu	
Italian	it	
Japanese	ja	
Korean	ko	
Norwegian	no	
Other/unknown	xu	
Polish	pl	
Portuguese	pt	
Russian	ru	
Simplified Chinese	zh	People's Republic of China (Simplified Chinese): zh-CN
Spanish	es	
Swedish	sv	
Traditional Chinese	zh	Taiwan (Traditional Chinese) : zh-TW
Turkish	tr	

System.capabilities.localFileReadDisable

Availability

Flash Player 7.

Usage

```
System.capabilities.localFileReadDisable
```

Description

Read-only property; a Boolean value that specifies whether Flash Player attempts to read anything (including the first SWF file that Flash Player launches with) from the user's hard disk.

System.capabilities.manufacturer

Availability

Flash Player 6.

Usage

```
System.capabilities.manufacturer
```

Description

Property; a string that indicates the manufacturer of Flash Player, in the format "Macromedia *OSName*" (*OSName* could be "Windows", "Macintosh", "Linux", or "Other OS Name"). The server string is M.

System.capabilities.os

Availability

Flash Player 6.

Usage

`System.capabilities.os`

Description

Property; a string that indicates the current operating system. The `os` property can return the following strings: `"Windows XP"`, `"Windows 2000"`, `"Windows NT"`, `"Windows 98/ME"`, `"Windows 95"`, `"Windows CE"` (available only in Flash Player SDK, not in the desktop version), `"Linux"`, and `"MacOS"`. The server string is `OS`.

System.capabilities.pixelAspectRatio

Availability

Flash Player 6.

Usage

`System.capabilities.pixelAspectRatio`

Description

Property; an integer that indicates the pixel aspect ratio of the screen. The server string is `AR`.

System.capabilities.playerType

Availability

Flash Player 7.

Usage

`System.capabilities.playerType`

Description

Property; a string that indicates the type of player. This property can have the value `"StandAlone"`, `"External"`, `"PlugIn"`, or `"ActiveX"`. The server string is `PT`.

System.capabilities.screenColor

Availability

Flash Player 6.

Usage

`System.capabilities.screenColor`

Description

Property; indicates whether the screen is color (`color`), grayscale (`gray`), or black and white (`bw`). The server string is `COL`.

System.capabilities.screenDPI

Availability

Flash Player 6.

Usage

```
System.capabilities.screenDPI
```

Description

Property; indicates the dots-per-inch (dpi) resolution of the screen, in pixels. The server string is DP.

System.capabilities.screenResolutionX

Availability

Flash Player 6.

Usage

```
System.capabilities.screenResolutionX
```

Description

Property; an integer that indicates the maximum horizontal resolution of the screen. The server string is R (which returns both the width and height of the screen).

System.capabilities.screenResolutionY

Availability

Flash Player 6.

Usage

```
System.capabilities.screenResolutionY
```

Description

Property; an integer that indicates the maximum vertical resolution of the screen. The server string is R (which returns both the width and height of the screen).

System.capabilities.serverString

Availability

Flash Player 6.

Usage

```
System.capabilities.serverString
```

Description

Property; a URL-encoded string that specifies values for each `System.capabilities` property, as in this example:

```
A=t&SA=t&SV=t&EV=t&MP3=t&AE=t&VE=t&ACC=f&PR=t&SP=t&SB=f&DEB=t&V=WIN%207%2C0%2C0
%2C226&M=Macromedia%20Windows&R=1152x864&DP=72&COL=color&AR=1.0&OS=Windows%20
XP&L=en&PT=External&AVD=f&LFD=f
```

System.capabilities.version

Availability

Flash Player 6.

Usage

```
System.capabilities.version
```

Description

Property; a string containing the Flash Player platform and version information, for example, `"WIN 7,0,0,231"`. The server string is `V`.

System.security object

Availability

Flash Player 6.

Description

This object contains methods that specify how SWF files in different domains can communicate with each other.

Method summary for the System.security object

Method	Description
`System.security.allowDomain()`	Allows SWF files in the identified domains to access objects and variables in the calling SWF file, or in any other SWF file from the same domain as the calling SWF file.
`System.security.allowInsecureDomain()`	Allows SWF files in the identified domains to access objects and variables in the calling SWF file, which is hosted using the HTTPS protocol.

System.security.allowDomain()

Availability

Flash Player 6; behavior changed in Flash Player 7.

Usage

```
System.security.allowDomain("domain1", "domain2, ... domainN")
```

Parameters

domain1, domain2, ... domainN   Strings that specify domains that can access objects and variables in the file containing the `System.Security.allowDomain()` call. The domains can be formatted in the following ways:

- `"domain.com"`
- `"http://domain.com"`
- `"http://IPaddress"`

Description

Method; allows SWF files in the identified domains to access objects and variables in the calling SWF file, or in any other SWF file from the same domain as the calling SWF file.

In files playing back in Flash Player 7 or later, the parameter(s) passed must follow exact-domain naming rules. For example, to allow access by SWF files hosted at either www.domain.com or store.domain.com, both domain names must be passed:

```
// For Flash Player 6
System.security.allowDomain("domain.com");
// Corresponding commands to allow access by SWF files
// that are running in Flash Player 7 or later
System.security.allowDomain("www.domain.com". "store.domain.com");
```

Also, for files running in Flash Player 7 or later, you can't use this method to allow SWF files hosted using a secure protocol (HTTPS) to permit access from SWF files hosted in nonsecure protocols; you must use System.security.allowInsecureDomain() instead.

Example

The SWF file located at www.macromedia.com/MovieA.swf contains the following lines.

```
System.security.allowDomain("www.shockwave.com");
loadMovie("http://www.shockwave.com/MovieB.swf", _root.my_mc);
```

Because MovieA contains the `allowDomain()` command, MovieB can access the objects and variables in MovieA. If MovieA didn't contain this command, the Flash security implementation would prevent MovieA from accessing MovieB's objects and variables.

System.security.allowInsecureDomain()

Availability

Flash Player 7.

Usage

```
System.Security.allowInsecureDomain("domain")
```

Parameters

domain   An exact domain name, such as "www.myDomainName.com" or "store.myDomainName.com".

Returns

Nothing.

Description

Method; allows SWF files in the identified domains to access objects and variables in the calling SWF file, which is hosted using the HTTPS protocol.

By default, SWF files hosted using the HTTPS protocol can be accessed only by other SWF files hosted using the HTTPS protocol. This implementation maintains the integrity provided by the HTTPS protocol.

Macromedia does not recommend using this method to override the default behavior because it compromises HTTPS security. However, you may need to do so, for example, if you must permit access to HTTPS files published for Flash Player 7 or later from HTTP files published for Flash Player 6.

A SWF file published for Flash Player 6 can use `System.security.allowDomain()` to permit HTTP to HTTPS access. However, because security is implemented differently in Flash Player 7, you must use `System.Security.allowInsecureDomain()` to permit such access in SWF files published for Flash Player 7 or later.

Example

In this example, you host a math test on a secure domain so that only registered students can access it. You have also developed a number of SWF files that illustrate certain concepts, which you host on an insecure domain. You want students to be able to access the test from the SWF file that contains information about a concept.

```
// This SWF file is at https://myEducationSite.somewhere.com/mathTest.swf
// Concept files are at http://myEducationSite.somewhere.com
System.Security.allowInsecureDomain("myEducationSite.somewhere.com")
```

See also

System.security.allowDomain(), `System.exactSettings`

targetPath

Availability

Flash Player 5.

Usage

`targetpath(movieClipObject)`

Parameters

movieClipObject   Reference (for example, _root or _parent) to the movie clip for which the target path is being retrieved.

Returns

A string containing the target path of the specified movie clip.

Description

Function; returns a string containing the target path of *movieClipObject*. The target path is returned in dot notation. To retrieve the target path in slash notation, use the _target property.

Example

This example displays the target path of a movie clip as soon as it loads.

```
onClipEvent(load){
    trace(targetPath(this));
}
```

See also

`eval()`

tellTarget

Availability

Flash Player 3. (Deprecated in Flash 5; use of dot notation and the with action is recommended.)

Usage

```
tellTarget("target") {
    statement(s);
}
```

Parameters

target   A string that specifies the target path of the Timeline to be controlled.

statement(s)   The instructions to execute if the condition evaluates to true.

Returns

Nothing.

Description

Deprecated action; applies the instructions specified in the *statements* parameter to the Timeline specified in the *target* parameter. The tellTarget action is useful for navigation controls. Assign tellTarget to buttons that stop or start movie clips elsewhere on the Stage. You can also make movie clips go to a particular frame in that clip. For example, you might assign tellTarget to buttons that stop or start movie clips on the Stage or prompt movie clips to jump to a particular frame.

In Flash 5 or later, you can use dot notation instead of the tellTarget action. You can use the with action to issue multiple actions to the same Timeline. You can use the with action to target any object, whereas the tellTarget action can only target movie clips.

Example

This tellTarget statement controls the movie clip instance ball on the main Timeline. Frame 1 of the ball instance is blank and has a stop() action so that it isn't visible on the Stage. When the button with the following action is clicked, tellTarget tells the playhead in ball to go to Frame 2 where the animation starts.

```
on(release) {
   tellTarget("ball") {
     gotoAndPlay(2);
   }
}
```

The following example uses dot notation to achieve the same results.

```
on(release) {
   ball.gotoAndPlay(2);
}
```

If you need to issue multiple commands to the ball instance, you can use the with action, as in the following statement.

```
on(release) {
   with(ball) {
     gotoAndPlay(2);
     _alpha = 15;
     _xscale = 50;
     _yscale = 50;
   }
}
```

See also

with

TextField class

Availability

Flash Player 6.

Description

All dynamic and input text fields in a SWF file are instances of the TextField class. You can give a text field an instance name in the Property inspector and use the methods and properties of the TextField class to manipulate it with ActionScript. TextField instance names are displayed in the Movie Explorer and in the Insert Target Path dialog box in the Actions panel.

The TextField class inherits from the Object class.

To create a text field dynamically, you can use `MovieClip.createTextField()`.

Method summary for the TextField class

Method	Description
TextField.addListener()	Registers an object to receive notification when the `onChanged` and `onScroller` event handlers are invoked.
TextField.getFontList()	Returns names of fonts on the player's host system as an array.
TextField.getDepth()	Returns the depth of a text field.
TextField.getNewTextFormat()	Gets the default text format assigned to newly inserted text.
TextField.getTextFormat()	Returns a TextFormat object containing formatting information for some or all text in a text field.
TextField.removeListener()	Removes a listener object.
TextField.removeTextField()	Removes a text field that was created with `MovieClip.createTextField()`.
TextField.replaceSel()	Replaces the current selection.
TextField.setNewTextFormat()	Sets a TextFormat object for text that is inserted by a user or by a method.
TextField.setTextFormat()	Sets a TextFormat object for a specified range of text in a text field.

Property summary for the TextField class

Property	Description
TextField._alpha	The transparency value of a text field instance.
TextField.autoSize	Controls automatic alignment and sizing of a text field.
TextField.background	Indicates if the text field has a background fill.
TextField.backgroundColor	Indicates the color of the background fill.
TextField.border	Indicates if the text field has a border.
TextField.borderColor	Indicates the color of the border.

Property	Description
TextField.bottomScroll	The bottommost visible line in a text field. Read-only.
TextField.embedFonts	Indicates whether the text field uses embedded font outlines or device fonts.
TextField._height	The height of a text field instance in pixels. This only affects the bounding box of the text field, it does not affect the border thickness or text font size.
TextField._highquality	Indicates the rendering quality of the SWF file.
TextField.hscroll	Indicates the horizontal scroll value of a text field.
TextField.html	Indicates the current maximum scrolling position of a text field.
TextField.htmlText	Contains the HTML representation of a text field's contents.
TextField.length	The number of characters in a text field. Read-only.
TextField.maxChars	The maximum number of characters that a text field can contain.
TextField.maxhscroll	The maximum value of TextField.hscroll. Read-only.
TextField.maxscroll	The maximum value of TextField.scroll. Read-only.
TextField.menu	Associates a ContextMenu object with a text field.
TextField.mouseWheelEnabled	Indicates whether Flash Player should automatically scroll multiline text fields when the mouse pointer is positioned over a text field and the user rolls the mouse wheel.
TextField.multiline	Indicates if the text field contains multiple lines.
TextField._name	The instance name of a text field instance.
TextField._parent	A reference to the instance that is the parent of this instance; either of type Button or MovieClip.
TextField.password	Indicates if a text field hides the input characters.
TextField._quality	Indicates the rendering quality of a SWF file.
TextField.restrict	The set of characters that a user can enter into a text field.
TextField._rotation	The degree of rotation of a text field instance.
TextField.scroll	Indicates the current scrolling position of a text field.
TextField.selectable	Indicates whether a text field is selectable.
TextField._soundbuftime	The amount of time a sound must prebuffer before it streams.
TextField.tabEnabled	Indicates whether a movie clip is included in automatic tab ordering.
TextField.tabIndex	Indicates the tab order of an object.
TextField._target	The target path of the specified text field instance. Read-only.
TextField.text	The current text in the text field.
TextField.textColor	The color of the current text in the text field.

Property	Description
TextField.textHeight	The height of the text field's bounding box.
TextField.textWidth	The width of the text field's bounding box.
TextField.type	Indicates whether a text field is an input text field or dynamic text field.
TextField._url	The URL of the SWF file that created the text field instance. Read-only.
TextField.variable	The variable name associated with the text field.
TextField._visible	A Boolean value that determines whether a text field instance is hidden or visible.
TextField._width	The width of a text field instance in pixels. This only affects the bounding box of the text field, it does not affect the border thickness or text font size.
TextField.wordWrap	Indicates whether the text field word-wraps.
TextField._x	The x coordinate of a text field instance
TextField._xmouse	The x coordinate of the pointer relative to a text field instance. Read-only.
TextField._xscale	The value specifying the percentage for horizontally scaling a text field instance.
TextField._y	The y coordinate of a text field instance.
TextField._ymouse	The y coordinate of the pointer relative to a text field instance. Read-only.
TextField._yscale	The value specifying the percentage for vertically scaling a text field instance.

Event handler summary for the TextField class

Event handler	Description
TextField.onChanged	Invoked when the text field is changed.
TextField.onKillFocus	Invoked when the text field loses focus.
TextField.onScroller	Invoked when one of the text field scroll properties changes.
TextField.onSetFocus	Invoked when the text field receives focus.

Listener summary for the TextField class

Method	Description
TextField.onChanged	Notified when the text field is changed.
TextField.onScroller	Notified when the scroll or maxscroll property of a text field changes.

TextField.addListener()

Availability

Flash Player 6.

Usage

```
my_txt.addListener(listener)
```

Parameters

listener An object with an onChanged or onScroller event handler.

Returns

Nothing.

Description

Method; registers an object to receive notification when the onChanged and onScroller event handlers have been invoked. When a text field changes or is scrolled, the TextField.onChanged and TextField.onScroller event handlers are invoked, followed by the onChanged and onScroller event handlers of any objects registered as listeners. Multiple objects can be registered as listeners.

To remove a listener object from a text field, call TextField.removeListener().

A reference to the text field instance is passed as a parameter to the onScroller and onChanged handlers by the event source. You can capture this data by putting a parameter in the event handler method. For example, the following code uses txt as the parameter that is passed to the onScroller event handler. The parameter is then used in a trace statement to send the instance name of the text field to the Output panel.

```
myTextField.onScroller = function (txt) {
   trace (txt._name + " changed");
};
```

Example

The following example defines an onChange handler for the input text field myText. It then defines a new listener object, myListener, and defines an onChanged handler for that object. This handler will be invoked when the text field myText is changed. The final line of code calls TextField.addListener to register the listener object myListener with the text field myText so that it will be notified when myText changes.

```
myText.onChanged = function (txt) {
   trace(txt._name + " changed");
};
myListener = new Object();
myListener.onChanged = function (txt) {
   trace(txt._name + " changed and notified myListener");
};

myText.addListener(myListener);
```

See also

TextField.onChanged, TextField.onScroller, TextField.removeListener()

TextField._alpha

Availability

Flash Player 6.

Usage

`my_txt._alpha`

Description

Property; sets or retrieves the alpha transparency value of the text field specified by `my_txt`. Valid values are 0 (fully transparent) to 100 (fully opaque). The default value is 100.

Example

The following code sets the `_alpha` property of a text field named `text1_txt` to 30% when the button is clicked:

```
on(release) {
   text1_txt._alpha = 30;
}
```

See also

`Button._alpha, MovieClip._alpha`

TextField.autoSize

Availability

Flash Player 6.

Usage

`my_txt.autoSize`

Description

Property; controls automatic sizing and alignment of text fields. Acceptable values for autoSize are `"none"` (the default), `"left"`, `"right"`, and `"center"`. When you set the `autoSize` property, `true` is a synonym for `"left"` and `false` is a synonym for `"none"`.

The values of `autoSize`, `multiline`, and `wordWrap` determine whether a text field expands or contracts to the left side, right side, or bottom side. You can use the following code and enter different values for `autoSize`, `multiline`, and `wordWrap` to see how the field resizes when these values change.

```
createTextField("my_txt", 1, 0, 0, 200, 20);
with (my_txt) {
   border = true;
   borderColor = 0x000000;
   multiline = false;
   wordWrap = false;
   autoSize = "none";
   text = "Here is a whole bunch of text that won't fit in the field ";
}
```

Example

The following sets the autosize property of the text field my_txt to "center".

```
my_txt.autosize = "center";
```

TextField.background

Availability

Flash Player 6.

Usage

my_txt.background

Description

Property; if true, the text field has a background fill. If false, the text field has no background fill.

TextField.backgroundColor

Availability

Flash Player 6.

Usage

my_txt.backgroundColor

Description

Property; the color of the text field background. Default is 0xFFFFFF (white). This property may be retrieved or set, even if there currently is no background but the color is only visible if the text field has a border.

See also

TextField.background

TextField.border

Availability

Flash Player 6.

Usage

my_txt.border

Description

Property; if true, the text field has a border. If false, the text field has no border.

TextField.borderColor

Availability

Flash Player 6.

Usage

`my_txt.borderColor`

Description

Property; the color of the text field border, the Default is `0x000000` (black). This property may be retrieved or set, even if there is currently no border.

See also

`TextField.border`

TextField.bottomScroll

Availability

Flash Player 6.

Usage

`my_txt.bottomScroll`

Description

Property (read-only); an integer (one-based index) that indicates the bottommost line that is currently visible in `my_txt`. Think of the text field as a "window" onto a block of text. The property `TextField.scroll` is the one-based index of the topmost visible line in the window.

All the text between lines `TextField.scroll` and `TextField.bottomScroll` is currently visible in the text field.

TextField.condenseWhite

Availability

Flash Player 6.

Usage

`my_txt.condenseWhite`

Description

Property; a Boolean value that specifies whether extra white space (spaces, line breaks, and so on) in an HTML text field should be removed when the field is rendered in a browser. The default value is `false`.

If you set this value to `true`, you must use standard HTML commands such as `<BR>` and `<P>` to place line breaks in the text field.

If `my_txt.html` is `false`, this property is ignored.

See also

`TextField.html`

TextField.embedFonts

Availability

Flash Player 6.

Usage

`my_txt.embedFonts`

Description

Property; a Boolean value that, when `true`, renders the text field using embedded font outlines. If `false`, it renders the text field using device fonts.

TextField.getDepth()

Availability

Flash Player 6.

Usage

`my_txt.getDepth()`

Parameters

None.

Returns

An integer.

Description

Method; returns the depth of a text field.

TextField.getFontList()

Availability

Flash Player 6.

Usage

`TextField.getFontList()`

Parameters

None.

Returns

An array.

Description

Method; a static method of the global TextField class. You don't specify a specific text field (such as `my_txt`) when you call this method. This method returns names of fonts on the player's host system as an array. (It does not return names of all fonts in currently loaded SWF files.) The names are of type `string`.

Example

The following code displays a font list returned by `getFontList()`.

```
font_array = TextField.getFontList();
for( i in font_array){
    trace(font_array[i]);
}
```

TextField.getNewTextFormat()

Availability

Flash Player 6.

Usage

`my_txt.getNewTextFormat()`

Parameters

None.

Returns

A TextFormat object.

Description

Method; returns a TextFormat object containing a copy of the text field's text format object. The text format object is the format that newly inserted text, such as text inserted with the `replaceSel()` method or text entered by a user, receives. When `getNewTextFormat()` is invoked, the TextFormat object returned has all of its properties defined. No property is `null`.

TextField.getTextFormat()

Availability

Flash Player 6.

Usage

`my_txt.getTextFormat()`

`my_txt.getTextFormat(index)`

`my_txt.getTextFormat(beginIndex, endIndex)`

Parameters

`index` An integer that specifies a character in a string.

`beginIndex, endIndex` Integers that specify the starting and ending locations of a span of text within `my_txt`.

Returns

An object.

Description

Method; Usage 1: returns a TextFormat object containing formatting information for all text in a text field. Only properties that are common to all text in the text field are set in the resulting TextFormat object. Any property which is *mixed*, meaning that it has different values at different points in the text, has its value set to null.

Usage 2: Returns a TextFormat object containing a copy of the text field's text format at *index*.

Usage 3: Returns a TextFormat object containing formatting information for the span of text from *beginIndex* to *endIndex*.

See also

```
TextField.getNewTextFormat(), TextField.setNewTextFormat(),
TextField.setTextFormat()
```

TextField._height

Availability

Flash Player 6.

Usage

```
my_txt._height
```

Description

Property; the height of the text field, in pixels.

Example

The following code example sets the height and width of a text field.

```
my_txt._width = 200;
my_txt._height = 200;
```

TextField._highquality

Availability

Flash Player 6.

Usage

```
my_txt._highquality
```

Description

Property (global); specifies the level of anti-aliasing applied to the current SWF file. Specify 2 (best quality) to apply high quality with bitmap smoothing always on. Specify 1 (high quality) to apply anti-aliasing; this will smooth bitmaps if the SWF file does not contain animation. Specify 0 (low quality) to prevent anti-aliasing.

See also

```
_quality
```

TextField.hscroll

Availability

Flash Player 6.

Usage

```
my_txt.hscroll
```

Returns

An integer.

Description

Property; indicates the current horizontal scrolling position. If the `hscroll` property is 0, the text is not horizontally scrolled.

For more information on scrolling text, see "Creating scrolling text" on page 357.

Example

The following example scrolls the text horizontally.

```
on (release) {
  my_txt.hscroll += 1;
}
```

See also

`TextField.maxhscroll`, TextField.scroll

TextField.html

Availability

Flash Player 6.

Usage

```
my_txt.html
```

Description

Property; a flag that indicates whether the text field contains an HTML representation. If the `html` property is `true`, the text field is an HTML text field. If `html` is `false`, the text field is a non-HTML text field.

See also

`TextField.htmlText`

TextField.htmlText

Availability

Flash Player 6.

Usage

`my_txt.htmlText`

Description

Property; if the text field is an HTML text field, this property contains the HTML representation of the text field's contents. If the text field is not an HTML text field, it behaves identically to the `text` property. You can indicate that a text field is an HTML text field in the Property inspector, or by setting the text field's `html` property to `true`.

Example

In the following example, the text in the text field `text2` is rendered bold.

```
text2.html = true;
text2.htmlText = "<b> this is bold text </b>";
```

See also

`TextField.html`

TextField.length

Availability

Flash Player 6.

Usage

`my_txt.length`

Returns

A number.

Description

Property (read-only); indicates the number of characters in a text field. This property returns the same value as `text.length`, but is faster. A character such as tab ("\t") counts as one character.

TextField.maxChars

Availability

Flash Player 6.

Usage

`my_txt.maxChars`

Description

Property; indicates the maximum number of characters that the text field can contain. A script may insert more text than `maxChars` allows; the `maxChars` property only indicates how much text a user can enter. If the value of this property is `null`, there is no limit on the amount of text a user can enter.

TextField.maxhscroll

Availability

Flash Player 6.

Usage

`my_txt.maxhscroll`

Description

Property (read-only); indicates the maximum value of `TextField.hscroll`.

TextField.maxscroll

Availability

Flash Player 6.

Usage

`TextField.maxscroll`

Description

Property (read-only); indicates the maximum value of `TextField.scroll`.

For more information on scrolling text, see "Creating scrolling text" on page 357.

TextField.menu

Availability

Flash Player 7.

Usage

`my_txt.menu = contextMenu`

Parameters

`contextMenu`   A ContextMenu object.

Description

Property; associates the ContextMenu object *contextMenu* with the text field *my_txt*. The ContextMenu class lets you modify the context menu that appears when the user right-clicks (Windows) or Control-clicks (Macintosh) in Flash Player.

This property works only with selectable (editable) text fields; it has no affect on nonselectable text fields.

Example

The following example assigns the ContextMenu object menu_cm to the text field news_txt. The ContextMenu object contains a custom menu item labeled "Print" with an associated callback handler named doPrint(), which performs printing operations (not shown):

```
var menu_cm = new ContextMenu();
menu_cm.customItems.push(new ContextMenuItem("Print...", doPrint));
function doPrint(menu, obj) {
  // "Print" code here
}
news_txt.menu = menu_cm;
```

See also

Button.menu, ContextMenu class, ContextMenuItem class, MovieClip.menu

TextField.mouseWheelEnabled

Availability

Flash Player 7.

Usage

my_txt.mouseWheelEnabled

Description

Property; a Boolean value that indicates whether Flash Player should automatically scroll multiline text fields when the mouse pointer is positioned over a text field and the user rolls the mouse wheel. By default, this value is true. This property is useful if you want to prevent mouse wheel scrolling of text fields, or implement your own text field scrolling.

See also

Mouse.onMouseWheel

TextField.multiline

Availability

Flash Player 6.

Usage

my_txt.multiline

Description

Property; indicates whether the text field is a multiline text field. If the value is true, the text field is multiline; if the value is false, the text field is a single-line text field.

TextField._name

Availability

Flash Player 6.

Usage

```
my_txt._name
```

Description

Property; the instance name of the text field specified by *my_txt*.

TextField.onChanged

Availability

Flash Player 6.

Usage

```
my_txt.onChanged = function(){
    // your statements here
}
```

Parameters

None.

Returns

The instance name of the text field.

Description

Event handler; invoked when the content of a text field changes. By default, it is undefined; you can define it in a script.

A reference to the text field instance is passed as a parameter to the onChanged handler. You can capture this data by putting a parameter in the event handler method. For example, the following code uses txt as the parameter that is passed to the onChanged event handler. The parameter is then used in a trace() statement to send the instance name of the text field to the Output panel.

```
myTextField.onChanged = function (txt) {
    trace (txt._name + " changed");
};
```

TextField.onKillFocus

Availability

Flash Player 6.

Usage

```
my_txt.onKillFocus = function(newFocus){
    // your statements here
}
```

Parameters

newFocus The object that is receiving the focus.

Returns

Nothing.

Description

Event handler; invoked when a text field loses keyboard focus. The onKillFocus method receives one parameter, *newFocus*, which is an object representing the new object receiving the focus. If no object receives the focus, *newFocus* contains the value null.

TextField.onScroller

Availability

Flash Player 6.

Usage

```
my_txt.onScroller = function(textFieldInstance){
    // your statements here
}
```

Parameters

textFieldInstance A reference to the TextField object whose scroll position was changed.

Returns

Nothing.

Description

Event handler; invoked when one of the text field scroll properties changes.

A reference to the text field instance is passed as a parameter to the onScroller handler. You can capture this data by putting a parameter in the event handler method. For example, the following code uses txt as the parameter that is passed to the onScroller event handler. The parameter is then used in a trace() statement to send the instance name of the text field to the Output panel.

```
myTextField.onScroller = function (txt) {
    trace (txt._name + " scrolled");
};
```

See also

TextField.hscroll, TextField.maxhscroll, TextField.maxscroll, TextField.scroll

TextField.onSetFocus

Availability

Flash Player 6.

Usage

```
my_txt.onSetFocus = function(oldFocus){
    // your statements here
}
```

Parameters

oldFocus   The object to lose focus.

Returns

Nothing.

Description

Event handler; invoked when a text field receives keyboard focus. The *oldFocus* parameter is the object that loses the focus. For example, if the user presses the Tab key to move the input focus from a button to a text field, *oldFocus* contains the text field instance.

If there is no previously focused object, *oldFocus* contains a null value.

TextField._parent

Availability

Flash Player 6.

Usage

```
my_txt._parent.property
_parent.property
```

Description

Property; a reference to the movie clip or object that contains the current text field or object. The current object is the one containing the ActionScript code that references _parent.

Use _parent to specify a relative path to movie clips or objects that are above the current text field. You can use _parent to climb up multiple levels in the display list as in the following:

```
_parent._parent._alpha = 20;
```

See also

Button._parent, MovieClip._parent, _root, targetPath

TextField.password

Availability

Flash Player 6.

Usage

`my_txt.password`

Description

Property; if the value of `password` is `true`, the text field is a password text field and hides the input characters. If `false`, the text field is not a password text field.

TextField._quality

Availability

Flash Player 6.

Usage

`my_txt._quality`

Description

Property (global); sets or retrieves the rendering quality used for a SWF file. Device fonts are always aliased and, therefore, are unaffected by the `_quality` property.

Note: Although you can specify this property for a TextField object, it is actually a global property, and you can specify its value simply as `_quality`. For more information, see `_quality`.

TextField.removeListener()

Availability

Flash Player 6.

Usage

`my_txt.removeListener(listener)`

Parameters

`listener` The object that will no longer receive notifications from `TextField.onChanged` or `TextField.onScroller`.

Returns

If `listener` was successfully removed, the method returns a `true` value. If `listener` was not successfully removed (for example, if `listener` was not on the TextField object's listener list), the method returns a value of `false`.

Description

Method; removes a listener object previously registered to a text field instance with `TextField.addListener()`.

TextField.removeTextField()

Availability

Flash Player 6.

Usage

`my_txt.removeTextField()`

Description

Method; removes the text field specified by `my_txt`. This operation can only be performed on a text field that was created with `MovieClip.createTextField()`. When you call this method, the text field is removed. This method is similar to `MovieClip.removeMovieClip()`.

TextField.replaceSel()

Availability

Flash Player 6.

Usage

`my_txt.replaceSel(text)`

Parameters

`text` A string.

Returns

Nothing.

Description

Method; replaces the current selection with the contents of the `text` parameter. The text is inserted at the position of the current selection, using the current default character format and default paragraph format. The text is not treated as HTML, even if the text field is an HTML text field.

You can use the `replaceSel()` method to insert and delete text without disrupting the character and paragraph formatting of the rest of the text.

You must use `Selection.setFocus()` to focus the field before issuing this command.

See also

`Selection.setFocus()`

TextField.replaceText()

Availability

Flash Player 7.

Usage

```
my_txt.replaceText(beginIndex, endIndex, text)
```

Description

Method; replaces a range of characters, specified by the *beginIndex* and *endIndex* parameters, in the specified text field with the contents of the *text* parameter.

TextField.restrict

Availability

Flash Player 6.

Usage

```
my_txt.restrict
```

Description

Property; indicates the set of characters that a user may enter into the text field. If the value of the restrict property is null, you can enter any character. If the value of the restrict property is an empty string, you can't enter any character. If the value of the restrict property is a string of characters, you can enter only characters in the string into the text field. The string is scanned from left to right. A range may be specified using the dash (-). This only restricts user interaction; a script may put any text into the text field. This property does not synchronize with the Embed Font Outlines check boxes in the Property inspector.

If the string begins with ^, all characters are initially accepted and succeeding characters in the string are excluded from the set of accepted characters. If the string does not begin with ^, no characters are initially accepted and succeeding characters in the string are included in the set of accepted characters.

Example

The following example allows only uppercase characters, spaces, and numbers to be entered into a text field:

```
my_txt.restrict = "A-Z 0-9";
```

The following example includes all characters, but excludes lowercase letters:

```
my_txt.restrict = "^a-z";
```

You can use a backslash to enter a ^ or - verbatim. The accepted backslash sequences are \-, \^ or \\. The backslash must be an actual character in the string, so when specified in ActionScript, a double backslash must be used. For example, the following code includes only the dash (-) and caret (^):

```
my_txt.restrict = "\\-\\^";
```

The ^ may be used anywhere in the string to toggle between including characters and excluding characters. The following code includes only uppercase letters, but excludes the uppercase letter Q:

```
my_txt.restrict = "A-Z^Q";
```

You can use the \u escape sequence to construct restrict strings. The following code includes only the characters from ASCII 32 (space) to ASCII 126 (tilde).

```
my_txt.restrict = "\u0020-\u007E";
```

TextField._rotation

Availability

Flash Player 6.

Usage

my_txt._rotation

Description

Property; the rotation of the text field, in degrees, from its original orientation. Values from 0 to 180 represent clockwise rotation; values from 0 to -180 represent counterclockwise rotation. Values outside this range are added to or subtracted from 360 to obtain a value within the range. For example, the statement my_txt._rotation = 450 is the same as my_txt._rotation = 90.

See also

Button._rotation, MovieClip._rotation

TextField.scroll

Availability

Flash Player 6.

Usage

my_txt.scroll

Description

Property; defines the vertical position of text in a text field. The scroll property is useful for directing users to a specific paragraph in a long passage, or creating scrolling text fields. This property can be retrieved and modified.

For more information on scrolling text, see "Creating scrolling text" on page 357.

Example

The following code is attached to an Up button that scrolls the my_txt text field.

```
on (release) {
  my_txt.scroll = myText.scroll + 1;
}
```

See also

TextField.hscroll, TextField.maxscroll

TextField.selectable

Availability

Flash Player 6.

Usage

my_txt.selectable

Description

Property; a Boolean value that indicates whether the text field is selectable (editable). The value true indicates that the text is selectable.

TextField.setNewTextFormat()

Availability

Flash Player 6.

Usage

my_txt.setNewTextFormat(*textFormat*)

Parameters

textFormat   A TextFormat object.

Returns

Nothing.

Description

Method; sets a TextFormat object for newly inserted text, such as text inserted with the replaceSel() method or text entered by a user in a text field. Each text field has a new text format. When text is inserted, the new text is assigned the new text format.

The text format is set in a new TextFormat object. It contains both character and paragraph formatting information. Character formatting information describes the appearance of individual characters; for example, font name, point size, color, and associated URL. Paragraph formatting information describes the appearance of a paragraph; for example, left margin, right margin, indentation of the first line, and left, right, and center alignment.

See also

TextField.getNewTextFormat(), TextField.getTextFormat(), TextField.setTextFormat()

TextField.setTextFormat()

Availability

Flash Player 6.

Usage

```
my_txt.setTextFormat (textFormat)
my_txt.setTextFormat (index, textFormat)
my_txt.setTextFormat (beginIndex, endIndex, textFormat)
```

Parameters

textFormat   A TextFormat object, which contains character and paragraph formatting information.

index   An integer that specifies a character within my_txt.

beginIndex   An integer.

endIndex   An integer that specifies the first character after the desired text span.

Returns

Nothing.

Description

Method; sets a TextFormat object for a specified range of text in a text field. You can assign each character in a text field a text format. The text format of the first character of a paragraph is examined to perform paragraph formatting for the entire paragraph. The setTextFormat() method changes the text format applied to individual characters, to groups of characters, or to the entire body of text in a text field.

The text format is set in a new TextFormat object. It contains both character and paragraph formatting information. Character formatting information describes the appearance of individual characters, for example, font name, point size, color, and associated URL. Paragraph formatting information describes the appearance of a paragraph, for example, left margin, right margin, indentation of the first line, and left, right, and center alignment.

Usage 1: Applies the properties of *textFormat* to all text in the text field.

Usage 2: Applies the properties of *textFormat* to the character at position *index*.

Usage 3: Applies the properties of the *textFormat* parameter to the span of text from the *beginIndex* parameter to the *endIndex* parameter.

Notice that any text inserted manually by the user, or replaced by means of TextField.replaceSel(), does not assume the formatting specified in a call to setTextFormat(). To set the default formatting for a TextField object, use TextField.setNewTextFormat().

Example

This example creates a new TextFormat object called myTextFormat and sets its bold property to true. It then calls setTextFormat() and applies the new text format to the my_txt text field.

```
myTextFormat = new TextFormat();
myTextFormat.bold = true;
my_txt.setTextFormat(myTextFormat);
```

TextField.setNewTextFormat(), TextFormat class

TextField._soundbuftime

Availability

Flash Player 6.

Usage

my_txt._soundbuftime

Description

Property (global); an integer that specifies the number of seconds a sound prebuffers before it starts to stream.

TextField.StyleSheet class

Availability

Flash Player 7.

Description

The TextField.StyleSheet class lets you create a style sheet object that contains text formatting rules such as font size, color, and other formatting styles. You can then apply styles defined by a style sheet to a TextField object that contains HTML- or XML-formatted text. The text contained by the TextField object is then automatically formatted according to the tag styles defined by the style sheet object. You can use text styles to define new formatting tags, redefine built-in HTML tags, or create style classes that can be applied to certain HTML tags.

To apply styles to a TextField object, assign the style sheet object to a TextField object's styleSheet property.

For more information, see "Formatting text with Cascading Style Sheets" on page 343.

Method summary for the TextField.StyleSheet class

Method	Description
TextField.StyleSheet.getStyle()	Returns a copy of the style sheet object associated with a specified style name.
TextField.StyleSheet.getStyleNames()	Returns an array that contains the names of all of the styles registered in the style sheet object.
TextField.StyleSheet.load()	Begins loading a CSS file into the style sheet object.
TextField.StyleSheet.parseCSS()	Parses a string of CSS text and creates the specified style.
TextField.StyleSheet.setStyle()	Adds a new style to the style sheet object.

Event handler summary for the TextField.StyleSheet class

Method	Description
`TextField.StyleSheet.onLoad`	Callback handler invoked when a TextField.StyleSheet.load() operation has completed.

Constructor for the TextField.StyleSheet class

Availability

Flash Player 7.

Usage

```
new TextField.StyleSheet()
```

Returns

Nothing.

Description

Constructor; creates a TextField.StyleSheet object.

TextField.StyleSheet.getStyle()

Availability

Flash Player 7.

Usage

```
styleSheet.getStyle(styleName)
```

Parameters

styleName   A string that specifies the name of the style to retrieve.

Returns

An object.

Description

Method; returns a copy of the style object associated with the style named *styleName*. If there is no style object associated with *styleName*, *null* is returned.

Example

Suppose a style sheet object named `textStyles` loads an external style sheet file named styles.css that contains a single style named `heading`, which defines `font-family`, `font-size`, and `font-weight` properties, as shown below.

```
// In styles.css
heading {
  font-family: Arial;
  font-size: 24px;
  font-weight: bold;
}
```

The following code loads the styles from the CSS file, and then displays each property name and its value in the Output panel.

```
var styleSheet = new TextField.styleSheet();
styleSheet.load("styles.css");
var sectionStyle = styleSheet.getStyle("heading");
for(property in sectionStyle) {
  var propName = property;
  var propValue = sectionStyle[property];
  trace(propName + " : " + propValue);
}
```

This would display the following in the Output panel:

```
fontfamily : Arial
fontsize : 24px
fontweight : bold
```

See also

```
TextField.StyleSheet.setStyle()
```

TextField.StyleSheet.getStyleNames()

Availability

Flash Player 7.

Usage

```
styleSheet.getStyleNames()
```

Parameters

None.

Returns

An array.

Description

Method; returns an array that contains the names (as strings) of all of the styles registered in this style sheet.

Example

This example creates a style sheet object named styleSheet that contains two styles, heading and bodyText. It then invokes the style sheet object's getStyleNames() method, assigns the results to the array names_array, and displays the contents of the array in the Output panel.

```
var styleSheet= new TextField.StyleSheet();
styleSheet.setStyle("heading", {
  fontsize: '24px'
});
styleSheet.setStyle("bodyText", {
  fontsize: '12px'
});
var names_array = styleSheet.getStyleNames();
trace(names.join("\n"));
```

The following is displayed in the Output panel:

```
bodyText
heading
```

See also

TextField.StyleSheet.getStyle()

TextField.StyleSheet.load()

Availability

Flash Player 7.

Usage

```
styleSheet.load(url)
```

Parameters

url   The URL of a CSS file to load. The URL must be in the same domain as the URL where the SWF file currently resides.

Returns

Nothing.

Description

Method; starts loading the CSS file into *styleSheet*. The load operation is asynchronous; use the TextField.StyleSheet.onLoad callback handler to determine when the file has finished loading.

The CSS file must reside in exactly the same domain as the SWF file that is loading it. For more information about restrictions on loading data across domains, see "Flash Player security features" on page 392.

Example

The following example loads the CSS file named styles.css (not shown) into the style sheet object styleObj. When the file has finished loading successfully, the style sheet object is applied to a TextField object named news_txt.

```
var styleObj = new TextField.StyleSheet();
styleObj.load("styles.css");
styleObj.onLoad = function (success) {
  if(success) {
    news_txt.styleSheet = styleObj;
  }
}
```

See also

TextField.StyleSheet.onLoad

TextField.StyleSheet.onLoad

Availability

Flash Player 7.

Usage

```
styleSheet.onLoad = function (success) {}
```

Parameters

success   A Boolean value indicating whether the CSS file was successfully loaded.

Returns

Nothing.

Description

Callback handler; invoked when a TextField.StyleSheet.load() operation has completed. If the style sheet loaded successfully, the *success* parameter is true. If the document was not received, or if an error occurred in receiving the response from the server, the *success* parameter is false.

Example

The following example loads the CSS file named styles.css (not shown) into the style sheet object styleObj. When the file has finished loading successfully, the style sheet object is applied to a TextField object named news_txt.

```
var styleObj = new TextField.StyleSheet();
styleObj.load("styles.css");
styleObj.onLoad = function (success) {
  if(success) {
    news_txt.styleSheet = styleObj;
  }
}
```

See also

TextField.StyleSheet.load()

TextField.StyleSheet.parseCSS()

Availability

Flash Player 7.

Usage

```
styleSheet.parseCSS(cssText)
```

Parameters

cssText   The CSS text to parse (a string).

Returns

A Boolean value indicating if the text was parsed successfully (true) or not (false).

Description

Method; parses the CSS in *cssText* and loads the style sheet with it. If a style in *cssText* is already in *styleSheet*, the properties in *styleSheet* are retained, and only the ones in *cssText* are added or changed in *styleSheet*.

To extend the native CSS parsing capability, you can override this method by creating a subclass of the TextField.StyleSheet class. For more information, see "Creating subclasses" on page 366.

TextField.StyleSheet.setStyle()

Availability

Flash Player 7.

Usage

```
styleSheet.setStyle(name, style)
```

Parameters

name A string that specifies the name of the style to add to the style sheet.

style An object that describes the style, or null.

Returns

Nothing.

Description

Method; adds a new style with the specified name to the style sheet object. If the named style does not already exist in the style sheet, it is added. If the named style already exists in the style sheet, it is replaced. If the *style* parameter is null, the named style is removed.

Flash Player creates a copy of the style object that you pass to this method.

Example

The following code adds a style named emphasized to the style sheet myStyleSheet. The style includes two style properties: color and fontWeight. The style object is defined with the {} operator.

```
myStyleSheet.setStyle("emphasized", {color:'#000000',fontWeight:'bold'});
```

You could also create a style object using an instance of the Object class, and then pass that object as the *style* parameter, as the next example shows.

```
var styleObj = new Object();
styleObj.color = '#000000';
styleObj.fontWeight = 'bold';
myStyleSheet.setStyle("emphasized", styleObj);
delete styleObj;
```

Note: The last line of code (delete styleObj) deletes the original style object passed to setStyle() While not necessary, this step reduces memory usage, because Flash Player creates a copy of the style object you pass to setStyle().

See also

{} (object initializer)

TextField.styleSheet

Availability

Flash Player 7.

Usage

`my_txt.styleSheet = TextField StyleSheet`

Description

Property; attaches a style sheet to the text field specified by `my_txt`. For information on creating style sheets, see the TextField.StyleSheet class entry and "Formatting text with Cascading Style Sheets" on page 343.

TextField.tabEnabled

Availability

Flash Player 6.

Usage

`my_txt.tabEnabled`

Description

Property; specifies whether `my_txt` is included in automatic tab ordering. It is `undefined` by default.

If the `tabEnabled` property is `undefined` or `true`, the object is included in automatic tab ordering. If the `tabIndex` property is also set to a value, the object is included in custom tab ordering as well. If `tabEnabled` is `false`, the object is not included in automatic or custom tab ordering, even if the `tabIndex` property is set.

See also

`Button.tabEnabled, MovieClip.tabEnabled`

TextField.tabIndex

Availability

Flash Player 6.

Usage

`my_txt.tabIndex`

Parameters

None.

Returns

Nothing.

Description

Property; lets you customize the tab ordering of objects in a SWF file. You can set the `tabIndex` property on a button, movie clip, or text field instance; it is `undefined` by default.

If any currently displayed object in the SWF file contains a `tabIndex` property, automatic tab ordering is disabled, and the tab ordering is calculated from the `tabIndex` properties of objects in the SWF file. The custom tab ordering only includes objects that have `tabIndex` properties.

The `tabIndex` property must be a positive integer. The objects are ordered according to their `tabIndex` properties, in ascending order. An object with a `tabIndex` value of 1 precedes an object with a `tabIndex` value of 2. If two objects have the same `tabIndex` value, the one that precedes the other in the tab ordering is `undefined`.

The custom tab ordering defined by the `tabIndex` property is *flat*. This means that no attention is paid to the hierarchical relationships of objects in the SWF file. All objects in the SWF file with `tabIndex` properties are placed in the tab order, and the tab order is determined by the order of the `tabIndex` values. If two objects have the same `tabIndex` value, the one that goes first is `undefined`. You shouldn't use the same `tabIndex` value for multiple objects.

See also

`Button.tabIndex, MovieClip.tabIndex`

TextField._target

Availability

Flash Player 6.

Usage

`my_txt._target`

Description

Property (read-only); the target path of the text field instance specified by `my_txt`.

TextField.text

Availability

Flash Player 6.

Usage

`my_txt.text`

Description

Property; indicates the current text in the text field. Lines are separated by the carriage return character ('\r', ASCII 13). This property contains the normal, unformatted text in the text field, without HTML tags, even if the text field is HTML.

See also

`TextField.htmlText`

TextField.textColor

Availability

Flash Player 6.

Usage

my_txt`.textColor`

Description

Property; indicates the color of the text in a text field.

TextField.textHeight

Availability

Flash Player 6.

Usage

my_txt`.textHeight`

Description

Property; indicates the height of the text.

TextField.textWidth

Availability

Flash Player 6.

Usage

my_txt`.textWidth`

Description

Property; indicates the width of the text.

TextField.type

Availability

Flash Player 6.

Usage

my_txt`.type`

Description

Property; Specifies the type of text field. There are two values: `"dynamic"`, which specifies a dynamic text field that cannot be edited by the user, and `"input"`, which specifies an input text field.

Example

```
my_txt.type = "dynamic";
```

TextField._url

Availability

Flash Player 6.

Usage

`my_txt._url`

Description

Property (read only); retrieves the URL of the SWF file that created the text field.

TextField.variable

Availability

Flash Player 6.

Usage

`my_txt.variable`

Description

Property; The name of the variable that the text field is associated with. The type of this property is String.

TextField._visible

Availability

Flash Player 6.

Usage

`my_txt._visible`

Description

Property; a Boolean value that indicates whether the text field `my_txt` is visible. Text fields that are not visible (`_visible` property set to `false`) are disabled.

See also

`Button._visible, MovieClip._visible`

TextField._width

Availability

Flash Player 6.

Usage

`my_txt._width`

Description

Property; the width of the text field, in pixels.

Example

The following example sets the height and width properties of a text field:

```
my_txt._width=200;
my_txt._height=200;
```

See also

```
MovieClip._height
```

TextField.wordWrap

Availability

Flash Player 6.

Usage

```
my_txt.wordWrap
```

Description

Property; a Boolean value that indicates if the text field has word wrap. If the value of wordWrap is true, the text field has word wrap; if the value is false, the text field does not have word wrap.

TextField._x

Availability

Flash Player 6.

Usage

```
my_txt._x
```

Description

Property; an integer that sets the *x* coordinate of a text field relative to the local coordinates of the parent movie clip. If a text field is on the main Timeline, then its coordinate system refers to the upper left corner of the Stage as (0, 0). If the text field is inside a movie clip that has transformations, the text field is in the local coordinate system of the enclosing movie clip. Thus, for a movie clip rotated 90 degrees counterclockwise, the enclosed text field inherits a coordinate system that is rotated 90 degrees counterclockwise. The text field's coordinates refer to the registration point position.

See also

```
TextField._xscale, TextField._y, TextField._yscale
```

TextField._xmouse

Availability

Flash Player 6.

Usage

`my_txt._xmouse`

Description

Property (read-only); returns the *x* coordinate of the mouse position relative to the text field.

See also

`TextField._ymouse`

TextField._xscale

Availability

Flash Player 6.

Usage

`my_txt._xscale`

Description

Property; determines the horizontal scale of the text field as applied from the registration point of the text field, expressed as a percentage. The default registration point is (0,0).

See also

`TextField._x, TextField._y, TextField._yscale`

TextField._y

Availability

Flash Player 6.

Usage

`my_txt._y`

Description

Property; the *y* coordinate of a text field relative to the local coordinates of the parent movie clip. If a text field is in the main Timeline, then its coordinate system refers to the upper left corner of the Stage as (0, 0). If the text field is inside another movie clip that has transformations, the text field is in the local coordinate system of the enclosing movie clip. Thus, for a movie clip rotated 90 degrees counterclockwise, the enclosed text field inherits a coordinate system that is rotated 90 degrees counterclockwise. The text field's coordinates refer to the registration point position.

See also

`TextField._x, TextField._xscale, TextField._yscale`

TextField._ymouse

Availability

Flash Player 6.

Usage

`my_txt._ymouse`

Description

Property (read-only); indicates the *y* coordinate of the mouse position relative to the text field.

See also

`TextField._xmouse`

TextField._yscale

Availability

Flash Player 6.

Usage

`my_txt._yscale`

Description

Property; the vertical scale of the text field as applied from the registration point of the text field, expressed as a percentage. The default registration point is (0,0).

See also

`TextField._x`, `TextField._xscale`, `TextField._y`

TextFormat class

Availability

Flash Player 6.

Description

The TextFormat class represents character formatting information.

You must use the constructor `new TextFormat()` to create a TextFormat object before calling its methods.

You can set TextFormat parameters to `null` to indicate that they are undefined. When you apply a TextFormat object to a text field using `TextField.setTextFormat()`, only its defined properties are applied, as in the following example:

```
my_fmt = new TextFormat();
my_fmt.bold = true;
my_txt.setTextFormat(my_fmt);
```

This code first creates an empty TextFormat object with all of its properties undefined, then sets the `bold` property to a defined value.

The code `my_txt.setTextFormat(my_fmt)` only changes the `bold` property of the text field's default text format, because the `bold` property is the only one defined in `my_fmt`. All other aspects of the text field's default text format remain unchanged.

When `TextField.getTextFormat()` is invoked, a TextFormat object is returned with all of its properties defined; no property is `null`.

Method summary for the TextFormat class

Method	Description
`TextFormat.getTextExtent()`	Returns text measurement information for a text string.

Property summary for the TextFormat class

Property	Description
`TextFormat.align`	Indicates the alignment of a paragraph.
`TextFormat.blockIndent`	Indicates the block indentation, in points.
`TextFormat.bold`	Indicates whether text is boldface.
`TextFormat.bullet`	Indicates whether text is in a bulleted list.
`TextFormat.color`	Indicates the color of text.
`TextFormat.font`	Indicates the font name of the text with a text format.
`TextFormat.indent`	Indicates the indentation from the left margin to the first character in the paragraph.
`TextFormat.italic`	Indicates whether text is italicized.
`TextFormat.leading`	Indicates the amount of vertical space (called *leading*) between lines.
`TextFormat.leftMargin`	Indicates the left margin of the paragraph, in points.
`TextFormat.rightMargin`	Indicates the right margin of the paragraph, in points.
`TextFormat.size`	Indicates the point size of text.
`TextFormat.tabStops`	Specifies custom tab stops.
`TextFormat.target`	Indicates the window in a browser where a hyperlink is displayed.
`TextFormat.underline`	Indicates whether text is underlined.
`TextFormat.url`	Indicates the URL to which the text links.

Constructor for the TextFormat class

Availability

Flash Player 6.

Usage

```
new TextFormat([font, [size, [color, [bold, [italic, [underline, [url,
   [target, [align, [leftMargin, [rightMargin, [indent, [leading]]]]]]]]]]]]])
```

Parameters

font   The name of a font for text as a string.

size   An integer that indicates the point size.

color   The color of text using this text format. A number containing three 8-bit RGB components; for example, 0xFF0000 is red, 0x00FF00 is green.

bold   A Boolean value that indicates whether the text is boldface.

italic   A Boolean value that indicates whether the text is italicized.

underline   A Boolean value that indicates whether the text is underlined.

url   The URL to which the text in this text format hyperlinks. If *url* is an empty string, the text does not have a hyperlink.

target   The target window where the hyperlink is displayed. If the target window is an empty string, the text is displayed in the default target window _self. If the *url* parameter is set to an empty string or to the value null, you can get or set this property, but the property will have no effect.

align   The alignment of the paragraph, represented as a string. If "left", the paragraph is left-aligned. If "center", the paragraph is centered. If "right", the paragraph is right-aligned.

leftMargin   Indicates the left margin of the paragraph, in points.

rightMargin   Indicates the right margin of the paragraph, in points.

indent   An integer that indicates the indentation from the left margin to the first character in the paragraph.

leading   A number that indicates the amount of leading vertical space between lines.

Returns

Nothing.

Description

Constructor; creates a TextFormat object with the specified properties. You can then change the properties of the TextFormat object to change the formatting of text fields.

Any parameter may be set to null to indicate that it is not defined. All of the parameters are optional; any omitted parameters are treated as null.

TextFormat.align

Availability

Flash Player 6.

Usage

my_fmt.align

Description

Property; indicates the alignment of the paragraph, represented as a string. The alignment of the paragraph, represented as a string. If "left", the paragraph is left-aligned. If "center", the paragraph is centered. If "right", the paragraph is right-aligned. The default value is null which indicates that the property is undefined.

TextFormat.blockIndent

Availability

Flash Player 6.

Usage

my_fmt.blockIndent

Description

Property; a number that indicates the block indentation in points. Block indentation is applied to an entire block of text; that is, to all lines of the text. In contrast, normal indentation (TextFormat.indent) only affects the first line of each paragraph. If this property is null, the TextFormat object does not specify block indentation.

TextFormat.bold

Availability

Flash Player 6.

Usage

my_fmt.bold

Description

Property; a Boolean value that indicates if the text is boldface. The default value is null, which indicates that the property is undefined.

TextFormat.bullet

Availability

Flash Player 6.

Usage

my_fmt.bullet

Description

Property; a Boolean value that indicates that the text is part of a bulleted list. In a bulleted list, each paragraph of text is indented. To the left of the first line of each paragraph, a bullet symbol is displayed. The default value is null.

TextFormat.color

Availability

Flash Player 6.

Usage

my_fmt.color

Description

Property; indicates the color of text. A number containing three 8-bit RGB components; for example, 0xFF0000 is red, 0x00FF00 is green.

TextFormat.font

Availability

Flash Player 6.

Usage

my_fmt.font

Description

Property; the name of the font for text in this text format, as a string. The default value is null, which indicates that the property is undefined.

TextFormat.getTextExtent()

Availability

Flash Player 6. The optional *width* parameter is supported in Flash Player 7.

Usage

my_fmt.getTextExtent(*text*, [*width*])

Parameters

text   A string.

width   An optional number that represents the width, in pixels, at which the specified text should wrap.

Returns

An object with the properties `width`, `height`, `ascent`, `descent`, `textFieldHeight`, `textFieldWidth`.

Description

Method; returns text measurement information for the text string *text* in the format specified by *my_fmt*. The text string is treated as plain text (not HTML).

The method returns an object with six properties: `ascent`, `descent`, `width`, `height`, `textFieldHeight`, and `textFieldWidth`. All measurements are in pixels.

If a *width* parameter is specified, word wrapping is applied to the specified text. This lets you determine the height at which a text box shows all of the specified text.

The `ascent` and `descent` measurements provide, respectively, the distance above and below the baseline for a line of text. The baseline for the first line of text is positioned at the text field's origin plus its `ascent` measurement.

The `width` and `height` measurements provide the width and height of the text string. The `textFieldHeight` and `textFieldWidth` measurements provide the height and width required for a text field object to display the entire text string. Text fields have a 2-pixel-wide "gutter" around them, so the value of `textFieldHeight` is equal the value of `height` + 4; likewise, the value of `textFieldWidth` is always equal to the value of `width` + 4.

If you are creating a text field based on the text metrics, use `textFieldHeight` rather than `height` and `textFieldWidth` rather than `width`.

The following figure illustrates these measurements.

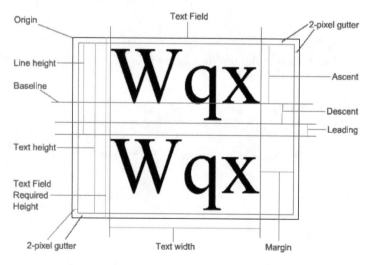

When setting up your TextFormat object, set all the attributes exactly as they will be set for the creation of the text field, including font name, font size, and leading. The default value for leading is 2.

Example

This example creates a single-line text field that's just big enough to display a text string using the specified formatting.

```
var text = "Small string";

// Create a TextFormat object,
// and apply its properties.
var txt_fmt = new TextFormat();
with(txt_fmt) {
   font = "Arial";
   bold = true;
}

// Obtain metrics information for the text string
// with the specified formatting.
var metrics = txt_fmt.getTextExtent(text);

// Create a text field just large enough to display the text.
this.createTextField ("textField", 0, 100, 100, metrics.textFieldWidth,
   metrics.textFieldHeight);
textField.border = true;
textField.wordWrap = true;
// Assign the same text string and
// TextFormat object to the TextField object.
textField.text = text;
textField.setTextFormat(txt_fmt);
```

The following example creates a multiline, 100-pixel-wide text field that's high enough to display a string with the specified formatting.

```
// Create a TextFormat object.
var txt_fmt:TextFormat= new TextFormat();

// Specify formatting properties for the TextFormat object:
txt_fmt.font = "Arial";
txt_fmt.bold = true;
txt_fmt.leading = 4;

// The string of text to be displayed
var textToDisplay:String = "Macromedia Flash 7, now with improved text
   metrics.";

// Obtain text measurement information for the string,
// wrapped at 100 pixels.
var metrics:Object = txt_fmt.getTextExtent(textToDisplay, 100);

// Create a new TextField object using the metric
// information just obtained.
this.createTextField ("textField", 0, 50, 50-metrics.ascent, 100,
   metrics.textFieldHeight)
textField.wordWrap = true;
textField.border = true;
// Assign the text and the TextFormat object to the TextObject:
textField.text = textToDisplay;
textField.setTextFormat(aformat);
```

TextFormat.indent

Availability

Flash Player 6.

Usage

my_fmt.indent

Description

Property; an integer that indicates the indentation from the left margin to the first character in the paragraph. The default value is null, which indicates that the property is undefined.

See also

TextFormat.blockIndent

TextFormat.italic

Availability

Flash Player 6.

Usage

my_fmt.italic

Description

Property; a Boolean value that indicates whether text in this text format is italicized. The default value is null, which indicates that the property is undefined.

TextFormat.leading

Availability

Flash Player 6.

Usage

my_fmt.leading

Description

Property; the amount of vertical space (called *leading*) between lines. The default value is null, which indicates that the property is undefined.

TextFormat.leftMargin

Availability

Flash Player 6.

Usage

my_fmt.leftMargin

Description

Property; the left margin of the paragraph, in points. The default value is null, which indicates that the property is undefined.

TextFormat.rightMargin

Availability

Flash Player 6.

Usage

my_fmt.rightMargin

Description

Property; the right margin of the paragraph, in points. The default value is null, which indicates that the property is undefined.

TextFormat.size

Availability

Flash Player 6.

Usage

my_fmt.size

Description

Property; the point size of text in this text format. The default value is null, which indicates that the property is undefined.

TextFormat.tabStops

Availability

Flash Player 6.

Usage

my_fmt.tabStops

Description

Property; specifies custom tab stops as an array of non-negative integers. Each tab stop is specified in points. If custom tab stops are not specified (null), the default tab stop is 4 (average character width).

TextFormat.target

Availability

Flash Player 6.

Usage

my_fmt.target

Description

Property; indicates the target window where the hyperlink is displayed. If the target window is an empty string, the text is displayed in the default target window _self. If the TextFormat.url property is an empty string or null, you can get or set this property, but the property will have no effect.

TextFormat.underline

Availability

Flash Player 6.

Usage

my_fmt.underline

Description

Property; a Boolean value that indicates whether the text that uses this text format is underlined (true) or not (false). This underlining is similar to that produced by the <U> tag, but the latter is not "true" underlining, because it does not skip descenders correctly. The default value is null, which indicates that the property is undefined.

TextFormat.url

Availability

Flash Player 6.

Usage

my_fmt.url

Description

Property; indicates the URL that text in this text format hyperlinks to. If the url property is an empty string, the text does not have a hyperlink. The default value is null, which indicates that the property is undefined.

TextSnapshot object

Availability

Authoring: Flash MX 2004.

Playback: SWF files published for Flash Player 6 or later, playing in Flash Player 7 or later.

Description

TextSnapshot objects let you work with static text in a movie clip. You can use them, for example, to lay out text with greater precision than that allowed by dynamic text, but still access the text in a read-only way.

You don't use a constructor to create a TextSnapshot object; it is returned by MovieClip.getTextSnapshot().

Method summary for the TextSnapshot object

Method	Description
TextSnapshot.findText()	Returns the position of the first occurrence of specified text.
TextSnapshot.getCount()	Returns the number of characters.
TextSnapshot.getSelected()	Specifies whether any of the text in the specified range has been selected by TextSnapshot.setSelected().
TextSnapshot.getSelectedText()	Returns a string that contains all the characters specified by TextSnapshot.setSelected().
TextSnapshot.getText()	Returns a string containing the characters in the specified range.
TextSnapshot.hitTestTextNearPos()	Lets you determine which character within the object is on or near specified coordinates.
TextSnapshot.setSelectColor()	Specifies the color to use when highlighting characters that have been selected with the TextSnapshot.setSelected() command.
TextSnapshot.setSelected()	Specifies a range of characters to be selected or deselected.

TextSnapshot.findText()

Availability

Authoring: Flash MX 2004.

Playback: SWF files published for Flash Player 6 or later, playing in Flash Player 7 or later.

Usage

`my_snap.findText( startIndex, textToFind, caseSensitive )`

Parameters

`startIndex` An integer specifying the starting point in `my_snap` to search for the specified text.

`textToFind` A string specifying the text to search for. If you specify a string literal instead of a variable of type String, enclose the string in quotation marks.

`caseSensitive` A Boolean value specifying whether the text in `my_snap` must match the case of the string in `textToFind`.

Returns

The zero-based index position of the first occurrence of the specified text, or -1.

Description

Method; searches the specified TextSnapshot object and returns the position of the first occurrence of `textToFind` found at or after `startIndex`. If `textToFind` is not found, the method returns -1.

See also

`TextSnapshot.getText()`

TextSnapshot.getCount()

Availability

Authoring: Flash MX 2004.

Playback: SWF files published for Flash Player 6 or later, playing in Flash Player 7 or later.

Usage

`my_snap.getCount()`

Parameters

None.

Returns

An integer representing the number of characters in the specified TextSnapshot object.

Description

Method; returns the number of characters in a TextSnapshot object.

See also

`TextSnapshot.getText()`

TextSnapshot.getSelected()

Availability

Authoring: Flash MX 2004.

Playback: SWF files published for Flash Player 6 or later, playing in Flash Player 7 or later.

Usage

`my_snap.getSelected(from, to)`

Parameters

`from` An integer that indicates the position of the first character of `my_snap` to be examined. Valid values for `from` are 0 through `TextSnapshot.getCount()` - 1. If `from` is a negative value, 0 is used.

`to` An integer that is 1+ the index of the last character in `my_snap` to be examined. Valid values for `to` are 0 through `TextSnapshot.getCount()`. The character indexed by the `to` parameter is not included in the extracted string. If this parameter is omitted, `TextSnapshot.getCount()` is used. If this value is less than or equal to the value of `from`, `from+1` is used.

Returns

A Boolean value of `true`, if at least one character in the given range has been selected by the corresponding TextSnapshot.setSelected() command, `false` otherwise.

Description

Method; returns a Boolean value that specifies whether a TextSnapshot object contains selected text in the specified range.

To search all characters, pass a value of 0 for `from` and `TextSnapshot.getCount()` (or any very large number) for `to`. To search a single character, pass a value of `from+1` for `to`.

See also

`TextSnapshot.getSelectedText()`, `TextSnapshot.getText()`

TextSnapshot.getSelectedText()

Availability

Authoring: Flash MX 2004.

Playback: SWF files published for Flash Player 6 or later, playing in Flash Player 7 or later.

Usage

`mySnapshot.getSelectedText( [ includeLineEndings ] )`

Parameters

`includeLineEndings` An optional Boolean value that specifies whether newline characters are inserted into the returned string where appropriate. The default value is `false`.

Returns

A string that contains all the characters specified by the corresponding TextSnapshot.setSelected() command.

Description

Method; returns a string that contains all the characters specified by the corresponding TextSnapshot.setSelected() command. If no characters are selected, an empty string is returned.

If you pass a value of true for *includeLineEndings*, newline characters are inserted in the string returned where deemed appropriate. In this case, the return string might be longer than the input range. If *includeLineEndings* is false or omitted, the selected text is returned without any characters added.

See also

TextSnapshot.getSelected()

TextSnapshot.getText()

Availability

Authoring: Flash MX 2004.

Playback: SWF files published for Flash Player 6 or later, playing in Flash Player 7 or later.

Usage

mySnapshot.getText(*from, to* [, *includeLineEndings*])

Parameters

from   An integer that indicates the position of the first character of *my_snap* to be included in the returned string. Valid values for *from* are 0 through TextSnapshot.getCount() - 1. If *from* is a negative value, 0 is used.

to   An integer that is 1+ the index of the last character in *my_snap* to be examined. Valid values for *to* are 0 through TextSnapshot.getCount(). The character indexed by the *to* parameter is not included in the extracted string. If this parameter is omitted, TextSnapshot.getCount() is used. If this value is less than or equal to the value of from, from+1 is used.

includeLineEndings   An optional Boolean value that specifies whether newline characters are inserted into the returned string where appropriate. The default value is *false*.

Returns

A string containing the characters in the specified range, or an empty string if no characters are found in the specified range.

Description

Method; returns a string that contains all the characters specified by the *from* and *to* parameters. If no characters are selected, an empty string is returned.

To return all characters, pass a value of 0 for *from* and TextSnapshot.getCount() (or any very large number) for *to*. To return a single character, pass a value of from+1 for *to*.

If you pass a value of true for *includeLineEndings*, newline characters are inserted in the string returned where deemed appropriate. In this case, the return string might be longer than the input range. If *includeLineEndings* is false or omitted, the selected text is returned without any characters added.

See also

TextSnapshot.getSelectedText()

TextSnapshot.hitTestTextNearPos()

Availability

Authoring: Flash MX 2004.

Playback: SWF files published for Flash Player 6 or later, playing in Flash Player 7 or later.

Usage

```
my_snap.hitTestTextNearPos(x, y [, maxDistance] )
```

Parameters

x   A number that represents the x coordinate of the movie clip containing the text in *my_snap*.

y   A number that represents the x coordinate of the movie clip containing the text in *my_snap*.

maxDistance   An optional number that represents the maximum distance from *x*, *y* that can be searched for text. The distance is measured from the centerpoint of each character. The default value is 0.

Returns

An integer representing the index value of the character in *my_snap* that is nearest to the specified *x*, *y* coordinates, or -1 if no character is found.

Description

Method; lets you determine which character within a TextSnapshot object is on or near specified *x*, *y* coordinates of the movie clip containing the text in *my_snap*.

If you omit or pass a value of 0 for *maxDistance*, the location specified by the *x*, *y* coordinates must lie inside the bounding box of *my_snap*.

See also

MovieClip.getTextSnapshot(), `MovieClip._x`, `MovieClip._y`

TextSnapshot.setSelectColor()

Availability

Authoring: Flash MX 2004.

Playback: SWF files published for Flash Player 6 or later, playing in Flash Player 7 or later.

Usage

```
mySnapshot.setSelectColor(hexColor);
```

Parameters

hexColor   The color used for the border placed around characters that have been selected by the corresponding TextSnapshot.setSelected() command, expressed in `0xRRGGBB` format.

Returns

Nothing.

Description

Method; specifies the color to use when highlighting characters that have been selected with the TextSnapshot.setSelected() command. The color is always opaque; you can't specify a transparency value.

TextSnapshot.setSelected()

Availability

Authoring: Flash MX 2004.

Playback: SWF files published for Flash Player 6 or later, playing in Flash Player 7 or later.

Usage

mySnapshot.setSelected(*from, to, select*)

Parameters

from   An integer that indicates the position of the first character of *my_snap* to select. Valid values for *from* are 0 through TextSnapshot.getCount() - 1. If *from* is a negative value, 0 is used.

to   An integer that is 1+ the index of the last character in *my_snap* to be examined. Valid values for *to* are 0 through TextSnapshot.getCount(). The character indexed by the *to* parameter is not included in the extracted string. If this parameter is omitted, TextSnapshot.getCount() is used. If this value is less than or equal to the value of from, from+1 is used.

select   A Boolean value that specifies whether the text should be selected (true) or deselected (false).

Returns

Nothing.

Description

Method; specifies a range of characters in a TextSnapshot object to be selected or deselected. Characters that are selected are drawn with a colored rectangle behind them, matching the bounding box of the character. The color of the bounding box is defined by TextSnapshot.setSelectColor().

To select or deselect all characters, pass a value of 0 for *from* and TextSnapshot.getCount() (or any very large number) for *to*. To specify a single character, pass a value of from+1 for *to*.

Because characters are individually marked as selected, you can issue this command multiple times to select multiple characters; that is, using this command does not deselect other characters that have been set by this command.

this

Availability

Flash Player 5.

Usage

```
this
```

Description

Identifier; references an object or movie clip instance. When a script executes, this references the movie clip instance that contains the script. When a method is called, this contains a reference to the object that contains the called method.

Inside an on event handler action attached to a button, this refers to the Timeline that contains the button. Inside an onClipEvent() event handler action attached to a movie clip, this refers to the Timeline of the movie clip itself.

Because this is evaluated in the context of the script that contains it, you can't use this in a script to refer to a variable defined in a class file:

```
// in file applyThis.as
class applyThis{
  var str:String = "Defined in applyThis.as";
  function conctStr(x:String):String{
    return x+x;
  }

  function addStr():String{
    return str;
  }
}

// Use following code in FLA to test movie
import applyThis;

var obj:applyThis = new applyThis();
var abj:applyThis = new applyThis();
abj.str = "defined in FLA";

trace(obj.addStr.call(abj,null));    // defined in FLA
trace(obj.addStr.call(this,null));   // undefined
trace(obj.addStr.call(obj,null));    // Defined in applyThis.as
```

Similarly, to call a function defined in a dynamic class, you must use this to scope the function:

```
// incorrect version of simple.as
dynamic class simple{
  function callfunc(){
    trace(func());
  }

}

// correct version of simple.as
dynamic class simple{
  function callfunc(){
    trace(this.func());
  }
}
```

```
// statements in FLA file
import simple;
var obj:simple = new simple();
obj.num = 0;
obj.func = function():Boolean{
  return true;
}
obj.callfunc(); // syntax error with incorrect version of simple.as
```

Example

In the following example, the keyword this references the Circle object.

```
function Circle(radius) {
  this.radius = radius;
  this.area = Math.PI * radius * radius;
}
```

In the following statement assigned to a frame, the keyword this references the current movie clip.

```
// sets the alpha property of the current movie clip to 20
this._alpha = 20;
```

In the following statement inside an onClipEvent() handler, the keyword this references the current movie clip.

```
// when the movie clip loads, a startDrag() operation
// is initiated for the current movie clip.

onClipEvent (load) {
  startDrag (this, true);
}
```

See also

on(), onClipEvent()

throw

Availability

Flash Player 7.

Usage

throw *expression*

Description

Statement; generates ("throws") an error that can be handled ("caught") by a catch{} or finally{} code block. If an exception is not caught by a catch or finally block, the string representation of the thrown value is sent to the Output panel.

Typically, you throw instances of the Error class or its subclasses (see the following examples).

Parameters

expression   An ActionScript expression or object.

Example

In this example, a function named `checkEmail()` checks whether the string that is passed to it is a properly formatted e-mail address. If the string does not contain an @ symbol, the function throws an error.

```
function checkEmail(email:String) {
    if (email.indexOf("@") == -1) {
        throw new Error("Invalid email address");
    }
}
```

The following code then calls the `checkEmail()` function within a `try` code block, passing the text in a text field (`email_txt`) as a parameter. If the string parameter does not contain a valid e-mail address, the error message is displayed in a text field (`error_txt`).

```
try {
    checkEmail("Joe Smith");
} catch (e) {
    error_txt.text = e.toString();
}
```

In this example, a subclass of the Error class is thrown. The `checkEmail()` function is modified to throw an instance of that subclass. (For more information, see "Creating subclasses" on page 366.)

```
// Define Error subclass InvalidEmailError
// In InvalidEmailError.as:
class InvalidEmailAddress extends Error {
    var message = "Invalid email address.";
}

function checkEmail(email:String) {
    if (email.indexOf("@") == -1) {
        throw new InvalidEmailAddress();
    }
}
```

See also

Error class, `try..catch..finally`

toggleHighQuality()

Availability

Flash 2; deprecated in favor of `_quality`.

Usage

`toggleHighQuality()`

Parameters

None.

Returns

Nothing.

Description

Deprecated function; turns anti-aliasing on and off in Flash Player. Anti-aliasing smooths the edges of objects and slows down SWF playback. This action affects all SWF files in Flash Player.

Example

The following code could be applied to a button that, when clicked, would toggle anti-aliasing on and off:

```
on(release) {
    toggleHighQuality();
}
```

See also

`_highquality`, `_quality`

trace()

Availability

Flash Player 4.

Usage

`trace(expression)`

Parameters

expression An expression to evaluate. When a SWF file is opened in the Flash authoring tool (via the Test Movie command), the value of the *expression* parameter is displayed in the Output panel.

Returns

Nothing.

Description

Statement; evaluates the expression and displays the result in the Output panel in test mode.

Use this action to record programming notes or to display messages in the Output panel while testing a movie. Use the *expression* parameter to check if a condition exists, or to display values in the Output panel. The `trace()` action is similar to the `alert` function in JavaScript.

You can use the Omit Trace Actions command in Publish Settings to remove `trace()` actions from the exported SWF file.

Example

This example is from a game in which a draggable movie clip instance named my_mc must be released on a specific target. A conditional statement evaluates the `_droptarget` property and executes different actions depending on where my_mc is released. The `trace()` action is used at the end of the script to evaluate the location of the my_mc movie clip and to display the result in the Output panel. If my_mc doesn't behave as expected (for example, if it snaps to the wrong target), the values sent to the Output panel by the `trace()` action will help you determine the problem in the script.

```
on(press) {
  my_mc.startDrag();
}

on(release) {
  if(eval(_droptarget) != target) {
    my_mc._x = my_mc_xValue;
    my_mc._y = my_mc_yValue;
  } else {
    var my_mc_xValue = my_mc._x;
    var my_mc_yValue = my_mc._y;
    target = "_root.pasture";
  }
  trace("my_mc_xValue = " + my_mc_xValue);
  trace("my_mc_xValue = " + my_mc_xValue);
  stopDrag();
}
```

true

Availability

Flash Player 5.

Usage

```
true
```

Description

Constant; a unique Boolean value that represents the opposite of `false`.

See also

```
false
```

try..catch..finally

Availability

Flash Player 7.

Usage

```
try {
    // ... try block ...
} finally {
    // ... finally block ...
}
try {
    // ... try block ...
} catch(error[:ErrorType1]) {
    // ... catch block ...
} [catch(error[:ErrorTypeN]) {
    // ... catch block ...
}] [finally {
    // ... finally block ...
}]
```

Parameters

error   The expression thrown from a *throw* statement, typically an instance of the Error class or a subclass thereof.

ErrorType   An optional type specifier for the *error* identifier. The catch clause only catches errors of the specified type.

Description

Keywords; enclose a block of code in which an error can occur, and then respond to the error. If any code within the try code block throws an error (using the throw action), control passes to the catch block, if one exists, then to the finally code block, if one exists. The finally block always executes, regardless of whether an error was thrown. If code within the try block doesn't throw an error (that is, if the try block completes normally), then the code in the finally block is still executed. The finally block executes even if the try block exits using a return statement.

A try block must be followed by a catch block, a finally block, or both. A single try block can have multiple catch blocks but only one finally block. You can nest try blocks as many levels deep as desired.

The *error* parameter specified in a catch handler must be a simple identifier such as e or theException or x. The variable in a catch handler can also be *typed*. When used with multiple catch blocks, typed errors let you catch multiple types of errors thrown from a single try block.

If the exception thrown is an object, the type will match if the thrown object is a subclass of the specified type. If an error of a specific type is thrown, the catch block that handles the corresponding error is executed. If an exception that is not of the specified type is thrown, the catch block does not execute and the exception is automatically thrown out of the try block to a catch handler that matches it.

If an error is thrown within a function, and the function does not include a catch handler, then the ActionScript interpreter exits that function, as well as any caller functions, until a catch block is found. During this process, finally handlers are called at all levels.

Example

The following example shows how to create a `try..finally` statement. Because code in the `finally` block is guaranteed to execute, it is typically used to perform any necessary "clean-up" code after a `try` block executes. In this example, the `finally` block is used to delete an ActionScript object, regardless of whether an error occurred.

```
var account = new Account()
try {
  var returnVal = account.getAccountInfo();
  if(returnVal != 0) {
    throw new Error("Error getting account information.");
  }
}
finally {
  // Delete the 'account' object no matter what.
  if(account != null) {
    delete account;
  }
}
```

The following example demonstrates a `try..catch` statement. The code within the `try` block is executed. If an exception is thrown by any code within the `try` block, control passes to the `catch` block, which displays the error message in a text field using the `Error.toString()` method.

```
var account = new Account()
try {
  var returnVal = account.getAccountInfo();
  if(returnVal != 0) {
    throw new Error("Error getting account information.");
  }
} catch (e) {
  status_txt.text = e.toString();
}
```

The following example shows a `try` code block with multiple, typed `catch` code blocks. Depending on the type of error that occurred, the `try` code block throws a different type of object. In this case, `myRecordSet` is an instance of a (hypothetical) class named RecordSet whose `sortRows()` method can throw two different types of errors: RecordSetException and MalformedRecord.

In this example, the RecordSetException and MalformedRecord objects are subclasses of the Error class. Each is defined in its own AS class file. (For more information, see Chapter 9, "Creating Classes with ActionScript 2.0," on page 359.)

```
// In RecordSetException.as:
class RecordSetException extends Error {
  var message = "Record set exception occurred."
}
// In MalformedRecord.as:
class MalformedRecord extends Error {
  var message = "Malformed record exception occurred.";
}
```

Within the RecordSet class's `sortRows()` method, one of these previously defined error objects are thrown depending on the type of exception that occurred. The following code snippet shows how this code might look.

```
// Within RecordSet.as class file...
function sortRows() {
  ...
  if(recordSetErrorCondition) {
    throw new RecordSetException();
  }
  if(malFormedRecordCondition) {
    throw new MalformedRecord();
  }
  ...
}
```

Finally, in another AS file or FLA script, the following code invokes the `sortRows()` method on an instance of the RecordSet class. It defines `catch` blocks for each type of error that is thrown by `sortRows()`.

```
try {
  myRecordSet.sortRows();
} catch (e:RecordSetException) {
  trace("Caught a recordset exception");
} catch (e:MalformedRecord) {
  trace("Caught a malformed record exception");
}
```

See also

Error class, `throw`, `class`, `extends`

typeof

Availability

Flash Player 5.

Usage

```
typeof(expression)
```

Parameters

expression   A string, movie clip, button, object, or function.

Description

Operator; a unary operator placed before a single parameter. The typeof operator causes the Flash interpreter to evaluate *expression*; the result is a string specifying whether the expression is a string, movie clip, object, function, number, or Boolean value. The following table shows the results of the typeof operator on each type of expression.

Parameter	Output
String	string
Movie clip	movieclip
Button	object
Text field	object
Number	number
Boolean	boolean
Object	object
Function	function

undefined

Availability

Flash Player 5.

Usage

```
undefined
```

Parameters

None.

Returns

Nothing.

Description

A special value, usually used to indicate that a variable has not yet been assigned a value. A reference to an undefined value returns the special value `undefined`. The ActionScript code `typeof(undefined)` returns the string `"undefined"`. The only value of type `undefined` is `undefined`.

In files published for Flash Player 6 or earlier, the value of `undefined.toString()` is `""` (an empty string). In files published for Flash Player 7 or later, the value of `undefined.toString()` is `undefined`.

The value `undefined` is similar to the special value `null`. When `null` and `undefined` are compared with the equality operator, they compare as equal.

Example

In this example, the variable x has not been declared and therefore has the value `undefined`. In the first section of code, the equality operator (`==`) compares the value of x to the value `undefined` and the appropriate result is sent to the Output panel. In the second section of code, the equality operator compares the values `null` and `undefined`.

```
// x has not been declared
trace ("The value of x is " + x);
if (x == undefined) {
  trace ("x is undefined");
} else {
  trace ("x is not undefined");
}

trace ("typeof (x) is " + typeof (x));
if (null == undefined) {
  trace ("null and undefined are equal");
} else {
  trace ("null and undefined are not equal");
}
```

The following result is displayed in the Output panel.

```
The value of x is undefined
x is undefined
typeof (x) is undefined
null and undefined are equal
```

unescape

Availability

Flash Player 5.

Usage

```
unescape(x)
```

Parameters

x   A string with hexadecimal sequences to escape.

Returns

A string decoded from a URL-encoded parameter.

Description

Function; evaluates the parameter *x* as a string, decodes the string from URL-encoded format (converting all hexadecimal sequences to ASCII characters), and returns the string.

Example

The following example illustrates the escape-to-unescape conversion process.

```
escape("Hello{[World]}");
```

The escaped result is as follows:

```
("Hello%7B%5BWorld%5D%7D');
```

Use unescape to return to the original format:

```
unescape("Hello%7B%5BWorld%5D%7D");
```

The result is as follows:

```
Hello{[World]}
```

unloadMovie()

Availability

Flash Player 3.

Usage

```
unloadMovie(target)
```

Parameters

target   The target path of a movie clip.

Returns

None.

Description

Function; removes a movie clip that was loaded by means of loadMovie() from Flash Player. To unload a movie that was loaded by means of loadMovieNum(), use unloadMovieNum() instead of unloadMovie().

Example

The following example unloads the movie clip `draggable_mc` on the main Timeline, and loads `movie.swf` into level 4.

```
on (press) {
    unloadMovie ("_root.draggable_mc");
    loadMovieNum ("movie.swf", 4);
}
```

The following example unloads the movie loaded into level 4.

```
on (press) {
    unloadMovieNum (4);
}
```

See also

loadMovie(), MovieClipLoader.unloadClip()

unloadMovieNum()

Availability

Flash Player 3.

Usage

unloadMovieNum(*level*)

Parameters

level   The level (_level*N*) of a loaded movie.

Returns

Nothing.

Description

Function; removes a movie that was loaded by means of loadMovieNum() from Flash Player. To unload a movie that was loaded by means of loadMovie(), use unloadMovie() instead of unloadMovieNum().

See also

loadMovie(), loadMovieNum(), unloadMovie()

updateAfterEvent()

Availability

Flash Player 5.

Usage

```
updateAfterEvent()
```

Parameters

None.

Returns

Nothing.

Description

Function; updates the display (independent of the frames per second set for the movie) when you call it within an `onClipEvent()` handler or as part of a function or method that you pass to `setInterval()`. Flash ignores calls to `updateAfterEvent` that are not within an `onClipEvent()` handler or part of a function or method passed to `setInterval()`.

See also

`onClipEvent()`, `setInterval()`

var

Availability

Flash Player 5.

Usage

```
var variableName [= value1] [...,variableNameN [=valueN]]
```

Parameters

`variableName`   An identifier.

`value`   The value assigned to the variable.

Returns

Nothing.

Description

Statement; used to declare local or Timeline variables.

- If you declare variables inside a function, the variables are local. They are defined for the function and expire at the end of the function call.
- If variables are not declared inside a block ({ }) but the action list was executed with a call() action, the variables are local and expire at the end of the current list.
- If variables are not declared inside a block and the current action list was not executed with the call() action, the variables are interpreted as Timeline variables. However, you don't have to use var to declare Timeline variables.

You cannot declare a variable scoped to another object as a local variable:

```
my_array.length = 25;      // ok
var my_array.length = 25; // syntax error
```

When you use `var`, you can strictly type the variable; see "Strict data typing" on page 242

Note: Classes defined in external scripts also support public, private, and static variable scopes. See Chapter 9, "Creating Classes with ActionScript 2.0," on page 359 and `private`, `public`, and `static`.

Video class

Availability

Flash Player 6; the ability to play Flash Video (FLV) files was added in Flash Player 7.

Description

The Video class lets you display live streaming video on the Stage without embedding it in your SWF file. You capture the video by using `Camera.get()`. In files published for Flash Player 7 and later, you can also use the Video class to play back Flash Video (FLV) files over HTTP or from the local file system. For more information, see "Playing back external FLV files dynamically" on page 401, NetConnection class, and NetStream class.

A Video object can be used like a movie clip. As with other objects you place on the stage, you can control various properties of Video objects. For example, you can move the Video object around on the stage by using its `_x` and `_y` properties; you can change its size using its `_height` and `_width` properties, and so on.

To display the video stream, first place a Video object on the Stage. Then use `Video.attachVideo()` to attach the video stream to the Video object.

To place a Video object on the Stage:

1 If the Library panel isn't visible, select Window > Library to display it.
2 Add an embedded Video object to the library by clicking the Options menu on the right side of the Library panel title bar and selecting New Video.
3 Drag the Video object to the Stage and use the Property inspector to give it a unique instance name, such as `my_video`. (Do not name it Video.)

Method summary for the Video class

Method	Description
Video.attachVideo()	Specifies a video stream to be displayed within the boundaries of the Video object on the Stage.
Video.clear()	Clears the image currently displayed in the Video object.

Property summary for the Video class

Property	Description
Video.deblocking	Specifies the behavior for the deblocking filter that the video compressor applies as needed when streaming the video.
Video.height	Read-only; the height of the video stream, in pixels.

Property	Description
Video.smoothing	Specifies whether the video should be smoothed (interpolated) when it is scaled.
Video.width	Read-only; the width of the video stream, in pixels.

Video.attachVideo()

Availability

Flash Player 6; the ability to work with Flash Video (FLV) files was added in Flash Player 7.

Usage

my_video.attachVideo(*source*)

Parameters

source   A Camera object that is capturing video data or a NetStream object. To drop the connection to the Video object, pass null for *source*.

Returns

Nothing.

Description

Method; specifies a video stream (*source*) to be displayed within the boundaries of the Video object on the Stage. The video stream is either an FLV file being displayed by means of the NetStream.play() command, a Camera object, or null. If *source* is null, video is no longer played within the Video object.

You don't have to use this method if the FLV file contains only audio; the audio portion of an FLV files is played automatically when the NetStream.play() command is issued.

If you want to control the audio associated with an FLV file, you can use MovieClip.attachAudio() to route the audio to a movie clip; you can then create a Sound object to control some aspects of the audio. For more information, see MovieClip.attachAudio().

Example

The following example plays live video locally.

```
my_cam = Camera.get();
my_video.attachVideo(my_cam); // my_video is a Video object on the Stage
```

The following example plays a previously recorded file named myVideo.flv that is stored in the same directory as the SWF file.

```
var nc:NetConnection = new NetConnection();
nc.connect(null);
var ns:NetStream = new NetStream(my_nc);
my_video.attachVideo(ns); // my_video is a Video object on the Stage
ns.play("myVideo.flv");
```

See also

Camera class, NetStream class

Video.clear()

Availability

Flash Player 6.

Usage

my_video.clear()

Parameters

None.

Returns

Nothing.

Description

Method; clears the image currently displayed in the Video object. This is useful when, for example, you want to display standby information without having to hide the Video object.

See also

Video.attachVideo()

Video.deblocking

Availability

Flash Player 6.

Usage

my_video.deblocking
my_video.deblocking = *setting*

Description

Property; specifies the behavior for the deblocking filter that the video compressor applies as needed when streaming the video. The following are acceptable values for *setting*:

- 0 (the default): Let the video compressor apply the deblocking filter as needed.
- 1: Never use the deblocking filter.
- 2: Always use the deblocking filter.

The deblocking filter has an effect on overall playback performance, and it is usually not necessary for high-bandwidth video. If your system is not powerful enough, you might experience difficulties playing back video with this filter enabled.

Video.height

Availability

Flash Player 6.

Usage

my_video.height

Description

Read-only property; an integer specifying the height of the video stream, in pixels. For live streams, this value is the same as the `Camera.height` property of the Camera object that is capturing the video stream. For FLV files, this value is the height of the file that was exported as FLV.

You may want to use this property, for example, to ensure that the user is seeing the video at the same size at which it was captured, regardless of the actual size of the Video object on the Stage.

Example

Usage 1: The following example sets the height and width values of the Video object to match the values of an FLV file. You should call this code after NetStream.onStatus is invoked with a `code` property of `NetStream.Buffer.Full`. If you call it when the `code` property is `NetStream.Play.Start`, the height and width values will be 0, because the Video object doesn't yet have the height and width of the loaded FLV file.

```
// Clip is the instance name of the movie clip
// that contains the video object "my_video".
_root.Clip._width = _root.Clip.my_video.width;
_root.Clip._height = _root.Clip.my_video.height;
```

Usage 2: The following example lets the user press a button to set the height and width of a video stream being displayed in the Flash Player to be the same as the height and width at which the video stream was captured.

```
on (release) {
  _root.my_video._width = _root.my_video.width
  _root.my_video._height = _root.my_video.height
}
```

See also

`MovieClip._height`, `Video.width`

Video.smoothing

Availability

Flash Player 6.

Usage

my_video.smoothing

Description

Property; a Boolean value that specifies whether the video should be smoothed (interpolated) when it is scaled. For smoothing to work, the player must be in high-quality mode. The default value is `false` (no smoothing).

Video.width

Availability

Flash Player 6.

Usage

```
my_video.width
```

Description

Read-only property; an integer specifying the width of the video stream, in pixels. For live streams, this value is the same as the `Camera.width` property of the Camera object that is capturing the video stream. For FLV files, this value is the width of the file that was exported as an FLV file.

You may want to use this property, for example, to ensure that the user is seeing the video at the same size at which it was captured, regardless of the actual size of the Video object on the Stage.

Example

See the examples for `Video.height`.

void

Availability

Flash Player 5.

Usage

```
void (expression)
```

Description

Operator; a unary operator that discards the *expression* value and returns an undefined value. The `void` operator is often used in comparisons using the `==` operator to test for undefined values.

while

Availability

Flash Player 4.

Usage

```
while(condition) {
   statement(s);
}
```

Parameters

condition   The expression that is reevaluated each time the `while` action is executed.

statement(s)   The instructions to execute while the condition evaluates to `true`.

Returns

Nothing.

Description

Statement; tests an expression and runs a statement or series of statements repeatedly in a loop as long as the expression is `true`.

Before the statement block is run, the `condition` is tested; if the test returns `true`, the statement block is run. If the condition is `false`, the statement block is skipped and the first statement after the `while` action's statement block is executed.

Looping is commonly used to perform an action while a counter variable is less than a specified value. At the end of each loop, the counter is incremented until the specified value is reached. At that point, the `condition` is no longer `true`, and the loop ends.

The `while` statement performs the following series of steps. Each repetition of steps 1–4 is called an *iteration* of the loop. The `condition` is retested at the beginning of each iteration, as in the following steps:

1 The expression `condition` is evaluated.

2 If `condition` evaluates to `true` or a value that converts to the Boolean value `true`, such as a nonzero number, go to step 3.

   Otherwise, the `while` statement is completed and execution resumes at the next statement after the `while` loop.

3 Run the statement block `statement(s)`.

4 Go to step 1.

See also

`do while`, `continue`, `for`, `for..in`

with

Availability

Flash Player 5.

Usage

```
with (object) {
   statement(s);
}
```

Parameters

`object`   An instance of an ActionScript object or movie clip.

`statement(s)`   An action or group of actions enclosed in curly braces.

Returns

Nothing.

Description

Statement; lets you specify an object (such as a movie clip) with the `object` parameter and evaluate expressions and actions inside that object with the `statement(s)` parameter. This prevents you from having to repeatedly write the object's name or the path to the object.

The *object* parameter becomes the context in which the properties, variables, and functions in the *statement(s)* parameter are read. For example, if *object* is my_array, and two of the properties specified are length and concat, those properties are automatically read as my_array.length and my_array.concat. In another example, if *object* is state.california, any actions or statements inside the with action are called from inside the california instance.

To find the value of an identifier in the *statement(s)* parameter, ActionScript starts at the beginning of the scope chain specified by the *object* and searches for the identifier at each level of the scope chain, in a specific order.

The scope chain used by the with action to resolve identifiers starts with the first item in the following list and continues to the last item:

- The object specified in the *object* parameter in the innermost with action.
- The object specified in the *object* parameter in the outermost with action.
- The Activation object. (A temporary object that is automatically created when a function is called that holds the local variables called in the function.)
- The movie clip containing the currently executing script.
- The Global object (built-in objects such as Math and String).

To set a variable inside a with action, the variable must have been declared outside the with action or you must enter the full path to the Timeline on which you want the variable to live. If you set a variable in a with action without declaring it, the with action will look for the value according to the scope chain. If the variable doesn't already exist, the new value will be set on the Timeline from which the with action was called.

In Flash 5 or later, the with action replaces the deprecated tellTarget action. You are encouraged to use with instead of tellTarget because it is a standard ActionScript extension to the ECMA-262 standard. The principal difference between the with and tellTarget actions is that with takes a reference to a movie clip or other object as its parameter, while tellTarget takes a target path string that identifies a movie clip as its parameter, and cannot be used to target objects.

Example

The following example sets the _x and _y properties of the someOther_mc instance, and then instructs someOther_mc to go to Frame 3 and stop.

```
with (someOther_mc) {
   _x = 50;
   _y = 100;
   gotoAndStop(3);
}
```

The following code snippet shows how to write the preceding code without using a with action.

```
someOther_mc._x = 50;
someOther_mc._y = 100;
someOther_mc.gotoAndStop(3);
```

You could also write this code using the tellTarget action. However, if someOther_mc were not a movie clip, but an object, you could not use the with action.

```
tellTarget ("someOther_mc") {
    _x = 50;
    _y = 100;
    gotoAndStop(3);
}
```

The with action is useful for accessing multiple items in a scope chain list simultaneously. In the following example, the built-in Math object is placed at the front of the scope chain. Setting Math as a default object resolves the identifiers cos, sin, and PI to Math.cos, Math.sin, and Math.PI, respectively. The identifiers a, x, y, and r are not methods or properties of the Math object, but since they exist in the object activation scope of the function polar(), they resolve to the corresponding local variables.

```
function polar(r) {
    var a, x, y;
    with (Math) {
        a = PI * r * r;
        x = r * cos(PI);
        y = r * sin(PI/2);
    }
    trace("area = " +a);
    trace("x = " + x);
    trace("y = " + y);
}
```

You can use nested with actions to access information in multiple scopes. In the following example, the instance fresno and the instance salinas are children of the instance california. The statement sets the _alpha values of fresno and salinas without changing the _alpha value of california.

```
with (california){
    with (fresno){
        _alpha = 20;
    }
    with (salinas){
        _alpha = 40;
    }
}
```

See also

tellTarget

XML class

Availability

Flash Player 5 (became a native object in Flash Player 6, which improved performance significantly).

Description

Use the methods and properties of the XML class to load, parse, send, build, and manipulate XML document trees.

You must use the constructor new XML() to create an XML object before calling any of the methods of the XML class.

Method summary for the XML class

Method	Description
XML.addRequestHeader()	Adds or changes HTTP headers for POST operations.
XML.appendChild()	Appends a node to the end of the specified object's child list.
XML.cloneNode()	Clones the specified node and, optionally, recursively clones all children.
XML.createElement()	Creates a new XML element.
XML.createTextNode()	Creates a new XML text node.
XML.getBytesLoaded()	Returns the number of bytes loaded for the specified XML document.
XML.getBytesTotal()	Returns the size of the XML document, in bytes.
XML.hasChildNodes()	Returns true if the specified node has child nodes; otherwise, returns false.
XML.insertBefore()	Inserts a node in front of an existing node in the specified node's child list.
XML.load()	Loads a document (specified by the XML object) from a URL.
XML.parseXML()	Parses an XML document into the specified XML object tree.
XML.removeNode()	Removes the specified node from its parent.
XML.send()	Sends the specified XML object to a URL.
XML.sendAndLoad()	Sends the specified XML object to a URL and loads the server response into another XML object.
XML.toString()	Converts the specified node and any children to XML text.

Property summary for the XML class

Property	Description
XML.contentType	Indicates the MIME type transmitted to the server.
XML.docTypeDecl	Sets and returns information about an XML document's DOCTYPE declaration.
XML.firstChild	Read-only; references the first child in the list for the specified node.
XML.ignoreWhite	When set to true, text nodes that contain only white space are discarded during the parsing process.
XML.lastChild	References the last child in the list for the specified node.
XML.loaded	Read-only; checks if the specified XML object has loaded.
XML.nextSibling	Read-only; references the next sibling in the parent node's child list.
XML.nodeName	The node name of an XML object.
XML.nodeType	The type of the specified node (XML element or text node).
XML.nodeValue	The text of the specified node if the node is a text node.
XML.parentNode	Read-only; references the parent node of the specified node.

Property	Description
XML.previousSibling	Read-only; references the previous sibling in the parent node's child list.
XML.status	A numeric status code indicating the success or failure of an XML document parsing operation.
XML.xmlDecl	Specifies information about a document's XML declaration.

Collections summary for the XML class

Method	Description
XML.attributes	Returns an associative array containing all of the attributes of the specified node.
XML.childNodes	Read-only; returns an array containing references to the child nodes of the specified node.

Event handler summary for the XML class

Event handler	Description
XML.onData	An event handler that is invoked when XML text has been completely downloaded from the server, or when an error occurs downloading XML text from a server.
XML.onLoad()	An event handler that returns a Boolean value indicating whether the XML object was successfully loaded with XML.load() or XML.sendAndLoad().

Constructor for the XML class

Availability

Flash Player 5.

Usage

```
new XML([source])
```

Parameters

source   The XML text parsed to create the new XML object.

Returns

Nothing.

Description

Constructor; creates a new XML object. You must use the constructor to create an XML object before calling any of the methods of the XML class.

Note: The createElement() and createTextNode() methods are the "constructor" methods for creating the elements and text nodes in an XML document tree.

Example

Usage 1: The following example creates an new, empty XML object.

```
my_xml = new XML();
```

Usage 2: The following example creates an XML object by parsing the XML text specified in the *source* parameter, and populates the newly created XML object with the resulting XML document tree.

```
anyOtherXML = new XML("<state>California<city>san francisco</city></state>");
```

See also

```
XML.createElement(), XML.createTextNode()
```

XML.addRequestHeader()

Availability

Flash Player 6.

Usage

```
xml.addRequestHeader(headerName, headerValue)
xml.addRequestHeader(["headerName_1", "headerValue_1" ... "headerName_n",
    "headerValue_n"])
```

Parameters

headerName   An HTTP request header name.

headerValue   The value associated with *headerName*.

Returns

Nothing.

Description

Method; adds or changes HTTP request headers (such as `Content-Type` or `SOAPAction`) sent with `POST` actions. In the first usage, you pass two strings to the method: *headerName* and *headerValue*. In the second usage, you pass an array of strings, alternating header names and header values.

If multiple calls are made to set the same header name, each successive value replaces the value set in the previous call.

You cannot add or change the following standard HTTP headers using this method: `Accept-Ranges`, `Age`, `Allow`, `Allowed`, `Connection`, `Content-Length`, `Content-Location`, `Content-Range`, `ETag`, `Host`, `Last-Modified`, `Locations`, `Max-Forwards`, `Proxy-Authenticate`, `Proxy-Authorization`, `Public`, `Range`, `Retry-After`, `Server`, `TE`, `Trailer`, `Transfer-Encoding`, `Upgrade`, `URI`, `Vary`, `Via`, `Warning`, and `WWW-Authenticate`.

Example

This example adds a custom HTTP header named `SOAPAction` with a value of `Foo` to an XML object named `my_xml`.

```
my_xml.addRequestHeader("SOAPAction", "'Foo'");
```

This next example creates an array named `headers` that contains two alternating HTTP headers and their associated values. The array is passed as a parameter to the `addRequestHeader()` method.

```
var headers = ["Content-Type", "text/plain", "X-ClientAppVersion", "2.0"];
my_xml.addRequestHeader(headers);
```

See also

LoadVars.addRequestHeader()

XML.appendChild()

Availability

Flash Player 5.

Usage

```
my_xml.appendChild(childNode)
```

Parameters

`childNode`   The child node to be added to the specified XML object's child list.

Returns

Nothing.

Description

Method; appends the specified child node to the XML object's child list. The appended child node is placed in the tree structure once removed from its existing parent node, if any.

Example

The following example clones the last node from `doc1` and appends it to `doc2`.

```
doc1 = new XML(src1);
doc2 = new XML();
node = doc1.lastChild.cloneNode(true);
doc2.appendChild(node);
```

XML.attributes

Availability

Flash Player 5.

Usage

my_xml.attributes

Parameters

None.

Returns

An array.

Description

Property; an associative array containing all attributes of the specified XML object.

Example

The following example writes the names of the XML attributes to the Output window.

```
str = "<mytag name=\"Val\"> intem </mytag>";
doc = new XML(str);
y = doc.firstChild.attributes.name;
  trace (y);
doc.firstChild.attributes.order = "first";
z = doc.firstChild.attributes.order
  trace(z);
```

The following is written to the Output panel:

```
Val
first
```

XML.childNodes

Availability

Flash Player 5.

Usage

`my_xml.childNodes`

Parameters

None.

Returns

An array.

Description

Property (read-only); an array of the specified XML object's children. Each element in the array is a reference to an XML object that represents a child node. This is a read-only property and cannot be used to manipulate child nodes. Use `XML.appendChild()`, `XML.insertBefore()`, and `XML.removeNode()` to manipulate child nodes.

This property is undefined for text nodes (`nodeType == 3`).

See also

`XML.nodeType`

XML.cloneNode()

Availability

Flash Player 5.

Usage

`my_xml.cloneNode(deep)`

Parameters

deep   Boolean value specifying whether the children of the specified XML object are recursively cloned.

Returns

An XML node.

Description

Method; constructs and returns a new XML node of the same type, name, value, and attributes as the specified XML object. If *deep* is set to `true`, all child nodes are recursively cloned, resulting in an exact copy of the original object's document tree.

The clone of the node that is returned is no longer associated with the tree of the cloned item. Consequently, `nextSibling`, `parentNode`, and `previousSibling` all have a value of `null`. If a clip copy is not performed, `firstChild` and `lastChild` are also `null`.

XML.contentType

Availability

Flash Player 6.

Usage

`my_xml.contentType`

Description

Property; the MIME type that is sent to the server when you call the `XML.send()` or `XML.sendAndLoad()` method. The default is *application/x-www-form-urlencoded*.

See also

`XML.send()`, `XML.sendAndLoad()`

XML.createElement()

Availability

Flash Player 5.

Usage

`my_xml.createElement(name)`

Parameters

name   The tag name of the XML element being created.

Returns

An XML element.

Description

Method; creates a new XML element with the name specified in the parameter. The new element initially has no parent, no children, and no siblings. The method returns a reference to the newly created XML object representing the element. This method and `createTextNode()` are the constructor methods for creating nodes for an XML object.

XML.createTextNode()

Availability

Flash Player 5.

Usage

my_xml.createTextNode(*text*)

Parameters

text   The text used to create the new text node.

Returns

Nothing.

Description

Method; creates a new XML text node with the specified text. The new node initially has no parent, and text nodes cannot have children or siblings. This method returns a reference to the XML object representing the new text node. This method and createElement() are the constructor methods for creating nodes for an XML object.

XML.docTypeDecl

Availability

Flash Player 5.

Usage

my_xml.XMLdocTypeDecl

Description

Property; specifies information about the XML document's DOCTYPE declaration. After the XML text has been parsed into an XML object, the XML.docTypeDecl property of the XML object is set to the text of the XML document's DOCTYPE declaration. For example, <!DOCTYPE greeting SYSTEM "hello.dtd">. This property is set using a string representation of the DOCTYPE declaration, not an XML node object.

The ActionScript XML parser is not a validating parser. The DOCTYPE declaration is read by the parser and stored in the docTypeDecl property, but no DTD validation is performed.

If no DOCTYPE declaration was encountered during a parse operation, XML.docTypeDecl is set to undefined. XML.toString() outputs the contents of XML.docTypeDecl immediately after the XML declaration stored in XML.xmlDecl, and before any other text in the XML object. If XML.docTypeDecl is undefined, no DOCTYPE declaration is output.

Example

The following example uses XML.docTypeDecl to set the DOCTYPE declaration for an XML object:

my_xml.docTypeDecl = "<!DOCTYPE greeting SYSTEM \"hello.dtd\">";

See also

XML.toString(), XML.xmlDecl

XML.firstChild

Availability

Flash Player 5.

Usage

`my_xml.firstChild`

Description

Property (read-only); evaluates the specified XML object and references the first child in the parent node's children list. This property is `null` if the node does not have children. This property is undefined if the node is a text node. This is a read-only property and cannot be used to manipulate child nodes; use `appendChild()`, `insertBefore()`, and `removeNode()` to manipulate child nodes.

See also

`XML.appendChild()`, `XML.insertBefore()`, `XML.removeNode()`

XML.getBytesLoaded()

Availability

Flash Player 6.

Usage

`XML.getBytesLoaded()`

Parameters

None.

Returns

An integer indicating the number of bytes loaded.

Description

Method; returns the number of bytes loaded (streamed) for the XML document. You can compare the value of `getBytesLoaded()` with the value of `getBytesTotal()` to determine what percentage of an XML document has loaded.

See also

`XML.getBytesTotal()`

XML.getBytesTotal()

Availability

Flash Player 6.

Usage

```
XML.getBytesTotal()
```

Parameters

None.

Returns

An integer.

Description

Method; returns the size, in bytes, of the XML document.

See also

```
XML.getBytesLoaded()
```

XML.hasChildNodes()

Availability

Flash Player 5.

Usage

```
my_xml.hasChildNodes()
```

Parameters

None.

Returns

A Boolean value.

Description

Method; returns `true` if the specified XML object has child nodes; otherwise, returns `false`.

Example

The following example uses the information from the XML object in a user-defined function.

```
if (rootNode.hasChildNodes()) {
  myfunc (rootNode.firstChild);
}
```

XML.ignoreWhite

Availability

Flash Player 5.

Usage

```
my_xml.ignoreWhite = boolean
XML.prototype.ignoreWhite = boolean
```

Parameters

boolean   A Boolean (true or false) value.

Description

Property; default setting is false. When set to true, text nodes that contain only white space are discarded during the parsing process. Text nodes with leading or trailing white space are unaffected.

Usage 1: You can set the ignoreWhite property for individual XML objects, as in the following code:

```
my_xml.ignoreWhite = true
```

Usage 2: You can set the default ignoreWhite property for XML objects, as in the following code:

```
XML.prototype.ignoreWhite = true
```

XML.insertBefore()

Availability

Flash Player 5.

Usage

```
my_xml.insertBefore(childNode, beforeNode)
```

Parameters

childNode   The node to be inserted.

beforeNode   The node before the insertion point for the *childNode*.

Returns

Nothing.

Description

Method; inserts a new child node into the XML object's child list, before the *beforeNode* node. If the *beforeNode* parameter is undefined or null, the node is added using appendChild(). If *beforeNode* is not a child of *my_xml*, the insertion fails.

XML.lastChild

Availability

Flash Player 5.

Usage

my_xml.lastChild

Description

Property (read-only); evaluates the XML object and references the last child in the parent node's child list. This method returns null if the node does not have children. This is a read-only property and cannot be used to manipulate child nodes; use appendChild(), insertBefore(), and removeNode() to manipulate child nodes.

See also

XML.appendChild(), XML.insertBefore(), XML.removeNode()

XML.load()

Availability

Flash Player 5; behavior changed in Flash Player 7.

Usage

my_xml.load(*url*)

Parameters

url   The URL where the XML document to be loaded is located. If the SWF file issuing this call is running in a web browser, *url* must be in the same domain as the SWF file; for details, see "Description," below.

Returns

Nothing.

Description

Method; loads an XML document from the specified URL, and replaces the contents of the specified XML object with the downloaded XML data. The URL is relative, and is called via HTTP. The load process is asynchronous; it does not finish immediately after the load() method is executed.

In SWF files running in a version of the player earlier than Flash Player 7, *url* must be in the same superdomain as the SWF file that is issuing this call. For example, a SWF file at www.someDomain.com can load variables from a SWF file at store.someDomain.com, because both files are in the same superdomain of someDomain.com.

In SWF files of any version running in Flash Player 7 or later, *url* must be in exactly the same domain (see "Flash Player security features" on page 392). For example, a SWF file at www.someDomain.com can load variables only from SWF files that are also at www.someDomain.com. If you want to load variables from a different domain, you can place a *cross-domain policy file* on the server hosting the SWF file that is being accessed. For more information, see "About allowing cross-domain data loading" on page 394.

When load() is executed, the XML object property loaded is set to false. When the XML data finishes downloading, the loaded property is set to true, and the onLoad() method is invoked. The XML data is not parsed until it is completely downloaded. If the XML object previously contained any XML trees, they are discarded.

You can specify your own event handler in place of the onLoad() method.

Example

The following is a simple example using XML.load():

```
doc = new XML();
doc.load ("theFile.xml");
```

See also

XML.loaded, XML.onLoad()

XML.loaded

Availability

Flash Player 5.

Usage

my_xml.loaded

Description

Property (read-only); determines whether the document-loading process initiated by the XML.load() call has completed. If the process completes successfully, the method returns true; otherwise, it returns false.

Example

The following example uses XML.loaded in a simple script.

```
if (doc.loaded) {
    gotoAndPlay(4);
}
```

XML.nextSibling

Availability

Flash Player 5.

Usage

my_xml.nextSibling

Description

Property (read-only); evaluates the XML object and references the next sibling in the parent node's child list. This method returns null if the node does not have a next sibling node. This is a read-only property and cannot be used to manipulate child nodes. Use appendChild(), insertBefore(), and removeNode() to manipulate child nodes.

See also

XML.appendChild(), XML.insertBefore(), XML.removeNode()

XML.nodeName

Availability

Flash Player 5.

Usage

my_xml.nodeName

Description

Property; the node name of the XML object. If the XML object is an XML element (nodeType == 1), nodeName is the name of the tag representing the node in the XML file. For example, TITLE is the nodeName of an HTML TITLE tag. If the XML object is a text node (nodeType == 3), the nodeName is null.

See also

XML.nodeType

XML.nodeType

Availability

Flash Player 5.

Usage

my_xml.nodeType

Description

Property (read-only); takes or returns a nodeType value, where 1 is an XML element and 3 is a text node.

See also

XML.nodeValue

XML.nodeValue

Availability

Flash Player 5.

Usage

my_xml.nodeValue

Description

Property; the node value of the XML object. If the XML object is a text node, the nodeType is 3, and the nodeValue is the text of the node. If the XML object is an XML element (node type is 1), it has a null nodeValue and is read-only.

See also

XML.nodeType

XML.onData

Availability

Flash Player 5

Usage

```
my_xml.onData = function(src) {
   // your statements here
}
```

Parameters

src   The raw data, usually in XML format, that is sent by the server.

Returns

Nothing.

Description

Event handler; invoked when XML text has been completely downloaded from the server, or when an error occurs downloading XML text from a server. This handler is invoked before the XML is parsed and therefore can be used to call a custom parsing routine instead of using the Flash XML parser. The XML.onData method returns either the value undefined, or a string that contains XML text downloaded from the server. If the returned value is undefined, an error occurred while downloading the XML from the server.

By default, the XML.onData method invokes XML.onLoad(). You can override the XML.onData method with your own behavior, but XML.onLoad() will no longer be called unless you call it in your implementation of XML.onData.

Example

The following example shows what the onData method looks like by default:

```
XML.prototype.onData = function (src) {
   if (src == undefined) {
     this.onLoad(false);
   } else {
     this.parseXML(src);
     this.loaded = true;
     this.onLoad(true);
   }
}
```

The XML.onData method can be overridden to intercept the XML text without parsing it.

XML.onLoad()

Availability

Flash Player 5.

Usage

```
my_xml.onLoad = function (success) {
  //your statements here
}
```

Parameters

success   A Boolean value indicating whether the XML object was successfully loaded with a `XML.load()` or `XML.sendAndLoad()` operation.

Returns

Nothing.

Description

Event handler; invoked by Flash Player when an XML document is received from the server. If the XML document is received successfully, the *success* parameter is `true`. If the document was not received, or if an error occurred in receiving the response from the server, the *success* parameter is `false`. The default implementation of this method is not active. To override the default implementation, you must assign a function containing your own actions.

Example

The following example creates a simple SWF file for a simple e-commerce storefront application. The `sendAndLoad()` method transmits an XML element containing the user's name and password, and installs an `onLoad` handler to handle the reply from the server.

```
function myOnLoad(success) {
  if (success) {
    if (e.firstChild.nodeName == "LOGINREPLY_xml" &&
        e.firstChild.attributes.status == "OK") {
      gotoAndPlay("loggedIn")
    } else {
      gotoAndStop("loginFailed")
    }
  } else {
    gotoAndStop("connectionFailed")
  }
}
var myLoginReply_xml = new XML();
myLoginReply_xml.onLoad = myOnLoad;
my_xml.sendAndLoad("http://www.samplestore.com/login.cgi",
            myLoginReply_xml);
```

See also

`function`, `XML.load()`, `XML.sendAndLoad()`

XML.parentNode

Availability

Flash Player 5.

Usage

my_xml.parentNode

Description

Property (read-only); references the parent node of the specified XML object, or returns null if the node has no parent. This is a read-only property and cannot be used to manipulate child nodes; use appendChild(), insertBefore(), and removeNode() to manipulate children.

XML.parseXML()

Availability

Flash Player 5.

Usage

my_xml.parseXML(*source*)

Parameters

source   The XML text to be parsed and passed to the specified XML object.

Returns

Nothing.

Description

Method; parses the XML text specified in the *source* parameter, and populates the specified XML object with the resulting XML tree. Any existing trees in the XML object are discarded.

XML.previousSibling

Availability

Flash Player 5.

Usage

my_xml.previousSibling

Description

Property (read-only); returns a reference to the previous sibling in the parent node's child list. The property has a value of null if the node does not have a previous sibling node. This is a read-only property and cannot be used to manipulate child nodes; use XML.appendChild(), XML.insertBefore(), and XML.removeNode() to manipulate child nodes.

XML.removeNode()

Availability

Flash Player 5.

Usage

my_xml.removeNode()

Parameters

None.

Returns

Nothing.

Description

Method; removes the specified XML object from its parent. All descendants of the node are also deleted.

XML.send()

Availability

Flash Player 5.

Usage

my_xml.send(*url*, [*window*])

Parameters

url   The destination URL for the specified XML object.

window   The browser window to display data returned by the server: _self specifies the current frame in the current window, _blank specifies a new window, _parent specifies the parent of the current frame, and _top specifies the top-level frame in the current window. This parameter is optional; if no *window* parameter is specified, it is the same as specifying _self.

Returns

Nothing.

Description

Method; encodes the specified XML object into an XML document and sends it to the specified URL using the POST method.

XML.sendAndLoad()

Availability

Flash Player 5; behavior changed in Flash Player 7.

Usage

my_xml.sendAndLoad(*url*, *targetXMLobject*)

Parameters

url   The destination URL for the specified XML object. If the SWF file issuing this call is running in a web browser, *url* must be in the same domain as the SWF file; for details, see "Description," below.

targetXMLobject   An XML object created with the XML constructor method that will receive the return information from the server.

Returns

Nothing.

Description

Method; encodes the specified XML object into a XML document, sends it to the specified URL using the POST method, downloads the server's response and then loads it into the *targetXMLobject* specified in the parameters. The server response is loaded in the same manner used by the load() method.

In SWF files running in a version of the player earlier than Flash Player 7, *url* must be in the same superdomain as the SWF file that is issuing this call. For example, a SWF file at www.someDomain.com can load variables from a SWF file at store.someDomain.com, because both files are in the same superdomain of someDomain.com.

In SWF files of any version running in Flash Player 7 or later, *url* must be in exactly the same domain (see "Flash Player security features" on page 392). For example, a SWF file at www.someDomain.com can load variables only from SWF files that are also at www.someDomain.com. If you want to load variables from a different domain, you can place a *cross-domain policy file* on the server hosting the SWF file that is being accessed. For more information, see "About allowing cross-domain data loading" on page 394.

When load() is executed, the XML object property loaded is set to false. When the XML data finishes downloading, the loaded property is set to true, and the onLoad() method is invoked. The XML data is not parsed until it is completely downloaded. If the XML object previously contained any XML trees, they are discarded.

See also

XML.load()

XML.status

Flash Player 5.

Usage

my_xml.status

Description

Property; automatically sets and returns a numeric value indicating whether an XML document was successfully parsed into an XML object. The numeric status codes and a description of each are listed as follows:

- 0 No error; parse was completed successfully.
- -2 A CDATA section was not properly terminated.
- -3 The XML declaration was not properly terminated.
- -4 The DOCTYPE declaration was not properly terminated.
- -5 A comment was not properly terminated.
- -6 An XML element was malformed.
- -7 Out of memory.
- -8 An attribute value was not properly terminated.
- -9 A start-tag was not matched with an end-tag.
- -10 An end-tag was encountered without a matching start-tag.

XML.toString()

Availability

Flash Player 5.

Usage

my_xml.toString()

Parameters

None.

Returns

A string.

Description

Method; evaluates the specified XML object, constructs a textual representation of the XML structure including the node, children, and attributes, and returns the result as a string.

For top-level XML objects (those created with the constructor), XML.toString() outputs the document's XML declaration (stored in XML.xmlDecl), followed by the document's DOCTYPE declaration (stored in XML.docTypeDecl), followed by the text representation of all XML nodes in the object. The XML declaration is not output if XML.xmlDecl is undefined. The DOCTYPE declaration is not output if XML.docTypeDecl is undefined.

The following code is an example of `XML.toString()` that sends `<h1>test</h1>` to the Output panel.

```
node = new XML("<h1>test</h1>");
trace(node.toString());
```

See also

`XML.docTypeDecl, XML.xmlDecl`

XML.xmlDecl

Availability

Flash Player 5.

Usage

`my_xml.xmlDecl`

Description

Property; specifies information about a document's XML declaration. After the XML document is parsed into an XML object, this property is set to the text of the document's XML declaration. This property is set using a string representation of the XML declaration, not an XML node object. If no XML declaration was encountered during a parse operation, the property is set to `undefined.XML`. The `toString()` method outputs the contents of `XML.xmlDecl` before any other text in the XML object. If `XML.xmlDecl` contains the `undefined` type, no XML declaration is output.

Example

The following example uses `XML.xmlDecl` to set the XML document declaration for an XML object.

```
my_xml.xmlDecl = "<?xml version=\"1.0\" ?>";
```

The following is an example of XML Declaration:

```
<?xml version="1.0" ?>
```

See also

`XML.docTypeDecl, XML.toString()`

XMLNode class

Availability

Flash Player 5.

Description

The XMLnode class supports the following properties, methods, and collections; for information on their usage, see the corresponding XML class entries.

Property, method, or collection	Corresponding XML class entry
appendChild()	XML.appendChild()
attributes	XML.attributes
childNodes	XML.childNodes
cloneNode()	XML.cloneNode()
firstChild	XML.firstChild
hasChildNodes()	XML.hasChildNodes()
insertBefore()	XML.insertBefore()
lastChild	XML.lastChild
nextSibling	XML.nextSibling
nodeName	XML.nodeName
nodeType	XML.nodeType
nodeValue	XML.nodeValue
parentNode	XML.parentNode
previousSibling	XML.previousSibling
removeNode()	XML.removeNode()
toString()	XML.toString()

See also

XML class

XMLSocket class

Availability

Flash Player 5.

Description

The XMLSocket class implements client sockets that allow the computer running Flash Player to communicate with a server computer identified by an IP address or domain name. The XMLSocket class is useful for client-server applications that require low latency, such as real-time chat systems. A traditional HTTP-based chat solution frequently polls the server and downloads new messages using an HTTP request. In contrast, an XMLSocket chat solution maintains an open connection to the server, which allows the server to immediately send incoming messages without a request from the client.

To use the XMLSocket class, the server computer must run a daemon that understands the protocol used by the XMLSocket class. The protocol is as follows:

- XML messages are sent over a full-duplex TCP/IP stream socket connection.
- Each XML message is a complete XML document, terminated by a zero byte.
- An unlimited number of XML messages can be sent and received over a single XMLSocket connection.

The following restrictions apply to how and where an XMLSocket object can connect to the server:

- The XMLSocket.connect() method can connect only to TCP port numbers greater than or equal to 1024. One consequence of this restriction is that the server daemons that communicate with the XMLSocket object must also be assigned to port numbers greater than or equal to 1024. Port numbers below 1024 are often used by system services such as FTP, Telnet, and HTTP, thus XMLSocket objects are barred from these ports for security reasons. The port number restriction limits the possibility that these resources will be inappropriately accessed and abused.
- The XMLSocket.connect() method can connect only to computers in the same domain where the SWF file resides. This restriction does not apply to SWF files running off a local disk. (This restriction is identical to the security rules for loadVariables(), XML.sendAndLoad(), and XML.load().) To connect to a server daemon running in a domain other than then one where the SWF resides, you can create a security policy file on the server that allows access from specific domains. For more information on creating policy files for XMLSocket connections, see "About allowing cross-domain data loading" on page 394.

Setting up a server to communicate with the XMLSocket object can be challenging. If your application does not require real-time interactivity, use the loadVariables() action, or Flash HTTP-based XML server connectivity (XML.load(), XML.sendAndLoad(), XML.send()), instead of the XMLSocket class.

To use the methods of the XMLSocket class, you must first use the constructor, new XMLSocket, to create a new XMLSocket object.

Method summary for the **XMLSocket** class

Method	Description
XMLSocket.close()	Closes an open socket connection.
XMLSocket.connect()	Establishes a connection to the specified server.
XMLSocket.send()	Sends an XML object to the server.

Event handler summary for the **XMLSocket** class

Event handler	Description
XMLSocket.onClose()	An event handler that is invoked when an XMLSocket connection is closed.
XMLSocket.onConnect()	An event handler that is invoked by Flash Player when a connection request initiated through XMLSocket.connect() has succeeded or failed.
XMLSocket.onData()	An event handler that is invoked when an XML message has been downloaded from the server.
XMLSocket.onXML()	An event handler that is invoked when an XML object arrives from the server.

Constructor for the **XMLSocket** class

Availability

Flash Player 5.

Usage

```
new XMLSocket()
```

Parameters

None.

Returns

Nothing.

Description

Constructor; creates a new XMLSocket object. The XMLSocket object is not initially connected to any server. You must call XMLSocket.connect() to connect the object to a server.

XMLSocket.close()

Availability

Flash Player 5.

Usage

`myXMLSocket.close()`

Parameters

None.

Returns

Nothing.

Description

Method; closes the connection specified by XMLSocket object.

See also

`XMLSocket.connect()`

XMLSocket.connect()

Availability

Flash Player 5; behavior changed in Flash Player 7.

Usage

`myXMLSocket.connect(host, port)`

Parameters

host   A fully qualified DNS domain name, or an IP address in the form *aaa.bbb.ccc.ddd*. You can also specify `null` to connect to the host server on which the SWF file resides. If the SWF file issuing this call is running in a web browser, *url* must be in the same domain as the SWF file; for details, see "Description," below.

port   The TCP port number on the host used to establish a connection. The port number must be 1024 or higher.

Returns

A Boolean value.

Description

Method; establishes a connection to the specified Internet host using the specified TCP port (must be 1024 or higher), and returns `true` or `false` depending on whether a connection is successfully established. If you don't know the port number of your Internet host machine, contact your network administrator.

If you specify `null` for the *host* parameter, the host contacted will be the host where the SWF file calling `XMLSocket.connect()` resides. For example, if the SWF file was downloaded from http://www.yoursite.com,specifying `null` for the host parameter is the same as entering the IP address for www.yoursite.com.

In SWF files running in a version of the player earlier than Flash Player 7, *url* must be in the same superdomain as the SWF file that is issuing this call. For example, a SWF file at www.someDomain.com can load variables from a SWF file at store.someDomain.com, because both files are in the same superdomain of someDomain.com.

In SWF files of any version running in Flash Player 7 or later, *url* must be in exactly the same domain (see "Flash Player security features" on page 392). For example, a SWF file at www.someDomain.com can load variables only from SWF files that are also at www.someDomain.com. If you want to load variables from a different domain, you can place a *cross-domain policy file* on the server hosting the SWF file that is being accessed (it must be placed on the HTTP server running on port 80 in the same domain as the socket server). For more information, see "About allowing cross-domain data loading" on page 394.

When `load()` is executed, the XML object property `loaded` is set to `false`. When the XML data finishes downloading, the `loaded` property is set to `true`, and the `onLoad()` method is invoked. The XML data is not parsed until it is completely downloaded. If the XML object previously contained any XML trees, they are discarded.

If `XMLSocket.connect()` returns a value of `true`, the initial stage of the connection process is successful; later, the `XMLSocket.onConnect` method is invoked to determine whether the final connection succeeded or failed. If `XMLSocket.connect()` returns `false`, a connection could not be established.

Example

The following example uses `XMLSocket.connect()` to connect to the host where the SWF file resides, and uses `trace` to display the return value indicating the success or failure of the connection.

```
function myOnConnect(success) {
   if (success) {
     trace ("Connection succeeded!")
   } else {
     trace ("Connection failed!")
   }
}
socket = new XMLSocket()
socket.onConnect = myOnConnect
if (!socket.connect(null, 2000)) {
   trace ("Connection failed!")
}
```

See also

`function, XMLSocket.onConnect()`

XMLSocket.onClose()

Availability

Flash Player 5.

Usage

```
myXMLSocket.onClose() = function() {
    // your statements here
}
```

Parameters

None.

Returns

Nothing.

Description

Event handler; invoked only when an open connection is closed by the server. The default implementation of this method performs no actions. To override the default implementation, you must assign a function containing your own actions.

See also

function, XMLSocket.onConnect()

XMLSocket.onConnect()

Availability

Flash Player 5.

Usage

```
myXMLSocket.onConnect(success)
    // your statements here
}
```

Parameters

success   A Boolean value indicating whether a socket connection was successfully established (true or false).

Returns

Nothing.

Description

Event handler; invoked by Flash Player when a connection request initiated through XMLSocket.connect() has succeeded or failed. If the connection succeeded, the *success* parameter is true; otherwise the *success* parameter is false.

The default implementation of this method performs no actions. To override the default implementation, you must assign a function containing your own actions.

The following example illustrates the process of specifying a replacement function for the onConnect method in a simple chat application.

The function controls which screen users are taken to, depending on whether a connection is successfully established. If the connection is successfully made, users are taken to the main chat screen on the frame labeled startChat. If the connection is not successful, users go to a screen with troubleshooting information on the frame labeled connectionFailed.

```
function myOnConnect(success) {
   if (success) {
      gotoAndPlay("startChat")
   } else {
      gotoAndStop("connectionFailed")
   }
}
```

After creating the XMLSocket object using the constructor method, the script installs the onConnect method using the assignment operator:

```
socket = new XMLSocket();
socket.onConnect = myOnConnect;
```

Finally, the connection is initiated. If connect() returns false, the SWF file is sent directly to the frame labeled connectionFailed, and onConnect is never invoked. If connect() returns true, the SWF file jumps to a frame labeled waitForConnection, which is the "Please wait" screen. The SWF file remains on the waitForConnection frame until the onConnect handler is invoked, which happens at some point in the future depending on network latency.

```
if (!socket.connect(null, 2000)) {
   gotoAndStop("connectionFailed")
} else {
   gotoAndStop("waitForConnection")
}
```

See also

function, XMLSocket.connect()

XMLSocket.onData()

Availability

Flash Player 5.

Usage

```
XMLSocket.onData = function(src) {
   // your statements here
}
```

Parameters

src   A string containing the data sent by the server.

Returns

Nothing.

Description

Event handler; invoked when a message has been downloaded from the server, terminated by a zero byte. You can override XMLSocket.onData to intercept the data sent by the server without parsing it as XML. This is a useful if you're transmitting arbitrarily formatted data packets, and you'd prefer to manipulate the data directly when it arrives, rather than have Flash Player parse the data as XML.

By default, the XMLSocket.onData method invokes the XMLSocket.onXML method. If you override XMLSocket.onData with your own behavior, XMLSocket.onXML will no longer be called unless you call it in your implementation of XMLSocket.onData.

```
XMLSocket.prototype.onData = function (src) {
  this.onXML(new XML(src));
}
```

In the above example, the *src* parameter is a string containing XML text downloaded from the server. The zero byte terminator is not included in the string.

XMLSocket.onXML()

Availability

Flash Player 5.

Usage

```
myXMLSocket.onXML(object) = function() {
  // your statements here
}
```

Parameter

object   An XML object that contains a parsed XML document received from a server.

Returns

Nothing.

Description

Event handler; invoked by Flash Player when the specified XML object containing an XML document arrives over an open XMLSocket connection. An XMLSocket connection may be used to transfer an unlimited number of XML documents between the client and the server. Each document is terminated with a 0 (zero) byte. When Flash Player receives the 0 byte, it parses all of the XML received since the previous 0 byte, or since the connection was established if this is the first message received. Each batch of parsed XML is treated as a single XML document and passed to the onXML method.

The default implementation of this method performs no actions. To override the default implementation, you must assign a function containing actions that you define.

Example

The following function overrides the default implementation of the onXML method in a simple chat application. The function myOnXML instructs the chat application to recognize a single XML element, MESSAGE, in the following format.

```
<MESSAGE USER="John" TEXT="Hello, my name is John!" />.
```

The onXML handler must first be installed in the XMLSocket object as follows:

```
socket.onXML = myOnXML;
```

The function displayMessage() is assumed to be a user-defined function that displays the message received by the user.

```
function myOnXML(doc) {
   var e = doc.firstChild;
   if (e != null && e.nodeName == "MESSAGE") {
     displayMessage(e.attributes.user, e.attributes.text);
   }
}
```

See also

```
function
```

XMLSocket.send()

Availability

Flash Player 5.

Usage

```
myXMLSocket.send(object)
```

Parameters

object   An XML object or other data to transmit to the server.

Returns

Nothing.

Description

Method; converts the XML object or data specified in the object parameter to a string and transmits it to the server, followed by a zero byte. If object is an XML object, the string is the XML textual representation of the XML object. The send operation is asynchronous; it returns immediately, but the data may be transmitted at a later time. The XMLSocket.send() method does not return a value indicating whether the data was successfully transmitted.

If the myXMLSocket object is not connected to the server (using XMLSocket.connect()), the XMLSocket.send() operation will fail.

Example

The following example illustrates how you could specify a user name and password to send the XML object my_xml to the server:

```
var my_xml = new XML();
var myLogin = my_xml.createElement("login");
myLogin.attributes.username = usernameTextField;
myLogin.attributes.password = passwordTextField;
my_xml.appendChild(myLogin);
myXMLSocket.send(my_xml);
```

See also

```
XMLSocket.connect()
```

Macromedia Flash MX 2004 and Macromedia Flash MX Professional 2004 provide enhanced compile-time error reporting if you specify ActionScript 2.0 (the default) when you publish a file. The following table contains a list of error messages that the Flash compiler can generate.

Error number	Message text
1093	A class name was expected.
1094	A base class name is expected after the 'extends' keyword.
1095	A member attribute was used incorrectly.
1096	The same member name may not be repeated more than once.
1097	All member functions need to have names.
1099	This statement is not permitted in a class definition.
1100	A class or interface has already been defined with this name.
1101	Type mismatch.
1102	There is no class with the name '<ClassName>'.
1103	There is no property with the name '<propertyName>'.
1104	A function call on a non-function was attempted.
1105	Type mismatch in assignment statement: found [lhs-type] where [rhs-type] is required.
1106	The member is private and cannot be accessed.
1107	Variable declarations are not permitted in interfaces.
1108	Event declarations are not permitted in interfaces.
1109	Getter/setter declarations are not permitted in interfaces.
1110	Private members are not permitted in interfaces.
1111	Function bodies are not permitted in interfaces.
1112	A class may not extend itself.
1113	An interface may not extend itself.

Error number	Message text
1114	There is no interface defined with this name.
1115	A class may not extend an interface.
1116	An interface may not extend a class.
1117	An interface name is expected after the 'implements' keyword.
1118	A class may not implement a class, only interfaces.
1119	The class must implement method 'methodName' from interface 'interfaceName'.
1120	The implementation of an interface method must be a method, not a property.
1121	A class may not extend the same interface more than once.
1122	The implementation of the interface method doesn't match its definition.
1123	This construct is only available in ActionScript 1.0.
1124	This construct is only available in ActionScript 2.0.
1125	Static members are not permitted in interfaces.
1126	The expression returned must match the function's return type.
1127	A return statement is required in this function.
1128	Attribute used outside class.
1129	A function with return type Void may not return a value.
1130	The 'extends' clause must appear before the 'implements' clause.
1131	A type identifier is expected after the ':'.
1132	Interfaces must use the 'extends' keyword, not 'implements'.
1133	A class may not extend more than one class.
1134	An interface may not extend more than one interface.
1135	There is no method with the name '‹methodName›'.
1136	This statement is not permitted in an interface definition.
1137	A set function requires exactly one parameter.
1138	A get function requires no parameters.
1139	Classes may only be defined in external ActionScript 2.0 class scripts.
1140	ActionScript 2.0 class scripts may only define class or interface constructs.
1141	The name of this class, '‹A.B.C›', conflicts with the name of another class that was loaded, '‹A.B›'.
1142	The class '‹ClassName›' could not be loaded.
1143	Interfaces may only be defined in external ActionScript 2.0 class scripts.
1144	Instance variables cannot be accessed in static functions.
1145	Class and interface definitions cannot be nested.

Error number	Message text
1146	The property being referenced does not have the static attribute.
1147	This call to super does not match the superconstructor.
1148	Only the public attribute is allowed for interface methods.
1149	The import keyword cannot be used as a directive.
1150	You must export your movie as Flash 7 to use this action.
1151	You must export your movie as Flash 7 to use this expression.
1152	This exception clause is placed improperly.
1153	A class must have only one constructor.
1154	A constructor may not return a value.
1155	A constructor may not specify a return type.
1156	A variable may not be of type Void.
1157	A function parameter may not be of type Void.
1158	Static members can only be accessed directly through classes.
1159	Multiple implemented interfaces contain same method with different types.
1160	There is already a class or interface defined with this name.
1161	Classes, interfaces, and built-in types may not be deleted.
1162	There is no class with this name.
1163	The keyword '<keyword>' is reserved for ActionScript 2.0 and cannot be used here.
1164	Custom attribute definition was not terminated.
1165	Only one class or interface can be defined per ActionScript 2.0 .as file.
1166	The class being compiled, '<A.b>', does not match the class that was imported, '<A.B>'.
1167	You must enter a class name.
1168	The class name you have entered contains a syntax error.
1169	The interface name you have entered contains a syntax error.
1170	The base class name you have entered contains a syntax error.
1171	The base interface name you have entered contains a syntax error.
1172	You must enter an interface name.
1173	You must enter a class or interface name.
1174	The class or interface name you have entered contains a syntax error.
1175	'variable' is not accessible from this scope.
1176	Multiple occurrences of the 'get/set/private/public/static' attribute were found.
1177	A class attribute was used incorrectly.

Error number	Message text
1178	Instance variables and functions may not be used to initialize static variables.
1179	Runtime circularities were discovered between the following classes:%1
1180	The currently targeted Flash Player does not support Debugging.
1181	The currently targeted Flash Player does not support the releaseOutside event.
1182	The currently targeted Flash Player does not support the dragOver event.
1183	The currently targeted Flash Player does not support the dragOut event.
1184	The currently targeted Flash Player does not support dragging actions.
1185	The currently targeted Flash Player does not support the loadMovie action.
1186	The currently targeted Flash Player does not support the getURL action.
1187	The currently targeted Flash Player does not support the FSCommand action.
1188	Import statements are not allowed inside class or interface definitions.
1189	The class '‹A.B›' cannot be imported because its leaf name is already being resolved to the class that is being defined, '‹C.B›'.
1190	The class '‹A.B›' cannot be imported because its leaf name is already being resolved to imported class '‹C.B›'.
1191	A class's instance variables may only be initialized to compile-time constant expressions.
1192	Class member functions cannot have the same name as a superclass's constructor function.
1193	The name of this class, '‹ClassName›', conflicts with the name of another class that was loaded.
1194	The superconstructor must be called first in the constructor body.
1195	The identifier '‹className›' will not resolve to built-in object '‹ClassName›' at runtime.
1196	The class '‹A.B.ClassName›' needs to be defined in a file whose relative path is '‹A.B›'.
1197	The wildcard character '*' is misused in the ClassName '‹ClassName›'.
1198	The member function '‹classname›' has a different case from the name of the class being defined, '‹ClassName›', and will not be treated as the class constructor at runtime.
1199	The only type allowed for a for-in loop iterator is String.
1200	A setter function may not return a value.
1201	The only attributes allowed for constructor functions are public and private.

APPENDIX B
Operator Precedence and Associativity

This table lists all of the ActionScript operators and their associativity, from highest to lowest precedence.

Operator	Description	Associativity
	Highest precedence	
+	Unary plus	Right to left
-	Unary minus	Right to left
~	Bitwise NOT	Right to left
!	Logical NOT	Right to left
not	Logical NOT (Flash 4 style)	Right to left
++	Post-increment	Left to right
--	Post-decrement	Left to right
( )	Function call	Left to right
[ ]	Array element	Left to right
.	Structure member	Left to right
++	Pre-increment	Right to left
--	Pre-decrement	Right to left
new	Allocate object	Right to left
delete	Deallocate object	Right to left
typeof	Type of object	Right to left
void	Returns undefined value	Right to left
*	Multiply	Left to right
/	Divide	Left to right
%	Modulo	Left to right
+	Add	Left to right

Operator	Description	Associativity
add	String concatenation (formerly &)	Left to right
-	Subtract	Left to right
<<	Bitwise left shift	Left to right
>>	Bitwise right shift	Left to right
>>>	Bitwise right shift (unsigned)	Left to right
<	Less than	Left to right
<=	Less than or equal to	Left to right
>	Greater than	Left to right
>=	Greater than or equal to	Left to right
instanceof	Instance of	Left to right
lt	Less than (string version)	Left to right
le	Less than or equal to (string version)	Left to right
gt	Greater than (string version)	Left to right
ge	Greater than or equal to (string version)	Left to right
==	Equal	Left to right
!=	Not equal	Left to right
eq	Equal (string version)	Left to right
ne	Not equal (string version)	Left to right
&	Bitwise AND	Left to right
^	Bitwise XOR	Left to right
|	Bitwise OR	Left to right
&&	Logical AND	Left to right
and	Logical AND (Flash 4)	Left to right
||	Logical OR	Left to right
or	Logical OR (Flash 4)	Left to right
?:	Conditional	Right to left
=	Assignment	Right to left
*=, /=, %=, +=, -=, &=, |=, ^=, <<=, >>=, >>>=	Compound assignment	Right to left
,	Comma	Left to right

Lowest precedence

The following tables list all of the keys on a standard keyboard and the corresponding ASCII key code values that are used to identify the keys in ActionScript. For more information, see the Key class entry in Chapter 12, "ActionScript Dictionary," on page 409.

Letters A to Z and standard numbers 0 to 9

The following table lists the keys on a standard keyboard for the letters A to Z and the numbers 0 to 9, with the corresponding ASCII key code values that are used to identify the keys in ActionScript.

Letter or number key	Key code
A	65
B	66
C	67
D	68
E	69
F	70
G	71
H	72
I	73
J	74
K	75
L	76
M	77
N	78
O	79
P	80
Q	81
R	82

Letter or number key	Key code
S	83
T	84
U	85
V	86
W	87
X	88
Y	89
Z	90
0	48
1	49
2	50
3	51
4	52
5	53
6	54
7	55
8	56
9	57

Keys on the numeric keypad

The following table lists the keys on a numeric keypad, with the corresponding ASCII key code values that are used to identify the keys in ActionScript.

Numeric keypad key	Key code
Numbpad 0	96
Numbpad 1	97
Numbpad 2	98
Numbpad 3	99
Numbpad 4	100
Numbpad 5	101
Numbpad 6	102
Numbpad 7	103
Numbpad 8	104
Numbpad 9	105

Numeric keypad key	Key code
Multiply	106
Add	107
Enter	108
Subtract	109
Decimal	110
Divide	111

Function keys

The following table lists the function keys on a standard keyboard, with the corresponding ASCII key code values that are used to identify the keys in ActionScript.

Function key	Key code
F1	112
F2	113
F3	114
F4	115
F5	116
F6	117
F7	118
F8	119
F9	120
F10	121
F11	122
F12	123
F13	124
F14	125
F15	126

Other keys

The following table lists keys on a standard keyboard other than letters, numbers, numeric keypad keys, or function keys, with the corresponding ASCII key code values that are used to identify the keys in ActionScript.

Key	Key code
Backspace	8
Tab	9
Clear	12
Enter	13
Shift	16
Control	17
Alt	18
Caps Lock	20
Esc	27
Spacebar	32
Page Up	33
Page Down	34
End	35
Home	36
Left Arrow	37
Up Arrow	38
Right Arrow	39
Down Arrow	40
Insert	45
Delete	46
Help	47
Num Lock	144
; :	186
= +	187
- _	189
/ ?	191
` ~	192
[{	219
\ |	220

Key	Key code
] }	221
" '	222

APPENDIX D
Writing Scripts for Earlier Versions of Flash Player

ActionScript has changed considerably with the release of Macromedia Flash MX 2004 and Macromedia Flash MX Professional 2004. When you create content for Flash Player 7, you'll take advantage of the full power of ActionScript. You can still use Flash MX 2004 to create content for earlier versions of Flash Player, but you won't be able to use every ActionScript element.

This chapter provides guidelines to help you write scripts that are syntactically correct for the player version you are targeting.

About targeting older versions of Flash Player

While writing your scripts, use the Availability information for each element in the ActionScript dictionary (see Chapter 12, "ActionScript Dictionary," on page 409) to determine if an element you want to use is supported by the Flash Player version you are targeting. You can also determine which elements you can use by displaying the Actions toolbox; elements that are not supported for your target version are highlighted in yellow.

If you are creating content for Flash Player 6 or Flash Player 7, you should use ActionScript 2.0, which provides a number of important features that aren't available in ActionScript 1, such as improved compiler errors and more robust object-oriented programming capabilities.

For a review of differences in how certain features are implemented when publishing files for Flash Player 7 versus how the features are implemented in files published for earlier versions of the player, see "Porting existing scripts to Flash Player 7" on page 219.

To specify the player and ActionScript version you want to use when publishing a document, select File > Publish Settings and then make your selections in the Flash tab. If you need to target Flash Player 4, see the next section.

Using Flash MX 2004 to create content for Flash Player 4

To use Flash MX 2004 to create content for Flash Player 4, specify Flash Player 4 in the Flash tab of the Publish Settings dialog box (File > Publish Settings).

Flash Player 4 ActionScript has only one basic primitive data type, which is used for both numeric and string manipulation. When you author an application for Flash Player 4, you must use the deprecated string operators located in the Deprecated > Operators category in the Actions toolbox.

You can use the following Flash MX 2004 features when you publish for Flash Player 4:

- The array and object access operator ([])
- The dot operator (.)
- Logical operators, assignment operators, and pre-increment and post-increment/ decrement operators
- The modulo operator (%), and all methods and properties of the Math class

The following language elements are not supported natively by Flash Player 4. Flash MX 2004 exports them as series approximations, which creates results that are less numerically accurate. In addition, because of the inclusion of series approximations in the SWF file, these language elements take up more room in Flash Player 4 SWF files than they do in Flash Player 5 or later SWF files.

- The for, while, do..while, break, and continue actions
- The print() and printAsBitmap() actions
- The switch action

For additional information, see "About targeting older versions of Flash Player" on page 999.

Using Flash MX 2004 to open Flash 4 files

Flash 4 ActionScript had only one true data type: string. It used different types of operators in expressions to indicate whether the value should be treated as a string or as a number. In subsequent releases of Flash, you can use one set of operators on all data types.

When you use Flash 5 or later to open a file that was created in Flash 4, Flash automatically converts ActionScript expressions to make them compatible with the new syntax. You'll see the following data type and operator conversions in your ActionScript code:

- The = operator in Flash 4 was used for numeric equality. In Flash 5 and later, == is the equality operator and = is the assignment operator. Any = operators in Flash 4 files are automatically converted to ==.
- Flash automatically performs type conversions to ensure that operators behave as expected. Because of the introduction of multiple data types, the following operators have new meanings:

  +, ==, !=, <>, <, >, >=, <=

  In Flash 4 ActionScript, these operators were always numeric operators. In Flash 5 and later, they behave differently depending on the data types of the operands. To prevent any semantic differences in imported files, the Number() function is inserted around all operands to these operators. (Constant numbers are already obvious numbers, so they are not enclosed in Number()).

- In Flash 4, the escape sequence \n generated a carriage return character (ASCII 13). In Flash 5 and later, to comply with the ECMA-262 standard, \n generates a line-feed character (ASCII 10). An \n sequence in Flash 4 FLA files is automatically converted to \r.

- The & operator in Flash 4 was used for string addition. In Flash 5 and later, & is the bitwise AND operator. The string addition operator is now called add. Any & operators in Flash 4 files are automatically converted to add operators.

- Many functions in Flash 4 did not require closing parentheses, for example, Get Timer, Set Variable, Stop, and Play. To create consistent syntax, the getTimer function and all actions now require closing parentheses. These parentheses are automatically added during the conversion.

- In Flash 5 and later, when the getProperty function is executed on a movie clip that doesn't exist, it returns the value undefined, not 0. The statement undefined == 0 is false in ActionScript after Flash 4 (in Flash 4, undefined == 1). In Flash 5 and later, solve this problem when converting Flash 4 files by introducing Number() functions in equality comparisons. In the following example, Number() forces undefined to be converted to 0 so the comparison will succeed:

```
getProperty("clip", _width) == 0
Number(getProperty("clip", _width)) == Number(0)
```

Note: If you used any Flash 5 or later keywords as variable names in your Flash 4 ActionScript, the syntax returns an error when you compile it in Flash MX 2004. To solve this problem, rename your variables in all locations. See "Keywords" on page 237 and "Naming a variable" on page 245.

Using slash syntax

Slash syntax was used in Flash 3 and 4 to indicate the target path of a movie clip or variable. In slash syntax, slashes are used instead of dots; also, to indicate a variable, you precede it with a colon:

```
myMovieClip/childMovieClip:myVariable
```

To write the same target path in dot syntax (see "Dot syntax" on page 234), which is supported by Flash Player 5 and later, you would use the following code:

```
myMovieClip.childMovieClip.myVariable
```

Slash syntax was most commonly used with the tellTarget action, whose use is also no longer recommended. The with action is now preferred over tellTarget because it is more compatible with dot syntax. For more information, see tellTarget and with in Chapter 12, "ActionScript Dictionary," on page 409.

Object-Oriented Programming with ActionScript 1

The information in this appendix was excerpted from the Macromedia Flash MX documentation and provides information on using the ActionScript 1 object model to write scripts. It is included here for the following reasons:

- If you want to write object-oriented scripts that support Flash Player 5, you must use ActionScript 1.

- If you already use ActionScript 1 to write object-oriented scripts and aren't ready to switch to ActionScript 2.0, you can use this appendix to find or review information you need while writing your ActionScript 1 scripts.

If you have never used ActionScript to write object-oriented scripts and don't need to target Flash Player 5, you should not use the information in this appendix, because writing object-oriented scripts using ActionScript 1 is deprecated; instead, see Chapter 9, "Creating Classes with ActionScript 2.0," on page 359 for information on using ActionScript 2.0.

Note: Some of the examples in this appendix use the `Object.RegisterClass()` method. This method is supported only in Flash Player 6 and later; don't use this method if you are targeting Flash Player 5.

About ActionScript 1

ActionScript is an object-oriented programming language. Object-oriented programming uses *objects*, or data structures, to group together properties and methods that control the object's behavior or appearance. Objects let you organize and reuse code. After you define an object, you can refer to the object by name without having to redefine it each time you use it.

A *class* is a generic category of objects. A class defines a series of objects that have common properties and can be controlled in the same ways. Properties are attributes that define an object, such as its size, position, color, transparency, and so on. Properties are defined for a class, and values for the properties are set for individual objects in the class. Methods are functions that can set or retrieve properties of an object. For example, you can define a method to calculate the size of an object. Like properties, methods are defined for an object class, and then invoked for individual objects in the class.

ActionScript includes several built-in classes, including the MovieClip class and others. You can also create classes to define categories of objects for your applications.

Objects in ActionScript can be pure containers for data, or they can be graphically represented on the Stage as movie clips, buttons, or text fields. All movie clips are instances of the built-in class MovieClip, and all buttons are instances of the built-in class Button. Each movie clip instance contains all the properties (for example, _height, _rotation, _totalframes) and all the methods (for example, gotoAndPlay(), loadMovie(), startDrag()) of the MovieClip class.

To define a class, you create a special function called a *constructor function*. (Built-in classes have built-in constructor functions.) For example, if you want information about a bicycle rider in your application, you could create a constructor function, Biker(), with the properties time and distance and the method getSpeed(), which tells you how fast the biker is traveling:

```
function Biker(t, d) {
  this.time = t;
  this.distance = d;
  this.getSpeed = function() {return this.time / this.distance;};
}
```

In this example, you create a function that needs two pieces of information, or parameters, to do its job: t and d. When you call the function to create new instances of the object, you pass it the parameters. The following code creates instances of the object Biker called emma and hamish.

```
emma = new Biker(30, 5);
hamish = new Biker(40, 5);
```

In object-oriented scripting, classes can receive properties and methods from each other according to a specific order; this is called *inheritance*. You can use inheritance to extend or redefine the properties and methods of a class. A class that inherits from another class is called a *subclass*. A class that passes properties and methods to another class is called a *superclass*. A class can be both a subclass and a superclass.

An object is a complex data type containing zero or more properties and methods. Each property, like a variable, has a name and a value. Properties are attached to the object and contain values that can be changed and retrieved. These values can be of any data type: String, Number, Boolean, Object, MovieClip, or undefined. The following properties are of various data types:

```
customer.name = "Jane Doe";
customer.age = 30;
customer.member = true;
customer.account.currentRecord = 000609;
customer.mcInstanceName._visible = true;
```

The property of an object can also be an object. In line 4 of the previous example, account is a property of the object customer and currentRecord is a property of the object account. The data type of the currentRecord property is Number.

Creating a custom object in ActionScript 1

To create a custom object, you define a constructor function. A constructor function is always given the same name as the type of object it creates. You can use the keyword this inside the body of the constructor function to refer to the object that the constructor creates; when you call a constructor function, Flash passes it this as a hidden parameter. For example, the following is a constructor function that creates a circle with the property radius:

```
function Circle(radius) {
  this.radius = radius;
}
```

After you define the constructor function you must create an instance of the object. Use the new operator before the name of the constructor function and assign the new instance a variable name. For example, the following code uses the new operator to create a Circle object with a radius of 5, and assigns it to the variable myCircle:

```
myCircle = new Circle(5);
```

Note: An object has the same scope as the variable to which it is assigned.

Assigning methods to a custom object in ActionScript 1

You can define the methods of an object inside the object's constructor function. However, this technique is not recommended because it defines the method every time you use the constructor function, as in the following example, which creates the methods area() and diameter():

```
function Circle(radius) {
   this.radius = radius;
   this.area = Math.PI * radius * radius;
   this.diameter = function() {return 2 * this.radius;}
}
```

Each constructor function has a prototype property that is created automatically when you define the function. The prototype property indicates the default property values for objects created with that function. Each new instance of an object has a __proto__ property that refers to the prototype property of the constructor function that created it. Therefore, if you assign methods to an object's prototype property, they are available to any newly created instance of that object. It's best to assign a method to the prototype property of the constructor function because it exists in one place and is referenced by new instances of the object (or class). You can use the prototype and __proto__ properties to extend objects so that you can reuse code in an object-oriented manner. (For more information, see "Creating inheritance in ActionScript 1" on page 1007.)

The following procedure shows how to assign an area() method to a custom Circle object.

To assign a method to a custom object:

1 Define the constructor function Circle(), as follows.

```
function Circle(radius) {
   this.radius = radius;
}
```

2 Define the area() method of the Circle object. The area() method calculates the area of the circle. You can use a function literal to define the area() method and assign the area property to the circle's prototype object, as follows:

```
Circle.prototype.area = function () {
    return Math.PI * this.radius * this.radius;
};
```

3 Create an instance of the Circle object, as follows:

```
var myCircle = new Circle(4);
```

4 Call the area() method of the new myCircle object, as follows:

```
var myCircleArea = myCircle.area();
```

ActionScript searches the myCircle object for the area() method. Since the object doesn't have an area() method, its prototype object Circle.prototype is searched for area(). ActionScript finds it and calls it.

Defining event handler methods in ActionScript 1

You can create an ActionScript class for movie clips and define the event handler methods in the prototype object of that new class. Defining the methods in the prototype object makes all the instances of this symbol respond the same way to these events.

You can also add an `onClipEvent()` or `on()` event handler action to an individual instance to provide unique instructions that run only when that instance's event occurs. The `onClipEvent()` and `on()` actions don't override the event handler method; both events cause their scripts to run. However, if you define the event handler methods in the prototype object and also define an event handler method for a specific instance, the instance definition overrides the prototype definition.

To define an event handler method in an object's prototype object:

1 Place a movie clip symbol with the linkage ID `theID` in the library.

2 In the Actions panel (Window > Development Panels > Actions), use the `function` action to define a new class, as shown here:

```
// define a class
function myClipClass() {}
```

This new class will be assigned to all instances of the movie clip that are added to the application by the Timeline, or that are added to the application with the `attachMovie()` or `duplicateMovieClip()` method. If you want these movie clips to have access to the methods and properties of the built-in MovieClip object, you'll need to make the new class inherit from the MovieClip class.

3 Enter code like the following:

```
// inherit from MovieClip class
myClipClass.prototype = new MovieClip();
```

Now the class `myClipClass` inherits all the properties and methods of the MovieClip class.

4 Enter code like the following to define the event handler methods for the new class:

```
// define event handler methods for myClipClass class
myClipClass.prototype.onLoad = function() {trace ("movie clip loaded");}
myClipClass.prototype.onEnterFrame = function() {trace ("movie clip entered
    frame");}
```

5 Select Window > Library to open the Library panel if it isn't already open.

6 Select the symbols that you want to associate with your new class, and select Linkage from the pop-up menu in the upper right of the Library panel.

7 In the Linkage Properties dialog box, select Export for ActionScript.

8 Enter an identifier in the Identifier box.

The identifier must be the same for all symbols that you want to associate with the new class. In the `myClipClass` example, the identifier is `theID`.

9 Enter code like the following in the Script pane:

```
// register class
Object.registerClass("theID", myClipClass);
_root.attachMovie("theID","myName",1);
```

This registers the symbol whose linkage identifier is `theID` with the class `myClipClass`. All instances of `myClipClass` have event handler methods that behave as you defined them in step 4. They also behave like all instances of the class MovieClip, because you told the new class to inherit from the class MovieClip in step 3.

```
function myClipClass(){}

myClipClass.prototype = new MovieClip();
myClipClass.prototype.onLoad = function(){
   trace("movie clip loaded");
}
myClipClass.prototype.onPress = function(){
   trace("pressed");
}

myClipClass.prototype.onEnterFrame = function(){
   trace("movie clip entered frame");
}

myClipClass.prototype.myfunction = function(){
   trace("myfunction called");
}

Object.registerClass("myclipID",myClipClass);
_root.attachMovie("myclipID","ablue2",3);
```

Creating inheritance in ActionScript 1

Inheritance is a means of organizing, extending, and reusing functionality. Subclasses inherit properties and methods from superclasses and add their own specialized properties and methods. For example, reflecting the real world, Bike would be a superclass and MountainBike and Tricycle would be subclasses of the superclass. Both subclasses contain, or *inherit*, the methods and properties of the superclass (for example, wheels). Each subclass also has its own properties and methods that extend the superclass (for example, the MountainBike subclass would have a gears property). You can use the elements prototype and __proto__ to create inheritance in ActionScript.

All constructor functions have a prototype property that is created automatically when the function is defined. The prototype property indicates the default property values for objects created with that function. You can use the prototype property to assign properties and methods to a class. (For more information, see "Assigning methods to a custom object in ActionScript 1" on page 1005.)

All instances of a class have a __proto__ property that tells you what object they inherit from. When you use a constructor function to create an object, the __proto__ property is set to refer to the prototype property of its constructor function.

Inheritance proceeds according to a definite hierarchy. When you call an object's property or method, ActionScript looks at the object to see if such an element exists. If it doesn't exist, ActionScript looks at the object's __proto__ property for the information (myObject.__proto__). If the property is not a property of the object's __proto__ object, ActionScript looks at myObject.__proto__.__proto__, and so on.

The following example defines the constructor function Bike():

```
function Bike (length, color) {
   this.length = length;
   this.color = color;
}
```

The following code adds the roll() method to the Bike class:

```
Bike.prototype.roll = function() {this._x = _x + 20;};
```

Instead of adding `roll()` to the MountainBike class and the Tricycle class, you can create the MountainBike class with Bike as its superclass:

```
MountainBike.prototype = new Bike();
```

Now you can call the `roll()` method of MountainBike, as shown in the following:

```
MountainBike.roll();
```

Movie clips do not inherit from each other. To create inheritance with movie clips, you can use `Object.registerClass()` to assign a class other than the MovieClip class to movie clips. See `Object.registerClass()` in Chapter 12, "ActionScript Dictionary," on page 409.

For more information on inheritance, see the `Object.__proto__`, `#initclip`, `#endinitclip`, and `super` entries in Chapter 12, "ActionScript Dictionary," on page 409.

Adding getter/setter properties to objects in ActionScript 1

You can create getter/setter properties for an object using the `Object.addProperty()` method.

A getter function is a function with no parameters. Its return value can be of any type. Its type can change between invocations. The return value is treated as the current value of the property. A setter function is a function that takes one parameter, which is the new value of the property. For instance, if property x is assigned by the statement x = 1, the setter function is passed the parameter 1 of type Number. The return value of the setter function is ignored.

When Flash reads a getter/setter property, it invokes the getter function, and the function's return value becomes a value of prop. When Flash writes a getter/setter property, it invokes the setter function and passes it the new value as a parameter. If a property with the given name already exists, the new property overwrites it.

You can add getter/setter properties to prototype objects. If you add a getter/setter property to a prototype object, all object instances that inherit the prototype object inherit the getter/setter property. This makes it possible to add a getter/setter property in one location, the prototype object, and have it propagate to all instances of a class (much like adding methods to prototype objects). If a getter/setter function is invoked for a getter/setter property in an inherited prototype object, the reference passed to the getter/setter function will be the originally referenced object, not the prototype object.

For more information, see `Object.addProperty()` in Chapter 12, "ActionScript Dictionary," on page 409.

The Debug > List Variables command in test mode supports getter/setter properties that you add to objects using `Object.addProperty()`. Properties that you add to an object in this way are displayed alongside other properties of the object in the Output panel. Getter/setter properties are identified in the Output panel with the prefix `[getter/setter]`. For more information on the List Variables command, see "Using the Output panel" on page 281.

Using Function object properties in ActionScript 1

You can specify the object that a function is applied to and the parameter values that are passed to the function, using the `call()` and `apply()` methods of the Function object. Every function in ActionScript is represented by a Function object, so all functions support `call()` and `apply()`. When you create a custom class using a constructor function, or when you define methods for a custom class using a function, you can invoke `call()` and `apply()` for the function.

Invoking a function using the Function.call() method in ActionScript 1

The `Function.call()` method invokes the function represented by a Function object.

In almost all cases, the function call operator (`()`) can be used instead of the `call()` method. The function call operator creates code that is concise and readable. The `call()` method is primarily useful when the `this` parameter of the function invocation needs to be explicitly controlled. Normally, if a function is invoked as a method of an object, within the body of the function, `this` is set to `myObject`, as in the following:

```
myObject.myMethod(1, 2, 3);
```

In some situations, you may want `this` to point somewhere else, for example, if a function must be invoked as a method of an object but is not actually stored as a method of that object.

```
myObject.myMethod.call(myOtherObject, 1, 2, 3);
```

You can pass the value `null` for the *thisObject* parameter to invoke a function as a regular function and not as a method of an object. For example, the following function invocations are equivalent:

```
Math.sin(Math.PI / 4)
Math.sin.call(null, Math.PI / 4)
```

For more information, see `Function.call()` in Chapter 12, "ActionScript Dictionary," on page 409.

To invoke a function using the Function.call method:

- Use the following syntax.

  ```
  myFunction.call(thisObject, parameter1, ..., parameterN)
  ```

  The method takes the following parameters:

  - The parameter *thisObject* specifies the value of `this` within the function body.
  - The parameters *parameter1...*, *parameterN* specify parameters to be passed to *myFunction*. You can specify zero or more parameters.

Specifying the object to which a function is applied using Function.apply() in ActionScript 1

The `Function.apply()` method specifies the value of `this` to be used within any function that ActionScript calls. This method also specifies the parameters to be passed to any called function.

The parameters are specified as an Array object. This is often useful when the number of parameters to be passed is not known until the script actually executes.

For more information, see `Function.apply()` in Chapter 12, "ActionScript Dictionary," on page 409.

To specify the object to which a function is applied using Function.apply():

- Use the following syntax.

  ```
  myFunction.apply(thisObject, argumentsObject)
  ```

  The method takes the following parameters:

  - The parameter *thisObject* specifies the object that *myFunction* is applied to.
  - The parameter *argumentsObject* defines an array whose elements are passed to *myFunction* as parameters.

Index

Q-R

real world. real training. real results.

Get more done in less time with Macromedia Training and Certification.

Two Types of Training

Roll up your sleeves and get right to work with authorized training from Macromedia.

1. Classroom Training

   Learn from instructors thoroughly trained and certified by Macromedia. Courses are fast-paced and task-oriented to get you up and running quickly.

2. Online Training

   Get Macromedia training when you want with affordable, interactive online training from Macromedia University.

Stand Out from the Pack

Show your colleagues, employer, or prospective clients that you have what it takes to effectively develop, deploy, and maintain dynamic applications—become a Macromedia Certified Professional.

Learn More

For more information about authorized training or to find a class near you, visit **www.macromedia.com/go/training1**

macromedia®
TRAINING AND CERTIFICATION